Touched by Greatness

The story of Tom Graveney, England's much-loved cricketer

ANDREW MURTAGH

Touched by Greatness

Greatness

The story of Tom Graveney, England's much-loved cricketer

ANDREW MURTAGH

First published by Pitch Publishing, 2014

Pitch Publishing

A2 Yeoman Gate

Yeoman Way

Durrington

BN13 3QZ

www.pitchpublishing.co.uk

A CIP catalogue record is available for this book from the British Library.

ISBN 978 1 90962 623 2

Typesetting and origination by Pitch Publishing

Printed and bound by CPI Group (UK) Ltd, Croydon, CR0 4YY

Contents

Foreword..6

Preface...8

Spiritual Home... 15

Acknowledgements....................................... 31

1. Early Days 1927–45 33

2. Army 1945–48.. 48

3. The Young County Player 1948–51....................... 55

4. Playing For England 1951–54............................ 74

5. Family Life And Cricket 1950–61 92

6. Seasoned International – The First Incarnation 1954–59..... 105

7. The Day Job – Gloucestershire 1954–60.................. 127

8. County Champions – Worcestershire 1961–70 148

9. Out Of The Wilderness – England 1966–69 179

10. Life After Cricket 1970–94 227

11. Mr President 1994–2006 251

Foreword

by Sir Michael Parkinson

Old men forget, but not everything. We have a secret hoard of memories stored like golden guineas which the passing years cannot contaminate.

If I close my eyes and think of all I have seen in a lifetime of playing and watching cricket, I see Fred Trueman bowling to Tom Graveney at New Road, Worcestershire, in 1962. Tom had just qualified for the home county and he celebrated the move by scoring 1,539 runs at an average of 48.09. At the same time, playing for England against the Pakistan tourists, he scored 401 runs at an average of 100.25. In the same season Fred Trueman was England's main wicket-taker in Tests with 22 at under 20 each and in county cricket 106 wickets at 17.82.

But statistics are not why I remember that day. It was the perfect setting for Tom Graveney. His elegance at the crease and his languid strokeplay deserved the setting of cathedral and river. And Fred, for all the fire and brimstone of his personality, had an action of such purity and grace that watching him bowling and Tom batting in that setting was a never-to-be-forgotten sight. Tom batted better than Fred bowled and his 80-odd on a seaming wicket was a masterpiece.

Twenty years later and Tom Graveney, now in his 60s and long retired, came to my local cricket club at Bray in Berkshire. His son Tim was first-team captain and we were having a fun game to raise funds. Tom sportingly agreed to turn up and venture into the middle although he had not played for a good number of years. I was umpiring as he took guard and hoped our first bowler, a tearaway from Australia, might have enough sense to give Tom a courtesy one off the mark. At it was he came charging in at full tilt and bowled a quick bouncer which Tom swayed away from and then gave the bowler what is often described as an old-fashioned look.

A further bouncer followed but this time Tom moved forward and inside the line and flicked the ball into the adjoining churchyard for six. The next ball went even further into the gravestones and when the bowler pitched up Tom unfurled (there is no other way to describe it) a cover drive of such grace and elegance he should have been wearing a powdered wig and silk knee breeches.

At the end of the over our bowler said, 'Jeez, the old bugger can bat. Who is he?'

'Tom Graveney,' I said.

It meant nothing.

'Who did he play for?' asked the bowler.

'Gloucester, Worcestershire and England,' I said.

I cannot repeat the Aussie's reply.

If I analyse my most lasting memories of cricket they all feature players of graceful manner. Tom Graveney in full flow was effortless and unfeigned. There were no curlicues or flourishes. The beauty of his play was its simplicity, its lack of vanity. What you learn about style is it can't be taught. Those who try look like frauds. Those who possess such a gift simply can't help it.

Andrew Murtagh has written Tom's story with thorough research and sympathetic understanding of a man who was often misunderstood and sometimes controversial except in one regard: everyone agreed he was a batsman of unique style, and not the kind of cricketer who fades from memory.

Preface

I saw Tom Graveney bat once. I wonder how many times that observation has been made the length and breadth of the cricketing world. I have heard it often enough during the course of writing this book. And the odd thing is that it is usually accompanied by a glazing over of the eyes and a settling of the facial expression into a warm glow of nostalgia, rather like the recollection of a pleasant meal, together with a nice bottle of wine, during a particularly intense holiday romance.

Clearly, to the transfixed onlookers, a Graveney innings was much more than the sum of its parts. It transcended the number of runs that he had scored, even the context of the match in which it had been played. Frequently the teller of the anecdote was hazy about the exact details of the game itself – 'It was against the Australians in 1956…or was it the West Indies in 1957? Anyway, he was batting at Lord's…oh, hang on a minute, was it the Oval? Never mind – what I remember is the cover drive for four…'

Sport can do this to you. A moment of supreme skill, matchless artistry, breathtaking athleticism and surpassing grace can make you blink in disbelief and the memory of it stays with you forever.

Can it therefore be taken as read that a thing of transient beauty can be more important than the result of the game? Can a delicate chip over the goalkeeper, an outrageous dummy by a wing three-quarter, a cross-court bullet of a backhand take on any the more or less significance if the match is lost?

The long-suffering fan, ardent for success, would say no. But the two elements – the artistic and the prosaic – do not have to be mutually exclusive. Kelly Holmes, when she won Olympic gold in the 1,500 metres in Beijing in 2008, seemed to be floating effortlessly over the track while her competitors huffed and puffed and went backwards. The Spanish football team won the World Cup by simply passing the ball to each other, weaving intricate patterns all over the pitch, while their opponents chased shadows. Roger Federer is like liquid as he moves around the court, producing elegant winners, barely breaking sweat.

It is said that Tom Graveney never played an ugly stroke. A rash one perhaps, or a false one, or even not one at all, but never one that offended the eye. The trouble is that when a stylish batsman gets out playing a languid shot, he is accused of being 'loose' and failing to concentrate. Whereas, if the stroke results in the ball being caressed to the boundary, a collective sigh of appreciation goes up from the spectators, who turn to each other and say, 'Did you see *that*?'

A batsman of more recent vintage but of similar gracefulness to Tom Graveney was David Gower. He suffered from the same sort of criticism in his career, that he was too nonchalant at times, but he always had his answer ready. 'I scored 8,231 Test runs,' he would retort. 'So I must have been doing something right.' Tom's response to the charge that he was too carefree for the rigours of Test cricket is not so pointed but equally pertinent. 'I scored a few,' he grinned. 'And I didn't bat too badly, did I?'

I should say so. By 'a few', he meant 47,793 first-class runs, with 122 centuries. Of course, bald statistics do not tell the whole story. In Tom Graveney's case, it is not just the runs on the board, nor the numbers in the record books, which cricket lovers prefer to remember, but the manner in which he made them.

Nevertheless, it is illuminating to keep his career figures in mind when we try to assess his impact on the history of post-war English cricket. He was a serious player in a golden age of English bats-manship, who started his England career batting with Len Hutton and ended it with another Yorkshireman, Geoff Boycott. The runs he scored were beautifully crafted but, my goodness, they were as invaluable as anyone's to the cause of Gloucestershire, Worcestershire and England. He was as worthy of his place at the top table of English batsmen in the 1950s and 60s as Hutton, Compton, May, Cowdrey, Dexter and Barrington and anyone else you care to mention.

But was he a 'great' batsman, as opposed to a very, very good Test player? Greatness as a sobriquet is much bandied about – too much, one might say – and we need to be quite clear what we are talking about here. Many English kings were given epithets – Ethelred the Unready, Edward the Confessor, William the Conqueror – but only one, Alfred, was termed the Great, for rather more, one imagines, than his expertise in the kitchen.

In most people's estimation, Shakespeare was a great dramatist but could the same be said of his contemporaries – Marlowe, Jonson, Kyd – who arguably wrote great plays too? Beethoven was a great composer but Elgar could bang out a tune to knock your socks off and Haydn wrote nearly as many symphonies as Graveney scored hundreds. Were they great too? All of a sudden, defining 'greatness' throws up all sorts of caveats and complications.

There are a certain handful of cricketers in the history of the game who, without argument, are placed in the pantheon, the elite, the premier league: Grace, Bradman, Hammond, Sobers, Warne and…then it starts to get tricky. Barnes? Headley? Hobbs? Hutton? Pollock? Tendulkar? Richards (Viv or Barry)? Lara? Muralitharan? Already, I hear you taking issue with me and arguing the case for other, equally worthy candidates. In the end, of course, it is no more than a pleasant, but pointless, exercise. Does it really matter? And how can you compare one player to another from different eras? Or a bowler to a batsman?

Was Tom Graveney a great batsman? Some say he was. Others baulk at the ultimate accolade. But just to satisfy an inward curiosity, I decided to put the question to the man himself. He frowned as he gave the matter some thought. 'No, I wouldn't say that I was a great batsman.' And then a slow smile spread across his face. 'But I would say that I played some great innings!'

If you saw him bat, doubtless you have already made up your mind. If you didn't, listen to the opinions of others in this book and form your own judgement. That he was touched by greatness is indisputable and in this, friend and foe, team-mate and opponent, all are agreed. Tom Graveney played some of the most perfect, most accomplished, most graceful innings of anyone who has taken guard.

I saw Tom Graveney bat once. I really did. He was 76 not out at the time. Years that is, not runs. The date was 2 May 2003. The occasion was the formal opening of the new, all-weather cricket nets at Malvern College. They were to be dedicated to George Chesterton, a lifetime stalwart of the college, master in charge of cricket and a former opening bowler for Worcestershire.

'Would you like me to bring along my old friend Tom Graveney to help with the show?' he asked me. I considered this offer for two seconds and accepted. As it happened, Tom Graveney was George's maiden first-class victim, in the 1949 season, one an undergraduate playing for Oxford, the other a young and rising star for Gloucestershire. Later, much later, George had become president of Worcestershire CCC and Tom had succeeded him. They had become firm friends.

It was a delightful little scene. The cricket ground at Malvern College is pleasantly situated on the slopes of the Malvern Hills, with a panoramic view out over the Severn Valley and the Vale of Evesham. On a clear day, the Cotswolds can be seen in blue outline across the valley.

A small crowd of interested spectators had gathered: boys, masters, groundsmen, parents, press, passers-by. Tom had been an easy guest, effortlessly mingling with, and chatting to, all and sundry. Suddenly, he grabbed a spare bat. 'How about a net, George?' he loudly suggested. George needed no second bidding and picked up a ball. I cannot pretend that I was not a little perturbed. George was 81 and Tom 76. I was responsible for these two elderly men. And they were going to have a net!

'Come on, George,' urged Tom, taking guard. 'Put it on the spot, as you always did.' George paced out his run. Not the ten yards that it used to be in his pomp, admittedly – more like a hop and a step. But the arm came over, ramrod straight, and the ball was delivered, as requested, on a length and at off stump. Tom leaned forward and with perfect timing, stroked it into the side-netting. A Graveney cover drive. Has there ever been a more famous stroke in the history of the game? A discernible purr of appreciation from the onlookers suggested there had not. It was a lovely moment. Poignantly, it was the last time George Chesterton ever bowled a ball and the last time Tom Graveney picked up a bat.

Following this encounter with Tom, I made it a point to visit him whenever I was in Cheltenham, which is where he lives. He was generous with his time and only too willing to recount stories about his career, which I was only too willing to listen to. Slowly, it dawned on me that I would like to record these memories and anecdotes before they were lost forever; in other words, I felt impelled to write the story of his life. But would he agree?

Tentatively, I broached the subject and surprisingly, he readily agreed. 'I've been done before, you know,' he warned me. Of course he has been 'done' before. How foolish of me to think otherwise. 'How many times?' I asked, my heart sinking. 'Oh, three or four. I forget exactly.' With more confidence than I felt, I assured him that my version would be….well, *different*. 'Of course it will,' he said. Not the least attractive trait of this man is a willingness to praise and to encourage rather than to throw a damp towel over things.

Accordingly, I would drive down to Cheltenham every week to see him and to record the narrative of his life. He had a fund of stories and tales to tell of his cricketing career and I was gripped. Two things intrigued me. It is well documented that he had two notorious brushes with MCC, at the time the governing body of cricket, which had resulted in bans, of one form or another. How come? Tom is the least confrontational man I know. His easy-going charm and geniality are well known. And why was he left out of the England side for long stretches of time when players of lesser ability were chosen ahead of him? These were conundrums that I was anxious to explore.

Did I uncover the truth of the controversies? I really don't know. Often one man's account is set against another's and you just have to make up your own mind on the balance of probability and on the evidence before you. The trouble was that these incidents happened a long time ago and many of the principal characters are now dead.

But did it really matter who was in the right? I came to realise that I only had, for the most part, Tom's side of the story and, frankly, that was all that interested me. This was not going to be a history book, nor a no-holds barred, sensationalised biography, but a chronicle of changing social and sporting times seen through his eyes.

He was *there*, you see. He was in the team that won back the Ashes in 1953 after 19 years of disappointment. He played in the fixture when the fledgling state of Pakistan won their first Test match against the mother country in 1954. He played against Garry Sobers when Sobers made his Test debut as a 17-year-old in 1954. He was fielding at slip when Tyson blew away the Aussies in 1954/55. He hit a majestic 258 (his highest score) against the West Indies in 1957. He was on the infamous tour of Australia in 1958/59, marred by the throwing controversy.

He was banned from county cricket for the whole of the 1961 season because he wanted to move from Gloucestershire to Worcestershire after having been sacked as captain. He was part of the Worcestershire side that won back-to-back County Championships in 1964 and 1965.

He made a triumphant return to the England side at the age of 39 in 1966, scoring a memorable 165 in a famous eighth-wicket partnership of 217 with John Murray to beat the West Indies at the Oval. He played the innings of his life on a wicked turner at Lord's in 1967 against the masterful Indian spinners Chandrasekhar, Bedi and Prasanna.

He was in that famous photo when Underwood claimed the last Australian wicket at the Oval in 1968 to beat Australia, with everyone on the pitch, save the square leg umpire, in shot. This was the same match in which D'Oliveira scored 158 and then was shockingly left out of the touring party that winter to South Africa, which led to the tour's cancellation and South Africa's isolation from Test cricket for the next two decades. Graveney was great friends with D'Oliveira and stood shoulder to shoulder with him as the affair took its acrimonious and fateful course.

He was on the ill-fated tour of Pakistan of 1968/69, which was abandoned mid-Test because the country was in the throes of a violent civil war. And, finally, he was disciplined and dropped by England (for the last time) for playing in a benefit match on the Sunday of a Test match. All in all, his was an eventful career.

He reckons, what, with one thing or another, he was robbed of six years of playing for England. 'I was unlucky enough to get on the wrong side of people in charge,' he says. 'But what's the point of getting upset about it? That's life. You just have to get on with it.'

He maintains that he was fortunate to play in a golden age of English cricket. 'Most of the England players in the 50s would have got into a World XI,' he avers. 'We beat Australia three times in a row, you know. And they were a bloody good side!'

In the 60s, it was the West Indies who were the team to beat and this was the period of his 'second coming', if you like, when his talent was seen in its full flower, the glorious autumn of his career. Fulfilment came to him late.

A backbone of steel runs down his body, whatever Len Hutton said about his ruddy cheeks and his too-cheerful demeanour. Listen to this story of his son's. 'I was playing golf with Dad,' recounts Tim. 'It was a foursomes and as we walked down the first fairway, a furious row erupted between father and son over which club I should use for the next shot. I stuck to my guns, selected the club I wanted and he retreated, muttering and cursing under his breath. Well, you can guess what happened. He was right and I was wrong. We took a five and lost the hole. No son should be subjected to the thunderous look he gave me. But we won! And all was well. You know, Dad is so competitive he would go head to head with his granny to win a game.'

Bear that in mind as the narrative of Tom Graveney's life gently unfolds.

Spiritual Home

Lord's
17 June 1966

'Shove over,' he told them.

Dutifully, his team-mates shuffled along the bench to make room for him. They did so, unhesitatingly, unthinkingly, for two reasons. Tom Graveney, at 39 years of age, was the senior player in the team. And he was next in to bat.

The dressing room at Lord's is spacious and well appointed – 'unlike a few others I could mention', he thought grimly – but by contrast the balcony is small and does not permit all 11 players at the same time to sit out there and watch the cricket. That is, if they want to. Graveney had a habit of not watching proceedings until he was next in and then he would go out and sit on the end – always one of the ends – of the bench until it was time for him to enter the fray.

He was superstitious, in common with many cricketers, a man of unyielding habit and routine, and as he was batting at number three, he went straight out, once he had put on his pads, to watch the first ball of England's innings. He was pleased to be at three. Your best batsman usually occupies that berth and he was sure that he was England's best batsman. He was in the form of his life and he was confident that three was where he should be.

In the past, during his long and chequered career at international level, he had never been *entirely* convinced that the selectors and the captain were wholly persuaded by his value to the team, despite his weight of runs, so he had been shifted up and down the batting order, as if no one quite knew where to put him.

Once, in New Zealand, Hutton had told him, right out of the blue, 'Come on, Tom, you're opening with me.' He hated opening. But what could you do, he reasoned at the time – you do what your captain tells you. Today, however, he was at three and that suited him fine. He felt grateful to Colin Cowdrey, who had just been made captain, for this gesture of confidence.

He sat down at the end of the bench, balanced his bat carefully against the wrought iron railing, checking that his chewing gum was exactly where it should be; stuck on to the splice at the back of the bat.

The first over of an innings is always a tense affair, especially for those watching on the team balcony. Even those who could not squeeze on to the balcony were peering anxiously through the windows. The one or two who were deliberately not watching had their ears pinned back. A shouted appeal and a roar from the crowd usually meant bad news; what everyone wanted was a nice, quiet, uneventful over.

There was perhaps a touch more anxiety and anticipation than usual. Everyone remembered what the West Indian fast bowlers had done to England the last time they were here in 1963. Four of this England team – Barrington, Cowdrey, Parks and Titmus – had been playing in that famous Test. Wes Hall had broken the arm of Cowdrey, who came to the wicket for the last over of the game, arm in plaster, with all four results still possible.

So, let's see if Hall and Griffith are as fearsomely quick as they were three years ago. Hello! Garry's taking the first over from this end. That's a bit of a surprise. Since the last time the West Indies were in England, Sobers's new-ball bowling had increased in effectiveness; he was now the genuine article as an all-rounder. So, perhaps it was not so much of a surprise to see him marking out his run.

'Let's hope he bowls lots and lots of overs,' said Tom, to no one in particular.

'Why's that, Tom?'

'Then he'll be too tired to bat.'

'Don't you believe it.'

'Well, at least we wouldn't see him until lower down the order.'

Conversation lapsed as they watched the first over, negotiated without alarm. Now it was Hall from the Nursery End. Had he lost pace over the past year or so, they wondered. The first few balls settled the matter. No, it seemed he was as quick as ever, careering in like a runaway train off that long run of his, all flailing arms and wicked intent.

Graveney's mind flitted back to another Test match at this same ground, against the Australians in 1953. He was batting with Len Hutton. As it happened, he bowed to no one in his admiration for Hutton as a batsman, 'a great player' he would say, 'even after the war, with one arm shorter than the other'. But on this occasion, he felt that he played every bit as well as Hutton.

Together, the two of them had put the Australian attack – Lindwall, Miller, Johnston, Davidson, Benaud – to the sword, in an exhibition of batsmanship that *Wisden* described as 'glorious to behold'. Even now, Graveney savoured the memory. At the close of play they strode off, masters of the situation, Hutton unbeaten on 83 and Graveney on 78. The next morning, 'Len being Len, he told me I mustn't get out and that we should build up a big lead.'

Upon resumption, Lindwall immediately bowled Graveney. 'Len rarely showed his emotions but I knew he was furious,' Tom repeatedly recounted afterwards. 'But I tell you it was the best ball I ever received, a fast in-swinging yorker. I jabbed down on it and hit it quite hard actually, but it squeezed in underneath and castled me.' Later, Lindwall confirmed that he had never bowled a better delivery.

Tom smiled to himself. *That was 15 years ago! Then, I was playing with Hutton. Now it's Boycott out there. I've straddled two generations. Two generations? It feels like two centuries.*

He took a deep breath. He was nervous, he didn't mind admitting. All batsmen are nervous before they go into bat, he knew that as well as anyone, but this was different. After a three-year gap, during which England had played 37 Test matches, he had been recalled to the side.

The news had come like a bolt from the blue. After a disappointing Ashes tour to Australia in 1962/63, he had been dropped. He believed that his international career was at an end. At his age, he was unlikely to earn a reprieve. He had long since given up any hope of it and had instead concentrated on scoring runs – lots of them – for Worcestershire.

The irony was that he felt that, in spite of the fact that he was in his late 30s, he was batting better than ever. This Indian summer of form he could ascribe to nothing other than a conviction, at last, of his being valued in the team as the number one batsman, someone upon whom everybody else relied. He preferred to have this responsibility thrust upon him; it gave him a sense of his own worth and he enjoyed having to rise to the challenge. Hitherto, he had never felt *totally* trusted by a succession of England captains, from Hutton down to Dexter. Now he had the opportunity, albeit a little late in his career, to put that right and he had jolly well better not squander the chance.

He took a deep breath. *Come on, have confidence in yourself. You love this ground, you've played here often enough and scored runs. You normally do well against the West Indies. What about that 258 you scored against them at Trent Bridge in 1957? No need for nerves. Not now, of all days. It was your birthday yesterday. Take that as a good omen.*

The trouble with waiting to go into bat, unlike a trip to the dentist, is that you never know when the precise moment will come when you are called. It could be in the next few seconds; it could be hours. *I could be up here all afternoon and evening. And I probably will be, if Boycott has his way. He likes to 'book in for bed and breakfast', as he never tires of saying.* Tom rather hoped that would not be the case and that he would be batting sooner rather than later. Not that he wanted a wicket to fall.

He didn't have long to wait. With only eight runs on the board, a great shout went up from Wes Hall and the rest of the West Indian fielders, Milburn was the batsman and the umpire's finger went up. Immediately, Graveney was on his feet, picking up his bat, popping the chewing gum into his mouth and putting on his gloves.

As he made his way across the dressing room floor to the door, he donned his blue England cap, vaguely aware of muttered expressions of good luck from his team-mates as he exited the room. Most people associate cricketers coming downstairs with the clatter of studded boots on concrete. But Lord's is different. There is an almost funereal hush as the footsteps are muffled by carpet and rubber underlay. Usually, at the bottom of the stairs, Tom would have turned right into the Long Room. For Test matches, however, the England team occupied the home dressing room, normally the domain of Middlesex, and it was on the other staircase. He turned left, quickening his stride. He wanted to get out there as quickly as possible.

The Long Room was jam-packed, as it usually was for Test matches. On this occasion, the members were all on their feet, cheering loudly. Tom had never heard that before and was for a moment nonplussed. *Why are they making such a din?* It then dawned on him that they were cheering him. Embarrassed, he put his head down and stepped through the throng, which dutifully parted to make way for him, applauding and acclaiming him all the while. *What's going on? MCC members just don't do this. At best, it's just a smattering of polite clapping.*

He strode through the open French windows and down the steps and became aware that the whole pavilion, members in their blazers and egg and bacon ties, were on their feet, clapping and cheering. The attendant at the bottom of the steps was standing back, holding the gate ajar as Tom walked through, a ridiculous grin splitting his face.

Like all cricketers who play at Lord's, Tom experienced that familiar frisson of pleasure and anticipation as he set foot on the grass, no longer taken aback by the pronounced slope, left to right, of the outfield, as he was on his first outing on this ground, way back in 1949.

He was aware that every single spectator in the ground on that Friday afternoon was on their feet, applauding his every step to the middle. *My God, what a reception! And I haven't even scored a run yet.* He gulped, trying to get rid of that lump in his throat. England were 8/1 and he needed to concentrate. He touched and tugged at his cap, familiar gestures to Graveney watchers.

As he took guard, he was aware of Seymour Nurse racing from slip to have a word with Wes Hall, the bowler. It was a long sprint. Hall started his run-up from the boundary's edge, it seemed. It often looked as if he was pushing off from the sightscreen. *I know what you're saying to him, Seymour. You're telling him I'm a front-foot player and that he should test me with a short one. As if Wes doesn't know that by now! Right then, let's get straightaway on to the back foot.*

It is always a gamble to second-guess a bowler's intention but sure enough, Tom was correct in his prediction. First ball, Hall sent down a rapid bouncer and Tom was ready for it, swaying out of the way.

At the end of the over, the two batsmen sauntered down the wicket, with every appearance of studied nonchalance, to exchange a few words.

'Flippin' 'eck!' said Boycott, tapping down a few imaginary divots with the heel of his bat. 'That were a helluva reception you got there, Tom. What's oop, your birthday or summat?'

'No. But it's bloody terrifying, Geoffrey.'

'Good look.'

'Don't worry, I will.'

Boycott shook his head and wandered off, once again enveloped in his cocoon of single-minded concentration. Then Tom realised that he might have misunderstood his Yorkshire partner. *I think probably he said 'good luck'.*

For the first few overs or so, Tom played well within himself. He was seeing the ball well enough but he was being cautious. Then he leant in to a couple of drives, which found the middle of the bat, the ball streaking across the outfield most satisfactorily for four, and he was away. His feet were moving well and he seemed to be timing the ball nicely. All initial nerves melted away and he believed that he was set for a big score, provided he didn't do anything stupid.

Jim Parks, England's wicketkeeper, remembers the innings very well. 'I was at the other end for a while. Tom was such an elegant batsman. He seemed to have so much time to play the ball. He made it look effortless and easy. And the West Indies had the best attack in the world, don't forget. He was like Colin Cowdrey – he didn't have to smash the ball to the boundary, he just eased it off the face of the bat with enough timing for it to reach the boundary without hitting the boards and bouncing halfway back to the wicket. And this was his first Test back after a break of three years. Amazing!'

Tom lost his partner Boycott for 60 just before the close of play, with the score at 123, but there were no further setbacks before the umpires removed the bails. He was batting so well that he was a little sad that he couldn't continue but he was happy enough with his 65 not out as he walked off. The ovation that he received from the crowd was every bit as warm as his reception when he came out. This time, he raised his bat to acknowledge the applause and hurried up the pavilion steps to seek the sanctuary of the dressing room. *At least I've done myself justice and not let the supporters down.*

Later, soaking his tired muscles in a hot bath, he allowed himself a sigh of deep satisfaction. He was in good form and he had managed to transfer that feeling of confidence to the grand stage, which was an immense relief. He had also wrested the initiative away from his opponents and he knew only too well how that West Indian attack could rip apart an innings once they got within sniffing distance of an opening. He and Boycott had slammed shut that opening. *Hopefully, we can consolidate tomorrow and build up a significant lead. And I want a hundred, I really do.*

But most of all, he was thankful once again to be in the international arena, where he felt he belonged.

He reached for his towel. *Yes, it's good to be back.*

Lord's
19 June 1969

'Morning, Tom.'

'Good morning, sir. How are you?'

'Fine, thank you. Good luck today.'

He knows why I'm here, thought Tom Graveney, as he walked through the Grace Gates. Tom had always got on with the gatemen at Lord's and had never been refused admission, which is almost a rite of passage for cricketers, of whatever country or team. *They always seem to recognise me.* He might have added had he thought about it that gatemen the length and breadth of the country recognised Tom Graveney. He was that sort of man, always prepared to share a cheery word with even the most humble of staff members. Doormen, barmen, waitresses, stewards, groundsmen, paper sellers, dressing room attendants… You would be hard pressed to find anyone who worked at a cricket ground who had a bad word to say about him. A man of the people, you might say.

But not of MCC, it seemed. The gateman knew, the doorman at the entrance to the pavilion, he knew too, judging by the look on his face, the steward who escorted him upstairs, he knew too – 'everyone bloody knows why I'm here,' thought Tom, bitterly.

In the lavatory – *It's funny that I didn't know where it was, seeing that I've played here countless times* – he checked his tie in the mirror, trying to stem a rising tide of panic as he contemplated what was ahead of him. *Lindwall and Miller – I could cope with them. Heine and Adcock too. Hall and Griffith. They held no terrors. But committees, legal people, MCC bigwigs, all articulate and slippery, well, that's not my cup of tea. I prefer to play the game, when your opponent is visible and in front of you, not all this political stuff, when you don't know who is your enemy and who is your friend.*

He took a deep breath, opened the door and made his way to the committee room, affecting a nonchalance that he did not feel. *Usually, in this building, I'm in my whites and everything is fine. Whenever I have to wear a suit, I seem to be in trouble.* Once more, he nervously fingered the knot of his tie.

For the umpteenth time, he went over in his mind the events that had led to this state of affairs. Worcestershire had agreed to grant him a benefit for the 1969 season. Every professional cricketer had need of the money raised during his benefit year (that is, if he was lucky enough to be awarded one); cricket was not a lucrative trade, neither was it a lengthy one.

Tom was 42 and had been fortunate to survive so long in the game but he had to think of the future; he had a wife and two children, he had no qualifications outside cricket and he couldn't go on playing for ever. His benefit was important to him. Through mutual friends, he had been introduced to Tony Hunt, the chairman of Luton Town Football Club. He was a sports fanatic and wanted to organise a charity match in Luton, with a number of guest celebrities in the two teams. Knowing that it was Tom's benefit year, he offered him £1,000 to take part.

These benefit matches, usually on a Sunday, were a familiar feature of the cricketing landscape hitherto. Professional cricketers played two three-day matches during the week, with Sundays off, thereby freeing them to take part in these harmless, though lucrative, jamborees. The trouble was that this year, 1969, saw the inauguration of the new Sunday League. Consequently, the number of free Sundays had become severely restricted.

One of the two Sundays when Worcestershire did not have a match was Sunday 15 June. That was the date scheduled for the Luton match. However, herein lay a problem. It fell on the rest day of the first Test match against the West Indies and Tom was likely to be playing. He was in a quandary and unsure what to do.

But they know all this. They won't be quizzing me about the background. All they will be interested in is what happened between Alec and me in that phone call.

Alec Bedser was the chairman of the England selectors. He and Tom knew each other well. They had played in the same England team in the early 1950s. Tom had immense respect and admiration for Bedser. *He carried the England bowling almost single-handedly in those difficult post-war years. What a bowler! What stamina! What courage! I'll always say that – and I mean it.*

Though they were not bosom pals, Tom considered that they were good friends and understood each other. Accordingly, when the clash of dates became apparent, Tom rang Bedser to seek his advice. Bedser told him that he would not be able to play in the benefit game as it was in the middle of a Test match. Tom explained that financially he could not afford to say no and that in fact he was already committed. Bedser once again voiced his disapproval and urged Tom to withdraw. 'Well, if that's the case,' said Tom, 'don't pick me.' *I said that. I know I said that. I couldn't have made it plainer.*

When the team was announced for the first Test, Graveney's name was included so he assumed that the selectors had come to some sort of accommodation about his commitment to the Luton game and that he was free to play.

Tom turned up at Old Trafford for the Test and no one, not Bedser, nor any of the other selectors, nor Ray Illingworth, the captain, mentioned Luton. England won the toss and batted. Progress was slow, Boycott occupying the crease for much of the day in scoring 128. *It was strange seeing Geoffrey out there without glasses. Still, a hundred proves that he can see just as well through those new contact lenses of his.*

Tom was 53 not out at stumps and felt that he had played pretty well, though he would be the first to admit that the West Indian attack was not as fearsome as it was when Hall and Griffith were in their pomp. He was lying in the bath, soaking his tired limbs as he always did, when Bedser came in and told him that he was not, under any circumstance, to play on the Sunday at Luton.

I now regret swearing. I shouldn't have lost my temper. But it was a shock. I was bitterly disappointed, I have to admit, and conscious that only trouble lay ahead. I had to go to Luton and that was the long and the short of it.

The next morning, perhaps distracted by the coming storm, Graveney only added 24 to his score before being bowled by Holder. *Hmm, Vanburn did me. That's gratitude for you, especially after I had arranged for him to come and play for us at Worcester! Still, I've made a mighty good signing there. I'm sure he'll take a lot of wickets for us.*

On the rest day on Sunday, Tom travelled down to Luton as arranged and played in the benefit match, as he had promised. Despite his gloomy mood, Tom smiled at the memory. *Richie Benaud and Bob Simpson were bowling to me – gentle leggies! I don't think I could have got injured if I tried.* He returned to the team hotel in Manchester in good time and hardly battle-weary.

The next morning, Bedser informed him that he had reported him to Lord's and that he would be expected to attend a disciplinary hearing on the 19th of the month. *And here I am. I'm really not looking forward to this. The MCC will find against me, I know they will. They always do. We players don't stand a chance. What rights have we got? None!*

At the time, when Bedser had told him that he had to report to Lord's, he hadn't been too worried. He had expected no less. But what happened that afternoon really rankled. *Whoever it was who made that announcement on the Tannoy when we were in the field that T.W. Graveney would be attending a disciplinary hearing at Lord's on the 19th of June, should be shot. I could have been underneath a catch – and then dropped it.*

He hadn't been underneath a catch at the time but he was certainly under a cloud. All his team-mates knew about Luton and his brush with Bedser but whatever they had thought about Tom's actions, they had been appalled that he had been subjected to such public ridicule. People in the crowd had booed at the announcement, but whether that was in support of Tom or not, he really didn't know. *I bet that damned announcer doesn't get hauled over the coals, just like I'm about to.* His mood of dark foreboding had intensified. He felt sure that he was about to be hung out to dry.

He was ushered into the committee room. He remembered all too vividly the last time he was escorted into a Lord's committee room. On that occasion, MCC officials were also sitting in judgement of him, his cricketing future in their hands. He felt equally powerless then as he felt now. It was in 1960 and they were banning him from county cricket for one year, as a period of registration, because he had wanted to move from Gloucestershire to Worcestershire, after his home county had sacked him as captain. *How long will it be this time? Because they're bound to take Alec's word and not mine.*

It was 11am sharp when he was shown into the committee room. He counted eighteen members seated around a large table. *Eighteen! That's more than a cricket team.* Some of the members he recognised – Doug Insole, Donald Carr and one or two other familiar faces. Some looked downwards, attentively shuffling their papers. Others regarded him with interest.

He knew that curious stare well; he almost expected them to come over to ask for his autograph. 'For my grandson, Tom. Not for me, you understand.' The chairman of the committee swiftly called the meeting to order and politely invited Tom to give his version of the story. Tom did, as clearly and as concisely as he could, omitting nothing but taking care not to embellish either. When he had finished, the chairman thanked him and asked him to leave the room while the committee members pondered what he had said.

Tom went and sat on the balcony outside. A match was taking place. He noticed the players, recognised a few and remembered that it was a county game between Middlesex and Lancashire. An extraordinary match was unfolding. This he knew because his customary scrutiny of the cricket scores in the paper had told him that both sides had been bowled out on the first day for 91.

They don't seem to be making much of a better fist of it second time round. Oh that's out! Come on, umpire; it hit him plumb in front. He's not going to give it. Not out. Well, well, well.

Gloomily, he pondered the fact that this would be just about the first time since he was a kid that he could remember watching a county game that he wasn't playing in. *I'd much rather be batting out there than sitting up here. Wicket's doing a bit. That would be a challenge. I'd back myself though. Much more than I would back myself in there.*

Although Bedser had not spoken, Tom had been aware of the looming presence of the man as he gave evidence. Once again, he reflected on his decision to tell the truth to the committee. In spite of everything, he felt sorry for his friend and former team-mate. The conversation between them on the phone *had* taken place and he *had* told Bedser not to pick him if he wasn't to be allowed to play at Luton.

He guessed that Bedser had forgotten to inform the other selectors what had happened (Alan Smith, Billy Sutcliffe and Don Kenyon had all expressed surprise when it became clear that he was committed to play at Luton on the Sunday) and that the matter had just drifted until it was too late. *I could just say that it was a misunderstanding, that the conversation with Alec hadn't taken place, and I'll just take whatever punishment they dish out. It would save all this bother and get Alec off the hook.* But as he went through that scenario in his mind yet again, he knew that he couldn't have done it. It wasn't the truth. It wouldn't be right.

He was aware of a figure beside him. It was Donald Carr, who told him that the committee were now ready to see him. The chairman told him that they had made their decision. *I recognise him now. It's Edmund King, chairman at Warwick. He looks as if he'd rather be anywhere than sitting in that chair.*

King told Tom that they had found in favour of Alec Bedser and that he, Tom Graveney, had been informed at practice on the Wednesday before the start of the Test that he would not be allowed to play at Luton and that he had disregarded this plain instruction. Of the telephone conversation, not a word was said. Silence. Tom realised that that was it. He had been found guilty and now he was expected to leave.

He stood up. With as much composure as he could muster, he said, 'That's not true,' and walked out.

Lord's
5 October 2004

'Mr Graveney?'

'Yes.'

'Your car is ready, sir.'

'Thank you. I shall be right out.'

As he stepped out of his modest home in Cheltenham, Tom Graveney gave a little shiver. It was half past six in the morning, not yet quite light and the October weather had turned chilly. He had made sure to wear a cardigan under his blazer, for he was now 77 and felt the cold. He had never put on much weight even after he had stopped playing; he was still tall and upright and his frame was spare. But the shiver could not be wholly ascribed to the brisk morning; he had to confess to a little frisson of excitement too.

The traffic was reasonably light at this time in the morning. The meeting that he was going to was scheduled for half past eight, an early start, he thought, but he didn't mind; he had always been a man of punctuality, first in the dressing room before play, never late, always prepared. *Two hours. We should be there in plenty of time.* He settled down and watched the familiar landmarks pass by.

The gateman leaned forward, the better to see the occupant of the car. Tom pressed the button and the window noiselessly opened.

The gateman recognised Tom immediately. 'Good morning, Mr President.'

Tom gave a little laugh. 'Good morning, sir. A little early I think but you'll let us in, I hope. I need a quick net.'

The Grace Gates were obligingly opened and the car purred through.

'You can pull over, just on the right here,' he told his chauffeur. 'That'll be fine.'

To Tom's surprise, the chauffeur ignored his instructions and headed for a parking bay with the word 'President' clearly displayed on the wall. *Fair enough. At least now I haven't got to worry about finding a parking spot.* An MCC member of staff was holding open the door for him. Stiffly, he got out.

'Good morning, Mr President.'

'Morning. Thank you.'

I think I could get quite used to this.

'The pavilion is out of use,' said the liveried MCC attendant. 'The meetings are held in the Warner Stand. Shall I escort you there?'

'That's very kind of you but I don't think that will be necessary. I've been here a few times, you know.' *So often, it's become almost my second home.*

He made his way around the back of the pavilion. Refurbishment work had started the day after the last game of the season and the sound of sawing and hammering could clearly be heard as he approached the Warner Stand. Upstairs, he was greeted by Roger Knight, the MCC secretary. Tom got on well with him. Tom got on well with most people.

'Good morning, Mr President,' beamed Knight. 'Good trip up?'

'Uneventful, Roger,' he replied. 'Very like my presidency, I hope.'

Knight laughed. No doubt he hoped so too. Coffee was served and quickly the room filled. Some of the faces Tom knew but many he did not. Ever since the announcement that he was to become MCC president had been made public in April, he had been attending these meetings 'to run you in', as Knight had said to him, but he was still surprised how many people were present, all with their different jobs and areas of responsibility. *I've only got a year. How on earth am I going to get to know them all?* He may not have been able to put names to faces but they all knew him and almost without exception they came up to welcome him as their president and to wish him well. *I wish they'd stop calling me Mr President. Plain Tom will do.*

As the chairman, Charles Fry, called the meeting to order and everyone slowly took his seat, Tom allowed himself a glance out of the window, towards the pavilion to his right. The familiar Victorian frontage was covered in green tarpaulin. Tom had taken a peek at what was going on during a previous visit and been taken aback by the mess and the shambles that assailed his eyes. And the beginning of the 2005 season was only six months away. *They'll never finish it in time. And the Aussies are here next year.*

He tried to make out where the bench was where he had sat watching Middlesex play Lancashire all those years ago while a disciplinary committee determined his fate. He smiled to himself. *And now I am president of that institution that treated me so badly. Well, well, well – wonders never cease.*

The invitation to become president had been a total surprise. He had met Charles Fry in Bombay and had got along with him very well. The appointment of the next MCC president is entirely in the gift of the outgoing president and Fry had asked him. He was dumbfounded but greatly honoured. Not only on his own behalf, though that was a source of great pride to him, but for all professional cricketers up and down the land. The distinction between gentlemen and players had long since been abolished but Tom still counted himself as one of those who came from the professional ranks.

The presidents of MCC since its inception had traditionally come from the ruling class, the great and the good of the country. Tom had looked up the list of his predecessors. He had counted nine barons, six viscounts, one duke, one lord, one prime minister, one High Court judge…and Prince Philip, Duke of Edinburgh. *And now plain old Tom Graveney. The world has truly changed.* Indeed it had. In recent years former cricketers had served – Mike Brearley, Colin Cowdrey, Ted Dexter, Peter May, Tony Lewis to name a few – but their status was what Tom would still call 'amateur'. *I am the first professional president of MCC.* Once more he had to pinch himself.

He was roused from his reverie by the voice of Charles Fry as chairman welcoming Tom Graveney in his official capacity for the first time, saying how pleased everyone was to see him there and wishing him well in his term of office. A murmur of appreciative endorsement went round the table. *I ought to say something here.* He took a deep breath.

'I've only got 12 months in the job but I promise I'll do the best I can.'

Will that do? That is my intention, after all. Yes, I think it'll do.

Acknowledgements

What is history? That's a good question. I ask it because the answer is pertinent to this book. The matter came to mind following an interview by Joan Bakewell of Dominic Sandbrook, the popular social historian, in which she posed that very question. His answer was revealing. He said that he never relied on personal recollection for his research for the simple reason that it was unreliable. He depended on the written word – documents, diaries, memoranda, logbooks, notes, official papers, articles, newspaper reports – for his investigative study.

People's memories, you see, are often at fault. The police know this. One witness says the hit and run car was black; another will swear it was blue. How often have we ourselves had to eat our words, or our hat, when we have been proved wrong over something that we *knew* to be right?

So, in that sense, this book is unequivocally *not* an historical account of English cricket in the 1950s and 1960s. I have shamelessly relied on personal account, not least that of my subject. It has been my intention to record one man's memory of his cricket career that was right at the centre of the national and international game during this period. It may be of interest to cricket and social historians but it is not history.

I have tried, as far as I can, to verify dates, scores, incidents where possible and occasionally I have employed the recollections of others – family, friends, team-mates, opponents, colleagues – to add some depth and perspective to my subject's account. But mostly it is Tom Graveney's voice that you hear. From time to time, I have utilised my own voice – to question, to prompt, to delve – but I hope it does not detract from the narrative.

Tom and I met every week for over a year, spending many hours in deep conversation, which spawned the informal tone of the book. Tom said that it sounded like two old friends having a natter about life in front of a sitting room fire, and he was fine with that. For the most part, his memory was impeccable. As his friend and former Worcestershire team-mate, Duncan Fearnley, said of him, 'Tom Graveney can remember every blade of grass he ever played cricket on.'

It goes without saying that Tom's recollections are no doubt selective. How could they be otherwise? We all, to a greater or lesser extent, are tempted to re-write the past in a more favourable light to ourselves. But, by and large, his memories are not markedly self-serving. He regrets and he forgives. He bears little animosity to those who might have wronged him or misjudged him. In fact, he is remarkably generous and kind in his assessment of others. 'Look,' he said, 'I'm in my 80s now. What's the point of harbouring grudges or blaming other people at my age?'

Towards the end of the process of writing this book, his health declined and his memory faltered. For the latter events in his life I had to rely more and more on the help of his children, Becky and Tim. For this, I am grateful and let me say now that it was a privilege to be allowed into the Graveney family without let or hindrance. I could not have completed the task – indeed, I would not have attempted it – without their full cooperation and encouragement.

Others to whom I owe a debt of gratitude for helping me write this book include Duncan Fearnley, Jim Parks, Ken Graveney, David Graveney OBE, George Chesterton MBE, Peter Richardson, John Mortimore, David Allen, Tony Brown, David Courtney, Rodney Cass, Norman Gifford OBE, Mark Pougatch, Peter Baxter, Nick Hunter, Rev Mike Vockins OBE, Charles Fry, Roger Knight OBE, Sir Tim Rice, Baroness Rachel Heyhoe-Flint OBE, Sir Michael Parkinson, Lin Murtagh and Tim Jones.

1

Early Days 1927–45

'Did you ever smoke, Tom?'
'Yes, I did. Gave up when I was five.'

'Yer gan oot tha dor, oop tha rerd an farl in tha hurl.'

I beg your pardon, Tom?

'Yer gan oot tha dor, oop the rerd an farl in the hurl.'

I had no idea you could speak Anglo-Saxon.

'It's Geordie, mun. A lot of people forget I was born in North-umberland.'

A lot of people forget; in fact I would go as far as to say that a lot of people didn't know that Tom Graveney is actually a Geordie, born in Riding Mill, a small village between Hexham and Newcastle, in 1927. I guess that most people, myself included, had it in their mind's eye that Tom Graveney, with his ruddy cheeks, his open face and his genial demeanour, was the archetypal West Countryman, his roots deeply embedded in the green grass of Gloucestershire's cricket grounds.

'I supported Newcastle United as a boy,' he said by way of affirmation. 'Still do, in fact.' Fair enough. I wasn't going to take issue. They are all a bit emotional and volatile up there, especially where their football is concerned.

It transpires that Tom does not actually come from old Northumberland stock – 'To tell you the truth,' he confessed with a grin, 'those are the only words of Geordie I know' – but from antecedents firmly based in London.

His father, Alfred John, known to everyone as Jack, was actually a chorister at St Paul's when a schoolboy, and it is difficult to imagine a more London background than that. Jack married comparatively late in life, to Mary Bella Strachan, who was 15 years his junior. She came from a solid country background – her father ran a local pub – and was a brilliant cook, according to her son.

We all think that no one can cook as well as our mother, isn't that so, Tom? But Tom had a faraway look in his eyes as he told me this and seemed disinclined to enter into any metaphysical discussion on mothers and sons and Sunday roasts. 'She was a strong woman, you know,' he said at length. 'Must have been to have five children in 12 years. And we were a pretty lively bunch. Sport all day, every day.'

The five in order of age were Margaret, Ken, Tom, Maurice and Dorothy. Margaret died many years ago, Maurice died in 2008 but three are still alive at the time of writing. Dorothy married a rugby player, Gordon Lovell, who was for a while scrum-half for Bristol, and now lives in south Wales. Maurice was a good cricketer and played club cricket to a reasonably high standard but was three years younger than Tom and therefore not as close to him as his other brother, Ken, who was only two years older. By all accounts, Ken and Tom were inseparable as children, and they remain close to this day, sharing a love of all games, particularly cricket.

Of course, in the world of county cricket, Ken Graveney is almost as well known as his brother, having played for Gloucestershire, becoming captain in the 1963 and 1964 seasons. Necessarily, he features large in this account of his brother's life owing to their parallel careers in cricket and to Ken being such a formative influence on Tom, especially when they were younger. 'Ken is a great man,' Tom said, and then he fixed me with a droll grin that I soon came to recognise as a characteristic expression, 'but very *naughty!* Whenever we came home after playing outside, and I was trailing along ten yards behind, Mum would immediately know he'd been up to mischief.'

Were you ever in trouble yourself? 'Oh no,' he said virtuously. 'I was a good boy.' And again, there was that comical wince, as if to suggest that he wasn't going to admit to anything, whatever others might say.

It seemed to me at this point that it would be a good idea to contact brother Ken to confirm these boyhood memories and to give a different perspective on Tom's early life. That was easier said than done. He lives in Texas and is of course elderly now – two years Tom's senior – and not in the best of health.

To help me, I enlisted the services of Ken's son, David. He and I are old friends, our association going back many years to when we used to play cricket against each other. In fact, on my first-class debut for Hampshire against Gloucestershire, the scorecard makes dismal reading: Murtagh ct Graveney b Sadiq 0. He has never let me forget it. David of course went on to have a successful career for Gloucestershire and Durham and latterly became chairman of selectors of the England team.

'Ah, nephew David,' said Tom fondly when I told him I had contacted him, 'Gloucester had a terrific record with the Graveneys as captains, you know. Sacked all three of us!' Hmm, now there's a story for a later chapter, I thought. 'That's right,' confirmed David. 'My father got the bullet too. He's had three wives, you know, so you could say that Dad has had a… *full* life!'

So it came to pass that a transatlantic telephone conversation was scheduled and a slightly tremulous but unmistakeably Graveney voice came on the line. 'Those games of cricket we used to have outside the back door,' said Ken. 'You know, I could never get the little blighter out!' It was abundantly clear to the elder brother that the intransigent batsman at the other end of the pitch was possessed of a rare talent, even at that early age.

'He had a level of hand-eye coordination that was exceptional. It allowed him to play the ball off the wicket. He would hook the world's fastest bowlers off the front foot! I remember once when…' He then went on to marvel at some of the innings that Tom played in his career, all of which will be appraised in later chapters.

I gently tried to steer Ken back to their childhood. 'I was the rebel, you know.' I had guessed as much. 'Tom was the gentle one. He wasn't as competitive as me.' Now that surprised me. Of course Tom was competitive. You can't become one of the world's best batsmen without competitive blood coursing through your veins.

But Ken was adamant. Perhaps it was just a question of degrees, not absolutes.

'All three of us were very different, you know,' Tom told me. He paused, and I expected him to give me a thumbnail sketch of each brother, his strengths, weaknesses, personality traits and emotional contrasts.

But no. Listen to this quick analysis of the Graveney boys: 'Ken bowled fast, right hand and batted left-hand. Maurice was a slow left-armer and batted right-hand. And I bowled and batted right-handed. Curious, eh?' I laughed out loud. If ever there was any doubt in my mind that here was a man whose whole life had been informed by his love of cricket, then it was banished in that instant. And that suited me down to the ground. It reminded me a little of me, as it happens.

Jack was an engineer who worked for Vickers Armstrong, situated on the Tyne, which explains the move up north from London. 'He made the 16-inch shells for the battleships *Rodney* and *Nelson*,' said Tom proudly. 'Look – one's over there.' I cast my eyes around his small, cosy sitting room in his house in Cheltenham but could see nothing that resembled an instrument of death and destruction. Trophies, cups, silver salvers, cricket memorabilia abounded but no ordnance from a mighty ship of the line.

'There,' he pointed, 'the lamp stand.' There it was indeed, bronze, diligently polished and gleaming in the morning sun, acting as a base for a lamp, a thing of strange, stark beauty, notwithstanding its deadly function. I was impressed. Of course it wasn't a 16-inch shell – they are nearly as big as a man – but a three-and-a-half-inch shell used for a smaller gun but it looked lethal enough.

Maybe HMS *Rodney* had not fired this particular shell during her pursuit of the German battleship *Bismarck* in May 1941 but she must have fired many similar ones in one of the most famous naval engagements of the war. I fell into a reverie. *Sink The Bismarck* was the first ever film I had seen and as a young boy I had been fascinated by this story and other accounts of momentous clashes of iron leviathans at sea.

'Keen sportsman he was. Golfer, cricketer, anything.' Tom brought me back to the here and now. Idly, I assumed he was not referring to Prussia's Iron Chancellor, or to the brave commander of HMS *Rodney*, but to his father. 'Never without a fag in his mouth, rolling it from one side to the other.'

Did you ever smoke, Tom? This was not such an odd query as it might seem. Extraordinary to relate, especially from the perspective of these disapproving and health conscious times, many first-class cricketers *did* smoke in those days. 'Yes, I did,' he replied, without missing a beat. 'Gave up when I was five!'

I looked up from my notepad. His eyes were twinkling. 'It's true. Five I was when I had my first drag and there and then I decided it wasn't for me. It was all Ken's fault.'

What had happened was that their father had decided to pay the two boys a visit when they were away at Cub Scout camp in Wallsend. He was clearly a man of style because he arrived in a sleek, chauffeur-driven Armstrong Siddeley. What other car would it be for an employee of Vickers Armstrong?

With carefree benevolence, he handed the two boys 6d each, for sweets he naively believed. Ken had other ideas. He immediately went to the nearest tobacconists and purchased five Woodbines for tuppence. With commendable fraternal consideration, he encouraged his younger brother to light one up. It was not a success. 'He did me a favour really,' Tom said, 'I never touched another cigarette again.'

Another early memory he has is that the two of them used to have wrestling matches at home in front of guests before they went in to dinner. 'We were the cabaret, you could say, the warm-up act.'

Who won? He wasn't saying. 'But I do recall the golf match we had to play, with a brand-new golf bag from my dad as the prize.' He remembered who won that tussle all right. They played with special, cut-down clubs and Ken won – two and one. 'He got the bag and I got nothing,' Tom said ruefully.

An important lesson learnt early – first is first and second is nowhere. Any professional sportsman has to embrace this ruthless philosophy to succeed and Tom did not score 4,882 Test runs without having the cold glint in his eyes of the hired gun. The trick that he mastered, and this conundrum I hoped to tease out of him over the succeeding months of our conversations, is that he managed to do it with such an easy-going and good-natured personality. His enemies in the game were apparently thin on the ground. And how did he manage to convince even his brother that he wasn't competitive?

He ran away from school. I seized upon this proffered piece of information with eagerness as evidence perhaps of a future rebel and an anti-authoritarian figure. 'It was my second day, at break time. Hated it.' He remembers running home in a desperate race with his brother, who had been deputed to keep an eye on him, to reach the comforting and enfolding arms of his mother before Ken caught up with him. But it was but a blip on a generally happy childhood; he maintains without irony that his schooldays were enjoyable ones. 'How could they be anything else,' he averred, 'with all that sport?'

The family moved to a bigger house in Jesmond, a suburb of Newcastle, near to Northumberland Cricket Club, where a lot of good Minor Counties cricket was played. He remembers being taken to watch visiting touring teams at Sunderland, including India, South Africa and Australia and was struck by players such as 'Chuck' Fleetwood-Smith, Len Darling and Bill Woodfull.

One incident remains firmly fixed in his mind. The fielders applauded the Australian captain, Woodfull, to the wicket (this must have been in 1934) and immediately retreated to give him one off the mark.

Did they do that to all the incoming batsmen? 'No, only the captain. A gesture of sportsmanship, I suppose, a mark of respect. Extraordinary. Wouldn't happen nowadays.'

Something else that probably wouldn't happen nowadays was that if one of the five Graveney children caught any of the childhood diseases of the day, such as mumps or chickenpox, they were all unceremoniously bundled into the same room in the hope and expectation that the germs would be unselfishly portioned out, the better to build up resistance. It seemed to work. What with all the sport and physical activity, they were a pretty healthy family.

With the exception, that is, of their father. Inevitably, his heavy smoking took a terrible toll and he died of cancer of the lungs at the age of 51, when Tom was only six. Tom remembers the funeral and his bewilderment that everyone seemed to be laughing and getting drunk. His father was a respected and popular local figure and he could not get his young head around the adult concept of seeing off a good friend with a pint or two and a few cheerful memories. Funerals were meant to be sad and solemn affairs, he thought, and somehow laughter seemed inappropriate.

How did you get on with your dad, so far as you can remember? 'Oh, very well,' he answered without a hint of hesitation. 'He was strict but fair.'

By this time, the family had moved to Fenham, on the Gosford Road. The house backed on to the moor and the two boys, Ken and Tom, helped by their father, used to cut and roll, with great ceremony and labour, a cricket pitch on the grass outside the back door. Endless hours were spent bowling and batting – and fielding, presumably, as the ball needed retrieving after any good shot – while hotly contested matches took place.

What were they? England v Australia? Yorkshire v Lancashire? Northumberland v Durham? He grinned. 'No, just me against him. Tough enough.' *Were you at all aware at this stage of your latent talent?* He shook his head. 'Never gave it a thought. All I wanted to do was play – all day if possible.'

The death of his father did not seem to impact too gravely on the six-year-old. At least, if it did, any emotional repercussions have clearly dissipated over so many years. In any case, the mind at that age is not given to introspection and the water soon closes over unpleasant memories. That is if the family environment is a happy and caring one, which it evidently was.

The period of mourning in the household was not a protracted one. A distant cousin took a shine to their mother at the funeral and in no time at all, it seemed, had taken on the whole family. Bob Gardner was his name. Immediately, a quotation from *Hamlet* floated into my mind, 'The funeral bak'd meats / Did coldly furnish forth the marriage tables.'

Was Tom, I wondered, equally consumed with resentment of his new stepfather, and his o'er hasty marriage to his mother, as was the eponymous hero of Shakespeare's most famous play? Not a bit of it.

Tom was very fond of Uncle Bob and got on with him famously. In fact, he is full of admiration for him for looking after the family so well.

'To take on my mother, together with five kids, was quite an undertaking. I don't know how we would have coped otherwise.' Tom has nothing but good memories of the man. 'He treated us all very well. I liked him. He was no games player himself but he encouraged us and supported us.' Plainly, there were no family skeletons rattling in this cupboard.

Schooling was at the Royal Grammar School, Newcastle. Tom had no problems settling in and coped well enough with his studies. He spoke fluent Geordie then, he maintains, though there is no trace of the accent left now, of course. 'I'm pretty good at accents, you know,' he told me. 'You should have heard my Queensland accent when I was playing for them!'

Perhaps this talent to mimic accents tells us much about his ability to blend in with his surroundings, to feel comfortable and at home wherever he found himself – schools, barracks, dressing rooms, social gatherings, commentary boxes, committee rooms, pubs. He has always been clubbable man. When I asked him about the masters at RGS and what influence they had on him, he started to giggle. And then out came this, 'Buggy Little did a piddle on the coast of France. Bertie tried to do the same but did it in his pants.' The tears were rolling down his cheeks. 'They were masters at the school,' he gasped. 'Everyone used to sing it. Silly, isn't it? But it still tickles me.'

I assured him that as a former teacher I was well aware of the paroxysms of mirth that naughty little ditties can give rise to in the young. 'Don't put that in,' he implored me. 'Nonsense,' I assured him, 'no one can possibly be offended. Mr Little and Bertie won't come back from the grave and put you into detention.' By then his chortles had got to me and we had to pause for a while.

The family then moved across the country to Fleetwood in Lancashire where their mother and new stepfather opened a shop, selling anything and everything, from sweets to knitting needles. Tom attended Arnold School, where presumably he soon adopted a Lancashire accent and quickly settled into the sporting ethos of the place, which counted England footballers Jimmy Armfield and George Eastham among its old boys.

It was at this time that his mother suffered a horrific car accident. She was rushed to hospital in Manchester where she remained unconscious for four days. Tom's memories of this time are hazy – he was only seven – but he does say, with sadness in his voice, that though she survived, she was never quite the same thereafter.

By this time, war clouds were beginning to gather over Europe, something of which the young Tom was aware but not so much that it interfered with games. Uncle Bob was a very good accountant and had got a job in the building trade, cranes and suchlike. This explained yet another move for the family, this time to Avonmouth, Bristol, in 1938. In the ensuing conflict, which seemed to be fast approaching, cranes were going to be of the utmost importance in Britain's docks and Bristol was of huge strategic importance to the country.

Tom was sent to Bristol Grammar School. He was now 11 years of age. The first problem was into which of the school's houses he was going to be placed. One of the housemasters gave him a little quiz. If you can spell Strachan House (pronounced 'Strawn', as it happens), then you can come here. Tom knew the answer; of course he did. Mary Bella Strachan (also pronounced 'Strawn') was his mother's maiden name. He rattled off the answer and the die was cast – Strachan House it was and he never looked back.

Was your housemaster a helpful influence on your early life? Sometimes, you know… 'Lovely man. He was a good housemaster and I liked him.' His indulgence of his new pupil must have been sorely tested very early on. First days at a new school did not seem to have a happy effect on Tom. You will remember that he didn't even make it to break on the second morning at primary school. This time he had a fight, with a boy whom he considered was throwing his weight around too much and bullying some poor unfortunate.

Who won? Tom grimaced. 'A score draw, I think you could call it.' He then went on to say that his opponent in the schoolyard scrap later became his best friend. I looked at him but there was no hint of irony in his eyes and not for the first time I wondered at the warm-heartedness of the man. Was there no limit to his affability?

I knew that there had been moments of controversy and bitterness that had stalked his career but it was a mystery to me how any disagreeableness could loiter outside his door – it was always so hospitably wide open. No doubt the telling of the story would eventually unravel the puzzle.

In the meantime, let us delight in a young boy enjoying the opportunities to play sport that came his way at Bristol Grammar School. Rugby was the main winter game and he had never played rugby. He was a round ball man so he was sent to join the spear-carriers on a side pitch, well away from the main stage, for a peripheral game of football. He scored six goals before half-time.

A passing master spotted his potential and he was immediately drafted into the prep school team as scrum-half, a position it was felt best suited his diminutive stature. So it was no more football for him.

Rugby became his game and as he made his way up the school, and he began to shoot up, he was moved into the centres and then to blindside flanker, finally ending up as full-back for Bristol. 'Gloucester soon put paid to that,' he said ruefully. 'They didn't want one of their players getting injured in the off-season playing a dangerous game.'

Early on, he learned to kick with both feet. He used to enjoy breaking away from the scrum and making darting runs, going for drop goals if ever he was in range. Naturally, he took all the kicks. He played in a good side. Eight of them went on to play for Bristol, and one, Bobby MacEwan, became a Scottish international hooker.

The fixture list was impressive, it has to be said. Opponents included Prior Park, KES Bath, Queen Elizabeth's Hospital, Bristol and Cotham School (who counted among their alumni future team-mates Arthur Milton, David Allen and John Mortimore). The cricket was of a good standard too, he reckoned, and of course he was in the first XI at a young age.

Were you the captain? 'No, a chap called David Dalby was the captain, and a very good one too. He later went on to become the chief executive at Kent.'

How many hundreds did you score at school? He shook his head. 'None, surprisingly enough. I was more of a bowler then, an out and out quickie. Well, *I* thought I was fast!'

Do you remember any of the masters? Your cricket coach? He laughed. 'Mr Tulloch! He had a whistle tied to a length of string around his neck. If you did anything wrong, he'd wheel it around in his hand and catch you on the backside! Good coach though. In fact, I got on well with most of the masters.' Now, there's a surprise.

And how were you academically? 'All right. I was quite bright and coped well enough.' He failed his School Certificate, as it happened, because he narrowly missed out on the pass mark for one of the subjects – English Language – and as the rules applied then, that wiped out the whole exam but he put that right the next term and passed with five credits.

I wondered how the family had managed to pay the fees. His father, with commendable foresight, had set up a trust before he died which funded his education. 'I thoroughly enjoyed my time at school,' Tom said, finally. 'They were good times and I made many friends in all the teams I played.'

I believe in the truism that team sport engenders friendship and camaraderie. And if you're good at playing games, unless you are a thorough going scoundrel, of course, the respect that you are afforded is usually assured. This may seem unfair to social commentators and champions of equality but it does seem to be an inescapable fact of life. Tom Graveney is patently a case in point. Certainly his childhood was remarkably stable and carefree.

This idyll came to a shuddering halt in September 1939, when war with Germany was declared. Or, to be more precise, it was in November of 1940 when the Luftwaffe turned its attention on the city of Bristol. It was an obvious target, not only for its docks but also because of the nearby aerodrome at Filton, home to the Bristol Aeroplane Company, which manufactured the Blenheim, Beaufort and Beaufighter aircraft, among others.

For the next six months, Bristol took a fearful pounding. Indeed, it was calculated that the city was the fifth most heavily bombed target in Britain during the war, behind London, Hull, Birmingham and Southampton. After one particularly heavy raid, the Lord Mayor of Bristol said, 'The city of churches in one night became the city of ruins.'

Tom was now 13, still not of an age when much introspection is going on but old enough to see and understand what was happening all around. He didn't believe all the good stories and the propaganda pushed out by the news and information services. Coventry had been severely bombed just ten days previously and it had been widely reported by the newspapers. Fearing a disastrous collapse of public morale, the government chose not to make known the full extent of the blitz on Bristol, referring vaguely to a raid on 'a town in the west'.

The evidence of Tom's own eyes told a different story as he made his way daily to and from school in those dark days. He remembers one intense night of bombing and being appalled at the scenes of destruction and devastation the next morning. He has a recollection of exploding bombs getting louder and nearer, one dropping on a property not far up the road from where they lived. An Anderson shelter took a direct hit and all those inside were pulverised. The fuel tanks down in the docks exploded and lit up the night sky. He remembers being on fire-watching duties at school and a visit by Queen Mary just before Christmas in 1940, when he was dressed in his best bib and tucker as a sergeant in the Combined Cadet Corps.

Into the New Year and still Bristol suffered. On 3 January, during a 12-hour raid, a 4,000lb bomb was dropped, the largest in the Luftwaffe's armoury. It did not explode. After being made safe it was dug out (it had penetrated to a depth of 30 feet) and was eventually used in the victory parade in London in 1945. Bristolians gave it the name of 'Satan'.

In March, following yet another heavy raid, a report from the Mass Observation Unit noted, 'People are getting worn out with the continual bombardment in a place where every bomb is a bomb somewhere quite near you and at you. The irregular, sporadic sudden switching of heavy raids here has a strongly disturbing effect.'

The infamous and so-called Good Friday raid was one of the worst, though thankfully also one of the last. The suburbs of the city were hit, probably by mistake, as it was believed that nearby Filton was the target. In all, Bristol was bombed 77 times, 1,300 people lost their lives and the damage to buildings and dwellings was incalculable.

I make these observations – shocking though they undoubtedly are – for no other purpose than to try to gauge the effect of relentless bombardment in a time of war on a 13-year-old boy.

How were you affected, Tom? He shrugged his shoulders. 'You just got on with it, I suppose.' And that was all he said. Or was prepared to say.

Most young boys, no matter how straitened their circumstances, usually find casual opportunity for fun and games. Ken used to collect the most extraordinary and hazardous paraphernalia and hide it all under the house. A city that is being bombed provides rich pastures for the accumulation of the detritus of war, especially for kids with recklessness in their veins and not an ounce of fear in their hearts.

Tom used to follow his brother home on these occasions, trailing the obligatory ten yards behind, not at all sure of the wisdom of some of Ken's additions to his collection. One such was a canister that had been dropped by the Luftwaffe, one of thousands of parachute flares. He had watched it come down and knowing the terrain round about, he knew exactly where it had landed. Careful searching located its whereabouts and, proudly, he bore it home, to take pride of place in the secret stash under the house.

Tom shuddered at the memory. 'God knows what we had under there. Must have been a fire risk. But Ken was like that – fearless.' Ken remembers the occasion well. Apparently he used to collect a lot of these flares that had for one reason or another failed to ignite. He would sell them to the fire brigade at 6d a time. This one was special. The silk parachute was still intact.

Who did you sell that to, Ken? He replied that he had absolutely no intention of telling me. 'But let's just say,' he finally revealed, 'that I was of an age that knew the birds from the bees!'

They remembered rationing. What healthy teenager with a bottomless stomach wouldn't? Although Tom believes that in some ways they were able to avoid the worst of it. A US naval commander was billeted at their house and frequently bore gifts and presents from Uncle Sam. This American liked his golf and many were the times when Tom would creep into his room and look admiringly at the set of new golf balls in his bag. In wartime, you see, you couldn't afford to lose many balls. 'But I never took any,' said Tom with an innocent look on his face that suggested he had been sorely tempted.

Mention of golf set him off on one of his stories. As we have seen, he loved his golf and had played ever since he was old enough to stand up. A member at the club where he used to hack around watched a few strokes and was clearly impressed. He asked him to play with him in the Easter Handicap. They went to see the club secretary who wanted to know Tom's handicap. Of course, he didn't have one. 'What do you usually go round in?' he was asked. Tom airily replied, 'Oh, about 80.' 'Right then – your handicap will be eight.' At which point in the story, Tom started off on one of his uncontrollable giggles. 'We thrashed them,' he chortled. 'My handicap was soon reduced to five, as you can imagine.'

What was your handicap when you were playing at your best? 'One,' he replied without a trace of conceit. 'Could have been scratch if I'd been able to play more regularly.' To anyone ignorant of the game, it need only be said that a scratch golfer is a seriously good player.

The gods apportion sporting prowess with occasional unreasonable inequality. Knowing that a contemporary of his, Ted Dexter, was a golfer who could just as easily have made his name on the fairway as at the crease, I asked him if he had ever played the great man. Many times apparently. After retirement, both men worked for the BBC commentating on Test matches and they frequently went for a round of golf before broadcasting began. 'Beat him six and four once,' Tom announced proudly. Though he did acknowledge that Dexter was the better player.

School life came to an end when he was 17. 'Seventeen and a half, to be precise,' said the mathematician. This is no mere quip. He was good at maths and it was expected that he would end up in accountancy, like his stepfather. But a few days' work experience in an office put paid to that. A nine-to-five job in a suit and tie certainly didn't appeal.

'So I joined up on the very day that I was old enough.' This was in January 1945 and the war was far from over. His brother had gone into the Royal Marines, becoming a lieutenant in 42 Commando and had seen 128 consecutive days of active service on the front line at the D-Day landings and thereafter through the killing fields of northern France. He had been invalided home with battle exhaustion, just before the Battle of Walcheren.

In the breakout from Normandy, the supply lines of the Allied forces had become stretched further and further. The capture of Antwerp, a deep-water port, was crucial. Walcheren Island stood at the mouth of the estuary and it was heavily fortified by German troops. It was a bloody battle to secure it. Ken was lucky to have missed it. His platoon was wiped out. So his younger brother could not possibly be joining up in a spirit of naive jingoism.

So why did you volunteer? He pursed his lips. 'I don't know,' he said. 'I'd been in the CCF at school and it seemed the logical thing to do, to join the Army. I just wanted to get involved. What I was sure about was that I didn't want to be an accountant!'

So he did not put away his school uniform and don a suit and a white collar. No, it was to be a uniform of an altogether rougher cloth.

2

Army 1945–48

'If it hadn't been for my brother, I'd have been a general!'
(Capt T.W. Graveney)

Early one morning in January 1945, Adolf Hitler was awakened by one of his lackeys.

'Entschuldigung, mein Fuhrer.'

Hitler rubbed his eyes. He hadn't been getting much sleep in recent months.

'Ja?'

'A secret communique has just reached us. It says that…that…'

The adjutant was clearly agitated.

'What is it, man? Spit it out!'

'Apparently Tom Graveney has just volunteered for service in the British Army.'

Hitler sank back on his pillow. Suddenly, he looked careworn and drained.

'Then the war is lost,' he said simply.

In actual fact, when Tom accepted the King's shilling in January 1945, there was no guarantee that the war was going to finish any time soon. We know now that the tide had already turned decisively in the Allies' favour by then but if you were a serving soldier – or, for that matter, a suffering civilian – in any of the battle zones, you might be forgiven for thinking that ultimate victory, and peace, was hardly just over the horizon.

In Europe, the Battle of the Bulge, the German counter-offensive in the heavily forested mountains of the Ardennes, was still raging. The bitter conflict on the Eastern Front saw no abatement. US Marines had not yet landed on Iwo Jima. The destructive and controversial bombing of Dresden had not yet taken place. The fateful crossing of the Rhine by the combined forces of British and American armies did not happen until March.

The point is that no one volunteering to join the armed services at that stage of the war could possibly have stated with any certainty that he would not see battle.

Were you worried, Tom, at the possibility of having to fight? 'Never thought about it.' I pressed him. Was he being deliberately reticent here or was there actually no thought of danger in his mind, in the same way that a young man can feel indestructible once he gets behind the wheel of a car? 'I think it was just a case of wanting to do your duty,' he finally conceded. 'Most people felt like that during the war.'

Fair enough. Ordinary people of my generation who were – thankfully – never put to the test, can have nothing but respect and gratitude for those who fought for our nation's freedom and way of life. As it happened, Tom Graveney did not see active service – the war ended just as he completed his training – but he was not to know that. 'They also serve who only stand and wait.' John Milton's words resonated just as much in 1945 as they did in 1665.

In any event, 364610 Private T.W. Graveney presented himself at the 22nd Primary Training Battalion in Derby for six months of basic training. He claims he enjoyed the experience, belying the popularly held belief that army training is marginally less agreeable than a cross-country run at prep school on a wet and windswept day in February.

In any event, if one of the training details was flogging himself over sodden fields in full kit, he cannot have been lagging too far at the back; some officer spotted latent promise in the young lad to the extent it was thought that he might have officer potential and he was sent to the Officer Cadet Training Unit. 'I just got on with it,' he said modestly, 'and by the time I passed out as a 2nd Lieutenant, I was just 19. Not bad, eh?' By this time, the Japanese had surrendered and the war was over, with the Army trying to come to terms with its reduced peace-time role and the fact that it had nearly three million men in its ranks, many of whom had to be repatriated and demobilised, a huge logistical exercise in itself.

There was less need for battle training and more time was devoted to sorting out the problems of general administration, man management and recreational organisation. As we shall see, Tom showed himself to be particularly suited to this role. Not that he wouldn't have been a crack shot with a Lee Enfield rifle in his hands if the occasion had demanded but recreational training (i.e. cricket) was right up his street.

On his birthday, 16 June 1946, he was sent abroad, first to Heliopolis, near to Cairo, for two weeks and then to Athens, where he joined the 2nd/4th Battalion, the Hampshire Regiment.

The Hampshire Regiment? I thought you were by this stage a firm son of Gloucestershire? He grimaced. It was all to do with re-organisation, he maintained, the breaking up of brigades and the necessity for a number of officers to be transferred, as it were. He and three other lieutenants were sent to Egypt to join the Artillery. Tom hated it.

Why? What's wrong with the Artillery? Nothing personal, he maintained. 'You see, I was a soldier. That is what I had been trained for – not to be a gunner.' I let that one pass. I have never been in the Army so the tensions and rivalries between the various arms of that institution are a bit obscure to me. I guess it's a bit like being told to teach physics when you have taken your degree in biology.

His displeasure was made known in a subtle but effective way. He resolutely continued to wear his Gloucestershire cap badge instead of the Hampshire one. His commanding officer hauled him over the coals but Tom was not for turning. I was beginning to register that a streak of healthy stubbornness – well hidden, for the most part – lay beneath the skin of the genial elder man opposite me. 'In that case,' exclaimed his exasperated boss, 'you'd better go and find yourself another job.'

So it was not the glasshouse for Tom but it might just as well have been. He was to be sent to Kenya to keep an eye on Jewish terrorists who were imprisoned there. That came as a surprise to me. Not that

Tom was to be sent to Nairobi but that there were Jewish terrorists in Kenya. But the socio-political intricacies of post-war Zionism do not concern us here. Nor did they Tom then. Before he set sail, an officer recognised him. 'You were here last year, weren't you? I seem to remember that you played a lot of cricket. We're looking for a sports officer. Do you fancy it?' Tom bit off his hand.

At the outbreak of war, Britain, under the terms of an old treaty, claimed the right to full occupation of Egypt. So the country became a battle area and a base, accommodating hundreds of thousands of troops. By the end of the war, Egypt had become a gigantic staging post. GHQ Middle East Command was lodged in Cairo with immense problems on their hands with the continuing crises in Palestine and the evacuation of troops from India. In short, there were a lot of soldiers hanging around with not a lot to do.

This is where Lieutenant Graveney earned his stripes. His job was to organise recreational sport for the troops. But that wasn't his true role. In fact, that was just a cover for the stealthy recruitment to HQ Company of talented sportsmen passing through the base. It goes without saying that HQ Company pretty well cleaned up in all the competitions and most of the regimental silver ended up in their mess. Tom does not admit as much but I bet his promotion to captain at the tender age of 20 was expedited by a grateful, sports-mad commanding officer.

Were you proud of the promotion? 'Yes I was. Not bad for someone who had joined up as a private only two and a half years previously.'

He gave me a picture of his daily routine. He would rise at 6am, have breakfast then march his parade up and down for about half an hour. Then it would be sport for the rest of the day. Squash, tennis, basketball, hockey, football and, of course cricket – even boxing.

Boxing? I never had you down as a pugilist. 'I was six foot by this time and only nine and a half stone. Never had much meat on me, even later on in my career.' Anyway, like Muhammad Ali, he reckoned he was quick enough to steer clear of trouble in the ring and his long reach meant that he could jab away at will. That is until he came up against a true boxer. 'He hit me once and I felt a great shudder pass down through my body. And that was the end of my boxing career.'

He had more success when a ball came into play. He was challenged to a game of squash by one of his superior officers. Now, Tom had never played squash. But he soon worked out that the game was not dissimilar to fives, which he had played at school. 'I wiped the floor with him!' Never mind the floor; Tom had to wipe his cheeks from the tears of laughter at the memory. There was no re-match, apparently.

Cricket unsurprisingly took up the majority of his time. He played for the Army, Egypt and the Combined Services. He reckons that the standard was good. His memory of team-mates is a little vague but he does recall one player who was 'bloody good' and for a short time on the books at Arsenal.

The wickets were on matting. They used to dig out the mud from the Suez Canal and lay down a strip and roll it. It baked hard in the sun and rolled out like a billiard table and when the matting was laid down, wickets of pace and true bounce were produced. He enjoyed batting on mats. Once he got used to the bounce, he found that the ball came on to the bat nicely.

And what about your bowling? You used to bowl seamers, you told me. He gave me an old-fashioned look. 'Too damned hot!' he announced. Matches would periodically be abandoned because of sandstorms. The conditions may have been harsh but the cricket was great fun and competitive enough to satisfy him. The hostilities had blown away much of the fustiness and snobbery of the pre-war years and everyone got on well, officers and men. It was to come as something of a shock to the easy-going Tom Graveney when he later took up the game for a living that he found the social distinctions between amateurs and players still persisted in pockets of resistance. And influential ones at that.

I asked him about life in the Army. Surely it wasn't all playtime. Yes it was, he maintained, just like one big holiday, and he loved it. They slept under canvas but the facilities and amenities were good. They even had carpets in their tents.

Did you have a batman? 'I did. Lovely chap. But he did get me drunk one night in the NCOs' mess. I wasn't a big drinker then. Obviously. Woke up at four o'clock the next afternoon. All I can remember was that there had been a lot of toasting going on.'

I probed him about relations with the locals and any involvement the troops might have had in the politics of the area. Not a great deal, it appears. These were soldiers who were, for the most part, on their way home after active service and wanted to keep well away from any local squabbles. Though there was a continual skirmish with the shoeshine boys. If you didn't engage their services, 'the little scoundrels would chuck polish all over your trousers'.

After a year in Egypt, he qualified for a month's leave in England. It was late summer in 1947, remembered as one of the sunniest and hottest on record. He discovered to his surprise that his brother Ken by now had joined Gloucestershire on his demobilisation from the Royal Marines. This was in the days before air mail, e-mails and mobile phones so I suppose it was on the cards that Tom in Egypt was unaware what his brother was up to in the west of England; both probably had other fish to fry than to pen letters, to be sent by ship, to their brother, no matter how close they were.

As it happened, Gloucestershire were playing Middlesex at Cheltenham at the time, a match in which Middlesex clinched the County Championship after winning a low-scoring game by 68 runs. Ken wasn't playing but he did suggest to Charlie Barnett, whose benefit season it was, that if he was short of players for one or two of his benefit matches then he might 'have a look at that brother of mine, who can play a bit'.

So it was that Tom found himself playing in an exhibition match at Stinchcombe, together with half a dozen Essex players. Tom remembers hitting a few fours through the covers in an innings of 30-odd. As he sat in the dressing room, unbuckling his pads, he was approached by Charlie Barnett, who engaged him in what he thought was no more than desultory conversation about his future in the Army. Barnett had played 20 Test matches for England, scoring two centuries, though, in common with many of his generation, the war had robbed him of his best years. Nevertheless, he was something of a legend in Gloucestershire and the young Graveney dutifully and politely answered his queries.

Tom was an Army captain by now, he had the perfect job, he was happy and his career seemed clearly mapped out for him. 'That is a pity,' said Barnett, 'because we think you'd make a decent cricketer.' Well, one thing led to another and soon Tom was offered a contract to turn pro. On the face of it, he was confronted by a difficult choice. He loved the Army, he was well paid and possibilities of promotion seemed limitless. 'So,' he drolly remarked, 'had it not been for my brother, I'd have been a general! I might have lost a few battles but our regiment would have won everything on the cricket pitch.'

In fact the choice was an easy one. He leapt at the chance of playing cricket for a living. In truth, he had never before considered the possibility. He had scored stacks of runs in Egypt but that was on matting and he had no real idea of his potential. His brother Ken had no such qualms. He believed that the matting wickets had taught Tom a great deal and the quality of those few cover drives at Stinchcombe was clear for all to see. Even a hardened pro such as Charlie Barnett. Mind you, the financial disparity between Army pay and Gloucestershire pay was a bit of a shock. He signed for £4 a week throughout the 12 months of the year.

And what were you getting in the Army? 'Can't really remember. But it was a lot more. And don't forget I didn't have any expenses. Everything was laid on for me.'

He returned to Egypt to see out the remaining six months of his commission. In January 1948, he returned home a civilian. Hitler had been right. Captain Graveney had won the war and now it was the turn of county bowlers up and down the land to sleep uneasily in their beds.

3

The Young County Player 1948–51

'They're not going to bowl you half-volleys all day like they did in the Army, you know.'
(Charlie Parker, Gloucestershire coach)

So the stage was set. True, it was more provincial rep than the West End – The Parks in Oxford is not Lord's or Old Trafford – but it was a significant moment for Tom Graveney as he embarked on his long and illustrious career in cricket. Together with George Emmett, he was opening the batting for Gloucestershire on the first day of the 1948 season. Note the date – 1 May. It seems strange, and frankly ludicrous, that these days the season is already well advanced by then.

Tom was nervous but anxious to get stuck in. The months since resigning his commission in the Army had dragged and like everyone else on county duty throughout the land, he'd had enough of pre-season training and nets and yearned for the season to get underway. Their opponents were Oxford University and lest anyone think that the students would be no more than a gentle pipe-opener, let me remind you that these fixtures were first-class and that in the immediate post-war years, university cricket was possibly as strong as it ever was.

On the Oxford side that day were three future Test players; A.H. Kardar, C.B. van Ryneveld and D.B. Carr, so no one thought – as sadly they came to in latter years – that the students were going to be pushovers. Certainly not Tom, as he ruefully pointed out. Even now, 60 years later, the wince was unaffected as he declaimed,

'Graveney caught Travis bowled Whitcombe 0!' Well, thought I, at least the great man and I share one distinction in common, a debut duck, even if our careers took wholly divergent paths after a similar discouraging start.

And it didn't get much better as the weeks rolled on into June and July. In 20-odd innings, he never scored a fifty. The wonder of it was that he remained in the side for so long. Ordinarily, you would have expected him to be dropped much earlier, no matter how much latent talent oozed from his bat. Clearly, some good judges of potential were rooting for him. Nevertheless, it must have been a wretched time. There is nothing worse than glumly sitting in the dressing room, day after day, no matter how sympathetic and encouraging your team-mates are, while others spend time in the middle doing what you should be doing.

Tom had given up a promising career in the Army for this. There was no guarantee that his contract at the end of the season would be renewed. Professional sport is a cruel, cut-throat business. If he didn't perform, he could find himself on the dole come September. He nodded when I put this to him and professed he had no idea why they persevered with him. Eventually, he was dropped and throughout June and July, he was in and out of the side, with runs proving to be as elusive as ever.

The nadir came at Bristol in mid-July against Derbyshire. Once again, his face took on a forlorn aspect as he recounted the sorry scores. 'First innings: Graveney caught Pope bowled Gladwin 0. Second innings: Graveney caught Dawkes bowled Jackson 0. The first and only time in my career that I bagged 'em. And in one day too!'

He was unimpressed with his captain on that occasion. It had been a low-scoring game. Derbyshire had batted first and had been bowled out for 207. Gloucestershire had replied with 202, Graveney out for a duck. In went Derbyshire again and were dismissed for 210. There were 15 minutes left to play that evening, a tricky period for the openers to negotiate at the best of times. Despite what any batsman may say to the contrary, no one fancies batting then one bit. The bowlers are fired up; they can steam in and throw everything at you in the few remaining overs, when the light is often not at its best.

If you survive, all well and good – you've done your job. But then you have to start all over again the next morning. Everything to lose and not much to gain, you think glumly as you take guard.

Tom would not have been worried about this as the Gloucestershire side trooped off the field that evening. He wasn't opening the batting. He was number five in the order and, barring disaster, he would not be required to bat until the next day. Probably a relief to him, considering his wretched form and his gloomy mood.

In the dressing room between innings however, the captain, B.O. Allen, dropped a bombshell. Both openers, Barnett and Emmett, were to be spared the ordeal. In their stead, 'sacrificial lambs' you might say, Lambert and Graveney were to be sent out to face the music. 'Go on,' he said to Tom. 'Get out there and score your run.' He knew that Tom was on a pair.

He must have known that the young man's confidence was low. He could have spared him the ordeal if he had had any sympathy for the poor chap. Perhaps he believed that Tom would either sink or swim in such a pressured situation and, in any case, professional cricket is a hard game played by hard men and if you can't stand the heat in the kitchen… Even if that were so and his decision had been intended to help Tom, he could at least have sent him on his way with words of encouragement. Tom's eyes rolled at the memory of it. 'B.O. Allen,' he said. 'Not a sympathetic man.'

In any event, the strange tactic failed miserably. Tom was out first ball. One can only imagine his desolation that evening. And the two regular openers, who had been saved for the next day, did not fare much better. Barnett was out for 12 and Emmett for six as wickets clattered and Gloucestershire were dismissed for 146, losing by 87 runs.

For Tom to be undone by bowlers of the calibre of Gladwin and Jackson – Test match bowlers both – was no disgrace but by now the captain had clearly lost confidence in him and the guillotine was about to fall. Tom Graveney would be consigned to the wilderness of second XI cricket, where he would no doubt dolefully consider the folly of his career choice.

So what had gone wrong? How had it come to pass that a batsman, whom such an experienced judge as Charlie Barnett had said could 'play a bit', had found himself so far out of his depth that he didn't know where his next run was going to come from?

Technique had quite a bit to do with it, initially anyway, before a succession of low scores had severely dented his confidence. 'Playing in Egypt, where I scored a lot of runs, I hadn't come across anyone really quick,' he said. And of course, in the professional game, most counties had at least one fast bowler who was always likely to test your technique – and courage – against the short ball.

The problem was not any failure of nerve against short-pitched bowling – Tom's Test record would firmly give the lie to that accusation – but that he was playing exclusively off the front foot. The accepted orthodoxy is that you will never flourish against quick bowling if you do not learn how to play off the back foot. A fraction more of a second to react and play your shot, you see. 'Charlie Barnett said to me early on, "They're not going to bowl you half-volleys all day, you know." So I had to adapt.'

You started to play back to the quicks, then? He shook his head. 'No, I remained essentially a front-foot player but I learned to play off the back foot a little bit more. Charlie taught me to play back more often.' Essentially therefore, he trusted in his own technique, his own style of play, but he knew that he had to adapt, to tinker with it when the occasion demanded. 'I only ever stayed rooted to the spot, instead of making an initial movement forward, when I faced left-arm quickies over the wicket – such as Sobers, Davidson, Bill Johnstone.'

The reason for this is technically complex. I really need to draw a diagram. But here goes… If you lunge forward to a ball swinging into you from left-arm over, it becomes unavoidable that you have to play around your front pad, therefore playing across the line and leaving you vulnerable to being hit on the pad and adjudged lbw if you miss it. Which is bound to happen eventually with bowlers of the calibre of Sobers, Davidson and Johnstone firing it in at you.

'So I used to put my weight on the toes of my front foot. That way I couldn't move, see?' That was another thing I was to learn about my friend sitting opposite. He made batting sound so easy. And I know it's so difficult.

I often reflect on the role that luck plays in a cricketer's career. Rarely is a century scored without a bit of luck. You can give a catch and the fielder drops it. You can go for a risky run in the nervous 90s and the throw can miss the wicket by inches while you are still yards out of your crease. You can be plumb lbw but the umpire had an insect in his eye. You can have your middle pole ripped out of the ground by an unplayable delivery but the bowler had overstepped the mark and a no-ball was called. I remember once getting out for 98. Then the scorer checked his arithmetic and, hey presto, I was a centurion.

By the same token, bad luck can stalk you. You can be given out caught behind when you didn't hit it. Or you can be given out lbw when you *did* hit it. Or your partner can call you for a run and at the last second change his mind, leaving you stranded halfway down the wicket. Or the umpire might be the bowler's father-in-law, in which case you shouldn't have bothered to strap on your pads.

And the cruellest cut of all is to be run out backing up, when the bowler deflects a straight drive on to the stumps. At times like that, you can be forgiven for thinking that King Lear must have played cricket in his younger days. For he it was who howled on the blasted heath after being unfairly dismissed, 'As flies are to wanton boys are we to the gods, they kill us for their sport.'

By the same token, good or bad luck can shadow a cricketer off the field. It is commonly believed that Peter Taylor was selected to play for Australia in the 1986/87 Ashes series instead of Mark Taylor in a comical case of mistaken identity. Peter 'Who' went on to take seven wickets in the match. In a tour of the West Indies, Chris Lewis ruled himself out of contention for selection by shaving his head and getting sunstroke. Glenn McGrath couldn't play in a vital Test match in England when he stepped on a cricket ball during an impromptu game of rugby during a warm-up session. In a game that I was playing in South Africa, our opening bowler turned his arm over as a loosener in the dressing room before play, shattered the light bulb and badly cut his wrist. One of our supporters took his place – and didn't perform at all badly. The game is littered with instances, bizarre and tragic, where one man's bad luck has been another's good fortune.

And so it happened that Tom Graveney's exile to the 'stiffs' at Gloucestershire was to be short-lived, owing to a curious twist of fate. Of all people, the England selectors came to his rescue – 'the first and only time they ever did me a favour', he remarked drily – when they dropped Len Hutton for the third Test against Australia. In his place, they chose George Emmett, Gloucestershire's opening batsman. There was a public outcry, not so much because Emmett had been selected, a fine player in his own right, but because the great Hutton had been omitted.

The experiment was not a success. Emmett scored ten and none and was promptly dropped for the next match, Hutton being restored to the side. The capricious moods of national selectors do not concern us here (though they will in later chapters); the point is that Gloucestershire had a very small playing staff and with Jack Crapp also on England duty, they really had no one else to play.

So Tom was recalled. A stroke of good fortune, you might say. Who can tell? Maybe he would have been summoned back into the fold in the fullness of time and made his mark, notwithstanding all that had gone on before. Somehow, I doubt that his genius would have lain dormant for long. Tom Graveney lost to the game in 1948, at the age of 21? It doesn't bear thinking about.

The turning point came at the pleasant, tree-lined, seaside ground in Bournemouth. He scored 47. On the face of it, that doesn't sound like a life-changing, or even a game-changing, innings. Sometimes, when you look at a scorecard, you have to interpret what's happening.

The trial was by spin. This is obvious, because the Hampshire seam bowlers, Herman and Hill, bowled only eight overs between them, before the spinners were let loose. And this was on the first morning of the match, even before the holidaymakers had finished their breakfast in the boarding houses and hotels. Tom confirmed as much. It was a 'square turner'. Charlie Knott and Jim Bailey, 'as fine a pair of spinners on the circuit', bowled unchanged for the rest of the innings. Gloucestershire were dismissed for 187, and Tom's 47 was the highest score. Not only was it a masterly exhibition of how to play on a turning wicket but also it gave him the confidence that he could cut the mustard at this level. Gloucestershire may have lost the match by eight wickets but their young prodigy was up and away.

And he never looked back. In August, the runs flowed, 673 of them, as renewed confidence coursed through his veins. His maiden first-class century came against the Combined Services at the Wagon Works in Gloucester, not a particularly notable venue for this momentous occasion in his career. We agreed that the ground would be unlikely to make it into any shortlist of the game's most beautiful arenas. 'Sometimes they didn't even turn the showers on for us,' Tom noted waspishly but a hundred is a hundred. There were to be 121 more.

In the final match of the season against Kent, Gloucestershire were cruising to a nine-wicket victory. Tom was batting at the time with Charlie Barnett, who signed off with an unbeaten century, Tom finishing on 52 not out. As he was sitting in the dressing room, unbuckling his pads, no doubt reflecting that his decision to quit the Army and take up professional cricket for a living was not such a bad idea after all, he was hit on the head by a cap that had been flicked across the room. Bemused, he looked up. That was his captain's way of awarding him his county cap.

I was flabbergasted when I heard that. I know how cherished a county cap is. It is rather like being awarded your colours at school. Or getting your pilot's wings. Or stepping up to receive a gong from the Queen. It is a public endorsement of your personal achievement and as such is a very proud moment. In cricket, of course, it has added significance. It signals that you have arrived and that you are an integral part of the team. It also brings about a significant rise in pay ('from £4 a week to £5', he laughed) and entitles you to an all-important benefit in ten years' time.

The occasion should be special. Your captain should make a fuss of you in front of your team-mates. For Allen to present it in such an off-hand manner was unforgivable. That is my opinion, not Tom's. He just shrugged his shoulders at the memory. 'He never really did like me, that man.'

But why not, Tom? Everybody else in that dressing room got on with you. He shook his head. 'I really don't know.' He then went on to tell me another story about B.O. Allen that today seems scarcely credible.

Gloucestershire were playing against Cambridge University. This was in 1950 and a quick glance at the scorecard indicates the high standard of university cricket at the time; the first four in the batting order for the undergraduates were Dewes, Sheppard, Doggart and May. My eye was also caught by the presence of Oliver Popplewell in the Cambridge side. Later he was to become MCC president and a well-known High Court judge, who presided over the famous Jonathan Aitken libel case, which led to the imprisonment of the former Tory MP for perjury. He also led the official inquiry into the Bradford City stadium fire and probably left his most lasting impression on the British public's consciousness by innocently asking in another libel case concerning Linford Christie, 'What is Linford's lunchbox?'

Lunches for county cricketers come not in boxes but on china plates and there was little doubt that the Cambridge batsmen, Doggart and Sheppard, were looking forward to theirs after a satisfying morning's work. As the Gloucestershire fielders made way for them to trot up the pavilion steps first, Tom was moved to say to Sheppard as he passed, 'Well played, David.'

Once inside, he was hauled aside by his captain and given a stern dressing-down. 'You *never* address an amateur by his Christian name,' he was told. 'You either call him Mr or Sir.' He was told that an apology to the person concerned would be required. Tom looked at his captain to make sure that he wasn't joking but B.O. Allen didn't do irony.

The vexed question of amateurs and professionals in the game at that time, gentlemen and players, if you like, is one that greatly interests me and will be examined in a later chapter. But let us take stock for a moment to probe into this little scene. Tom was no longer a callow youth, a naughty schoolboy who had forgotten his manners; he was a capped player, an established figure within the team and on the circuit. And he was being told to go and apologise to a student (David Sheppard, later the Bishop of Liverpool, was not yet even a reverend) for not calling him Sir.

What was David Sheppard's reaction when you told him? 'He was aghast,' said Tom simply. 'For goodness' sake, we had been out to dinner with each other the night before!'

As I say – scarcely credible, even in those days. 'B.O. Allen was a bit like that, standing on his own dignity.' It was noticeable that in all his references to Allen, Tom never failed to give him both his initials, as if he were letting him have it with both barrels. 'Mind you,' he added, with characteristic fairness, 'he wasn't a bad player and was worth his place in the side.'

Were they all like that, the amateurs, a bit pompous? 'Not all,' Tom hastened to reassure me. 'There were a few who were a bit...*funny*, but most of them were perfectly fine with me.'

As an example, he cited his selection at the end of that first summer in 1948 for the annual fixture of North versus South at the Hastings festival. It was public recognition for a promising first season, one that surprised him, plucking him from what he believed to be obscurity. 'I played for the North, even though I played for Gloucester. And Roly Jenkins, from Worcester, played for the South! Work than one out.'

I was less concerned about the selectors' shaky grasp of geography than how the amateurs and professionals socialised in the evenings at a festival. 'Never saw much of them,' he said, referring to the amateurs. 'Bill Edrich – he was p***** for the whole three days.' This was said in something approaching a respectful tone of voice and it was no wonder, for Bill Edrich, sober or not, bowled Tom for a duck in the first innings.

But Edrich was like that. He had been a squadron leader in Bomber Command in the war and having survived against all the odds, a few days carousing on the south coast was small beer in comparison. So Edrich as an example of a typical amateur was not to be trusted. In any case, Tom was just pleased to be included and playing cricket with such good players and he did not spend too much time fretting about social distinctions.

It had been a satisfying debut season – well, the final month anyway – but he was under no illusions that he would have to improve his technique if he was to make further progress. Accordingly, he was a regular fixture in the indoor nets that winter at the County Ground in Bristol. Together with Charlie Parker and George Emmett, he worked hard to develop his back-foot play.

Did it work? Did you think all those hours practising indoors were fruitful? He thought that it all worked out in the end. He did not eschew his front-foot style but he did learn to take the ball at the top of its bounce.

Were you ever forced on to the back foot in your career? He shook his head. 'I still played forward and trusted in my technique.'

How did you play the bouncer then? He smiled. 'I hooked off the front foot,' he replied disarmingly. I whistled in disbelief. That sounded to me like a ticket for the Accident and Emergency department of the nearest hospital. But it was a fact confirmed by his brother, Ken. 'I told you about the incredible hand-eye coordination that my brother had,' he said. 'I remember him once hooking Wes Hall for six high up into the stands. Off the front foot!'

Tom put it all down to his unusual grip of the bat. Unlike most batsmen, he held it high up the handle and always picked it up dead straight behind him, rather than over third slip, or even gully. The only concession he made to the faster pace of the professional game was that he shortened the extravagant backlift that had served him so well on the sun-baked matting of Egypt. Anyway, it worked for him and few bowlers consistently got the better of him.

For the rest of his time he got himself a job at Bell & Nicholson, a big wholesale store in Bristol who loyally employed him in all manner of capacities every winter when he wasn't touring. They were very good to him, he acknowledged. 'I played a lot of golf with the boss,' he smiled.

The first match of the 1949 season was against Oxford University at The Parks, scene of that duck on his debut the previous year. 'They're not going to do that to me again,' he told himself as he took guard. He scored a couple then a single before facing up to a tall medium-pacer who was unknown to him. George Chesterton was unknown to many on the ground that day; he was making his first-class debut. He looked innocuous and it did not seem to any of the onlookers that he would pose much of a threat.

'And then I bowled him!' George told me some 60 years later. 'Tom obligingly left the merest chink of light between bat and pad and the ball nipped through it.' Tom chuckled at the memory. 'Mighty fine bowler George was. One of the best of the amateurs at that time.'

But you would say that, Tom – he'd just bowled you. But Tom was having none of it, reiterating that Chesterton could bowl all right, astonishing really when you consider that his teaching duties at Malvern College only allowed him to play a handful of games for Worcestershire every season. 'He got me in the second innings too,' said Tom admiringly. 'Not before he'd scored a hundred,' said George, putting the record straight. And thus began a friendship between the two, cemented by their successive terms as president of Worcestershire CCC in the 1990s, that remained until George's death in 2012.

Typically, Tom remembers only the manner of his dismissal that day, not the 108 runs that had gone before. Quite simply, it was one of the most astonishing catches that he ever succumbed to. He had struck Chesterton a mighty blow over mid-on. Fielding at deep mid-off was the Oxford captain, Clive van Ryneveld, already a South African Test player. He sprinted all of 30 yards and dived headlong, clutching the ball in his hands inches from the turf. 'Astonishing,' said Tom, 'I'd never seen anything like it.' George grinned. 'Tom was deceived by my slower ball,' was his verdict.

Deceived or not, Tom's confidence as he embarked on his second season was sky-high. Very often, young batsmen succumb to 'second season syndrome' after a promising first year; the bowlers work out their weaknesses and word soon gets around. The new kid on the block may have played almost exclusively off the front foot but there seemed precious little opposing bowlers could do about it.

Bill Edrich, he of the limitless capacity for roistering and high spirits, was shrewd enough to believe that he had the measure of the prodigy. Noting his fondness for the drive on the off side, he bowled exclusively at Tom's leg stump. His brother Ken told me about it, 'Leg side theory,' he called it, 'bit like bodyline but without the bouncers.'

Did it work? 'Yes it did.' And then the chuckle came down the trans-atlantic line. 'But not for long!'

The runs flowed. Tom scored three other centuries and finished the season with 1,506 Championship runs, a considerable haul. *Wisden* was moved to declare, 'His elegant stroke-play stamped him as one of the best young players in the country.' He was selected for the Players to play the Gentlemen at Lord's. It was a great honour but one that he was a little slow to appreciate. 'They plucked me from nowhere,' he said. 'And I didn't get any runs.' Perhaps he was a little overawed by the company he was keeping.

The batting order ran: Hutton, Langridge, Robertson, Compton, Graveney, Close. It was also his first visit to the headquarters of cricket. Like everyone else who takes his first look at the famous old ground, he was astonished at the pronounced slope, left to right, looking from the players' balcony. His inauspicious debut at Lord's can be overlooked. He was to play there a further 46 times, scoring eight centuries, and he came to love the place. In fact, with the exception of Bristol and Worcester, there is no other ground where he put down his cricket bag more often. Home from home, you might say.

He remembers two innings in particular that summer. He scored 132 out of an innings total of 239 against Surrey at the Oval and 159 against Somerset at Bristol. Arthur Wellard eventually bowled him. 'There you are,' Wellard announced to his team-mates as Tom turned for the pavilion. 'Told you he played across the line!'

This time, at the conclusion of the County Championship, Tom was invited to play in the Scarborough Festival, a notch up from Hastings. And you can understand why, when you listen to his description of festival cricket. 'Play started late, at 12noon. Lunch was taken at 1.30pm. Tea at 4pm. We didn't go into tea. Tea was brought out to us on the pitch. Waiters carried out the tables and we were served on the square. All the while the band played. And stumps were drawn at 6pm, so all the spectators could go back to where they were staying in time for their supper.' Or tea, as it is confusingly called up there.

Was the cricket taken seriously? 'I should say so! All the matches had first-class status, you know. And the touring side were invited every year. That year it was the New Zealanders. I had a wonderful time.' He was only 22, but he felt comfortable in his surroundings and he loved what he was doing – scoring runs.

The development of a county cricketer into a Test player proceeded at a stately rather than hurried pace in 1950. It was almost as if the batsman had played himself in, got the measure of the bowling and the wicket and had set himself to get his hundred, eschewing any mad dash through the 80s and 90s. Tom scored the statutory thousand runs in the season, generally reckoned to be the benchmark of a good county player – in fact he scored well in excess of that number, 1,892 to be precise – but his average still hovered around the late 30s.

You need to be averaging well into the 40s for journalists and selectors to sit up and take notice. There were highlights of course; he scored his first double hundred, against Sussex, as well as 197 against Nottinghamshire and 115 against Glamorgan. The season was the swansong, if you can call it that, of B.O. Allen, the captain, and his departure did not give Tom sleepless nights. 'Never did get on with him,' he confessed. 'We just didn't see eye to eye.'

The captaincy was given to pretty well the only amateur available, Sir Derrick Thomas Louis Bailey, 3rd Baronet and a decorated Second World War pilot. Tom's eyes widened at the memory. 'His cricket bag was a shambles! He was still wearing his father's old overcoat that had seen lengthy service before the war!' I started laughing and he looked at me quizzically. *I play tennis with his son, would you believe? And his kit is probably pre-war too!*

The breakthrough came in 1951. Tom started off like a train – I'm always amused by that cliché; all trains that I have ever travelled on start slowly – with a double hundred against Oxford University. He reached 1,000 runs by the middle of June and finished the season with 1,654 runs at an average of 48.64. Now, those figures, let alone the manner in which they were gathered, *would* make the national selectors sit up and take note. But it took an unfortunate injury to Denis Compton to open the door for Tom.

In a previous match, he had missed a full toss – 'just about the only full toss that Denis missed in his life!' – and had been hit full on the instep, which precluded his participation in the third Test against the South Africans. Tom privately harboured thoughts that he was in with a chance of being called up, so he was listening to the radio at lunchtime on the Sunday before the match, when the team was traditionally announced.

A letter from MCC came the following day, confirming his selection. Worth that decision to pass up on his chance of a field marshall's baton, he reflected, as he made his way north to Old Trafford. It is interesting to point out that another great batsman noted for his dashing style, the South African, Roy McLean, was also making his Test debut. Neither made his mark in this match but the South Africans kept their faith in their young man and the England selectors did not, as we shall see.

Tom was very nervous before he went into bat, as you would expect, and remembers later seeing a photo of himself on the players' balcony looking exceedingly green around the gills. There were several rain delays and he had a long time to wait, batting at number four. He scored only 15 before being bowled by the off-spinner, Athol Rowan.

He wasn't required to bat in the second innings as England wrapped up a nine-wicket victory but he does remembers being bemused by the proceedings as England cantered to their target of 142. Hutton was on 99 centuries in his career and what more fitting way was there to notch up his 100th hundred than in a Test match? But only 142 runs were required, so it was going to be a tall order, even if he did bat like a dream and hog the strike.

All was going swimmingly. Both targets steadily approached and it seemed, with considerable help from his partners, first Ikin and then Simpson, who resolutely and unselfishly eschewed any run-getting themselves, that he would do it. Eventually, he reached 94 but only four runs were needed for victory and of course the end of the game. At this point, even the South Africans lent a hand to manipulate the score. Mann deliberately bowled a leg-side full toss so that Hutton could hit it for six, gain his hundred and win the match. Hutton mistimed his heave at the ball and it dribbled for four and he was left stranded on 98 not out. Tom was watching from the balcony. Even now, he remains ambivalent about it all. 'It shouldn't really happen in a Test match,' he muttered.

He wasn't selected for the next Test.

Were you upset or angry that they dropped you after only one innings? He shook his head. He expected it. 'I wasn't going to take the place of the great Denis Compton, was I?' Perhaps not. But they did pick the young Peter May for his debut in the fourth Test. Once again, the generosity of spirit of my companion made itself manifest. 'Ah, but he did score a hundred, didn't he? And went on to have a pretty decent career!'

Notwithstanding his initial, unsuccessful, foray into the international arena, he had thoroughly enjoyed the experience and no doubt quietly resolved that he should not be a 'one-cap wonder'. The only thing for it was to return to Gloucestershire and to make as many runs as he could, which he did – by the sackful. In fact, the very next day after the Test match, he scored a hundred against Northamptonshire and followed that up with another in the second innings.

Sadly, 1951 marked the end of his brother's career. Ken had been bedevilled with injury and a slipped disc finally persuaded him that enough was enough. He bowled out-swingers at a lively pace but it has to be said that playing most of his home matches at Bristol did not exactly set his pulse racing as he ran in to bowl. The seamers would bowl half a dozen overs each, merely to remove the shine, before the spinners, Goddard and Cook, grasped the ball from their hands and didn't relinquish it for the rest of the day.

Unsurprisingly, Ken's greatest feat took place on a ground far from home, Chesterfield, traditionally one of the quickest wickets in the country. He took all ten Derbyshire wickets that day. There is something quite splendid about a scorecard when someone has taken all ten. I hope he has it framed somewhere in his house in Texas, though what Americans would make of it, I cannot imagine. But to any cricketer to see the phrase, 'bowled J.K.R. Graveney', repeated ten times takes the breath away. So it was a loss to the county that a bad back forced him from the game.

As it happened, that was not the end of his association with Gloucestershire. In 1963, he was persuaded to take over the captaincy of the county after the sacking of Tom Pugh, who had himself taken hold of the reins when Tom had been sacked in 1961 – a controversial episode in Tom's life which we will be discussing in a later chapter – a post Ken filled until *he* was sacked in 1964. It does seem that Gloucestershire had a period when they went through captains as much as Chelsea do managers these days.

So Tom, give me a flavour of what it was like to be a county cricketer in the 1950s. Your daily routine, for example. 'Two buses.' Momentarily, I was nonplussed. I wondered why it took *two* buses for the team to travel around the country. Cricketers have a lot of kit, I know, but surely one would have sufficed.

He explained. 'I lived in Stoke Bishop. I had to get two buses every morning to get to the ground. Nightmare when you had to lug your bag around.' Only four players in the team had a car. Tom didn't get his first car until 1955. So bus it was. Imagine an England player today catching a bus to work.

The team would gather in the dressing room at 10am and get changed to go and practise, during which banter would fly and tall stories would be told. 'I was the youngster in the side but the older players were very good to me and helped me a lot.' He has warm memories of Jack Crapp, the Cornishman in the side, who was always ready with an encouraging word or a sensible piece of advice. Andy Wilson, the diminutive wicketkeeper, was a positive influence and a gentleman to boot. Tom was struck by the size of Tom Goddard's hands, with fingers 'like bananas'. He was an enthusiastic appealer. 'That man would have appealed against his own grandmother!'

Tom was ever an assiduous and serious netter. It may seem strange to make this point that a professional sportsman would want to practise his craft in a sensible and dedicated manner. Consider, for example, how many hours a day a virtuoso violinist spends doing his scales and rehearsing his pieces. Or how long a ballerina spends at the barre, stretching and exercising. So it should be taken for granted that cricketers took their time in the nets seriously. Well, strange to relate, that is not always the case. Some players mess about, trying out all sorts of outrageous shots or 'mystery' balls. Others seem to regard their time in the nets as a challenge to knock as many tiles off the roof of the pavilion as they can, in the process losing many balls and engendering havoc on the road outside the ground. How many times they have their castles knocked over in the process never seems to bother them. Ian Botham and Andrew Flintoff were notoriously light-hearted netters. 'Ah well,' the coach would grumble, 'everyone's different and prepares in his own way. It's what happens in the middle that counts.'

Tom Graveney was most certainly not of this ilk. He would bat properly, taking time to hone his defensive technique and to play himself in before he would consciously set himself to be more expansive in his strokeplay. In other words, he would try to replicate, as far as that was possible, match conditions. Goddard and Cook, the two spinners, would always come to bowl in his net, confident that he would play properly and not try to slog them into the next county.

After a bit of catching practice, they would retire to the dressing room and prepare themselves mentally for what was to come, depending on who had won the toss and whether they were batting or bowling. Watching the captains bending over the rolling coin out in the middle to see whether it fell heads or tails was always a point of gathered interest, everyone attempting to analyse from the body language who had won and who was the happier. Some captains have fun at their team's expense, deliberately trying to mislead their colleagues with a shake of the head or a shrug of the shoulders. But the announcement over the crackling Tannoy would put paid to any further doubt. 'Matches in those days started at 11.30am,' he reminded me. And then it was down to business.

At the close of play, after a leisurely shower, both teams would usually gather for a drink or two in the pavilion bar. It should not be forgotten that many of the players were older and had lost the best part of their playing careers to the war. Unsurprisingly, they were determined to wring every last drop of enjoyment out of the time that was left to them in the game. Consequently, friendships were forged around the counties and fiercely nurtured. There was none of the animosity, real or manufactured, between sides that, sadly, you see today. They played it hard on the field of play but off duty, they socialised over pints of beer.

'Everyone was looking forward to better things,' Tom explained. 'We were playing cricket again after the terrible times in the war.' Being of an affable and gregarious disposition, Tom enjoyed these friendly get-togethers and loved listening to the old pros reminiscing and swapping stories. In the Army, he drank little. As a cricketer, he learned to refuel, always sensibly, he assured me, with a grin. He perspired a lot – 'the green dye from my Worcestershire cap used to run in rivulets down my neck and stain my shirt' – and therefore he needed to rehydrate. Beer was as good as anything. He turns his nose up at the concept of isotonic drinks. And as for ice baths!

If the game were at home, it would be two buses back to Stoke Bishop, that is if his entreaties for a lift had fallen on deaf ears. If they were on their travels, it would be taxis to the railway station. And as the junior pro, Tom would be responsible for ensuring that all the cricket bags were loaded and unloaded at the correct destinations. Just listen to this story of his and compare it with the more straightforward and painless journeys of today.

Gloucestershire were playing at home in Cheltenham. At stumps, it was a rapid change and a dash to the station to catch the train to London. Across town from Paddington to Victoria meant more taxis in order to catch the last train down to Dover, where they were due to play Kent the following morning. One imagines that they did not arrive much before midnight, travel-weary and desperate for a comfy bed – which they did not always get.

I say 'one imagines' because Tom cannot confirm this. He wasn't with them. In the scramble from the taxi to board the train before it set off for Dover, all his team-mates had dashed for their carriage leaving him to struggle with 12 large bags. He failed to make it. He was left on the platform with all the kit as the train snaked its way out of the station. He caught the milk train, much favoured by inebriated office workers and tardy undergraduates, arriving in Dover at four in the morning. And he had to play the next day. Not only that, Gloucestershire batted first and he found himself at the crease in the first over. He scored 73, 'through bleary eyes'.

They played 28 Championship matches as opposed to the 16 they play today. The schedule was relentless; two three-day matches every week, with Sundays off. If there was no exhibition match to be played on the Sunday for someone's benefit, Tom would play 36 holes of golf with his great friend, Arthur Milton.

There were no one-day matches, it is true, but the standard of county cricket in the 1950s was as high as it ever was and the crowds, starved of entertainment during the war, flocked to watch. It was tiring, and you had to be fit and resilient to survive, but Tom loved it.

4

Playing For England 1951–54

'I was next man in when the crowd invaded the pitch. There wasn't a blade of grass to be seen. We hadn't won the Ashes since Larwood and the Bodyline series.'

'Next day, was it an open-top bus tour of London and a visit to Downing Street?'

'You're joking. We were in Eastbourne playing Sussex. Straight back to the day job, you might say.'

One presumes that the young Tom Graveney was not responsible for all the kit and suitcases on the quayside as the MCC team made their way up the gangplank of the luxury liner SS *Chusan*, berthed at Tilbury Docks.

Following his outstanding season in 1951, he had been selected to go on the tour of India, Pakistan and Ceylon that winter. It was the first visit by an England side to the sub-continent since the war and as such was very much intended to be a public relations exercise, to foster goodwill and closer contact with the colonies through cricket. Except that it wasn't the England side in fact. It was very much the England second team. None of the first team wanted to tour. Several of them had been in India during the war and didn't want to go back.

Partition, and the granting of full independence to India and Pakistan, had only happened four years earlier and both cricket teams were still finding their way in international terms. The matches against Pakistan were not even granted Test status and of course Ceylon was not yet Sri Lanka. So the senior players judged that it was a good time to put their feet up for the winter and not put themselves through the ordeal of touring in countries where the conditions were traditionally very difficult.

Consequently, the MCC team set sail without regulars such as Hutton, Compton, Evans, Laker, Bedser, Bailey and others. Not that this weighed too much on Tom's mind as he got to know his team-mates on the two-week voyage across the Mediterranean, through the Suez Canal, where he must have cast a wistful eye to the west where he served in the Army, and down the Arabian Peninsula to India.

The food on board he described as 'deluxe', at a time, let us not forget, when there was still rationing in Britain, and which turned out to be a brutal contrast with what they had to eat when they got to India.

His room-mate was Don Kenyon, who was later to be his captain when he moved to Worcestershire. 'He was wretchedly homesick,' Tom commented. Some cricketers don't take to touring and find being away from home for months at a time an ordeal. It has to be said that Tom never felt like this. He lapped up the social and cricketing experiences. Mind you, even he was moved to remark on the poverty and filth of Bombay when they arrived, so much so that 'it made you want to turn straight round and go home'.

They didn't go home. They couldn't. There was nothing for it other than to knuckle down and get on with the job, no matter how alien the conditions. For touring and playing cricket in India is vastly different to what it is like back home and even experienced tourists find the going hard. Everything is an assault on the senses. The heat, the dust, the milling crowds, the incessant clangour and the absence of proper amenities can prove to be debilitating to even the hardiest of souls. The desperate poverty that often rubs shoulders with the most opulent wealth can grate on the soul; everything seems so chaotic and disorganised. There is no peace, no privacy; nothing is tranquil, nothing temperate. Added to which, you rarely feel completely well and in full control of your bowels.

The cricket is like nothing else that you have ever experienced. The wickets are usually dry and dusty, wholly unsuitable to quick bowling. The ball soon loses its shine and spin takes over. But it is not like spin in England. The conventional finger spinner finds it hard to make much of an impact; instead you are assailed by cohorts of wrist spinners who really do give it a big rip, supported by a cordon of expectant and noisy catchers close by. It is tough and a real test of character and technique.

Thankfully, Tom was not found wanting and soon settled into his groove, scoring heavily in the warm-up matches. Just before the first Test, he contracted dysentery and was in hospital as his colleagues battled hard to save the game. The crucial partnership that gained the draw was between Allan Watkins, who batted for nine hours for his unbeaten 137, and Donald Carr, who scored 76 not out. Carr greatly enjoyed his personal celebration of his brave innings; Tom remembers him merrily cycling around the hotel that night.

All well and good. The series was still level, even though the Englishmen had been vastly outplayed. But herein lay a problem. Who was going to make way for Graveney, now that he was out of hospital and raring to go? For the weight of runs that he had already scored on the tour had made it inconceivable that he should not play. And now the vexatious question of amateurs and professionals reared its head again.

The side was led by Nigel Howard, a very ordinary cricketer, 'and that's putting it kindly' said Tom. But the crucial point was that he was an amateur and it was considered unthinkable by MCC that anyone else other than an amateur would be equal to the social and diplomatic duties required of a captain leading a side abroad in their colours. By all accounts, he was a perfectly decent chap but it was becoming clear to everyone that he wasn't worth his place in the side.

Things came to a head at the selection meeting for the second Test, attended by the captain, Nigel Howard, the manager, Geoffrey Howard, and the senior professional, Allan Watkins. It was Watkins who stuck his head above the parapet and announced that, in his opinion, the captain should stand down. One can almost hear the collective intake of breath, still audible down the decades. Telegrams with MCC back at Lord's were exchanged and eventually the edict came down from on high: under no circumstances was the captain not to play. So poor Donald Carr got the chop. One imagines that he did not get on his bicycle when he heard the news.

Political rumblings or not, Tom concentrated on getting back on his bike as soon as he was fit and you can say that he didn't fall off for the remainder of the tour. Runs came aplenty, including a mammoth eight-hour 175 in the second Test. 'I couldn't get out,' he told me. 'There was no one ready to bat. They were all on the toilet!'

Conditions were fairly basic, he admitted, sleeping in dormitories, barracks and hotels that were conspicuously bereft of any stars. Sometimes they were billeted in the most splendid of maharajahs' palaces, 'but nothing worked!'

Coping with tribulation can sometimes bring a team closer together and that was certainly true of this touring party. They were a 'good bunch of blokes', Tom insisted, and they 'all stuck to the task'. He positively drooled about some of the Indian batsmanship. Merchant, Mankad, Hazare, Roy and Umrigar all scored heavily but it was the manner in which they made their runs that caught his eye. Perhaps it was a case of one stylish player admiring the artistry of others.

Mankad was also by far and away the best bowler on either side, managing to get the ball to bite and spin in a way that the Englishmen were unable to do. Despite all their travails, the series was squared at one apiece and *Wisden* reported accurately enough that 'taking everything into consideration…the team did as well as could have been expected'.

Travel was by train then. Long dusty journeys, eh? Tom looked at me with an expression perilously close to a smirk. 'We had our own plane, I'll have you know. A DC3 it was. And sometimes it was piloted by our manager, Geoffrey Howard.' Touring in those days wasn't all hardship, I thus conjectured.

Another curious fact was that they visited Pakistan in the middle of the Indian tour. The two matches against the national side were not official Tests but it was a tough interlude. The first in Lahore was played on grass, which is not to say that it was anything like the grass back home. Notwithstanding, Tom scored a not-out 109.

The second was played in Karachi on matting, tightened to the exact tension to suit their quick bowlers. 'Fazal Mahmood – on matting. Unplayable,' was Tom's uncompromising verdict. Maybe that was so for mere mortals but Graveney seemed to manage all right. He had omitted to mention his personal contribution and I had to look it up. He scored 123.

How did you compare the two sides, as opponents and men? 'The Pakistanis were tough and aggressive. That's more their culture, isn't it? But the Indians…well, they were *smoothies*!' He was grinning as he said this and I got what he meant. On the field of play, the Pakistanis may wield the scimitar but the Indians are just as effective with judicious use of the stiletto.

Did you enjoy the whole experience? He paused. 'We-ell,' he replied at length, 'I certainly found it…*fascinating*. And I came back a better player.'

Leeds is a long way north of Madras. To the Indians, on the return tour of England and battling it out in the first Test of the 1952 summer, it must have seemed a very long way north. On a different planet even. Only four months earlier, they had been putting England to the sword – or should I say the stiletto? – in hot and dusty Madras, winning by an innings. Now they were batting for their lives on a lively green top at Headingley.

And I use the phrase 'for their lives' advisedly. Steaming down the hill, his dark, lank hair flapping against his shirt collar was the young – and very fast – Fred Trueman. Tom was in a particularly favourable position to witness the Indians' discomfiture; he was fielding at silly mid-off, right in front of their faces.

'I was the only fielder in front of the bat,' he told me. 'The rest were spread out in the slips and gully.' Raised on the slow, lifeless pitches of the sub-continent, where fast bowlers, such as they were, only had one function in the team and that was to see off the shine of the new ball, the Indian batsmen were totally unprepared for, and manifestly ill-equipped to deal with, what had hit them. 'I remember seeing the whites if their eyes widen in horror as the ball went past their chin,' he said, with all the relish you bask in when the nasty fast bowler is on your side. 'They definitely didn't fancy it.'

Within the space of 14 balls, they were four wickets down for no runs. There had never been such a calamitous start to an innings in a Test match. This was the second innings and up until that point, the Indians had played pretty well and were in a reasonable position to press on and win the match. Trueman's pace put paid to any thoughts of that.

A bouncer to Roy hit the back of his bat and was caught at second slip by Compton. Mantri got an inside edge on to his stumps and Manjrekar was bowled neck and crop. In the meantime, at the other end, Bedser had dismissed Gaekwad. Tom remembers his friend, Polly Umrigar, playing Trueman from nearer the square leg umpire than the line of the ball. Trueman didn't get him but soon Umrigar was gone and the score was 26-5. There was no way back from that and India were eventually dismissed for 165, Trueman finishing with 4-27, to add to the three wickets he had taken in the first innings – on his debut. The 128 runs for victory were safely knocked off, Compton and Graveney undefeated at the end.

So a legend was born? 'Who, me?' Tom said disingenuously and we laughed. 'I knew Fred was a good bowler because I had played against him at Yorkshire. Funnily, he rarely got me out. I had far more trouble against Statham.'

Ah yes, Trueman and Statham, one of the most famous of the game's opening pairs of bowlers. The names trip off the tongue: Larwood and Voce; Lindwall and Miller; Adcock and Heine; Hall and Griffith; Lillee and Thomson; Waqar and Wasim, not to mention any combination of fearsome West Indians in the 1970s and 80s.

It was not surprising that, of the two, Trueman should be the better remembered. He was more flamboyant, more outspoken and more controversial. Statham, by contrast, was quiet and unassuming and simply got on with the job of bowling. 'He was double-jointed,' Tom reminded me. 'He could put his hands together behind his back and pull them right over his shoulders. He was very accurate – and bloody quick. Quite simply, he was a brilliant bowler. And such a lovely man.'

Tom takes full credit for teaching Brian Statham to – no, not how to play the cover drive but how to drink beer. In copious amounts too. It was on the Australian tour of 1954/55 and he reckoned fast bowlers needed liquid to quench their thirst after a long day in the field, 'not those dreadful liqueurs he used to drink!' Statham soon became – and remained throughout their playing days – one of Tom's closest friends in the game.

The Indians, who drank less beer and who left their best all-rounder, Vinoo Mankad, at home, were no match for the English on their home pitches and lost the four-match series by three Tests to one.

Tom is modest about his contributions to the team's success but he has no right to be. In fact, 1952 was something of an *annus mirabilis* in his early career. He scored over 2,000 runs in all first-class matches and was named as one of the *Wisden* Five Cricketers of the Year. I wonder how many times he would have been accorded that honour if it were not bestowed upon any individual just the once.

There was no overseas tour that winter, which was a pity, given the form that Tom was in. The following season, the Australians were in town and it seemed unlikely that such tough and battle-hardened competitors would be stepping on the square leg umpires' toes when they faced Trueman. In fact they were not to face Trueman at all until the final Test – he was on National Service – but there was plenty of riveting and exciting cricket on show, notwithstanding the absence of England's eye-catching young fast bowler.

The series of course is remembered for the emotional scenes when England finally, after 19 years of hurt and disappointment, regained the Ashes. The fact that it happened in the same year as Queen Elizabeth was crowned gave it added piquancy in the imagination of the British public. Tom played in all five Tests but he did not have a particularly productive time with the bat. 'Lucky to stay in the side,' he confessed. 'I did just enough to keep my place.'

Nevertheless, he has vivid memories of all five games as fortunes ebbed and flowed and the tension was ratcheted up until the euphoric finale at the Oval. 'To be honest, we were frightened of our batting, even before the series started.' I raised an inquisitive eyebrow. 'So the selectors, of whom Hutton was one, packed the side with batting, to the detriment of our bowling attack, I firmly believed.'

You would have thought that any five from a list of Hutton, Edrich, Watson, Compton, May, Graveney, Simpson, Bailey and Kenyon – all of whom played that summer – would have scored enough runs to enable them to pick another bowler. Apparently not. The averages for the series would seem to bear out the selectors' misgivings. Only Hutton (443 runs at 55.37 – a personal, as well as a national, triumph) averaged over 40. The Ashes were won largely by a bowler, Alec Bedser, who took 39 wickets. As well as one or two famous rearguard actions.

There was a lot of rain around that summer, three of the Tests being significantly affected by loss of play. The first Test at Trent Bridge is remembered for only one ball by our hero. In the first innings, England were 17/3, reeling in the face of an onslaught from the Australian fast bowler, Ray Lindwall. Tom, next man in, was relieved to get a half-volley on leg stump, which he appreciatively tucked away for three runs. He scored 22 in a stand with Hutton, who top scored with 43. Bedser took 14 wickets in the match and deserved to have his efforts rewarded with a victory but rain prevented any result.

'Oh yes,' said Tom, 'there was something else. Quite comical, really.' In the Australian second innings, wickets were tumbling and the light was bad. The talk in the visitors' dressing room was all about appealing against the light, which in those days, the batting side were allowed to do. The next man in, Don Tallon, the wicketkeeper, had been asleep during these discussions and clearly hadn't heard what was afoot. A wicket fell and he picked up his bat to go out to face the music.

'Give it a go, Don,' were the words from his captain, Lindsay Hassett, as he walked out of the room. Of course, Hassett meant 'give the light a go', as in 'appeal against the light'. Tallon was oblivious and believed that his captain's instruction to 'give it a go' meant 'have a slog'. Which he did, with spectacularly unsuccessful results. He was not well received by his team-mates when he returned a short time later and was dropped for the rest of the series, his place being taken by Gil Langley. You have to pick your moments to have a kip in the dressing room.

At Lord's for the second Test, Tom enjoyed a long stand with Hutton during the course of which there was a little incident, not important in itself, but, looking back on it, Tom is minded to believe that it encapsulated the difference between him and his captain and served as an illustration why Hutton did not wholly trust the young Graveney.

'Bill Johnstone was bowling,' he said. 'He had the ability to angle the ball across you. I followed one and it kept on going and I kept on following it. I didn't nick it but I nearly ruptured myself reaching for it. And then I started laughing. "That's the first time I've ever done that!" I said out loud. Len was not best pleased. Batting was no laughing matter for him.'

As the final hour of the day's play approached, with Tom seeing the ball like a football, Hutton came down the wicket and instructed his young partner to shut up shop – he didn't want to give the Australians another wicket that night. And as everyone knows, one wicket can lead to another, and another. Tom was flabbergasted. He sensed that the Australian attack was tiring and was there for the taking and that a century was well within his reach that evening. But his captain had spoken and who was he, a newcomer to the side, to take issue? It was in Hutton's nature to proceed with caution. Tom preferred to play what was in front of him, whatever the time on the pavilion clock. At the close of play, he was 78 not out.

The next morning, he was yorked by Lindwall without adding to his score. The best ball he ever bowled, Ray told me years later. I hit it hard but still it somehow squeezed under my bat.' At stumps on the fourth day, England, chasing an improbable target of 343, were 20/3 and staring down the barrel of defeat. The next morning, Compton was out at 12.40pm and a sparse crowd had already resigned themselves to the inevitable.

Willie Watson, a double international incidentally (he played football for England on four occasions), was defending obdurately and now he was joined at the wicket by Trevor Bailey. They were not parted until 5.50pm. They had shared a partnership of 163 runs but plainly that was an irrelevance. An improbable draw had been secured and the British public were captivated by one of the most astonishing backs-to-the-wall partnerships in cricket history.

Even the normally unexcitable *Times* newspaper compared the manner of it to Dunkirk. 'And guess what,' remarked my commentator. 'The very next day I was playing against the Aussies again, for Gloucestershire at Bristol.'

Did they relax? You know, take their foot off the gas? Tom gave me a withering look. 'You've got to be joking! It's Australians we're talking about here.'

The third Test at Old Trafford was a wet anti-climax. Almost half of the match was lost to rain. 'Mind you,' reminded my friend, 'we had 'em 35/8 in their second innings. We would have won had it not been for the rain.'

The fourth match of the series, at Headingley, was another nail-biter. Again, there was a lot of rain around and runs were not in plentiful supply. Graveney top scored with 55 in England's first-innings total of 167.

It all boiled down to the final day, with Australia needing to score 177 in 115 minutes. Hutton believed that the wicket would take spin and got Lock on to bowl early. But he was having one of those days when nothing much happened – 'in fact,' said Tom, 'he bowled badly.' The Australians were cruising to victory when Bailey grabbed the ball and proceeded to bowl so wide of the leg stump that the batsmen couldn't reach it and the runs dried up. The draw was secured by means of a brave piece of resourceful bowling or a shocking exhibition of negative cricket that harmed the game's image, depending on your point of view.

The Australians were not best pleased to be denied by Bailey's obduracy – for the second time – and the press were fiercely critical of England's tactics. Tom's opinion is illuminating. 'Well,' he said, 'you've got to do what you've got to do. Sometimes it isn't pretty.'

So the scene was set for the denouement at the Oval. With the series locked at 0-0, an extra day was set aside in order to get a result, which was rather sporting of the Aussies, I thought, as they only needed a draw to retain their grip on the Ashes. Tom's eyes widened when I told him about the extra day. 'Really? I never knew that.' And then he gave me a wolfish grin. 'In any case we didn't need it. Polished 'em off in four and a half days!'

It was nip and tuck in both first innings, Australia 275, England 306. Then the Surrey 'spin twins', Laker and Lock, set to work, bowling Australia out for 162. Laker took four and Lock five as the wicket took spin, hardly surprising really, as this was the Oval, their home turf. The canter to victory was a formality, especially as the Australians had no spinner in their side, and it was somehow fitting that the two old warhorses, Compton and Edrich, who had endured so much Ashes heartache over the years, stretching back to series before the war, should be at the crease when the winning runs were struck.

Tom was sitting on the players' balcony, with his pads strapped on, watching as a delirious crowd invaded the pitch. 'I was the next man in. There wasn't a blade of grass to be seen. We hadn't won the Ashes since Larwood and the Bodyline series.'

Next day, was it an open-top bus tour of London and a visit to Downing Street? He scoffed at the very thought. 'You're joking. We were in Eastbourne playing Sussex. Straight back to the day job, you might say.' He then fell quiet, lost in reverie. I waited for him to resume his narrative, possibly about the rest of the season or maybe the Australians, who were his opponents on no less than eight occasions that summer. 'I'm the last one alive from that team, you know,' he eventually said. 'They've all gone, now that Trevor's died.'

I looked at the England team for that historic match and it was true; Graveney is the last one standing from Hutton, Edrich, May, Compton, Bailey, Evans, Laker, Lock, Trueman, Bedser. One by one my boyhood heroes marched across my mind. To Tom, they were his team-mates and friends. It was a poignant moment.

On Boxing Day, the MCC team to the West Indies left Britain by plane, for the first time. They stopped off in Newfoundland to rest and refuel, only to be rudely awakened by the airline authorities who informed them that a major storm was imminent and they would be snowed in for a week if they didn't get going immediately. They escaped from one storm, you might say, and flew straight into another.

The 1953/54 tour of the West Indies was one of the most controversial, acrimonious and unhappy tours ever undertaken by an England side. Paradoxically, Tom enjoyed a successful time with the bat and found the wickets, the heat and the West Indian people very much to his liking. But the tour was riven with internal dissension, political wrangling, dreadful umpiring, arguments on the field and rioting off it.

As it happened, England fought back well from a 2-0 deficit to square the series but there was much soul-searching by both cricketing Boards of Control afterwards and the fall-out was considerable. Two players, Lock and Trueman, were heavily censured for their behaviour when they returned home and were controversially denied their tour bonus. 'But between you, me and the gatepost,' Tom told me, 'they carried the can for others who were equally guilty. Let's just say that one or two were better at covering their tracks! After all, no one was going to send home senior players like Compton and Evans, were they?' And then he put his hand comically over his mouth as if to say, er, sorry about that – it just slipped out.

West Indies cricket has been bedevilled by inter-island squabbling and political posturing pretty well ever since its inception in the 1890s as a loose confederation of the far-flung English-speaking countries in the Caribbean. It played its first Test match in 1928 and had only sporadic success until the 1960s, despite possessing within its ranks a succession of marvellously gifted players. It was not until Frank Worrell was appointed captain, and was able to put aside the rivalries from the different islands and persuade his players to believe in themselves as a team, that their fortunes started to soar. Later, under the captaincy of Clive Lloyd and then Viv Richards, the West Indies became the dominant force in world cricket in the 1970s and 80s.

Since those glory days, sadly, there has been a steady decline in harmony and performance, partly through lack of strong leadership, partly through incompetent management and partly through a nosedive in popularity of cricket in the islands, in the face of competition from football, athletics and basketball.

The point about internecine strife in the governing body of West Indies cricket at the time of this tour is given credence by one or two astonishing stories from our eponymous hero. For the first Test at Sabina Park in Kingston, Jamaica, the great George Headley, a Jamaican, was flown out from Dudley, where he had been playing in the Birmingham League, to make a wholly unexpected comeback at the age of 45, thereby becoming the oldest West Indian to represent his country. 'Of course, he was well past his sell-by date,' said Tom, 'but he had to play because the local press had made it very plain that no one would turn up to watch if he didn't!'

Although the West Indies won comfortably, Headley wasn't up to it, being dismissed twice by Lock. 'He didn't see Lock's quicker ball,' my informant told me. 'It knocked two stumps out of the ground! Mind you, not many did see Lockie's quicker ball.' And he gave me a wink. The implication was clear. For years, Tony Lock was plagued by arguments about the legitimacy of his action and my research reveals that he was actually called for throwing during this match. 'He was the quickest bowler we had!' said Tom with only a hint of hyperbole.

The bowler who instigated England's last innings collapse was a fellow called Esmond Kentish. He took 5-49. 'And we never saw him again on the tour!' remarked Tom, shaking his head. 'Local politics, see?'

During the match, the wife and son of the umpire were attacked following an unpopular decision, the first hint of crowd trouble that was later to flare up alarmingly and dangerously. The thorny problem of poor, not to say biased, umpiring reared up again in the second Test in Barbados. Facing a large first-innings deficit, thanks largely to Walcott's monumental 220, England batted as if time had stood still. During the third day, the West Indies bowled 114 overs and England scored only 128 runs. And this in conditions ideal for batting, as Walcott had so vigorously demonstrated.

In the stands, the crowd barracked furiously; in the press, England were vilified for these go-slow tactics. Tom tells a revealing story which illustrates further the captain's almost pathological safety-first mindset. Early on, he joined Hutton at the crease. He soon located the middle of the bat and the ball raced away for two successive fours. Hutton approached him at the end of the over and told him, 'We don't want any of that. We've got to grind it out.' The upshot of his captain's instructions was that Graveney scored 15 in two hours and five minutes. It just wasn't him. Eventually, he succumbed tamely to a Ramadhin full toss.

The crucial umpiring decision that cost England the game came in the second innings. Compton and Graveney were making a decent fist of saving the game (the target to win was an improbable 495) before Compton was given out lbw for 93 with the worst decision on a cricket field that Tom has ever seen. Incredibly, the team later discovered that the umpire was Clyde Walcott's brother! After that, the England innings fell away and they lost by 181 runs, despite Graveney carrying his bat for 64, and they were now 2-0 down in the series.

England won the third Test in Guyana (or British Guiana, as it was known then) but not before a full-scale riot had threatened to end the match prematurely. 'Georgetown was a rough old place,' said Tom. 'I went back there 14 years later and the hotel was exactly the same – awful.'

In keeping with powerful forces in local politics, a Guyanese favourite, Christiani, had to be selected and the Englishmen's reservations about the umpiring were in no way assuaged by the news that the groundsman would be donning the white coat. Almost inevitably, it was an umpiring decision that sparked the riot. McWatt was given out run out and, as he was a local Guyanese player, the crowd erupted in anger. A hail of bottles rained down on the outfield and things were getting perilously close to violent disorder, so much so that the mounted police were deployed.

The chairman of the West Indies Board, Sir Errol de Santos (my source rarely forgets a name, especially one as sumptuous as this), pleaded with Len Hutton to take his team off the pitch because it was becoming dangerous. But the pragmatic Yorkshireman was unmoved – England were in a favourable position and he wanted another wicket, he explained. Sonny Ramadhin, the incoming batsman, was making his unenthusiastic way to the crease and happened to be passing the two men at the time. 'You can have mine any time you like,' he said. Not very much later, he was as good as his word.

It was Jonny Wardle, the team joker, who restored calm. He picked up one of the many bottles strewn across the outfield and pretended to drink from it. A more than passing impersonation of a drunken man reeling on rubbery legs made the crowd laugh and soon their mood had lightened to the extent that some semblance of order was restored and the game resumed. England won at a canter.

But not before Hutton had made a bizarre and, some might say, entirely self-serving decision. With only 75 required, he sent in Graveney and May to open the batting, instead of Watson and himself. 'He didn't fancy it,' was Tom's uncompromising verdict. On this occasion, unlike the time when his Gloucestershire captain had done the same to him, Graveney survived to see off the deficit but the poor young May did not.

The fourth Test in Trinidad was unusual in that it was played on a jute mat. 'You got out when you got tired,' was how Tom described this batsman's paradise. Which might explain a rare show of public anger from our normally mild-mannered hero. When the batsmen are in the ascendancy, chances for a dismissal come along rarely and must be seized and not squandered. So it is infuriating when you believe you have been denied your just desserts by a bad decision. The Englishmen's unhappiness over the umpiring had been simmering throughout the series and here it boiled over.

On the last ball before lunch, Holt – 'who never walked' – drove at it and was caught by Tom who was fielding at slip. He threw the ball gleefully up in the air and strode off to tuck into his lunch. Behind him, he heard Hutton beseeching the umpire, 'Go on – give him out!' The umpire was unmoved. So was Holt. Graveney was not. 'I lost my temper,' he admitted. 'I just stalked off and the whole ground booed me.' The match was a dull draw, there being barely enough time to complete the first round of innings, scarcely surprising with totals of 681 and 537.

And so, for the deciding Test, it was back to Kingston. Tom admitted that, though he loved the West Indies and got on famously with the locals, he would never book a holiday in Jamaica.

Why not, Tom? 'The place…well, it's a bit wild, lawless.' 'Edgy', we agreed, so unlike the leisurely, relaxed atmosphere of the other islands. The atmosphere for the match was edgy all right. That is until the sting was taken out of the exchanges by a magnificent double century from Hutton, which secured a large first-innings lead for England and despite a fightback by the West Indians in their second innings, only 72 were required for victory.

Once again Hutton pulled rank and sent in Graveney in his stead. This time he did not survive, being bowled for a duck. May and Wardle knocked off the runs to win the match and square the series. There is a notable footnote to this game. The 17-year-old Garfield Sobers made his Test debut.

You all must have been pleased to pull it back to 2-2, having lost the first two games? 'We were. It was a hell of an effort. Len was magnificent. What a fine player! It was a tragedy that he, along with others, lost what would have been his peak years to the war. One arm was shorter than the other, you know.'

Actually, I didn't. When Hutton was in the Army as a PE instructor, he had a bad accident in one of the training exercises and several operations left him with one arm shorter than the other, by one and a half inches. 'That made him struggle against the quicks, and my God was he peppered later in his career, but somehow he coped and scored all those runs. Amazing. That's why he enjoyed giving it back to the Aussies in 1954/55 over there. He'd had to cope with Lindwall and Miller for years, with only Alec Bedser, a medium-pacer, to respond. And then we had Tyson and Statham and the boot was firmly on the other foot at last. I think he enjoyed that.'

Tom had cause to be grateful to his captain for one thing, in spite of the fact that he sent him in to open when he fancied putting his feet up. 'He put me at first slip,' he said, 'which I enjoyed, and made my own.'

Ken Graveney told me that his brother was a superb slipper who caught practically everything that came his way.

'I modelled myself on Neil Harvey,' Tom told me. 'He was a brilliant all-round fielder. He caught the ball with his fingers pointed skywards, unlike the traditional English way, with the fingers pointing downwards.'

So, it was first slip for you for the rest of your career, was it? 'We-ell, as I got older, I moved more square – first, then second, then third, then gully.'

And now you're dead square? We laughed at that.

Was he a good captain? 'Len? Yes, you could say that. He was accused of being a bit defensive at times but he was a Yorkshireman, don't forget. They don't give much away.'

And how was he with you? 'Fine. A bit uncommunicative. But he was like that with everyone. You never knew quite what was going on in his mind.'

I asked Tom about the controversy and antagonism that had dogged the tour. It was generally accepted that the umpiring had been substandard and it was decreed afterwards that panels of umpires would be drawn up for subsequent series, rather than appointing local umpires for each Test. Nonetheless, the England team had been given a bad press, by both West Indian and English newspapers, for openly showing their displeasure about the umpiring and for some of their behaviour off the field.

'Do you know who we reckoned was the mole, the one who spilt the beans?' I shook my head. 'Swanton!' That surprised me not at all. E.W. Swanton would have had the ears of Gubby Allen and all the other committee members of MCC back at Lord's.

What did you think of Swanton, the supreme being of all things cricket? 'Pompous a***! But he did take me on an unofficial tour of the West Indies two years later. It was a sort of bridge-building exercise between the two countries. It was his tour, so he could bat where he liked. Not a bad player actually. Of course he didn't play in the serious games. He nicked one in an early match and didn't walk!'

So much for the Corinthian values which he so strenuously espoused. No doubt Tom was taken back there because, easily and naturally, he got on with everyone – players, officials, press, fans, waiters. But also, I guess it would be fair to say that he had grown up and was now firmly fixed in the international cricket firmament, confident and comfortable in his surroundings. He had learnt what it takes. And this included off-the-field behaviour, even in an age when press and public scrutiny was not so intrusive as it is today.

Let me give you a case in point. During a rest day, Tom wanted to play some golf. He was invited to play in a pro-am tournament in Jamaica, which he would normally have accepted with alacrity. But discretion prompted him to decline. They had just lost a Test – heavily. 'It wouldn't have looked good,' he explained. That is a lesson that some professional sportsmen never learn, no matter how talented they are.

By way of preparation for the storm that was awaiting them back in England, a ferocious one assailed them on the journey home. They were travelling by sea, not by air. Their ship – Tom described it more as a 'banana boat' – was not luxurious. It wasn't very big either, only 7,000 tonnes, and it was tossed around in some very heavy seas like a cork in a whirlpool. 'There were times when it seemed to be standing on end,' said England's finest sailor.

Did you get seasick? 'No. I've got a pretty good stomach. Trueman and Lock were dreadfully sick. But they were sharing a cabin, so fortunately we didn't see much of them.' I bet they would have turned an even greener hue had they known that they were about to lose their tour bonus.

The ship docked in Avonmouth, Tom's home town. 'I was allowed ashore for one night only, to see my new-born little girl.'

What? You haven't told me you're married yet! He looked at me oddly. 'I've been married for 60 years. You know that.' What I meant was that his courtship and marriage had slipped past unnoticed in our narrative, and it was high time we put that right.

5

Family Life And Cricket 1950–61

'Were you a strict father, Tom?'
'Certainly was. When I was there!'

It was boxing, not cricket, that constituted the subject of the verbal sparring that Tom had with his future wife when he first met her in June 1950. He remembered a young lady sitting on the stairs of a pub called The Hole in the Wall, near his home in Westbury-on-Trym, on the outskirts of Bristol. She had just been playing tennis and her short skirt was 'showing a great deal more leg than it ought'. In answer to the question that I had not asked – but might well have – he said, 'Jackie had great legs. Always did.'

They fell into conversation and at the time a boxing match was being broadcast loudly on the radio. It was in fact a bout that had caught the public's attention. On the retirement of the world champion, Joe Louis, a contest for the vacant crown between the American, Lee Savold, and the British hope, Bruce Woodcock, had been set up at The White City. Over 50,000 spectators were present and the fight had prompted a great deal of national interest. So much so that our local Romeo started talking to the tennis player about uppercuts rather than late cuts. Jackie was clearly impressed with the young man's pugilistic scholarship and challenged him to a bet on the fight's outcome. 'I backed the American,' he said.

Who won? 'I did,' he replied, rather pleased with himself. *And what did you win?* 'A drink,' was the pious reply, as if to say, well, this is 1950 we're talking about here.

Several rounds later, they got married in Winchcombe on 30 August 1952. Tom had been given permission by Gloucestershire to miss the last match of the season. 'I think I managed to catch the Sec in a good mood,' he said.

Who was your best man? 'Brother Ken.' *I bet he gave a good speech.* Tom pulled a face, in that theatrically humorous way of his. 'Ken is a very entertaining man.'

For a while, they lived with her parents in Bristol. Jackie's father was a fanatical cricketer and was still playing at the age of 82. 'He was an amazing man. Died while he was decorating the ceiling. To tell you the truth, he had more to do with his daughter marrying me than she did!' Tom still has his father-in-law's watch, with a lovely inscription on the back honouring his 50-year playing career for the Bristol Schoolmasters' Cricket Club.

Becky, the Graveneys' first-born, arrived on the scene while Tom was on duty with MCC in the West Indies in 1954. The wives of three of the players – Hutton, Compton and Evans – had joined the team at some stage on the tour and considerately brought out a photo of the baby for the proud father to see. A round of rum and cokes would have been immediately ordered, I am sure – and one for the waiter too. Tim, number two in the batting order, was born in 1960.

Why the delay of six years? Too much touring? One of the great advantages of age is that poor hearing can come to your aid when necessary. But I persisted with the point about touring and being away from home and family for long periods of time. Was he ever homesick and did he find the prolonged absences a trial? He thought about that. He enjoyed touring and playing cricket in different countries and testing himself against the best in varying conditions.

'We just got on with it,' he concluded. 'Of course it didn't suit everyone and even recently there have been one or two well-publicised cases of England players being forced to come home because they couldn't cope. But I was fine. I just loved playing for England.'

So how did you manage to keep the home fires burning from a distance? He smiled. 'A lot of letter writing.'

It set me thinking. International cricket tours are not so long these days – two or three months rather than the five or six they used to be – and mobile phones, texting and Skype make communication easier, but an international cricketer in the 21st century still spends an awful lot of time away from home. Separation from family is just as hard, in whatever era you played. So where do your priorities lie? In the emotional make-up of any professional sportsman, there must reside more than a trace of selfishness. Your livelihood depends upon your being successful; if, for whatever reason, success eludes you, the axe is poised over your neck. It is a cruel fact of life that you are only as good as your last game. Like politics, it always ends in tears.

Few retire from the game – whatever game it might be – fully content and fulfilled. If you are good at what you do, and genuinely love the life, and are ambitious to fulfil your talent, you will do all that it takes to be successful. In other words, you have to be dedicated and single-minded in your pursuit of glory, or else you fall by the wayside, soon to pick up your P45 slip.

Ruthlessness is part of it, though I would contend that team games, when you have to play with, and for, other people, rather than the solitary sports, like tennis, golf and athletics, does help to provide some sort of understanding of other people's perspective. But still, personal sensitivities invariably have to be sacrificed on the altar of success.

What has this got to do with Tom Graveney, generally regarded as one of the nicest men in the game? Well, there are two points to be made here. First, he saw no reason to bring real or simulated animosity on to the field of play. Famously companionable off the field, in the pavilion and in the bar after the game, he was able to face up to his opponents whenever he stepped on to the pitch and let his skill do the talking. He would seek to dominate a bowler and showed no mercy when he was on top.

But it was never personal. To him, the bowler was just that, someone who delivered the ball so that he could hit it. It was never that man Smith from Wessex who had upset him last year by refusing to declare or that nasty fast bowler Jones from Loamshire who always tried to knock his block off. It was a game, played by certain rules, within which you did your damnedest to win. And then, afterwards, you would all have a drink and chat affably about it all.

Were you ever sledged when you were batting? 'No, never,' he answered. 'Lindwall, Miller, Hall, Statham, Sobers, Davidson – they never said a word. I just got on with my job and they got on with theirs.' Different times, admittedly, but even nowadays, with the emphasis on histrionic appealing and personal confrontation – what Steve Waugh used to call 'mental disintegration' – there are certain batsmen, the very best, admittedly, who don't seem to get sledged. Richards (either of them), Lara, Tendulkar, Dravid, Laxman or Chanderpaul rarely had abuse hurled at them.

Perhaps there are certain players with an inner peace, a phlegmatic temperament and an innate decency that do not rub people up the wrong way. Tom Graveney was such a person. But that doesn't mean that he was soft. He didn't give his wicket away. He wanted to score runs, as many as he could, and nothing, no one would stand in his way. Is this selfishness? Of a sort, I suppose. No professional sportsman can survive without that single-minded impulse to survive.

Anyone who sings for his supper – and I include all professional entertainers and peripatetic breadwinners – has to square with his conscience being away from home and abandoning his family. Tom Graveney was no different. There were times when he felt guilty about being an absent father for long stretches of time and he did his best to make up for it during the infrequent and intermittent periods when he was at home. His daughter, Becky, recounts one incident from her childhood, which poignantly illustrates the point.

'Dad came back from touring somewhere or other. I was, what, four or five at the time. Apparently, I ran away from this strange man who approached me with a funny looking doll in his hand. I locked myself in the loo and it took two hours for them to get me out.'

With a rueful smile, Tom admitted that he remembered the occasion very well. 'It was not a doll. It was a koala bear. So it must have been after the 1958/59 tour of Australia.' 'I've got about 80 foreign dolls,' said Becky, laughing. 'But I was away at school,' she added, 'and kept very busy, so it wasn't too bad most of the time. I always hated saying goodbye. Still do, as a matter of fact.'

Her brother, Tim, remembers watching from the top floor of their house in Winchcombe for the returning hero to make his appearance at the far end of the street. He was aware that his father was a famous person in the neighbourhood but didn't really know why. In point of fact, stressed Tom, his children were remarkably unaffected by their father's fame. He did his best to keep firmly separate his role as a celebrated national sportsman from that as a family man.

'I know he was away a lot,' said Tim, 'but I don't remember him coming very often to watch me play cricket, for example, at school.' This was not said with any resentment; Tim just accepted that that was the way things were. 'That's probably true,' conceded Tom. 'But I was desperate for it not to become the Tom Graveney Show whenever I made an appearance. As soon as I would set foot anywhere in the school or on the pitches, everybody would rush up to me and ignore the children. It wasn't right. I wanted to avoid that.'

And you have to see his point. Tim is sanguine about his father's prominence in the public eye. 'Having a famous father has its disadvantages, certainly, but it also opens up a lot of doors. How many times in my life has someone said to me, "Your name is Graveney? You must be Tom's son. I remember when I watched your dad play at…" And away we'd go. That person, who revered Dad's memory and the pleasure he had given him, would be my friend too. And more often than not, I'd make very useful contacts.' Tom laughed when I told him this. 'That son of mine has a bulging address book, the biggest I've ever seen!'

Tell me, were you a strict father? 'Certainly was.' And then the slow, wide grin. 'When I was there!' One story he tells has obviously gone down in family folklore. He was cross with Tim for some long-forgotten misdemeanour and was fully intending to deliver physical chastisement of one form or another to the errant youngster. That is, if he could catch him. 'The house was built in a sort of circular style so the little blighter could run round and round, in one door and out the other, and I could never corner him. Bit like a farce, really.'

The obvious person to talk to therefore, the one on whom the burden largely fell for looking after the family and bringing up the children, is, needless to say, his wife, Jackie. But sadly that is not possible. She now lives in a nursing home once Tom had eventually been persuaded by his children that he was no longer able to look after her single-handedly. The strain was having an alarming effect on his own health and his friends were becoming concerned by his weight loss and obvious decline. She was not well and he saw it as his duty to care for her, at whatever personal cost.

Amateur psychologists might nod their heads here and point to this as a classic case of expiation for past neglect, feelings of guilt for being away so often when he was needed. There may be something in this. But who knows? It is not my job to peer too closely into another man's marriage. We all cope with life's vicissitudes as best we can.

What I have gleaned from the recollections of Tom's numerous friends and colleagues is that he has *always* been very loyal to Jackie, long before she required the specialised care that she now has. Happily, she lives in a home right next door to where Tom lives, so he is able to potter across to see her every day and have lunch with her three times a week. By all accounts, she is content and well cared for and the improvement in Tom's health and vigour is thankfully apparent. The stress of a full-time carer is not one for an 85-year-old.

Nevertheless, Tom's regular absences from the home – and don't forget that a professional cricketer's life is largely spent on the road during the summer too, quite apart from the winter tours – did have a dispiriting effect on Jackie. That much is admitted by Becky and, tacitly, by her father.

'Fortunately, there was a tight-knit family network in support,' she said. 'That's why we moved to Winchcombe. My mum's sister, Marjorie Newton, and her husband, Roy, lived there and managed a coaching inn, The George. It was quite famous for having a secret passage connected to Sudeley Castle, to enable the monks to make their escape during the Reformation and King Henry VIII's Dissolution of the Monasteries. My aunt and uncle became like my second parents.'

Tom knew that it was difficult for his wife, bringing up two young children often on her own, but felt reassured by the support of a loyal and extended family. It was a state of affairs that wasn't ideal but it was one shared by countless other families in a not so distant world war. 'We just got on with it,' said Tom. 'That was my job. Wasn't any good at anything else, was I?'

Becky laughed at this. 'Don't run away with the impression that touring was all hard work and lonely hotel rooms for Dad. He had a whale of a time – all those cocktail parties and receptions in maharajahs' palaces!'

Tom gave an enigmatic smile, as if to say, 'Well, touring is not all champagne and canapés, I'll have you know. There was a fair bit of serious cricket to be played as well. But perhaps, from time to time, there was a grain of truth in what you are saying.'

Both Becky and Tim are agreed that their mother struggled with their father being away for long periods. Becky remembers wistfully family holidays in the Isle of Wight but of course one person was always missing. 'Anyway,' she said philosophically, 'Dad would have been hopeless on those holidays. He hates the sea and the sand.'

So what sort of social life did you have? 'Mainly, it revolved around cricket,' she answered. 'That's true,' agreed Tom, 'it takes over your life, doesn't it?'

Did the family come to watch you play? 'To home matches, yes, a fair bit. Usually at Cheltenham, which is a lovely ground. Bristol wasn't so easy. It can be a soulless place. The facilities were not so good and viewing isn't the best. When I moved to Worcester…well, it felt like home. Still does, as a matter of fact.'

Becky remembers going to watch her father play twice at Lord's. On both occasions, he scored runs. But Jackie seemed to have a hoodoo on him. As soon as she entered a ground, no matter how unobtrusively, he would get out. Tim remembers less of any particular innings. He was younger and busied himself for hours, during the intervals and after stumps, playing on the outfield at Worcester with the Headley children and Basil D'Oliveira's son, Damian. Sometimes, Becky would join them. 'My goodness!' exclaimed one onlooker from the bar in the pavilion. 'Just look at that girl bowling. She's better than all of them!'

Tell me about your mother. A bit fiery at times, people tell me. 'Feisty', said Tim. 'Strong,' said Becky, 'but her bark was worse than her bite.' Tom just smiled sphinx-like. His love for her is unconditional and in any case, it's difficult to get an entirely dispassionate judgement of a wife from a husband. Or vice versa, for that matter. Jackie Graveney intrigued me, not because I like peering into other people's private lives but because I was interested in how she dealt with Tom's fame, the vicissitudes of a professional sportsman's career and the effect it had on family life.

What is it like to have a husband who is almost universally revered, even 45 years after he stopped playing? How do you cope with having perfect strangers coming up to you all the time and telling you, with a dreamy look in their eyes, that they remember when Tom Graveney played a cover drive in 1953? Or was it 1954? No, possibly it was 1955… I bet she could have a story or two to tell, if only she were in a position to tell them.

But then Becky made an interesting point. She felt her mother was not always made to feel comfortable by other wives and committee members at receptions and social gatherings. Even though the world beyond cricket was changing, there was still a fair amount of snobbery around when Tom was playing. Jackie was always intensely protective of her husband's reputation as a cricketer and especially in the earlier days of his career, when the England selectors did not seem to appreciate his deeds as much as the general public, she suffered for him. And furthermore she didn't mind who knew it. There was the suspicion, an intuition that hardened into certainty after Tom was sacked as captain at Gloucestershire (a story that we shall deal with in due course), that her husband suffered at the hands of amateur prejudice. You see, Tom was a player and gentlemen ran the game.

The distinction had been around ever since the birth of cricket and was enshrined in the annual Gentlemen v Players fixture that was first played in 1806. In simple terms, the players were paid to play cricket; the gentlemen were not. The difference was shaped by the English class system. The gentry had private means and therefore could play the game as amateurs whereas the workers had to be paid for their employment and thereby became professionals.

Lord's was built as a private club and opened in 1787, later named Marylebone Cricket Club (MCC), which soon saw itself as the sole custodian of the game and its laws, in England and elsewhere. The ranks of amateur players were swelled by a steady influx of players from the public schools and the universities, with the professionals almost exclusively coming from the working class. The status quo remained pretty much unchanged, with the clear social divide between gentlemen and players, up until the Second World War.

As in many facets of life, that social and political upheaval changed people's perceptions of how a fairer society ought to be organised and though cricket was slower to adapt than other institutions, it could no more stand in the way of progress than the horse in the way of the motor car. Or buckles on pads being replaced by Velcro.

When Tom started playing, there were still pockets of resistance to change that survived in the game, such as the belief that an amateur captain was usually a better bet than a professional. True, Hutton was the first professional to captain England in 1952 but I'm sure had Peter May – an amateur – been ten years older, he would have been asked to take on the job rather than Hutton. As it was, after Hutton retired, MCC reverted to type and appointed May as captain in 1955. The scorecards of the day still persisted with the distinction of status: it would be P.B.H. May, Esq or Mr P.B.H. May but it would be Graveney T.W.

Finally, in 1962, the whole ridiculous charade was done away with, largely because of the confusion over, and the abuse by, the 'shamateurs', the amateurs who were being covertly paid to play. 'Those shamateurs!' laughed Tom. 'They were getting paid more than we professionals!' In fact Tom played in the final Gentlemen and Players match at Lord's in 1962. Captaining the Gents was Ted Dexter. Captaining the Players was Fred Trueman. The match was drawn, a compromise that seems to be admirably English in its even-handedness.

What did you think of it all, the amateur and professional divide? 'Good riddance to it. We were all players. Let's just get on with playing the game without all these petty distinctions. The abolition of amateur status had become inevitable, just as the power of MCC in running the game worldwide was beginning to seep away. It was a change long overdue.'

Did you have to come out on to the field of play through different gates when you started playing? 'No, that was done away with after the war.'

Did you ever have to change in separate rooms to the amateurs? 'No. I think Lancashire still had a captain's room but that was about it.'

Did you get on all right with the amateurs? 'With one or two exceptions, yes, I did. We all played the game because we loved it. It certainly had nothing to do with the salary we earned,' he laughed sardonically. 'Most of the amateurs were fine. Only one or two were a bit funny. We didn't have many at Gloucestershire. B.O. Allen, not my favourite person, as you know, was one. His successor, Sir Derrick Bailey, who was odd at times but a nice enough fella and not a bad captain. Other teams, like Somerset and Worcestershire, seemed to rely on amateurs more than we did. Some of them were good enough, some were not.'

And there's the rub. The less well-off clubs went through periods when they simply couldn't afford to have a fully professional staff and had to rely on a steady stream of amateurs to pull together 11 players and fulfil their fixtures.

I am reliant on the reminiscences of George Chesterton, a former teaching colleague of mine at Malvern College, for his perspective on amateurism. In the 1950s, he opened the bowling for Worcestershire. But only during the school holidays. He truly was an amateur. He wasn't paid to play; he was one of that rapidly diminishing breed of schoolmaster-cricketers who played when they could.

'It was extraordinary, really,' he told me, 'I would simply ring up the secretary of the club at the beginning of the season and let him know what games I was available to play. And I would just turn up on the morning of the match and… play.'

What? No training, no practice, no nets? 'Well, I had bowled a few at the boys in the nets at Malvern,' he conceded. 'On my debut for Worcestershire, I entered the dressing room – and this was in August, don't forget – and there were all these players that I had idolised as a boy staring back at me, an unknown amateur just down from Oxford. I was making my way to the furthest corner of the room when Reg Perks, the legendary fast bowler, cried out, "Come over and change next to me, George. There are plenty of pegs here." I never forgot that moment of kindness. The pros just accepted me straight away.'

Peter Richardson, a team-mate and a good friend of George's, takes up the story. 'Ah, yes, that was because George was good enough. We had a succession of Cambridge graduates or sons of committee members who played for us – all hopeless! But George was different. He was by far the best of the amateur bowlers. When I was captain, about two-thirds of the way through the season, everybody, especially the bowlers, were tired and started to moan.

'"Don't worry, lads," I would say. "Next week George will be back!" And that seemed to cheer everyone up. His value to Worcestershire in those difficult years was inestimable.'

The point is that George Chesterton earned his place in the side on merit. The professionals would never have accepted him otherwise. Tom Graveney concurred. 'Mighty fine bowler, George. I was his first first-class wicket you know – Oxford University v Gloucestershire in 1949.' Tom is like an elephant with cricket facts and figures.

True amateurs, such as Chesterton, were already a dying breed in the game; more and more of the so-called amateurs were finding it difficult to play full-time without financial remuneration and various and even more ingenious ways were being found to pay them. Eventually, the concept of amateurism was scrapped and the distinction between them and the players ceased to exist.

On paper perhaps the division between the classes had been abolished but did it still live on in people's minds, in a way that Jackie sometimes uncomfortably sensed? 'Not among the players. We all got on well. There was no friction at all,' Tom insisted. 'I have a theory, tried and tested all my life, and it pretty much holds true every time. All cricketers are decent people. There's something about the common bond that binds us all together. A few quarrels here and there but they're soon forgotten. Like one big family really.'

And then, by way of illustrating his premise, he told me a story about a Test match on the tour of the West Indies in 1967/68. Charlie Griffith bowled him a 'beamer'. Now, anyone who has played the game can vouch for the fact that a 'beamer' is the most dangerous delivery a bowler can bowl. It is aimed straight at the head of the batsman and because he is looking down at the pitch, expecting it to bounce – short or full – he is totally unprepared for the missile heading straight for his face at 90mph. It is not in his line of sight. It can cause horrific injury, especially in the days before helmets, and it is banned as a legitimate delivery. That does not stop one or two hotheads doing it of course, usually claiming that the ball 'slipped' out of the hand.

That is nonsense, as any batsman will tell you. A beamer is a beamer and is always delivered with malicious intent, no matter how profuse the subsequent apology. The trouble is that the damage has been done. If you are lucky enough to avoid being hit, you will always be looking for it and it upsets your rhythm and concentration. Such offenders are never well regarded in the game. One such reprobate was Charlie Griffith and I was unsurprised to hear from Tom that he occasionally let one go. 'I was as mad as a snake,' he said. 'I came as close as I ever had to losing it completely on the pitch. I went down the wicket and said to him, "If you ever do that to me again, you ****, I'll kill you!" This was said with my bat raised above my head. I would have done, you know. Fortunately, the umpire stepped in and a major scene was averted. Thank goodness, or I would have been banned for life.'

What happened afterwards, between you and Griffith? 'Oh, we patched it up, like you always do. But he never did that to me again.'

The point is, he was at pains to emphasise, that was one of the rare occasions when real animosity had soured a game of cricket that he had played in. 'Amateurs, professionals, aristocrats, coal miners, Test players, county players, black, white, brown – just didn't matter. It's a sort of brotherhood. So no, the abolition of amateurs and professionals didn't make any difference to me.'

What about the administrators, the committee men, MCC? Any residual prejudice or snobbery there? He wrinkled his nose sceptically. 'Well, there might have been *some*. But it never bothered me.'

The irony of it all is that Tom, a captain in the Army at the age of 20, and by his amused estimation probably a general by now, would have been in the officer class, firmly in the ranks of the amateurs. Yet here he was, playing as a professional for Gloucestershire. But it is an irony that is largely lost on him. To him, everyone was a fellow player and he found it easy to get on with anyone, whatever his social background.

After the game, over a pint or two, he was much more interested in discussing this shot or that ball or the crucial dropped catch that changed the course of the match than he was bothered by what school his companion had been to. All the Australians, for example, were 'amateurs', there being no professional set-up in that country, but it made not a jot of difference to Tom, whether he was ducking under a bouncer from Ray Lindwall or sharing a drink with him in the bar afterwards.

I persisted. *But what about the earlier days? At the festivals at the end of the season at Hastings and Scarborough?* He did admit that certain social distinctions pertained but he seemed quite unperturbed by it all. 'The amateurs stayed in the Grand Hotel and had to don dinner jackets in the evenings. We pros had to find ourselves a bed and breakfast somewhere. We didn't mix much. But that was fine. I was perfectly content getting to know my fellow pros over a meal and a few drinks.'

He was comfortable in his life as a professional cricketer and confident enough in his ability. After all, no one wore a black tie at 11.30am the next day at the start of play. Everyone was in flannels.

6

Seasoned International – The First Incarnation 1954–59

'Graveney's got a red face. And I don't like red faces.'
(Len Hutton, England captain)

There is a story about Len Hutton that, if only half-true, is revealing. Tom assures me that it did happen exactly as he describes and I have heard it from one or two other sources as well but I still find it difficult to credit that team selection for a national side can be conducted in such an off-hand and maladroit manner.

The custom was that the selection committee for an overseas tour would conduct their deliberations and then present their chosen team to MCC, who would then send out invitations to the players concerned. Of course the captain's opinions and wishes would be taken into consideration but the choice was not his alone. However, Hutton being Hutton, it is unlikely that his wishes would have been ignored. He knew whom he wanted in his team and whom he didn't.

Hutton may have been England's first professional captain but the game was still run by amateurs and there were those in the upper hierarchy of MCC who were deeply suspicious of anything that smacked of professionalism in its administration. In fact, following the controversial tour of the West Indies in 1953/54, a considerable faction within MCC had been deeply critical of Hutton's captaincy – the first by a professional abroad – and blamed him for the less than flattering public image that the England team had presented on tour. He remained as captain for the first Test that summer against

Pakistan but then physical and mental exhaustion, undoubtedly brought on by the troubles that winter, caused him to miss the second and third Tests.

The anti-Hutton cabal seized their moment and manoeuvred the amateur, David Sheppard, into the captaincy. Already advanced on his clerical career that would culminate in his becoming Bishop of Liverpool, he had to take leave of absence from his theological studies to resume playing for England. The old guard at Lord's saw him as a better candidate to take on the role of captaining the England side on the forthcoming Ashes tour to Australia that winter and he was asked to make himself available, which he did.

Hutton, a Yorkshireman let no one forget, was not to be so easily sidelined. He had not been sacked. He had merely been unfit and, in his opinion, Sheppard had been the stand-in captain only while he was away. And of course, his standing in the public's estimation was well nigh impregnable, to say nothing of his pre-eminent position as the country's leading batsman. Besides, he had unfinished business with the Aussies. He had defeated them in England. Now he wanted to beat them in their own backyard. All those years of hurt, stretching back before the war, had to be avenged before he hung up his boots. And he had a plan. More of that shortly.

In the face of strong public opinion, the anti-Hutton faction was routed and he was restored to the captaincy for the fourth Test and for the winter tour. As it happened, England lost that match, providing the fledgling state of Pakistan with their first victory in a Test match, provoking wild scenes of jubilation and celebration by their supporters in front of the pavilion at the Oval.

It really was an extraordinary and wholly unexpected result for, in truth, the Pakistan side were not that strong and had been pretty well outplayed all summer. For example, they had been heavily defeated – by an innings and 129 runs – in the second Test at Trent Bridge during which England had amassed a mammoth total of 558/6 declared, with Compton scoring 278. Tom Graveney had shared a fourth-wicket stand with him of 154, contributing a sublime but all-too-brief 84. *Wisden* reported, 'Well as Compton played, Graveney played even better.'

'Don't put that in,' Tom ordered me, 'it sounds boastful.' For once, I have gone against the great man's wishes. It needs to be emphasised from time to time how much the beauty and elegance of his strokeplay enchanted the watching public.

Though few begrudged the Pakistanis their triumph in the final Test that summer, Tom is adamant that it should never have happened. In a low-scoring game, it was nip and tuck as England chased a fourth-innings total of 167. With the score at 109/2, an England victory seemed a formality. But it was getting dark and Godfrey Evans persuaded Hutton that he should go in, chance his arm and get the match finished that night.

The plan backfired. Wickets tumbled and in the face of some fine medium-pace bowling from Fazal Mahmood (the same Fazal that Tom had described as 'unplayable' on his home surface of matting), the England innings crumbled. They lost by 23 runs, Fazal taking 12 of the 20 wickets to fall.

It was a blow to Hutton but not a grievous one. He still had his eye on the larger prize – getting one over the old enemy that winter. The plan that I referred to earlier had been germinating in his mind for a while. It was to do it with pace. Nothing radical about that. Australian pitches traditionally favoured fast bowling and Lindwall and Miller had been reminding him of that fact, often uncomfortably so, for many years. But this time it was different. He had up his sleeve a secret weapon by the name of Frank Tyson.

Well, perhaps it wasn't such a secret after all; those, including Tom Graveney, who had already faced him when he bowled for his native Northamptonshire, were in no doubt of his raw pace. But as yet he was untried and untested on the international stage. Hutton, however, believed in him and planned to build his attack around him. With Brian Statham sharing the new ball, Hutton was sure that, at long last, he had the firepower to outgun the Australians. Accordingly, he set about putting the pieces of the jigsaw in place.

The story goes that Tom, Statham and Jim Laker were having a drink in the bar when Hutton joined them. Not a naturally gregarious man, whom some found rather serious and impenetrable, he did take trouble with his team and looked after their interests. That is, if you were part of his plans. He engaged the young Statham in conversation, asking him whether he felt he would bowl well on hard, Australian wickets. Statham unsurprisingly replied that he believed that hard, Australian wickets would suit him just fine – indeed he was very much looking forward to the opportunity of bowling on them.

Hutton assured him that he would have that opportunity, as he would be picked for the tour. He turned to Tom and asked him whether he fancied his chances Down Under with the bat. Tom replied with commendable enthusiasm; who wouldn't relish batting on hard, Australian wickets? He too was promised a berth in the touring team. Then Hutton moved on to Laker. 'Jim,' he said, 'go and get the drinks, will you?'

And in such a way did England's premier spin bowler discover that he would not be touring that winter. Trueman and Lock, two members of the Ashes-winning side of 1953, were also controversially omitted. 'Len was a bit funny like that,' commented Tom. 'You never really knew what was in his mind.' He maintained that he had a good relationship with his captain, though others found him a bit stiff and uncommunicative. His authority in the side was unquestioned, even if the amateur lobby at Lord's, and elsewhere, would have preferred Sheppard at the helm.

It was felt that a professional leader, whose Pudsey accent was sometimes too flat for their liking, would be unable to fulfil the social and diplomatic functions of an MCC captain abroad. Fortunately, there were little or no murmurings from within the team itself. Of the amateurs, Edrich was a contemporary and had been a professional with him before the war and the others, Bailey, Simpson, May and Cowdrey, were much younger and no threat to his leadership.

Tom did voice a slight criticism of him as a skipper, believing that he was a bit cautious in his tactics and seemed more concerned in holding on to what advantage he had rather than pressing on to ram home that advantage. Neither was Tom alone in this reservation; the press too thought that England were negative in their play and deliberately slow in their over rate. But the ends justified the means, as we shall see, and there were few naysayers when he returned home with the Ashes.

Tom also admitted to a vague and unspoken conviction that his captain was losing faith in him. 'Could never quite put my finger on it,' he said, 'but I had the distinct feeling that he couldn't trust me in a crisis.' Perhaps it went back to that dismissal at Lord's in 1953, he mused, when he was 78 not out overnight. The following morning, remember, Lindwall had yorked him without adding to his score, with a disapproving Hutton watching from the non-striker's end. If that is so, then it was a pitiless judgement for it was a brute of a ball and would probably have done for anyone, Hutton included. But Hutton was a Yorkshireman and came from the school of hard knocks.

More revealing was the comment that Hutton made about Tom, no doubt in an unguarded moment, but cutting enough. 'Graveney's got a red face,' he said, 'and I don't like red faces.' Later on, when the tour of Australia was well advanced, he confided in the tour manager, Geoffrey Howard, 'I am a bit afraid that he is not quite the chap for the big occasion when the heat is on.'

Tom shrugged his shoulders when reminded of this. 'Let's not forget,' he generously pointed out, 'there were some mighty fine players knocking about at the time, all vying for their places; Hutton himself; Edrich; Simpson; May; Compton; Bailey. And Cowdrey was developing into a fine, fine player.' That was true enough; it was a golden age of English batsmanship. But not to be classed in the same category because you had a 'red face' is a bit harsh.

'Or maybe it was when I got him out,' he added suddenly. I must have widened my eyes in disbelief, for he continued, 'I got 80 first-class wickets, you know.' I had to admit that my knowledge of his bowling prowess was less extensive than that of his batting.

Having decided in the heat of Egypt that quick bowling was a mug's game, he started to flirt with a mixture of leg spin and googlies and with a lot of practice in the nets at Gloucestershire – after all, what else is there to do in a net session when you're not batting? – he turned himself into a useful part-time bowler. 'Took 5-28 against Derbyshire in 1953,' he told me proudly.

A quick rooting about in the record books confirmed this fact – as if I ever doubted it – and in only seven overs too. What a devastating exhibition of the ancient and unfathomable craft of wrist spin that must have been. And that wasn't the end of it, either; few batsmen can resist waxing lyrical over their sporadic successes with the ball. 'Anyway,' he continued, 'when we were playing Yorkshire in 1954, I got Len out. Bowled him. He wasn't very happy.'

He can't have been that cross. After all, he took you to Australia that winter. Perhaps he took you as a bowler. We both laughed. You could tell that there was no lingering animosity on his part towards Hutton. On the contrary, the respect he felt for the man was palpable. 'Even after the war, and his injury, he was still a great player.'

Whatever reservations anyone might harbour over Hutton's less-than-tactful man-management, there can be no denying the clear-sighted formulation of his tactics to beat Australia and the courageous way that he stuck to his guns. Especially after the disastrous loss of the first Test, in which he had famously put them in, suffering as they amassed 601/8 declared to condemn England to an innings defeat plus plenty. The press hung him out to dry but he still believed in his strategy and was convinced that Tyson would come good, even though the fast bowler had failed thus far to make the impact that was expected of him.

This was all to change at Sydney in the second Test. As recounted by Tom, the story had me rapt, as it must have had those watching all those years ago. He hadn't played in the first Test owing to illness but returned for this game. 'Frank had a long run, about 38 paces. It seemed too long, especially in that heat. And don't forget, we had eight-ball overs in Australia then.'

Tyson, under advice from his captain and others, decided to shorten it, and the results were electrifying. England were well behind when they started their second innings and found themselves staring defeat in the face when they were reduced to 55/3 before May (104) and Cowdrey (56) put together a stand of 116 precious runs. The England total of 296 was respectable but the target for the Australians of 223 was not considered too difficult. But then Tyson took hold of the new ball and proceeded to deliver one of the most devastating spells of fast bowling ever seen in a Test match.

'I was fielding at first slip,' said Tom. 'There was a 40-mile-an-hour gale blowing down the ground. I was standing 40 yards back, nearer the boundary behind me than the stumps. And still the snicks were flying over my head. It was frightening.'

I guess the Aussies didn't fancy it too much then, did they? Tom pulled a face that seemed to hint he had considerable sympathy for the opposing batsmen on this occasion – even if they were Australian.

'But don't forget the brave contribution of my old mate, Brian Statham,' he stressed. 'He played a crucial part in the victory. Nineteen overs – eight-ball overs, remember – and took three for 40-odd, into the teeth of that howling gale. Incredible! Such stamina! Such accuracy!'

Australia were dismissed for 184 (Tyson 6-85 and ten wickets in the match) and England had won by the narrow margin of 38 runs, to bring the series level at 1-1. Defeat, and a 2-0 deficit, would have been hard to stomach and would have meant, in all probability, the loss of the Ashes.

'The Toast is Typhoon Tyson' was the headline in one of the papers the next morning and debate raged as to whether anyone had ever, in the history of the game, bowled as fast as Tyson that day. The debate still goes on to this day. Tom is adamant that he has never seen anyone, in his playing days or since, who has bowled faster. And no less an authority than Sir Don Bradman, who had faced Larwood, let us not forget, and who later witnessed Lillee and Thomson in their pomp, always said that Tyson, on that tour in 1954/55, was the fastest of the lot.

By now, Tyson had the Indian sign on his opponents and once again, in the next Test, blew away the Australian second innings with figures of 7-27 to give England victory by 128 runs and a 2-1 advantage in the series. His bowling was every bit as fearsomely fast as in the previous match and his reputation as a sporting legend was now sealed. Tom was a mere spectator this time – Hutton had decided to drop him – and the same happened for the fourth Test, which decided the rubber and the Ashes.

England won by five wickets, though not without a nervous wobble at the very end. Left with only 94 to win, they were reeling at 18/3 in the face of a furious onslaught from Keith Miller, dismissing Hutton, Edrich and Cowdrey in short order.

In the dressing room, Hutton gloomily observed that Miller 'has done for us again'. Compton was strapping on his pads. 'Hang on,' he said. 'I haven't batted yet.' He went out and saw the team home, a proper and fitting moment, perhaps, for England's most charismatic batsman to be at the crease when the Ashes were retained, as he had been at the Oval some 18 months earlier when England won them back after all those years.

I read somewhere that 56 bottles of champagne were consumed that night. And that Bill Edrich climbed one of the marble pillars of the hotel and sang 'Ginger'. Can you confirm this? Tom smiled. 'I wouldn't be surprised. In fact, I wouldn't be surprised at anything Bill did. I remember once he was politely asked to extinguish his cigarette. He did so by jumping fully clothed into the hotel swimming pool.'

Delighted as he was, Tom was chomping at the bit to make his own mark on this historic tour. His chance came in the fifth Test. 'Edrich was finished,' he said. 'Exhausted. Shot his bolt.' Hardly surprising really. His cricket career had started before the war. After joining up with the RAF, there were many times when he was flying Blenheim bombers in missions over Germany – for which he was awarded the DFC – when he firmly believed that he would never see a cricket ground again but the gods deemed otherwise. Against all the odds, he survived and continued to serve his country on the cricket field, and in the bar afterwards, with distinction up until this moment.

Victory had been assured, he was tired and he stood down, never to play for his country again. Tom was set to take his place. All right, the series had already been won but this was a Test match and it was against Australia.

It rained. Solidly, for three days. Eventually, the rain abated enough for the two captains to go out on to the field to toss with only 13 hours of scheduled play remaining. But back in the England dressing room, no one knew who was in the team; characteristically, Hutton was playing his cards very close to his chest. When he returned, having won the toss, he turned to our hero and said, 'Get your pads on, Tom; you're opening with me.' Tom was flabbergasted. 'I didn't even know I was playing. And I certainly wasn't an opener.'

Did you, er, remonstrate? He shook his head. 'We did as we were told. He was the captain and what he said, you did. You wanted to play, see. No rocking the boat. You just got on with it.'

So he strapped on his pads and joined his captain on their walk to the middle from the famous green-roofed and ornately designed pavilion of the Sydney Cricket Ground.

Apparently it had been Bradman's idea. He had offered the observation to Hutton in desultory conversation that Graveney would make a good opener. Tom had never opened in his life and was understandably nervous as he took guard to face Lindwall. His third ball, on leg stump, he glanced off his legs and was relieved to see it race away for four. The nerves were settled.

Hutton, who *had* opened in his life – in 76 Tests up to this point, to say nothing of his 500-odd matches for Yorkshire – did not last long, caught Burge, bowled Lindwall for six. Peter May joined Graveney at the crease and together they put on a stand of 182. Tom effortlessly stroked his way to 111. *Wisden* commented, 'Graveney, when the tension had gone, finished in a blaze of glory.' Thereafter, the game petered out in an inevitable draw.

Let us look again at that phrase of the *Wisden* correspondent, 'when the tension had gone', faintly damning in its praise, I think you will agree. It is a strange but inescapable fact that this hundred of Tom's was the only one he scored against Australia. Dare I whisper it aloud that he had a bit of a 'thing' with the old enemy? In much the same way, Ian Botham, despite – or maybe because of – his great friendship with Viv Richards, never really performed against the West Indies with the same panache that he did against other countries, and faced the same criticism. Did Hutton's unvoiced reservations about Graveney's temperament have a ring of truth about it?

I tentatively broached the subject with him. His reply was instantaneous and illuminating. 'Every time I hit the ball in the air against that lot,' he said, 'someone caught it.' Sometimes sport can be made too complicated, 'paralysis by analysis', as someone cleverly coined it. Perhaps that was just the way it was. He never had much luck against Australia, and it can happen like that.

'Never got any runs against your old county,' he said by way of explanation of things that are inexplicable. And it is true. For Gloucestershire against Hampshire, he averaged only 21.69, as opposed to an average of 43.02 overall. It wasn't as if Hampshire at that time possessed a frightening attack. 'Aaargh, Derek Shackleton,' he groaned at the memory of that county's medium-pace bowler. 'He'd bore you out!'

Similarly, there is a wide discrepancy in his favourite and less-favoured grounds. 'You always like the grounds where you make runs,' he assured me, a trifle unnecessarily. 'Never got runs at Old Trafford or Headingley. But I always seemed to get runs at Chesterfield, Trent Bridge, the Oval and of course Lord's.' Now explain that. I can't. As Geoff Boycott has said on numerous occasions: 'It's a foonny old game, creeckit.'

So, it was back home to take on the visiting South Africans? 'Hang on a minute.' Tom held up his hand. 'There was still the New Zealand leg of the tour to get through.' I had forgotten that. They were long tours in those days and there must have been, within the party, following the dramas of the Australian leg, a sense of 'after the Lord Mayor's Show'.

It was decided to persist with the experiment of using Tom as an opener and on the face of it, it didn't seem to be such a bad idea after all, despite his misgivings – in four matches, he scored two hundreds.

There is a lovely story he tells about Hutton, in the second Test, which proved to be his swansong in international cricket. 'Typical Len, really,' said Tom, chuckling. Just a brief glance at the scorecard discloses the story of a remarkable game. New Zealand scored 200 in their first innings; England replied with 246. As he led his team on to the field for the New Zealand second innings, Hutton announced, 'We've got a lead of 46. Just enough to beat them by an innings.'

'And we did!' Tom guffawed. 'Bowled 'em out for 26! It was all over in one and a half hours.' He did admit that the wicket was a 'bit dodgy'. But still – all out for 26! It smacks of a one-sided school house match more than a Test. And it remains the lowest total ever recorded in a Test match.

Notwithstanding the need to move the narrative forward, I now wanted to linger with the 1954/55 tourists. It had, in the main, been a frustrating time for Tom but it had been an engrossing series, it had produced a fast-bowling hero in Frank Tyson, fit to rank with the greats of the game, and the Ashes had been retained away from home, and that doesn't happen very often. In fact, since the war, only four England captains have matched Hutton's feat – Illingworth, Brearley, Gatting and Strauss.

As we have seen, Hutton was physically and emotionally spent following his exertions and retired soon afterwards. Other players too – Edrich, Bedser, Compton, Simpson – were either at the end, or nearing the end, of their Test careers so you could sense a sort of a changing of the guard was in the offing. I was interested in the next generation of England cricketers who would form the backbone of the national side, contemporaries of Tom and more his age.

Peter May, the vice-captain – I suppose he was the obvious candidate to take over from Hutton? Tom nodded. 'He was a tough competitor – a hard man on the field. Probably the best post-war batsman we've had. The way he used to punch the ball wide of mid-off…' While he was calling to mind the potency of May's strokeplay, he was playing the shot in his armchair, the way all cricketers do when describing what happened.

Suddenly, the imaginary bat was put away. 'Hated the press,' he said, and then he hastened to soften the utterance. 'That is to say, he was very suspicious of them and always felt uncomfortable in their presence and giving interviews. He used to leave all that stuff to the manager.' He then fell into a reverie. 'What a player! Such a shame he retired early.'

And Colin Cowdrey? 'Wonderful eye! Wonderful touch. If only he'd had the temperament and ruthlessness of Peter May, he would have been a superb player. As it was, he was still a bloody good player, wasn't he?'

Any rivalry between the two of you? Any edge to your relationship? After all, he was keeping you out of the side. He laughed. 'Edge? Colin? He was my son's godfather.' Enough said.

I know that MCC didn't go in for open-top bus parades and stuff like that but surely there was some welcoming party on your return? Freedom of the City of Bristol? A year's free sausages from your local butcher? A bench named after you at the College ground in Cheltenham? 'I bought myself a car,' he told me. 'My first, a Ford Anglia, for £635. Registration number THT 428.' It's funny how you never forget the number plate of your first car. No more bus journeys to the county ground at Bristol, we can therefore assume for England's finest. Nowadays, I believe the England players are given a sponsored Jaguar. That is, one each, I hasten to add, not one to share among them.

The experiment of using him as an opener survived the journey home from the Antipodes. In fact, you could say it gained in momentum and credibility; MCC asked Gloucestershire to use him as an opener in their early matches as practice for the forthcoming series against South Africa.

Unwilling but uncomplaining, Tom did as he was told. The ploy met with only fitful success. Despite a productive season in the County Championship, he failed to score a hundred in the five Tests against the South Africans, averaging only 24.33, with a highest score of 60.

What did you think of the South Africans? He hesitated. 'Some of them were OK. Roy McLean and Johnny Waite were fine but the others…a bit grim and humourless, I found them.' Strangely enough, there was no opportunity in the future to get to know them better and to change his mind perhaps. He never again encountered them on the field of play, though, as we shall see later, they were to feature large in his life with events off the field.

He then told me about Heine and Adcock, possibly the most feared, and certainly the most fearsome, opening attack in the 1950s. 'Adcock was a bloody good bowler. Heine – he wasn't interested in getting you out. All he wanted to do was hit you!'

Before the first Test, when practising in the nets, the England players had been casting an interested and possibly concerned look across at their opponents who were limbering up in the adjoining nets, noting how Heine was making his own team-mates jump around in discomfort when facing him. They couldn't believe it when they returned to the pavilion to learn that he hadn't been picked – a mistake that the South Africans did not repeat in the second Test.

This business of opening Tom – how long did you persist with it? He gave me a knowing look. 'I soon knocked that one on the head.' By the time the Australians were back, the following season, he had reverted to his normal spot at number four in the order.

The year of 1956 will always be firmly etched in people's minds for the Test at Old Trafford in which Jim Laker took 19-90, an astonishing feat that is unlikely ever to be repeated. Tony Lock, bowling more and more furiously as history was being made at the other end, took the one other wicket. The story has gone down in Ashes folklore but it does not, alas, concern us here. It was events back in the pavilion that proved to be far more contentious for our protagonist.

After the first two matches, in which Tom had scored 8, 10*, 5 and 18, he was dropped, reviving once more the debate over his record against Australia. In 14 innings against them, he had scored one century and two fifties and was only averaging 26.30.

Whether the Australians were catching everything that Tom hit at them or not, it has to be admitted that the selectors had a point. Tom nodded his head when this was put to him. 'They were quite right to drop me – no question about it.' His place was taken by the 41-year-old Cyril Washbrook, who had retired from international cricket and who was, believe it or not, one of the selectors! The irony of the situation was that Tom was in superlative form that summer.

Let me quote from *Wisden*, 'Graveney was outstanding… Often in unhelpful conditions, he stood alone, scoring masterfully while most of his colleagues failed.'

One innings in particular will serve as an example of his ascendancy. Against Glamorgan, he scored 200 out of the team's total of 298. Only two other batsmen made double figures. When he was eventually out, Wilf Wooller, the Glamorgan captain, cried out, tongue in cheek one firmly hopes, 'Graveney, that's the worst double hundred I've ever seen!'

The value to his team of this innings can be gauged by the fact that, despite being bowled out for 81 in the second innings, Gloucestershire still won by 37 runs.

There were other brilliant innings too during the course of the season, including five more hundreds, and he easily topped the County Championship averages at 52.55. And this in a wet summer when no one else had averaged in the 50s. So, what went wrong?

Why was he only picked for the first two Tests and why was he so controversially omitted for the winter tour of South Africa when he was in the form of his life?

Tom takes up the story. 'In actual fact, I was recalled for the fourth Test, the one in which Laker took 19 wickets. But in the match before, against Lancashire, Brian Statham had bowled me a bouncer and hit me on the hand. I told Cyril Washbrook, one of the selectors, who was playing in the match, what had happened and that I would probably not be fit for the forthcoming Test.'

It would seem that the message was not passed on to the other selectors. When Tom reported to the team hotel and told Gubby Allen, the chairman of the selection committee, what had happened, the reaction he got was a frosty one. Hastily, Alan Oakman was summoned as cover from Sussex and on the morning of the match, he took the field instead of Tom. These things happen in professional sport. Unforeseen injury, resulting in a belated change of personnel and game plan, is a fact of life in a dressing room.

But Allen was vexed, not so much by the late and enforced drafting in of Oakman but more by the fact that all his private doubts about Graveney's temperament had resurfaced, at a crucial moment in an Ashes series to boot. In short, Allen didn't trust Tom and though the accusation was never voiced, at least not in Tom's hearing, the implication was clear; Graveney was using an excuse not to play.

In Allen's mind, it was obvious what he was up to. If Graveney played and failed, he would run the risk of being dropped again and left out of the winter touring party to South Africa. Better to cry off and rely on the overwhelming weight of runs he was scoring for Gloucestershire to secure his berth on the boat. So Allen left Graveney out of the team for the fifth Test and didn't select him for the South African tour.

And it wasn't his only controversial decision; he also left Fred Trueman at home. All hell broke loose in the press. Graveney had headed the batting averages that summer and Trueman the bowling and neither of them were in the team. If Graveney was one of the best 11 cricketers in the country at the end of July, which obviously the selectors believed he was because they had selected him for the fourth Test, then why did they not consider him to be in the top 17 players when the touring party was announced a month later?

It wasn't as if Graveney had lost form. He had continued to score heavily as he had done all season. As Alice cried in *Alice in Wonderland*, 'Curiouser and curiouser.' Though I doubt the popular newspapers of the time – *The Mirror*, *The Mail* and *The Sketch* – would have put it quite like that. Charlie Barnett, Tom's old coach at Gloucestershire, put it succinctly enough in an article in the local rag, which was then followed up and quoted by one of the Sunday broadsheets, 'What a disgrace!' Certainly, on cricket grounds alone, the decision was a bizarre one.

I am surmising what was in Gubby Allen's mind, but of course that is impossible to verify. All the selectors at that meeting are now dead and even when they were alive, they remained tight-lipped about the affair, as they had every right to be.

Tom is adamant that he reported the injury to Washbrook when it occurred during the Lancashire game and that Washbrook failed to pass on the message to Allen. He shakes his head in puzzlement at the suggestion that he was trying to pull a fast one. He never shirked a challenge in his career and he didn't on this occasion.

Peter Richardson, who was playing in the England side at the time – in fact he scored a vital hundred in this very game, on a wicket that the Australians found unplayable – offered another perspective on the affair. 'Tom is a lovely fella,' he told me, 'but in the dressing room – well, this one anyway – he was a bit quiet. He wasn't one to voice his opinion easily and there were a few of us who didn't hold back. He wasn't what you would call a natural leader. I can well imagine that there was a breakdown in communication between him and the selectors.'

That is quite possibly true. On his own admission, Tom never felt entirely trusted by the England team management during his first incarnation as a Test player and believed he suffered from their lack of confidence in him. He suspected, though he had nothing like any concrete evidence to support it, successively, Hutton, May and Dexter, as captains, did not fully trust him as a batsman when the chips were down. He always said that he thrived when given the responsibility of being the side's leading batsman, who is expected to get the runs. And his career for Gloucestershire, Worcestershire and, in his latter years, for England would seem to bear that out.

So, were you upset at being left out? 'Yes. But there was nothing I could do. I deserved to be dropped in the first place. I felt I deserved to be recalled when I was. And I should have been on that tour.' Gubby Allen, it has to be said, was not everybody's cup of tea. He ran MCC as his personal fiefdom and some felt that he laid himself open to charges of snobbery and favouritism. 'I don't know about that,' said Tom, 'but if it came to a choice between this player or that and they had more or less equal ability then, yes, you did feel that he would…' He didn't finish the sentence so I did.

He was happier in the company of public school types? Tom sort of nodded. Then he added with rare warmth, 'Gubby Allen! He did me no favours as a selector. He was born in Australia, you know. Should've stayed there!' Now, Tom is a gentle soul whose natural instinct is generosity of spirit and few people – a very few – provoke disfavour in his soul. But even Jesus was known to have lost his temper, when expelling the moneychangers from the temple, so it would be extraordinary if Tom Graveney, a man of flesh and blood, went through his career without having one or two clashes with those in authority. One was Gubby Allen; another was B.O. Allen, his captain at Gloucestershire. There was no chance that Tom was ever going to name his son Alan.

I am sure he would rather have been in South Africa but as he sipped his rum and coke on a verandah overlooking the milky blue Caribbean Sea, his mind must have pondered on the way things sometimes turn out for the best. Instead of weaving out of the way of well-directed bouncers from Heine and Adcock, he was enjoying a pleasant tour of Jamaica with the Duke of Norfolk's team.

Not that the cricket was a doddle: Jamaica boasted several Test players in their side and the matches were first-class. The Duke was fanatical about his cricket but a hopeless player. He was allowed to play – and captain – in one of the less serious matches and put himself on to bowl. Tom sidled up to the batsman and suggested *sotto voce* that it would be enormously gratifying to the visiting side, if not the entire nobility of the Mother Country, if he were to sacrifice his wicket in the face of the Duke's, admittedly incompetent, bowling.

The batsman, no doubt already picturing himself on bended knee in front of his sovereign at Buckingham Palace, obliged by running down the wicket to the Duke's gentle delivery and missing it by a country mile. Colin Ingleby-MacKenzie – captain of Hampshire – was keeping wicket. Not very well, it seemed, for he fumbled the ball badly and the batsman had no option but to regain, somewhat sheepishly, his ground. 'Ingleby,' rang out the unmistakeably patrician tones of His Grace. 'You are for the Tower!'

The sunshine and rum and cokes must have done Tom the world of good for his form for Gloucestershire on his return to county duty at the start of the 1957 season was eye-catching, to the selectors as well as the cricketing public. Five hundreds and a 99 earned him a recall to the colours for the second Test against the visiting West Indies at Lord's. He scored a duck. No matter. In the third match, at Trent Bridge, he made 258. It was a stupendous innings and proved to be his highest score in Test cricket, or in any form of cricket, for that matter.

'I was lucky,' he said 'The wicket was a beauty and everything just clicked.' When he reached his hundred – his first for England in 22 matches – he looked up at the players' balcony to see his captain, Peter May, signalling to him by tapping his head. 'The message was clear,' said Tom, 'I had to get my head down and score another.' Which he did. He shared a stand of 266 with Peter Richardson, who scored 126 himself.

Peter recalls Tom's batting with clarity and admiration. 'Tom – he was such a graceful player,' he told me. 'Mr Elegance, we called him.'

Wisden was equally fulsome in its praise for the strokeplay on display, 'Graveney drove with tremendous power, making full use of his height.' At last, following another stand of 207 with Peter May, who made a faultless 104, he quit the scene, having been at the crease from 11.45am on the Friday until 2.20pm on Saturday. The West Indies were on their knees when May declared at 619/6.

Was this the best innings of your career, do you think? He shook his head. 'I played better on one or two other occasions. There was that innings of 151 against India at Lord's on a square turner. And they had all those marvellous spinners – Chandrasekhar, Venkat, Bedi, Prasanna.'

Ah yes. That was in 1967. We're not there quite. 'I'll tell you another thing about that innings, the 258, not the 151. That is, if I'm not boring you.' I leaned forward. Bored? I hadn't been yet and it was unthinkable that I would be now.

'I always had my little routines and habits. You know, some people put on their left pad first or refuse to change their gloves when they're scoring runs, that sort of thing.' I nodded. I never knew a single cricketer who was not superstitious in some way, whatever he may have claimed to the contrary. One chap when I was at school refused to wear a box while batting, for the simple reason that he had forgotten to don it one day and scored a fifty. And he never flinched!

Tom continued. 'I always chewed gum when I was batting. I never chewed gum at any other time. If I was not out at lunch or tea or close of play, I would stand my bat upright against the bench and stick the gum on the splice, ready for when I resumed my innings. Anyway, it was obviously a long innings, with quite a few intervals, including one overnight. At lunch on the Saturday, I was 258 not out. When I went out for the afternoon session, the gum had gone! Probably dried out and fallen off on to the floor in the dressing room. Five minutes later, I was bowled by Smith without adding to my score.' We nodded at each other. We both know that the cricketing gods toy with us in such ways.

Speaking to Peter Richardson about this match unearthed an interesting footnote. His brother, Dick, was also in the side, the first – and only – time that two brothers have represented England in the same Test. If you look at the scorecard, you will see that Dick made 33, not a significant score in view of the mammoth team total but hardly a failure. *Wisden* was moved to comment, 'His innings left no one in any doubt of his promise.' Strange indeed that he was discarded for the next Test and never played for England again.

The Rev David Sheppard, by now only a part-time cricketer on account of his ecclesiastical career, was preferred for the remaining two Tests. The list of One-Test Wonders, as the unlucky players are known, is much longer than you might imagine and contains some oddly familiar names. Joining Dick Richardson are: Fred Grace (brother of W.G.); Fred Tate (father of Maurice); Vic Stollmeyer (brother of Jeff); Merv Harvey (brother of Neil); Alan Butcher (father of Mark); 'Father' Marriott; Charlie Parker; Stuart Law; Arnie Sidebottom (father of Ryan); Andy Lloyd and, perhaps the strangest of the lot, Darren Pattinson (who was picked for England and is the brother of the current Australian fast bowler, James).

Tom Graveney may have felt on occasions in his career that he was at the mercy of the whims of the selectors but not in this prolific season. He scored another century in the fifth Test and finished with a series average of 118, positively Bradman-esque in its magnitude. But cricket is a cruel mistress and form can desert you just as quickly as it can find you.

He looked at his record for the 1958 season and quoted the pronouncement of a contemporary columnist in sombre tones that would not have done disservice to Richard Dimbleby describing Winston Churchill's funeral. 'The 1958 season was not one of Graveney's better years.'

'Hmm… Scored 900 runs less than the year before. Funny… don't seem to remember much about 1958.' I pressed him. The New Zealanders were here. 'Oh yes, so they were. Bert Sutcliffe… By far their best player. But we smashed 'em. Trueman and Statham were in their pomp and they were no match for them. Dull series. I was rested for the last Test, in readiness for the forthcoming tour of Australia.'

Ah yes, the infamous 1958/59 Ashes series. It was calamitous. At that time, I was at an age when I was beginning to fall in love with cricket and old enough to realise that something had gone terribly wrong with England. It wasn't just that we were thrashed 4-0, though that was shameful enough. Reports coming back from Down Under were hinting, even to my immature ears, that the series had been a disgrace. I hadn't really understood why and I was keen to get it from the horse's mouth, as it were.

On paper, and by popular consent, the team that set sail from Tilbury aboard the P&O liner, SS *Iberia*, on 20 September 1958 (the last MCC team to travel by ship, incidentally) was one of the strongest ever assembled. Just look at the list of who's who in a golden age of

English cricket: May (captain); Cowdrey; Bailey; Evans; Graveney; Laker; Loader; Lock; Milton; Richardson; Statham; Subba Row; Trueman; Tyson; Watson. In addition, replacements Dexter and Mortimore were called for on account of injuries to Subba Row and Watson. What a team! It seemed inconceivable that they would not return with the Ashes. But not only did they surrender the urn, they were humiliated.

Before we examine the vexed and controversial subject of throwing which bedevilled the tour, it is important to point out that, in pretty well every department of the game, England were outplayed by a resurgent Australian side, shrewdly captained by Richie Benaud. It was felt that the experienced England players should have been at their peak; on reflection, it was easy to see that many of them were just past it. Furthermore, the Australians quickly bonded into a cohesive and focussed unit. The Englishmen, by contrast, gave every appearance of being disunited and at odds with each other.

'We were not a team,' was Peter Richardson's opinion. 'We'd been together for too long and quite frankly we'd all got fed up with each other.' Tom agreed with this assessment. 'It wasn't a happy team. I can truthfully say that it was the most disappointing and depressing tour I've ever been on.'

Listen to these words of Arthur Milton, a friend and team-mate of Tom's at Gloucestershire, on his first – and only – trip with MCC. I quote from Mike Vockins's book on Arthur Milton, *The Last of the Double Internationals*. Milton told him, 'It was a team that had one or two disruptive individuals… Unfortunately, it wasn't the best of tours… I think, and I really don't like saying it, but, as a new tourist, I don't think the management seemed a real part of the team.'

Tom was not a new tourist – it was his fourth in MCC colours – so he was perhaps a little more forthright in his assessments of what went wrong. 'Peter May had his fiancée with him, together with their family,' he said, 'and that probably distracted him from his job. The traditional Saturday evening party was abandoned, as I recall, and that was a pity. Team spirit suffered as a result.'

Though May enjoyed almost universal respect and loyalty among his players, it was generally felt he was outmanoeuvred tactically by the more astute Richie Benaud. 'Perhaps Peter was a little too defensively minded at times,' conceded Tom, though he yielded to no one in his admiration for May as a great batsman and a tough competitor.

And then there was the problem with the manager. Freddie Brown was hugely popular in Australia. He had captained the England side on the 1950/51 tour, largely regarded as a very weak side coming out of the Mother Country, exhausted and debilitated by six years of war. His combative style and never-say-die attitude won him a lot of friends. By now, at the age of 47, he clearly had a drink problem.

'He was the worse for wear most of the time,' said Tom. 'Halfway through the tour, he had to be sent off for a fortnight somewhere to dry out!' That must have caused a stir, even in an age when some hard drinking went on at the close of play, so unlike the more abstemious and regulated regimes that obtain for modern-day cricketers. 'He was a hopeless, hopeless manager,' Tom sighed, more in sadness than condemnation. With the officers on the bridge so distracted, it was no wonder the good ship England was headed for trouble.

The iceberg that loomed out of the darkness was throwing. Controversies such as bribery, betting scandals, spot fixing, 'shamateurism' and illegal bowling actions plagued the game for many years – and that was just in Victorian times! So the quarrel that was about to engulf the tour was not new. Like the officers on the bridge of the *Titanic* who knew that icebergs were in the vicinity, the cricket authorities were well aware that throwing was already a blight on the game's reputation. But a strange inertia seemed to envelop the law-makers and the administrators, and the England players felt – whatever they were constrained to say publicly – that they were left high and dry in the firing line.

Four of the Australian bowlers – Meckiff, Rorke, Slater and Burke – were by common consent 'chuckers'. You only have to look at photos of their actions at the moment of delivery to be dumbfounded that they were never called in any of the Tests. Mind you, the problem was not exclusively an Australian one; umpires in England had already been encouraged to no-ball bowlers who contravened the law on illegal deliveries. Indeed, Tony Lock, whose faster ball had long since raised more than a few eyebrows (if very few backlifts from surprised batsmen), was shocked when he saw newsreel of his action and took steps to re-model it in a smoother groove.

But the Australian Board of Control kept their heads firmly in the sand and denied there was a problem. The England players were not of the same opinion. Tom took up the story. 'We played against Meckiff in one of the State games before the Tests. He was useless. Then suddenly, in the Test matches, he was a completely different kettle of fish. Left-arm over too, which made him more awkward. "Chuckiff", the English press called him. And Gordon Rorke was another. He ran in, and from 18 yards, because of his exaggerated drag, he'd suddenly stand upright in all of his six foot four inches – and throw it at you!'

Didn't you complain? Was there no channel of appeal? After all, this was totally contrary to the laws, to say nothing of the spirit, of the game. He shook his head mournfully. 'Peter May said it would sound like sour grapes.'

Peter Richardson agreed. 'It just wasn't a fair contest. There was nothing we could do about it. We would have liked to make our point somehow but Freddie Brown wouldn't let us. Said we can beat this lot anyway, chuckers or no chuckers. Well, we didn't.'

Arthur Milton recalled, in Mike Vockins's biography, 'We encountered not only Meckiff and Rorke but there were two others playing for South Australia in Adelaide. Hitchcock and Trethewey – "Pitchcock and Trethrowy" we nicknamed them!'

The throwing controversy rumbled on for a few years but the fall-out from the disastrous tour was immediate and brutal, signalling the end of some very distinguished Test careers. Bailey, Watson, Laker, Evans and Tyson never played for England again. Lock, Milton and Graveney were jettisoned as well.

'It was the end of an era,' said Peter Richardson. As for Tom, at the age of 32, he wasn't at all convinced that, as far as Test cricket was concerned, it wasn't the end for him too. He looked thoughtful and disconsolate when he admitted as much to me, in his sitting room, with unseasonable rain lashing at the windows. Then suddenly, he perked up. 'That was before the Second Coming!' he beamed.

7

The Day Job – Gloucestershire 1954–60

'Gloucester! They sacked all the Graveneys.'
(Ken Graveney)

'**D**on't give up the day job' is the sardonic cliché usually directed at a star-struck ingenue aching for overnight success. Tom Graveney had achieved success on the international stage and it hadn't happened overnight but he could not have given up the day job, even if he had wanted to.

The current England set-up, structured around central contracts, means that the Test players of today rarely see their counties. Indeed, in one or two cases, it is arguable whether any allegiance to a county exists at all. It wasn't the same for the England players in the 1950s and 60s. We have seen from Tom's descriptions of his routine during a normal summer that very often he would be turning out for Gloucestershire on the morning following the completion of a Test match. That was just the way it was.

How did you find returning to the county game after a Test match? 'No problem at all. Slipped back into it very easily, in fact. I loved scoring runs, you see. And I scored one or two, didn't I?'

I should say so. By one or two, he meant 19,705 runs for Gloucestershire alone, including 50 centuries. And that was only half his career. As we shall see, in 1961, he moved to Worcestershire, for the 'Second Coming', as he calls it, a period when he seemed to bat even better than ever.

What sort of team were Gloucestershire when you played for them?
'We were a mid-table team, I suppose, but we had some good
players. Jack Crapp and George Emmett were good pros and knew
the game.'

Following the resignation of Sir Derrick Bailey as captain in
1952, Gloucestershire broke with tradition and appointed their first
professional, the Cornishman Jack Crapp, to lead the side. Another
professional, George Emmett, who remained in situ until Tom's
appointment in 1959, followed Crapp as captain in 1955.

Clearly Tom had enormous respect for both his predecessors
and maintained, with some vigour – unsurprisingly in view of what
happened later when he was in charge – that none of the players had
the slightest problem with having a professional as captain. 'They
were the best men for the job,' he said, 'whatever certain members of
the committee may have been thinking.'

Crapp, Emmett, plus the emerging talent of Arthur Milton,
as well as Graveney's immense contributions when he wasn't on
England duty, meant that runs were rarely in short supply. George
Lambert was a useful seamer but the traditional strength of
Gloucestershire's attack lay in their spinners. Tom Goddard (off
breaks) and Sam Cook (slow left-arm) would get 30 wickets each
every time they played in the Festival Week at Cheltenham, Tom
asserted.

And waiting in the wings were David Allen and John Mortimore,
two very different but effective off-spin bowlers. 'David fired it in
and spun it sharply. Morty was not such a big spinner of the ball but
relied more on guile and flight. Both bloody good bowlers.'

The England selectors were obviously in agreement with this
assessment; Allen played in 39 Tests and Mortimore nine. In addition,
David Smith, a quick bowler, and Tony Brown, an all-rounder, arrived
on the scene and it was felt, not just by Tom, that Gloucestershire
had a side capable of beating anyone in the championship.

'And we had a joker in the pack,' Tom pointed out, 'Bomber Wells.'
He meant in both senses. Bomber Wells was indeed an exceedingly
funny man but he was also an unorthodox and unpredictable off-
spinner and often provided another, very useful, option to his

TWG with new England cap and sweater.

Two little boys in blazers and whites. I have not shown this photo to anyone who has not been enchanted by this delightful picture of the two Graveney brothers – Ken is on the left and Tom on the right. Even now, Tom still chuckles when he sees it.

Capt. Graveney driving the desk. Egypt 1947. Tom loved his time in the Army and would have made it his career had not Gloucestershire come calling.

Graveney raises his bat after one of his earlier centuries. Egypt 1947. The ground was situated alongside the Suez Canal. Mud from the canal would be laid down and rolled. Baked hard by the sun, it would become as smooth as a billiard table and when matting was put down, wickets of pace and true bounce were produced. "The standard was pretty good," Tom asserted. "See, we're all in shorts. Goodness, there wasn't much of me, was there?"

Playing for Gloucestershire at Westbury-on-Trym 1948. The balance and poise were there for all to see at the outset. Tom has stepped out of his crease to play the ball off his front foot, familiar territory for him.

Graveney launches a trademark cover drive 1948. All right, the delivery was a wide half-volley – look how far outside the off stump the wicketkeeper has had to move – but it is still a stroke of power and elegance. Unusually, Tom is hatless. But, as usual, he is immaculately turned out – look at those gleaming white boots.

Tom marries Jackie in Winchcombe, 30th August 1952. "And so began sixty years of hard labour," he joked. In fact their marriage proved to be remarkably durable until Jackie's death in June 2013.

Graveney walks out to bat at Bristol for Gloucestershire. The time, you will note, is ten past six, never a good time to go into bat. Nowadays, spectators are not allowed on the playing area, so this file of appreciative onlookers is a thing of the past. It is a shame. It seems that the players have become isolated from the paying public. Incidentally, I should love to know what's inside that schoolboy's case.

Graveney on the defensive. Gloucestershire v Somerset 1953. Tom has always made a point about his grip high up the bat handle. Here, several inches of rubber can clearly be seen below the bottom hand.

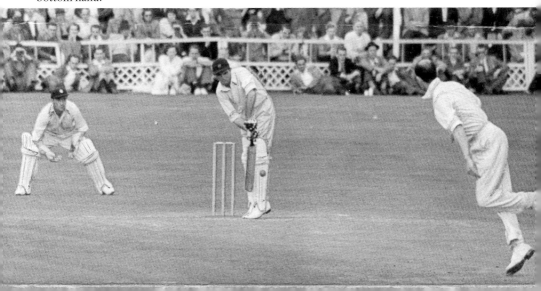

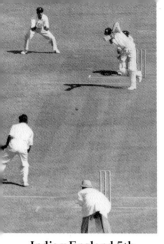

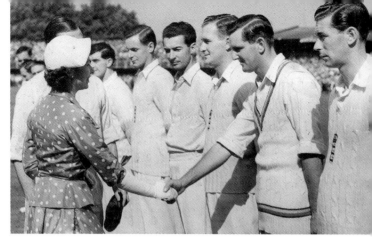

India v England 5th Test at Madras 1952. Graveney straight drives. "Just look at that left elbow pointing to the heavens!" Tom commented. Even he thought it was a touch exaggerated.

Graveney is introduced to the Queen at Lord's during the 2nd Test v India 1952. Hutton (mainly obscured) introduces Tom to Her Majesty. "It's funny," remarked Tom, "but Len always struggled to remember my name at official functions." Also in shot, from left to right are Fred Trueman, Peter May, Reg Simpson, Jim Laker, TWG, Derek Shackleton. Just look at those partings!

Graveney resumes his partnership with Hutton at Lord's v Australia 1953. Graveney was on 78* and Hutton on 83*. The evening before, Tom reckoned they had the Australians on the ropes. But instead of taking advantage of a spent bowling attack, Hutton advised caution and instructed Tom to shut up shop. "I would have got my hundred that evening," he asserts. "As it was, two balls later, I was making the return journey. Lindwall bowled me with a fast in-swinging yorker, the best ball he ever bowled, he told me. Len was not happy!"

Graveney and Statham bound for Australia and the 1954-55 Ashes series. "Brian was my biggest mate on tour," Tom said. "Taught him to drink. Beer, not those fancy cocktails he used to have."

Graveney and Cowdrey return – with the Ashes – from Australia 1955. "Colin was a fine, fine player," was Tom's verdict on his team-mate. "If only he'd had the ruthless streak of Peter May, what a great batsman he would have been."

Graveney mounts the pavilion steps at Trent Bridge during his mammoth innings of 258 against the West Indies, 3rd Test 1957. When he reached his hundred – his first for England for 22 matches – Tom looked up at the players' balcony to see his captain, Peter May, signalling to him by tapping his head. "The message was clear," said Tom, "I had to get my head down and score another."

Gloucs v Surrey at the Wagon Works, Gloucester, 1959. Graveney facing, Lock is the bowler, Swetman the wicketkeeper. Note the fact that Tom has not stirred a muscle, not even picked up his bat, even though Lock is on the point of releasing the ball. It is as if he is in an impenetrable bubble of concentration and serenity, totally confident in his quick reactions. Most batsmen would have been on the move by now, either forward or back, depending on what their 'trigger movement' was. I am convinced that only the great batsmen stay this still for so long before committing themselves to the stroke.

At the time, Gloucestershire were in the running for the championship, so they had prepared a turning wicket to suit their spinners. A thoroughly ill-considered decision. Surrey had two of the best spinners in the world and between them, Laker and Lock took 19 wickets, bowling Gloucs out for 101 and 71. The home side's aspirations of winning their first championship lay in tatters.

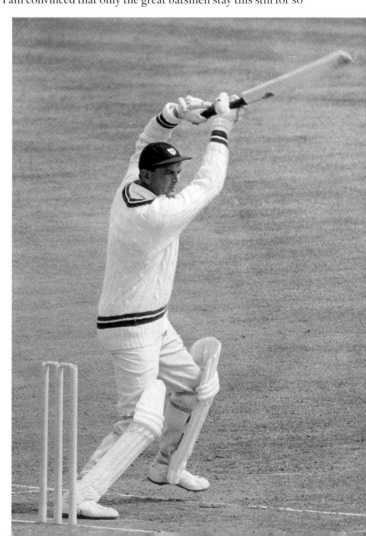

Graveney forces the ball away through the covers off the back foot. "Tom was predominantly a front-foot player," commented his Gloucestershire team-mate, Tony Brown, "but that is not to say he *couldn't* play off the back foot." Note how far back in his crease is Tom's back foot. And look at that elegant follow-through!

Graveney on the pull Middx v Gloucs at Lord's 1960 (© *Sport and General, Press Agency Ltd, 2-3 Gough Street, Fleet Street, London, EC4*) Freddie Titmus was the bowler and John Murray the wicketkeeper, both team-mates of Tom's in the England side. Pity the poor fielder at short leg. He was all right though; Tom has spared him a clattering and placed the ball wide of him to his left.

Graveney on the drive (© *TR Beckett, The Flat, GCCO, Upton Lane, Gloucester)* Barrie Mayer of Gloucestershire is the wicketkeeper. This shot perfectly illustrates the Graveney technique. In his own words: "The back of my top hand faced between mid-off and extra cover and the wrist acted as a pendulum. The bat went back straight and came down straight. Very simple." This photo was taken from square on and the full face of the bat is directly visible, indicating that he has picked it up straight, not over third slip or gully, like most batsmen. If that sounds too technical, just admire the poise, balance and elegance of the stroke.

Graveney is applauded off the pitch at Lord's during his innings of 153 v Pakistan, 1962. 1962 was the year of his return to first-class cricket after his year's ban. It was an auspicious return to the highest level of the game – he averaged 100.25 that summer in Tests. "I came back hungry," he said.

The modern term for this shot is the slog-sweep. It seems almost sacrilegious to use such an ugly phrase to describe any stroke of Graveney's. Notwithstanding, the perfect balance is still very much in evidence and the characteristically high grip up the bat handle can be clearly seen.

Graveney and Horton after a record partnership of 314 Worcs v Somerset at New Road, Worcester, 1962 (© *Berrows Newspapers, the Trinity, Worcester*). Martin Horton scored 233 and Tom 164*, a club record third wicket partnership. "After my ban, Worcestershire was the obvious side to go to. I knew quite a few of the boys and it had always struck me as a friendly club. And I never regretted my decision for one moment."

The Worcestershire team v Middx at Lord's, 1962. Top, left to right: Jim Standen, Len Coldwell, Dick Richardson, Norman Gifford, Ron Headley, Brian Booth (w-k), W Powell (masseur). Seated, left to right: Martin Horton, Jack Flavell, Don Kenyon (capt), Bob Broadbent, TWG. The young Norman Gifford, seen skulking at the back, has obviously forgotten his blazer. I wonder what he would have said about that when he later became captain himself. Worcs won a thrilling run chase by six wickets, thanks to an imperious innings from Tom of 119.

Graveney hooks. England v Pakistan at Lord's 1962 *(© Sport and General).* Tom's brother, Ken, said this of him: "He had a level of hand-eye co-ordination that was exceptional. He would hook the world's fastest bowlers off the front foot!" This shot perfectly illustrates his point.

Worcestershire celebrate winning the championship for the second year running. Hove, 1965 *(© Birmingham Post).* Left to right: Martin Horton, Jack Flavell, Norman Gifford, Brian Booth, Len Coldwell, Don Kenyon (capt), Doug Slade, Alan Ormrod, Ron Headley, Brian Booth, Dick Richardson, Basil D'Oliveira. TWG can be seen swinging from the rafters. "My goodness, we were a thirsty lot!" was Tom's appraisal of the team.

Graveney square cuts. The wicketkeeper is Jimmy Binks of Yorkshire. *(© Berrows Newspapers, Worcester).* The word that is most often used to describe Tom's batting is 'elegant'. You do not need to be a student of the coaching manual to admire the perfect balance and gracefulness of movement in this shot of him as he executes the square cut. Beautifully timed – four runs, I should say.

Tom meets the Queen at Lord's 1966. Colin Cowdrey makes the introductions. Left to right: Colin Milburn (head turned aside), Basil D'Oliveira, Geoff Boycott and TWG. It was the first time Boycott had replaced glasses with contact lenses.

This was the scene of Tom's comeback to Test cricket at the age of 39. The entire ground rose as one to applaud him to the wicket when he came into bat. They did the same when he returned to the pavilion, having narrowly missed, by three runs, an emotional hundred.

Engineer c Graveney b Brown 32. Third Test v India at Edgbaston 1967 *(© Central Press Photos).* Amiss (third slip), Barrington (second slip), TWG (first slip), Murray (wicketkeeper), Milburn (short leg). "I reckoned if I got my hands to it, I'd catch it," said Tom. It is often overlooked what a fine slip fielder Tom was. He took 554 catches in his career, and dropped very few.

Tom and Ken Graveney, suitably blazered. "Ha, got one over my brother there," remarked Tom, "I'm wearing my MCC blazer."

TW Graveney OBE 1968. Becky, Tom, Tim and Jackie Graveney leave the Clarendon Hotel on their way to the Palace for his investiture. *"You must have been getting to know Her Majesty pretty well by now. What did she say to you?"* He fixed me with an unwavering stare. "If I told you that," he said, "I'd end up in the Tower."

The captains toss for innings. England v Australia, Headingley, 1968. Tom only captained his country once. An injury to Colin Cowdrey meant that Tom, his vice-captain, had to step into the breach. By an odd coincidence, the Australian vice-captain, Barry Jarman, also had to stand in for his injured skipper, Bill Lawry. Tom remembers the moment as pure comedy. "All the press, radio and TV people were milling about, with the groundsmen putting the final touches to the wicket. And no-one noticed us! I don't know who the photographer was but he was the only one to capture the moment."

Graveney plays the ball to leg. *(© Patrick Eagar).* The unmistakeable figure crouching behind the stumps is Alan Knott, "quite the most complete and talented 'keeper I've ever seen", was Tom's verdict.

Tom Graveney in animated discussion with his great friend Everton Weekes, on tour with the International XI World Tour, 1962. *(© John McGeorge, Salisbury, S Rhodesia)*

Ron Roberts, the tour manager, Ray Lindwall, the Australian fast bowler, Everton Weekes, the West Indian batsman and Tom were in a car driving from Bulawayo to Salisbury in Rhodesia. It was very hot and they stopped off at a bar for a drink, ordering four gins and tonic. The woman behind the bar said to Weekes, "You get out. You're not allowed in here." There was a colour bar operating in the country. "We were shocked," remembered Tom. "We all marched out and told her what to do with her gin and tonic. It was terrible." A precursor possibly of what was to come with the D'Oliveira affair and South Africa's isolation from world sport.

England team v West Indies, Old Trafford 1969 *(© Central Press and Photos Ltd).* Standing, left to right: Phil Sharpe, Barry Knight, John Snow, David Brown, Basil D'Oliveira, Derek Underwood. Seated, left to right: Alan Knott (w-k), TWG, Ray Illingworth (capt), John Edrich, Geoff Boycott. This was Tom's final Test match.

The Graveney cover drive (© *Ken Kelly*). Has there ever been a more famous stroke in the history of the game? It has often been compared with that famous photo of Wally Hammond cover driving, the handkerchief hanging stylishly out of his hip pocket. But Hammond's shot, though technically perfect, is all muscular power and explosiveness. By contrast, Graveney's drive is all about poise, balance, elegance, timing. It is undeniably a thing of beauty.

Graveney and D'Oliveira walk out to bat at Old Trafford against West Indies 1969. This was Tom's last innings in Test cricket. It is a poignant image, not least because he is accompanied to the wicket by his great team-mate and lifelong friend, Basil D'Oliveira.

The final curtain. Worcs v Warwicks, New Road, Worcester, 1970. Graveney is applauded off the pitch by both sides at the conclusion of his last match as a county cricketer. The old cathedral looks on approvingly. "It was a strange feeling," remembers Tom. "At home, we were already packing for Australia."

Three Graveneys, three captains of Gloucestershire. Left to right: Ken 1963-64, David 1981-88, Tom 1959-60. "Gloucester! They sacked all the Graveneys." (Ken Graveney)

The publican. From 1974-84, Tom was the landlord of the Royal Oak in Prestbury, Cheltenham. It became a popular watering hole and meeting place for cricketers the land over. Judging by this photo, Tom pulled pints off the front foot too. "Every night was party night," said Tom, "but it was bloody hard work!"

The 40th anniversary reunion of the Worcestershire side that won the 1964 championship, 19th August 1984 at New Road. Left to right: Bob Carter, John Elliott, Duncan Fearnley, Dick Richardson (mostly obscured), Basil D'Oliveira, Martin Horton, Tom Graveney showing Jack Flavell how to bowl, Don Kenyon, Brian Brain, Doug Slade, Roy Booth, Joe Lister (secretary in 1964), Len Coldwell. "It was a bloody good side," remembered Tom. "Looking around the team in the dressing room, you couldn't see a weak link anywhere."

Brothers in arms. Tom (left) and brother Ken share a fraternal moment at the picturesque ground at Cheltenham College during festival week. Tom is proudly wearing his Worcestershire tie. Ken is proudly wearing…well, no-one is at all sure what club that is.

Graveney the golfer. Tom was a highly accomplished golfer. The elegance of the drive is in every way familiar to Graveney watchers. Here he is sharing a round with his great friend, Garry Sobers, at the Royal Westmoreland Golf Club in Barbados, a week before it was officially opened.

The left-handed scissors. To his astonishment and great honour, Tom was invited to become the president of the MCC in 2004-05, the first professional to be so honoured. Here he is officially opening the newly refurbished pavilion, just in time for the Ashes series in 2005. "Where are the left-handed scissors?" he demanded. Using scissors was the only thing he ever did left-handed. A pair of left-handed scissors was hastily produced to everybody's amusement and he duly cut the ribbon.

captains when Gloucestershire decided to go with three spinners. Whether his captains fully appreciated his unorthodox antics on the field of play is a moot point but Tom was convulsed with laughter when he was telling me one or two of the many stories that abound about Bomber Wells.

He was nicknamed 'Bomber' after the British heavyweight boxer, Bombardier Billy Wells, who is the man forever enshrined on celluloid in people's memory hitting the huge gong at the beginning of films made by Rank. 'He was half-blind, you know,' Tom said of his team-mate. 'He couldn't see the scoreboard. He would always be sidling up to you asking what the score was.'

John Mortimore confirmed that Bomber did not much like exercise, so he employed a run-up of one pace – if that, sometimes. 'When he first played,' said Mortimore, 'I'm convinced the captain at the time, Sir Derrick Bailey, didn't know what was going on. He was fielding at mid-off and he liked to walk in a few paces while the ball was being delivered. The umpire called "Over" and Sir Derrick looked bemused. We reckoned he had actually only seen three balls and thought the umpire couldn't count.'

Eventually, Sir Derrick became exasperated by Bomber bowling his overs too quickly and shouted at him to take the game more seriously and to take a proper run-up. Tom takes up the story. 'Bomber purposefully strode back half-a-dozen paces. "Far enough, Skip?" Sir Derrick grumpily agreed that it was. And then, before you could bat an eyelid, he delivered the ball from where he was standing! And he pitched it! Of course, we all fell about laughing.'

Did Sir Derrick also find it amusing? Tom made a face. 'Sir Derrick didn't have much of a sense of humour.'

On one occasion, with the connivance of Roly Jenkins of Worcestershire, who was batting at the time, he completed an over in the time that it took the bells of the famous old cathedral in Worcester to strike 12. I'm told that takes 34 seconds.

'He would never deliberately bowl when a batsman wasn't ready,' claimed Mortimore, 'but many a time, people got out to him when they were, shall we say, not *entirely* set. I remember John Langridge, from Sussex, letting a ball go through to the wicketkeeper.

'Arthur Milton was at slip and whistled in disbelief. "Were you ready for that, John?" he asked. "Watching, yes," answered Langridge. "Ready, no."'

Both Graveney and Mortimore were agreed that Bomber, who had an agricultural style as a batsman, was a menace to bat with. 'His calling was atrocious,' said Tom. 'On one occasion, Sam Cook was exasperated after having been run out by Bomber. "For heaven's sake, say *something*!" he shouted. Quick as a flash came back the answer, "Goodbye."'

For all that, Bomber Wells could bowl all right. Eventually, frustrated by lack of opportunity at Gloucestershire where Mortimore and Allen took precedence, he moved to Nottinghamshire, retiring in 1965 with 999 first-class wickets to his name. He declined to play in the last match of that season so that he could have the opportunity of taking his 1,000th wicket. 'Plenty of people have taken 1,000 wickets,' he said, 'but no one has taken 999!'

Later on, a trawl through the record books unearthed the fact that he had actually only taken 998 wickets but he never accepted the statisticians' evidence and claimed to his dying day that it was truly 999.

Cricket, more than most games, seems to throw up such endearing and enduring characters and somehow you expect one of the West Country teams to have more than their fair share. In the same way, you somehow feel that such oddballs would never flourish at, say, Surrey or Yorkshire. 'Yes, we were a happy team,' confirmed Tom.

David Allen, who was awarded his county cap by Tom when he was captain in 1959, describes Graveney as a batsman thus, 'Tom was a front-foot player, typical of batsmen who were brought up on West Country pitches that were generally low and slow.'

Tony Brown, another team-mate of Tom's at Gloucestershire, also pointed out to me that Tom favoured the front foot. 'His cricketing career with Gloucestershire, with years of playing on the front foot to combat variable bounce, usually low, meant that to some extent he did not play many shots off the back foot.

'But that did not mean to say that he couldn't. He could play the short ball expertly enough because his record against the West Indies was as good an anybody's and five of his 11 Test hundreds were made against that country.'

All the ex-players I have spoken to about Tom remarked on the fearless way he used to hook bouncers off the front foot. That demands bravery, a keen eye and, above all, time, the hallmark of any great player. As his brother Ken said, he may have been blessed with exceptional hand-eye coordination but he never took this gift for granted. Everyone who knew him made mention of his constant and regular net practices, what today is termed his 'good work ethic'.

'For all that he was such an elegant batsman,' said Allen, 'he worked very hard at his game and never missed a net.' John Mortimore concurred. 'Tom practised every day,' he said. 'This didn't suit everyone. Arthur Milton, for example, would only go in the nets when he felt he needed to work on a particular chink in his technique.'

Tom shrugged when quizzed about his practice routine. 'I just felt that I wanted to stay in the groove. What's that famous quote by Gary Player, "The more I practise, the luckier I seem to get"? Well, that was my view too. Good for sweating off the previous night's beer too!'

Brown goes on about the compulsion to practise. 'One particular incident sticks in the mind and that was on Tom's return from the West Indies tour of 1953/54. Gloucestershire players were practising in the indoor nets in April, preparing for the 1954 season and Graham Wiltshire, who was fast-medium, was bowling to Tom who was, as usual, keen to come into the nets and practise even though he had been playing cricket all winter. The indoor nets at Bristol were not terribly good, the lighting was poor and "Wilt" bowled this delivery, which hit the edge of the matting halfway down. The ball went at some pace straight for Tom Graveney's head.

'Tom, as ever on the front foot, hooked it off his nose, looked up with a broad grin and said, "Good job I've had some practice against those in the winter!"'

Those indoor sessions were recalled clearly by Allen. 'If you went into the same net as Tom had just been using,' he said, 'you'd find yourself standing in a pool of sweat.' Mortimore recognised and valued Tom's dedicated approach to practice. He liked to bowl to him in the nets because, first, it was always 'good to pit yourself against the best, and Tom was by this time an established Test player' and, secondly, he would play properly and methodically, 'so you too could work on bowling strategies'.

Brown observed, 'To bat with him in the middle was the ultimate... A truly wonderful experience to be able to study and witness at first hand the languid style of Tom Graveney.'

Professionals are naturally wary of flair and gracefulness; what counts in their book is not pretty shots but runs on the board. But if that stylishness is backed up with a solid technique and a tough streak of competitiveness, then even the most curmudgeonly and hard-bitten of them are as capable of purring with delight at an elegant stroke as any spectator in the stands.

Geoff Boycott used to marvel at David Gower's delicate timing and could be heard to laud to the heavens Michael Vaughan's cover driving. 'Boycott!' exclaimed Tom when I mentioned him. 'I'm his favourite player!'

How come? 'When I first batted with him. I think I hit a couple of cover drives and he must have been impressed.' Mention of the cover drive is never far from people's lips when they talk about Tom Graveney. It was his hallmark stroke but in fact, say all his contemporaries, he had all the shots.

Listen once more to Tony Brown, 'Gloucestershire had never been short of stroke-makers and over the years batsmen of the calibre of W.G. Grace, Gilbert Jessop, Wally Hammond, Charlie Barnett and George Emmett had pleased the crowds around the country but the elegant play of T.W. Graveney was to give added pleasure to those people.'

He wasn't the only one to compare Graveney to the great Wally Hammond. John Mortimore talks of conversations in the dressing room as to who was the better player, Hammond or Graveney. To some, it would be unthinkable to mention them both in the same breath but to others, the sheer class of Tom's batting bore comparison with the great man.

Tom's own assessment of Hammond is revealing.

Did you ever see him bat? 'I watched him play when I was a young boy. It was worth the two bob to get into the ground just to watch him walk out to bat. He had a presence about him. And don't forget he could bowl too. Bloody quick, before the war. He was a majestic player. Incomparable.'

He was momentarily lost in nostalgic thought. Time for me to look up Hammond's record. He finished his Test career (interrupted by the war, let us not forget) with an average of 58.45.

The benchmark for 'greatness' in a batsman is usually set at the average of 50. In the pantheon of all-time 'great' batsmen, Hammond stands at eighth in the list. On top is Graeme Pollock with an average of 60.67. Just below Hammond lie Garfield Sobers with 57.78 and Jack Hobbs with 56.94. Just a minute, I hear you cry, what about Bradman? Ah, but he doesn't really count. How can you evaluate someone who inhabits a completely different stratosphere? Do I really need to tell you that his Test average was 99.94?

So, by any standards, Wally Hammond was up there with the best of them. And then Tom stirred. 'I played with him, you know. It was in 1951 against Somerset. He had been persuaded to come out of retirement for this match, to increase the gate and swell the club's coffers, probably. We all watched him bat from the balcony. After two overs, I went back inside. I couldn't watch anymore. He'd lost it. He couldn't play. So sad.'

For all his talent, for all his dashing strokeplay and international success, for all his physical prowess and matinee idol looks, Hammond's was a sad life right until the end. George Chesterton, already mentioned as one of the best of the schoolmaster-cricketers of Tom's early career, recalls playing with Hammond for MCC and being disheartened because he was so withdrawn and morose, sitting alone in the dressing room, nursing his Scotch and refusing to join the others for lunch in the pavilion. 'All in all,' said Chesterton, 'he cut an unattractive figure, so unlike the handsome sportsman of his younger days.'

Hammond was generally regarded as being a difficult man, moody and fractious, and his later years, blighted by the effects of a serious car crash and innumerable failed business ventures, were not happy ones and he died at the relatively early age of 62. Whenever anyone who knew him or played with him mentions his name, the note of pleasure in the voice as great deeds are recalled is always accompanied by a clouding of the eyes as the personal and social problems are brought to mind. That never happens when anyone talks about Tom Graveney. The expression of delight is instantaneous and genuine and there is no ambivalence in the regard in which he is held; his Test match average may have been inferior to Hammond's but as a man, there can be no comparison.

And it is as a man, as one of their team-mates, that people such as Allen, Mortimore and Brown speak most fondly of him. When David Allen broke into the England side, he and Tom would travel to representative matches together, always with Tom driving. They were invariably convivial journeys.

One took longer than it should. Bristol to Scarborough is a beast of a journey at the best of times; after a long day in the field and another match to play the next morning, it becomes a test of endurance. Especially before the advent of motorways. And even more so with Tom at the wheel. 'Sam Cook needed a lift to Tetbury, so we stopped at The Eight Bells to say our farewells. Then Tom had to go home to Winchcombe, where we had a drink at The George before setting off for our destination. We arrived at The Salisbury Hotel in Scarborough at 3.30am. The night porter had to be wakened to let us in. He was not best pleased!'

Although Tom was a senior player in the Gloucestershire side – 'One did not usually speak until spoken to!' remembers Brown – everyone found him very approachable. 'He was wonderful to us younger players,' said Mortimore, 'relaxed and easy going and always helpful.' Brown agreed. 'He was very happy to be with us,' he said, 'and to help in any way he could. Also, he was generous.'

He went on to stress that bats were (still are!) expensive, especially for young pros. 'A bat would cost a fiver, and that was a week's wages.' Tom used to give him bats. 'And to have a bat that was rejected by Tom Graveney was far better than having one from your local supplier.'

Indeed, it might seem from what Brown told me that his cricket bag was full of equipment mostly given to him by Tom. 'Mind you, we had to do one or two things in return.' One of these was to run errands for him, usually returning 'bags of clothes to the stores on Park Street and Queen's Road in Bristol that Mrs Graveney had "on approval" from some of the fashion houses'. These were errands that the lads were only too happy to carry out it would appear, if only for the excuse to escape the cricket ground and waste some time doing a bit of shopping themselves. 'But only *after* practice,' Brown virtuously insisted, 'not instead of!'

The summer of 1959 was a glorious one in which batsmen up and down the country flourished as the wickets baked hard and true. As we have seen, Graveney had paid the price, with others, for that disastrous tour of Australia the previous winter by not being selected to play for England against the touring Indians. His great friend, Arthur Milton, was chosen instead but sadly failed to nail down his place. Others were tried – Ken Taylor, Martin Horton, Gilbert Parkhouse, Geoff Pullar, Brian Close, Ramon Subba Row – all good cricketers but none, you would have thought, in Graveney's league.

However, Tom was not greatly exercised by any snub, real or imagined, and returned to Gloucestershire to concentrate his mind and talent happily enough on playing for his county. He was now captain, he had a good side under him, the sun was shining, it was his benefit year and Gloucestershire came within a whisker of winning the championship for the first time in their history, a prize that still eludes them.

All was well in the world, you would think. Sadly not. Tom had broken his finger, which put him out for a crucial period of a month mid-season and George Emmett had to come out of retirement to lead the side in his absence.

The broken finger – who hit you? 'No, I did it fielding. Never got hit batting. Well, not seriously.'

Were you ever 'sweded'? 'Only hit on the head once, in 1951, in Pakistan, by Khan Mohammed. It was Hanif Mohammed's first Test – at the age of 16! They had a swivel roller, which put a shine on the wicket. I lost sight of the ball against this sheen. Hit me on the head.

At the time we were 319/1! Wasn't going to come off, was I? No harm done anyway. Too thick for any lasting damage!' In all, he missed ten championship matches that summer and failed to break the 1,000-run barrier for the first time since he started playing in 1948.

To be injured and out of action is extremely frustrating for a professional sportsman. It must be doubly so if you are captain. You are faced with the dilemma of whether to remain 'hands on', influencing strategy and decisions as much as you can from the sidelines, or making yourself scarce and trusting in your lieutenants. If you try to keep a high profile, you run the risk of queering your vice-captain's pitch and undermining his authority. But if you take time out to mow the lawn and paint the shed, you can quickly become the forgotten man, surplus to requirements.

George Emmett had been captain for the previous four years. He knew the ropes, his team knew him and how he operated and no doubt they all got along fine. So can you imagine the mixed feelings the new captain had as he saw his team functioning perfectly well without him? Furthermore, Emmett had a totally different style to Tom. He had been in the Army, he was neat, organised, rigorous, stern and authoritative; Tom was more easy-going, preferring to get his message across with encouragement and courtesy. He took the view that everyone was a professional and knew his role in the team and his job, as captain, was to provide the emotional and competitive environment for the team to flourish. Two quite different philosophies, you might say.

For all that, Gloucestershire performed admirably that season and very nearly were the ones to bring to an end Surrey's long dominance of the County Championship in the 1950s. During a purple patch late on in the season, with Graveney back at the helm, they defeated Yorkshire – the eventual champions – by an innings and 77 runs. The crucial game was against Surrey at Gloucester. The pitch took spin from the outset. Gloucestershire had three very capable spinners – Cook, Mortimore and Allen – in their ranks. But Surrey could call upon two of the finest spinners of the era in Laker and Lock and they duly put the home side to the sword to win a low-scoring game by 81 runs. And that was it. Yorkshire were crowned champions, with Gloucestershire second and Surrey, their long reign having been brought to an end, third. So near, yet so far. One can only speculate whether they would have carried off the pennant had Graveney been fit throughout the season and contributed the vital runs that he assuredly would have done.

Having just had the most successful season in their history, you would have thought that all ambition, purpose and enterprise at the club would have been bent up to go one better the following season. Yet it appears that unity of commitment was far from the minds of more than a few of the members of the committee.

Cricket clubs, even today, are strange hybrid organisations, managed in ways that would be entirely recognisable to their Victorian forebears. One or two have reorganised themselves on a more modern business model, dispensing with unwieldy committees and time-serving functionaries but in the majority, the committee, especially the cricket committee, still holds sway. And committees, largely comprised of club stalwarts with time on their hands to serve, tend to be deeply conservative in their outlook.

Certainly Gloucestershire, at the turn of the decade, still hankered after the good old days when cricket clubs were made up of professionals, with a sprinkling of talented amateurs within the ranks and, of course, with an amateur at the helm. Sometime in 1959, Tom recollects that Sir Percy Lister, the chairman of the committee, announced to all and sundry that he had unearthed 'the new Ted Dexter'. Tom spluttered and choked on his coffee as he told me this, 'The new Ted Dexter! Tom Pugh was no Ted Dexter let me assure you. Ted was the most extraordinarily talented games player I have ever seen and though Tom Pugh was a mighty fine rackets player, he was no more than an average cricketer.' Nonetheless, Tom Pugh, an old Etonian, recommended to Gloucestershire by Percy Fender, joined the club in 1959, playing a few games.

In 1960, he played in the side more regularly, revealing himself to be a batsman of limited technical ability but with considerable pluck and guts. In one of the most poignant ironies of Tom Graveney's career, Pugh shared in a stand of 256 with him at Chesterfield against Derbyshire. Tom scored 135 and Pugh 137, his one and only first-class hundred. The irony of it was that Pugh had already been promised the captaincy and moves were afoot, even then, to have Graveney removed and Pugh installed in his place. Tom was completely unaware of the machinations that were being conducted behind his back. And so, it would seem, were many of his team-mates.

'To this day,' maintains Tony Brown, 'not many of the players who were playing at the time knew much about it all.'

David Allen was a newcomer, only having been presented with his county cap the previous year, and claimed to be out of the loop. John Mortimore, now a regular in the side, said, 'I didn't know what was going on at the time. Not many of the players did either.'

A few years afterwards, Tom was playing golf with Tom Pugh – there was never any personal animosity between the two – and Pugh admitted that he had been sounded out by members of the Gloucestershire committee as to his willingness to take over the captaincy *before* he had even signed on for the county. That was why he played in those few games in 1959. Graveney as captain had not wanted him in the side, arguing that a professional would have to make way – and lose his match fee – for an amateur who was no better. But his views were not heeded; Tom being Tom, he accepted the decision and thought no more about it. Nor did he sense anything untoward as the 1960 season proceeded.

Although results did not match those of the previous year, a position of eighth in the championship hardly merited a wholesale rush for the lifeboats. After the final match of the season, a victory against Essex by seven wickets, Tom was summoned by Sir Percy Lister to lunch, during which he dropped the bombshell; it was the committee's intention to replace Tom as captain for the 1961 season with Tom Pugh. Tom never saw it coming.

'I was flabbergasted,' he said. 'The team hadn't been playing badly. Not as well as the previous year, admittedly, but we'd had one or two significant injuries which hadn't helped. As far as I was aware, there was no mutiny in the ranks.'

It was claimed later by members of the committee that they had been made aware of the fact that there were one or two murmurings within the dressing room about Tom's captaincy. Now, there is not a dressing room on God's earth, even if captained by St Peter himself, where one or two murmurings cannot be heard about the captain's decisions. All the great captains in history have had their critics, both within and without the four walls of the dressing room.

The Grand Old Man himself, W.G. Grace, Warwick Armstrong, Douglas Jardine, Don Bradman, Len Hutton, Richie Benaud, Frank Worrell, Clive Lloyd, Mike Brearley, Steve Waugh – every one of them did not get every decision right and not everyone in their team was wholly in agreement with what was going on all of the time.

One or two people at the club felt that Graveney was a trifle defensive in his tactics and tended to let things drift a little. Even Mortimore, a supporter of Tom's, suggested that he could have changed the bowling a bit more frequently. 'The attack was experienced. Brown, Smith, Mortimore, Allen, Cook – we all knew our job and rarely would we bowl badly. So none of us would want to come off. What bowler does? Perhaps, on one or two occasions, Tom could have rotated us a bit more, rather than leaving us on. It's difficult for a captain and you can't always get it right. Tom would ask, "Feeling OK? Tired? Want a rest?" None of us wanted a rest!'

I asked him whether he was aware of wholesale dissatisfaction within the team with Tom's captaincy, whether there was a strong desire for a change of leader. Mortimore looked askance and shook his head.

On reflection, Tom admits, he wasn't the best captain in county cricket. But neither was he the worst. 'They were not an easy side to captain, you know,' he said. I raised an eyebrow. My impression, buttressed by the recollections of Tony Brown, John Mortimore and David Allen, was that they were a decent side, cheerful in each other's company and in no mood to effect a palace revolution.

'Our attack was based on the spinners,' he explained, 'so we bowled our overs quickly, often more than 20 an hour. Bomber Wells, remember, could bowl an over in one minute!'

That was true, and immediately I saw what he meant. In the days when county matches were of three days' duration instead of the four that we have now, many a stalemate had to be unravelled with judicious, not to say imaginative, use of the declaration. If the wicket was good or if the weather had intervened, it was often difficult to get four innings over and done with in three days and a draw would result.

There are times when a draw is welcome and hard fought for but there are other times, especially when you are chasing points, when a draw will not do. The sight of the two captains huddled together in a quiet corner of the pavilion, haggling over timing of declarations on the third day of a county game, somehow trying to engineer a result out of an unpromising deadlock, was not an uncommon phenomenon in those days. As a captain, you wanted to offer the bait but you also needed to have the means at your disposal to put the brakes on and to stop your opponents running away with it if things started to go wrong. The best means of frustrating a run chase that is getting out of hand is to have two fast bowlers with enormously long run-ups who bowl their overs at a funereal pace.

Tom did not have this luxury. He had Bomber Wells who didn't even have a run-up! So one can sympathise with his reluctance to throw caution to the wind and make challenging declarations. And if you draw more matches than you would like, you are labelled a negative captain. Sometimes it is as well to remember that the best captains usually have the best and most effective players for the job at their disposal.

For all that, decisions such as this are rarely made on cricketing grounds alone. Tom has two possible explanations for his sacking. In common with many of the counties, with the exception of the larger clubs whose grounds staged Test matches, Gloucestershire were struggling financially in the late 1950s and early 60s. After the post-war boom, attendances at county games had been steadily dwindling and not until the advent of the Gillette Cup in 1963, followed by various formats of the one-day game, did the health of the game improve.

Gloucestershire were running at an annual loss, to the extent that some thought the club was in real danger of going out of business. The ground at Bristol was becoming dilapidated and the amenities were in dire need of renovation, to say nothing of the cost of maintaining a presence at the 'out' grounds – Gloucester, Stroud and Cheltenham.

'Tom Pugh's father was a pretty wealthy businessman,' Tom told me. 'He owned a large firm of motor mowers.' Nothing more was said but I made the obvious inference.

So some sort of financial donation was promised if his son was made captain? He gave me the kind of Gallic shrug that would not have done Napoleon a disservice. To be fair to Tom Pugh, in my research about this rumour it would seem that he always disputed this, saying that no such payment was promised or given.

John Mortimore offers a more likely explanation. Some influential members of the committee still hankered after the good old days of amateur captains and in Tom Pugh they believed they had found the right man. 'He was a competitive player, not in Tom's class, obviously, but a perfectly decent bloke,' said Mortimore. 'He fitted the bill for what the committee wanted as an amateur captain.'

But they might just as well have been trying to stem the tide rushing up the Severn Estuary. The days of the amateur captain were numbered. The amateur, as a breed, was practically extinct by 1960, a fact acknowledged by the abolition of the distinction between amateurs and players only two years later.

But the committee were set on their course. The farcical steps they had to go to in their desire to keep their plans a secret amused Mortimore. 'Apparently, they were driving around the back lanes of Gloucestershire trying to find a quiet pub to hold their clandestine meetings.' He was adamant that the players were unaware of what was afoot. The news, when it broke, came as much as a surprise to them as it did to Tom.

So, Tom, how did you react when the coup de grace *was delivered?* 'I went on the golf course and slogged a few.'

Were you upset? Silence. What a stupid question, I said to myself. 'They wanted me to stay, you know.'

Well, of course they did, in view of the number of runs you scored for them each season. 'And then I thought, b***** it, I'm going. I didn't see why I should have to resign the captaincy when the results were not bad. It wasn't as if there were calls for my resignation from the players or the members. And if they were short of money, well, that was hardly my fault, was it?'

According to daughter, Becky, and son, Tim, Jackie was deeply upset by what had happened and never forgave the club for the slight to her husband's reputation and good name. The writing was on the wall. Tom informed the committee of his intention to leave.

He remembers being 'invited' to a council of war by the club's president, the Duke of Beaufort, at his country seat at Badminton. The meeting was attended by Sir William Grant, chairman of the club, and Sir Percy Lister, chairman of the cricket committee. For moral support, Tom took along his brother. 'Ken's always a good man for a crisis.'

During that meeting, they offered to increase Tom's wages if he stayed and played under the new captain, and this would be confirmed in a letter. 'And do you know what?' Tom laughed sardonically. 'I'm still waiting for that letter.' But the die was cast. He felt that he could not go back. The club now appeared to accept the inevitable and told him that he could leave 'with their good wishes'.

It was at this stage that things turned nasty. For reasons that were not at all clear to Tom, the committee decided to renege on their agreement to allow him to move without let or hindrance to another county and wrote to MCC to that effect, saying that they would block any attempt at such a move. In those days, not so long ago, let us remind ourselves, MCC would only agree to the transfer of a player from one county to another if they had both clubs' consent. Failing that, the player concerned would have to serve a qualification period of one year, during which he would not be allowed to play in any County Championship matches. In effect, Tom would be banished from the first-class game for 12 months. He appealed, a forlorn gesture, he knew, but the whole thing seemed so unfair. Why had Gloucestershire gone back on their word?

The hearing was held at Lord's. This time he took along a QC to plead his case but it was to no avail. The vote was 5-1 in favour of the employer; Tom was to be consigned to the cricketing wilderness for one year. He remembers sitting on a balcony looking out over the green outfield while the MCC sub-committee deliberated before being summoned inside for the verdict. 'That was how cricket was run then,' he told me. 'The players had no power. MCC were our masters. We just had to do what we were told.'

The case raised a great deal of public interest; no less a luminary in the national press than E.W. Swanton was appalled at the way the whole business had been handled. Ay, but there's the rub, as our hero might have said. He didn't in fact but what he did say was this. 'It wasn't so much that they wanted to change their captain. That was their right, I suppose. But what stuck in the throat was the way that they changed their tune, not allowing me to go to another county when they said they would.'

No mention of restraint of trade and freedom of players to move from one club to another. The George Eastham court case, the Packer revolution, the Bosman ruling – all these landmarks in the shift of power from the employers to the players were still over the horizon.

He had played his last game for Gloucestershire. He had scored 21 run out in the first innings and 21 not out in the second – not a particularly glittering farewell, not that he was to know that it was the end, but at least he signed off with a victory, by seven wickets against Essex. And into exile he went, axed by his country and sacked by his county. At the age of 33, he might have been forgiven for believing that his best years were behind him.

Did you ever think, well, that could be it, there's no way back now? He smiled. 'The second part of my career was better than the first!' Be that as it may, for Gloucestershire he had scored nearly 20,000 runs and stood shoulder to shoulder, in most people's opinion, with those other greats of the county, W.G. Grace, Gilbert Jessop and Wally Hammond. And the committee had sacked him!

The story has an interesting footnote. Tom Pugh's leadership lasted barely two years. Although his captaincy was adequate, his batting wasn't and it soon became obvious to all and sundry that he wasn't worth his place in the team. So he was shown the door and in his place the committee asked Tom's brother, Ken, to take up the reins. It was another extraordinary decision, yet again prompted by their obsession with amateur captains.

The amateur, as a concept, had been abolished the previous year but Ken fitted the bill because he would not be paid for his services. He had no need. He was a wealthy man in his own right. And Gloucestershire were desperately short of money. But in all other respects, one would be hard pressed to think of a more bizarre choice. He was 38, he had not played first-class cricket since 1951 and he had a bad back. Time to talk to his son, David, I decided, in an attempt to unravel this curious piece of strategic thinking.

'Dad has led a very colourful life,' said David. 'I should say so,' Tom added later. 'He's had three wives, you know.' And he gave an indulgent smile. 'We're quite different characters, you know.'

This I had already gathered. More forceful and assertive than Tom, Ken had made a name for himself in the world of commerce after retiring from cricket; indeed, you might even say that, as a captain of industry, he was ideally suited to become captain of a county cricket team. And in many ways, you would be right.

'He loved it,' said David. 'But really it came to him ten years too late.' Of course it was too late. His bad back prevented him from bowling, he batted down the order and no one in his late 30s was going to fling himself around in the field. Furthermore, the new one-day format, the Gillette Cup, was up and running and it soon became clear that higher standards of athleticism were going to be called for than hitherto. Ken was a leader of men, there can be no doubt about that, but physically he wasn't up to the task.

Not that he would have admitted it. All his life, he had been bucking the odds. After leaving school, he had gone into the Army and trained as a Marine. He was in one of the advanced commando units to land on the beaches of Normandy on D-Day. 'He never spoke about it,' said David, 'but I know it must have been terrible.'

As he was telling me this, I reflected that we cricket lovers sometimes need to take a cold shower of realism. Heroism is not really facing a fast bowler and getting hit. Fear is not really crouching down close in at short-leg. Danger is not really a wet wicket. Luck is not really getting dropped in the slips. 'All he ever said about it,' went on David, 'was that the opening scenes in *Saving Private Ryan* were just as it was.'

Tom told me that his brother was wounded in the murderous battle for Caen but continued to fight with his unit, 42 Commando, through Normandy towards the German border. 'He saw 128 consecutive days' front-line combat. His unit was practically wiped out. When he was sent home, he was suffering from battle exhaustion.' From the tone of his voice, it was clear that Tom had immense respect for his brother. 'Mind you,' he said, in an effort to lighten the tone, 'Ken always reckoned he was in more danger from the trigger-happy Yanks than he was from the Germans.'

David's mother died when he was young. His father did what many men seem to do when left bereft by bereavement – he married his secretary who was 25 years his junior. 'That lasted five years,' Tom snorted. 'By this time he was playing a lot of golf. One day his partner dropped dead on the course. Eventually, Ken married his widow and she's kept him alive ever since. They now live in the US. Ken – what a lad!' It is no wonder that David holds especial affection for his uncle. He was like a surrogate father when he was growing up.

After the war, Ken started working as a trainee manager in catering in Bristol and quickly worked his way up the ladder to become CEO and eventually managing director of Sutcliffe Catering, a firm started by colleagues in the Royal Marines. Now it becomes clearer why the committee at Gloucestershire believed that in Ken they had recruited the right man, someone with considerable energy, authority and force of personality. He was also a prominent sportsman in his own right – though no longer at cricket. He was captain of the Gloucestershire golf team.

'So Dad was captain – and later president – of Gloucestershire in two different sports,' said David. 'Unique, I think.' So who was the better golfer, Ken or Tom, I wondered. 'Tom had problems with his putting!' shouted Ken down the transatlantic telephone line. 'Ken was a bit wild off the tee but was magnificent around the greens,' maintained Tom.

'Dad won the Gloucestershire championship,' pointed out referee David. 'Uncle Tom never did.' 'That's because I was playing cricket,' was the riposte from Tom.

Competitiveness courses through the Graveney dynasty, that much is evident. 'Do you know what?' Tom added. 'Ken rang me up when I was on tour in Queensland and told me that they'd offered him the captaincy. Asked me whether I minded! Of course not, I told him. Don't worry about what happened to me. Go ahead and accept. And he did a pretty good job, under the circumstances.'

John Mortimore, who played under him and succeeded him as captain, confirmed this. 'He was outgoing and extrovert and didn't mind ruffling a few feathers. I think he enjoyed it.' But they sacked him too.

When I asked Ken about this, there was a pause on the line and then he exclaimed, 'Gloucester! They sacked all the Graveneys.' All? More than two? And then I remembered. David had been appointed captain in 1982. Towards the end of the 1988 season, he discovered that he had been relieved of his duties in the strangest, and some might say the most insensitive, of circumstances.

The reasons for his dismissal do not concern us here but let David take up the sequence of events. 'It was at Bristol. We were playing Worcester. I'd just come off the field having taken 6-38 in the second innings, after taking eight in the first, and I was told I'd been sacked as captain. Imagine! I'd just taken 14 wickets in the match! And the season hadn't finished.'

Tom was deeply upset for his nephew. 'David is such a nice bloke and he deserved better than that.' The fact that the scenario had so closely resembled his back in 1960 was to him bitterly ironic. Jackie was furious, needless to say, having all her suspicions and seething resentments about Gloucestershire confirmed.

By that time, Tom had been appointed president of Worcestershire and one of his duties – more of a pleasure in fact to Tom – was to represent the club at away fixtures as a guest of the opponents' committee. Going back to his old club had been a bittersweet experience but his natural affability and bonhomie had seen him through. Jackie, however, had found it impossible and had steadfastly refused to go back.

At length, Tom had talked her round. Let bygones be bygones, he had said; what happened was a long time ago and now we should support our nephew. Reluctantly, she agreed, but would only join them later in the afternoon. Lunch with the enemy would be too stressful, she reasoned. She arrived at the ground at about 5pm that very day that we have been describing. Immediately, she became aware that rumours that David had been sacked were spreading around the ground like wildfire. It was true, she soon discovered. 'And do you know what?' said Tom. 'She never set foot in that ground again.'

And what about you, Tom? Do you ever go back, for social occasions…you know, ex-players' reunions? He waggled his head in a quandary. 'Yes. Now and then.'

Is it awkward for you? 'A little. I feel much more at home at Worcester. Well, it is my home really.'

8

County Champions – Worcestershire 1961–70

'People say the bowlers won us the championship in 1964 and 1965. No we didn't. That bloke over there won it for us.'
(Len Coldwell, gesturing to Tom Graveney)

'In retrospect, my year off from the game in 1961 was the best thing that ever happened to me,' Tom confided in me. 'When I came back, I was determined to make up for lost time.'

His move from Gloucestershire a short distance up the M5 to Worcestershire was an obvious one. The family were now living in Winchcombe and in fact it was a shorter journey to Worcester than it was to Bristol. 'It was Sir George Dowty, the president of Worcestershire, who got me to play for them. His business was in Cheltenham and he said to me, "Come and play for us!" The idea greatly appealed, so I did. And I never regretted it for one second.'

It helped that he knew a few of the Worcestershire players well – Don Kenyon, Norman Gifford and the Richardson brothers – and he had always enjoyed playing against them, finding them to be a friendly bunch.

Part of the terms of his registration for Worcestershire was that he would have to take up residence in his new county.

Where did you live? He grinned. 'Winchcombe.'

Winchcombe? But that's in Gloucestershire, isn't it? 'Well, yes, but it's close. Only a few…' I nodded. His secret was safe with me. 'I did have a postal address in Broadway, which *is* in Worcestershire, where all my mail was sent,' he added by way of mitigation.

His suspension from county cricket for a year did not mean that he could therefore swan off on a luxury cruise, even if that was what he would have wanted to do. The thrill of overseas tours had begun to pall a little. As a contracted player, he still had to report for duty with his new employers on 1 April 1961. The surroundings may have changed but the routine didn't. He found the atmosphere very welcoming and any disquiet he may have felt was immediately dispelled.

He was prohibited from playing in the County Championship but he could still have his daily net and he was allowed to play against the visiting Australians and the two universities. For the rest of the time, he turned out for the Second XI and played for Dudley on Saturdays in the Birmingham League. He was also invited on a very pleasant, but not-too-taxing, three-week tour of Bermuda with Stuart Surridge's team.

'It was like a breath of fresh air, this year away from the bright lights,' he told me. 'I was 35, I'd been playing non-stop for 13 years and I needed a break. Also, I'd been on lots of overseas tours in the winter and had hardly seen my family. It gave me a chance to re-charge the old batteries.'

How did you find playing at a lower level? Did it ever frustrate you? He shook his head as if surprised by the question. 'No, not at all. A game of cricket is a game of cricket. You've still got to go out there and perform.' Spoken like a true professional.

Every day, every match, every pitch, every opponent brings its own challenges; to relax, to ease off, to take the foot off the pedal, is simply not allowed for in the professional cricketer's psyche. Well, it may be in some – Ian Botham did not always feel that he could operate at full throttle – but in Tom's case, the very idea of putting his feet up for a year while drawing his salary was as anathema to him as not buying his round in the bar at the close of play.

Duncan Fearnley – he of the bat-making firm – can vouch for this diligence of Tom's when at work. As a 21-year-old, he joined Worcestershire on the same day as Tom. He is proud of the fact that their numbers in the records of Worcestershire players should be sequential: Graveney 307 and Fearnley 308. 'We were a young side in that second XI team,' he said. 'Playing were Fred Rumsey, Alan Ormrod, Ron Headley, Norman Gifford, Doug Slade, Jim Standen – the nucleus, if you like, of the team that went on to win back-to-back championships in the mid-60s. And it was wonderful to have Tom Graveney, an established international, in the same side.'

He went on to praise Tom's exemplary preparation and attitude throughout his time in the stiffs. 'He was first in the dressing room in the morning, reading the newspaper before changing, whatever he had been up to the previous night. Every day he had a net, match days or practice days. We youngsters watched and learned.' According to Fearnley, Tom never gave his wicket away, whether it was a second XI game or a Test match. Even when playing for Dudley, he made sure he got 50 before essaying a few extravagant shots.

His routine never varied. Fearnley again, 'Batting at number four, he never watched a ball until the first wicket down. And then he'd come out on to the balcony, sit down and watch that partnership closely, whether it lasted one ball or most of the day. And then, when it was time for him to bat, he would don his cap, put on his gloves and make his way out to the middle tugging at his cap in that unhurried yet confident manner of his.

'And when he came back into the dressing room at whatever break of play, whether he was ten not out or 100 not out, his habits remained unchanged. He would sit down, quietly take off his pads, put his bat upright against the bench and carefully attach his chewing gum to the splice.'

Tom's explanation for this strict adherence to routine? 'It helps to keep you focussed, in the groove. It's just the way I was, I suppose. Everyone's different and has their own way of doing things. That was mine.'

At the beginning of the 1962 season, the pressure was on. It was all very well timing the ball sweetly for Worcestershire's seconds and Dudley but would he be able to repay the faith that his new county had invested in him once he returned to the first-class game?

I don't believe that even a batsman of Tom's class would not have had one or two butterflies in his stomach as he bade his team-mates good morning as they arrived one by one in the dressing room at Worcester on 2 May. As tradition dictated, their first opponents were the visiting Pakistanis. Tom was anxious to do well. Somehow, life seems a lot easier if you get off to a good start. His calamitous first few months, all those years ago, when he started out at Gloucestershire must have been nagging away at him but being the experienced pro that he was, he would have given them short shrift.

He had been fortunate having had a little pre-season tour with a side put together by Ron Roberts, the distinguished cricket correspondent. I say a 'little' tour but I ought to give it its full name, An International XI World Tour, and it was significant for much more than giving Tom Graveney a bit of batting practice. It was the first multi-racial cricket tour ever undertaken, with 25 players from all countries flying in and flying out at various stages to take part.

Eight first-class matches were played in Rhodesia, New Zealand, East Pakistan (now, of course, Bangladesh), India and Pakistan. The mixed race composition of the team makes this story of Tom's all the more shocking and an ominous portent of what was to come in the cricketing world. They were travelling from Bulawayo up to Salisbury, in Rhodesia. In Tom's car were Ron Roberts, the manager, Ray Lindwall, the Australian fast bowler and Everton Weekes, the West Indian batsman. They were parched and stopped for a drink. They ordered four gins and tonic.

'The woman behind the bar,' recounted Tom, 'said to Everton, "You get out. You're not allowed in here." We all marched out and told her what to do with her gin and tonic. There was a colour bar, you see. It was terrible.'

On an excursion further north into Kenya, they played a match in Nairobi and were blown away by the batting of a Cape Coloured, who was part of the team but not well known to them. They would not have heard of him because of the restrictive laws in his native South Africa, which prevented him from playing with, or against, white cricketers.

'He was on 80 not out,' remembered Tom, 'and the new ball was taken. Far from being intimidated by the fast bowlers, he raced to 150 in no time at all. He smashed it everywhere. I've never seen hitting like it. They ran out of new balls because he kept on hitting them into the bush.'

Later, Everton Weekes was moved to describe it as the best innings he had ever seen. And the name of the unknown batsman? Basil D'Oliveira. As we shall see, D'Oliveira was to play a principal role in the remainder of Tom's cricketing career as well as becoming one of his closest and most enduring friends for the rest of his life.

Tom caught up with him a couple of years later playing in a Commonwealth team on a tour of Pakistan. By now, D'Oliveira had secured for himself a position as a professional for Middleton in the Lancashire League. 'Late one night in Karachi, back at the hotel, we polished off a couple of bottles of Scotch,' admitted Tom, a little shame-facedly. 'I said to him that he was wasting his time in the leagues. What he needed to do was to play the first-class game. Come to Worcester, I urged him.'

When he got home, Tom was as good as his word and recommended him in the strongest possible terms to the committee. Worcestershire grabbed him with both hands and the rest, as they say, is history.

But to return to the International World XI Tour. It gave Tom more than casual batting practice. He played in all eight first-class games and made two centuries, as well as three scores in the 90s. His confidence, if ever it needed boosting, was sky-high as he faced the Pakistanis in the first match of the 1962 season. He got off to a flyer, making the almost inevitable hundred in the second innings. And of course, he didn't stop there. I am reminded of a phrase – from where I know not – which described his batting in this, the second stage of his career, 'as if the iron had entered his soul'. He certainly had a point to prove and he admits that he felt like a man reborn. 'I was run-hungry,' he succinctly put it.

Tim, his son, has a typically straightforward explanation for the change in him. 'I think he wanted to put two fingers up to the Gloucestershire committee.' Mike Vockins, in his history of Worcestershire CCC, described the metamorphosis in more evocative language, 'It was a more purposeful Graveney that spectators saw. The classical grace and timing were still there but to this grace was added a steel-like dimension.'

In whatever way onlookers, press, committee members, team-mates and opposing bowlers preferred to describe the new Graveney, the figures tell a plain but remarkable story. He scored over 2,000 runs that season, at an average of 54.02, and finished second in the national averages to Reg Simpson.

An indication of how well he was playing is given by this story he recounted to me. Worcestershire were playing Somerset, at home, at New Road. The wickets at Worcester were known to be a little spicy, a far cry from the dead pitches at Bristol. The fact that Tom flourished on these wickets when others faltered spoke volumes for his technique and his new-found appetite for the contest. But the prepared wicket was a shocker. Glumly, both captains, Don Kenyon for the home side and Harold Stephenson for the visitors, cast their eyes over it before the toss and both came to the conclusion that it was unfit for play.

'It did look awful,' confirmed Tom. Hasty telephone calls were made to Lord's in an effort to get the game postponed but the powers that be at headquarters were adamant in their ruling; the game must proceed as scheduled at all costs. Then Tom started laughing. 'Unplayable?' he spluttered. 'We scored 520/3 declared and they were 70/1. Nothing wrong with it.' Tom made 168 and Martin Horton 233, his highest first-class score. Mind you, Worcestershire did bowl Somerset out twice, to win by 264 runs.

'Don't forget that we played on uncovered wickets in those days,' he reminded me. I too had been brought up on uncovered wickets and was not alone in my belief that they presented a searching examination of a batsman's technique as well as providing variety and fascination to the game which today's covered, bland surfaces tend not to. 'Sometimes it was a struggle to bat on a rain-affected wicket,' he said, 'especially if the opposition had a decent spinner, which they invariably did. It was a battle for survival.'

Interestingly enough, Tom's nephew, David Graveney, added a relevant comment in the course of discussing Tom's career about the wickets at Worcester. 'He wasn't the only one to leave the lifeless pitches at Bristol to improve their batting,' he told me. 'Chris Broad moved from Gloucestershire to Nottinghamshire for the same reason. And look what happened to him. He got picked for England. So you could say his decision was vindicated.'

'Ah,' I remarked, a little impishly, 'is that why you left Gloucester too?' He gave me a look that was as close to a dirty one as he could manage. 'The point is,' he went on, 'that my uncle became a better player on the sporting wickets at Worcester. For that reason alone, apart from all the other stuff, it was a good move for him.'

I should say so. Even the national selectors recognised that a new Graveney was among them. He was recalled – at last – to the England team.

Why now? What made them change their minds? He shrugged his shoulders. 'Sheer weight of runs, I suppose.' He was hugely amused by the paperwork of the MCC bureaucracy when they informed him of his recall to the national team. 'They sent the letter to Gloucestershire!'

The joining instructions from the selectors may have gone astray but he knew the way to Edgbaston well enough, where he made his comeback against Pakistan and scored 97. Oh for those extra three runs. It doesn't seem much but it means a great deal. Never mind.

Wisden described the innings as 'a classical display' and Tom was happy enough to be back on the world stage, scoring runs. On his return to Lord's in the second Test, he made sure of his century this time and added another, in the fourth at Trent Bridge, for good measure. All in all, with a series average of 100.25, you could say that he had made his point all right.

'We should have won the championship that year, too,' he claimed, even now the irritation in his voice all too pronounced. My memory failed me here so I dived back into the record books. They revealed that Worcestershire finished second in 1962 and came so close to pipping Yorkshire to the post. In the event, much rain in August robbed them of cricket, time, points and possibly victories but by the time of their final match of the season, against Nottinghamshire at Worcester, they would go to the top of the table if they secured a win. This they duly did and only a victory by Yorkshire against Glamorgan at Harrogate could deny them the title.

'There was a lot of rain around,' said Tom, 'and the whole of the second day's play of Yorkshire's game was wiped out. The ground was still waterlogged on the third day but all the Yorkshire supporters were out on the pitch prodding the grass with the points of their umbrellas to allow most of the water to drain away. They played and bowled Glamorgan out twice in the day.'

Couldn't happen today, spectators helping to dry out the ground, could it? Mournfully, he agreed, before reminding me that the same thing happened in 1968, at the Oval, when the boot was on the other foot, allowing Derek Underwood to bowl out the Aussies in a famous last-ditch win. Now that I do remember…but we are getting ahead of ourselves.

Tom was of course a shoo-in for the forthcoming Ashes tour Down Under. Ted Dexter was the captain, the batting was strong, particularly so with Graveney back in the side, and hopes were high that England could regain the urn.

Tom, at 35, was the oldest in the party but he was in prime form and this, his third tour of Australia, would surely lay to rest the ghosts of previous disappointments against the old enemy. The answer came concealed in the curious fact that he wholly omitted any mention of the tour in his initial recollections of this stage of his career. When pressed, he gave a little grimace. 'Ah yes,' he said, 'the Sussex tour.'

This cutting comment was so uncharacteristic of the generous tone of his reminiscences that I decided to do a little research of the 1962/63 MCC tour of Australia. The Duke of Norfolk was the manager. He was a great cricket lover and his family seat is at Arundel Castle, which is in Sussex. Was there any personal friction there? 'The Duke? He was a lovely chap, utterly charming. In fact I played quite regularly in his teams and got on very well with him.'

The English cricket season traditionally opened with the Duke of Norfolk's XI playing against the summer tourists in the grounds of the Castle and to be asked to play was considered an honour as well as a good career move. Tom appreciated his annual invitation. 'Played against the Duke of Edinburgh there once,' he remembered.

Oh yes, I've seen a photo of him bowling in his younger days. Was he any good? 'He was no mug, you know. He bowled off-spinners. Got me out once. "I hope you didn't do that deliberately," he remarked as

I walked past him. I assured him that I had not. He must have believed me because, in the next New Year's honours list, I was awarded the OBE!' He roared with laughter. I think we can safely say that Tom had no issues with dukes.

David Sheppard? He too was on that tour. He had taken a sabbatical from his ministry in the Church to play and there had been a large faction at Lord's eager to make him captain but in the end Ted Dexter had been confirmed as MCC's choice of leader.

Undeterred, Sheppard had still made himself available to tour and during the course of the team's travels around the country, he 'filled the Anglican cathedral of every state capital from Perth to Brisbane', wrote E.W. Swanton. Or as Tom wryly put it, 'David put a thousand on the gate whenever he preached.'

Sheppard played for Sussex. So was there a problem there? Only in the sense, it seems, that his presence kept Tom out of the side in the first Test. However, as Sheppard made runs in that game, following it up with a century in the second – which England won – and, all things considered, did not have a bad tour, on the basis of runs scored, his place in the side was not really a bone of contention. 'No, David and I were good friends,' Tom hastened to assure me. 'Mind you, he dropped a few,' he chortled.

Sheppard's long absence from the game, while a source of admiration when he was batting, did mean that his reactions in the field were not as sharp as they might have been and gave rise to a fund of amusing stories. One that gained increased prominence in the years that followed was Fred Trueman's exasperated response when Sheppard shelled one off his bowling, 'For ****'s sake, Reverend, keep your hands together like you do on Sundays!' Even Sheppard's wife was moved to comment, when she was asked whether her husband would christen a child, 'I shouldn't, if I were you. He's bound to drop it.'

So, what about the captain, Ted Dexter, another man of Sussex? There was a ruminative pause. While Tom was thinking about his response, I remembered an earlier conversation we had had about 'Lord Ted'. It was fairly evident that Tom had unswerving admiration for Dexter as a batsman; he rated him as the best all-round games player he has ever seen. But as a captain of England, he wasn't so sure. At the very least, Dexter seemed to show less than wholehearted confidence in Tom on this tour. 'I was left out for the first Test.'

Why? Not fit? Not well? Not in great nick? He pulled a face. 'I don't know why. I really don't. I didn't then and I don't now.' His form in the warm-up games had not been remarkable but he had scored 99 against South Australia and a fifty against Queensland and it should not be forgotten that he had just had an outstanding series against Pakistan. Once again, he felt, rightly or wrongly, that his captain was ambivalent about his value, and role, in the team.

And Tom flourished when he believed his influence was needed and valued. He found it hard to bat in a self-contained bubble, like Barrington, Boycott, Tavare, Trott, Kallis, Chanderpaul et al. 'Ted's a funny chap,' he said. 'You never quite knew what plan or tactic he was hatching in his mind.' Hmm, not the greatest communicator then, I surmised. Often, the great players do not find it easy to understand why less gifted team-mates sometimes struggle and suffer from crises of confidence.

Dexter's batting on this tour was imperious but after a bright start and a victory in the second Test to level the series, his captaincy became increasingly introspective and defensive. Notoriously a man of mercurial moods and quixotic theories, he was difficult to read and prone to gamble if he became bored or if he felt the game was drifting.

'Once, we couldn't find him,' Tom disclosed, 'until someone looked out of the dressing room window and noticed him out on the outfield. He was practising how to throw a boomerang!'

I sensed from what Tom reluctantly revealed about the tour that he believed Dexter wouldn't trust him in a crisis, convinced that he was a fair-weather sailor who cut and ran when the weather turned nasty. I believe that there is evidence enough in Graveney's career to give the lie to this view but the thing was that Tom, though dismissing this judgement himself, never really did himself justice when he suspected his captain was thinking along those lines.

He played in only three Tests that winter – he missed the third with a bad dose of flu – and never got going, his bafflement at the selection policy further exacerbated by being asked – instructed, really – to bat at number six in two of the Tests, hardly a ringing endorsement of his captain's faith in him. His top score in the series was only 41.

Ironically, a former team-mate – and driving companion – of his at Gloucestershire, David Allen, was also in the touring party and shared Tom's equivocal opinion of Dexter as a captain. 'I had a sneaking feeling,' he told me, 'that Tom and I were not at the top of the hit parade on the tour and the captain preferred other players.'

Instinctively, Dexter didn't really trust the spinners in his bowling attack, preferring to use the quick bowlers as his spearhead, with a spinner – or himself as a third seamer – to contain things until the quicks were rested and ready to fire again. On this tour, he had the celebrated opening pair of Trueman and Statham to lead the attack but though they were both still capable of significant spells, they were nearing the ends of their careers, had lost some of their pace and therefore were less effective.

Allen was considered at this time to be the senior spinner but he was passed over in favour of Fred Titmus. Titmus, as it happened, had a good tour but many onlookers, including some of the Australian team, believed that had Allen been allowed a more significant role in the series, England might well have won the Ashes. To be fair to Dexter, he did later acknowledge his misjudgement, admitting that he had 'deprived the side of a great bowler for much of the tour'.

One beneficial off-shoot of their periods of idleness meant that Graveney and Allen could renew their partnership behind the wheel of a car. Allen recollects one agreeable drive to the Barossa Valley in South Australia to visit the famous vineyards. They had been warned by friends about the dangers of exceeding the speed limit but the lovely scenery and one or two glasses of Australia's finest had lowered their guard. Twice they were stopped by the police and issued with warnings.

'On the third occasion,' Allen relates, 'the policeman was very angry. He seemed nonplussed when Tom gave his name and address but the interview calmed down when Tom offered to leave tickets for him and his family for the game next day.'

Tom takes up the story. 'It was Richie Benaud who saved our bacon. He was in the car behind us and he stopped to see what help he could give us. I think the copper listened more to the captain of Australia than he did to me!'

Notwithstanding these pleasant interludes – Tom has always loved Australia and Australians – it was another miserable tour. He was surplus to requirements on the New Zealand leg and returned home early, convinced that this time his Test career was over for good. 'That was it. Dropped for the third time. There was no way back. Look, I was in my mid-30s. My time had passed.'

So, it was back to the day job. 'Yes. I just concentrated on enjoying playing for Worcester.'

His pessimism about his England career seemed well founded as the 1963 season unfolded. Tom had scored a typically resourceful 73 (out of a total of 119) for Worcestershire against the West Indies in the opening match of the season but it soon became apparent that the national selectors had all but discarded him for good as one by one a succession of reputable but uninspiring county players were preferred, with only fitful success.

The likes of Brian Bolus, Phil Sharpe, Mickey Stewart, Brian Close and Peter Richardson would all have had their advocates but surely none of them could have been considered to be in the same class as Graveney.

Did it rankle with you that lesser players were being favoured? He shook his head. 'Never gave it a thought. I'd had my time in the sun. And besides, that season wasn't a good one, for me or the team.' Indeed it wasn't. After the heady successes of 1962, Worcestershire suffered something of an inexplicable collapse, from second to 14th, in the championship. They didn't win a match until mid-July, which was not the form of potential champions. And their champion batsman was out of sorts too. His average fell by 20 runs for the season and he only made a single century all summer.

There was however one highlight. The year of 1963 was one of great change in domestic cricket. One exciting innovation was the launch of the first limited overs competition, the Gillette Cup. It proved to be an instant and popular success and Worcestershire made up for their disappointing show in the three-day game with a successful run in the knock-out form, which saw them reach the final, at Lord's, against Sussex. It was a nail-biting affair, which Sussex won by a mere 14 runs. Worcestershire may have again finished as runners-up but they won many admirers for their decision to field all three of their spinners and to play attacking cricket to the last.

In the end, Ted Dexter, the Sussex captain, lined most of his fielders around the boundary and Worcestershire were restricted to scampering for singles when boundaries were needed. Dexter received a mixed press for his tactics. Some berated him for this negative ploy; others lauded him for his strategic genius. Certainly, he was the first to latch on to the concept that limited overs cricket was more about saving runs than seeking to take wickets.

Tom was typically phlegmatic about the furore. 'You've got to do what it takes to win,' he said. Certainly, the proof of the pudding was in the eating, as far as Dexter was concerned; Sussex retained the cup the following year.

Did you enjoy the one-day game? 'Yes I did. You see, when the Gillette Cup started, it was 65 overs per side, which I felt was long enough to build a decent innings. We had some good games.'

And the fielding? You were no longer a spring chicken. How did you cope? 'I managed OK,' he assured me. 'I always kept myself fit and I was rarely injured. I drank a fair bit but I felt that the fluid was a fair replacement for all that I had sweated out on the field.' I must have looked a little sceptical because he added, with a wry grin, 'But I always knew when to stop.' Incidentally, his career average in the Gillette Cup was 48.54. He knew when it was time to go to bed, clearly.

One thing, Tom – I notice that you don't seem to be playing in those end-of-season festivals anymore. How come? He grimaced. 'You would have thought,' he eventually said, 'that they would have invited me during my year away from county cricket, seeing that I had so few opportunities to play. Well, they didn't. Probably because it was felt I was persona non grata, I suppose. I was upset, I have to say. Especially as I had been a loyal supporter down the years. So I refused any invitation after that and never went again.'

Tom is a genial and gentle soul but he bleeds like any man and he can dig his heels in when he feels he has been wronged. 'I find it easy to forgive,' he once told me in the course of our many conversations, 'but I don't forget.'

It must have become increasingly obvious to the informed onlooker that Worcestershire, in the early 1960s, were assembling a team that could match any in the country. A batting line-up of Kenyon, Horton, Headley, Graveney and Dick Richardson, with D'Oliveira waiting in the wings, serving his year's qualification period, had the technique and the skill to thrive on any wicket. The opening attack of Flavell and Coldwell was the best around and the spin department was well stocked with bowlers of the calibre of Gifford and Slade, and Horton too.

'But you know what?' Tom stressed. 'Where we scored over other counties was in the quality of our back-up players.'

With Kenyon sometimes absent on Test selecting duties and others in the team at various times being called up to play for England (though this did not include Graveney, as we have seen), as well as the usual injuries that always take their toll, the reserves were frequently called upon to step into the breach.

Bob Carter and Brian Brain were fine bowlers in their own right, Alan Ormrod was slowly establishing himself in the side and Jim Standen, when football commitments permitted, was often an inspirational presence.

'Jim Standen,' said Tom admiringly, 'was our "phantom seamer". But what a fielder! Sometimes he was our only man in front of square on the off side, he was that good. As you would expect of a First Division goalkeeper.'

It is a curious fact, one that shall never be repeated, that Standen won the FA Cup with West Ham United in 1964 and the County Championship with Worcestershire in the same year. In those days it was possible to combine the two careers; nowadays, the seasons are far too congested and overlap too much.

If the pundits were backing Worcestershire to achieve great things and their supporters were hoping that, after the near miss in 1962, the team would go one better, the critical point was whether the players themselves believed they had it in them to become champions.

That they answered this question so emphatically could be put down to the leadership and influence of one man, according to Tom Graveney. 'Don Kenyon was a superb captain,' he said, 'the best I ever played under. He did it all on his own, you know. He had his own mind and rarely asked for advice. But he seemed to have this quiet authority and was able to get the best out of his players. And we had a few fiery characters in that dressing room, I can tell you.'

Actually he didn't tell me much, still adhering loyally to the sanctity and privacy of the dressing room. But it doesn't take the investigative tenacity of a *Sunday Times* journalist to unearth the fact that Jack Flavell had a temper to match his red hair, that Dick Richardson lived life to the full on and off the field, that Ron Headley had an effervescent personality, that Basil D'Oliveira could be a handful, that Jim Standen was no shrinking violet and that Kenyon's team comprised almost exclusively internationals who reckoned they knew a thing or two about the game. Tom did not include himself among this number. 'I was a good boy,' he said virtuously, 'I only had six pints before I drove home.'

The qualities that Don Kenyon exhibited as a captain were extolled by everyone to whom I spoke who had played with him. George Chesterton, one of the great amateur bowlers from a previous generation, reckoned that the captaincy was the making of him. 'He was a little dour and as an opening batsman almost totally wrapped up in his own performances,' he said. 'But when he became captain, it forced him to emerge from his shell and think of others. Thus he grew into the job in the side and became a better man for it.'

Norman Gifford, a young left-arm spinner not long of course a future championship-winning captain himself, agreed wholeheartedly. 'Don was brilliant. There were some huge personalities in that side but Don handled them superbly. He was a quiet man but he had presence. He ran the show and there was no back-chat from anyone.'

Duncan Fearnley concurred. 'Oh aye. He was a great captain, tactically very astute,' he said simply. 'Bit tight though. He used to walk away with all the sponsors' cigarettes!'

Tom added this observation with a laugh. 'He was a miserable bugger. "How are you this morning, Don?" we'd ask him and invariably he would come back the reply, "Didn't sleep so well last night" or, "Not feeling so good today" or, "Me back's killing me." Not the happiest man in the world was our Don.'

The captain may not have always been happy but the team was, a fact clearly evident to anyone with eyes to see. It has to be said, for all that, it is always easier to engender a good team spirit when you're winning.

By mid-July 1964, it had become clear that the championship was going to be a two-horse race between Warwickshire and Worcestershire. Huge crowds were in attendance at Edgbaston when the contending sides clashed for the second time that summer (the first at New Road having been drawn). The wicket was substandard and a disappointment to neutral observers who believed that the best two teams in the country deserved a better surface on which to slug it out.

The way the match progressed offered a microcosm of the whole season. To put it simply, Worcestershire batted better – or at least Tom Graveney did – on a pitch made for bowlers, one that the visiting seamers, Flavell and Standen, took full advantage of in the first innings and the spinners, Horton and Gifford, did the same in the second.

Warwickshire were dismissed for 72 and 86, and lost by the emphatic margin of 219 runs. Graveney batted for more than two hours to salvage 32 not out in the midst of the wreckage of a total of only 119 in the first innings and in the second, he batted imperiously, when all around him were struggling, to score 95 over five hours. 'I played well,' he conceded, 'but it was the bowlers who won it for us. Plus some wonderful catching.'

Fair enough. The old adage that bowlers, not batsmen, win you matches still holds as good today as it ever did. But let me offer you another perspective. It was Rodney Cass who told me the story. Cass came to the club in 1968 to succeed Roy Booth as wicketkeeper. He remembers vividly a cocktail party at the county ground at which a number of old Worcestershire players were present. Conversation came round to the exploits of the great side of 1964 and 1965.

'People say the bowlers won us the championship in 1964 and 65,' declared the Devonian, Len Coldwell, one of the members of that famous attack.t 'No we didn't. That bloke over there won it for us.' And he gestured across the room to Tom Graveney. 'They prepared the wickets to suit our bowlers,' said Cass, 'in the full knowledge that Tom could get runs on any surface.'

His argument stands up to a scrutiny of the figures. That summer, Graveney had as good a season as he had ever had, scoring 2,271 runs at an average of 55.39. Second in the team's averages was Ron Headley, who managed only 35.35 per innings. Yes, it is true that bowlers have to bowl sides out or games cannot be won. But the batsmen have to score enough runs to give them something to bowl at. Time and time again, Graveney's batting shored up the Worcestershire innings and the bowlers did the rest. And all this on poor pitches.

'No, that's not quite true,' Tom begged to differ. 'We won more matches away from home than at Worcester.' Well, that may be so. But nothing can detract from the majesty of Graveney's batting that summer, the number of runs he scored and the grace and elegance with which he scored them.

Don't listen to me; heed the words of the fabled cricket writer, Neville Cardus, 'An innings of Graveney's remains in the memory... He has no equal as a complete and stylish stroke-maker... When in form, he makes batsmanship look the easiest and most natural thing in the world.'

Or, to put it another way, as Rodney Cass did, 'He was one of the greats, no question. The talent he had...well, it just wasn't fair to the rest of us!'

After the ruthless dispatch of their nearest rivals, the title was only Worcestershire's to lose. Which they very nearly did, losing three of their next four matches. The collywobbles were banished by a convincing win over Leicestershire and in their following game, a draw with Northamptonshire, Graveney scored his 100th hundred, at home, in front of his adoring fans. It was a remarkable achievement and he joined a select band of only 14 men to have done it. That list has now grown to 24 with Mark Ramprakash scoring his in 2008 but it is unlikely that the feat will ever be equalled again, now the County Championship has been divided into two and fewer matches are played.

Do you remember the innings? 'David Larter was bowling badly. I'd got to 99 and then suddenly, out of the blue, he bowled me a really good over. After I had been beaten a couple of times, Keith Andrew, their wicketkeeper, said to me, "Do you want us to give it to you?" Of course I said no, but inside I wanted to say yes! On the last ball of the over, Larter bowled me a bouncer. I went to hook it, got a bottom edge, it bounced over short leg and we scrambled the single. Not the most elegant way to reach the milestone but I was happy enough.'

How did you celebrate? 'I was waving my bat in the air all the way to the other end. Not quite in the Kevin Pietersen style but perhaps still a bit over the top.'

Any special commemorations, festivities, official jamborees? He shook his head. 'Not like when Graeme Hick got his. I was president of the club then. We took out bottles of champagne to the middle with glasses on a silver salver to drink a toast. I was so excited, I dropped my glass and broke it, the champagne spilling all over the wicket.'

There was no time for resting on laurels; there was a championship to be won. The race went down to the wire. For Tom, it was wholly ironic that the defeat of Gloucestershire eventually yielded them the title, the first in the club's history.

Ken Graveney remembers the occasion well. He was captain of Gloucestershire at the time and he was at the crease when victory was secured. Or, more strictly speaking, he was *not* at the crease when it happened. There is a lovely photo of Roy Booth gleefully whipping off the bails with Graveney well down the wicket and giving a rather resigned look behind him.

'We were about to lose by an innings and we were close to making Worcestershire bat again,' Ken said. 'When we were only two short of the target, I turned to Roy and said, "Get ready. I don't want to field."' Gifford tossed one up, Graveney charged, missed and Booth did the rest. 'Ken!' said brother Tom, laughing, 'There was no way he was going to come out again to field.'

Joy was unconfined when news filtered back to Worcester that Warwickshire had lost to Hampshire. The title was definitely theirs. There was no time for extensive celebration for the team however; county cricket is a treadmill and they were soon on their way to Eastbourne to take on Sussex the next day.

At the season's end, Graveney's value to this historic triumph was underlined by the fact that he finished third in the national averages, and one of those above him, Basil D'Oliveira, had only played in eight innings while he served his year's qualification. Yet the England selectors had resolutely ignored him for the Test matches against Australia that summer and neither was he picked for the forthcoming winter tour of South Africa.

When quizzed about this extraordinary state of affairs, Tom could only shake his head dolefully. 'I should have gone to South Africa in 1956/57. Why I wasn't picked I shall never know. And this tour in 1964/65? I was in my late 30s and I had given up hope of ever being picked again.'

The batsmen who were chosen to tour were the captain, Mike Smith, Parfitt, Barrington, Dexter, Barber, Brearley and Boycott. Surely that line-up would have been strengthened by the inclusion of Graveney, playing at the top of his form. *Curiouser and curiouser.*

That the championship pennant should be fluttering proudly in the breeze on the flagpole atop the New Road pavilion throughout the 1965 season would have seemed wholly appropriate to the Worcestershire members and supporters. It was the club's centenary. The prospect of back-to-back championships would not have been wholly fanciful either; the team was settled, experienced and full of confidence. There was also the addition of Basil D'Oliveira to their ranks, now having served his year's qualification and available for all county matches.

'It was a helluva side,' remarked Tom, 'there were no weaknesses. Wherever you looked, there were match-winners. It was a pleasure to be part of it all.' The pleasure was mutual, Norman Gifford assured me.

Mind you, they scarcely played like champions in the earlier part of the season, recording only one win in May and one in June, to languish well down the table. Graveney was batting with all the imperious poise and commanding presence that Worcestershire supporters had come to expect but the overall performances of the side were uncharacteristically lacklustre.

One exception was the outstanding form of D'Oliveira. In his first two matches, he scored 106 and 163. 'Keep this up, Basil,' remarked Dick Richardson to him as they drove up to Leeds, 'we want you to score a hundred every game you play.' A century was not forthcoming against Yorkshire but the impression he made was considerable.

At long last, he had achieved his dream of playing first-class cricket, a dream that must have seemed preposterous and out of the question growing up and learning the game in apartheid South Africa.

It is clear from any mention that Tom made of Basil throughout our extensive conversations that an immediate and unshakeable bond was formed between the two men and they became the firmest of friends. It was a friendship that was to endure a lifetime, until Basil died in 2011.

'He was a good pal,' said Tom quietly. 'Basil became almost like one of the family,' Becky, Tom's daughter told me. Tim, his son, offered this observation, 'I think Basil respected Dad. And that wasn't always the case with others.' Whatever the dynamics between these two great characters in the English game, it was certain that the elder man took particular pleasure in his protégé's immediate impact on the field of play.

Ah, but wait just a moment… Who actually *was* the elder man? And here we stumble upon one of the most enduring and disputed mysteries in recent cricket history. At this time, Graveney was 38 years old: that fact has never been challenged. D'Oliveira's age was given as 34, and that fact has frequently been challenged.

D'Oliveira was always wilfully vague about his date of birth. It was popularly assumed that he had subtracted several years, firmly believing that no one would give him a contract if his true age were revealed. He never let his guard down and the secret went with him to the grave. And his family always deflected any serious enquiry with amused but impenetrable equivocation. Up and down the country, it became something of standing joke.

Who cared, so long as he was scoring runs, which he did aplenty for most of his career? Certainly not the Worcestershire supporters, who flocked to see the muscular savagery of his batting. And in time – a very short time, as it happened – when he was selected to play for England, this nebulous business of his age only served to enhance the legend and to deepen the affection and respect that he was held in by the British public.

Here was a man who, against all the odds, had overcome such enormous social and political barriers in order to play the game that he loved, at a level commensurate with his gifts. Just think of the number of runs he would have scored had he been born an Englishman.

Form is temporary but class is permanent goes the old cliché and at last Worcestershire hit their stride and thereafter carried all before them. One supreme example of the manner in which they turned their fortunes around was in the game against Gloucestershire in mid-August. Tom remembers the match with total clarity. 'It was at Cheltenham on a wicket tailor-made for their spinners, Allen and Mortimore. In the last innings, we needed 131 to win. Doesn't sound much but believe me, that wicket was a shocker and we didn't think we'd make 50.'

His worst fears appeared well founded as Worcestershire slumped to 19/3 in very short order, the ball turning square. D'Oliveira joined Graveney at the wicket. Tom admitted to his partner that the Gloucestershire spinners were all but unplayable and the only chance he had of surviving was to chance his arm, run down the wicket at them and hope for the best. D'Oliveira, schooled on the patchy and unreliable surfaces of a deprived community in the Cape, preferred to rely on his eye and the strength of his forearms and play off the back foot.

It was a fascinating technical and mental struggle, one recalled almost ball by ball by another of the protagonists, John Mortimore. He explained that bowling to the two of them involved a completely different strategy. 'Tom played every ball off the front foot; Basil went back to everything. If you strayed in width, Tom would put you away every time. But if you bowled straight, he wouldn't look to hit you. I always felt that if you bowled well at Tom, you could maintain a level of control over the situation. Basil was different. He was on the back foot and played the ball late and consequently was more difficult to bowl to.' And then he laughed, as if remembering himself. 'I said Tom was easier to bowl to, not to get out!'

No one got either of them out. The required total was reached – improbably – without further loss of wickets, Graveney not out 59 and D'Oliveira not out 55. Worcestershire were on their way. Norman Gifford had this to say about that extraordinary exhibition of batsmanship. 'Later on, in my coaching career, I always tried to keep in mind that partnership of theirs on a nigh-unplayable wicket – Tom playing forward and Basil playing back. The point to get across to young players is that sometimes there is no single, right way of doing things. There can be an alternative which is just as effective.'

Worcestershire's late charge to the retention of their title comprised ten victories in their last 11 matches. The penultimate game of the season, against Hampshire, which Worcestershire had to win to have any chance of catching Northamptonshire, was a nail-biter. Rain severely curtailed playing time but both captains, Kenyon (obviously) and Ingleby-MacKenzie (because he was that type of man) were determined, notwithstanding, to make a game of it.

Two strategic declarations set up the contest nicely. Hampshire were asked to score 147 in 160 minutes, a not unreasonable target. But the sun had come out, the damp pitch began to dry out and it became virtually unplayable as Flavell and Coldwell ran through them. They were all out for 31, Flavell 5-9 and Coldwell 5-22. Amazing.

The victory that got hold of the necessary points to pip Northamptonshire to the post was secured at Hove against Sussex. It was no stroll in the park. Many an anxious moment was endured before Worcestershire prevailed, to win by four wickets with only 11 minutes of the season remaining. The championship pennant was to remain aloft on the flagpole at New Road for another year.

And what of Tom's recollection of this triumph of one of the smaller and less fancied counties in the championship? 'Good players who knew how to do the business. Good catching. Good team spirit.

And an excellent captain.' Don Kenyon was equally sure of the secret of their success. 'Complete team spirit and effort and a happy side,' were his words at the end of the campaign.

But what about your contribution, Tom, 1,648 runs at an average of 48.11? It seemed you were batting as well as ever. He remained silent for a while. 'Do you know what?' he said at last. 'I thought I was the best batter in the country during these three years. Perhaps I wasn't but the point is that I thought I was. The responsibility was for me to get the runs so that the bowlers had a decent total to bowl at. And I thrived on it. As for getting back into the England side… Well, I was getting on in age and thought I had no chance. I just concentrated on playing for Worcestershire and enjoying it.'

Nevertheless, it is strange to relate that the England selectors continued to ignore the best player in the country in the form of his life (not just Tom's opinion; it was shared by many commentators and shrewd onlookers) for any of the Tests that summer, against New Zealand and South Africa.

And what a bizarre fact that the South Africans, a force in world cricket, continued to elude him. The only time he played against them was on his debut in 1951 and in the five-match series in 1955. He was selected for the tour of that country in 1968/69 but, as we shall see, that tour never took place for reasons far removed from mere cricket politics. Furthermore, he was ignored for the winter tour of Australia, a batsman who had come fifth in the national batting averages, one of whom above him was a South African, Graeme Pollock.

Let's leave aside the blinkered policy of the selectors for the moment. Tell me a little about your team-mates in this 'helluva' side, as you called it. 'Gladly,' he said, and he was away. 'Don Kenyon was a great captain. But don't forget what a top-class batsman he was. I thought he was unlucky whenever he played for England. As an opener, he always seemed to come up against the great fast bowlers of the day – Lindwall, Miller, Adcock, Heine.'

Flavell and Coldwell – they were a handful as an opening attack, weren't they? 'Do you know, Jack Flavell never congratulated you if you caught one off his bowling! He'd come down the wicket and it didn't matter whether you were still lying flat out on the turf having taken a blinder with one hand, he would always say, in that Black Country accent of his, "What a pearler!" Always. Without fail.'

Tom shook his head in amused bafflement and then went on, 'He bowled wicket to wicket. Sometimes, he'd brush against the stumps as he delivered the ball, which shows how close in he'd get in his delivery stride. If you came out to bat after he'd bowled, you'd find yourself standing in a hole where his front foot had been landing!'

As any batsman knows, it is very disconcerting to take guard in a hole. The essence of batsmanship is balance and it is very hard to stand perfectly poised when one foot is an inch or two lower than the other, whatever the best efforts of the groundsman have been to fill the crater.

Was he quick? Tom's response was a theatrical shudder. I think that we can deduce that Flavell was indeed quick. 'Coldwell was different. He bowled inners at a lively pace, with the odd one straightening. Very accurate. Wonderful bloke.'

And the spinners? 'Once again, a contrast in styles, though they both bowled left arm. Gifford used to fire it in, Slade had more of a loop. And we had Horton's off spinners too, for some variety.'

And let's not forget your occasional leg spinners. 'Very occasional,' he corrected me.

It was perhaps expecting too much that this team of all the talents would make it a hat-trick of championships in 1966. That they came so close, runners-up to Yorkshire, says much about their enduring qualities but, as a side, they were getting old. Kenyon was 41, Booth 39, Graveney 38, Flavell 36, D'Oliveira 33 (though probably more) and Coldwell 32.

One by one, the stalwarts retired, though Graveney continued to defy the years and 1966 was yet another prolific season for him, as was 1967. The Indian summer of his career seemed to go on and on. In 1968, he succeeded Don Kenyon as captain of the county side. He had of course stood in for Kenyon many times when injury or Test selection duties interfered and he was now a vastly experienced and greatly respected county pro, so there were no problems with any of the players about the appointment or the way he handled the job.

'The younger players worshipped him,' Rodney Cass, Booth's successor as wicketkeeper, assured me. Norman Gifford agreed. 'What it was to have the great Tom Graveney as your skipper! He would encourage us and pass on useful tips, quietly, you know. You'd be bowling to him in the nets and he'd give you a little nod if you managed to get one past his bat. Which was very rarely. And in the middle, when I was bowling and he'd be standing at silly mid-off, he'd get hold of the ball, turn and lob it back to me with a little smile or a word of encouragement.'

Tom says that he was not of the histrionic school of captaincy. He didn't go in for rousing Churchillian exhortations before play; he would simply stand up when the umpires were on their way to the middle, put on his cap and say to everyone, 'Come on then, troops,' and off they would go. He took the view that they were all professionals, so they should all know their jobs. 'You know the form,' he would say, and if they didn't, or were not prepared to learn, they wouldn't last very long in that environment.

He saw no point in losing his temper, ruling by fear. In any case, it wasn't in his nature. He preferred to lead by example. And in this, the evidence is overwhelming that his influence was infectious. Even now, in the twilight of his career, the dedication to practice never wavered. His contemporaries refer to it time and time again, almost with awe.

'It didn't matter whether the nets were worn and old, Tom would still go in there every day for half an hour, on match days or practice days,' said Gifford. 'I loved bowling to him. You cannot help but learn your craft if you're bowling every day to one of the greats of the game.'

Tom laughed ruefully when asked about his net routine. 'Some of the nets provided up and down the country were shocking,' he said. 'I remember going into the nets at Northants. Brian Brain was bowling – off 20 yards, as usual! He hit me on the ear. The *left* ear,' he emphasised, turning his head sideways as he did so. Of course! The point he was making was that, as ever, his technique was intact and that he was batting sideways, not square on. 'Anyway, it must have shaken me up a bit because on the way home, I became a bit confused and got lost. I ended up somewhere in the Malvern Hills, not having a clue where I was.'

'He was a pro's pro,' said Cass, 'a wonderful role model for us youngsters.' Gifford concurred. 'Great player that he was, he never stopped working at it. He never relaxed, as if to say I've got this game cracked. For example, he never gave his wicket away, whether he was playing for England or Dudley in the Birmingham League or in the nets. Even in charity games, he would make sure he got 50 before getting out. He'd played for England, you see, and he was proud of that fact and jealous of his reputation. It was almost as if he was saying – you're not going to get the better of me, whether it was a club bowler or Wes Hall.'

'Some people said that Tom Graveney was a selfish batsman,' Duncan Fearnley announced during one of our conversations, quite out of the blue. 'Rubbish!' he declared, his Yorkshire vowels accentuating his passion. He went on to tell me a story to discredit that viewpoint, one that, incidentally, I had never come across.

During Tom's enforced leave of absence from county cricket in 1961, he came to the crease during the morning session of a second XI match to join Fearnley, who was batting rather well. In fact he was in with a shout of scoring a hundred in the session before lunch, a feat not often accomplished in any form of the game.

'Tom strolled up the wicket and said to me that he would give me the strike so that I'd have the best chance of doing it. I didn't quite manage it, but never mind. Anyway, several years later, we were playing Derby at Chesterfield and Tom and I were batting together. It was a run chase. Tom came up to me and said, "Remember that time I gave you the strike? Well, if you do the same for me now, I think we can win." And we did! He could place the ball wherever he liked. The point is he didn't farm the strike for his own benefit, like a few great players I could mention. He only did it for a purpose – to win the match.'

Oddly enough, John Mortimore raised the same subject when he was talking about another great man of Gloucestershire, Wally Hammond, who certainly did pinch the strike, frequently and unashamedly. 'But Tom was never like that,' he said, 'he was a gentleman and played fair.'

That epithet crops up repeatedly when Tom's former team-mates talk about him. 'He was the perfect gent,' Fearnley assured me, 'he never sledged and he was always the first in the bar at the close of play to buy the opposition a drink.' And this from Gifford, 'He was just a lovely, lovely bloke. Very popular with team-mates and opponents alike. Buy everyone a drink and we'd listen to the great man telling stories about Test matches and overseas tours. And then, a bit later, we youngsters would go out for a meal and maybe to a pub or a club and come back to the hotel later and Tom would still be there at the bar, supping his pints and reminiscing with all the other older players.'

No one denies that Tom Graveney liked his beer, least of all the man himself. But no one ever saw him drunk. 'Tom could handle his drink,' said Gifford. 'He knew when he'd had enough and would slip off to bed. And he was always first in the dressing room the next morning, as bright as a button.' Tom laughed at this. 'I never got a hangover. I was lucky I suppose. I was young, I was fit, I never put on weight and I steered clear of injury.'

'Don't forget his fielding,' Cass was keen to bring to my attention. 'He fielded at first slip, right next to me keeping wicket. He had a great pair of hands and caught nearly everything.' That was a fact underlined by his brother Ken, who believed that even at an early age, his younger brother displayed a remarkable level of hand-eye co-ordination. 'He was very critical of himself if one went down,' said Cass, '"I should have got that", he'd mutter. And mostly he did.'

Tom was matter-of-fact about his slip fielding. 'I reckoned if I got my hands on it, I'd catch it.' Indeed he did, 554, to be precise.

By the by, who was the best slipper you ever saw? 'Bobby Simpson,' he answered without a moment's hesitation.

Opinions vary about Tom Graveney's period of captaincy at the club. No one was in any doubt that he was the obvious candidate to succeed Don Kenyon. His seniority, his experience and his status in the game made it unthinkable that anyone else should be appointed, even if the committee, the way committees do, hummed and hawed before announcing their decision.

The admiration and respect in which he was held throughout the club meant that it was hardly going to be a controversial choice.

That Worcestershire were unable to repeat the successes of the Kenyon era was no great surprise. The team were going through a painful period of transition and Graveney had to plead for patience from everybody; players of the calibre of Kenyon, Horton, Headley, Richardson, Booth, Flavell and Coldwell could not be replaced overnight. Added to which, Graveney himself and D'Oliveira were frequently away on Test duty.

Still, positions of seventh in 1968 and sixth in 1970 were scarcely ruinous but 1969 was a bad year, it has to be said; the county ground flooded in May, the team finished a disappointing 14th, crowds dwindled and bankruptcy was not such an unimaginable possibility. Joe Lister, the club's secretary, was moved to announce publicly, 'I doubt whether we have ever had a more disastrous season financially.'

None of this, of course, was Tom Graveney's fault. So, what is the verdict on his three-year tenure of the captaincy? He is modest about his impact but felt the need to reiterate that the great team that won back-to-back championships had broken up and it would take time to build another. But he said he thoroughly enjoyed the experience and believed that he did his bit to bring on the youngsters.

He is very proud of two signings he made, to add to that of D'Oliveira. During his tour of the West Indies in 1967/68, Tom had encountered a tall, gangling fast bowler by the name of Vanburn Holder and so impressed was he at the potential of the young man that he got the club to sign him up without further ado. 'Not a bad signing, eh?' said Tom. 'And the blighter got me out in my very last Test innings. That's gratitude for you!'

The acquisition of Glenn Turner was not quite so straightforward. He had first tried his luck at Warwickshire. But they already had their full quota of overseas players, so the New Zealander drove down the M5 to have a trial at Worcestershire. Tom took a brief look at him in the nets and immediately said, 'Sign him up!'

The necessary paperwork was completed and the rest is history; Turner went on to join Tom on the illustrious roll of honour of batsmen who have scored 100 first-class hundreds. You might say, therefore, that Tom had done his bit to secure the immediate well-being of the club and to pave the way for its future success.

There were, it has to be admitted, one or two rumblings about his tactical aptitude ('But not from the younger players,' Cass stressed). Some felt that he changed the field too much; others that he under-bowled Doug Slade. I asked Norman Gifford about this. 'Well,' he said with a knowing smile, 'Tom was a batsman, wasn't he?'

And here an ancient quarrel in the game stirred. Bowlers never believe that batsman-captains understand them and the pressures under which they operate. And historically, the captains were invariably amateurs, and therefore batsmen. The hard graft of bowling was usually the sole preserve of the working class. Bowlers were convinced that they were second-class citizens, there to do the bidding of their captains and social superiors. Old habits die hard and even in the modern game, the suspicion lingers that batsman-captains find it hard to know when a bowler really needs a rest. I doubt that Gifford was being wholly serious but it remains a diverting argument.

Whatever the final judgement on Tom's captaincy, all are agreed that he was unlucky to succeed Don Kenyon – a hard act to follow – and that he was hampered by not having at his disposal the firepower enjoyed by his predecessor.

For all that, these were heady days for Tom and his family. In the autumn of his career, he was batting as well as he had ever done. At last, he had found his niche on the national and international stage, a place where he felt comfortable and which was rightfully his. The public cherished him as a sportsman with a rare and graceful talent, who rarely failed to entertain. 'He used to empty the bars and pubs when he came out to bat,' Cass told me, and as a Yorkshireman, he is never one prone to gild the lily. 'The supporters flocked in their thousands just to watch him play.'

They also respected him for his obviously decent demeanour and lack of airs and graces. They also, as is often the way with the British public, honoured him for his longevity; he had started his career in the dreary post-war years and now he was ending it in the bright, gaudy Swinging Sixties. For his part, he was only too happy to respond with grace and friendliness to his numerous fans and an army of autograph hunters. At Worcestershire, he felt totally in his element. 'As soon as I walked through those gates the first day I was here, I knew I'd made the right choice,' he said. 'I felt at home immediately. Everyone was so kind to me.'

It seemed entirely appropriate and fully deserved that he was awarded the OBE in 1968 'for services to cricket'. He went to the Palace in May, together with Jackie and his children, Becky and Tim, to receive his award from the Queen. 'I didn't miss a match,' he was keen to tell me.

Describe to me what happened. 'The Queen and I were good friends,' he said with a grin, 'I'd met her before. She used to come to tea on the Monday of the Lord's Test. The players would have to go into the committee room and share a cuppa with her. A delightful woman.'

But you really did know Prince Philip quite well, didn't you? 'I did. We played cricket a few times together – charity matches and stuff.'

Did the Queen recognise you when she pinned the medal to your chest? 'We had quite a long chat actually.'

What did she say? He gave me a sideways look. 'If I told you, I'd end up in the Tower.'

It helped that his wife, Jackie, was happier while he was at Worcestershire, appreciating and basking in the high regard that everyone had for her husband. At Gloucestershire and at other grounds, she had not felt totally at ease but the friendly and family-oriented atmosphere at New Road on match days helped her to relax and enjoy her time with friends and the other wives of the players.

Tim, their son, has nothing but joyful memories of sunlit evenings playing cricket on the outfield after the close of play, with Basil's son, Damian, and other children. 'We used to play for hours until it got dark,' he said. 'Meanwhile Dad and Basil used to drink steadily in the bar. But Dad never got drunk. Basil was sometimes the worse for wear but Dad could handle himself. He was never late on parade the next day.'

His sister, Becky, used to join in heartily with these impromptu games of cricket and would catch the eye of more than one onlooker from the pavilion with her immaculate bowling action. She too loved the limelight as the daughter of a famous cricketer. Now 15, she relished meeting and getting to know all the players.

Glenn Turner and Rodney Cass were two of her favourites. 'And Basil too,' she said. 'He was hilarious.' She then recounted a story about him – to go with all the better known ones – that gives a little insight into the fun and humour that went hand in hand with the more serious business of playing cricket for a living in those days.

During an advantageous hiatus in the 1969 season, Tom went on a short tour of Devon and Cornwall as part of the schedule for his benefit year. He asked Basil to come with him. Basil was never going to say no. They played four or five games for the Whitbread Wanderers. The managing director of the brewing company was very keen on his cricket and had agreed to help with Tom's benefit if he agreed to turn out for his team as a guest player.

'It was a very alcoholic tour,' Tom admitted. 'Dad and Mum had decided that eventually they ought to go to bed,' said Becky, taking up the story. 'Basil remained in the bar and continued drinking. When he too made his way to his room, he was, how shall we put it, a little unsteady on his feet. He hammered on my parents' door to wish them good night. Actually, what he was shouting was, "Tom – I love you!" Mum shouted back, "Basil! Go to bed – you're p****d!" The next night, the same rigmarole took place, Basil reassuring Dad, in the loudest possible tones, of his undying affection, "Tom – I love you!" Now there was a myna bird somewhere about obviously belonging to the hotel. The next night when Basil hammered on my parents' door, a voice, perfectly mimicking Basil's, loudly intoned, "Tom – I love you!" Basil was… well, somewhat put out.'

Tears of laughter were streaming down Tom's face as he recalled the footnote to the story. 'The next morning we found on the footpath a dead myna bird.'

And was the culprit ever exposed and brought to book? Tom's shoulders were heaving so much, it was difficult to tell whether he was nodding or shaking his head. After a lengthy recovery period, he offered this appraisal of his Worcestershire team, 'My goodness, we were a thirsty lot!'

9

Out Of The Wilderness – England 1966–69

'Tom missed out a lot. He would never have been out of an Australian side during my Test career.'
(Richie Benaud, Australian captain)

When the call came – or recall, should I say – it came as a bolt out of a clear blue sky. The selection of D'Oliveira for the first Test of the 1966 summer against the West Indies had caused a stir of interest because of his South African background and the circumstances surrounding his decision to become a naturalised Englishman. But his form for Worcestershire had made his selection a perfectly reasonable decision. In the event, he didn't play, as he was made 12th man on the morning of the match, the selectors favouring another bowler, a disastrous decision as it turned out.

Tom Graveney was not too worried, however; he knew that sooner or later his great friend would gain his first cap. As for his own chances of playing in the Test side – well, he counted them as practically zero and had long given up entertaining any hopes that he might somehow, sometime, be recalled, no matter how many runs he was scoring.

He took a detached interest, as all England supporters did, in the team when it was announced at lunchtime on the Sunday before the game and was wholly unprepared for the shock of hearing his own name read out. 'I was astonished,' he admitted. 'Totally bowled over.'

And that didn't happen very often, did it? 'Eh?' *Getting bowled…oh, never mind.* 'Surprised wasn't the word. All right, I was batting better than I had ever done in my life but I was 39 – hardly the future, was I? I kept wondering – yes, but why now?'

The fact that England had just suffered a humiliating defeat at Old Trafford, by an innings and within three days, might have had something to do with it. And Tom had a record of playing well against the West Indies. In addition, Colin Cowdrey had supplanted Mike Smith as captain and Cowdrey had always been a Graveney fan. Still, it was a brave decision. Tom had been in the wilderness for three years, during which England had played 38 Tests. And the West Indies were the acknowledged world champions.

Excited? 'Not 'arf! Here was my chance.' He climbed into his car at the completion of Worcestershire's match against Middlesex and set off for London. The second Test was at Lord's, a place he knew well. In fact the car could probably have driven itself to St John's Wood.

Tell me, were you nervous when you walked out to bat on that second afternoon? 'Frightened to death! Especially when all the MCC members stood up and cheered me all the way to the wicket.' After initial edginess, he settled down and played well. 'I had Boycott at the other end. I think that's why he always said I was his favourite batsman, because of the way I played on my comeback.'

Just think about this for a moment. Tom had opened the batting in a Test match with Len Hutton. Now he was batting with Geoffrey Boycott. His career was spanning two generations. 'Two generations? It felt like two different centuries!' Sadly, a century in his first match back for so long was to be denied him by just four runs. The acclamation he received however on his return to the pavilion was as emotional as if he had three figures to his name. 'Yes, it was a good game for me. I was back on the world stage and it felt…right.'

He was pleased that Basil D'Oliveira made his debut in the same match. 'I thought Basil was unlucky. He was run out when going well.' In fact the dismissal was a bizarre one. His partner, Jim Parks, drove a ball straight and hard back down the wicket. It ricocheted off D'Oliveira's heel and cannoned into the stumps. That is not out. But with commendable speed of thought, Hall, the bowler, gathered the ball into his hands and pulled out a stump, with D'Oliveira still out of his ground. And that *is* out.

He had done enough, however, to convince everyone that his class and temperament were ideally suited to this level and he went on, as we all know, to have a successful and distinguished career for England.

Why did you bat at number six in the second innings? 'Wes Hall had hit me on the hand and I couldn't really hold the bat. I wasn't going to bat but we lost two wickets in successive balls and were in danger of losing the match which we had fought so hard to win.' He averted the hat-trick and stayed with Colin Milburn until the draw was secured, his 30 not out being achieved virtually one-handed.

That hundred by Milburn? It must have been thrilling to watch it from 22 yards away. 'I've rarely seen hitting like it. Some of those sixes were out of this world. Almost literally.'

He wasn't just a slogger, was he? 'Certainly not! He was a proper batsman and it was such a tragedy when that car accident robbed him of an eye and pretty well finished his career.'

What about his fielding? After all, he was nicknamed 'Ollie' after the rotund Oliver Hardy. 'You know, he was a brave fielder at short leg and surprisingly nimble on his feet for a big man. Such a shame. He only played nine Tests.'

A week's rest to enable his bruised hand to heal and then it was the third Test at Trent Bridge, another of his favourite hunting grounds. Sure enough, he secured the century that was denied him at Lord's and you might say his comeback was complete. He had steered England to a first-innings lead of 90 but the West Indies extricated themselves from this unpromising position to win by 139 runs. 'Basil played really well in both innings,' Tom said, 'That pleased me a lot.' The match was also significant for marking Derek Underwood's debut.

The West Indies underlined their total superiority in the fourth Test at Headingley with another innings victory. 'Never liked Headingley,' announced Tom. 'My highest score there was…what, 71?' Later research substantiated that assertion.

The series may have been lost – disastrously so – but there was one last act to be played out in this West Indian summer. The final Test at the Oval delivered one of the most memorable matches Tom has ever played in. It made no difference to the rubber but it helped substantially to salvage some English pride in the summer game after such a disappointing season, especially as the national football team had just won the World Cup only a few months earlier. It was also a personal triumph for Tom Graveney to round off in splendid style what was possibly his best season. Certainly the most satisfying.

'Yes,' he said, '1966 was a great year for me. Who would have believed it – at my age! And I was batting so well. Everything seemed to come so easy.'

The selectors had made wholesale changes to the side, including appointing their third captain, Brian Close, of the series. This demonstrated the turmoil that English cricket was in at the time. In the event, the choice of Close was a shrewd one; he distinguished himself with his field placing, his bowling changes and, not least, his fearless fielding at short leg.

'Brian did some odd things. He'd go and stand in some very strange positions,' Tom admitted. 'But he was a good captain and more often than not, his tactics would work.'

Some said he was a difficult man to work with, strong-minded but obstinate. 'I know. He had a reputation as being awkward and disruptive, a trouble-maker. But that was unfair – he wasn't.' Tom did agree that Close held no truck with the stuffed shirts at MCC and around the counties. 'We were playing together for the Players against the Gentlemen at Lord's in 1949.'

Crikey, Tom, we're in 1966, a lifetime later. Don't tell me – you remember how many Close scored. 'Sixty-five,' he answered, without a moment's hesitation. 'Anyway, when he got to his fifty, Billy Griffith, who was keeping wicket and later was to become secretary of MCC, said to him, "Well played, Brian." Closey, all of 18 years of age, turned to him and said, "Thank you, Billy." Griffith was a bit taken aback, I can tell you. Professionals were expected to address the amateurs as "Sir".'

By now, the Players, Graveney and Close, were the elder statesmen of the England side. And their country was indebted to these two as events unfolded in the Test. Close husbanded his bowling resources skilfully to dismiss the West Indies for only 268. But then a familiar story seemed to be repeating itself. England lost quick wickets and when Graveney made his way to the middle, they were 85/3, soon to become 166/7, and staring at another humiliating defeat.

At first, Tom had concentrated solely on survival in the face of the West Indian onslaught until he found in John Murray a stalwart partner. Now, Murray was no tail-end Charlie; he could bat properly and had already hit a century off the tourists earlier in the summer playing for MCC.

'He was so nearly out first ball,' Tom recounted. 'Wes Hall hit him on the pad plumb in front. But fortunately he had got just the faintest tickle of an inside edge. Otherwise that would have been curtains for us.'

Slowly, but with increasing fluency, the two batsmen wrested back the initiative. At close of play, they walked off undefeated to an ovation from a packed Oval crowd, Graveney on 132 and Murray on 81. There is a well-known photo of them both, Graveney with his cap pushed back on his head and both looking tired but elated as they acknowledge the applause. Alongside, and slightly to the rear, Sobers, ever the sportsman, is looking at Graveney, smiling and applauding. That says it all.

Certain defeat had been averted but could they kick on the next day and build an imposing lead? Yes they could. Graveney was eventually run out for 165 and Murray dismissed for 112. The tail wagged furiously and England closed their innings on 527.

Come on Tom, that must have been one of your greatest moments on a cricket field, the way you turned the game on its head. What an innings! Your best? Second best? He was not to be enticed by such a claim. 'I still argue that the truly great innings are played on bad wickets, where your skill and technique are examined to the last degree. This wicket was a belter. One that Geoffrey would say that you should book in for bed and breakfast.' Boycott, incidentally, only made 20.

For the first and only time in the series, West Indies were up against it. The English players believed that only one man stood between them and victory, the greatest all-round cricketer in the history of the game – Garry Sobers. That is not my contention; it is Tom's. 'Garry was the best player ever,' he asserted. 'He could do anything. And in this series, he did – frequently.'

Sobers captained the side, he bowled a mixture of orthodox and unorthodox left-arm spinners, he was developing into one of the most dangerous new ball bowlers in the world, he caught blinders close to the wicket and of course his batting was peerless. When he came to the wicket, he was averaging in excess of 100 for the series and all West Indian hopes rested on his shoulders.

'Do you know,' Tom announced, 'in a funny way, we were always pleased when Garry had bowled a lot of overs. It meant that he would be tired and would come in down the order.' Sobers had bowled 54 overs in England's innings and had come in at number seven. But he still had to be dismissed. Close had a theory. He believed Sobers would not be able to resist hooking at a bouncer, even if the situation demanded caution, at first anyway.

Close was correct in one sense; Sobers didn't do 'cautious'. The ball was as likely to end up on the roof of the stand as in the hands of an English fielder but Close instructed John Snow to give him a short one, prepared to gamble on the outcome. I remember vividly what happened next; I was watching on an old black and white television. Snow bounded in and duly delivered a quick bouncer, Sobers hooked impulsively, got a bottom edge and the ball ricocheted off his thigh pad and dollied into Close's hands at short leg. Joy was unconfined in my household, to say nothing of the reaction inside the Oval.

'People say it was the easiest of catches,' Tom was at pains to point out, 'but you have a look at the replay. Brian was standing a couple of feet away when one of the most ferocious hookers in the game swung hard at it. And he didn't move! He didn't duck or take evasive action of any kind. He didn't even blink. And the ball gently lobbed into his hands. I tell you that was a *fabulous* catch, showing tremendous bravery. No helmet and protective armour in those days. Madness really.'

England duly secured the victory by an innings and 34 runs, which put more of a gloss upon the summer. But there was no doubt who were the better side. Indeed the West Indies had further enhanced their status as the best side in the world and Sobers was now at the peak of his powers. 'I played a lot of golf with him,' Tom told me. 'My God, he could whack it!'

How good a player was he? Good as you? Tom nodded. 'He played off scratch. But he could hit it further than me.' They were to continue their rivalry on the golf course as well as the cricket pitch that winter.

As part of the festivities to mark the independence of Barbados from direct British rule in 1966, a cricket match was arranged (what else in that cricket-mad island?): Barbados against the Rest of the World. And in case you're thinking that is a mighty piece of overweening hubris for a tiny island 21 miles in length and 14 miles in breadth, with a population of only 282,000, to take on the rest of the cricketing world, you need to think again.

At various times in their recent history, they have produced a glittering array of renowned cricketers and at this particular time, they had in their side Test players Conrad Hunte, Seymour Nurse, Wes Hall, Charlie Griffith, David Holford and of course the incomparable Garfield Sobers.

Tom Graveney, that seasoned tourist, was invited to go, 'the only Englishman in the party'. Perhaps he was forgetting the presence of his Worcestershire and England team-mate, Basil D'Oliveira, or else he wasn't counting him strictly as an Englishman because of his South African roots.

Mention of South Africa raised the thorny problem of apartheid and the increasing isolation of South African cricket that was shortly to explode into a full-scale political and diplomatic conflagration, one that was to badly burn these two most genial of cricketers. Three South Africans – Graeme Pollock, Denis Lindsay and, Tom thinks but isn't sure, Barry Richards – who were selected for the Rest of the World team were refused entry into the island because of their country's repressive and colour-segregated domestic policies. Shades of things to come. Rohan Kanhai, Bob Barber and John Murray were flown in rapidly as replacements.

'Bill Lawry was our captain,' said Tom. 'At the official dinner, when he was making a speech, he turned to me and said, "I see Gubby Allen is here, Tom, to check up on you." It brought the house down. Gubby Allen was there because he ran the MCC and everyone knew of my problems with that man.' He rolled his eyes. 'Gubby Allen – he did me no favours in my career.'

Notwithstanding the presence of his nemesis, Tom regarded the whole thing as 'a great little tour'. They spent ten days at the Hilton Hotel 'practising hard'.

Were there nets at the hotel then? He gave me a funny look. 'I didn't say that we were practising cricket!' The Rest of the World won comfortably as it turned out but the game was marred by the news that Frank Worrell had died. Few could believe it at first. He had recently retired after the successful 1963 tour of England and was only 42. He had been the first black man to captain the West Indies and is largely held responsible for uniting that disparate band of far-flung islands into a cohesive and effective unit that paved the way for their dominance of world cricket in the 1970s and 80s. He was also a wonderful batsman in his own right and his premature death from leukaemia cast a pall on proceedings.

There was no MCC tour that winter, Tom. What did you do apart from improve your golf handicap? 'At the time, Don Kenyon and I had a sports shop in Redditch. I used to drive up there every day. It ticked over nicely.' That was until another sports shop opened up nearby in direct competition. Tom knew the owner. His name was David Courtney. He remembers giving lifts to the young David, who was 13 at the time and an avid cricket fan, to and from the cricket in Cheltenham in his Vauxhall. As a matter of courtesy, Courtney went to introduce himself to Tom, wondering whether the great man would remember him.

'Tom was leaning on the counter doing the invoices,' David told me. 'He did recognise me and we got chatting and there was absolutely no animosity between us whatsoever. Indeed, when his shop closed, he came to work for me – when he wasn't playing cricket! – and did so for the next 20-odd years. He was great at chatting to customers about artificial wickets, which my company, 3D Sports, was developing. Tom will talk to anyone, as long as it's about cricket! And I am proud to say that to this day we have remained the greatest of friends.'

The summer of 1967 had two countries on tour consecutively, India and Pakistan, each playing three Tests. Unlike in previous seasons, Tom now believed that he was an automatic choice for the England team. His form remained as good as ever, making it even more unfathomable why the selectors had turned their backs on him for so long.

Something has been troubling me for some time, Tom, on this vexed issue of the wilderness years. Don Kenyon was one of the selectors. He was your county captain. He could see, week in, week out, how well you were playing. So why didn't he pick you? Or, at the very least, recommend your name strongly to his co-selectors? Tom gave me another one of those looks. 'Don? He didn't want me going off to play for England. He wanted me to stay and continue scoring runs for Worcester!'

I looked at him closely but was unable to discern whether he was being serious or not. The fact that his admiration for Don Kenyon is unwavering suggests that he probably wasn't. In any event, the selectors, belatedly no doubt, were indebted to Graveney in both series; he averaged 50.20 against the Indians and 54 against the Pakistanis.

'You asked me what my greatest innings was. Well, let me tell you about it.' I settled back comfortably in my chair, spellbound. It must be the 151 he scored at Lord's, I thought to myself, against the Indians. I was correct.

'It had rained overnight. No covers in those days – at least, they did cover the ends, but the wicket was left exposed to the elements. The next morning, the ball was turning square and taking great chunks out. And India had three of the best spinners in the world – Chandrasekhar, Prasanna and Bedi. Remember my contention that an innings can only be judged "great" if it's made on a difficult wicket against the best bowlers? Well, this pitch was difficult all right, damn near unplayable.'

Later, I searched *Wisden* for elaboration on the engrossing contest that was going on between bat and ball. 'A crowd of 12,000 watched almost silently as Barrington, Graveney and D'Oliveira treated Chandrasekhar and the two left-armers, Bedi and Surti, with the utmost respect… While D'Oliveira struggled to find his form – he only added six in an hour – Graveney never looked in the slightest trouble.'

The great batsmen always make it look easy, no matter how taxing the conditions. They seem to have so much time to play their strokes when everybody else is hurried and under pressure.

'Do you know what Basil said to me when we were out there? He came up the wicket and told me to p*** off because I was making him look stupid!' Once Graveney was out, wickets predictably tumbled but he had given England an unassailable lead and the match was won by an innings and 124 runs.

It is interesting to note that this hundred, his ninth in Tests, had come 15 years after his first, also against India in Bombay. Once again, his contribution had been crucial. It didn't matter whether he was taking on the fearsome pace of Hall and Griffith or the wily arts of the three Indian spinners; he had proved truly that he was a man for all seasons.

Graveney not a man for a crisis? That charge can be dismissed as definitively as a half-volley outside off stump by one of his cover drives. Elegantly but disdainfully.

And all this at 40 years of age. 'I know,' he agreed, a little ruefully. 'But I was enjoying my cricket, I kept myself fit and I was at the top of my game.'

Looking back, do you think your technique had changed? Did you have to adapt, as you got older? He smiled. 'After a truly disastrous start in my first season, when I doubted everything about my batting, I put trust in my technique and didn't change a thing. And it served me pretty well, don't you think?'

England tours of the Caribbean always seem to be dogged by controversy and the one in the winter of 1967/68 was no exception. Except that on this occasion it all started to kick off *before* the team had left these shores. Brian Close had acquitted himself well as captain during the summer and both India and Pakistan had been dispatched comfortably enough. It was inconceivable that he would not lead the side to the West Indies.

That is, until he lost his temper. The row took place on the last day of the game between Warwickshire and Yorkshire at Edgbaston towards the end of the season. Warwickshire needed 142 runs to win in 100 minutes. They fell short by only nine runs. That they had failed to reach their target was blamed largely on the tardy Yorkshire over rate and when you consider the facts – Yorkshire only bowled 24 overs in the time available, including just two overs in the last 15 minutes – you would have to agree that the critics had a point.

Brian Close was the Yorkshire captain and did not take too kindly to the accusations that he had orchestrated this blatant piece of gamesmanship by deliberate time-wasting. In fact, one Warwickshire member made his feelings known, loudly and colourfully, as the Yorkshire side walked off the pitch. Close went over to berate him and a furious exchange took place. Later on, it was claimed that Close had got the wrong man but the damage had been done. The team for the West Indies, with Close as captain, had already been picked but MCC overruled the selectors, stripped Close of the captaincy and appointed Colin Cowdrey in his stead.

As it transpired, Cowdrey proved to be a great success, notwithstanding the fact that he had not been the selectors' first choice. Hitherto, he had had a mixed record as captain of England; no doubt because he never felt that he had been given the job with any assurance of permanency. This time, with a whole tour to mould the team as he saw fit, he truly believed he was captain of his own ship, and it showed. Tom noticed a significant change in his friend's demeanour.

'Colin was usually such a gentle and nice man. In fact I always used to say that if only he had half of Peter May's ruthlessness, he would have been an even better player. But on this tour he was quite strict.'

This is a view shared by Jim Parks, England's wicketkeeper. 'I always thought that Colin was too nice a fellow to be a successful captain. But he did all right on this tour.' They both believed that the tour manager, Leslie Ames, kept things ticking over nicely, smoothing ruffled feathers – and there were a few – whenever a clear head and a composed voice were required. 'The Kent Mafia they were!' said

Tom, and on this occasion, unlike his allusion to the Sussex Mafia on Dexter's tour of Australia, the respect in his voice was obvious.

Before the series started, news arrived from home that he had been awarded the OBE in the New Year's honours list 'for services to cricket'. It was a singular honour for someone still active on the field of play and, as if to prove that he could still cut the mustard at the ripe old age of 40, he scored 118 in the first Test. 'And then I didn't score another run all tour,' he pointed out.

Before we try to unearth reasons for his collapse in form, it is as well to remember what a brilliant innings it was. *Wisden* described it as 'a glorious exhibition of cultured batting' and importantly it helped England to a massive total of 568, a clear statement of intent by the Englishmen in the first innings of the series. He shared a big stand with Ken Barrington.

Tell me about Barrington. 'The thing about Kenny was that he hated to get out. I know all batsmen hate getting out – of course they do – but he wouldn't sell his wicket for love or money.' When Tom first saw him playing for Surrey, he was a stroke-maker from the outset. But in the 1950s, Surrey, by far the strongest county in England, were chock-full of fine batsmen. So, in order to cement his place in the side, he cut out some of his shots to improve his run-making record.

Thereafter, his primary objective at the crease was to stay there, forever and a day. England had cause on many an occasion to give thanks for his powers of endurance and concentration. Wally Grout, the Australian wicketkeeper, reckoned that when Ken Barrington came out to bat, it seemed that he trailed the Union flag behind him.

His career average of 58.67 in Tests underlines how effective he was at just amassing runs. However, there was one controversial incident in his career when he was dropped from the team for slow scoring in the first Test at Edgbaston in 1965 against the New Zealanders. When you appreciate that he scored 137 in 437 minutes, almost bringing the game to a standstill, you might be tempted to have some sympathy for the selectors in their brave decision. 'But he could hit the ball when he wanted to,' said Tom. 'He had this strange compulsion to bring up his hundred with a six. He did it a lot.'

He did it four times in Tests, including the innings for which he was disciplined. By chance, Tom found himself sharing a room with him on this tour.

Originally, Barrington and John Edrich were put together, but Barrington was a fitful and fidgety sleeper and Edrich found that he was forever being disturbed and getting no sleep. He appealed to the management for a change of 'roomie' and Tom was nominated to take his place.

Did you get any sleep then? 'Nothing keeps me awake!' he replied.

So what happened to your form after that? You had been batting so well for so long. He shrugged his shoulders. Even the best players suffer from fluctuations in form. If the reason were apparent, cricket would be a much simpler game – and no doubt the poorer for it. All you can do is scrutinise your technique, practise hard to iron out the flaws and trust in your ability. And, as we know, Tom was ever an assiduous practiser.

Then he exclaimed in anguished tones, in much the same way he had done when calling to mind another of his nemeses, Derek Shackleton of Hampshire, 'Aaargh – Lance Gibbs! He could get me out with an orange.' Reassuring somehow to hear that. 'Let me give you an example,' he said, warming to his theme. 'In the last Test in Guyana, he bowled me a ball on leg stump. I flipped it – really middled it – about an inch off the turf. It hit Sobers, who was taking evasive action, on the steel cap of his boot, ricocheted up and the wicketkeeper snaffled it. Graveney caught Murray bowled Gibbs 0!' For a moment, I thought he was going to cry.

'Then there was the riot,' he said, perking up. *Was there always a riot when England played the West Indies in the Caribbean?* 'It seemed so,' he agreed and reminded me of the comical antics of Johnny Wardle, who picked up one of the bottles thrown on to the pitch by an unruly crowd on Hutton's tour in 1953/54 and pretended to drink from it, thus averting possible bloodshed.

Jim Parks remembers very well the incident that sparked all the trouble. 'Basil D'Oliveira was bowling and Basil Butcher was batting. I was standing up to Basil – D'Oliveira, that is – as I always did. We noticed that Butcher had a habit of glancing the ball very fine on the leg side, often in the air. So Basil suggested that I stand back and see what happened.

'He bowled one down the leg side, Butcher glanced it in the air and as I was already going that way, I dived and caught it. It was definitely out. But Butcher didn't walk. So the umpire correctly and bravely gave him out. And then all hell broke loose.'

Bottles were thrown and the police waded in. 'There was tear gas and someone had a gun,' said Tom. 'Unfortunately, when the police let off the tear gas canisters,' said Parks, 'they misjudged the wind and it blew into our faces. We all had to make a mad dash for the dressing room to splash water on to our streaming eyes.' England were in a good position at the time and might well have gone on to win the match but the 75-minute delay before it was deemed safe to resume play seemed to unnerve the England players and they ceded the initiative, Sobers playing one of his great innings. In the end, England hung on grimly for a draw, their plight not eased by some very strange umpiring.

So the standard of umpiring had not greatly improved since your last visit there 13 years previously? 'It had not,' Tom replied in a tone of voice that brooked no argument.

The result of the series hinged on a quixotic declaration made by Sobers in the fourth Test in Trinidad, which even today provokes much argument and debate. Out of the blue, with his team on 92/2, he declared, challenging England to score 215 in two-and-three-quarter hours. It was a gamble but Sobers was ever the gambler.

Nonetheless, he must have weighed up the odds and concluded that England couldn't manage that and would probably perish in the attempt. And indeed there was some discussion in the England dressing room as to whether it was a realistic target and whether they should go for it. In the end they decided to pick up the gauntlet and thanks to some magnificent batting from Cowdrey and Boycott, they made it with three minutes to spare.

Celebration in the England camp was unrestrained. For Sobers however, national opprobrium was heaped upon his head and even now, he hasn't really lived it down. He was pilloried by the media and execrated by the public. 'They were burning effigies of him in the streets of Georgetown, where we played the last Test,' Tom remembers.

So why do you think he declared? 'I think he was sticking two fingers up at us.'

Why? 'Well, it was said that he was fed up with our negative attitude. If we'd shut up shop and played for a draw, he could turn round and say, there you are, all England are interested in is avoiding defeat. But who knows and who cares – we won.' And hung on to draw the last Test, thus winning a series in the Caribbean for only the second time.

The tour is also remembered for a bizarre and horrific boating accident that befell England's off-spinner, Fred Titmus. He had jumped off a small boat for a swim and on clambering aboard again, his foot came into contact with the propeller and four toes were sliced off. 'He was very lucky,' remembered Tom. 'A surgeon with the Canadian ice hockey team happened to be on holiday at the time and was on the beach. He undoubtedly saved Fred's career by ensuring that the big toe wasn't amputated, as it probably would have been with any of the local doctors.'

The boat was of an unusual design, with the propeller set immediately under the middle of the hull instead of the stern. Titmus, unaware of this, had put his foot into the propeller as he was scrambling back into the boat over the side. Tom remembers having to phone Titmus's wife to assure her that her husband was not in any danger and that she should not fly out to be at his side. Of course, his tour was over and he returned home. Fortunately, the Canadian surgeon had done such a good job that he continued to play for Middlesex for many years.

Titmus had been Cowdrey's vice-captain; that role now fell to Graveney and he led the side when the captain rested for a couple of games. 'So I captained MCC on tour, against Barbados and Guyana.'

Did you enjoy the experience? 'Not 'arf,' he smiled. 'There was a young Guyanese who made quite an impact on the series. His name was Clive Lloyd.'

How would you describe his batting? 'Frightening,' was the brisk reply. 'What a fielder! Before he became captain and went into the slips, he fielded at cover. He always used to shy at the stumps. We'd get eight overthrows every innings!'

How did your friend Basil D'Oliveira fare on tour? 'Basil had a shocker. It was his first overseas tour and between you and me, he probably socialised too much. I don't think Rohan Kanhai was a very good influence on him.'

Jim Parks took up this point when he told me of his memories of the tour. 'He was a man of colour touring with the England cricket team and as such, he was the focus of much attention. The West Indians loved him and proffered him hospitality wherever he went. And Basil being a sociable man, he accepted!'

Both Graveney and Parks remember it as a happy tour. 'Everyone got on,' said Tom. 'We were a real team, unlike the previous time I was there in 1953/54.' Parks agreed. 'I had a great time, even though I lost my place in the Test side. I broke my finger and a certain Alan Knott took my place. And that was the end of my Test career!' He told me that they would slip away to play nine holes of golf early in the morning before start of play. 'Don't see them doing that these days,' he laughed.

He then spoke about Graveney as a fellow tourist. 'He's such a nice man, Tom. Very easy to get on with. I remember playing against him first in 1951, when I was with the RAF. And there was that occasion when I was playing against him for Sussex. He cut at a spinner and edged the ball into the roll of my pad, where it stuck. Ha ha! He wasn't best pleased.'

'I remember that freakish dismissal,' countered Tom. 'No, I wasn't happy. You see, Jim and I, we were both *competitors*.' Poignantly, that was to be their last tour together.

The following summer, the Aussies were in town and surely this would provide Tom Graveney with the opportunity to lay to rest the ghost of his poor record against the old enemy. He continued to enjoy the warm sunshine of his Indian summer and now he could feel assured that he was a fixture in the England team, a confidence that he believed was denied him in other series between the two countries.

To some extent, he answered his critics with some good innings, notably a fine 96 in the third Test, finishing the series with an average of 42.12. If he was slightly disappointed with his aggregate of runs, it was nothing compared with the sense of anti-climax that everyone felt about a substandard and lacklustre series. By common consent, the Australian side was one of their weakest to come to these shores and having, to everybody's surprise, snatched the first Test from under the home side's noses, they sat back and played for the draws that would enable them to retain the Ashes.

In this, they demonstrated virtues of obduracy and determination and were ultimately successful in their objective – the rubber was squared at one apiece – but it hardly made for riveting cricket.

The Australian team, as ever, took their lead from their captain, Bill Lawry. He was the linchpin of their batting – he made the only Test hundred by the tourists – and he handled his limited resources in the field shrewdly. He was also lucky to win a crucial toss in the first Test to help them win the match and, as it turned out, the series. 'We batted badly though,' was Tom's verdict.

Wholesale changes were made by the England selectors for the second Test at Lord's, including the axing of D'Oliveira, a strange decision seeing that he had single-handedly defied the Australians in the second innings, carrying his bat for 87. The match was ruined by rain, however, Tom scoring 14 in his only innings. 'We would have won,' said Tom confidently, 'but we ran out of time.'

The third match was notable as the occasion of Colin Cowdrey's 100th Test. He celebrated by scoring a century and was so nearly joined in that distinction by Tom, who fell agonisingly short, out for 96. A first Test hundred against the Australians on home turf was denied him by a smart piece of bowling. 'I was batting really well,' he said, 'and then Connolly went round the wicket to change his angle of attack. I misjudged the line and he knocked back my leg stump.' It was a great shame but *Wisden* agreed with his assessment of his form, describing his innings as 'masterly'.

Once again, rain ruined England's chances of forcing a victory. Cowdrey pulled a muscle during the game and was unable to play in the next Test. For the first time in his career, Tom was asked to captain the national side. He was hugely honoured and resolved to enjoy every minute of the occasion, even if it were for only one match before Cowdrey returned. Coincidentally, Lawry was nursing a broken finger so his place as skipper was taken by his vice-captain, Barry Jarman, the wicketkeeper.

'I put on my blazer and sought out Jarman to go out to the wicket to toss,' Tom described. 'All the press, TV and radio people were milling about, with the groundsmen putting their finishing touches to the playing surface. And no one recognised us! We tossed up with hardly anyone taking any notice.'

The match was a damp squib. 'The Aussies played for a draw from the outset,' he said, 'because a draw meant that we couldn't win the series and thus they would retain the Ashes.' During the game, especially in their second innings, the Australian batsmen were rendered almost strokeless in their quest to keep the bowlers at bay. Eventually, they were bowled out leaving England to make 326 to win in five hours. Enterprisingly though Edrich, Dexter and Graveney batted, the tall order turned into a skyscraper and by the time Tom fell for 41, caught and bowled by Connolly, the run chase had petered out and the Ashes remained in Australian hands. 'All very disappointing,' was the captain's verdict.

Between the fourth and fifth Tests, Tom had a phone call, the repercussions of which were later to reverberate around the world. 'It was Colin Cowdrey. Roger Prideaux was injured and he wanted to know my opinion about a suitable replacement.'

Following his dismissal from the side earlier in the summer, Basil D'Oliveira had returned to Worcestershire and suffered a torrid time in the County Championship. It was almost as if the stuffing had been knocked out of him as single-figure score followed single-figure score.

A hint that he had regained some of his form was shown with a typically resourceful 51 (out of 105) against Yorkshire, an 89 against Warwickshire and a 40 not out against Middlesex. Tom, without hesitation, recommended his friend, Basil. 'He's back to his best,' he assured Cowdrey, gilding the lily a trifle. 'Fine,' was the reply. 'We'll stick him back in.'

As we shall see, it was a fateful decision. On cricketing grounds, it was a perfectly sound one but a few administrators at MCC with finely attuned political antennae were probably already sipping uneasily at their gins and tonic. The tour the following winter was to South Africa. That country operated a strict apartheid policy. Basil D'Oliveira was a Cape Coloured and as such would not be able to travel and to tour with the England team without let or hindrance.

Perhaps, reasoned the fretful blazers, the South African government would relax the law and make an exception in D'Oliveira's case. He was, after all, a naturalised Englishman. The trouble was that the South African Prime Minister, John Vorster, led a government that staunchly upheld the policy of apartheid and was not known for making exceptions or changing their minds.

Ah well, maybe it won't come to that, the anxious committee men at MCC might well have consoled themselves, as they reached for another gin and tonic; perhaps D'Oliveira will fail in this match and then we won't have to go to all that trouble of picking him for the tour. If they did think that then they didn't know Basil D'Oliveira. He had spent his whole life bucking the odds and proving people wrong. He was determined to seize this chance to play well in this Test and cement his place in the touring party to his home country.

Not that the political ramifications of having D'Oliveira in the side would have particularly concerned Graveney and his team-mates as they gathered for their customary pre-match dinner. Cricketers are by nature a fairly insular breed and attempt to reduce outside distraction to a minimum, the better to concentrate on the game. It is after all their job. Tom was just pleased to see his friend back in the side. Although the Ashes had gone, the England players were keen to make a point. They felt that they had been the better side throughout the series and that rain had robbed them of two realistic opportunities of squaring the rubber. This they could still do at the Oval.

Unlike some of the cricket that had preceded it, this match was an absorbing contest from first to last. England, taking first knock, endured some testing moments until Graveney joined Edrich and slowly, but with ever-increasing confidence, they wrested the initiative from their opponents. Edrich was as determined and obdurate as ever, nudging and dabbing judiciously, with the odd savage cut, accumulating runs soundly and effectively. Graveney, by contrast, was all elegant drives and pulls, making run-gathering appear easy and uncomplicated. Tom scored 63 and Edrich 164.

Tell me about John Edrich. This was his fourth hundred against Australia in thirteen Tests. I fancy he was a little underestimated, don't you? 'Not by us,' Tom assured me. 'He was a terrific player. Phlegmatic, solid, dependable. Such a different character to his uncle Bill. I got on well with him – such a lovely fella.'

D'Oliveira held the middle of the innings together. In Tom's words, it was 'an absolutely magnificent innings'. In view of the fact that he had only just got back into the side and was playing for his place on the forthcoming tour, to say nothing of the importance within the context of the match itself, it was a supreme exhibition of controlled and well-judged strokeplay. 'He had such powerful forearms,' Tom said. 'He struck the ball so cleanly that it would rocket to the boundary. He hooked and drove so commandingly.'

D'Oliveira's innings of 158 boosted England's total to a commanding 494. Australia in reply made 324 and were wholly indebted to their captain, Bill Lawry, who batted all day for his 135, the only century scored by an Australian throughout the series. 'Lawry,' offered Tom, unbidden. 'Happy fellow,' his wicked grin belying the sentiment of his words.

The follow-on having been averted, England went in search of quick runs (how else would you explain our hero being run out for 12?) and made 181 in short order. Australia had a mountain to climb. At 85/5 on the last day, the end seemed inevitable.

Then, at lunch, a sudden and violent storm engulfed south London. In no time at all, the Oval was flooded and once more during that benighted summer, it looked as if rain was going to thwart the Englishmen. After lunch, when the deluge had ceased, Cowdrey donned his blazer and went out to inspect the damage. He could have saved himself the bother. It was obvious to Graveney and other onlookers from the pavilion that play would be impossible; where the wicket had been now stood a huge lake.

'The Aussies were laughing and joking in their dressing room,' remembered Tom. 'They were convinced that that was it for the day.

And frankly, so were we.' Be that as it may, the Oval groundstaff had other ideas. Aided and abetted by an army of volunteers, they set about removing the surface water with brooms, mops, blankets, buckets, anything that came to hand.

'The Surrey members were walking about spearing the ground with the tips of their umbrellas to drain the water away,' Tom chuckled. 'Wouldn't be allowed today.'

Certainly not. But new technology has made obsolete the umbrella as a groundsman's tool; in its place there would be underground drainage and a huge motorised water squeegee. Quite what the Australians thought about the remarkable drying-up process that took place can only be imagined but at 4.45pm, the umpires deemed that the conditions were fit for play and the Australians had no option but to resume their innings.

In a nutshell, England needed to take five wickets in 75 minutes. For a while, Inverarity and Jarman held on without too much in the way of alarms. Then Cowdrey turned to D'Oliveira and his medium-pacers. 'Basil was quite a good partnership breaker,' Tom informed me, 'so it was a shrewd move by Colin.' Sure enough, D'Oliveira bowled Jarman. 'It came back,' said Tom, 'and clipped Jarman's pad on its way to hitting the stumps while he was padding up. It was the wicket we wanted.'

Immediately Cowdrey removed D'Oliveira from the Pavilion End and replaced him with Underwood. By now, the wicket was drying out. In these conditions, bowling his left-arm spinners at medium pace, Underwood was unplayable. The Australians, unused to playing on wet wickets, were all at sea. Surrounded by a cordon of predatory fielders close to the bat, they succumbed spectacularly.

Underwood took the last four wickets in 27 balls for only six runs. There is a famous photograph of the last ball of the match with the whole England team going up in unison for an lbw shout and the umpire's finger pointing to the sky. Inexplicably, Inverarity, who had defied them for four hours, had shouldered arms to a straight one and it had hit him on the pads plumb in front. Every single person on the field of play, save the square leg umpire, is in shot. There were not more than six minutes left to play.

Connolly got you out three times in the series. Was he a problem?
'No, not specifically. I just got out to him. The one who gave me the
most trouble was Gleeson.' Jackie Gleeson was an unorthodox leg-
spinner. He flicked the ball out of his hand with the middle finger.
Just try doing that with a tennis ball and you'll soon see how difficult
it is to control.

'Normally, leggies were meat and drink for me – I always fancied
them. But Gleeson I just couldn't pick. At least, if the light was good,
I could see which way the ball was rotating. But if it wasn't, I couldn't
read him. So I never really got after him.'

How did you get on with the Aussies? 'Oh, famously. They were a
good bunch.' It begs the question whether Tom didn't get on with
any of his opponents, such is his generosity of spirit and natural
gregariousness, but then I remember that he wasn't too keen on the
South Africans, finding them a bit arrogant and stand-offish.

But that was way back in 1955. The tour that he should have
been on but was inexplicably omitted from, the one to South Africa
in 1956/57, might have changed his mind but alas, for one reason
or another, he had played against them in only six Tests. This was
to change, surely, in the forthcoming tour, which he and his ally,
Basil D'Oliveira, were so much looking forward to. It was said that
an Ashes tour to Australia was unquestionably the apogee of any
cricketer's career but one to South Africa, where the steaks, as well
as the hospitality, are king-sized, was the most enjoyable.

In point of fact, it later emerged that MCC, both through
official and unofficial channels, had already been in contact with
the cricket authorities in South Africa before the touring party
was selected, seeking clarification of the situation if in the event
D'Oliveira were selected. The exchanges seem to have been vague
and inconclusive.

At best, MCC dragged its heels and gave the impression of an
organisation paralysed by vacillation and ambivalence, incapable of
deciding what was morally right and acting on it. At worst, it was
accused of bending to political pressure and taking whatever steps
were needed to ensure that the tour went ahead, come what may.
Whatever furtive machinations were going on in the dusty corridors

of Lord's, it can be safely assumed that D'Oliveira's critical innings of 158 at the Oval was nothing less than a huge inconvenience.

Tom takes up the story of what happened next. 'We were playing Sussex at New Road and at six o'clock, we gathered round the radio in the dressing room to listen to the announcement of the touring party to South Africa. Basil came in and the dressing room fell quiet as we listened to the names being read out. Basil's name wasn't on it. I was stunned.'

D'Oliveira himself later said that you could hear a pin drop in the room as the incredible news was digested. Then the air turned blue. It was Tom swearing. 'I said to him, "I never thought they'd do this to you, Bas." It was clear he was deeply upset.' Tom took him into the physiotherapist's room where he broke down and cried. Tom thought it best that he should immediately excuse him from anything further to do with the match and told him to go home. Later, D'Oliveira admitted that he had been deeply hurt and for some time afterwards felt as if his world had caved in. 'The stomach had been kicked out of me,' he said.

Tom was incandescent. He told everyone, press included, that if Basil wasn't going to South Africa, then neither was he. 'I meant it, you know,' he told me.

And how was that received by the authorities? 'Don't know. Don't care. I was that furious.'

He wasn't the only one. The news of D'Oliveira's omission was roundly condemned in the newspapers, MPs asked questions in the Commons, several MCC members resigned, others called for a Special General Meeting to discuss the affair and the Rev David Sheppard went on record to say that MCC had made 'a terrible mistake'.

Very few people, it seemed, believed the selection committee when they released a statement denying that their choice had been politically motivated. D'Oliveira had been omitted, they said, 'on cricketing grounds – and by a whisker'. The defence of the decision, such as it was, lay in the claim that Tom Cartwright, who ostensibly was chosen in D'Oliveira's place, was the better medium-pace bowler who would be more likely to flourish on South African wickets. It was also hinted that D'Oliveira had not behaved terribly well on the previous winter tour by MCC in the West Indies.

This was true. Even Tom, his staunchest ally, had conceded that Basil had not exactly distinguished himself in the Caribbean but it could be said that he had learnt his lesson and that his behaviour, to say nothing of his performances, had been immaculate in the two Tests he had played that summer. Furthermore, he was a batsman who could bowl; Cartwright was a bowler who could bat, a little. The defence did not wholly stack up and many suspected a conspiracy.

Tom remains deeply sceptical of the official MCC line, even to this day. 'To score 158 and then get *dropped?* Nonsense! It was political. They even tried to bribe him, you know.' D'Oliveira did admit later that he had been put under pressure, even to the extent of being offered a lucrative coaching post in the country, with free accommodation, to declare himself unavailable to tour. He angrily declined.

Tom is unwilling to criticise personally the members of the selection committee, all of whom were honest men, he believes. Of their number – Doug Insole, Alec Bedser, Peter May, Don Kenyon and Colin Cowdrey – only Insole is still alive and he has never wavered from his claim that they were put under no outside pressure whatsoever. It is interesting to note that the minutes of that meeting mysteriously disappeared soon after and have never been found. Graveney knew all of the selection panel, of course, from his playing days and has never had an issue with any of them personally but he remains adamant, an opinion overwhelmingly supported by the public, that this was not MCC's finest hour.

And what of the man in the eye of the storm? If this was not the finest hour in MCC's history, it certainly was D'Oliveira's. Overnight, he had been raised from the usual limited prominence of an England cricketer to the status of an international figure, symbolising the struggle for freedom of a repressed people in apartheid South Africa. But it was a role that he had neither sought nor felt at all comfortable with. He decided that the best course of action was to keep his mouth shut and to remain aloof from the furore that was raging all around him.

It was a wise decision. In keeping his own counsel, he unwittingly secured for himself an unassailable, heroic status in the eyes of the British public, far beyond the boundaries of international cricket. The respect and affection in which he was held remained undiminished until his death in 2011. In the tributes that poured in from the four corners of the earth after he died, mention was made repeatedly of the quiet dignity and restrained integrity with which he conducted himself during these hectic weeks and the difficult years thereafter. As Pat Murphy said on Radio 5 Live in a moving eulogy following D'Oliveira's death, 'He became a leading light for the instruments of change, without saying a word.'

In private, unsurprisingly, he opened up to close friends, including Graveney. He admitted he was deeply hurt by his omission and perplexed by the explanations given, that the decision had been arrived at 'on purely cricketing grounds'. 'He was top of the batting averages for the Test series and second in the bowling,' Tom pointed out, 'and yet he was considered not to be one of the best 16 players in the country. Ridiculous! The whole thing stank.'

Be that as it may, Basil felt that he had no option but to accept the snub and to quietly get on with his life. There was still one match left in the County Championship that season, against Surrey at New Road. His public demeanour may have been restrained but the same could not be said of his batting. It seemed that, once at the crease, he could unburden himself of all his frustrations and it just so happened that it was the poor Surrey bowlers who suffered. 'He always hit it hard,' said Tom, 'but that day he hit it harder. I had to declare when he was on 92 because we wanted to try and force a victory. Nearly did too, because we had 'em 75/8. It was a shame though I couldn't let him get his hundred.'

If D'Oliveira hoped that the harsh light of public scrutiny would soon flicker and die, he was in for another rude shock. In the meantime, Tom Cartwright had finally told the selectors that a long-standing shoulder injury would prevent him from joining the touring party. Whether they bowed to media pressure and the overwhelming wishes of cricket lovers up and down the country or whether he was really their first reserve all along, the selectors immediately announced D'Oliveira as Cartwright's replacement. Thus substituting a batsman for a bowler, as the more sceptical commentators pointed out. No matter. Basil was to get his lifetime wish, to travel to his homeland as a member of the English cricket team.

Or would he? It must have become increasingly apparent, even to the most myopic MCC member or cricket fan, that what would later come to be known as the D'Oliveira Affair was now bringing about international diplomatic consequences. The following day (17 September), an angry Prime Minister, John Vorster, denounced the instatement of D'Oliveira into the England side. 'We are not prepared to receive a team thrust upon us by people whose interests are not in the game but to gain certain political objectives.'

He followed that up with this scathing criticism of the cricket authorities in England, 'The MCC team is not the team of MCC but of the anti-apartheid movement.' Not much wriggle room there for MCC, though they had at the last tried hard to explore every avenue to save the tour. In the end, after much fruitless negotiating, they bowed to the inevitable and called it off. Basil was not to realise his ambition and Tom was not to tour South Africa – again.

Tell me, Tom, what was Colin Cowdrey's role in all this? He was the England captain and must have been at the centre of things. He was criticised for a less than straightforward approach with Basil. Is it true that he caved in to pressure from those above? Tom was silent for a minute, collecting his thoughts. And then he gave a little, sad smile. 'Colin wasn't always the most plain-speaking of fellows.' And he left it at that.

And Basil. How did he take it, his cup being dashed from his lips a second time? 'I think he was resigned to not going. He didn't seem surprised when it was called off. None of us was. He was just upset that his team-mates couldn't go on tour, all because of him.'

For a man who valued his privacy and was most happy in the company of his own, and the wider, family of cricketers, the media attention that assailed D'Oliveira was intolerable. The press were camped outside his home, his wife was deeply depressed and his children were being hassled. His Worcestershire team-mate, Rodney

Cass, felt sorry for him and offered him a couple of days' sanctuary in his flat. 'There was quite a famous artist, named Waldron West, who was the landlord,' said Cass. 'He came up to me and said, "Is that the bloke whose face is splashed all over the papers?" Guardedly, I said yes. "Tell you what," he said. "If you get him to sit for me to have his portrait done, I'll do one of you." The result of that arrangement is the large portrait of Basil that now hangs in the pavilion at New Road. And the one hanging over there is me. A bit younger, but it's not bad, is it?' Indeed not. Both portraits are imposing and impressive.

Swiftly, MCC moved to organise a replacement tour, which wasn't easy at such short notice. A combined visit to India, Pakistan and Ceylon was arranged but the Indian leg was cancelled owing to lack of funds. Ceylon (later Sri Lanka) at that time did not have Test match status and only one game, in Colombo, was scheduled as a prelude to the main business in Pakistan. Tom had already been to Pakistan twice, with MCC in 1951/52 – his first overseas tour – and in 1963/64 with a Commonwealth team.

It would not have been his destination of choice. He had been looking forward – as indeed they all had – to a full tour of South Africa but that seemed like an ever-decreasing prospect as the political row rumbled on. In fact, it was not long before all official sporting links were cut with South Africa. This was a tragedy for all concerned, not least the disadvantaged sections of society in that deeply divided country, but in the long run, the political aims of enforced isolation did the trick and apartheid was defeated. So you could say the pain was worth it.

But you cannot help but spare a sympathetic thought, whatever your political and moral convictions, for the poor South African cricket team. At this time, they had every right to consider themselves the number one team in the world but after their last hurrah against Australia in 1970 – whom they thrashed 4-0 – they were never again to strut their stuff on the world stage. The likes of Graeme Pollock, Peter Pollock, Eddie Barlow, Barry Richards, Mike Procter et al were to be cast into the international wilderness and the game was poorer for it. For Tom, it was a huge disappointment but it was not the end of his Test career.

Actually, he was fairly sanguine about the change. If, instead of steak on the barbecue, it was going to be curry, so be it. He was an England player and he would play wherever and whenever he was selected. 'I cannot understand how anyone can retire from international duty,' he said to me once. 'You've been selected for your country and it should be a great honour. You don't turn your back on your duty.'

He was commenting on recent arguments about central contracts and players wanting to pick and choose what Tests they played in so that they could maximise their earnings in the Indian Premier League. He was shaking his head sadly. 'We weren't paid much, so it wasn't the money that drove us. It was the game – all about winning.'

Just as a matter of interest, Tom, what did you get per Test? 'Two hundred pounds.' Two hundred pounds! Goodness me! No wonder Kerry Packer succeeded in turning the game upside down a few years later. He was pushing on a half-opened door.

Never mind what was happening on the political front in South Africa, it soon became apparent that MCC's choice of Pakistan as a substitute could not have been more ill-judged. The country was in chaos after a bitterly contested general election. There was conflict between parliament and the military, between elected politicians and the generals, and it seemed to the general public, as well as to outsiders, that one side was as corrupt as the other. This conflict would lead to the breakdown of law and order, massacres, civil war, ten million refugees, one million dead, war with India, military humiliation and the secession of East Pakistan, which would reinvent itself as a new country, Bangladesh. Not the place, nor the time, to send a team of cricketers.

It became clear as soon as they touched down on Pakistani soil after a pleasant 12-day stay in Ceylon that all was confusion and turmoil. The tour schedule had been changed before they arrived and continued to change while they were there, in an increasingly desperate attempt by the authorities to appease the warring factions.

The Pakistani Cricket Board was anxious for the tour to continue despite the mayhem and violence that were being unleashed all around. They hoped that the cricket would prove a distraction from the riots. All it did in fact was provide a focal point for the agitators and none of the games was spared disorder and lawlessness. MCC, back at Lord's, were desperate, for their part, not to call off the tour for fear of upsetting their hosts. And the cricketers were caught uncomfortably in the middle of all this.

The Army was out in force, there was gunfire, buildings were set alight and the team felt exposed and vulnerable, pawns in a wider political struggle. The irony was not lost on Tom that politics was the very reason that the South African tour had been cancelled. 'We shouldn't have been there,' he said. 'It was a young team and we had guys like Cottam, Prideaux, Fletcher, Hobbs, at the start of their Test careers, and they were inexperienced and frankly intimidated by this violent atmosphere.'

How the players – on both sides – managed to concentrate on a Test match while anarchy raged about them beggars belief. Trouble broke out in Lahore and the match was reduced to four days. Unsurprisingly, it was an unspectacular draw, noteworthy only for Cowdrey's fine century and the leg-break bowling of Intikhab Alam.

But if Lahore was a hotbed of student unrest, worse was to follow in Dacca. The trip to East Pakistan had been originally left off the schedule but now the tourists discovered that it had been restored at the behest of the politicians. 'The only reason we went,' said Tom, 'was that the students in Dacca, who had control of the city, threatened to burn down the British consulate if we didn't come.'

He remembers a meeting with the president's right-hand man that he, as vice-captain, attended. Rapidly, he realised that the tour management were about to capitulate to the political pressure before he stuck his oar in. 'I was convinced we shouldn't go – and said so. As the vice-captain, I was only expressing the views of the players, especially the younger ones, who felt they couldn't speak out. But I was a lone voice.'

They went. When they stepped off the plane, there were no police to be seen. They had retreated outside the city and left it in the control of left-wing agitators and rioting students. The game took place with this surreal backdrop of insurrection and simmering violence. Rather like the social fabric of the country, the pitch of rolled mud soon began to break up and England were only saved from capitulation by a superb unbeaten century by D'Oliveira.

How was Basil after the traumas of the previous season? 'Oh, he was fine. He soon regained his good spirits. I think it helped being away on tour, thrown in among his fellow tourists.' The match, marred throughout by protests and disturbances, was drawn and back they all came to West Pakistan. But there was to be no respite from the country's upheaval.

When it became apparent that the tension, and the violence, had abated not a jot – in fact it seemed to the tourists it had got a lot worse – things came to a head in the team room at the hotel in Karachi, where they were now based. There was no doubt that certain members of the side feared for their safety and were frankly terrified of taking the field because of he raised level of tension. It seemed to Tom and the others that the city was as volatile as a tinderbox and any spark, such as a controversial incident at the cricket, would set the whole place alight.

Once again, Tom brought these fears to the attention of the management, Cowdrey and Ames – the same two that Tom thought had done a good job in the West Indies the previous year when there had been crowd trouble. But this felt entirely different. People were getting killed. 'There was a…discussion,' Tom said enigmatically.

Did you get on with the two of them? 'They were both close friends of mine. That's what made it so difficult. Anyway, things got a bit heated, I said my piece and left them to decide what to do. We shouldn't have been there. It was dangerous.'

Their decision was that the tour went ahead. Tom felt that Ames had been put under pressure by MCC to continue at all costs and to pull all diplomatic strings – and he was very good at that – to get the authorities to guarantee that the Test would be properly policed. Assurances of safety had been coming thick and fast since the tour started but it had become increasingly obvious to the players that the authorities, and the police, had lost control and were unable to guarantee anything.

Nonetheless, the game started. Tom gave a hollow laugh when he talked about it. 'As far as I know, it is the only Test, putting aside interruptions from the weather, where only one innings out of the four was completed!' England won the toss and Colin Milburn, recently flown in from Australia as a replacement, scored a typically robust hundred and when he reached his milestone, hundreds of excitable people poured on to the pitch and surrounded him.

'It was quite frightening,' said Tom. 'You never knew what some lunatic might do. I had to wade in with my bat flailing to get them off him.' And then he added with that wicked grin of his, 'That was my training – to run round Colin!'

Milburn was famously well built. Some even called him fat. Tom gave no mention of his own contribution and it was only when I looked up the records that I discovered that he had scored 105. It was a remarkable innings, not so much for its graceful strokeplay but for its duration and its obstinate refusal to give way. He batted for five hours, in searing heat, with riots raging outside the ground, which threatened at any moment to spill into the stadium and on to the pitch. How did he manage to concentrate? 'I didn't play well. It was a struggle. I'd just had an argument with my two friends and there was mayhem around the boundary,' he recalled. 'But I stuck at it.'

It gives the lie to those who claimed, if still they did, that he was too much of a dilettante as a batsman, too unreliable to be a successful Test player. Somewhat bemused by these strictures, he said to me, almost as an example of this suspicion some people had of him: 'Jack Fingleton once said about me that he didn't think that my smiling face fitted in with the seriousness of Test cricket.' Because he was friendly with his opponents after close of play and liked to share a beer with them, he was suspected of not being ruthless enough.

B.O. Allen, Gubby Allen, Hutton, May, Dexter, all harboured their reservations about his appetite for battle. But he could get his head down and grind out the runs, if that was what his team needed and the situation demanded. All I can say is that Tom Graveney's record speaks for itself and underlines that he was as hard-nosed as they come, despite his ruddy complexion and genial countenance.

Poignantly, it was to be his last, the 11th, Test hundred. It wasn't his most fluent or his most dazzling innings but given the game's context and the myriad distractions that assailed him, it was one of his bravest and most resolute. When he came off the field, he was exhausted and dehydrated and he sat for ages on the bench, unable to move or speak. It, and everything else that was swirling around, had mentally and physically exhausted him.

By lunch on the third day, England had amassed 502/7, with Alan Knott stranded agonisingly four runs short of his maiden Test century. Any team that has scored 500 can be forgiven for relaxing and enjoying their lunch but the mood in the England dressing room was anxious and fearful. And I doubt it was much different in the Pakistan dressing room either.

At last, the powder keg exploded, as it had been threatening to do for days. A full-scale riot erupted inside the ground, the tents and marquees surrounding the boundary were set alight and the Army massed on the outfield, guns aimed and ready to fire at the uncontrollable mob. The game was immediately abandoned.

Who actually decided to call it off? 'Don't know. It was sort of a collective decision to get out of there as soon as possible. That is, with one exception.' He added, with a wry smile, 'Knotty wanted to stay to get his hundred!' Quickly, they piled into a bus, that already had its windows smashed, and lay down on the floor while the hazardous journey back to the hotel was completed.

That night, they flew out of the country, the tour having been abandoned with immediate effect. There wasn't a single member of that MCC party, player or management, who did not let out a sigh of relief as they cleared Pakistan air space. 'Horrible, horrible,' said Tom mournfully. 'What a way to end a tour.'

Before we left the sorry tale of Pakistan in 1968, I was keen to quiz him about the report of the ill-fated tour published in *Wisden*. One sentence caught my eye, 'Graveney, who otherwise did little in Pakistan, followed with a sparkling century of his own.'

Yet Tom had himself admitted that his hundred was not one of his most sparkling; in fact it had been a struggle throughout. Had the correspondent been at the same match? And what's this about doing little else? A quick look at the tour averages reveals that Graveney's average for matches other than Tests was 70.50! In Tests it was 44 and on the tour as a whole it was 52.83. I know that statistics do not always tell the full story but neither, on the other hand, can they be ignored. The *Wisden* correspondent is plain wrong here. And there is another quotation, 'Graveney was a sad disappointment as vice-captain.' Ouch!

What did he mean by that, Tom? 'I suppose word got out about my strong views about the ill-advisedness of the tour and how dangerous it was to carry on. I was only expressing the opinion of the team, especially the younger ones. After all, that's what a vice-captain is supposed to do, isn't it?'

How was your relationship with Cowdrey on tour? 'Colin found it all a bit much, what with the riots and all the political goings-on off the field. And who wouldn't? But he seemed unsure how to play it.'

And Ames, the manager? 'He was a lovely man. I got on with him very well. We did have that one bust-up before the Karachi Test but…' He tailed off. 'It was all a long time ago.' Perhaps, but I could not help but speculate what was in the manager's confidential report on the tour when he reported back to his masters at Lord's and whether its contents might have had a bearing on subsequent events the following season.

Quickly, Tom hurried home to organise his benefit. Worcestershire had awarded him one for the 1969 season and he had need of it. It may seem strange to us who have got used to England players driving Jaguar cars and earning enough money to count themselves millionaires but Tom needed the money that he hoped a benefit would bring.

He had played 78 Test matches but he was by no means a wealthy man. Perhaps others in his era had made a bit more money and shrewdly invested for the future but cricket was not a well-paid profession. This wouldn't change until the Packer revolution of the mid-70s.

Tom was no businessman and he wasn't particularly careful with his money (another way of saying that he always bought his round, and more, I guess) so his finances were perpetually in a state of crisis. 'We never had any money,' admitted his son, Tim. 'We weren't poor and we never went without but neither were we comfortably off.'

Tom shrugs his shoulders whenever the subject comes up. He maintains that he was never in it for the money; the sheer joy of playing cricket every day was enough reward for him. As long as he had enough to get by, he was content.

If I may be so bold, can I ask you how much were you actually paid? 'A few quid short of £2,000 a year.'

You were filling grounds all over the country you were only, and let's not forget, paid £200 a Test match? Where was all the money going? He shrugged his shoulders. 'Certainly not into our pockets. In those days we did as we were told, turned up and played. MCC ran the game and we were the paid retainers.'

While we were on the subject of finances, I thought I would chance my arm and ask about his two benefits, one for Gloucestershire and now this one for Worcestershire.

How much did you make? He answered without hesitation. 'Five thousand pounds at Gloucester, £7,000 at Worcester.'

Was that good, bad or about par for the course? He waggled his head, thinking about it. 'About average for small clubs like Gloucester and Worcester.' I could not help but ponder the anomalous fact that one of England's foremost batsmen since the war was only rewarded with an 'average' benefit when others of lesser ability and length of service at the richer clubs made considerably more. He then grinned. 'It was damned useful at the time. Helped to pay off the national debt!'

Against this backdrop of financial need was the final controversy of his career played out. It was a chance meeting that set off the chain reaction of events. At the Cricketers' Club in London, Tom was having a quiet drink with Colin McDonald, the Australian opening bat, who introduced him to Tony Hunt, the chairman of Coventry City Football Club.

'Tony was what you might call a sports nut,' said Tom, 'crazy about any game.' He knew who Tom Graveney was (who didn't?), admired him immensely as a player (who didn't?) and engaged him in conversation. Tom being Tom was only too happy to talk cricket. He was used to strangers approaching him for a chat and he usually responded warmly. He had the common touch in an era when elitism was only being grudgingly ceded by the ruling classes. The so-called Swinging Sixties was a time of great social upheaval and some of our major institutions, not least MCC, were slow to adapt.

In any event, the conversation soon turned to Tom's benefit at Worcestershire. Hunt offered him there and then £1,000 to play in a charity match at Luton on a Sunday during the forthcoming season. Having choked on his pint of bitter, Tom regained his composure and readily accepted. 'I needed the money,' he explained simply.

Put in the context of a total of £7,000 for his benefit, a one-off payment of £1,000 takes on a substantial significance, particularly when you bear in mind that his benefit match against Gloucestershire only raised a paltry £400. Now in past years, the date of the game, provided it was on a Sunday, would not have mattered; two county games were always scheduled for weekdays during the season and the players would have Sundays off.

If he wasn't turning out for a fellow professional's benefit jamboree, Tom was usually to be found on the golf course. It so happened that 1969 was the inaugural year of the John Player League, a new competition of 40 overs each that was expected to bring the crowds flocking to the grounds on a Sunday afternoon. Thus the number of available Sundays to organise benefit matches was severely limited.

The Luton match was scheduled for the Sunday – a rest day – in the middle of the first Test against the West Indies. Tom's successful return to Test cricket meant that he was certain to be picked; after all, his most recent innings had been that century in Karachi. He also appreciated that the players were forbidden to play cricket on the rest day of a Test. Those in charge would look a bit stupid if a player had got injured – say, broken a finger or some such accident – while playing in a charity game of no consequence and was unable to take the field for his country on the next morning. But that £1,000 was critical to Tom's finances and besides, he had already given his word. He was in a cleft stick and he was unsure what to do.

In the meantime, an unfortunate injury to the England captain had muddied the waters. A couple of weeks before the first Test,

Colin Cowdrey had snapped his Achilles tendon while playing for Kent. This was a cruel blow for him. After several years of uncertainty about his role in the England side, he felt that at last he was established in the post and that he was beginning to mould the team around him. Clearly it would be many months before he could even think of playing again and by then the captaincy would have been passed on, perhaps for good.

The selectors had to appoint a new captain. Speculation in the press was rife, with first one candidate being thrown up and then another almost daily. Tom had been Cowdrey's vice-captain in Pakistan and indeed had deputised for him when he was injured in the third Test against the Australians the previous season. Many felt that he was the obvious candidate and it was only a matter of waiting for the selectors to convene for the investiture to be confirmed. Tom was not so sure, though he kept his doubts to himself.

His scepticism was well founded. The chairman of selectors, Alec Bedser, whatever admiration he may have had for Tom's batting, was harbouring doubts about his suitability as a captain. In addition a new and likely candidate now hove into view. Ray Illingworth had left his native Yorkshire to join Leicestershire as captain and was now making a name for himself, leading a vibrant and talented side that would soon challenge for the championship and win it in 1975.

'He was on a hot streak,' Tom told me. 'Of course he was going to be a candidate.' In the end, Tom was passed over and the selectors (Bedser, A.C. Smith and Billy Sutcliffe) settled on Illingworth. That Illingworth went on to regain the Ashes in Australia in 1970/71, the first England captain to do so since Hutton in 1954/55, would seem to demonstrate that it was a shrewd decision but at the time much was made of the perceived slight to Tom Graveney. Whatever his public comments at the time, and he would not have been human if he had not endured private disappointment, Tom has always insisted that he harboured no grudge.

What was your opinion of Illingworth as a captain? Do you think he deserved the honour? 'I had no problems whatsoever with him as captain. He was doing a good job at Leicester and I think it was a good choice.'

What about all this media talk about a great rivalry between you two? 'That's all it was – talk.'

Notwithstanding the flap over the captaincy, Tom was no further forward in his dilemma over the benefit game at Luton. He decided to ring Bedser and lay out his cards on the table. When he had explained the situation, Bedser reminded him that it was forbidden to play in even a charity match on the rest day of a Test. Tom reiterated the financial implications for him if he were to cry off; quite simply he could not afford to say no. Bedser was immovable. He couldn't play and that was that. Then Tom said, 'Well, if that's the case, don't pick me.' He is adamant that those were the words that he used; he says he could not have made it plainer.

Alec Bedser is now dead so I have only heard one side of the story. In subsequent years, whenever Bedser was asked about that particular exchange during their telephone conversation, he claimed that he had no recollection of it. To be fair to Bedser, he was at the time busy sorting out the England captaincy issue so it could have been that he was distracted.

Nonetheless, Tom said that Bedser was aware of the game at Luton and knew that it was a problem because he had told Tom he couldn't play. What actually was said between the two of them, the importance of which will become clear later, will probably never be indisputably determined.

But wait a minute. There was another witness, albeit hardly a disinterested one. Becky, Tom's daughter, heard what was said. 'I remember it clearly as if it happened yesterday,' she told me. 'Mum and I were listening to the conversation while we were sitting on the stairs. Dad said, "If I'm not allowed to play, then don't pick me." I heard it!'

At lunch on the Sunday before the Test, Tom listened to the announcement of the team on the radio and was surprised, but relieved, to hear his name read out. He naturally assumed that Bedser had discussed the matter with his co-selectors and that somehow they had come to an accommodation about the Luton match. Tom turned up at Old Trafford on Wednesday 11th June for the usual net practice and nothing was said. All was well, he told himself.

On the Thursday, the new captain, Illingworth, performed his first service to his country by winning the toss. Naturally, he chose to bat and the first day was dominated by a century from Geoff Boycott, playing for the first time in contact lenses. Tom shared in a 128-run stand with Boycott, both batting circumspectly, determined to make the best use of a good wicket. At close of play, Tom was 56 not out. He had batted 'pretty well', he said, but as the country was sweltering in a heat wave, he felt more than usually tired as he soaked himself in the bath afterwards.

In came Alec Bedser. 'You know you're not allowed to play on Sunday,' he told the recumbent Tom.

Well…what was your reaction? 'I was disappointed.'

Oh, come on, Tom. What did you really say? 'The air turned blue,' he finally admitted. 'Later, I regretted my outburst but I was angry. I knew immediately that there was going to be trouble.'

It would have been good to record that, the next day, in this, his last Test innings, he scored a hundred but alas, he was bowled by Vanburn Holder for 75.

Were you cross at getting out when you were set? 'I was always cross at getting out. On this occasion, it was worse because I'd just signed Vanburn to play for us at Worcester. There's gratitude for you!'

He did not know of course that this was his swansong – there was after all a second innings (in which he did not bat) – but he must have guessed that the match at Luton could jeopardise his Test career. 'Even if I'd known that that was it, I still would have gone,' he made it plain. 'I needed the money and I had promised to go.'

Accordingly, he slipped away from Manchester on the Sunday, arrived at Luton, changed into his whites, went into bat when it was his turn, faced a few overs of the most gentle leg-breaks that Richie Benaud and Bobby Simpson could toss up and when the medium-pacer came on, he made sure he got out immediately. 'And I fielded at third man,' he said. 'Honestly, I don't think I could have got injured if I'd tried.'

Tell me, why did you actually play? Why didn't you just go down there to meet and greet, to stroll round the boundary signing autographs and making yourself available to the public? 'Because the deal was that I batted. That's what people wanted to see. And I'd given my word.'

That evening, he reported back to the team hotel in Manchester in plenty of time to get a good night's sleep. But of course by then the cat was out of the bag. The next morning, Bedser told him that he was going to report him to the disciplinary committee at Lord's. Tom was expecting no less. What he was not expecting, and it is something that rankles with him to this day, was that an announcement came over the Tannoy that afternoon while England were in the field, informing the crowd that T.W. Graveney had been reported to MCC over a disciplinary matter and that he was instructed to report to Lord's on 19 June, thus missing the next game for Worcestershire against Surrey. No consideration was given that he was the county captain.

A few people in the stands jeered but whether it was in support of Tom or not, he was unsure. I was appalled when he told me this. Whatever the rights and wrongs of the case, that is no way to treat a junior county second XI player let alone a senior and respected member (with an OBE) of the Test team. And what if he had been under a steepling catch at the time? But he wasn't. He just shrugged his shoulders.

And the rest of the team? They were all out there with you. What did they say? 'Well, everybody knew what was going on. But they were as shocked as me that it was announced so publicly.'

England won the match comfortably by ten wickets but Tom, on his 42nd birthday, was in no mood to celebrate. The next day when he should have been leading his team out against Surrey, he stayed at home and his anxiety grew. The more he thought about it, the more convinced he was that he had already been tried and found guilty in the corridors and committee room of MCC. 'In those days, yes even 1969, the players had no rights. MCC ran the game. I was on to a loser from the start.'

It has to be said that his misgivings had some basis in fact. MCC had banned him from county cricket for one year because he no longer felt that he could play for Gloucestershire. One of the best batsmen in the country was forced to play second XI cricket all summer – that was myopic management for you. But those were their rules and MCC dispensed them fearlessly. Whatever the true nature of the manoeuvring behind the scenes, Tom believed that he had few friends at Lord's.

It was time to ask a difficult question. The comment by the *Wisden* reporter that 'Graveney was a sad disappointment as vice-captain' resurfaced in my mind.

Wisden is not the mouthpiece of MCC but it is – or it was – regarded as an 'Establishment' publication. Do you think that your outspokenness on the Pakistan tour counted against you in the corridors of power? He gave it some thought. 'MCC liked people to speak their mind,' he eventually said, 'until that is anyone spoke out against them!'

The whole case hinged on that fateful telephone conversation between Tom and Alec Bedser. One person claimed his version and the other denied all knowledge of it. I decided to approach Alan Smith, one of Bedser's co-selectors (the other being Billy Sutcliffe, who died in 1998) to see whether he could shed any light on the matter. 'Neither I, nor Billy, had any idea what was going on,' said Smith. 'The first we heard about a potential problem was when we all got to Old Trafford.'

So Bedser had not mentioned anything to you about Tom's clash of commitments? He shook his head. 'Alec said nothing about it to me. Mind you, we were holed up in Leicester at the time, as I remember, negotiating with Illy about the captaincy. It was a busy period.'

What he seemed to be saying therefore was that, if the conversation had taken place, it was perfectly feasible that informing the other selectors had slipped Bedser's mind. But would Bedser admit that to the disciplinary committee? Tom's fate hung on the word of his old friend and team-mate.

Accordingly, sprucely turned out as usual, he reported to Lord's on the designated day, 19 June.

He was ushered into the committee room. 'There were 18 people there, sat round the table,' he said, the amazement in his voice still unmistakeable after all these years. As simply and as clearly as he could, he told his side of the story. 'I thought about lying,' he told me. It took a second or two for me to grasp the point of what he was saying.

He meant that he was tempted to throw in the towel and agree with Bedser's version and take whatever consequences would come his way.

Why didn't you? It might have saved all this trouble. 'Because it wasn't right,' he averred. 'It wasn't what happened.' He was then invited to step outside while the committee considered his evidence.

Did Bedser speak? 'No. I wasn't present when he gave them his report.'

So you had no opportunity to challenge any part of his statement? He shook his head.

Who was the chairman? 'A chap called Edmund King. Ever such a nice man. He was, I think, chairman of Warwickshire. I think he felt a bit sorry for me.' Nonetheless, Tom sensed that the odds were stacked against him.

Outside there was nothing better to do than sit on a bench and watch the game that was being played. 'Middlesex against Lancashire,' he remembered.

I guess that was the first time that you had watched a county game that you had not been involved in. Glumly, he agreed. It was almost as if he was sitting on that bench again, pondering the unequal position he was in. Who were the committee going to believe? Alec Bedser, the indefatigable servant of English cricket and the chairman of the selection committee or Tom Graveney, the gifted, yet maverick, batsman who always did things his way?

His reverie was cut short by a hand on his shoulder and a quiet request to rejoin his judges. He was told, in respectful tones he had to admit, that the committee had found Bedser's evidence more compelling and that they had therefore found in his favour. Graveney would be disciplined. To Tom it was a shock but hardly a surprise. He took a second or two to compose himself before saying, 'That's not true,' and turned on his heels and walked away, as if the umpire had delivered an unwelcome – and incorrect – decision. There was nothing for it but to quit the scene.

A statement was issued by MCC. 'The disciplinary sub-committee of the TCCB have considered the facts relating to the appearance of

T.W. Graveney in the match at Luton on Sunday 15 June, while a Test match in which he was taking part was in progress. They have ruled that Graveney be severely reprimanded and the selectors have been informed that he must not be considered for selection for England for the next three Test matches.'

What did you do next? 'I went for lunch to The Cricketers' Club with Crawford White.' That name rang a bell.

He was a journalist, wasn't he? 'The *Daily Mail*. Or was it *The Express*? I forget.'

And you spilled the beans? 'I did. Gave him his scoop. I did it because it wasn't right what they had done to me.'

The whole thing caused quite a stir, didn't it? Can you remember the press coverage? Was the general mood supportive or hostile? 'Generally kind, I think. Certainly most of the ex-players who wrote about it were on my side. And more people came over when the full facts came out.'

Sadly, my time was up. And it seemed like an appropriate moment to cut short our conversation. I was mindful that I should not tire him out. As we shook hands, he said, 'He told a fib, you know.'

Who? 'Alec. I felt sorry for him, actually. It wasn't like him at all. I think he had boxed himself into a corner and there was no way out.' As generous epilogues go, that takes some beating.

'I'll walk with you,' he said, as we made our way to the front door. 'Time to go and visit Mother.' He meant Jackie, his wife, who resided in the nursing home adjacent. As he opened the front door, a violent squall of wind and rain rushed through the corridor. 'Uh oh. Perhaps I won't,' he reconsidered.

The following week, I revisited Tom and revisited the subject. I wanted to discover whether, at the time, he knew that was the end of his international career or whether he still harboured hopes of yet another recall.

'No – that was it,' he said, unhesitatingly, 'I had been banned for three Tests, two against the West Indies and one against New Zealand, who were very weak, probably the weakest team in world cricket. It was obvious they were going to blood a few youngsters for those Tests. At 42, I wasn't going to be part of the future.'

But could you have carried on playing at the highest level? Did you still believe you could cut the mustard? 'I reckon I had another two years left in me. I was still seeing the ball well and my technique was holding up.'

What a shame. For you and the England supporters. 'It was a sad way to end,' he ruefully agreed. 'It would have been nice to…' He never elaborated but he probably didn't need to.

It set me thinking. Had he not been banned, had his form remained intact, had his body withstood another two years at the top, he would have played in the series the following summer against the Rest of the World. What a mouth-watering prospect that would have been, Graveney pitting himself against bowlers such as Procter, Peter Pollock, Sobers, Barlow, Intikhab and Gibbs. And how about comparing his style and technique with batsmen of the class of Barlow, Barry Richards, Kanhai, Graeme Pollock, Lloyd and the incomparable Sobers? I cannot help but think that the cricketing public was poorer for it.

And then, he might have gone to Australia that winter with Illingworth's team, who regained the Ashes, and – you never know – he might finally have laid to rest a few ghosts of his record against the old enemy. All ifs and buts, sadly. Tom was more concerned about what he was going to do for the rest of his life.

Whether it was a fortuitous turn of fate or not – that will become clear in the next chapter – a chance meeting during that fateful Test match at Old Trafford was to give Tom the opportunity of gainful and rewarding employment post retirement, something that had concerned him for some time.

Clem Jones was mayor of Brisbane from 1961–1975, to this day, the longest-serving mayor in Brisbane's history. A controversial and abrasive figure, he is credited with transforming the city from a backwater that had few municipal facilities to the thriving metropolis it is today. Not the least of his many achievements was to pave the city and to build an effective sewerage system. He had a reputation as a man 'who got things done'.

He was also a cricket fanatic. Tom had met him on the MCC tour of Australia in 1958/59 and they renewed their acquaintance at this

Test at Old Trafford. Jones was the unelected overlord of Queensland cricket; indeed, he ran its affairs as if it was his personal fiefdom. It so happened that he was on the lookout for a coach for the State cricket team and once he heard that Tom Graveney might be in the market for such a job, he immediately offered it to him.

Tom was sorely tempted. His Test career had come to an abrupt end. He could struggle on for a few more years at Worcestershire but that didn't appeal. He always remembered with sadness Wally Hammond playing for Gloucestershire long past his sell-by date and looking a pale shadow of his former self. Tom was determined not to cut such a sorry sight in the twilight of his career. And he had always loved Australia. But it meant moving to Brisbane lock, stock and barrel, dislocating the family and starting a new life. Would Jackie agree? They discussed it at length and eventually gave in to Jones's repeated exhortations to 'come out next winter and give it a whirl'.

They landed at Brisbane Airport in the new year of 1970 to be knocked backwards with a temperature of 100 degrees, with 100 per cent humidity. The welcome was warm and hospitable, as Tom had become accustomed to from Australians. The coaching side of the job did not faze him; he had been looking forward to it and he was keen to get stuck in. Queensland were the weakest of the states in the Sheffield Shield and it soon became evident to him that Jones – whose word was law – had employed him as a player-coach, not as a non-playing supervisor of the team, as Tom had been expecting. 'I was 42!' he exclaimed. 'Straight out of a cold and dark English winter. And they expected me to play! In those conditions! I didn't want any of that.'

But he had no choice. It seemed that you simply did not say no to the mayor. In his first match against South Australia, he scored 15, snared by Lance Gibbs – 'again!' he groaned. The second game confirmed all his worst fears. 'The mayor had his finger in all the pies,' he told me. 'He ran Queensland cricket like a mafia boss. He even prepared the wicket – badly!'

How badly soon became apparent. 'The pitch was unpredictable, to say the least. Thomson was bowling.' My eyes must have widened, for he quickly clarified himself. 'Not Jeff. He was a far better bowler. No, Froggy Thomson.' I remembered him. He had a whirlwind action, he bowled off the wrong foot, he sprayed it around like an out of control hosepipe and his career was brief. But he was distinctly rapid, people said.

'First up,' said Tom, 'he bowled me a short one, which hit me a painful blow on my forearm. After a while, I sort of recovered and faced up to the second ball. Here, I fell foul of the worst piece of bad luck that a cricketer has ever had. Froggy *never* bowled two balls in the same spot. He did now. It broke my arm.'

That was just about the only time you were ever pinned by a bowler. He agreed. 'I broke fingers. But that was fielding. No, I don't think I was ever seriously hurt by a fast bowler. It told me – as if I didn't know already – that I was too old for this lark.' He remembers walking back home to his lodgings at the end of the day, his arm in plaster. There was an old man smoking a pipe on his verandah, sitting on a chair. 'Hey, Tom!' he called out. 'Looks like yer bust yer wing!' Australians notoriously call it as they see it.

After one month, they returned home. Despite one or two misgivings, his mind was made up. He would play one more season for Worcestershire and then the family would emigrate to Australia.

That final season for Worcester must have been emotional, touring around the country and bidding farewell to all those grounds you had graced for 22 years? 'I don't know about emotional,' he chortled, 'but it was fairly alcoholic!'

You scored over a thousand runs at an average of 62.66. Wasn't the decision to retire a little premature? Now the chortles became guffaws. 'Second in the national averages to a certain G. St. A. Sobers. What a way to bow out!' Indeed. 'Ah, but look,' he said. 'See how many not outs I had.' Thirteen was the answer.

How come? 'I decided I should drop down the order. It was ridiculous Basil coming in at number five. So I swapped. He went in four and I went in five. Hence all those stars against my scores.'

That may be so but it remains a remarkable achievement nonetheless. At the age of 43, he was batting as well as ever. During the course of the season, he scored his 121st and 122nd first-class centuries, against Kent and Yorkshire respectively. His last away match was against Surrey at the Oval. He scored 50 not out and 82 not out.

Did you have a bit of a party? 'A bit of a party!' he said, 'I didn't go to bed for three days.'

How did you manage to score those runs then? 'I'm not sure. Entirely from memory, I guess.' And, as everyone knows, Tom Graveney is possessed of an uncommon memory.

And your swansong, at your beloved New Road, against Warwickshire? 'I got a few in the first innings. And Lance Gibbs, him again, got me out for 12 in the second.' Needless to say, he was cheered all the way to the wicket and all the way back. 'It was a strange feeling,' he described. 'On the one hand, it *was* very emotional. On the other hand, at home we were already packing and my mind was on Australia.'

Before we join him on the boat bound for Brisbane, let us pause for a moment and put into perspective this third and most satisfying term in the England team. The first had been from his debut in 1951 until he was jettisoned, with a few others, after the catastrophic tour of Australia in 1958/59. He was recalled in 1962 against the Pakistanis but was dropped after another disappointing tour of Australia in 1962/63. And the last, golden spell lasted from 1966 to 1969.

Now, here's an interesting fact. His overall Test average was 44.38, placing him firmly in the 'very good' category of international batsmen. But if you look at his record in that last spell, after his 39th birthday, from 1966–69, he averaged 49.30, a fraction short of the level when we start talking about the 'greats' of the game. So it was no idle boast of his when he maintained that during this period of his career, he was batting as well as he ever had.

'Tom Graveney was one of those batsmen – Graham Gooch was another – who played better the older he got.' Thus spake Alan Smith, the same A.C. Smith who was one of the selectors at the time of the Luton match. 'He had his own technique – unique, really. To play predominantly off the front foot like he did and prosper at the highest level of the game was extraordinary.'

Not only was his front-foot technique rare, his grip of the bat was out of the ordinary too – and let him not hear from you that it was unorthodox, for he will not entertain the idea of it. In fact, he believes that his technique adhered to all the tenets of orthodoxy that in recent years have been sadly neglected.

To explain what he meant, he seized an old bat that was to hand and showed me where on the handle he held it. At the top, I noted, with the top hand facing towards mid-off, more so than most. 'No one anymore seems to hold the bat the way I did,' he said, picking it up and starting to play an imaginary stroke. 'They hold it right down the bottom of the handle. My grip is right at the top – see? That way, the bat is like a pendulum. I picked it up straight behind me, not over third slip or gully, like so many players do nowadays. With this grip, it's impossible *not* to pick it up straight.' Who was I to argue?

It is misguided to assert that the beauty of his batsmanship was entirely God-given. He thought deeply about the game, ceaselessly analysing his opponents and his own responses to the challenges they posed. And, as we know, he was a relentless practiser, forever honing his technique and searching for perfection. He did have a singular talent, what his brother, Ken, called 'exceptional hand-eye coordination'. But there was a lot of work involved in order to make the fullest use of that natural talent. I lost count of the number of friends and acquaintances I talked to who told me about his dedicated practice routine.

As for the other characteristic of his batting style, the sheer elegance of his strokeplay, well…here we do have to give credit to the Almighty. Poise and gracefulness cannot be taught; you either have it or you don't. All we can do is observe and recognise it when we see it, and give thanks for having been in the presence of something special. People flocked to watch him bat, bars would empty, stands would fill, just in the hope that their day would be elevated by the beauty of how he could hit a leather ball with a lump of wood.

For those not fortunate enough ever to have seen him play let me allow the distinguished cricket writer, Neville Cardus, to paint a picture in words, 'In form and out of form, Graveney has rendered tribute to the graces of cricket…he has no equal as a complete and stylish stroke-maker.'

If you find the old wordsmith a little too poetical and idealised for your tastes, then permit me to bring to your attention the estimation of a cricket correspondent of much more recent vintage. Mike Selvey, writing in *The Guardian* in 2010, cast his mind back to 1968 when, as a callow 20-year-old playing for Surrey, he was bowling to Tom Graveney at New Road. 'The delivery, such as it was, contained no particular merit… It was lively enough in pace and not badly directed at around middle and off… Tom eased himself forward and the bat came down straight. Then, without hitting around his front pad, which had remained inside the line of the ball, he turned his top hand (not the bottom hand shovel that many use now) and caressed the ball away to the leg side. There was no crack of leather on willow, no explosion from the blade. The ball was eased with precision to the left of the fellow at mid-wicket and to the right of mid-on… Four runs then, and of what consequence to him? What, to him, were four more runs to set aside almost 48,000?'

Selvey then went on to list all the great batsmen that he had either played against or witnessed from the sidelines – Sobers, Pollock, Gavaskar, Richards, Barry and Viv, Lara, Tendulkar, Ponting, Kallis and others. 'But that late August boundary of Tom's in the twilight of his career remains the single most sublime, beautiful cricket stroke I have ever seen.'

10

Life After Cricket 1970–94

'There you are. It just goes to show that the big fella can get it up whenever he wants.'
(Tom Graveney describing to the nation, on BBC Television, Joel Garner bowling)

The shelf life of a professional sportsman is short. Sometimes brutally short. Imagine if you were a doctor, an inventor, a lawyer, a banker, an artist, an engineer, a musician, or indeed a butcher, a baker, a candlestick maker, and you were told that at the age of 35 your career was over. Overnight, you lose your source of income, your daily routine, your standing in the community, your self-worth, your *raison d'etre*, your passion most likely. If you are sensible, you might have planned for this eventuality but that is doubtful; what young man in his 20s thinks about retirement? It is a huge problem for those who have known nothing but sport in their lives, often from a very early age.

It is no different for cricketers. In fact, I would contend that it is considerably worse. It is no statistical coincidence that there is a higher incidence of suicides among cricketers than in most comparable sports. The reasons are complex and no doubt disputable but there is something in the nature of the game, its all-consuming character, that makes its termination so abruptly unwelcome. The closest parallel I can draw is the same sense of loss when members of the armed forces are made redundant. I have heard that belonging to a regiment is a bit like being part of a family and when the protective cloak of fellowship is cast off, the winds that then blow can be mighty chilly.

Cricketers too belong to a clan, except that it's not a regiment, it's a team. And cricket throws you together with your team-mates for long periods at a time. County games lasted three days (now four) and Test matches five. The season is long and unrelenting, with little time spent at home. And then there are the tours overseas in the winter, lasting months at a time. For many players, the dressing room *is* home. That is why the privacy, the sanctity, of the dressing room is so jealously guarded. For the intruder, accidental or otherwise, beware the volley of abuse as soon as he crosses the threshold.

And, like any home, there is potential for elation and despair, merriment and bad temper, camaraderie and friction, reassurance and jealousy. Cricket strips you bare emotionally and only someone who has been there and done that, a fellow pro, can fully understand the stress and the intensity within such a febrile and confined space. Some cope with it better than others. Some are ready to give up and eagerly embrace the release from the pressure. But more dread the day when the door of the dressing room finally shuts in their face.

I think we can take it as read that Tom Graveney missed first-class cricket. It had been his life for 22 years and though, with the introduction of the one-day game and the greater reliance on athletic outfielding, he could see that the writing was on the wall, you can bet your bottom dollar he wished he were 20 again. But time is a merciless mistress and he had to make provision for his family once the end of the good times was nigh. As he reflected on his long career, he accepted that he had had his disappointments but on balance he was happy that he had fulfilled his talent. He wouldn't have changed a thing.

In one sense, he believed that he was fortunate; he had a challenging and exciting coaching job to go to. Quite a few ex-pros were not so lucky. He became a Ten Pound Pom, taking advantage of the Australian government's scheme of assisted passage of only £10 for citizens of the Commonwealth. In this he was following in the exalted footsteps of Harold Larwood and Frank Tyson, though his leg breaks had not struck fear into Australian hearts as they had done. He was looking forward to his new life in Australia; his children, Becky and Tim, were beside themselves with excitement. The only fly in the ointment was that Jackie was still not well. It was hoped that a change of environment and some sunshine on her back would effect an improvement in her spirits.

The immediate problem facing Tom was the inferiority complex of the Queensland cricket team. In the Sheffield Shield, the domestic first-class competition in Australia, they had had a torrid time for several seasons. 'They were perpetual wooden spoonists,' said Tom, 'and it didn't take me long to find out why. In truth, they were not a very good side.'

But Clem Jones, the mayor of Brisbane and the driving force at the Gabba, the ground and the headquarters of the Queensland Cricket Association, was a man in a hurry. He liked to deliver quick solutions to problems and he wasn't too worried how many toes he stepped on in the process. That was why he had appointed Tom Graveney as the state cricket coach. He had gone to England to secure his man, a legend in the Test arena, *ergo* the results of the team would take an immediate turn for the better.

Tom knew as well as anyone that Rome wasn't built in a day. Addressing the deep-rooted problems of a failing team would take time; there was no instant fix. Coaching would have to start lower down the age groups and this would take years to come to fruition. He wasn't fazed by the task. He was anxious to get started and keen to start the process of rebuilding.

The first sign of trouble came with the mayor's insistence that Tom should turn out for the Shield side. Tom's luckless foray into Shield cricket the year before, when Froggy Thomson had broken his arm, cut no ice with Jones. Tom had assumed that this mishap had proved to all and sundry that he was too old to be taking on fast bowlers on hard, fast, bouncy Australian wickets. His job, he believed, was to act as a coach, manager, advisor, call it what you will, off the field and behind the scenes in the dressing room. Jones would have none of it. Tom was going to play and that was unnegotiable.

Why did you cave in and agree? Tom winced. 'Clem Jones was not a man who brooked any argument.'

Did you enjoy it? 'Well, I've always enjoyed playing cricket. But I have to admit that I had mentally switched off from playing.' He knew he wasn't up to it and no one enjoys the spotlight of public scrutiny turned on him when his powers are in decline. During the 1970/71 season, he batted in seven innings, scoring 102 runs at an average of 17. That just wasn't good enough and it depressed him. 'And I had to keep wicket!' he exclaimed.

Good God, I never knew that you donned the gloves. 'Lance Gibbs had done me yet again in the first innings but I got my own back by stumping him!'

Were you any good at it? Modestly, he screwed up his face. 'I struggled a bit down the leg side. I didn't keep regularly. I soon put a stop to that.' When I referred to the archives, I saw that Greg Chappell had scored a century in both innings, an indication that a new era was dawning in the game and that rationally, Tom Graveney ought not, at his age, to have been playing.

How about the coaching? Did you enjoy that? He said that he loved it and felt that he was getting through to the youngsters in particular during his time there. When there were no matches, he would coach, in schools and clubs throughout the state, in the mornings and evenings. 'All schools cricket was played on matting over concrete wickets,' he told me.

Pretty bouncy? He nodded.

Not much played off the front foot then? 'As you know, I was brought up on the low, slow wickets at Bristol. That's why I played off the front foot a lot. But I found myself teaching them how to play back. There aren't many Australians who are front-foot players,' he added knowingly.

Would you, do you think, have made a good coach? I mean a successful coach as a career, had the cards fallen differently for you? He thought about that and then answered, without a hint of arrogance, 'I think so – yes.'

But it was tough going. The weather was *hot*, and the humidity was draining. Becky believes that it took more out of him than he is prepared to admit. 'Coaching all those hours outside in 98 degrees.' She pulled a face. The distances were vast too. On one occasion, he travelled up to the Gold Coast, some 300 miles north, before setting out on a 1,500-mile trek inland to Mount Isa, the middle of nowhere it seemed to him.

What on earth for? He grinned. 'Teaching the kids to play cricket and the miners how to drink!' I would have thought taking on Aussies in the consumption of alcohol was a mug's game. 'They only drunk halves,' he said scornfully. 'The beers would get too hot otherwise. But I drank only pints. To refuel, of course.' It was stiflingly hot, very humid and he has always admitted to sweating profusely.

His descriptions of the inhospitable, sub-tropical climate led me to ask, almost as an afterthought, what he did in the winter. 'Winters were much more pleasant. Perfect for playing cricket, actually. So, although all first-class cricket in Australia is played in the summer, in the Brisbane winter cricket still went on in the clubs and schools.' That solved the problem of winter employment, always a worry for cricket coaches. That is, before the age of well-lit, artificial wickets, practice facilities, vast training centres and indoor cricket.

Tim put me right, however. 'He wasn't well paid, you know. We were always hard up.' When I put this to his father, he agreed. 'Money was always a problem. I got a job parking cars in a garage during the afternoons.' Coaching – outdoors – all morning, working in a garage in the afternoons and coaching again in the evenings. No wonder Becky thought it put a strain on her father. But he is adamant that he enjoyed it, despite the long hours.

And what about the children? I was curious to find out how they got on Down Under. It seems that Becky had the time of her life. She was of an age when the social side of the game was beginning to exert as much of a draw as the playing of it (remember her smooth bowling action that had elicited much admiration from onlookers as she played with the boys in front of the pavilion at New Road). She went to secretarial college and got a job as secretary to the chief executive of the Greyhound Racing Club at the Test cricket ground, the Gabba.

The fact that their offices were at the Gabba and that the actual racing track ran round the perimeter of the cricket pitch suited her down to the ground. 'We were celebrities and I met so many people,' she said. 'The Queensland cricketers looked after me exceptionally well.' Not the least aspect of her happiness in her new environment was that the family were together at last. 'Up until our time in Queensland,' she said, 'we had never spent more than two months all together without Dad disappearing on some tour or other.'

Tim swiftly adapted to his new environment, the way children can. It helped that he enjoyed the sporting and outdoor environment in which Australians grew up. 'The school he went to,' said his father, 'was a very good one.' It was the Church of England Grammar School, twinned with Geelong Grammar. 'The headmaster was the brother of Geoffrey Fisher, the Archbishop of Canterbury.'

So your spiritual needs were taken care of then, Tim? Like his father, Tim doesn't rise to the bait if he's not of a mind to do so. He too, it seemed, loved it in Australia.

Their social life was vibrant. There was, of course, the network of cricketing friends and acquaintances that Tom had built up throughout his four tours to the country. Ray Lindwall was particularly kind to them. 'He had a flourishing florist business that he set up when he retired from cricket. We spent Christmas with his family. He treated me like a son.' Ron Archer and Tony Dell were two more good friends. In fact, Tom claims, all the old Australian players were good to him.

Becky had numerous admirers amongst the Queensland team and elsewhere through her job at the greyhound club and Tim was soon speaking with an Aussie accent. All was rosy, you might imagine, in their new garden.

But it wasn't. Jackie had not really perked up in the different surroundings and now had what can only be described as a total and catastrophic emotional breakdown. She spent eight weeks in hospital. 'She nearly died,' Tom sombrely told me. 'It was a worrying time for all of us.'

Becky believes, looking back on the whole experience, that her mother never settled in her new country. 'It was difficult for Dad. He felt guilty, as if his long absences from home had caused all this trouble.'

As gently as I could, I raised this hypothesis with Tom and asked whether, even subconsciously, there could be some truth in it. He paused, conflicting emotions crossing his face. At that moment, one of Jackie's carers knocked on the door. 'Mr Graveney,' she said, 'your wife is calling for you.' Immediately, Tom raised himself from his supine position and asked for his Zimmer frame. 'Still together,' he said jovially, as he picked up speed down the corridor. 'Sixty years this month. Not many can say that, eh?'

Prolonged absences from home throughout his playing career there may have been. 'But that's the life of a cricketer,' he shrugged, as if to say there was nothing he could have done about that. And no one can deny that he has remained loyal and dutiful to his wife through good times and bad.

A source of increasing frustration and tension for Tom was the interference by Mayor Jones in the day-to-day conduct of his job. Jones was passionate about Queensland cricket and found their perennial lack of success difficult to stomach. 'But we were a poor side,' Tom said again. 'Just look at the team we had.'

I had. Victoria could boast Lawry, Stackpole, Redpath, Sheahan and Walker. New South Wales had Walters, O'Keeffe and Gleeson. For Western Australia there was Inverarity, Marsh, Massie, McKenzie and Lillee. And South Australia could field the two Chappells, Mallett and Jenner. There were only two names in the Queensland side that I recognised – Sam Trimble and Rusi Surti.

'That's right. Trimble went on one tour of the Caribbean but never played in a Test. Surti, an Indian, was our overseas player. Good chap. I liked him. He was a bit of a trailblazer, you know.' No, I didn't, so I asked why. 'At that time, Australia operated a kind of apartheid, a white-only immigration policy. So he was a sort of figurehead for the coloureds in the country.' That raised the knotty problem of Australia's equivocal relationship with its indigenous population, the Aborigines.

Were there many Aborigines in Queensland? 'Oh many.'

Did you have anything to do with them as far as coaching went? He shook his head. He had more pressing concerns than historically complex race relations.

One way that a disparity between two cricket sides can be evened up is to doctor the wicket. This of course has been going on since time immemorial and is what provides the endless variety and fascination of the game. India traditionally provide low, slow, dusty wickets to suit their spinners. England is better known for the green, seaming wickets favoured by a posse of medium- and fast-medium-pacers. In the West Indies, you would encounter (or that used to be the case) hard, bouncy wickets ideal for their fast bowlers. It would be a dull game if all wickets were uniform and without character.

The preparation of wickets to suit the home team is a perfectly legitimate stratagem; in the end, true class will prevail and the best cricketers have to master all different conditions. Tom Graveney scored five of his 11 Test hundreds battling the pace of the West Indies but his finest innings, as he has told us, was against the Indian spinners on a wickedly turning wicket.

But there is a world of difference between a wicket that traditionally favours the home side and a *bad* wicket. There might occasionally be a wicket that has fallen foul of accident or freakish weather conditions; normally, however, there is little or no excuse for preparing a wicket that is substandard. It is the result either of incompetence or worse still, sharp practice, the rationale being that poor playing conditions make the game more of a lottery. And you have a better chance of winning a lottery than competing with a better side.

Tom knew that Mayor Jones took a close interest in the preparation of the Brisbane wicket. In fact he considered himself to be an expert groundsman (or curator, as it is known in Australia) and later actually took control of a Test match wicket at the Gabba. Tom believed that his influence over the official groundsman at the Gabba was inappropriate and unprofessional and resulted in a succession of poorly prepared wickets.

Tom was trying to *raise* the standard of cricket in the state. How could he do that if the players had to perform on third-rate pitches? He stopped short of intimating that the wickets had been deliberately sabotaged but he certainly distrusted the mayor's motives. Becky agreed. As a secretary for the Greyhound Racing Club, on the actual

Gabba, she often had to stay on in the evenings. 'There was a rumour going the rounds that Jones used to creep out under the cover of darkness to put water on the wicket.'

There were other irritating incidences where the mayor 'stuck his oar in' and slowly, Tom's patience began to wear thin. 'I've always considered myself to be easy-going and tolerant, keen to avoid confrontation,' he said. And as he did so, I was reminded of the words of his brother, Ken, 'Tom was never a rebel. I was!' But every man has his breaking point. Tom was getting more and more exasperated by Jones's meddling and it was only a matter of time before the dam burst.

One day, he was busy picking a colts side, together with their coaches. There were three secretaries in the room, clacking and hammering away at their typewriters, so loudly that he could scarcely hear himself think. He suggested they repair to somewhere a little quieter. The only room they could find was the mayor's office. Tom settled himself in the chair and the selection meeting resumed.

He was suddenly aware of the door opening. Then it was slammed violently shut. It was Mayor Jones. In loud and intemperate language, he berated Tom for having the audacity to use his office. 'Something in me snapped,' Tom said. 'I shouted back and a fearful slanging match ensued. I'd had enough and I didn't care what happened.' He resigned on the spot.

The cricket was becoming harder and harder, which is no surprise for a man who was now 45. The coaching in the heat was draining. And the interference of the mayor at every step of the way was becoming intolerable. He was not sad to go. As he recalled those events some 40 years previously, a roguish chuckle rolled out. 'For some reason,' he said, 'Tim was there. He was sitting in the corridor outside while we were having this selection meeting and must have heard the exchange. Later, he said to me, "Dad, I've never heard you use language like that before." Well, I was angry.'

Having resigned, presumably you had to find a new job? He gave a cynical laugh. 'There weren't any. The mayor soon saw to that.'

What about in the other states? He shook his head. 'It was halfway through the season. All the posts had been filled.'

So what did you do? 'We packed up and came home. All the furniture and cases went back on the boat. We travelled by air. And I can tell you it cost more than £10!'

Jackie was not displeased to be making the return journey but the children were mortified. Tim had settled down and loved the lifestyle. Becky had been forging a thriving and energetic social scene for herself as well as enjoying the independence that a paid job gave her. She dug her heels in and threatened to stay.

'Between you and me,' Tom told me, 'I think she was in the grip of a love affair. I wasn't – how shall I say – completely in favour of the person concerned, so I put my foot down.' I checked with Becky. 'Well, I was a teenager. It was difficult for me, all this moving and changing. Dad said I was only 18. If I was still keen to come back to Australia when I was 21, then he would pay for me to go.'

And did you? She shook her head. With a little smile, it has to be said.

The journey home must have been a bit depressing? 'Miserable. When we were six hours into the flight, the captain came on and told us we could say goodbye to Australia.' The look on his face hinted at the wretchedness he must have felt. Becky thought that six hours in an aeroplane meant that they were nearly home! It was only when they were nearly home that the gloom lifted.

I tried to probe a little deeper here. Looking back on it, what perspective could he put on his Australian adventure? 'I felt a failure,' he said despondently. 'I thought I'd let everyone down. Including myself.' I was dumbfounded. There had been disappointments in his life but there had always been outside influences to mitigate the regrets. And, to the detached observer, it could be claimed that his career had been one of almost uninterrupted success.

He was, after all, revered the length and breadth of the cricketing world for his bewitching batsmanship and his modest demeanour. It seemed to me he was everyone's favourite cricketer. And here he was, confessing to sentiments of *failure*. It wasn't put on either. It was clear that he genuinely felt diminished by the experience.

Back in England, living in a converted garage of the George Inn in Winchcombe, owned by Jackie's sister and her husband, with no job and few prospects, he could perhaps have been forgiven for having a few regrets. Moreover, jobs in the world of cricket – and cricket was the only world he knew – were conspicuous by their absence in the middle of winter.

He put out a few feelers but they all came to nothing. How depressing for such a distinguished servant of the game that he should have been in such dire straits. Once again, I am reminded of the riches on offer for the modern player in comparison, but that was the way it was then for many cricketers. He was indebted – the whole family was – to the kindness of his brother and sister-in-law. At least they had a roof over their heads. Nevertheless, he knew that this was a state of affairs that could not endure for long. He would have to get a job, suitable or not – anything.

Out of the blue came a telephone call from an old friend and compatriot. Trevor Bailey knew of a position as manager of a recently opened squash and leisure club in Thorpe Bay, near Westcliff-on-Sea. Was he interested? It wasn't ideal but there was little alternative and Tom accepted. So, once more, the family was on the move.

Essex was not his natural hunting ground; he had played once at Westcliff and once at nearby Southend and that was about it. It felt a long way from family and friends in the West Country. Becky got a job with British Air Ferries, which operated out of the airport at Southend. Tim went to Westcliff High School, which was as different from Brisbane Grammar School as you could get. He was a tanned and fair-headed youth, who was used to the outdoor life. He had an Aussie accent, which he assured me he lost pretty rapidly, and he felt as isolated and as out of place as a vicar in a lap-dancing club. There were no lap dancers at the Courtlands Squash and Country Club but there were plenty of celebrities in evidence.

Becky remembers Roy Castle performing there and Tom recalls that the British number one squash player practised on the courts. Tom was no mean squash player himself and soon involved himself in the playing side of the club. Once, on court, he chased down a drop shot only to hear a crack accompanied by a searing pain in his ankle from a blow he believed came from his opponent's racket. He wheeled round but no one was anywhere near him. He hadn't been hit. He'd snapped his Achilles tendon. Six weeks in plaster but he still had to clear up and lock up at midnight every night. Jackie was furious with him. He should not, in her opinion, have been playing squash against much younger men at his age.

No longer able to compete on the squash court, he soon found the job as manager of the club wearisome and humdrum. 'Dad wasn't happy there,' Becky told me. 'He wasn't suited to it at all. He stuck it out for as long as he could but it was no life for him.'

Tom didn't dwell long on his memory of his time in Essex. 'I felt as if I lost three years of my life there,' he said gloomily. At length, he could stand it no longer and he resigned to take up a job as a travelling salesman, specialising in sporting goods. 'I'm no salesman,' he admitted, 'but people were very kind to me and I did all right.'

It is Tim's contention that he did better than 'all right'. 'Dad got Hi Tech the Lillywhite contract – a huge deal. But they never rewarded him. Always the way with Dad. Because he's so nice, people have taken advantage of him.' Tom admits that he never was much of a businessman but there was little else for him to do. 'What do you think is the worst part of being a salesman?' he asked me. I had no idea. 'Going into that first shop of the morning.'

Over a pint or two with an old friend, Frank Twiselton, the managing director of Whitbread in Cheltenham, he laid bare his misery with his life on the road with nothing but a suitcase to keep him company. How about taking over a pub, Twiselton suggested; in fact, he had the very one in mind. 'In a sense, you could say that running a pub was in the blood,' Tom said. 'We'd been living in one, after all, and we knew the ropes from Jackie's sister and her husband.'

Strings were pulled and the Graveneys leapfrogged over numerous people in the queue for the tenancy of the Royal Oak in Prestbury, just outside Cheltenham. 'And so began ten years of early mornings!'

Early mornings? Cricketers don't do early mornings. 'This one had to. Six-thirty, winter and summer.'

He felt that he had come home and he was much the happier for it. Mind you, there was much work to be done before the old coaching inn was made fit for business. 'It took three months to get it ready,' he said. 'It had been a rough old place and the lounge bar wasn't very...*loungy.*'

Eventually, they were ready and had planned a party for the opening night. 'And Bill Alley turned up a day early!' Alley was a former Somerset player and was now a first-class umpire.

Did you get your own back on the umpiring fraternity and send him on his way? 'No,' laughed Tom. 'We had two parties!'

It was hard going. He did everything himself, except cleaning the pipes, which was done by the brewers. Becky was on hand, a constant help and support. 'She came for six months,' Tom said, 'just to get us started, and she stayed for six years!' She told me that they all had their jobs; Tom ran the bar, Jackie supervised the cooking and Becky, being the personable girl she is, was front of house. 'It was a lovely little pub,' she said, 'Dad ran it well.'

At the back was a scrumpy bar – 'strong stuff' – populated by the rough and ready locals. 'They made sure there wasn't any trouble,' she said. 'They were very loyal and looked after us.' There was a skittle alley, which boasted seven teams. Matches took place every evening Monday to Thursday. 'And at the weekends, we would have parties. My God, we had some riotous times,' she added with a grin. During the summer, Becky would sunbathe on the grass outside the alley. 'I got a lot of drinks,' she laughed, 'as you can imagine.' I could.

The main bar, at the front, gradually became more decorated by memorabilia and old photos from his playing days. The pub became popular, a favourite watering hole of old friends and cricketers, past and present, passing through. As it was situated close to the Cheltenham Racecourse, it became very busy whenever there was a meeting on. 'Gold Cup week was manic,' remembers Becky. 'People were queuing up to get a drink, two or three deep at the bar. We made more money in those three days than we did in three months!'

And what of Tim? Tom had managed to secure for him a place as a day boy at Dean Close School in Cheltenham. 'Of course, Dad couldn't afford the fees,' he said. 'So to offset some of them, he did some coaching at the school.' During the school holidays, or whenever he was at home, his sister press-ganged him to help in the bar, which pleased him not at all. 'He became head boy,' Tom told me proudly. 'He was quite a useful off-spinner too. He took 42 wickets in one season up until the end of term. He played a lot of cricket. Still does. That's why he has such a bulging address book.'

The family soon adapted to village life and enjoyed it. Tom was now a different man. It was hard work but he loved the social side of what he was doing. The New Year's Eve parties were legendary, I've been told. Becky remembers her father dressed as Friar Tuck and her mother as a singing nun. Tom's friend, David Courtney, was a regular customer and brought a lot of friends and business associates – to say nothing of huge dollops of anarchic humour – to drink there. At one of these parties, he came in dressed as a schoolboy, even down to the untied laces and dirty knees. 'He had a satchel with him,' said Becky. 'Eventually we wanted to know what was in it. It was packed with condoms!'

I get the sense that there was a lot of laughter at the Royal Oak. It was probably for Tom an environment that most resembled the banter and high jinks that went on in a cricket dressing room. Whatever, he felt very much at home. 'But I couldn't have done it without Becky,' Tom was at pains to point out to me. 'She's a natural worker. She likes things done *properly*.'

Word soon spread that the Royal Oak was the pub to go to and it became a focal point for the cricketing and racing fraternity. One day, Harold Larwood, together with his mate and partner as opening bowler for England in the 1930s, Bill Voce, paid a visit. 'But I wasn't there,' groaned our publican, 'I was at a family wedding.' It also attracted the boffins from the nearby GCHQ for their lunch. Although the government communications and intelligence gathering centre was highly secret – indeed, it didn't officially exist – Becky was not fooled. 'We called it the Funny Farm, because they were an odd bunch, sitting there in the corner. If you asked them what they did, they just changed the subject.'

A measure of the success of the business was the award of Gloucestershire's Pub of the Year during the celebrations for the Queen's Silver Jubilee in 1977.

Did you make any money out of the pub? 'I made plenty of money. But most of it went to Whitbread. We were only tenants, you see.'

Tom was coming to rely on his daughter more and more. In fact, she was indispensable. He felt guilty because she was neglecting her own career and much as she enjoyed being at the centre of things, helping to run a pub had not really been in the script. Eventually, Ken, Tom's brother, waded in and told her a few home truths. He invited her to lunch at the Ladbroke Dragonora Hotel in Bristol, where he now lived; he was on the board for Sutcliffe Catering. Also invited was the hotel manager. Having introduced the two of them, Ken left it to them to talk about a job. The upshot of it was that she left the pub and moved down to Bristol and Tom had to fend for himself.

But you had Jackie by your side? There was a pause. He shook his head. 'In truth, Jackie did very little.' The family later told me that her health had taken another turn for the worse and that she was in and out of hospital. But as usual with Tom, he was anxious to deflect any awkwardness with an amusing story. 'She came back from shopping one afternoon. I was serving some Indian gentlemen in the bar. She erupted through the door, flung open the curtains and announced in a loud voice, "Heavens, it's dark in here!" There was an embarrassed hush for a moment or two. Then the Indian gentlemen burst out laughing and we all joined in.'

It was at this period in Tom's life that David Courtney gave him a helping hand, rather more so than drinking the pub dry. David was a director of 3D Sports, a cricket equipment and supplies company based in Cheltenham. Together with Brinton Carpets in Kidderminster, they had developed a new artificial wicket. He asked Tom to join the firm, knowing that his innumerable contacts within the cricket world would be of enormous benefit. Tom was only too happy to accept. He employed a manager to look after the pub while he toured the country selling artificial wickets. 'The two jobs gelled well,' he said. 'You know, a lot of people expected me to fall flat on my face. It was a source of some satisfaction that I proved them wrong.'

Most ex-professional cricketers miss the cricket, if not the actual game then certainly the sense of being fit and at the peak of their physical condition, to say nothing of the badinage and camaraderie of the dressing room. Tom Graveney was no different. He could reminisce behind the bar about his time in the game but down in deepest rural Gloucestershire, he was far removed from contemporary events in the Test match arena.

The World Cup of 1979 provided him with an unforeseen opportunity to reacquaint himself closely with the game he had left nine years earlier, something he had dearly loved and missed more than he was prepared to admit. The inaugural World Cup in 1975 had been a resounding success and it was expected that the second tournament four years later would provide equal entertainment. There were eight countries taking part and the BBC had undertaken to report on all the matches. They were in desperate need of experienced commentators, ex-players who knew the game.

It so happened that not long previously, Christopher Martin-Jenkins, the broadcaster and journalist, had invited Tom up to Regent Street in order to interview him for a piece that would be broadcast on the radio during an interval of one of the World Cup matches. 'I talked for one and a half hours,' Tom said. 'It was no great hardship.' Afterwards, they repaired for a drink to a pub over the road.

There, Peter Baxter, the producer of *Test Match Special*, who had been listening to the interview, told him that he had been very impressed with Tom's easy, conversational style and his razor-sharp recall of events and incidents. 'He was so good,' said Baxter, 'that we immediately took him on.' Needless to say, Tom was delighted and entered the broadcasting fray with great gusto.

'He fitted in very well and of course everyone loved him,' said Baxter. 'He had such an amazing memory about every game he'd played in. He wasn't very critical of the modern player – he was much too nice for that. By contrast, for example, Trevor Bailey was much more controversial in his opinions.' Tom did not stay with the TMS team for long; Baxter suggested that he might like to try television and a transfer was effected.

Before we leave the radio, Tom, tell me a little bit about John Arlott, the legend of the airwaves. Tom chuckled. 'Well, you always knew when he was coming. His battered briefcase used to tinkle with the bottles inside. Actually, he didn't do much behind the microphone after tea.'

Arlott was a renowned wine connoisseur and a good bottle of claret seemed to lubricate his poetical style as much as his deep, Hampshire vowels. He wrote once of his broadcasting career, 'Trevor Bailey and I were largely responsible for a fresh commentary noise, the popping of Champagne corks.'

The transfer from radio to television is not as easy as you might expect and not everyone, including much more experienced broadcasters than Tom, manages it successfully. What is that sardonic cliché – 'he has a perfect face for radio'? Nick Hunter, the boss of BBC TV cricket at the time, was pleased and surprised in equal measure at the adroitness with which Tom made the switch. 'It soon became clear that Tom was a natural in front of the camera,' he said. 'He was like he was in the middle, relaxed yet positive.'

Tom never gave the whole business of 'image' and 'screen persona' any thought; he just concentrated on being himself and talking about the cricket. 'I acted normally and chatted easily,' he said, 'and they seemed to be pleased with me.' Initially, he was tried out on a few one-day matches but he soon became part of the team.

And who was in the team? 'Peter West was the anchorman. He was a lovely fellow, so supportive and kind.'

And the others? 'Richie Benaud, Jim Laker, Tony Lewis – all friends from my playing days and terribly helpful to the newcomer.' As if you would need verification of the obvious, Hunter confirmed Tom's popularity with his co-commentators in the box: 'He got on well with everyone. He was a little tentative at first but he soon settled down and became a much valued member of the team.' Tom laughed when I reported this to him. 'It might have had something to do with the crate of white wine that was sent up every day.'

One thing he learnt quickly was impartiality. He took his lead from Benaud. 'Richie was as honest as the day is long. He was commentating on a side that wasn't his but he was always fair.' And then Tom screwed up his face. 'Well, except when we were playing Australia and then he was just the *tiniest, weeniest* bit biased.' Laker was as straight as a die and told it exactly as he saw it. Lewis spoke well, with a close knowledge of the game while West held it all together with great panache.

I got the impression that Tom felt privileged to be part of the team and pleased that his bosses seemed satisfied with his contributions. He was especially gratified to get a letter from Peter Alliss, the doyen of golfing commentators. 'Well done,' it said, 'you've cracked it.' They all received letters from viewers, most of them supportive and positive with the odd one lacerating in its criticism. It is a fact of life that those in the public eye receive nasty letters, always anonymous.

The best way to cope is to ignore them. But one greatly amused Tom and the rest of the team. It was simply addressed to 'Tom Graveney, Cricketer'. Somehow it found its way to Lord's on the very day of a Test match. It was sent upstairs to the BBC commentary box and handed to Tom. Inside, the terse message was, 'If this letter reaches you, the Post Office must have a higher opinion of you than I do.' Most people would have screwed it up and chucked it into the wastepaper basket. But not Tom. He kept it and produced it as the opening gambit of many of his after-dinner speeches. 'It usually did the trick,' he said. 'People found it very funny.'

How would you describe your style with the microphone? Did it differ in any way from your colleagues? He gave the question some thought but came up with nothing startling or controversial. 'I just tried to be myself,' he insisted. 'You can't be anything else – it never works.'

Nick Hunter, his producer, confirmed this. 'Tom didn't want to be negative about the modern players. He wasn't always carping on about how it was so much better in his day. They were fellow players, professionals like him, and he was loath to criticise.'

Peter Baxter offered an interesting and pertinent view on this very point. 'Tom's very "niceness" probably told against him in the end. Times were changing and a more contentious style seemed to be coming into vogue. Tom wasn't like that. Tom was just…well, Tom.'

So, what about the modern breed of commentators? What do you think of them? Yet again, Tom was reluctant to be drawn, as if criticism would sound like disloyalty. He would only say that they 'talk a bit too much'. Once more, he took his lead from Benaud, who believed there is no need to describe in great detail what the viewer can see perfectly well for himself. 'Let's face it,' said Tom, '25 per cent of the viewers do not have a great idea of what's really going on. So they might become bored by all the technical analysis and all these gizmos and toys and might be tempted to switch off the sound. Just let them watch and enjoy the game!'

There was perhaps the merest hint of disapproval at the 'characters' that are wheeled in to jazz up the broadcast. 'It's not a cabaret act,' he said archly. But then he swiftly sought to reassure me that his contemporaries were far from being devoid of a sense of humour. He remembers very well a match at Edgbaston when Mike Brearley, the England captain, was facing the giant West Indian fast bowler, Joel Garner, at 6ft 7in the tallest bowler around. Nothing much was happening. The wicket had gone dead and Brearley was making his way relatively serenely to his fifty. Suddenly, out of the blue, Garner sent one steepling past Brearley's nose. Tom was commentating at the time. 'There you are,' he declared to the nation. 'It just goes to show that the big fella can get it up whenever he wants.'

Behind him, in the box, mirth was with difficulty suppressed but he could hear the wheezes and snorts as everyone tried to keep a lid on the mayhem that threatened to break out. Beside him, his co-commentator, Tony Lewis, had his face buried in his handkerchief, unable to speak for several balls. It was a moment not unlike the famous 'leg over' incident with Brian Johnson that had the country in stitches, recently voted as the most memorable moment in radio history. This incident did not gain the same notoriety but it just goes to show that fun could be had in the commentary box without anyone being expected to put on a 'performance'.

He found the atmosphere in the box surprisingly relaxed yet everyone knew his job and performed it punctiliously. The 'batting order', as he called it, was pinned up on the board so you knew when you were 'on'. A commentator would do 20-minute slots throughout the day.

What did you do when you weren't on air? 'We just sat around, drinking the very nice white wine, and concentrated on the cricket.'

The relaxed yet professional tone was deliberately set by Nick Hunter. 'I would give them the basics,' he told me, 'and then I just let them get on with it. Too many rules can be intimidating. And the viewers seemed to like it. We got a lot of favourable feedback.' He was full of praise for Tom's contribution to the success of the programmes. For his part, Tom was only too happy to take his lead from the experienced media people around him.

And what differences in the game did you see from the days when you were out there in the middle? He gave me the look of ages. 'The game doesn't change much. The basics remain the same no matter what era you play in.'

Yes, but certain things have changed. Helmets, for example. Would you have worn one? 'Personally, I would have found them extremely uncomfortable. I sweated a lot when batting. It would have been like a sauna in there. In any case, I never thought about getting hit. I never thought I *would* get hit.'

So why do we hear so often these days the clang of ball on helmet? His answer was succinct. 'They take their eye off the ball.' With further prompting, he did accept that certain things had changed, some for the good but not all. The front foot law, which stopped bowlers dragging and delivering the ball from 19 yards, would have made a huge difference facing Lindwall and Miller. The restriction of the number of fielders to two behind square on the leg side was another significant change.

'When Cliff Gladwin was bowling – you know, those big in-swingers – there would be three catchers in your back pocket. Now you rarely see anyone fielding at backward short leg. My goodness,' he cried, suddenly animated, 'I would have scored another thousand runs without those short legs! I used to get out caught round the corner quite a lot.'

And then he made comment on the armour they all wear now when fielding at short leg. The sole protection that close-in fielders wore – and that was only sometimes – was a box. He mentioned two of his Worcestershire team-mates, Ron Headley and Dick Richardson, as arch exponents of the art and skill of close catching. Peter Sainsbury of Hampshire was another. 'And something else, they never have a third man now. So many runs go down there. We *always* had a third man.'

Had there been discernible improvement in fielding? 'Well, the best fielders in my day, like Colin Bland, Neil Harvey and our own Jim Standen, the West Ham goalkeeper, would have been outstanding in any era.'

But there were one or two carthorses around, weren't there? He laughed. 'Oh, each team had one. Bomber Wells with me at Gloucester. "Where's the ball gone?" he would cry, looking around desperately.'

Back to the commentating. *Did you socialise with the players much?* 'After the broadcast had finished and we'd packed up, there would always be the sponsor's tent to go to for a few drinks and a chat. Players, wives, umpires, media people – everyone mixed easily. They don't seem to do that anymore.' You could tell by the tone of his voice that he believed the loss of this aspect of the game, one that he loved and made the most of, was a regrettable development. Scuttling off home without having a beer with the opposition – the idea was unthinkable. And as for ice baths and isotonic drinks…well, I didn't dare broach that subject with him.

Who looked after the pub when you were away? 'I employed a manager.'

Dare I ask what sort of money did the BBC pay you? 'I think it was £150 a Test.' I raised an inquisitive eyebrow. 'Not a fortune but very welcome nonetheless.'

So money was a little less tight now? His son, Tim, gave a hollow laugh when he heard this.' We always seemed to be short of money. It cost us a fortune when Dad was away. You'd be amazed how big the slates got whenever he wasn't there. When the cat's away…'

Nonetheless, daughter Becky took the view that it was good for him to get away from the pub and their mother's travails with her health. In any event, it wasn't the money that was particularly important to him. Cricket was in his blood and he hadn't realised how much he had missed it since his retirement. And there was no better way to reacquaint himself with the game at the highest level than from the commentary box.

This passion has not dimmed over the years. In his mid-80s and terribly frail now, he still managed to make an appearance in the committee tent during Cheltenham week. Once, at the completion of our weekly chat, he suggested we turn on the television to see how the Test match was going – England v West Indies at Lord's.

Anderson was bowling, Edwards was the batsman. Anderson bowled a beauty, swinging in late and catching Edwards low down the pad on the back foot. 'That's out!' we both cried in unison. I had leapt out of my seat. I would like to say that Tom did likewise, but he would have done had he been any younger. 'Hitting leg stump, halfway up,' Tom announced authoritatively. No need for Hawkcyc when you have an experienced commentator by your side. And sure enough, Hawkeye confirmed the great man's opinion. No, Tom's love of cricket burns as fiercely now as it did in those Test matches with his brother outside the back gate in Newcastle.

He worked for the BBC for 14 years. The end, when it came, was no less a sadness than when he finished playing cricket. It is a fact of life, unwelcome no doubt, that each of us reaches our sell-by date at some time, whatever our job or calling. Fashions change, technology moves remorselessly forward, a new generation of young thrusters is anxious to make a mark, or perhaps we have got a little tired, a little stale, a little complacent. Whatever the reasons for Tom's removal from the team, he was never told.

'All that happened was that I didn't get the usual letter at the beginning of the season. After a while, I had to draw the inevitable conclusion.' Large organisations are notoriously bad at sympathetic personnel management and I doubt that the BBC were much better or worse than others in this regard. 'It was totally ironic too,' said Becky. 'He had been approached by Sky not long before and he had turned them down saying that he was a dyed in the wool BBC man.'

Tom made the observation that clearly the new team was going to have a Warwickshire hue about it, as Jack Bannister and Bob Willis – Warwickshire men both – had been drafted in but it is difficult to unearth any evidence of a palace coup. Perhaps Tom's time was up and that was the long and the short of it. Still, a letter of thanks for services rendered would have been nice. A better way to remember his long stint at the microphone would be this comment from his producer. 'Tom gave me a book,' said Hunter, 'and inside the front cover he'd written these words, "Thank you for helping me to enjoy my cricket again".'

In the meantime, the Royal Oak continued to flourish. Ten years after he had taken possession of it, ten years of success and good times but ten years of unflagging hard work too, it was time to take stock. Not of the casks and crisps but of his future. The toil was relentless, the responsibility worrisome, especially so after his linchpin, his daughter, moved on and he wasn't getting any younger.

As it happened, the landlords, Whitbread, had had their greedy eyes on the establishment for a while now. Tom had turned it into a bit of a cash cow and they wanted it back. However, Tom was the tenant and could not be simply ousted; a business agreement had to be brokered. Accordingly, an offer was made and, in truth, it had come at the right time. He had enjoyed the challenge of taking over a failing pub and making such a success of it but, my goodness, it had been 'bloody hard work'.

He accepted the offer and his time as a publican came to an end. Naturally, none of the locals and regulars wanted him to go and made strenuous representations to him to change his mind. But he was not for turning.

Would it be impertinent of me to ask how much Whitbread offered to buy you out? 'Ten grand,' he answered without hesitation. 'It was a good price and it kept the wolves from the door for a while.' He continued to work for his great friend, David Courtney, with 3D Sports and geared himself for a life on the road selling artificial wickets. At least it did not mean a 6.30am start every day. And it was probably no bad thing that Jackie was moved from the orbit of a pub and irregular hours.

I guess you clocked up thousands of miles? 'Not much different from being a professional cricketer, if you think about it.'

Ah, but you were no longer a young man. The routine must have grown a bit tedious after a while. Becky sought to put me right. She encouraged me to ask him about all the overseas cricket tours he was involved in at this time. 'Oh, I did about 17 of them,' he announced blithely. 'And terrific fun they were too.' Sometimes these tours were organised for cricket lovers following the national team abroad;

sometimes they were for club cricketers who wanted to experience playing in foreign climes. Tom's job was to meet and greet, keep the troops happy en route and in situ and in general to smooth the path with his affable company and his myriad contacts.

Bit of a sinecure then? 'Certainly not,' he protested, 'I had to organise deck games and…and quizzes…and…' Then he had the good grace to laugh. 'Anyway, someone had to do it. Several were on the *Canberra*. They all loved their cricket and they were very easy to manage.'

Did Jackie go too? He nodded. 'Yes, of course. Becky too, once or twice. I remember one tour with 90 cricketers and the two of them were the only women. They had a great time.'

You must have enjoyed those tours. He smiled, a little wistfully.

11

Mr President 1994–2006

'Oops, another one down!'
**(The president of MCC, Tom Graveney, drops his notes
while making a speech at the opening of the newly
refurbished Lord's pavilion)**

Player, publican, pundit, president… The progression is as straightforward as the alliteration. I had a friend who became the president of numerous cricket clubs and I remember asking him once what exactly were his duties. 'Oh, presidents are useless really,' he nonchalantly answered. 'They rally round, smile nicely and make the odd donation.'

There is no doubt that, as a president of a cricket club – and he was president of a few – Tom Graveney fitted the bill on all three counts. He is the first to rally round and help out, he has a nice smile and he is as generous as the day is long. But I beg to differ from my friend's assessment of the qualities needed to play the role effectively. There must have been good reason why so many clubs beat a path to their door.

First, you would expect that a president had stature and eminence in the game. Graveney is as well known and well regarded as anyone to set foot on a cricket ground. In fact, you would be hard pressed to name any ex-cricketer who is as dearly loved as he is. You would also hope that your president had useful contacts and friends in high places. Graveney had spent a lifetime in the game and had made it his business to remain on friendly terms with countless people in every cricketing nation on earth.

And then you would expect your man to be able to deliver a few words, often off the cuff, pitching a welcome or a thank you just at the appropriate level. Graveney can make a pretty speech as well as anyone. And finally, your figurehead should be able to climb down from the high table to mix freely with the hoi polloi. Graveney is the least pompous of men and loves nothing more than chatting about the game to gatemen or royalty; it makes no difference to him.

All of which makes the decision to ask Tom to become president of Worcestershire CCC an obvious and logical one. To find out how the committee at the club came to their judgement, I solicited the perspective of Mike Vockins, who was secretary at the time. Nowadays, the position would be known as 'chief executive'. Mike was quite happy with 'secretary'; everyone knew that he ran the club, cheerfully and efficiently, and he had no airs and graces.

'We had had a succession of local worthies as presidents,' he said, 'who were not well known on the public stage. We changed that when the Duke of Westminster was asked to do it from 1984–85. But he was a busy man and unable to attend many matches. It was he who suggested that we ask *names* in the cricket world.'

The appointment of Don Kenyon, a former captain and a legend of Worcestershire, proved to be a resounding success. He was followed by George Chesterton, one of those schoolmaster-cricketers, who played for the club in the 1950s as an amateur. He too was a popular choice. 'Both these men, in their separate ways,' said Vockins, 'had set the bar very high. Who were we to choose next?' The answer was staring them in the face. 'I was astonished when they asked me,' said Tom.

Who informed you that you were their choice? 'George. He was president and said that I would make a worthy successor. Whether I was or not, it's up to others to judge but I tried my best.'

There was never any doubt that he would be a success. Certainly not in the mind of Mike Vockins. 'Tom was superb,' he told me. 'He was so gifted, so relaxed and genial with everyone. The normal period of office was three years. Tom did it for five. I think that tells you all you need to know about our opinion of him.'

The role fitted him like a glove. A president of a cricket club is a figurehead rather than a mover and shaker but it is not all pouring the gin and tonic for guests in the committee room.

Influence can be exerted tactfully and judiciously, as Vockins explained. 'We had a young player, Reuben Spiring, who was at Durham University. We got wind that he had been tapped up by one or two other counties and we were concerned about losing him. However, we were not at all convinced he wanted to move. So I decided to travel up to Durham and thought it would be a good idea if the president accompanied me. We caught the train and what a memorable journey it was, what interesting recollections Tom had of his playing days! We met Reuben and in his quiet, gentle way, Tom talked him round and he stayed. Tom was excellent like that. None of "in my day" and all that when he talked to the current players. He was always positive and encouraging.'

Tom loved the job. Not that he would have regarded it as work. He attended committee meetings and offered up the benefit of his experience whenever he thought it was appropriate but the president did not drive the agenda. That duty fell to the chairman, who was none other than Duncan Fearnley, the same Duncan Fearnley who never tires of informing all and sundry that he (player number 308) joined the club on the same day as the great Tom Graveney (player number 307) in 1960. Both chairman and president got on well, then as now. 'Tom just loves talking about cricket,' Fearnley informed me, 'and of course his memory of every single one of his innings is legendary. So he was perfect for the job and was a great success.'

It was a period of change for the club during Tom's tenure as president. The championship-winning side of 1988 and 1989 was breaking up and new players were coming through. It was not his job to recruit and rebuild but he liked to keep in touch with the players and their families and they in turn enjoyed having him in their midst and never felt that his presence was an intrusion. It helped too that he had a warm and friendly professional relationship with Vockins, who ran the show on a daily basis. 'The thing about Tom,' Vockins pointed out, 'was that his love of Worcester was deep and genuine. People sensed this.'

For his part, Tom was only too happy to be once again closely involved in the first-class game. He acted as host during the home matches and attended as many of the away fixtures as he could, certainly those in the Midlands. There was a lot of driving involved but he was used to that with his job as a travelling salesman for 3D Sports. Visiting the grounds of other counties reinforced his view that very few rivalled Worcester for attractiveness, intimacy and friendly atmosphere.

What about Gloucestershire? How were you received when you went back there? 'My approach was to put past quarrels firmly behind me. The first time I went, my nephew David, now in charge of the Professional Cricketers' Association, was holding a breakfast function at the club, so that helped.' David Allen, a former colleague and team-mate of his was now the chairman and welcomed him 'with open arms'. Any potential embarrassment was immediately scotched. In fact, the friendly banter was as engaging as it was with any of the counties.

He was grateful for the 'five very happy years' that the presidency gave him and was actually anxious to serve another year but the club decided it was time for a change. Roy Booth, the county's wicketkeeper in Tom's time, succeeded him. 'He was a good choice,' Tom said, and then added mischievously in a not very good Yorkshire accent, 'but a bluidy Yorkie for all that!'

Before he handed over the reins of office, he had one final, sensitive task to perform. The Earl of Coventry fully expected to be appointed as his successor. Apparently, some impetuous and loose-tongued committeeman had informed Bill Coventry – erroneously as it turned out – that he was a shoo-in for the post. 'It was my tricky responsibility,' said Vockins, 'to put the good earl right, as diplomatically as was possible and again, Tom's gracious contribution proved invaluable. We were able to get Bill's understanding of the situation without ruffling too many feathers.'

Reluctant as he was for his tenure of office to be brought to a close, Tom maintained his ardent support for the club, attending matches regularly until quite recently when increasing immobility made it impracticable. It is a measure of the club, he asserts, that

Worcestershire has a thriving community of ex-players who meet regularly. 'It's like a family really,' he said. 'It was certainly where I felt most comfortable and at home when I was playing and in all the years since.'

He recounted some stories about Basil D'Oliveira, usually located in the members' bar at New Road, all bibulous and none repeatable. 'Just as well I lived in Cheltenham,' Tom confessed. 'It meant I could make my excuses and leave when I needed to.' His affection for his old friend and the D'Oliveira family was unwavering but he did admit that Basil was 'combustible' when in his cups. 'Funny really, because he didn't drink that much but it seemed to affect him. Whereas I was the opposite. I could down pints and it never affected me.'

As politicians seem to make the transition from the Commons to the Lords seamlessly, so you might be forgiven for thinking that Tom Graveney's journey from player to another Lord's would have been routine and unremarkable. But it wasn't at all like that. It is an archaic but jealously guarded tradition that the president of MCC chooses his own successor. No doubt there have been a few quixotic decisions down the years but the club would maintain that the system has in the main served them well.

Nonetheless, a quick glance at the roll call of past presidents demonstrates that the honour was bestowed on the great and the good exclusively, the gentlemen, not the players, the amateurs, not the professionals. Leaving aside the fair sprinkling of dukes, viscounts, barons and lords, to say nothing of Prince Philip, Duke of Edinburgh, the well known and the well connected of the game were heavily represented.

I refer to men like Lord Hawke, Lord Harris, Pelham Warner, Harry Altham and yes, Tom's old nemesis, Gubby Allen, all scions of cricket's ruling class. Former players such as Freddie Brown, Peter May, Colin Cowdrey, Ted Dexter and Tony Lewis are up there too but they would all be placed firmly in the amateur ranks. The likelihood of an ex-professional taking up the post must have seemed as improbable as a woman becoming prime minister.

Times they were a'changing, however. The distinction between professionals and amateurs had been blown away and a woman had walked through the front door of 10 Downing Street. And even more remarkably, a woman had walked through the front door of the pavilion at Lord's. Following a long campaign to allow women members of MCC, in 1999, former England captain Rachel Heyhoe-Flint and nine other women were elected full members of the club.

In recent years, it had made a conscious effort to throw off its fusty frock coat and to dress itself in a more fashionable suit – a suit, mind you, never jeans! – tailored for the 20th century. It used to be regarded, often scornfully, as a fixed bastion of autocracy, privilege and snobbery.

How many times did Tom Graveney raise his eyes to heaven when reflecting on his playing days and his brushes with the game's authorities and mutter, 'Well, that was MCC. They ran the game and we players had no say. We did as we were told.' That outlook sat uncomfortably with contemporary attitudes and, to its credit, MCC set about reforming itself. In Tom Graveney's opinion, one man was largely responsible for driving change and modernisation through the dusty corridors of Lord's.

Charles Fry, grandson of the legendary C.B. Fry, had had a long association with MCC, serving on numerous committees and working tirelessly behind the scenes to overhaul some of its outdated customs and practices. Roger Knight, who was the secretary of the club at the time, told me, 'Charles knew the club backwards and he definitely had an agenda!'

Nonetheless, despite his desire to shake up the administration and to streamline the governance, Fry was still at heart an Establishment figure and a stout defender of MCC's role as the guardian of the laws of the game and the spirit in which it should be played. He faced criticism for what some thought was his presidential style and his eagerness to set up a more efficient management structure but he was not one to fret over stepping on a few toes.

In 2003, he was asked to become president by the incumbent, Sir Tim Rice, the lyricist and theatrical producer and self-confessed cricket nut. During his year in office, Fry had accompanied Knight on a flight to Dacca to be present at Bangladesh's first Test match. En route, they had accepted an invitation to attend a function at the

Cricket Club of India in Mumbai. On the same plane were Tom and Jackie Graveney, also invited guests of India's most exclusive club.

Fry remembered playing against Tom when he was up at Oxford. 'I was fielding at cover when Tom was batting,' he grimaced, 'and I couldn't understand why, no matter where I stood, the ball kept on flashing past me for four.'

On a very hot evening, both he and Tom had to make a speech. Fry was impressed by the relaxed and straightforward delivery of his co-guest – unsurprising for a former television commentator – and, more importantly, that he kept it short and to the point, while at the same time appearing gracious and accommodating. The three of them, Graveney, Fry and Knight, got on famously during their brief stay.

'Hmm, Roger Knight,' Tom said to me when I brought up his name. 'Bowled me for 20-odd in 1968.' It is extraordinary that old players always bring up the story of their first duel when they meet each other. I looked up the records. Yet again, Tom's memory had not let him down. At the beginning of September, Worcestershire were playing Surrey at New Road. Knight was a Cambridge blue and had been nabbed by Surrey to play for them during his vacation. He did indeed bowl the great Tom Graveney for 23 – with a peach of a delivery or an innocuous straight one, depending on who is telling the story.

Fry was deliberating on his choice to succeed him as president and the conviction started to grow, following this chance meeting, that Tom was his man. Naturally enough, he discussed it with Knight, who was favourable to the idea, as was Sir Tim Rice, his immediate predecessor. I spoke to Sir Tim and asked him whether he remembered the circumstances surrounding Fry's favoured candidate. He certainly did.

Tom Graveney had been a hero of his ever since he had watched him as a young boy playing against the Australians in 1953. 'And he got better as he got older,' he marvelled. 'Was he a little impetuous as a batsman in the earlier stage of his career? Certainly, he batted imperiously later on when he had more responsibility.'

But was he the right choice to be president? 'Absolutely. He's such a charming and modest man that it would be impossible for anyone not to warm to him. Besides, he was so famous. Everybody's heard of Tom Graveney.'

So the die was cast. Charles Fry had made his decision and there was never a moment when he regretted it.

Why was he your choice? 'One: he was a cricketing hero. Two: he is a lovely man. Three: he is excellent with people. Four: it would be good for MCC.' Ah, might that be because he had been a professional and MCC were keen to shake off their elitist reputation?

Be that as it may, no one I spoke to about Tom's appointment was in the slightest doubt that the fact he had been a pro was utterly irrelevant. What counted was that now was the right time and that he was the right man. The appointment might surprise a few people but no one could possibly object. Many might even say 'and about time, too'.

One little seed of doubt then started to prey on Fry's mind. Tom was now 77. Although Tom was in good health, Fry knew from his own experience that the schedule was gruelling and the obligations many and none but a man of considerable stamina could cope. Was Tom fit enough?

It so happened that Sir Tim Rice knew Tim Graveney very well; he played regularly for his team, the Heartaches. Through Tim, Sir Tim had met Tom at Test matches at Lord's, become very friendly with the whole family and had even persuaded Graveney senior to turn out for the Heartaches on the odd occasion during his year as president of MCC.

Fry enlisted Rice's help to contact Tim to ascertain covertly whether he believed his father was up to the job. Tim misconstrued his role and, thinking the decision was a done deal, merely confirmed with his father that he could, and would, take on the post. Tom was flabbergasted but immensely honoured. Wild horses would not have deterred him from accepting. This was not quite what Charles Fry had intended but the cat was now out of the bag. Never mind – he was happy that his hand had been forced. Great secrecy had to be maintained however as the custom was that the announcement would not be made until the Annual General Meeting. Tom kept his mouth shut, as did his son.

When the news went public, it *did* cause a stir. 'Quite a few people were surprised,' Tom said, 'as I was the first professional to become president. It was quite ironic really, given my brushes with MCC over the years. But it didn't seem to be a problem. People were genuinely pleased for me and the support I got from everyone was truly wonderful.'

It was an exciting era of reorganisation and development at Lord's and the choice of president seemed to match the confident and changing mood of the times. The most obvious signs of this were of course the new buildings emerging on site. The new Mound Stand and Grandstand had been completed and the controversial, but strangely beautiful, Media Centre had been added in 1999. Now it was time to refurbish the old Victorian pavilion, a grade II listed building, at a cost of £8m. Completion was scheduled for the following season, in time for the visit of the Australians. Tom, for one, when he saw the chaos of the building site, doubted they would finish it in time.

Behind the scenes, the way the club was managed was also adapting. 'The role of the president was subtly changing,' Charles Fry told me. 'The donkey work used to be done by the treasurer, now redefined as the chairman. Together with the secretary, he would take over much of the admin from the president, thus freeing him up to be more of a figurehead.' This suited Tom; he was not, by any stretch of the imagination, a bureaucrat, a committee animal.

'It is a strange hybrid,' explained Roger Knight. 'The president is the top man but the business, on a day to day basis, is done by the secretary, who reports directly to the chairman, and between them, they are responsible for what happens. Meanwhile, the president can play it how he wants. He can get involved in the politics or he may not. Tom preferred not to but to stick to what he was good at – playing the role of figurehead and keeping everyone happy.' Fry agreed. 'Tom wasn't au fait with the workings of the committees. He didn't see that as his role. We tried to look after him and he repaid us by being an unqualified success.'

How did Tom see things and how much did he seek to influence decisions and shape future policy? His first move was a shrewd one. He persuaded his daughter to take a three-month sabbatical from her job to act as his right-hand woman and to make sure that social functions and official gatherings would run smoothly. He knew that she was an efficient and indefatigable organiser from their time together in the Royal Oak and he trusted her.

'I couldn't have done it without her,' he disclosed. Becky, for her part, took little persuading. She recognised that this was a tremendous honour for her father and wanted to help him make a success of it. And being a naturally gregarious girl, who knew cricketers and their world, she relished the challenge. Furthermore, she was painfully aware that her mother was not well enough to cope as Tom's helpmeet, though it was hoped that she would take a full part in the official receptions.

Did you have an agenda, Mr President? You know, plans to shake things up a bit? 'Ah…Mr President! Yes, I got used to that eventually. No longer Graveney T.W.! Plans? No, my only plan was to try to remember everybody's name. Actually, there was one thing I was keen on,' he offered as an afterthought, 'and that was youth cricket. I didn't think it was being given the priority it should have had. I'm glad that my words seemed to have some effect because youth cricket is much better organised and funded these days.'

Take me through your day. What was it like coming through the Grace Gates for the first time as president of MCC? He paused and shook his head at the wonder of it. 'Even now, it's difficult to believe. I would never have thought, at the beginning of my career all those years ago, that I, a mere county professional, would end up as president of MCC.' And then he started to laugh. 'I was wearing a suit. Of course I was wearing a suit. And it occurred to me that whenever I had to wear a suit to Lord's, I was usually in trouble.'

Not this time. Did the gateman recognise you and wave you through? Silly question. Gatemen *always* recognised Tom Graveney. 'They sent a car to pick me up, you know.'

From Cheltenham? 'Yes, from Cheltenham. Every time I went up to Lord's. I tried to attend as many committee meetings as I could.'

And there were all the dinners and receptions, as well as the matches. You must have been busy. 'It was exhausting. But I loved every minute of it. Everyone was so kind to me.'

It was hardly a surprise to me any more than it would have been to anyone who knows him that the new president made a point of greeting everyone in his usual affable manner as he made his way around Lord's on that first day. 'He was lovely with the staff,' confirmed Roger Knight. 'Everyone knew him, wherever he went. And he'd talk to anyone. He was a marvellous front man, a real pro's pro.'

For his own part, Tom was grateful for the help and support that Knight gave him. For on that first morning, Tom was nervous, he freely admits. He remembered looking around the table as they sat down for the meeting of the executive committee, seeing all those unfamiliar faces and worrying how he was going to get to know them.

'One or two I knew. But the chairmen of all the branches of cricket administered by MCC were there. There were about 20 of them. I had no idea there were so many committees.'

The meeting was called to order by the chairman, Charles Fry, who wasted no time in welcoming their new president. Tom, sensing that he should respond, said, 'I've only got 12 months to do anything but I'll do the best I can.' His impression was that those few words went down well enough.

Anything else you said by way of a contribution? He shook his head. 'Playing myself in gently,' he grinned. 'Len would have been proud of me!'

And then lunch? 'The lunches are always very good at Lord's.'

He was a diligent attender of committee meetings, being driven up to Lord's from Cheltenham every time, often twice a week. 'I couldn't have managed it without a car and driver,' he declared. A 6.30am start to be at Lord's at 8.30am sharp was a tough regimen for a man in his late 70s but it did mean that, usually, he could be back home with Jackie for lunch.

Did you enjoy those meetings? I got the impression from the look on his face that he never considered himself to be the one to engage in impassioned debate or political manoeuvring in committee but he said that he spoke up when the situation demanded or when his opinion was canvassed.

I quizzed Roger Knight about the president's contributions to discussion and strategy. He replied that Tom's year in the saddle was remarkable for its lack of controversy and bloodletting. 'Some presidents in the past have been subjected to hostile questioning from mutinous members who have an axe to grind. But it was an uneventful year. Tom was never subjected to any antagonism or nastiness. It was as if none of the members wanted to subject him to any hassle. He was so well regarded, you see.'

Tom was less anxious to take credit for the conciliatory style of his presidency; he maintained that Fry, as chairman, and Knight, as secretary, shouldered the burden of modernising the administration of the club, performed most of the donkey work and helped him on his way, shielding him from any political in-fighting.

Rachel Heyhoe-Flint, now a baroness, the first female member of the club, remembers these committee meetings very well. 'The chairman took the meeting,' she said, 'but would turn to the president out of courtesy to comment or to offer an opinion if the subject was of particular interest to him. Tom was very quiet in these meetings but he would speak when called upon and his contributions were wise and sensible. He was always listened to with great respect.'

He did, on one occasion, make a significant intervention. There was a house whose garden led directly into Lord's that belonged to MCC and was traditionally the grace-and-favour home of the club secretary. It used to belong to Gubby Allen and on his death it was bequeathed to…no, not his old friend Tom Graveney, but MCC, which had practically been his own fiefdom for so many years.

Roger Knight, the incumbent, currently resided there but he was due to retire from his post at the end of the year. His successor was to be Keith Bradshaw, an Australian. Now was a good time to lease out the property, it was felt, before the new man could have a chance to take up residence.

Tom was deeply unhappy about this; it just felt unfair and inconsiderate. So he surrendered the habit of a lifetime and went into bat for Australia. 'Look,' he argued. 'I've been here for six months and I don't know half the people who work here. So someone coming from Australia won't know *anyone*. We must keep the house for him. If he's forced to live somewhere else, away from Lord's, it won't be fair on him and it will make his job twice as difficult.' Fairness has always been important to Tom.

And what was the outcome? He allowed himself a little smile. 'They changed their minds and kept the house.'

If committee meetings were something to be endured, albeit with diligence and patience, entertaining the troops was right up his street. 'He was excellent at social functions,' Fry said. 'He was a superb host in the president's box,' agreed Knight. 'He was a top cricket man, everyone knew him and of course he knew, if not everyone, then all the ex-players down the years. He had a fund of stories to tell and everyone hung on his words. And what a memory he had for matches, scores, figures! We were lucky to have him.' Baroness Heyhoe-Flint underlined his popularity, 'He's just a lovely bloke, gentle, kind and caring.'

For his part, Tom loved every minute of it and only wished the honour had come ten years earlier, the better to cope with the relentless social merry-go-round. 'Lots of dinners,' he said, 'and lots of speeches. I got a bit nervous beforehand but I was all right once I got going. I had a captive audience, you see. They seemed to enjoy the cricket anecdotes.'

The going was tough, even he admitted, but he was reasonably sensible about the hours he kept and the amount of alcohol he consumed, for there was no net first thing the following morning to sweat off the evening's excesses. And Becky, of course, kept a watchful eye on him. Jackie enjoyed being at the centre of things once she had overcome her social unease and sense of not quite belonging and Becky and Tim, being social animals, thoroughly enjoyed the experience too.

All in all, it was an uneventful year. Off the field and in the committee rooms, that is. On the field, of course, it was one of the most eventful seasons in living memory. The year was 2005 and the Australians were in town. Everyone was hoping for a close series but not in anyone's wildest dreams could the riveting Ashes contest, that had the whole country on tenterhooks, have been predicted. 'But before then, there was the series against South Africa,' he reminded me. 'We had to go to Cape Town as guests of the South African Board.'

You had *to go to Cape Town? Poor you. You must have had a perfectly horrid time.* He continued as if he hadn't heard. 'All expenses paid. I was representing MCC. Charles Fry came, and Roger Knight.'

And Jackie? 'Jackie came too. Tim came out for the five days of the Test as well. Marvellous trip.' He remained baffled by the fact that, during a career spanning so many years, he had only played against South Africa in six Test matches (including his first in 1951) and had never toured there. Amid the euphoria of the summer Ashes series, it is often forgotten that England beat the South Africans on their own soil that winter and therefore were the first to take possession of the newly inaugurated Basil D'Oliveira Trophy.

'It was a poignant occasion,' Tim told me. 'Damian came out with me – we grew up together, don't forget – and he was there to represent his father when it was presented.' Winning the trophy outright gave the Englishmen the confidence that they could stand toe to toe with the mighty Australians in the forthcoming battle.

'First time I saw Pietersen bat,' he informed me. 'Bit of an "I" specialist, if you ask me.' Almost immediately, as if remembering himself, his wicked grin was replaced by a more conciliatory expression. 'But what a fabulous stroke-maker! Such a clean hitter of the ball!'

As promised, the pavilion was ready for the new season. Tom could scarcely believe it. Two weeks before, he had taken a look behind the green tarpaulin and it had resembled a 'bomb site'. Nonetheless, the contractors had been as good as their word, the extensive refurbishment had been completed and the official opening had been scheduled for the opening day of the first-class programme, traditionally MCC v the champion county, which happened to be Warwickshire.

Accordingly on a cold and drizzly day in early April, when no cricketer, especially a slip fielder, fancies taking to the field, the president stepped forward in front of a crowd of MCC members to make a little speech commemorating the occasion.

Do you remember what you said? He laughed. 'Well, during the usual thank yous, I dropped my notes. "Oops, another one down," I said. Brought the house down.' *I hope not, as it had only just been renovated.*

He made mention yet again of his sincere opinion that everyone at the club was bending over backwards to be kind to him, dutifully laughing in the right places, even if he had been reciting a page from the phone book. But I venture to disagree. I have heard some of his impromptu offerings and they are vignettes of charm and humour. 'And then there was the business with the left-hand scissors.' I looked blank. 'I had to cut the ribbon and I said I needed left-hand scissors.'

But there's no such thing. They're all the same. With commendable patience, he explained. 'I know. But oddly, using a pair of scissors is the only thing I do left-handed. Everything else, I'm right-handed.'

Except when you hold a bat. You lead with the top hand. 'That's right,' he smiled benignly, as if in encouragement to a hopeless youngster in the nets who doesn't know his top hand from his back leg. 'Anyway, a pair of left-hand scissors was produced and I cut the ribbon.' The spruced-up pavilion is very smart, we both agreed, sensitively and discreetly done without destroying the cosy feel of a members' club.

Before the Australians arrived, proper preparation had to be made for the inaugural Test match of Bangladesh in this country. Tom had booked the President's Box for his family on the Sunday of the game and was looking forward to a pleasant day entertaining his nearest and dearest. But it all went wrong for Bangladesh and the MCC president.

On a cloudy and damp morning, England won the toss and, unsurprisingly but a little unkindly, asked their opponents to bat. The Bangladesh batsmen could not possibly have feared anything worse than facing the England seamers in conditions that were bound to be favourable to the home team and alien to the visitors. But a Test match is a Test match, the England captain, Michael Vaughan, would have said, and being a Yorkshireman, there would have been little sympathy in his heart.

As anticipated, Bangladesh floundered against the four-pronged England seam attack (Harmison, Hoggard, Flintoff and Jones – a quartet that was to do England proud in the forthcoming Ashes series) and were bowled out for 108. As luck would have it, the sun came out when England batted, the conditions became benign and Trescothick (194) and Vaughan (120) filled their boots, the declaration coming at 528/3.

At one stage, it seemed quite possible that the match would not stretch into the third day, the Saturday, as Bangladesh wickets tumbled but in the event, they were able to stretch out the agony until noon the next day. Tom was crestfallen. He wanted to encourage the development of the game in Bangladesh (after all, he had played in that country and knew how fervent was their love of cricket) but he realised, as did many others, that this had been no contest.

Clearly, it would be a while before they could compete on an equal footing with the established Test nations. It took Sri Lanka time before they adapted. 'And look at them now,' said Tom. He tried to organise an exhibition match for the third day crowd but, in the end, it proved impossible.

And what happened to the family gathering on the Sunday? 'Cancelled,' he replied mournfully.

A Lord's Test match is a significant event in the cricket season as well as a fixture in the summer's social calendar. Particularly when the old enemy are visiting. One of the advantages of having an ex-player as president, especially one who had played against them in 22 Tests – undoubtedly a factor that Charles Fry had had in his mind when choosing his successor – was that the visiting Australians would be warmly welcomed and quickly put at their ease by the reassuring sight of Tom Graveney pouring the gin and tonic.

During the five days of the match, a regular stream of old friends and former adversaries beat a path to the president's door. 'A few survivors of the great Australian side of 1948 were there,' Tom said, 'Neil Harvey, Arthur Morris, Colin McDonald, Keith Miller, Sam Loxton…' He tailed off, lost in a warm, nostalgic glow. 'So many old friends…yes, it was a wonderful time. And I was president of MCC! I still find it difficult to believe.'

Anyone who was present in the pavilion that first morning of the match says that the atmosphere was electric, quite unforgettable. The series had been keenly anticipated by cricket lovers and the interest of the general public was enormous.

Unusually, the Lord's Test was the first of the five-match rubber and at lunch England trooped through the Long Room on their way back to their dressing room with Australia reeling at 97/5. Instead of the usual polite, restrained applause, the members were roaring their appreciation. Upstairs, in the dining room, the MCC president was enjoying the opportunity of reminding his Australian guests of the score.

'But not for long,' he grimaced. 'Do you remember the spell of bowling by McGrath later on in the day that wrecked our innings?' Do I indeed; McGrath took 5-21 – he always seemed to enjoy bowling at Lord's – to leave England in the perilous position of 92/7. And all in a day's play!

'There was plenty of banter, to and fro,' said Tom. 'All of it good-natured. It always was with the Aussies. We played hard but fair. And we always had a drink together in the dressing room at the close of play. Don't get me wrong. Those contests were bitterly fought but there was no nonsense on the field of play. We just got on with the game.'

The Australians got on with this game all right. They won by 239 runs. But England had shown that they were willing to stand up to their opponents and slug it out. The upshot was one of the most tense and exciting Ashes series in living memory.

And on your watch too, Tom. 'I know. It was out of this world. How blessed I was to be so lucky.'

On the Saturday of the game, the Australian Prime Minister was the guest of honour in the President's Box, together with John Major, an avid cricket fan. Earlier in the month, London had been rocked by a series of terrorists' bombs (events now known as 7/7) and security was pretty tight. Becky was struck by the differing levels of protection that the two men had. 'John Major had two bodyguards. The Australian Prime Minister had 12!'

Another guest was the larger-than-life figure of Peter Alliss. 'Tom, old boy,' he boomed, 'mine's a Pimm's!' The trouble was that it was not yet midday and the club rule was that no alcohol could be served before then.

So what happened? 'Er, we bent the rules a bit,' he sheepishly admitted. 'I don't think Roger Knight really approved.'

And so the series proceeded to its gripping finale at the Oval. When victory had at last been secured, it fell to the president of MCC to present the Ashes to the winning England captain, Michael Vaughan. 'It was a very proud moment,' Tom recalled, 'especially as my nephew David was there as well, in his capacity as chairman of selectors.'

What were the England players like? They had been up all night partying, as I remember. 'Tired!' was his response. 'As was I.'

That was pretty well it then? Your year in the saddle was nearly up. 'It was a momentous year for English cricket and I was proud to be part of it.'

When did you start thinking about who to name as your successor? 'Months before,' he laughed. 'Don't forget that the new president was announced at the committee meeting in April before he took up his post on 1 October. I can't tell you how many people's opinion I sought.'

Slowly a name took root in his mind and the more he thought about it, the more he was convinced that it would be a shrewd choice. 'It would have come as a bit of a surprise to some people but I had seen him at work in committee and I had been impressed. I felt he would stir things up a bit.'

The identity of the man who would 'stir things up a bit' had to remain a close secret until the April committee meeting. When Tom rang him to inform him of his choice, he was thunderstruck, so much so that he rang Tom back the following morning, just to check that it had not been a hoax. Indeed it was not, Tom assured him. 'And do you know what?' Tom told me. 'He said that it was the nicest phone call he had ever had in his life.'

The name of the next president was revealed at the Annual General Meeting. It was Robin Marlar. 'And I never really liked him,' Tom confessed. I must have expressed some surprise at this because Tom went to some pains to satisfy me that Robin Marlar was definitely not his favourite opponent in their playing days. 'But I just felt that he was the right man for the job. And in the event I think I was proved right.' Which makes his choice even more admirable.

Certainly, Tom was right on one point; Marlar stirred things up a bit all right. He had only been in the post for one day before he provoked an unholy row with his uncompromising opposition to mixed-sex games of cricket. For many years, for so long as he was the cricket correspondent of *The Sunday Times*, I had read his trenchant articles and was well acquainted with his strong opinions and controversial style. In fact, you would be hard pressed to think of a more direct contrast between his method of getting things done and Tom's naturally emollient and clubbable approach. In that sense, perhaps Tom was being more prescient with his choice of Marlar than he gives himself credit for.

And how are you with him now? 'With Robin? Oh, we're the best of friends.' Somehow, I would hardly have expected any other response.

And that was pretty much it. Having handed over the reins, he slipped away. He was tired, more tired than he cared to admit at the time. It had been a gruelling 18 months. 'Don't forget, you start getting to know the ropes in the six months between the announcement in April and when you take up the position in October.'

Despite the fact that he claims the year had passed all too quickly, he knew in his heart that he would not have been able to stand the pace for any longer. 'It took a lot out of him,' confirmed his nephew, David, 'and he wasn't the same man for some considerable time afterwards.'

Not that Tom would have missed a minute of it all. 'I was in close touch again with the game I love,' he said, 'and it was marvellous. Marvellous.' He also remarked on the strange feeling of loss immediately he handed over to Marlar. 'One minute you're the president; the next moment you're nobody.' A bit like the President of the United States when he quits the stage, I mused; suddenly the milling Secret Service personnel, the trappings of power, the presidential plane and the limousines are no longer at his beck and call. It was as if Tom recognised that, finally, his long career in the game was drawing to a close.

It was about this time in the narrative that his health deteriorated once more, worryingly so. His children moved him into the nursing home next door and it soon became apparent that there he was going to stay. For a while, he harboured hopes of a return to his own home, where he felt he could sustain his independence, surrounded by familiar things, but then he accepted the inevitable and surrendered to the expert and attentive care which was being administered.

I still visited him regularly and together we put some flesh on the passages of his story where the bones were a little bare. His memory was not as acute as it was but, with some prompting, he was still capable of recalling innings, matches, personalities. He maintained an interest in contemporary proceedings on the international cricket stage and watched the matches on the television.

'We've always been afraid of our batting,' he announced on one occasion. 'We're going into a game – in India, mind you – with only four bowlers. That's because we don't trust numbers one to five to get the runs. So we're playing with six batsmen. Same in my day, you know,' he added with a sad shake of the head. 'Always looking for a number six to shore up the batting.' Needless to say, he was proved right. With three ineffectual seamers and only one spinner, England lost that Test, heavily.

He seemed happy enough. Jackie was in a room but a short walk along the corridor and he continued to be ever solicitous of her. Everyone knew him and cheerfully greeted him. Unfailingly, he acknowledged these expressions of goodwill with openness and affability. It was his nature. But now it was nurses, carers, cleaners, workmen instead of gatemen, doormen, groundsmen, waitresses and dressing room attendants to whom he was being effortlessly friendly.

'They could do with you out there on the sub-continent, Tom,' said a painter, gesturing at him alarmingly with a dripping paintbrush. 'I've played out there, you know,' replied our hero, launching into a blow-by-blow account of the 1951/52 tour. Hang on, Tom, I brooded, we've done that tour; there's not much to add. But my impatience was short-lived. This is what he does best, lowering bucket after bucket into the deep well of his cricket memories. And what the hell,

(That this is true when the spring is extended by the weight in the equilibrium position should be clear from the argument that the tension due to the equilibrium extension just supports the weight, so that the restoring force is the *additional* tension due to the *additional* displacement. A mathematical argument is given in Appendix 1 to this chapter, p. 11). It follows that the equation of motion is

$$m\ddot{x} = -sx. \tag{1}$$

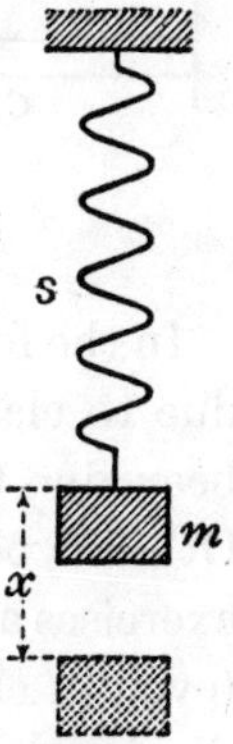

As a second example, consider the case of a mass M at the end of a thin metal strip, of length l and flexural rigidity EI, rigidly clamped at the other end. The first thing to do is to find the force acting on M, due to the elasticity of the metal strip, when M is displaced, say a distance y, from its equilibrium position. This force must be equal and opposite to the steady force F which would maintain a steady deflexion y when applied transversely at the end of the strip, as indicated in Fig. 2 (b). Now it is proved in books on strength of

FIG. 1

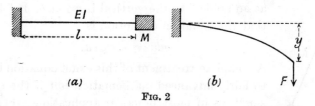

(a)   *(b)*

FIG. 2

materials, or theory of structures, that the end deflexion is given by the formula

$$y = Fl^3/3EI,$$

whence

$$F = (3EI/l^3)y. \tag{2}$$

It follows that the equation of motion of M is

$$M\ddot{y} = -F = -(3EI/l^3)y. \tag{3}$$

As a third example, consider a pulley of moment of inertia I at the end of a shaft of length l and torsional rigidity CJ, with the other end fixed. Then, using an argument very similar to that in the last paragraph, we first consider the steady torque T

which would maintain a steady angular deflexion θ of the pulley. As shown in books on strength of materials,

$$T = (CJ/l)\theta. \qquad (4)$$

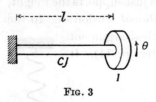

FIG. 3

The torque acting on the pulley when its deflexion is θ is equal and opposite to this, so that the equation of motion of the pulley is

$$I\ddot{\theta} = -T = -(CJ/l)\theta. \qquad (5)$$

In the foregoing three simple cases the restoring force has been due to elasticity, and the proportionality to displacement has been due to the tacit assumption that Hooke's law is obeyed. Other types of restoring force occur (examples are given in the exercises at the end of the chapter), and the restoring force is not (even in elastic systems) always accurately proportional to the displacement.

The last two statements are well exemplified by the well-known case of the simple pendulum. If m is the mass of the bob,

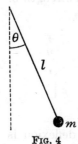

FIG. 4

then the restoring force when the string is inclined at an angle θ to the vertical is $mg \sin \theta$. It follows that the equation of motion is

$$ml\ddot{\theta} = -mg \sin \theta. \qquad (6)$$

A complete treatment of this exact equation leads to fairly advanced mathematics, but if the arc is small, as in most practical applications, then we may use an approximation which greatly simplifies, namely, that for small angles, θ and $\sin \theta$ are

approximately equal. When this is done, equation (6) becomes

$$ml\ddot{\theta} = -mg\theta, \qquad (7)$$

and its structure is exactly the same as that of equations (1), (3), and (5).

That simple electrical circuits have oscillatory properties analogous to those of simple mechanical systems may be shown by obtaining the equation satisfied by some quantity and verifying that the equation is of the same form as (1), (3), (5), and (7). The analogous circuit is the idealized one indicated in Fig. 5, consisting of a condenser of capacitance C, discharging through an inductance L. For the present we neglect (with less justice than when we neglected the mechanical resistances) the electrical resistance of the circuit. At any time let v be the voltage across the condenser, $+q$ and $-q$ the charges on the plates, and i the current in the inductance. The fact that current is due to charge flowing from or to the condenser plates is expressed by the equation

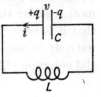

$$i = -dq/dt = -\dot{q}. \qquad (8)$$

Fig. 5

Faraday's law of induction gives

$$v = L\,di/dt, \qquad (9)$$

and the relation between charge and voltage is

$$q = Cv. \qquad (10)$$

From these equations it is quite easy to deduce that

$$L\ddot{q} = -q/C, \qquad (11)$$

which is an equation whose formal structure is precisely similar to that of (1), (3), (5), and (7). We conclude that inductance has in some sense inertial properties, and that a condenser is in some sense analogous to a spring; charge is analogous to displacement, and current to velocity. Later we shall see that this set of analogies can be further extended, but for the moment it may serve if we tabulate the electrical analogues of the elements of the mechanical systems we have so far considered; they are indicated by the corresponding equation.

Equation	Current	Inductance	Capacitance
(1)	$\dot{x}$	m	$1/s$
(3)	$\dot{y}$	M	$l^3/3EI$
(5)	$\dot{\theta}$	I	l/CJ
(7)	$\dot{\theta}$	ml	$1/mg$

1.3. Simple harmonic motion

The equations of the preceding section may, by division by the coefficient of the 'acceleration' term, all be reduced to the standard form

$$\ddot{x} = -\omega^2 x, \qquad (12)$$

in which ω^2 stands for one of the quantities s/m, $3EI/Ml^3$, CJ/Il, $mg/ml = g/l$, $1/LC$. Expressed in words, 'acceleration is proportional to displacement, and is directed towards the equilibrium position'. Books on elementary mechanics describe motion under these conditions as 'simple harmonic', and show that it is periodic, with period $2\pi/\omega$ or frequency $\omega/2\pi$. Alternatively, it may be verified that general solutions of the differential equation (12) are

$$x = A \sin \omega t + B \cos \omega t, \tag{13a}$$

$$x = a \sin (\omega t + \phi). \tag{13b}$$

Both of these represent motions with period $2\pi/\omega$, and indeed they are equivalent if

$$A = a \cos \phi, \qquad B = a \sin \phi, \tag{14a}$$

$$a = \sqrt{(A^2 + B^2)}, \qquad \tan \phi = B/A. \tag{14b}$$

The actual values of the constants A and B will depend upon the manner in which the motion is originated, that is, the initial velocity and displacement. The determination of the constants which occur in the solutions of linear differential equations is part of the technique explained and exemplified in texts on differential equations, and will not be further dealt with here. Some important examples are given in Chapter V and in the exercises thereon.

Although it may in practice be more usual to talk about the frequency (e.g. cycles per second), or the period, of vibration, it is clear from inspection of equations (12), (13a), and (13b) that the formulae and the mathematics will be greatly simplified by the use of the quantity we have denoted by ω. It is called the *pulsatance*, and is, as equations (13a) and (13b) clearly show, an equivalent angular velocity. In all theoretical work it is most convenient to use this pulsatance, converting to frequency or period only at a late stage (if at all).

The relation (13b) is susceptible of a simple and very useful geometrical interpretation since it shows that x can be represented by the projection of a line of length a rotating with uniform angular velocity ω. Thus if, in Fig. 6 a, OP is the position of a line of length a rotating at uniform angular velocity ω, starting at OP_0 when $t = 0$, and if OP_0 makes an angle ϕ with a datum radius OX, then, since the angle POP_0 is ωt, the perpendicular distance PN from P to OX is $a\sin(\omega t + \phi)$, and so represents x.

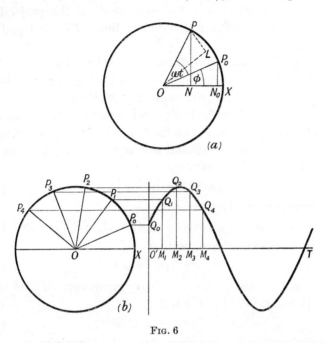

FIG. 6

The variation in the length of PN as OP rotates uniformly is easily visualized, and the construction may be extended so as to enable a time graph of the oscillation to be plotted without any calculations or reference to tables. Starting from P_0, equal arcs P_0P_1, P_1P_2, P_2P_3,...., corresponding to equal angles at O, and hence to equal increments of time, are marked along the circumference of the circle traced out by P (see Fig. 6 b). On a time-axis $O'T$, in OX produced, equal segments $O'M_1$, M_1M_2, M_2M_3,... are marked off, to represent these equal time intervals, and perpendiculars to $O'T$ are erected through the points M_1, M_2,... Finally, P_0, P_1, P_2,... are projected parallel to OX on to the corresponding perpendiculars, and through the set of points Q_0, Q_1, Q_2,... so obtained the time graph is drawn.

The alternative form (13 a) can be shown in the diagram, for if $P_0 N_0$ is drawn perpendicular to OX, as in Fig. 6 a, then $ON_0 = A$, $N_0 P_0 = B$. If the triangle $OP_0 N_0$ be imagined to rotate bodily, so that when OP_0 has turned to OP, N_0 is located at L, then it is clear that PN, considered as the projection, perpendicular to OX, of the broken line OLP, is equal to $A \sin \omega t + B \cos \omega t$.

The use of complex quantities as an aid to description and calculation of oscillating quantities is becoming increasingly common, on account of the manner in which it simplifies the mathematical treatment. For a brief account of the necessary basic ideas and results, Appendix 2 (p. 11) may be consulted.

For example, the right-hand side of equation (13 b) can be recognized as the imaginary component of

$$ae^{j(\omega t+\phi)} = ae^{j\phi}e^{j\omega t}. \tag{15}$$

We may also recognize that

$$ae^{j\phi} = a(\cos\phi + j\sin\phi) = A + jB, \tag{16}$$

upon use of (13 a). Hence, writing

$$C = A + jB = ae^{j\phi} \tag{17}$$

and using $\mathscr{I}$ to denote 'the imaginary component of', we may write (13 a) and (13 b) in the form

$$x = \mathscr{I}ae^{j(\omega t+\phi)} = \mathscr{I}Ce^{j\omega t}. \tag{18}$$

Finally, since in any sequence of equations involving complex quantities, we may at any stage equate either the real or the imaginary components, it is possible to drop the $\mathscr{I}$ throughout the work, on the understanding that (if necessary) the imaginary component must finally be taken. For many purposes (but *not* for all) this is unnecessary, since $Ce^{j\omega t}$ as it stands contains the information which we usually desire, namely the amplitude,

$$a = \text{modulus of } C = |C|, \tag{19}$$

and the phase, $\qquad \phi = \text{phase of } C. \tag{20}$

Finally, if, on this understanding, we write

$$x = Ce^{j\omega t}, \tag{21}$$

then we see that, for this form of x, we still have

$$\ddot{x} = -\omega^2 x.$$

Consequently, we shall frequently adopt (21) as a convenient way of describing a vibration, in the knowledge that results obtained from it do, when properly interpreted, give the solution of practical problems.

In view of the complete analogy between electrical and mechanical vibrations, the (so-called) vector diagrams used by the electrical engineer for solving alternating current problems could be used in connexion with mechanical vibrations, but we shall not make any considerable use of this technique.

1.4. Ubiquity of simple harmonic motion

In the case of the simple examples of vibrating systems examined in section 1.2 the restoring force turned out to be accurately or approximately proportional to the displacement, and equation (12), and its general solutions (13 a) or (13 b), apply strictly only when the proportionality is exact. In that event the pulsatance (and hence the frequency or the period) is independent of the amplitude, and the vibrations are accurately *isochronous*. The example of the simple pendulum shows, however, that for *small* oscillations the restoring force is very nearly proportional to the displacement, and becomes more nearly so as the displacement decreases. Indeed, the story goes that Galileo discovered the isochronous property of the simple pendulum by timing the swings of a hanging chandelier in Pisa cathedral against his heart-beats. That other vibrations, such as those mentioned in the Introduction, are at least approximately isochronous, is a matter of experience, and the reason for this is not far to seek.

The restoring force must depend in some manner on the displacement, that is, the force F must be a function of the displacement x, or

$$F = F(x). \qquad (22)$$

Now, except in the (rare) case when $F(x)$ has a 'singularity' at the origin, the function $F(x)$ will be expansible in a Maclaurin series,

$$F(x) = F(0) + xF'(0) + \frac{x^2}{2!}F''(0) + ..., \qquad (23)$$

where $F(0)$, $F'(0)$, $F''(0)$,... are the values of the function and its derivatives at $x = 0$; this expansion is valid for sufficiently small values of x. But if x is measured from the equilibrium position, $F(0) = 0$. Again, if x is small, the terms in x^2, x^3, ... are negligibly small compared with the term in x—provided that $F'(0)$ does not vanish—and this is true to any desired order of accuracy if x is small enough. Hence, for almost any system, $F(x)$ can, for sufficiently small values of x, be approximated to by the first surviving term in its Maclaurin series, namely, $xF''(0)$, or, for sufficiently small displacement, the restoring force is approximately proportional to the displacement, and we conclude that the small oscillations of *any* system may be expected to be very approximately simple harmonic, and so isochronous.

1.5. Determination of pulsatance

The most important quantity associated with a vibrating system and often the only one which it is desired to calculate is the pulsatance (frequency or period) of its free vibrations. For simple systems of the type already considered, systems whose configuration can be specified in terms of one variable (called a *coordinate*), most frequently (but not invariably) a linear or angular displacement from the equilibrium position—systems having *one degree of freedom*, as they are termed—this pulsatance can be determined quite simply if the equation of motion is written down. Making, if necessary, the approximations for small displacements, the equation can be reduced to the standard form (12) wherein the value of ω^2 can be clearly discerned, and whence ω (and, if needed, frequency and period) can be calculated. Numerous examples are given in the exercises at the end of this chapter.

Certain general conclusions are indicated by the results already obtained, and these conclusions will be further exemplified in the above-mentioned exercises, and in subsequent chapters. The formulae so far developed contain quantities representing the two fundamental essentials of a vibrating system, namely 'stiffness' (or its analogue), which causes a restoring force, and 'inertia' (or its analogue). Of these, the stiffness appears in the numerator, the inertia in the denominator, of the fraction which yields ω^2. Hence

(i) *an increase in the stiffness of a vibrating system results in an increased pulsatance (increased frequency, shortened period);*

(ii) *an increase in the inertia of a vibrating system results in a decreased pulsatance (decreased frequency, lengthened period).*

APPENDIX 1. SIMPLE SPRING SYSTEM

Fig. 7 represents (a) a light spring, of stiffness s, hanging unloaded; (b) the same spring, *in equilibrium,* supporting a mass m of weight $W = mg$, the extension of the spring being x_0; (c) the same spring with the mass, in motion, displaced a distance x from its equilibrium position. In (b), if the tension is P_0, then $P_0 = sx_0$, and also $P_0 = W$. In (c), since the total extension is now $(x+x_0)$, the tension P is given by $P = s(x+x_0)$. Moreover, the equation of motion is

$$m\ddot{x} = W - P.$$

Using the results of (b) and (c) we have

$$m\ddot{x} = sx_0 - s(x+x_0),$$

that is, $m\ddot{x} = -sx,$

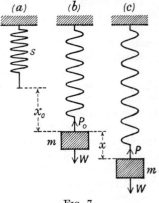

Fig. 7

an equation in which all reference to initial tension, initial extension, and weight have completely disappeared.

APPENDIX 2. COMPLEX NUMBERS

It is not the purpose of this appendix to enter into the philosophy of imaginary and complex numbers, but merely to recall the minimum amount of knowledge and technique necessary to the exploitation of their simplifying and labour-saving properties in dealing with vibrating systems.

Algebraic operations sometimes lead to formulae implying the need for the square root of a negative number, and suggest the introduction of an 'imaginary' unit, which we shall denote by j (many books of mathematics use i), which obeys the laws of ordinary algebra, and has in addition the property that

$$j^2 = -1.$$

From this it follows that

$$j^3 = j^2 . j = -j,$$
$$j^4 = (j^2)^2 = 1,$$
$$j^5 = j^4 . j = j,$$
$$\cdot \quad \cdot \quad \cdot \quad \cdot \quad \cdot \quad \cdot$$
$$1/j = j/j^2 = -j,$$
$$1/j^2 = -1,$$
$$\cdot \quad \cdot \quad \cdot \quad \cdot \quad \cdot$$

so that every integral power of j has one or other of the four values ± 1, $\pm j$. Thus no higher powers of j than the first need appear finally in any formula of complex algebra.

The fundamental entity of complex algebra, the complex number, may be regarded as compounded of multiples of the two units, 1 and j, and it is written in the form $a+jb$. In this a and b may be regarded as ordinary (called *real*) numbers; a is called the *real part* of the complex number, and jb is called the *imaginary part*.

For the algebraic manipulation of such numbers the ordinary laws of algebra, along with the fact that $j^2 = -1$, suffice, but a geometrical representation—the Argand diagram, often miscalled a 'vector diagram' by the electrical engineers—can be very helpful, because it allows a visualization of algebraic operations, and also because some of these operations can be carried out by actual drawing. It also helps to fix the idea—an essential idea—that the complex number can and must be regarded as *a single entity*.

On the Argand diagram the complex number

$$z = x+jy$$

is represented by the line joining the origin to the point P whose co-ordinates are (x, y), that is, OP in Fig. 8. The length, r, of this line is called the *modulus* of the complex number, often denoted by $|z|$. The angle θ which OP makes with the positive direction of the x-axis is termed the *phase* (sometimes *argument*, sometimes *amplitude*) of z. Clearly,

$$r = \sqrt{(x^2+y^2)}, \qquad \tan \theta = y/x,$$
$$x = r \cos \theta, \qquad y = r \sin \theta.$$

From this it follows that

$$z = x+jy = r \cos \theta + jr \sin \theta$$
$$= r(\cos \theta + j \sin \theta),$$

whence it appears that $(\cos \theta + j \sin \theta)$ is a *turning factor*, turning r through an angle θ. Since a turn through ϕ following a turn through θ results in a turn through $(\phi+\theta)$ we might expect that

$$(\cos\phi+j\sin\phi)(\cos\theta+j\sin\theta) = \cos(\phi+\theta)+j\sin(\phi+\theta).$$

This result is known as Demoivre's theorem, and is readily verified by expanding both sides.

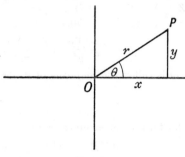

FIG. 8

Further, by use of the series for $\cos\theta$ and $\sin\theta$—or after noting that the derivative of $\cos\theta+j\sin\theta$ is $j(\cos\theta+j\sin\theta)$—it is seen that

$$\cos\theta+j\sin\theta = e^{j\theta}.$$

Hence we may write

$$z = re^{j\theta} \quad \text{(polar form)}$$

as alternative to $\quad z = x+jy \quad$ (cartesian form).

The rules for the fundamental algebraic operations are given below, and in these we write

$$z = x+jy = re^{j\theta},$$
$$Z = X+jY = Re^{j\phi}.$$

Addition and subtraction

$$z+Z = (x+jy)+(X+jY)$$
$$= (x+X)+j(y+Y)$$

and, similarly, $\quad z-Z = (x-X)+j(y-Y).$

If the complex numbers are given in the polar form, it is usually best to express them in cartesian form for addition or subtraction.

Multiplication

For this the polar form is simpler, since

$$zZ = re^{j\theta}.Re^{j\phi} = rRe^{j(\theta+\phi)}.$$

But direct multiplication of the cartesian expressions is possible and easy, and yields an equivalent result,

$$zZ = (x+jy)(X+jY)$$
$$= (xX-yY)+j(xY+yX).$$

Division

For this also the polar form is simpler, since

$$Z/z = Re^{j\phi}/re^{\theta} = (R/r)e^{j(\phi-\theta)}.$$

The cartesian forms can also be used, by 'realizing' the denominator, as follows:

$$\frac{Z}{z} = \frac{X+jY}{x+jy} = \frac{(X+jY)(x-jy)}{(x+jy)(x-jy)}$$

$$= \frac{Xx+Yy}{x^2+y^2}+j\frac{Yx-Xy}{x^2+y^2}.$$

The number $x-jy$ is called the *conjugate* of $z = x+jy$, and is often written $\bar{z}$.

Powers

For these the polar form is much superior, for

$$z^n = (re^{j\theta})^n = r^n e^{jn\theta}.$$

Roots

Simple inversion of the rule for powers suggests that

$$\sqrt[n]{z} = \sqrt[n]{r}.e^{j\theta/n}.$$

This is, however, only *one* of the values. It should be clear that

$$e^{j(\theta+2m\pi)} = \cos(\theta+2m\pi)+j\sin(\theta+2m\pi)$$
$$= \cos\theta+j\sin\theta = e^{j\theta},$$

if m is any (positive or negative) integer, so that we may write

$$z = re^{j(\theta+2m\pi)}.$$

From this, as above, we should conclude that

$$\sqrt[n]{z} = \sqrt[n]{r}.e^{j(\theta+2m\pi)/n}.$$

In this we can give m the values $0, 1, 2, ... (n-1)$, and derive n *distinct* values, each of which can claim to be an nth root of z. Putting $m = n$, $n+1, n+2, ..., -1, -2, ...,$ gives no new values, but repeats values in the above set. Hence we may say that there are n distinct nth roots of the complex number z, that is, two square roots, three cube roots, four fourth roots, and so on. Since the moduli of all these is $\sqrt[n]{r}$, while the phase increases by $2\pi/n$ in going from one to the next, it follows that the representative points are equally spaced round a circle on the Argand diagram.

EXERCISES ON CHAPTER I

1. A mass M is attached to the mid-point of a light string of length $2a$, fixed at its ends and stretched by a tension P. Find the frequency of transverse vibrations and the constants of the analogous circuit.

2. A mass M is attached to the end of a light bar of length l and flexural rigidity EI, clamped at the other end. Find the frequency of lateral vibrations.

3. Find the frequency of transverse vibrations for a mass attached to the centre of the bar in Ex. 2, (a) when supported at each end, (b) when clamped at each end.

4. A pulley, moment of inertia I, is attached to a shaft of length l dividing it into segments of lengths a and b. The shaft is clamped at both ends, and has torsional rigidity CJ. Find the frequency of torsional vibrations, neglecting the inertia of the shaft.

5. A piston of mass m closes a vessel of volume V containing air at pressure p. Find the frequency of vibration, given that the coefficient of volume elasticity of the air is γp, and that the area of the piston is A.

6. A uniform bar of mass m has equal transverse springs of stiffness s attached to its ends, the other ends of the springs being fixed. If the bar is pivoted at its mid-point, find the frequency of rotational vibration.

7. Find the approximate frequency of an acoustic resonator, the piston in Ex. 5 being replaced by air of density ρ in a neck of length l and area A. Give the numerical value for a litre flask with a neck of length 10 cm and diameter 1 cm, when $p = 1$ atm $= 10^6$ dynes/cm², $\rho = 0\cdot0013$ gm/cm³, and $\gamma = 1\cdot41$.

8. A body rests on an elastic support which deflects 1 in. under its weight. Find the frequency of vertical vibration.

9. A mass of 1 gm attached to the centre of a diaphragm reduces the frequency of vibration from 5,000 to 4,900 per sec. What is the effective mass of the diaphragm? What deflexion is produced by a normal central load of 1 gm wt?

10. A mass of 2 gm is attached to a light string 1 m long at a point 30 cm from one end. The string is fixed at its ends, and stretched by a tension of 100 gm wt. Find the frequency of transverse vibration.

II

ENERGY IN VIBRATING SYSTEMS

IT is possible to regard a vibration in any system as an inter-change of energies, a periodic transformation of energy from kinetic to potential and back again. This is helpful not only as a qualitative description in physical terms of an important feature of the phenomenon, but also, as we proceed to show, as a means of determining vibration frequencies. We note that the two energies, potential and kinetic, are associated respectively with the two essential features of vibrating systems, restoring force and inertia.

2.1. Kinetic energy

The specification of kinetic energy in mechanical systems is usually not difficult. If a mass m has a displacement x, and hence a velocity $\dot{x}$, the kinetic energy T is given by

$$T = \tfrac{1}{2}m\dot{x}^2. \tag{1}$$

Similarly, if a body with moment of inertia I about an axis has angular displacement θ about that axis, so that the angular velocity is $\dot{\theta}$, the kinetic energy is

$$T = \tfrac{1}{2}I\dot{\theta}^2. \tag{2}$$

These energies are expressed in dynamical units. If we desire to express them in gravitational (engineering) units, we replace m by W/g, W being the weight, and I by Wk^2/g, where k is the radius of gyration.

In the case of a rigid body in general motion we may have to use the fact that the total kinetic energy may be analysed into a sum of translational and rotational energies. Specifically if M is the total mass, V_G the speed of the mass-centre, Ω the resultant angular velocity, and I_G the moment of inertia about the axis through the mass-centre parallel to the instantaneous axis of rotation,

$$T = \tfrac{1}{2}MV_G^2 + \tfrac{1}{2}I_G\Omega^2. \tag{3}$$

It is also to be noted that the electrical circuit suggests the existence of an electrodynamic energy

$$T = \tfrac{1}{2}L\dot{q}^2. \tag{4}$$

2.2. Potential energy

The difference of potential energy between any two states or configurations of a system, denoted by suffixes 1 and 2, is the work done by the external forces in moving the system from the first state to the second. Using V to denote potential energy, and W to denote work, we may express this symbolically as

$$V_2 - V_1 = W_{12}. \tag{5}$$

It is to be noted that only *differences* of potential energy matter, and that the choice of a zero or datum is a matter purely of convenience. For vibrating systems the zero or datum state which is (always) the most convenient is that of *equilibrium*. With this convention we can define potential energy as the work done in displacing the system from its equilibrium position.

In the general case, when the force is proportional to the displacement, so that

$$F = sx, \tag{6}$$

where s is the equivalent stiffness,

$$V = \int_0^x sx\,dx = \tfrac{1}{2}sx^2. \tag{7}$$

By definition (or inverting the integration)

$$F = \frac{dV}{dx}. \tag{8}$$

We notice also that 　　$V = \tfrac{1}{2}Fx,$ 　　　　(9)

a very important result, which can be thought of as stating that the work done is the product of the average force and the total displacement. It must be borne in mind, however, that only when the relation between force and displacement is linear is the 'average force' the mean of initial and final values.

By using the fact that

$$x = F/s$$

we can derive a third formula for the potential energy, namely

$$V = F^2/2s, \tag{10}$$

where the energy is given in terms of the force. We notice that

$$\frac{dV}{dF} = \frac{F}{s} = x, \tag{11}$$

a result complementary to (8) above. It must be noted, however, that while (8) is true for *all* laws of force, (11) holds only for the linear law.

In many cases, as we shall see, the form involving the force (or its analogue) is that most readily obtainable. For statical purposes (e.g. theory of structures) it has many advantages, but for dynamical purposes we generally need V in terms of displacement. The above analysis shows that, having obtained V in terms of F, we may find x in terms of F, and hence F, and finally V, in terms of x.

Summarizing,

$$V = \tfrac{1}{2}sx^2 = \tfrac{1}{2}Fx = F^2/2s, \tag{12}$$

$$F = dV/dx, \qquad x = dV/dF. \tag{13}$$

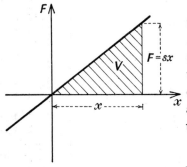

FIG. 9

It is instructive also to picture the above diagrammatically. If F is plotted against x, the work (P.E.) is represented by the area under the (F, x) curve. In the case of a linear law the area is a triangle, and the formula for this area gives immediately

$$V = \tfrac{1}{2}Fx, \tag{14}$$

whence the two others immediately follow. We may note also that (in the linear case only) the difference of potential energy due to increase in the deflexion from x_1 to x_2 is, by the formula for the area of a trapezium (see Fig. 10),

$$V_2 - V_1 = \tfrac{1}{2}(F_2 + F_1)(x_2 - x_1)$$

$$= \text{mean force} \times \text{increase of displacement.} \tag{15}$$

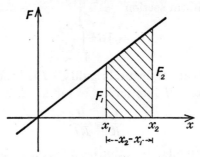

FIG. 10

2.3. Potential energy (*cont.*)

We continue first with some special examples. If a bar of sectional area A, length l, is stretched by a tension P, the extension e is given by

$$e = \frac{Pl}{AE},$$

whence
$$P = AE\frac{e}{l}. \tag{16}$$

It follows that

$$V = \tfrac{1}{2}Pe = \frac{P^2l}{2AE} = \frac{AEe^2}{2l}. \tag{17}$$

In such a case the energy is termed 'strain energy', and we shall use U generally to denote strain energy.

If the bar is non-uniform, so that A or E or both vary with the distance x from one end, then we consider an element of length dx, that is, replace l by dx, and then integrate from 0 to l so that

$$U = \tfrac{1}{2}P^2 \int\limits_0^l \frac{dx}{AE}. \tag{18}$$

Next we consider the torsion of a shaft of torsional rigidity CJ and length l. If θ is the twist, then the torque G is given by

$$G = \frac{CJ\theta}{l}, \tag{19}$$

and
$$U = \tfrac{1}{2}G\theta = \frac{G^2l}{2CJ} = \frac{CJ\theta^2}{2l}. \tag{20}$$

For non-uniform section

$$U = \tfrac{1}{2}G^2 \int_0^l \frac{dx}{CJ}. \tag{21}$$

Again, if a beam of flexural rigidity EI is bent by a constant bending moment M into an arc of radius R, it is known that

$$\frac{1}{R} = \frac{M}{EI}. \tag{22}$$

But, if θ is the angular deviation between the ends of the bent bar,

$$\theta = \frac{l}{R}, \tag{23}$$

so that

$$M = \frac{EI\theta}{l}. \tag{24}$$

Here

$$U = \tfrac{1}{2}M\theta = \frac{M^2 l}{2EI} = \frac{EI\theta^2}{2l}. \tag{25}$$

For non-uniform section, or non-uniform bending moment, this becomes

$$U = \int_0^l \frac{M^2}{2EI}\, dx. \tag{26}$$

As a simple instance of the process indicated at the end of the last section, consider the case of a cantilever beam of length l and

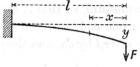

Fig. 11

constant flexural rigidity EI subject to a transverse end load F. The bending moment M at a distance x from F is Fx, so that

$$U = \int_0^l \frac{(Fx)^2}{2EI}\, dx = \frac{F^2 l^3}{6EI}. \tag{27}$$

Now the end deflexion, y, is given by

$$y = dU/dF = Fl^3/3EI. \tag{28}$$

Hence, also,
$$U = \frac{3EIy^2}{2l^3}. \qquad (29)$$

In the electrostatic analogy we find a complete agreement, for if q is the charge and v the voltage of a condenser of capacitance C, the formula for the energy is

$$V = \tfrac{1}{2}Cv^2 = \tfrac{1}{2}vq = q^2/2C. \qquad (30)$$

Coming to cases where results of the above form are approximations whose accuracy decreases with increasing displacement, we consider first the simple pendulum. If m is the mass of the bob, l the length of the string, then when the angular displacement is θ the potential energy (measured from the equilibrium position as datum) is, accurately,

$$V = mgl(1 - \cos\theta). \qquad (31)$$

If we use the cosine series, to two terms, we obtain the approximate quadratic formula

$$V = \tfrac{1}{2}mgl\theta^2. \qquad (32)$$

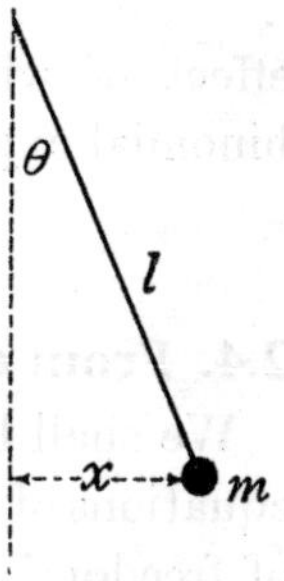

Fig. 12

Alternatively we may use, as a coordinate to specify the configuration of the system, the (horizontal) displacement, x, of the bob, so that

$$x = l\sin\theta \qquad (33)$$

and
$$V = mg\{l - \sqrt{(l^2 - x^2)}\}. \qquad (34)$$

Expanding the square root by the binomial theorem, retaining only two terms, we obtain the approximation

$$V = \tfrac{1}{2}mgx^2/l, \qquad (35)$$

again of the simple quadratic form.

Finally we consider the case of a stretched string, of length $2a$, tension P, fixed at the ends, with a central transverse deflexion y (see Fig. 13). Two points of view both lead to the same quadratic approximation:

(i) Suppose the string to be inextensible. Then the work done is the product of P and the shortening of AB, that is,

$$V = P\{2a - 2\sqrt{(a^2 - y^2)}\} \sim Py^2/a \qquad (36)$$

if the binomial expansion is stopped at the second term.

(ii) If the string stretches (the tension being assumed constant—it varies only by an amount of the second order, the

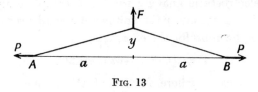

Fig. 13

effect of which is comparable with terms neglected in the binomial expansion), the work done is

$$V = P\{2\sqrt{(a^2+y^2)}-2a\} \sim Py^2/a. \tag{37}$$

2.4. From energy to equation of motion

We shall later use the energies of a system to construct the equations of motion, in the case of a system with several 'degrees of freedom', but for a system with a single degree of freedom (that is, whose configuration is specified by a single coordinate) this is particularly simple. The total energy of the system remains constant. In the (typical) case of a mass m controlled by a spring of stiffness s, the total energy

$$E = T+V$$

$$= \tfrac{1}{2}m\dot{x}^2+\tfrac{1}{2}sx^2 = \text{const.} \tag{38}$$

Differentiating with respect to time,

$$m\dot{x}\ddot{x}+sx\dot{x} = 0,$$

that is (unless $\dot{x} = 0$, when the system stays at rest),

$$m\ddot{x}+sx = 0, \tag{39}$$

the well-known equation of motion.

2.5. Energy method for the determination of pulsatance

Another aspect of the energy in a vibrating system is the periodic transformation of energy from potential to kinetic and vice versa. The total energy, of course, remains constant. At one moment—the end of the swing—it is *all* potential; at another—when passing through the equilibrium position—it is *all* kinetic.

Hence *the maximum kinetic energy is equal to the maximum potential energy*, that is,

$$\hat{T} = \hat{V}. \tag{40}$$

It is easy to show this formally. Considering again our mass and spring, with $\omega^2 = s/m$,

$$x = a \sin \omega t, \quad \text{and} \quad \hat{x} = a, \tag{41}$$

$$\dot{x} = \omega a \cos \omega t, \quad \text{and} \quad \hat{\dot{x}} = \omega a = \omega \hat{x}, \tag{42}$$

so that $\qquad \hat{T} = \tfrac{1}{2}m\hat{\dot{x}}^2 = \tfrac{1}{2}m\omega^2 a^2, \tag{43}$

$$\hat{V} = \tfrac{1}{2}s\hat{x}^2 = \tfrac{1}{2}sa^2. \tag{44}$$

Putting $\qquad\qquad\qquad \hat{T} = \hat{V}$

we derive $\qquad\qquad \tfrac{1}{2}m\omega^2 a^2 = \tfrac{1}{2}sa^2,$

so that $\qquad\qquad\qquad \omega^2 = s/m, \tag{45}$

agreeing with the previous result.

This method of equating maximum kinetic and potential energies affords a valuable means of obtaining pulsatances, which we shall exploit in later chapters. Although it yields, as in the above example and in the exercises at the end of the chapter, exact results for simple systems, it is especially useful as a means of obtaining approximate results for complicated systems for which exact formal results are difficult to obtain or to handle. We give a few simple examples of its use in this way.

2.6. Examples of the energy method

(i) The first example will be the allowance for the mass m of a spring which controls the vibration of a mass M at its end. Let the displacement of M from its equilibrium position be y. Then, if s is the stiffness of the spring, the potential energy is

$$V = \tfrac{1}{2}sy^2, \tag{46}$$

Fig. 14

since the *mass* of the spring has no effect upon V.

The kinetic energy of the mass M is

$$T_M = \tfrac{1}{2}M\dot{y}^2, \tag{47}$$

but since the spring also moves, it also has kinetic energy, and this we now calculate. If l is the (unstretched) length of the spring, the mass of a small element δx at a distance x from the fixed end is $(m/l)\delta x$, its displacement $(x/l)y$, and its velocity $(x/l)\dot{y}$; consequently, its kinetic energy is

$$\frac{1}{2}\frac{m}{l}\,\delta x\left(\frac{x}{l}\dot{y}\right)^2 = \frac{m\dot{y}^2}{2l^3}x^2\,\delta x.$$

The kinetic energy of the whole spring is thus

$$T_s = \frac{m\dot{y}^2}{2l^3}\int_0^l x^2\,dx = \tfrac{1}{6}m\dot{y}^2, \tag{48}$$

and the total kinetic energy of the system is

$$T = T_M + T_s = \tfrac{1}{2}(M + \tfrac{1}{3}m)\dot{y}^2.$$

Equating the maximum kinetic and potential energies, and using the fact that $\dot{\hat{y}} = \omega\hat{y}$, gives

$$\tfrac{1}{2}(M+\tfrac{1}{3}m)\omega^2\hat{y}^2 = \tfrac{1}{2}s\hat{y}^2,$$

whence

$$\omega^2 = s/(M+\tfrac{1}{3}m). \tag{49}$$

The meaning of this result is that the *effective mass* of the spring is one-third of its actual mass.

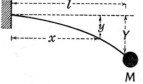

(ii) Allowance for the mass of a uniform cantilever when vibrating with a mass attached to the free end.

If the cantilever, of length l, mass m, and flexural rigidity EI has an end deflexion Y produced by a transverse force at the end, the strain energy (potential energy) is

Fig. 15

$$V = 3EIY^2/2l^3. \tag{50}$$

The kinetic energy of the mass M at the end is

$$T_M = \tfrac{1}{2}M\dot{Y}^2. \tag{51}$$

If y is the transverse deflexion of the cantilever at a distance x from the fixed end, the mass of an element of length δx is $(m/l)\delta x$, and its kinetic energy $\tfrac{1}{2}(m/l)\delta x\,\dot{y}^2$. It follows that the total kinetic energy of the cantilever is

$$T_c = \int_0^l \tfrac{1}{2}(m/l)\dot{y}^2 \, dx. \tag{52}$$

As before, we have $\hat{Y} = \omega \bar{Y}$, $\hat{y} = \omega \bar{y}$, so that

$$\hat{V} = 3EI\hat{Y}^2/2l^3, \tag{53}$$

$$\begin{aligned}\hat{T} &= \hat{T}_M + \hat{T}_c \\ &= \tfrac{1}{2}\omega^2\left\{M\hat{Y}^2 + (m/l)\int_0^l \bar{y}^2 \, dx\right\}.\end{aligned} \tag{54}$$

In order to proceed we need to know $\bar{y}$ as a function of x. An accurate solution can be obtained by the methods of Chapter XIV, and the theory of approximate methods will be given in Chapter XV, but here it may suffice to say that if m is small compared with M, a good approximation can be obtained by using the formula for the static deflexion due to a force at the end. From the theory of the bending of beams this is

$$\frac{y}{Y} = \frac{3lx^2 - x^3}{2l^3}. \tag{55}$$

From this,
$$\int_0^l y^2 \, dx = (Y/2l^3)^2 \int_0^l (9l^2x^4 - 6lx^5 + x^6) \, dx$$

$$= \frac{33}{140}lY^2. \tag{56}$$

Inserting this in (54) gives

$$\hat{T} = \tfrac{1}{2}\omega^2\hat{Y}^2(M + 33m/140), \tag{57}$$

so that equating $\hat{T}$ and $\hat{V}$ yields

$$\omega^2 = 3EI/l^3(M + 33m/140). \tag{58}$$

The meaning of this is that the inertia of the bar is equivalent to $33/140$ of its total mass at the end.

EXERCISES ON CHAPTER II

1. Find the free pulsatance of a mass M at the mid-point of a light string of length $2a$, stretched by a tension P, correcting for the mass of the string, m per unit length.

2. Find the free pulsatance of a pulley of moment of inertia I at the end of a shaft of torsional rigidity CJ, correcting for the mass of the shaft, of length l, radius r, and density ρ.

3. A mass M is attached to the centre of a light bar of length $2l$, mass m per unit length and flexural rigidity EI. Find the pulsatance of free transverse vibrations when the bar is freely supported at each end. (If y_1 is the central deflexion, the deflexion at x from one end is

$$y = y_1(3l^2x-x^3)/2l^3,$$

x being less than l.)

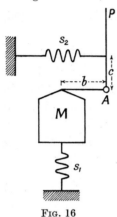

FIG. 16

4. A mass M is attached to one end of a bar of length l, pivoted at the other end. The bar is held horizontal in its equilibrium position by a spring of stiffness s attached at a distance a from the pivot. Find the pulsatance of free vibrations (a) neglecting the mass of the bar, (b) taking the mass m of the bar into account.

5. The sketch shows diagrammatically the parts of an amplitude meter. A considerable mass M is supported by a spring of stiffness s_1. To M is attached a bent lever pivoted at A and carrying the pointer P. This is kept in contact with M by a spring of stiffness s_2, attached at a distance c from A, the length of the other arm of the lever being b. The moment of inertia of the pointer system about A is I. Show that the system has the same frequency as a mass $M + I/b^2$ controlled by a spring of stiffness $s_1 + s_2 c^2/b^2$.

6. By means of the energy method deduce the pulsatances of the 'normal modes' of free vibration of two equal masses m at the points of trisection of a light string of length $3a$ fixed at the ends and stretched by a tension P, that is, those vibrations in which the displacements are (a) equal, (b) equal and opposite.

III

DISSIPATION OF ENERGY: DAMPED VIBRATIONS

In our earlier discussion of the essential requirements of a vibrating system we met the condition that friction must not be too great, and indeed came to the conclusion that in at least some systems friction might be regarded as a secondary effect. We now take up the question of applying a correction for this secondary effect, and of calculating the consequences of friction —not always small—in a vibrating system. The precise significance of the description 'not too great' will emerge from our discussion.

In the typical case of a mass m controlled by a spring of stiffness s, there will also be a force due to friction or 'resistance', F say, whose direction is always opposed to that of the velocity. Now the velocity may be towards or away from the equilibrium position for any particular displacement, according as the mass is travelling inwards or outwards, that is, the sign of the frictional force is *not* governed by the sign of the displacement x. Hence we must write our equation of motion

$$m\ddot{x} = -sx \mp F \tag{1}$$

(which is really *two* equations), the upper sign being taken if $\dot{x}$ is positive, the lower if $\dot{x}$ is negative. So long as the ambiguity of sign and the duplicity of equations persist, they will give rise to complications in the mathematics.

3.1. Laws of friction or resistance: equation of motion

One may distinguish between three classes of friction or resistance, commonly accepted in mechanics as agreeing reasonably well with experimental evidence:

  (a) solid sliding friction (Coulomb friction) constant in magnitude (so long as the normal reaction remains constant);

(b) viscous fluid friction—at relatively small speeds—proportional to the speed;

(c) 'hydraulic' friction—at greater speeds—proportional to the square of the speed.

Of these (b) has, from the mathematical standpoint, a dual advantage: (i) it is *automatically* self-reversing with the speed (which (a) and (c) are not); (ii) the resulting equation is *linear*, and therefore simple to handle (this applies also to (a) but not to (c)). For these reasons the law in (b) is almost universally used in a mathematical treatment, and does in fact represent an acceptably good approximation to what actually occurs in many mechanical systems, and is accurate in the electrical analogy.

If we introduce a 'resistance coefficient' r, so that the resistance F is given by

$$F = r\dot{x}, \tag{2}$$

then the typical equation of motion becomes

$$m\ddot{x} = -sx - r\dot{x},$$

or
$$m\ddot{x} + r\dot{x} + sx = 0. \tag{3}$$

In the first instance—*not* always—we may regard r as relatively small.

Before we develop the consequences of this equation, we may recall that if a condenser of capacitance C is discharged through a coil of resistance R and self-inductance L, the differential equation connecting the charge q with the time is

$$L\ddot{q} + R\dot{q} + q/C = 0, \tag{4}$$

which is seen to be of exactly the same form as (3), and where the electrical resistance R is seen to be analogous to the resistance coefficient r.

Other mechanical systems obeying the same law of resistance proportional to the speed will lead to an equation of exactly the same form.

It is convenient to reduce all these equations to a standard form. Dividing (3) by m (or (4) by L) we write ω^2, as before, for s/m (or for $1/LC$), and 2α for r/m (or for R/L). We shall term α

the 'resistance parameter'. We thus arrive at a standard equation for 'damped' (i.e. resisted) vibrations,

$$\ddot{x}+2\alpha\dot{x}+\omega^2 x = 0. \tag{5}$$

Before proceeding mathematically to solve this equation, it is well to consider qualitatively the sort of thing the solution might be expected to represent, in view of the physical meaning which underlies it. Friction may be expected to slow down the motion, and gradually to destroy it. Hence we should expect

(i) an increase in the period,
(ii) a steady decrease in the amplitude.

Which of these is the more marked, and their precise *quantitative* expression, are things which only a mathematical solution can show.

3.2. Solution of equation; damped vibrations

Many methods of solving the differential equation (5) are to be found in the textbooks of mathematics, and all (of course) lead essentially to the same result. The student is advised to refer to these textbooks, and to be familiar with methods other than the one to be outlined.

Recalling the properties of the exponential function, especially that its derivatives are multiples of itself, we realize that its behaviour makes it a possible type of solution for a linear differential equation with constant coefficients. Thus we adopt, as a trial formula,

$$x = Ae^{\lambda t}, \tag{6}$$

where A and λ are constants. From this,

$$\dot{x} = \lambda Ae^{\lambda t}, \qquad \ddot{x} = \lambda^2 Ae^{\lambda t}, \tag{7}$$

so that upon substitution in the equation we obtain

$$A(\lambda^2+2\alpha\lambda+\omega^2)e^{\lambda t} = 0. \tag{8}$$

Consequently the values of λ must be roots of the quadratic equation

$$\lambda^2+2\alpha\lambda+\omega^2 = 0, \tag{9}$$

and we are primarily interested in the case where α is small, so that the roots are complex, that is,

$$\lambda = -\alpha \pm j\sqrt{(\omega^2 - \alpha^2)}$$
$$= -\alpha \pm j\mu, \tag{10}$$

where $j^2 = -1$ (j is the 'imaginary' unit) and μ is an abbreviation for $\sqrt{(\omega^2 - \alpha^2)}$, that is,

$$\mu^2 = \omega^2 - \alpha^2. \tag{11}$$

A formal solution is therefore

$$x = A_1 e^{(-\alpha + j\mu)t} + A_2 e^{(-\alpha - j\mu)t}$$
$$= e^{-\alpha t}(A_1 e^{j\mu t} + A_2 e^{-j\mu t}). \tag{12}$$

Remembering the connexion between the imaginary exponential and the trigonometrical functions,

$$e^{j\theta} = \cos\theta + j\sin\theta,$$

we may write (12) in the 'real' form

$$x = e^{-\alpha t}(B\sin\mu t + C\cos\mu t) \tag{13 a}$$
$$= a e^{-\alpha t}\sin(\mu t + \phi). \tag{13 b}$$

But another way of regarding the result (12) is fruitful. It consists in considering the complex solution (in which z is written instead of x to avoid confusion)

$$z = A_1 e^{-\alpha t}e^{j\mu t} \tag{14}$$

plotted on an Argand diagram. If we put (since if we admit complex quantities at all, it is wise to do so thoroughly!)

$$A_1 = a e^{j\phi}, \tag{15}$$

then $\qquad\qquad z = a e^{-\alpha t}e^{j(\mu t + \phi)}. \tag{16}$

This represents a 'vector' of length $a e^{-\alpha t}$, at an angle $(\mu t + \phi)$ to the real axis. As t varies, the length of the vector varies according to the law $a e^{-\alpha t}$, while the 'vector' rotates with angular velocity μ. Its extremity thus describes a spiral (a so-called equi-angular spiral, in fact). A 'real' solution corresponds to a component or projection of the vector. The 'vertical' component —or 'imaginary part'—is $a e^{-\alpha t}\sin(\mu t + \phi)$, the horizontal component or real part is $a e^{-\alpha t}\cos(\mu t + \phi)$. The former is shown plotted, by horizontal projection of points at angular distance $45°$ (corresponding to time interval $\pi/4\mu$), in Fig. 17.

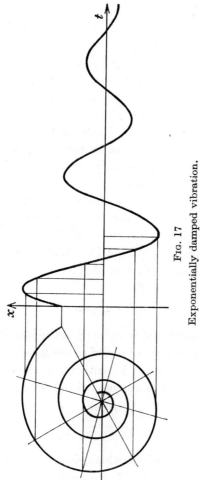

FIG. 17

Exponentially damped vibration.

All modes of attack yield essentially the same result, which, by (13 b), may be regarded as an oscillation of pulsatance μ (indicated by $\sin(\mu t + \phi)$, *but equally by* $e^{j\mu t}$), with an amplitude $ae^{-\alpha t}$ which decreases indefinitely with time, as indicated by the *decay factor* $e^{-\alpha t}$.

Noting that $\mu = \sqrt{(\omega^2 - \alpha^2)}$, and that the frequency of the vibrations is $\mu/2\pi$, or the period $2\pi/\mu$, we see that one effect of resistance is to *reduce the frequency*. Since, however, the effect depends upon α^2, this effect is of the second order, and is very small if the frictional resistance is small.

Far more important is the decay effect, since in this α occurs to the first power, and even if α is small, αt ultimately becomes very large. That oscillations in real systems do decrease in amplitude more or less gradually, or are *damped*, as we say, is a commonplace of observation.

As a measure of damping, the parameter α is one possible choice. It depends, however, upon an arbitrary unit of time. The vibrating system has its *own* inherent unit of time—its period $T = 2\pi/\mu$, and it is logical to refer to properties '*per period*' rather than 'per second'. One characteristic on this basis is the 'decay factor per period'

$$e^{-\alpha T} = e^{-2\pi\alpha/\mu}. \tag{17}$$

Another, more commonly employed, is the *logarithmic decrement*, δ, that is, the decrease *per period* of the logarithm of the amplitude. If we use natural logarithms, we have $\delta = 2\pi\alpha/\mu$. If (as is arithmetically more convenient) we use 10 as the base, we have
$$\delta = 0 \cdot 8686\pi\alpha/\mu$$
$$= 2 \cdot 7288\alpha/\mu. \tag{18}$$

Experimentally the logarithmic decrement can be regarded as the logarithm of the ratio of two successive maximum displacements on the same side of the equilibrium position, but when the damping is small it is necessary, if an accurate result is desired, to observe the decay over a number of periods, dividing the logarithm of the ratio of a maximum to that n periods later by n. In the case of ballistic measuring instruments, a knowledge of the rate of decay is necessary to correct for damping between the start of the motion from the equilibrium position and the observed first maximum displacement.

We return to the effect of damping upon the frequency. It has already been noted that, for small α, the difference between μ and ω is a small quantity of the second order. Indeed, unless the effect of damping is to produce decay so rapid that only a few vibrations are sensible, the effect upon the frequency is negligible unless unusually great accuracy is desired. To illustrate this, let us find the decay factor per period when the effect upon frequency is 1 per cent. Then

$$\mu = 0{\cdot}99\omega,$$

$$\mu^2 = \omega^2 - \alpha^2 = 0{\cdot}9801\omega^2,$$

$$\alpha^2 = 0{\cdot}0199\omega^2,$$

$$\alpha = 0{\cdot}1411\omega,$$

$$2\pi\alpha/\mu = 2\pi(0{\cdot}1411)/0{\cdot}99 = 0{\cdot}8953...,$$

$$e^{-2\pi\alpha/\mu} = e^{-0{\cdot}8953} = 0{\cdot}4085....$$

After 5 periods the amplitude is little more than one-hundredth of its initial value.

Thus, if damping is not very marked, its effect upon period or frequency is negligible unless really great accuracy is necessary.

3.3. Large damping

The condition for an oscillatory solution is that $\alpha^2 < \omega^2$. When this condition is not fulfilled, that is, when $\alpha > \omega$, the roots of the auxiliary equation (9) are both real, being

$$-\gamma_1 = -\alpha + \sqrt{(\alpha^2 - \omega^2)}, \quad -\gamma_2 = -\alpha - \sqrt{(\alpha^2 - \omega^2)}. \tag{19}$$

It should be clear that both these roots are negative.

The general solution of equation (5) is now

$$x = Ae^{-\gamma_1 t} + Be^{-\gamma_2 t}, \tag{20}$$

representing a solution which dies away asymptotically to zero. The values of A and B depend upon the initial displacement and velocity, and typical displacement-time graphs are given in Fig. 18.

One—and only one—passage through the equilibrium position is possible.

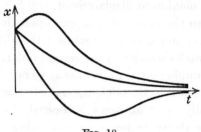

3.4. Critical damping

For some purposes it is desirable to make the system non-oscillatory, but clearly to apply more friction than is necessary is inefficient. The degree of damping which *just* makes a system non-oscillatory is therefore of importance. Moreover, the behaviour of the system then depends upon only *one* parameter, so that it is more easily and certainly calculable. The condition is termed *critical damping*.

The condition for critical damping is that μ should vanish, that is, that

$$\alpha = \omega,$$

or
$$r^2 = 4sm. \tag{21}$$

When this condition holds, the differential equation is

$$\ddot{x} + 2\alpha\dot{x} + \alpha^2 x = 0. \tag{22}$$

The auxiliary quadratic has two *equal* roots, both $-\alpha$, and so, by the theory of linear differential equations with constant coefficients, the general solution is

$$x = (A + Bt)e^{-\alpha t}, \tag{23}$$

with A and B constants to be determined by the initial conditions.

In a 'ballistic' instrument, for instance, an impulse causes departure from the equilibrium configuration with velocity V depending upon the magnitude of the impulse and the inertial properties of the system, that is, $x = 0$ and $\dot{x} = V$ when $t = 0$. Using these conditions to determine A and B we find

$$x = Vte^{-\alpha t}. \tag{24}$$

The displacement-time graph is indicated in the figure. The maximum swing is recorded, and is the measure of the applied

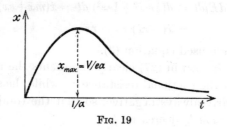

FIG. 19

impulse. We readily find that the condition for the maximum value of x ($\dot{x} = 0$) leads to $\alpha t = 1$, and hence to

$$x_{\max} = (V/\alpha)e^{-1}$$
$$= 0\cdot368(V/\alpha). \qquad (25)$$

The numerical factor $e^{-1} = 0\cdot368...$, which applies provided that the damping is critical, is independent of the constants of the system, and this circumstance is one reason for the importance of 'critical' damping.

3.5. Dissipation of energy

Besides its influence on pulsatance and amplitude, the presence of frictional resistance in a system has the effect of dissipating energy. That this is so is obvious since the direction of friction is always opposite to that of velocity, so that positive work must be done by the system in overcoming it. The fate of this lost mechanical energy is, possibly after intermediate transformation into other forms of physical energy, ultimately to be dissipated as heat.

Quantitatively, for the system considered in this chapter, the potential energy at any time t is, by (13 b),

$$V = \tfrac{1}{2}sx^2 = \tfrac{1}{2}a^2e^{-2\alpha t}\sin^2(\mu t+\phi). \qquad (26)$$

If t increases by a period, $2\pi/\mu$, V is reduced by a factor $e^{-4\pi\alpha/\mu}$. Similarly, as is easily shown, the kinetic energy $\tfrac{1}{2}m\dot{x}^2$ is reduced by the same factor. Thus we may describe $e^{-4\pi\alpha/\mu}$ as the *energy decay factor* per period. It is obviously the square of the (amplitude) decay factor given in (17).

Alternatively, we may consider the total energy, $E = T+V$. Its rate of change is

$$dE/dt = d(\tfrac{1}{2}m\dot{x}^2 + \tfrac{1}{2}sx^2)/dt = \dot{x}(m\ddot{x}+sx)$$
$$= \dot{x}(-r\dot{x}) = -r\dot{x}^2, \tag{27}$$

where we have used equation (3).

The form $\dot{x}(-r\dot{x})$ in (27) clearly represents the rate of doing work against the frictional resistance $r\dot{x}$, while the second form, $-r\dot{x}^2$, is clearly always negative, so that the total mechanical energy *continuously* decreases.

EXERCISES ON CHAPTER III

1. A diaphragm has effective mass 1 gm, stiffness $3\cdot97 \times 10^7$ dynes/cm, and resistance 200 dynes/cm/sec. Find the frequency of its damped vibrations, the logarithmic decrement, and the number of vibrations in which the amplitude is halved.

2. Find the capacitance of the condenser which, when discharged through a resistance of 10 ohms having an inductance of $0\cdot1$ henry, just makes the discharge non-oscillatory.

3. If the decay factor per period is $0\cdot9$, by how much per cent is the frequency reduced below that of the undamped frequency?

4. A lorry body oscillates on its springs at the rate of 30 vibrations per minute. The amplitude is halved in 2 sec. Find the differential equation for the vibrations, taking the second as the unit of time.

5. A mass of 5 gm, controlled by a spring, and subject to a resistance proportional to the velocity, executes free damped vibrations of frequency 5 per sec, and the decay factor per period is $0\cdot8$. Determine the stiffness of the spring and the resistance coefficient. (U.L.)

6. A mass of 100 gm executes damped vibrations. The period is observed to be $1\cdot85$ sec, and the amplitude is halved in 5 periods. Find the steady force necessary to maintain a displacement of 10 cm from the equilibrium position, and the frictional resistance at a speed of 10 cm/sec. (U.L.)

7. A vibrating system, with one degree of freedom, has mass m, resistance coefficient r, and stiffness s. Show that the energy decay factor per period is $e^{-2\pi r/\sqrt{(sm)}}$, approximately, when r is small.

If the frequency is less by $0\cdot5$ per cent than the undamped frequency, show that the amplitude decay factor per period is approximately $0\cdot53$. (U.L.)

MAINTAINED VIBRATIONS

4.1. Steady-state vibrations

W E have so far considered vibrating systems which, after some initial disturbance, were left to themselves and allowed to execute their free natural vibrations. These vibrations have a pulsatance depending on constants inherent in the system, and decay more or less rapidly on account of the frictional resistance which is always present. In many practical cases it is necessary to maintain a vibration for a considerable period of time with a constant (or at least not rapidly decreasing) amplitude, and with a pulsatance which is to be imposed upon the system, and is not necessarily the pulsatance natural to the system. To do this it is necessary to apply to the system a periodic force of the desired pulsatance, with a peak value such that the desired amplitude is maintained. The dissipation of energy due to friction is (as we shall see) made good by the work which the periodic force does on the system, and after the transient free vibrations which are also set up when the motion is initiated have died away, the system reaches a *steady-state vibration* in which a periodic force of constant peak value and pulsatance maintains indefinitely a vibration of constant amplitude and of the same pulsatance.

In this chapter we shall be concerned only with these ultimate steady-state vibrations, leaving for consideration in the next chapter the transients which occur in the early stages just after the force has commenced to act.

4.2. The equation of motion

We consider the typical case of a mass m controlled by a spring of stiffness s damped by a resistance proportional to the speed, with resistance coefficient r. Additionally we suppose that a force of peak value F and pulsatance β acts on the mass, and assuming the force to be sinusoidal,† we may represent it by $F \sin \beta t$. (We might use $F \cos \beta t$, which would mean only that we had chosen the zero time a quarter period later.) Hence the equation of motion is

$$m\ddot{x} = -sx - r\dot{x} + F \sin \beta t,$$

or $\qquad\qquad m\ddot{x} + r\dot{x} + sx = F \sin \beta t. \qquad\qquad (1)$

Dividing by m, and using the abbreviations $r/m = 2\alpha$ and $s/m = \omega^2$ of Chapter III, along with

$$f = F/m,$$

equation (1) may be rewritten in the form

$$\ddot{x} + 2\alpha\dot{x} + \omega^2 x = f \sin \beta t. \qquad\qquad (2)$$

(We may note that f can be interpreted as the *steady* acceleration which would be produced in the mass m by a *steady* force of magnitude F.)

For the time being we are concerned only with the steady-state solution of equation (1) or (2), that is, with the part depending on F, or, in mathematical parlance, with the particular integral.

It is, however, for most purposes mathematically most convenient to replace the sine (or cosine) by an imaginary exponential, the understanding being that, if necessary, the imaginary (or real) part of any resulting expression is to be taken.

4.3. Solution of the equation

We take the equation in the form

$$\ddot{x} + 2\alpha\dot{x} + \omega^2 x = fe^{j\beta t}. \qquad\qquad (3)$$

The steady-state solution which we seek is also of pulsatance β, so we assume that $\qquad\qquad x = Xe^{j\beta t} \qquad\qquad (4)$

with X, a constant, to be determined. As a consequence of this formula we have

$$\dot{x} = j\beta Xe^{j\beta t} = j\beta x, \qquad \ddot{x} = (j\beta)^2 Xe^{j\beta t} = -\beta^2 x. \qquad\qquad (5)$$

† If the force is periodic but not sinusoidal, it can be resolved into its Fourier components, each of which is sinusoidal, and which can be separately considered.

Substituting in the equation, we find that

$$x(-\beta^2+2j\alpha\beta+\omega^2) = fe^{j\beta t},$$

or
$$x = \frac{fe^{j\beta t}}{(\omega^2-\beta^2)+2j\alpha\beta}. \qquad (6)$$

For many purposes, however, we are interested in the velocity, $\dot{x}$, and writing equation (2) in terms of $\dot{x}$ we have

$$\dot{x}(j\beta+2\alpha-j\omega^2/\beta) = fe^{j\beta t},$$

or
$$\dot{x} = \frac{fe^{j\beta t}}{2\alpha+j(\beta-\omega^2/\beta)}. \qquad (7)$$

We may rewrite equations (6) and (7) in terms of the quantities m, r, s, F, obtaining

$$x = \frac{Fe^{j\beta t}}{(s-m\beta^2)+jr\beta}, \qquad (6\,a)$$

$$\dot{x} = \frac{Fe^{j\beta t}}{r+j(m\beta-s/\beta)}. \qquad (7\,a)$$

4.4. Meaning of solution: response curves

In discussing the formal solution just obtained, it is more convenient first to consider the velocity—mainly because β

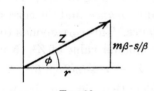

FIG. 20

occurs only in one component of the denominator. As is seen in the diagram, the denominator can be written in the form

$$r+j(m\beta-s/\beta) = Z\cos\phi+jZ\sin\phi$$
$$= Ze^{j\phi}, \qquad (8)$$

where
$$r = Z\cos\phi, \quad m\beta-s/\beta = Z\sin\phi, \qquad (9)$$

or
$$Z^2 = r^2+(m\beta-s/\beta)^2, \quad \tan\phi = (m\beta-s/\beta)/r. \qquad (10)$$

Hence we obtain
$$\dot{x} = \frac{Fe^{j\beta t}}{Ze^{j\phi}} = \frac{F}{Z}e^{j(\beta t-\phi)}. \qquad (11)$$

In real form the solution would be (if we take $F \sin \beta t$ as the maintaining force) the imaginary component of this, that is, we have

$$\dot{x} = (F/Z)\sin(\beta t - \phi). \tag{11a}$$

This gives us a maximum velocity

$$\hat{\dot{x}} = F/Z \tag{12}$$

and a phase lag ϕ of velocity behind force. It should be noted, however, that both these facts are equally evident in (11).

We next consider how this peak velocity $\hat{\dot{x}}$, which we shall call the *velocity response*, varies as the pulsatance of the maintaining force is altered. Rewriting (12) in full we have

$$\hat{\dot{x}} = \frac{F}{\sqrt{\{r^2 + (m\beta - s/\beta)^2\}}}. \tag{12a}$$

If β is very small, that is for very slow vibrations, the term s/β is very large, and so the velocity response (as would be expected for very slow vibrations) is very small. Also, for large values of β, that is for very quick vibrations, the term $m\beta$ is large, and again (as could perhaps be anticipated) the velocity response is very small. As β passes from very small to very large values, the response starts from zero, increases, attains a maximum, and then decreases to zero. The attainment of this maximum is termed *resonance*, and the corresponding value of β the *resonant* pulsatance. This corresponds to a minimum value of Z, and so to a minimum value of Z^2. Now

$$Z^2 = r^2 + (m\beta - s/\beta)^2, \tag{10 bis}$$

and it should be evident that, since the first term, r^2, is a constant, and the second, being a square, cannot be negative, the minimum occurs when the second term is zero, so that the condition for resonance is

$$m\beta - s/\beta = 0,$$

that is,

$$\beta^2 = s/m = \omega^2,$$

or

$$\beta = \omega. \tag{13}$$

Thus *the condition for resonance is that the pulsatance of the maintaining force should be the same as the pulsatance of free undamped vibrations.* At this pulsatance, $Z = r$, so that

$$\hat{\dot{x}}_{\max} = F/r, \tag{14}$$

and this clearly becomes greater if r is made smaller. Indeed the result (14) shows that the maximum velocity response is limited only by the frictional resistance.

Some typical velocity response curves are given in Fig. 21. From these, or directly from the formula (12 a), it is clear that for values of β either small or large compared with ω, the effect of the size of r is very slight, but that not only the maximum peak velocity but also the 'sharpness of resonance' depends entirely upon the (relative) value of r, From the facts exhibited in Fig. 21 two important conclusions emerge:

(i) 'sharp' resonance can be obtained only if the resistance is kept very small;

(ii) 'flat' resonance necessitates rather large damping, and thus inevitably entails a low efficiency.

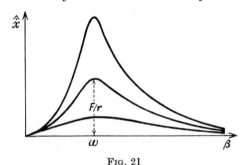

Fig. 21

Turning now to the consideration of the amplitude response, which is mathematically a little less simple, but for mechanical systems at least as important as the velocity response, we see, from (6 a), or from the general rule (for sinusoidal vibrations) that $\hat{x} = \beta\hat{x}$, that

$$\hat{x} = \frac{F}{\sqrt{\{(s-m\beta^2)^2+r^2\beta^2\}}} = \frac{F}{\beta Z}. \tag{15}$$

If β is very small, we see that

$$\hat{x} \sim F/s = x_{\text{eq}}, \tag{16}$$

where x_{eq} denotes the *steady* equilibrium displacement due to a *steady* force F, and so may be termed briefly the 'equilibrium displacement'. This agrees with the physical meaning of $\beta = 0$.

As β increases from zero, it is not immediately evident whether the denominator in (15) decreases or increases, because the first term, $(s-m\beta^2)^2$, does the former and the second term, $r^2\beta^2$, the latter. If the damping is small, however, we may expect the effect on the first term to be dominant, the denominator (initially) to *decrease*, and the amplitude $\hat{x}$ to *increase*. As soon as β has passed the value which makes $(s-m\beta^2)$ vanish, namely $\sqrt{(s/m)} = \omega$, both terms in the denominator of (15) steadily increase, and the amplitude steadily decreases, with increasing β. It thus appears that the maximum amplitude (for a constant value of F) occurs for a value of β less than ω. The actual value of β cannot be determined quite so simply as in the case of velocity response. To find the minimum value of the denominator of (15) we first equate to zero the derivative with respect to β of the quantity under the square-root sign, obtaining

$$2(s-m\beta^2)(-2m\beta)+2r^2\beta = 0,$$

whence *either*
$$\beta = 0, \tag{17 a}$$

or
$$\beta^2 = s/m - r^2/2m^2$$
$$= \omega^2 - 2\alpha^2. \tag{17 b}$$

It should be clear from the foregoing remarks that (17 a) corresponds to (relatively) large damping, and that for small damping (whenever $\omega^2 > 2\alpha^2$) the value of β given by (17 b) corresponds to the minimum denominator, and hence to the maximum amplitude. It is easy to verify by use of the rules for discriminating between maxima and minima depending on the sign of the second derivative, that

(i) if $\omega^2 > 2\alpha^2$ (so that (17 b) yields a *real* value of β), $\beta = 0$ gives a maximum denominator, and (17 b) a minimum;

(ii) if $\omega^2 < 2\alpha^2$ (so that (17 b) does not yield a real value of β), $\beta = 0$ gives a minimum denominator.

In either case $\hat{x}$ tends to zero as β increases indefinitely.

If the value of β^2 from (17 b) is substituted in the denominator of (15) it readily transpires that the maximum amplitude may be expressed in the form

$$\hat{x} = F/\mu r, \tag{18}$$

where, as in Chapter III, μ denotes the pulsatance of damped vibrations, and is given by $\mu^2 = s/m - r^2/4m^2$. When the damping is very small, the pulsatance for maximum amplitude response is very close to the resonance pulsatance ω and the maximum amplitude to $F/\omega r$.

The facts which have emerged from the preceding discussion are exhibited in Fig. 22, which shows typical amplitude response curves.

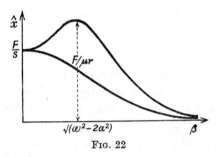

FIG. 22

It remains to consider the phase difference between the force and the motion produced. Reverting to (10) we have

$$\tan\phi = (m\beta - s/\beta)/r, \qquad (10 \ bis)$$

from which we see that $\tan\phi = 0$ (and so we may take $\phi = 0$) when $m\beta - s/\beta = 0$, that is, when $\beta = \omega$. Thus, at resonance, *velocity* and force are in phase. If β is less than ω, $\tan\phi$ is negative, and the velocity *leads* the force; as β tends to zero, $\tan\phi$ tends to $-\infty$, and hence the lead tends to $\frac{1}{2}\pi$ or a quarter period. If β is greater than ω, $\tan\phi$ is positive, so that velocity lags behind force; as β increases indefinitely, $\tan\phi$ tends to $+\infty$, and the lag to $\frac{1}{2}\pi$ or a quarter period. It is also clear from (10) that when r is small, β need differ from ω by only a comparatively small amount for the lag or lead to become very nearly equal to the limiting value $\frac{1}{2}\pi$, whereas for larger values of r the change of phase varies much more slowly with β.

Since displacement lags a quarter period behind velocity, it always lags behind the force, the phase lag varying from zero at zero pulsatance through $\frac{1}{2}\pi$ at resonance to π (that is, direct opposition) for very large pulsatances.

Curves showing the variation of ϕ with β are given in Fig. 23.

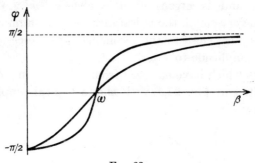

FIG. 23

The properties of a simple vibrating system have been humorously summed up by Sir Charles Inglis (*Vibrations of Railway Bridges*, Camb. Univ. Press (1934), p. x) as follows:

In this behaviour of the spring-supported mass there is something almost human; it objects to being rushed. If coaxed gently and not hurried too much, it responds with perfect docility; but if urged to bestir itself at more than its normal gait, it exhibits a mulish perversity of disposition. Such movement as it makes under this compulsion is always in a retrograde direction, and the more it is rushed the less it condescends to move. On the other hand, if it is stimulated with its own natural inborn frequency, it plays up with an exuberance of spirit which may be very embarrassing.

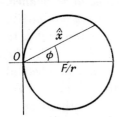

FIG. 24

An interesting representation of the connexion between peak velocity and phase is the Mallett circle diagram. Since $\hat{x}_{\max} = F/r$, and $r = Z\cos\phi$, we have

$$\hat{x} = \frac{F}{Z} = \frac{F}{r}\frac{r}{Z} = \hat{x}_{\max}\cos\phi. \quad (19)$$

If we regard $\hat{x}$ and ϕ as polar coordinates this is the equation of a circle of diameter $\hat{x}_{\max} = F/r$, passing through the origin and with its centre on the axis $\phi = 0$. The diagram is given in Fig. 24.

4.5. Some special cases

It is instructive to consider cases in which one control predominates, or in which one (resistance) is negligible.

(i) *Stiffness dominant*

In this case the equation of motion is

$$sx = F \sin \beta t,$$

whence
$$x = (F/s)\sin \beta t = x_{\text{eq}} \sin \beta t, \qquad (20\,\text{a})$$

$$\dot{x} = \beta(F/s)\cos \beta t, \qquad (20\,\text{b})$$

and
$$\hat{x} = F/s, \qquad \hat{\dot{x}} = (F/s)\beta. \qquad (21)$$

The corresponding response graphs are given in Fig. 25. The importance of this example is that it has a *constant amplitude response*, leading to the conclusion that in designing a system

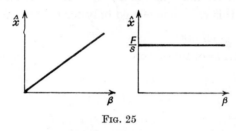

Fig. 25

required to have uniform amplitude response, inertia and friction must be kept subordinate to stiffness. Comparing Fig. 25 with Figs. 21 and 22, we see that for small pulsatances stiffness always dominates. Alternatively (since inertia cannot be entirely absent) we may say that uniform amplitude response can be achieved only by making the resonant frequency much higher than the working frequency.

(ii) *Resistance dominant*

The equation of motion is now

$$r\dot{x} = F \sin \beta t,$$

whence
$$\dot{x} = (F/r)\sin \beta t \qquad (22\,\text{a})$$

and
$$x = -(F/r\beta)\cos \beta t, \qquad (22\,\text{b})$$

or
$$\hat{x} = F/r\beta, \qquad \hat{\dot{x}} = F/r. \qquad (23)$$

The corresponding response curves are shown in Fig. 26, and comparison with Figs. 21 and 22 shows that they correspond to the portions of the complete response curves in the neighbourhood of resonance. The practical importance of this example is

the inference that uniform velocity response can be obtained
only by making resistance predominate, that is, at the expense

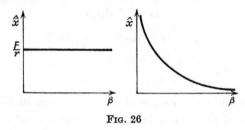

FIG. 26

of efficiency. It may also be inferred from (i) above and (iii)
below that this can be achieved only for medium frequencies.

(iii) *Inertia dominant*

The equation of motion is

$$m\ddot{x} = F\sin\beta t,$$

whence $$\dot{x} = -(F/m\beta)\cos\beta t \qquad (24\,\text{a})$$

and $$x = -(F/m\beta^2)\sin\beta t, \qquad (24\,\text{b})$$

or $$\hat{x} = F/m\beta^2, \qquad \hat{\dot{x}} = F/m\beta. \qquad (25)$$

The response curves are shown in Fig. 27, and comparison with
Figs. 21 and 22 shows that they correspond to the high-frequency

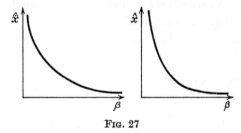

FIG. 27

ends of the complete response curves. We infer that at sufficiently high frequencies inertia will inevitably predominate, and
so limit velocity response, and to an even greater degree,
amplitude response.

(iv) *Negligible damping*

It has already been seen that, except when the pulsatance is
quite near to the resonant pulsatance, the effect of small damping

upon the response is insignificant. If we leave the damping term out of our equation, it reads

$$m\ddot{x} + sx = F\sin\beta t,$$

whence

$$x = \frac{F\sin\beta t}{s - m\beta^2} \tag{26 a}$$

and

$$\dot{x} = \frac{\beta F\cos\beta t}{s - m\beta^2}. \tag{26 b}$$

The first thing we notice about these formulae is that they give mathematically infinite results when $s - m\beta^2 = 0$, that is, when $\beta = \omega$. But we know, from our examination of the complete result, that at and near resonance neglect of r is not legitimate, although large (but not infinite) response is to be expected. We also note that if $\beta < \omega$, displacement and force have the same sign, whereas when $\beta > \omega$ they have opposite signs. This corresponds to the phase-lag variation from 0 at low frequencies to π at very high frequencies, the bulk of the variation occurring in a small range of β, including ω, when r is small.

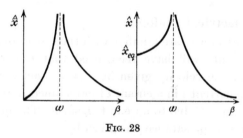

Fig. 28

The amplitude, $\hat{x}$, is the magnitude (regardless of sign) of the coefficient in (26 a), namely,

$$\hat{x} = \frac{F}{|s - m\beta^2|} \tag{27 a}$$

$$= \frac{F}{s|1 - \beta^2/\omega^2|} = \frac{x_{eq}}{|1 - \beta^2/\omega^2|}. \tag{27 b}$$

Graphs of $\hat{x}$ and $\hat{\dot{x}}$ are shown in Fig. 28. They should be compared with the graphs in Figs. 21 and 22 corresponding to small r. The final expression in (27 b) is a very useful result, and enables the amplitude of a maintained vibration to be rapidly determined from the parameters of the system and the peak value and pulsatance of the maintaining force—provided, of course, that the pulsatance is not too near that of resonance.

As an example, suppose that a mass of 100 lb is controlled by a spring so that it executes free vibrations at the rate of 150 cycles per minute, and is acted upon by a periodic force of peak value 5 lb wt at 120 cycles per minute, and (friction being small) we wish to calculate the amplitude of the maintained vibration.

Convenient units will be pounds, seconds, and inches. In terms of these,

$$\omega = 5\pi, \qquad \beta = 4\pi,$$

$$s = m\omega^2 = 2{,}500\pi^2 \text{ dynamical units}$$

$$= 2{,}500\pi^2/386 \text{ lb wt/in.}$$

Hence $\qquad x_{eq} = F/s = 5 \times 386/2{,}500\pi^2$ in.,

and finally, since $\beta^2/\omega^2 = 16/25$,

$$\hat{x} = \frac{5 \times 386}{2{,}500\pi^2} \times \frac{25}{9} = 0\cdot217 \text{ inch.}$$

4.6. The electrical analogue

Those readers who are familiar with the theory of alternating electric currents will have recognized that the form of the formulae for the velocity given in § 4.4 is exactly the same as that for the current i in a circuit of inductance L, resistance R, and capacitance C due to an e.m.f. $E \sin \beta t$. The impedance Z of the circuit at pulsatance β is given by

$$Z^2 = R^2 + (\beta L - 1/\beta C)^2, \tag{28}$$

the peak current by $\qquad \hat{i} = E/Z, \tag{29}$

the phase lag ϕ by

$$\tan \phi = (\beta L - 1/\beta C)/R, \tag{30}$$

and the current by

$$i = (E/Z)\sin(\beta t - \phi). \tag{31}$$

There is thus, as a comparison of these formulae with (10), (11 a), and (12) will show, a complete analogy between a vibrating system and an electric circuit. The analogous quantities, for translational and rotational mechanical systems, and for

electrical systems, are tabulated below. A further extension
to more complex systems will be made later, in Chapter X.

Mechanical		Electrical
Translation	*Rotation*	
linear displacement x	angular displacement θ	charge q
velocity $v = \dot{x}$	angular velocity $\omega = \dot{\theta}$	current $\dot{q}$
acceleration $\dot{v} = \ddot{x}$	angular acceleration $\dot{\omega} = \ddot{\theta}$	
mass m	moment of inertia I	inductance L
stiffness s (force per unit displacement)	stiffness s (torque per unit twist)	elastance $1/C$
flexibility $1/s$ (displacement per unit force)	flexibility $1/s$ (twist per unit torque)	capacitance C
resistance coefficient r	resistance coefficient r	resistance R
force F	torque G	e.m.f. E

4.7. Mechanical impedance; dynamic stiffness

The complete analogue of the preceding section makes it
possible to take over into the language of mechanical vibrating
systems terms which have been invented for use in electric
circuit theory. Actually, however, the fact that the electrical
engineer concentrates on current, while in mechanical vibrations
we are more often interested rather in displacement (the analogue
of electric charge) than in velocity (the analogue of electric
current), has meant that the borrowing has not been extensive
—and worse, that the borrowed term has not always been used
for the exact analogue. One such term *is* important—*mechanical
impedance*. Impedance, as used by the electrical engineer, means
the ratio of e.m.f. to current. It may apply to peak values, or it
may apply to the complex (vector) values. In the former, more
elementary, case, we have

$$Z = \hat{E}/\hat{i} = \sqrt{\{R^2 + (\beta L - 1/\beta C)^2\}}. \qquad (32)$$

The analogue of this is the ratio of peak force to peak velocity,
and we define mechanical impedance as the ratio of (peak) force
to (peak) velocity,

$$Z = \hat{F}/\hat{\dot{x}} = \sqrt{\{r^2 + (m\beta - s/\beta)^2\}}. \qquad (33)$$

E

In practice, it is rather the form

$$\hat{x} = \hat{F}/Z, \qquad (12\ bis)$$

corresponding to the electrical

$$\hat{\imath} = \hat{E}/Z, \qquad (29\ bis)$$

which is used.

From a peak velocity so determined an amplitude may be found, according to (15) above, but it is convenient to have a name for the divisor which converts (peak) force into amplitude. Now the *static* ratio of force to displacement is termed stiffness, so that the natural term for the ratio of peak force to amplitude is *dynamic stiffness* (sometimes called dynamic modulus). We thus define

$$\text{dynamic stiffness} = \hat{F}/\hat{x}$$
$$= \sqrt{\{(s - m\beta^2)^2 + r^2\beta^2\}}. \qquad (34)$$

We note that when $\beta = 0$, the dynamic stiffness reduces to s, the ordinary, or static, stiffness. Secondly we note that, when r is negligible (i.e. with small damping, and not too near resonance) the dynamic stiffness becomes $|s - m\beta^2|$ and the formula resulting from its use is (27 a).

4.8. Power supply

In the foregoing we have considered the 'steady-state' maintained vibration, and have obtained the constant amplitude of that vibration. When there is resistance in the system it is clear, from physical considerations, that energy is being dissipated, and that this dissipation of energy must be made good, by the force maintaining the vibrations. Now the *activity* (instantaneous rate of doing work) of a force is the force times the velocity of its point of application. Thus, in a simple system in which a force $F \sin \beta t$ produces a displacement $(F/Z)\sin(\beta t - \phi)$, the activity is

$$F \sin \beta t (F/Z)\sin(\beta t - \phi) = (F^2/Z)(\sin^2\beta t \cos\phi - \sin\beta t \cos\beta t \sin\phi).$$

Over a complete period the average value of $\sin^2\beta t$ is $\frac{1}{2}$, and that of $\sin\beta t \cos\beta t$ is zero. Hence the average activity, or the *power* supplied, is

$$\tfrac{1}{2}(F^2/Z)\cos\phi = \tfrac{1}{2}F\hat{x}\cos\phi. \qquad (35)$$

The result is, of course, precisely analogous to the well-known formula for power supply for alternating currents, and the well-known 'power factor', $\cos \phi$, makes its appearance equally in the mechanical case.

EXERCISES ON CHAPTER IV

1. Draw the velocity and displacement response curves for the action of a periodic force of peak value 1,000 dynes, acting on simple systems dominated by (a) a mass of 10 gm, (b) a spring of stiffness 10^7 dynes/cm, (c) a resistance of 1,000 dynes/cm/sec.

2. A system has effective mass 2 gm, stiffness 8×10^7 dynes/cm, and resistance coefficient 7,000 dynes/cm/sec. What are the frequencies of maximum velocity and displacement response?

3. Plot carefully the velocity and displacement response curves for the system in Ex. 2, for a periodic force of peak value 1,000 dynes, for frequencies up to 5,000/sec.

4. Obtain, where possible, the results of Exx. 2 and 3, (a) when the resistance coefficient is increased tenfold, (b) when it is decreased tenfold.

5. A vibrating system has mass 5 gm, resistance coefficient 3,000 dynes/cm/sec, and stiffness 4×10^7 dynes/cm. It is acted upon by a periodic force of peak value 10^4 dynes at 400 cycles/sec. Find the amplitude and peak velocity of the forced vibration, and the power exerted in maintaining it. (U.L.)

6. A mass of 100 lb is so supported that it executes free vibrations at the rate of 3 per sec. It is acted upon by a periodic force of peak value 5 lb wt. Find, neglecting friction, the amplitude of the forced vibrations (a) at 210, (b) at 300 cycles per minute.

7. A mass m is supported by a spring of stiffness s. The other end of the spring is constrained to vibrate with amplitude b and pulsatance β. Construct the differential equation for the displacement of m from its equilibrium position, and show that this is identical with that expressing the effect of a periodic force of peak value sb and pulsatance β on the mass m when the other end of the spring is fixed.

8. A spring of stiffness 20 lb wt/in., hanging vertically, supports a mass of 10 lb. If the support makes vertical oscillations of amplitude 0·1 in., find the amplitude of the forced vibrations at frequencies 2, 4, 6, and 10 per sec.

9. The support of a simple pendulum of length 1 m vibrates horizontally with amplitude 1 cm. Find the amplitude of the vibration of the bob at frequencies 15, 30, and 60 per minute.

10. A loud-speaker element has an effective mass of 10 gm and a resonant frequency 6,000 cycles/sec. Find the peak value of the periodic force necessary to maintain an amplitude of 0·01 cm at (a) 500, (b) 1,000, (c) 3,000 cycles/sec, neglecting friction.

11. Show that in any system the power necessary to maintain a given velocity response is independent of the forcing pulsatance, while that necessary to maintain a given amplitude response varies as the square of that pulsatance.

12. A diaphragm has an effective mass 1 gm, resistance coefficient 2,000 dynes/cm/sec, and resonant frequency 8,000 per sec. Find the power necessary to maintain an amplitude of 0·01 cm at 200 and at 2,000 cycles/sec. What power would be necessary to maintain the same velocity response at 2,000 cycles as occurs at 200?

13. A moving-coil loud-speaker has effective mass m, resistance coefficient r, and elastic stiffness s. The mechanical driving force is Ai when the current is i; A is a constant. If the current has pulsatance β show that the electrical effect of the speaker is that of an inductance A^2/s, a resistance A^2/r, and a capacitance m/A^2, in parallel, in series with the inductance L and resistance R of the coil.

14. If the velocity response of a simple damped vibrating system is the same for two different pulsatances β_1 and β_2, show that the resonant pulsatance is given by $\omega^2 = \beta_1\beta_2$.

15. Show that if r^2/ms is small, the pulsatance for maximum amplitude response is approximately $r^2\omega/4ms$ less than the resonant pulsatance. Show also that the pulsatances for which the velocity response is half of that at resonance are approximately $\omega \pm r\sqrt{3}/2m$.

16. A mass m is coupled to a platform by a spring of stiffness s, and relative motion is resisted by a force proportional to the relative velocity, the resistance coefficient being r. The platform oscillates with amplitude α and pulsatance β. Show that the amplitude of the vibration of the mass is greatest for a pulsatance given by $r^2\beta^2/s^2 = \sqrt{(1+2r^2/ms)} - 1$. (U.L.)

V

TRANSIENTS

5.1. Introduction

WE have just considered the steady-state vibration which a system can execute under the action of a periodic external force. It must, however, be clear that if such a force be applied to a system at rest, or if any change occur in the external forces acting on the system, some time must elapse before the system settles down to the new steady-state vibration. The motion which takes place in such a 'settling-down' period—or, more accurately, the difference between it and the steady-state motion—is termed a *transient*. This term seems to imply that the settling-down period is quite short, whereas it will transpire that it is mathematically infinite, since the approach to the steady state is asymptotic. However, the departure from the steady state does become insensible after a relatively short time.

The scope of this chapter is in fact wider than its title implies, for it is convenient to include in it topics to which the term transient does not strictly apply. In the first place, some consideration is given to undamped systems, where there is no 'settling down'. In the second place we consider external forces which are not just steady periodic ones.

The object of the chapter is to determine the effect of *any* change, sudden or continuous, in the external forces acting on a simple vibrating system.

5.2. General

So far we have examined two types of motion which a simple vibrating system can execute, namely the free vibrations of Chapter III and the maintained vibrations of Chapter IV. It is, however, possible for the system to move in a manner which is a combination of these two. In that case the magnitude of the maintained vibration is determined by the external force, but the amplitude and phase of the free (damped) vibration is not so determined, but depends also on the state of the system when the external force began to act. It thus appears, from this simple physical argument, that the transient is a damped free vibration, which does die away more or less rapidly, ultimately becoming insensible, and leaving the maintained vibration as the motion of the system.

Mathematically, our problem is that of finding the complete solution of the general differential equation of motion which, for a periodic external force, is

$$m\ddot{x}+r\dot{x}+sx = F\cos\beta t. \tag{1}$$

Now (as is shown in any textbook on the calculus, or on elementary differential equations) the solution of this equation may be regarded as consisting of two parts, namely a Particular Integral (P.I.), which is *any* solution of the equation as it stands, and a Complementary Function (C.F.), which is the general solution of the corresponding homogeneous equation, obtained by omitting all terms which do not contain x or its derivatives. The C.F. contains constants which cannot be determined from the differential equation, and whose number is equal to the order of the equation (in our case, two). Additional information, such as initial conditions, is needed to determine these constants, and in a practical problem this additional information is always available.

Applying all this to equation (1) above, it should be clear that a P.I. represents the maintained steady-state vibration which we studied in the last chapter, and the C.F. represents the free vibration which formed the subject of Chapter III; adding these corresponds to combining the motions. The constants in the C.F. can, in any particular case, be found by use of the initial conditions. The mathematical argument thus runs entirely parallel to the physical argument which commences this section.

5.3. Undamped system. Simple cases

It is worth while paying some attention to the undamped system, firstly on account of its mathematical simplicity, and secondly because, as we have seen, there are some aspects of our subject of study in which the effects of damping are relatively unimportant.

As a first case we consider the sudden application of a constant force to a mass controlled by a spring, and initially at rest. If, as usual, we denote by m the mass and by s the stiffness of the spring, and let F denote the magnitude of the force, then the differential equation, for $t > 0$, is

$$m\ddot{x} + sx = F, \tag{2 a}$$

subject to the conditions

$$x = 0 \quad \text{and} \quad \dot{x} = 0 \quad \text{when} \quad t = 0. \tag{2 b}$$

By any of the routine methods—or by the physical argument that the statical effect of a constant force is a constant displacement—a P.I. of this equation is readily found to be

$$\text{P.I.} = F/s. \tag{3}$$

The complementary function is the general solution of the equation
$$m\ddot{x} + sx = 0, \tag{4}$$

or if, as usual, we write $s/m = \omega^2$,

$$\ddot{x} + \omega^2 x = 0. \tag{4 a}$$

The general solution of this may be written, in the form most convenient for our present purpose,

$$\text{C.F.} = A \cos \omega t + B \sin \omega t. \tag{5}$$

The general solution of equation (2 a) is therefore

$$x = F/s + A \cos \omega t + B \sin \omega t. \tag{6}$$

We still have to determine A and B by use of the conditions (2 b). If $x = 0$ when $t = 0$ we must have

$$0 = F/s + A,$$

or $$A = -F/s. \tag{7 a}$$

The condition that $\dot{x} = 0$ when $t = 0$ gives

$$0 = B. \tag{7 b}$$

Collecting results, we have, finally,

$$x = (F/s)(1 - \cos \omega t). \tag{8}$$

A graph of x as a function of t is given in Fig. 29, and from this

—or immediately from the formula (8)—we see that it represents an oscillation of amplitude F/s about the new position of equilibrium, which is displaced a distance F/s from the old one. Another point of interest is that the maximum value of x is $2F/s$, which is twice the steady deflexion which would be produced by the steady force F. In any practical case, of course, the oscillation will be damped, so that the maximum displacement will then be somewhat less than $2F/s$. We thus arrive at

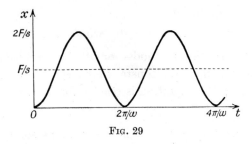

FIG. 29

the general principle for a simple vibrating system, that the maximum displacement produced by a steady force suddenly applied to the system at rest does not exceed twice the steady deflexion due to the force. (The exact solution for a damped system will be given in section 5.4.)

As our next example we will consider the case of a periodic force applied to the same undamped system, originally at rest, and will take the special case where the force is zero at the instant ($t = 0$) of application, so that if F is its peak value, it is represented by $F \sin \beta t$. The differential equation is

$$m\ddot{x} + sx = F \sin \beta t. \tag{9}$$

A P.I. of this equation is found to be

$$\text{P.I.} = \frac{F \sin \beta t}{s - m\beta^2} = X \sin \beta t, \tag{10}$$

where X is a temporary abbreviation for $F/(s - m\beta^2)$. As before, we have

$$\text{C.F.} = A \cos \omega t + B \sin \omega t. \tag{11}$$

The general solution of equation (9) is thus

$$x = X \sin \beta t + A \cos \omega t + B \sin \omega t. \tag{12}$$

The conditions (2 b) have still to be applied to determine A and B. The condition that $x = 0$ when $t = 0$ gives

$$0 = A, \tag{13}$$

and the condition that $\dot{x} = 0$ when $t = 0$ gives

$$0 = \beta X + \omega B. \tag{14}$$

Finally we have

$$x = \frac{F(\omega \sin \beta t - \beta \sin \omega t)}{\omega(s - m\beta^2)}. \tag{15}$$

This solution represents two oscillations of different amplitude and pulsatance, superposed. The resulting motion—except when β and ω are very simply related—appears very complex, despite the apparent simplicity of the formula, as the student may convince himself by drawing a few graphs: except when β and ω are commensurable, the motion is not periodic.

The foregoing clearly breaks down if $\beta = \omega$ (i.e. at resonance), for then $s - m\beta^2$ vanishes. In this case we find that

$$\text{P.I.} = -(F/2s)\omega t \cos \omega t, \tag{16}$$

so that now

$$x = -(F/2s)\omega t \cos \omega t + A \cos \omega t + B \sin \omega t. \tag{17}$$

The condition that $x = 0$ when $t = 0$ gives

$$0 = A, \tag{18}$$

and the condition that $\dot{x} = 0$ when $t = 0$ gives

$$0 = -F\omega/2s + \omega B. \tag{19}$$

Finally $\qquad x = (F/2s)(\sin \omega t - \omega t \cos \omega t). \tag{20}$

The term involving $\omega t \cos \omega t$ in the above represents an oscillation whose amplitude increases steadily without limit. In practice, of course, this indefinite increase will be checked by friction, but the solution we have just obtained, which is illustrated in Fig. 30, shows the early stages in the build-up of the large vibrations which are a feature of resonance.

(The result (20) can also be obtained from (15) as a limiting case, say by putting $\beta = \omega + \delta$ and letting δ tend to zero.)

We may note that in the absence of damping (as anticipated) the solutions of this section do not represent an asymptotic approach to a steady-state oscillation, so that the term 'transient'

is not strictly applicable to them. We proceed to deal with the
more practical—but mathematically more complicated—cases
similar to those of this section when the effects of damping are
taken into account.

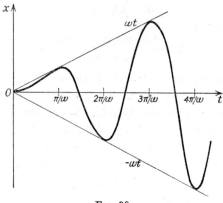

Fɪɢ. 30

5.4. Damped system. Simple cases

In this section results will be obtained for the damped system,
similar to those obtained in the last section for the undamped
system.

(a) *Constant force suddenly applied*

Let F be the magnitude of the force, and let time be measured
from the instant of its application. Then, if m, r, s, α, μ, and ω
have their usual meanings, the differential equation of motion is

$$m\ddot{x}+r\dot{x}+sx = F, \tag{21 a}$$

or
$$\ddot{x}+2\alpha\dot{x}+\omega^2 x = F/m. \tag{21 b}$$

The initial conditions are that $x = 0$ and $\dot{x} = 0$ when $t = 0$.

By any of the routine methods, or from physical considerations, we readily find that

$$\text{P.I.} = F/s = x_{\text{eq}}, \tag{22}$$

and
$$\text{C.F.} = e^{-\alpha t}(A \cos \mu t + B \sin \mu t), \tag{23}$$

so that
$$x = F/s + e^{-\alpha t}(A \cos \mu t + B \sin \mu t). \tag{24}$$

The condition that $x = 0$ when $t = 0$ gives

$$A = -F/s. \tag{25}$$

The condition that $\dot{x} = 0$ when $t = 0$ gives

$$-\alpha A + \mu B = 0,$$

or $\qquad\qquad\qquad B = -\alpha F/\mu s.$ (26)

Hence, finally,

$$x = \frac{F}{s}\left\{1 - e^{-\alpha t}\left(\cos \mu t + \frac{\alpha}{\mu}\sin \mu t\right)\right\}.$$ (27)

The meaning of this result is clearly that the system executes a damped free oscillation about a new position of equilibrium distant F/s from the original position.

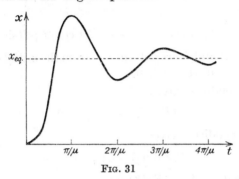

Fig. 31

It is of interest to consider the greatest deflexion which occurs in this case—and especially to verify that it is less than the value $2F/s$ which we found for the undamped system in the last section. It is easy to show from (27) that the condition for a stationary value of x, ($\dot{x} = 0$), reduces to $\sin \mu t = 0$, and that the condition for a maximum is satisfied if $\cos \mu t$ is negative. These are both satisfied when μt is any odd multiple of π. Physical reasoning suggests that to find the greatest of these maxima we should take the smallest (non-zero) value of t, that is, $\mu t = \pi$, giving

$$x_{\max} = (1 + e^{-\alpha \pi/\mu})x_{\mathrm{eq}},$$ (28)

which is less than twice x_{eq}.

A graph of x against t, illustrating the result (27), is given in Fig. 31.

The foregoing relates to lightly damped systems for which $\omega^2 > \alpha^2$; with greater damping it is found that x approaches x_{eq} asymptotically from below.

(b) Periodic force

Let the force $F \sin \beta t$ be applied at $t = 0$ to the simple (m, r, s) system, initially at rest. Then the differential equation is

$$m\ddot{x} + r\dot{x} + sx = F \sin \beta t. \tag{29}$$

A P.I. of this is given by the steady-state maintained vibration, that is,

$$\text{P.I.} = -(F/\beta Z)\cos(\beta t - \phi), \tag{30}$$

where Z, the mechanical impedance, and ϕ, the phase lag, have the same meaning as in section 4.4. The C.F. is still given by (23), so that

$$x = -(F/\beta Z)\cos(\beta t - \phi) + e^{-\alpha t}(A \cos \mu t + B \sin \mu t). \tag{31}$$

The values of A and B are determined from the initial conditions, $x = 0$ and $\dot{x} = 0$ when $t = 0$.

The first condition gives

$$-(F/\beta Z)\cos \phi + A = 0. \tag{32}$$

The second condition gives

$$-(F/Z)\sin \phi - \alpha A + \mu B = 0. \tag{33}$$

It follows that

$$A = (F/\beta Z)\cos \phi, \tag{34}$$

$$B = (F/\mu \beta Z)(\beta \sin \phi + \alpha \cos \phi). \tag{35}$$

Finally,

$$x = (F/\mu \beta Z)[e^{-\alpha t}\{\mu \cos \phi \cos \mu t + (\beta \sin \phi + \alpha \cos \phi)\sin \mu t\} - \\ -\mu \cos(\beta t - \phi)]. \tag{36}$$

The result appears complicated. It can be put into other forms by using the expressions for μ, $\cos \phi$, $\sin \phi$, and possibly also Z, in terms of α, ω, and β, but none of these is essentially simpler. The important thing is to realize that the result is nothing more than the combination of the maintained vibration with a 'transient', and that the latter is a damped free vibration characteristic of the system, with amplitude and phase such that the 'initial' displacement and velocity are both zero. Since the transient is here damped, and so asymptotically vanishes, the formula expresses the realistic result that the ultimate effect of the sustained external force is to produce the maintained vibration corresponding thereto, with an initial additional disturbance which dies out more or less rapidly according as the system is more or less dissipative.

5.5. The general disturbing force

So far we have considered cases in which the disturbing force is of a very simple form—either a constant or sinusoidal. If the force is periodic, but not simply sinusoidal, it may be resolved into its Fourier constituents; the above results may then be applied to the harmonics separately, and the final solution obtained by summation. There is, however, a general formula which can be applied to *any* disturbing force (which remains finite), represented by $F(t)$. It is convenient, however, to express the result in terms of the corresponding acceleration, $f(t)$, such that $f(t) = F(t)/m$. In effect, we seek the integral of the differential equation

$$\ddot{x} + 2\alpha\dot{x} + \omega^2 x = f(t), \tag{37}$$

subject to the conditions that $x(0) = 0$ and $\dot{x}(0) = 0$.

An instructive and quite simple way of obtaining the formula is to apply a physical argument, namely that the effect of a continuous force may be simulated by applying a series of small impulses. Assume the effect of the force acting in the small interval of time between T and $T + \delta T$ to be that of an impulse; the magnitude of this impulse must be $F(T)\delta T$. This would produce an instantaneous increase of velocity $\delta\dot{x}$, where

$$\delta\dot{x} = F(T)\delta T/m = f(T)\delta T. \tag{38}$$

The contribution to the total motion due to this impulse is $\delta x(t)$, a free vibration characteristic of the system, such that δx vanishes when $t = T$, and $\delta\dot{x}$ has the above value at that instant. The required result is to be attained by adding the effects of the impulses to which the system has so far been subjected—that is, in the limit of an indefinitely large number of indefinitely small impulses, by an integration between the limits 0 and t with respect to T. Further progress depends upon the nature of the particular system under consideration.

Let us first consider the simple case of the undamped system. For such a system, the displacement resulting from an 'initial' velocity v imparted at $t = 0$ to the system, starting from the equilibrium position, is easily found to be

$$x = (v/\omega)\sin \omega t$$

(see Ex. 2 below). It follows that the effect of the small impulse considered, applied at $t = T$, is

$$\{f(T)\,\delta T/\omega\}\sin \omega(t-T). \tag{39}$$

Hence the displacement at time t due to the disturbing force is

$$x = (1/\omega)\int_0^t f(T)\sin \omega(t-T)\,dT. \tag{40}$$

To illustrate how this formula produces results we apply it first to the case of a steady force F suddenly applied at $t = 0$. Here $f(t) = F/m$, a constant. The required result is then

$$\begin{aligned}
x &= (F/m\omega)\int_0^t \sin \omega(t-T)\,dT \\
&= (F/m\omega^2)[\cos \omega(t-T)]_0^t \\
&= (F/m\omega^2)(1-\cos \omega t), \tag{41}
\end{aligned}$$

which agrees with the result (8) obtained earlier in the chapter.

Secondly, let a force $F\sin \beta t$ be applied to the undamped system at $t = 0$, the system being initially at rest in the equilibrium position. Then the integral formula becomes

$$\begin{aligned}
x &= (F/m\omega)\int_0^t \sin \beta T \sin \omega(t-T)\,dT \\
&= (F/2m\omega)\int_0^t \{\cos[\omega t-(\omega+\beta)T]-\cos[\omega t-(\omega-\beta)T]\}\,dT \\
&= \frac{F}{2m\omega}\left[-\frac{\sin[\omega t-(\omega+\beta)T]}{\omega+\beta}+\frac{\sin[\omega t-(\omega-\beta)T]}{\omega-\beta}\right]_0^t \\
&= F(\omega \sin \beta t-\beta \sin \omega t)/m\omega(\omega^2-\beta^2), \tag{42}
\end{aligned}$$

again agreeing with the previously obtained result (15).

It should be clear from the above reasoning that the corresponding formula for the damped system will be obtained by replacing $\sin \omega(t-T)/\omega$ in (40) by the displacement produced by an impulse at $t = T$ giving unit velocity increment, which, as follows on putting $t-T$ for t in the answer to Ex. 4 below, part (ii), is

$$(1/\mu)e^{-\alpha(t-T)}\sin\mu(t-T),\qquad(43)$$

whence the integral expression becomes

$$x = (1/\mu)\int_0^t f(T)e^{-\alpha(t-T)}\sin\mu(t-T)\,dT.\qquad(44)$$

Formal derivation

The formula (40) above, as the solution of the mathematical problem, can be established by use of the formal methods of the theory of linear differential equations.

We recall that, if D denotes the differential operator d/dt, then

$$\frac{1}{D+a}f(t) = e^{-at}\int_0^t f(T)e^{aT}\,dT.\qquad(45)$$

The equation $\qquad\ddot{x}+\omega^2 x = f(t)$

has the symbolic solution

$$x = \frac{1}{D^2+\omega^2}f(t)$$

$$= \left\{\frac{1}{D-j\omega}-\frac{1}{D+j\omega}\right\}\frac{f(t)}{2j\omega}$$

$$= \int_0^t f(T)\frac{e^{j\omega(t-T)}-e^{-j\omega(t-T)}}{2j\omega}\,dT,$$

where the initial conditions have been satisfied by writing the lower limit of the integral as 0. By the use of the Euler formula for the sine in terms of exponentials, we recover the formula

$$x = (1/\omega)\int_0^t f(T)\sin\omega(t-T)\,dT.\qquad(40\ bis)$$

A similar method will produce the result for the damped system given in (44) above.

EXERCISES ON CHAPTER V

1. A non-dissipative system (m, s) is released from rest with an initial displacement a. Give the formula for the displacement after a time-interval t.

2. If the system in Ex. 1 is started from its equilibrium position with velocity v, give the displacement formula.

3. If the system in Ex. 1 has initial displacement a and initial velocity v, give the displacement formula, and verify that the total energy is constant and equal to $(mv^2 + sa^2)/2$.

4. Obtain results similar to those of Exx. 1 and 2 if damping proportional to the speed is also present, the resistance coefficient being r.

5. If an (m, s) system is in equilibrium under the action of a steady force F and the force is suddenly removed, find the ensuing motion.

6. Solve Ex. 5 when damping (coefficient r) is also present.

7. Use the integral formula to obtain the displacement of an (m, r, s) system, initially at rest, produced by the sudden application of (a) a constant force F, (b) a periodic force $F \sin \beta t$.

8. Use the integral formula to find the displacement of an (m, s) system, initially at rest, produced by the sudden application of the resonant force $F \sin \omega t$.

9. A constant force F acts from time 0 to time t_1 on an (m, s) system, initially at rest, and is then removed. Find the displacement (a) when $t < t_1$, (b) when $t > t_1$.

10. If a force $F \sin \beta t$ acts on an (m, s) system, initially at rest, for only (a) one complete period, (b) one half-period, beginning at $t = 0$ in each case, determine the subsequent motion of the system.

11. A particle of mass m is controlled by a spring so that it can perform oscillations of pulsatance ω. A force $F \cos \beta t$ is suddenly applied to the particle at an instant $(t = 0)$ when its displacement is zero and its velocity v. Show that the displacement at time t is

$$\frac{F(\cos \beta t - \cos \omega t)}{m(\omega^2 - \beta^2)} + \frac{v}{\omega} \sin \omega t. \qquad \text{(U.L.)}$$

MISCELLANEOUS EXERCISES ON CHAPTERS I TO V

1. A mass of 100 gm is controlled by a spring of stiffness 10,000 dynes/cm, and resisted by a force proportional to the speed. Determine the least value of the resistance coefficient which makes the motion non-oscillatory.

If the resistance coefficient has this value, what will be the maximum displacement of the mass after it has been set in motion from its equilibrium position with a speed of 10 cm/sec? (U.L.)

2. A particle which, in the absence of external forces, would be able to execute simple harmonic oscillations is moving under the action of a force $P\cos\beta t$. If its maximum speed is V, show that the period of the free oscillations would be $2\pi\sqrt{\{mV/(m\beta V \pm P)\beta\}}$, where m is the mass of the particle. (U.L.)

3. A vibrating system with negligible friction has mass m and stiffness s. The amplitudes of the displacement are a and b when it is acted upon by forces $F\sin pt$ and $F\sin qt$ respectively. If ω is the pulsatance of free vibrations of the system, show that

$$\omega^2 = \frac{ap^2 \pm bq^2}{a \pm b},$$

the upper signs being taken when ω is between p and q. (U.L.)

4. A uniform bar 15 in. long and of mass 1 lb can turn freely in a horizontal plane about a pivot 6 in. from one end; it carries a bob of mass 1 lb at the other. It is controlled by springs attached to points 6 in. on either side of the pivot, each of strength 12 lb wt/in. Find the frequency of free vibration, and the amplitude of the vibration of the bob when a periodic torque of peak value 1 lb wt-in. at 5 cycles/sec acts on the bar. (U.L.)

5. Two equal rough rollers rotate about fixed parallel horizontal axes at the same level, the directions being towards one another at the top. A uniform heavy bar rests on the cylinders, its length being perpendicular to the axes. Show that if the bar is displaced from the symmetrical position it will oscillate with pulsatance $\sqrt{(\mu g/a)}$, where μ is the coefficient of friction and $2a$ the distance between the axes.

6. Two pulleys, moments of inertia I_1 and I_2, are at the ends of a shaft of length l and torsional rigidity CJ. In the free vibration, in which the pulleys are in opposition, find the position of the section of zero motion (node) on the shaft, and the formula for the pulsatance.

7. A mass m vibrates under the action of a spring of compliance K (i.e. stiffness $1/K$) and a constant frictional force F—acting, of course, always in opposition to the velocity. Show that the displacement-time graph is the projection of a spiral composed of a number of semicircles with centres $2KF$ apart.

8. To simulate the effect of backlash in a vibrating system, consider a model where a mass m slides along a smooth horizontal rod, with springs of stiffness s, one on each side, and where there is a clearance c on each side of m when it is in its central position. Show that the period T varies with the amplitude a according to the formula

$$T = 2\pi\sqrt{\left(\frac{m}{s}\right)} \cdot \left\{1 + \frac{2c}{\pi(a-c)}\right\}.$$

Sketch the graph connecting T and a.

9. If the force-displacement graph for a system is as in Fig. 32, that is, the equation of motion is $m\ddot{x} = -(k+sx)$ when x is positive, and anti-

symmetrical with this when x is negative, show that the period T of an oscillation of amplitude a is given by

$$T = 4\sqrt{\left(\frac{m}{s}\right)}.\cos^{-1}\left(\frac{k}{k+sa}\right).$$

Draw the T–a graph, taking k, m, and s each unity, as far as $a = 10$, but paying special attention to values of a less than 1.

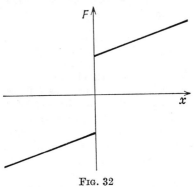

FIG. 32

10. In the 'electrostatic' loud-speaker, the force acting on the diaphragm is BE, where E is the instantaneous value of the voltage and B is a constant. If E has pulsatance β, show that the effect of the speaker on the electrical circuit is equivalent to a shunt across the capacitance C of the speaker, consisting of an inductance m/B^2, a resistance r/B^2, and a capacitance B^2/s, in series, where m, r, and s are the mechanical constants of the speaker.

11. The sound-box of a gramophone† can be represented by a mass M supported on a vertical spring of stiffness s, and of negligible mass. The lower end of the spring rests on the record. When reproducing a pure tone of pulsatance β, the record consists of 'hill and dale', the crests being h above, and the troughs h below, the average level of the groove. If y is the upward vertical displacement of M, show that

$$M\frac{d^2y}{dt^2} = -Mg+s(h\cos\beta t-y).$$

Find the particular integral of this equation, and show that Mg must not lie between $s(g/\beta^2+h)$ and $s(g/\beta^2-h)$ if the lower end of the spring is to maintain continuous contact with the record. (U.L.)

† Gramophone design has considerably improved since this question was set.

VI

LAGRANGE'S EQUATIONS

THE systems we have so far considered have been simple in the sense that only *one* quantity has been necessary to specify the position of the system. Usually this quantity has been a linear or angular displacement, but it might be, in the case of an electric circuit, the charge on a condenser. In more complex systems— a double pendulum, a car on its springs—more than one quantity is necessary to specify the position or configuration of the system. The next few chapters of the book are concerned with systems for which a finite number of such quantities suffices.

6.1. Coordinates: degrees of freedom

A coordinate may be described as any quantity in terms of which the position of an object or the configuration of a system is specified. It need not be a geometrical quantity such as a distance or an angle, although it will very often be convenient to use such quantities as coordinates.

As a very simple case we may consider a bar supported by springs at its ends (see Fig. 34, p. 70)—a highly idealized version of an automobile on its springs. Clearly the extensions of the two springs—the displacements x and y of the two ends—are possible coordinates and knowing them we know completely the position of the bar, that is, the configuration of the system. In terms of these the potential energy (strain energy of the springs) is easy to express, but the expression of the kinetic energy, although possible, is not quite so simple. For the latter, the displacement, z, of the mass-centre, and the angle of rotation, θ, are more convenient. But, if the length of the bar is $2l$, we have (approximately, for *small* displacements)

$$x = z - l\theta, \qquad y = z + l\theta, \tag{1}$$

whence
$$z = \tfrac{1}{2}(x+y), \qquad \theta = \tfrac{1}{2}(y-x)/l, \tag{2}$$

so that in fact each pair of coordinates is simply expressed in terms of the other pair.

It is important to notice that *two* quantities are needed in either case—one is not enough, more than two are super-fluous.

Again, in the case of the double pendulum (see Fig. 33, p. 70), an obvious choice is the angles θ and ϕ made by the strings with the vertical. Another possibility is the displacements x and y of the two bobs. We *could* choose x and ϕ, y and ϕ, or y and θ (but x and θ would *not* suffice). Here again, although many choices exist, the *number* of coordinates is always two.

For every system which may be thought of as made up of a finite number of discrete components, there is a minimum necessary number of coordinates, in terms of which any con-figuration of the system may be specified, and this is called the number of *degrees of freedom* of the system. The two systems already considered both have two degrees of freedom.

Thus a point moving on a plane, or on any other surface such as a sphere or cylinder, has *two* degrees of freedom. For example, in a plane we may use rectangular coordinates (x, y) or polar coordinates (r, θ) (or, indeed, other systems), but we always need two, and only two, coordinates. On a sphere, latitude and longitude are a possible choice—again *two* coordinates. A point in space has three degrees of freedom, a rigid body in space has six. Many other examples will be met and examined in this and later chapters.

To express these facts symbolically, let us denote the chosen coordinates in a system with n degrees of freedom by

$$q_1, \ q_2, \ q_3, \ ..., \ q_n.$$

Then if P is *any* point (particle) of the system, its space co-ordinates (x_P, y_P, z_P) are functions of the *independent* variables $q_1, q_2, ..., q_n$, in the sense that x is determined when $q_1, q_2, ..., q_n$ are all known, and that there is no *necessary* formal connexion between $q_1, q_2, ..., q_n$, i.e. that *any* combination of values of the q's (each within its possible range of variation, of course) corresponds to a possible configuration. For example, the displacement of a point distant αl from the centre of the rod of Fig. 34 is

$$z + \alpha l \theta \quad \text{(in terms of } z \text{ and } \theta\text{)}, \tag{3}$$

or $\quad \frac{1}{2}\{(1-\alpha)x + (1+\alpha)y\} \quad$ (in terms of x and y), $\tag{4}$

and these formulae are true for all (possible) values of z and θ, or of x and y.

In general, if (x_P, y_P, z_P) are the coordinates of a point P in a system,

$$x_P = X(q_1, q_2, ..., q_n),$$
$$y_P = Y(q_1, q_2, ..., q_n), \tag{5}$$
$$z_P = Z(q_1, q_2, ..., q_n).$$

It is also to be noted that we assume these relations to hold independently of time, that is, t does not occur explicitly in these formulae. In any *particular* motion possible to the system, from given initial conditions and under the action of prescribed forces, $x_P, y_P, z_P, ...$ and $q_1, q_2, ..., q_n$ are *all* functions of time—but the relationships expressed by (5) remain true *all the time*.

Two important equalities are needed in the next section, and we establish them here. Firstly, differentiating the formula

$$x = X(q_1, q_2, ..., q_n) \tag{6}$$

totally with respect to t, we have

$$\dot{x} = \frac{\partial X}{\partial q_1}\dot{q}_1 + \frac{\partial X}{\partial q_2}\dot{q}_2 + \cdots + \frac{\partial X}{\partial q_n}\dot{q}_n. \tag{7}$$

Now $\partial X/\partial q_1$ is independent of the velocities $\dot{q}_1, \dot{q}_2, ...$, so that, differentiating partially with respect to $\dot{q}_1$,

$$\frac{\partial \dot{x}}{\partial \dot{q}_1} = \frac{\partial X}{\partial q_1} = \frac{\partial x}{\partial q_1}, \tag{8}$$

and similarly for $q_2, ...$ and for y and z. Also

$$\frac{d}{dt}\left(\frac{\partial X}{\partial q_1}\right) = \frac{\partial^2 X}{\partial q_1^2}\dot{q}_1 + \frac{\partial^2 X}{\partial q_2\,\partial q_1}\dot{q}_2 + \cdots + \frac{\partial^2 X}{\partial q_n\,\partial q_1}\dot{q}_n, \tag{9}$$

and, from (7) (noting that $\dot{q}_1, ..., \dot{q}_n$ are independent of $q_1, q_2, ..., q_n$),

$$\frac{\partial \dot{x}}{\partial q_1} = \frac{\partial^2 X}{\partial q_1^2}\dot{q}_1 + \frac{\partial^2 X}{\partial q_1\,\partial q_2}\dot{q}_2 + \cdots + \frac{\partial^2 X}{\partial q_1\,\partial q_n}\dot{q}_n, \tag{10}$$

so that we have $\qquad \dfrac{d}{dt}\left(\dfrac{\partial x}{\partial q_1}\right) = \dfrac{\partial \dot{x}}{\partial q_1}, \tag{11}$

and similarly for $q_2, q_3, ..., q_n$, and for y and z.

6.2. The energies, and the work differential

Since the position of every point of a system of n degrees of freedom is known if we know the n coordinates $q_1, q_2, ..., q_n$, it follows that we can determine the potential energy V corresponding to any configuration also in terms of these coordinates. Thus V is a function of $q_1, q_2, ..., q_n$, in which these coordinates enter as independent variables, along, of course, with constants (parameters) expressing the forces in and geometry of the system.

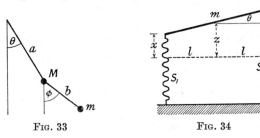

FIG. 33   FIG. 34

For example, in the double pendulum of Fig. 33, the mass M has risen (from its equilibrium position) a distance $a(1-\cos\theta)$ while m has risen a distance $a(1-\cos\theta)+b(1-\cos\phi)$. Hence

$$V = Mga(1-\cos\theta)+mg[a(1-\cos\theta)+b(1-\cos\phi)]$$
$$= (M+m)ga(1-\cos\theta)+mgb(1-\cos\phi). \tag{12}$$

Similarly, with the bar supported by two springs illustrated in Fig. 34,

$$V = \tfrac{1}{2}s_1 x^2+\tfrac{1}{2}s_2 y^2 \tag{13}$$
$$= \tfrac{1}{2}s_1(z-l\theta)^2+\tfrac{1}{2}s_2(z+l\theta)^2 \tag{14}$$

(the latter on the assumption that θ is small).

As regards kinetic energy, if (x, y, z) are the coordinates of a typical particle of mass m,

$$T = \sum \tfrac{1}{2}m(\dot{x}^2+\dot{y}^2+\dot{z}^2). \tag{15}$$

But, as we have seen,

$$\dot{x} = \frac{\partial X}{\partial q_1}\dot{q}_1+\frac{\partial X}{\partial q_2}\dot{q}_2+...+\frac{\partial X}{\partial q_n}\dot{q}_n, \tag{7 bis}$$

and similarly for $\dot{y}$ and $\dot{z}$. Using these, we see that the kinetic energy T is a homogeneous quadratic expression in the 'generalized velocities' $\dot{q}_1, \dot{q}_2, ..., \dot{q}_n$, in which the coefficients may involve the coordinates $q_1, q_2, ..., q_n$ as well (or may be only constants, of course).

Thus, with a uniform bar of mass m on springs (Fig. 34),

$$T = \tfrac{1}{2}m\dot{z}^2 + \tfrac{1}{2}m\frac{l^2}{3}\dot{\theta}^2$$

$$= \tfrac{1}{2}m\left(\frac{\dot{x}+\dot{y}}{2}\right)^2 + \tfrac{1}{2}m\frac{l^2}{3}\left(\frac{\dot{y}-\dot{x}}{2l}\right)^2$$

$$= \tfrac{1}{6}m(\dot{x}^2 + \dot{x}\dot{y} + \dot{y}^2). \tag{16}$$

Here the coefficients are constants.

In the case of the double pendulum, the velocity of M is $a\dot{\theta}$, perpendicular to the upper string. The mass m shares the motion of M, along with a velocity $b\dot{\phi}$ perpendicular to the lower string, relative to M. Thus the velocity v of m is compounded of $a\dot{\theta}$ and $b\dot{\phi}$ at an angle $(\phi-\theta)$ so that

$$v^2 = a^2\dot{\theta}^2 + 2ab\dot{\theta}\dot{\phi}\cos(\phi-\theta) + b^2\dot{\phi}^2,$$

and
$$T = \tfrac{1}{2}M(a\dot{\theta})^2 + \tfrac{1}{2}mv^2$$

$$= \tfrac{1}{2}\{(M+m)a^2\dot{\theta}^2 + 2mab\dot{\theta}\dot{\phi}\cos(\phi-\theta) + mb^2\dot{\phi}^2\}. \tag{17}$$

Here we see that the expression is again a homogeneous quadratic function of the velocities, but the coordinates appear in the coefficients.

Finally, if a force with components (X, Y, Z) acts on a particle at (x, y, z), then in a small displacement the work done is

$$X\,\delta x + Y\,\delta y + Z\,\delta z. \tag{18}$$

But since
$$\delta x = \frac{\partial x}{\partial q_1}\delta q_1 + \frac{\partial x}{\partial q_2}\delta q_2 + ...,$$

and similarly for δy and δz, the total work done by all forces,

$$\delta W = \sum (X\,\delta x + Y\,\delta y + Z\,\delta z), \tag{19}$$

when expressed in terms of $q_1, q_2, ..., q_n$, must assume the form

$$\delta W = Q_1\delta q_1 + Q_2\delta q_2 + ... + Q_n\delta q_n, \tag{20}$$

where, for example,

$$Q_1 = \sum \left(X\frac{\partial x}{\partial q_1} + Y\frac{\partial y}{\partial q_1} + Z\frac{\partial z}{\partial q_1}\right), \tag{21}$$

so that Q_1 is determined from the external forces and the geometry of the system.

In dealing with actual systems, however, it will usually be possible to express the work done in a general small displacement, by the external forces, directly in terms of $\delta q_1, \delta q_2, ...,$ and thus to determine (as the coefficients of the differentials) $Q_1, Q_2, ...$.

For example, if a force F acts transversely at a point on the bar of Fig. 34 at a point distant $\frac{1}{2}l$ from the right-hand end, the displacement of the point of application in terms of z and θ is $z + \frac{1}{2}l\theta$, so that

$$\delta W = F\delta(z + \tfrac{1}{2}l\theta) = F\delta z + \tfrac{1}{2}Fl\,\delta\theta, \qquad (22)$$

and hence the generalized forces corresponding to z (denoted by Z) and θ (denoted by Θ), obtained by comparing this with the general rule

$$\delta W = Z\,\delta z + \Theta\,\delta\theta, \qquad (23)$$

are

$$Z = F, \qquad \Theta = \tfrac{1}{2}Fl. \qquad (24)$$

(Note that, in fact, Θ is the moment of F about the mid-point.)

If we use as coordinates the displacements x and y of the ends (with the corresponding generalized forces X and Y) we have the displacement of the point of application $(\tfrac{1}{4}x + \tfrac{3}{4}y)$, so that

$$\delta W = F\delta(\tfrac{1}{4}x + \tfrac{3}{4}y) = \tfrac{1}{4}F\,\delta x + \tfrac{3}{4}F\,\delta y \qquad (25)$$

$$\equiv X\,\delta x + Y\,\delta y, \qquad (26)$$

whence

$$X = \tfrac{1}{4}F, \qquad Y = \tfrac{3}{4}F. \qquad (27)$$

(Note that these forces X and Y at the ends are equivalent to the applied force F in magnitude and position.)

It may be noted that while potential energy and work done are in many cases two different expressions for the same thing, it *is* in fact convenient to use *both*, and to make a distinction between 'internal' forces whose work contributes to the potential energy and 'external' forces, which contribute to δW. For instance, in studying the maintained vibrations of a mass m controlled by a spring of stiffness s and subject to a periodic force $\hat{F}\sin\beta t = F$, if we consider *only* the mass itself, the force acting is $-sx + F$; but we may profitably consider instead the mass-spring system characterized by kinetic energy $\tfrac{1}{2}m\dot{x}^2$, and potential energy $\tfrac{1}{2}sx^2$, acted on by the 'external' force F.

Indeed, there is also another class of forces which we can take account of as internal, namely resistances which are proportional to the speed. If $(r\dot{x}, r\dot{y}, r\dot{z})$ are the components of such a force, the work done in a small displacement $(\delta x, \delta y, \delta z)$ will be

$$-r(\dot{x}\,\delta x + \dot{y}\,\delta y + \dot{z}\,\delta z). \tag{28}$$

Now
$$r\dot{x}\,\delta x = r\dot{x}\left(\frac{\partial x}{\partial q_1}\,\delta q_1 + \frac{\partial x}{\partial q_2}\,\delta q_2 + \ldots\right)$$
$$= r\dot{x}\left(\frac{\partial \dot{x}}{\partial \dot{q}_1}\,\delta q_1 + \frac{\partial \dot{x}}{\partial \dot{q}_2}\,\delta q_2 + \ldots\right), \tag{29}$$

by (8), and similarly for $r\dot{y}\,\delta y$ and $r\dot{z}\,\delta z$. Thus if

$$2K = \sum r(\dot{x}^2 + \dot{y}^2 + \dot{z}^2) \tag{30}$$

= total rate of dissipation of energy of the system,

then these frictional forces contribute to δW an amount

$$-\delta H = -\left(\frac{\partial K}{\partial \dot{q}_1}\,\delta q_1 + \frac{\partial K}{\partial \dot{q}_2}\,\delta q_2 + \ldots\right). \tag{31}$$

The function K is called the *dissipation function* for these forces.

6.3. Lagrange's equations

The use of energy facilitates the solution of many problems in statics and dynamics. It does this mainly because of the simplification in the equations and the reduction in their number consequent upon the fact that all the internal forces which do no work will not appear in the equations. (It also follows that if it is desired to calculate these internal forces, then the principle of energy must be supplemented—usually by reference to Newton's laws.) While the single principle of conservation of energy alone is not a sufficient basis from which to determine the motion of a system with more than one degree of freedom, it *is*, however, still possible to use the energies in building up the equations of motion of a complex system, and the convenience and efficiency of the process are again essentially due to the explicit exclusion of 'internal' forces which do no work.

In order to deduce the appropriate formulae we start from the principle of d'Alembert that for any system in motion the set of actual forces and reversed mass-accelerations constitutes a force-system in equilibrium. We then apply the principle of virtual work which says that, for a force-system in equilibrium, the work done in any arbitrary small displacement is (to the first order of small quantities) zero.

If m is the mass of any particle, at a point (x, y, z) in space, and X, Y, Z are the components of force acting, and if the displacement has components $(\delta x, \delta y, \delta z)$, then (reversing the sign for later convenience) the two principles assert that

$$\sum \{m(\ddot{x}\,\delta x + \ddot{y}\,\delta y + \ddot{z}\,\delta z) - X\,\delta x - Y\,\delta y - Z\,\delta z\} = 0, \qquad (32)$$

where the sum is taken over all the particles of the system. We shall now express the various parts in terms of the generalized coordinates $q_1, q_2, ..., q_n$.

First we transform the simpler portion

$$- \sum (X\,\delta x + Y\,\delta y + Z\,\delta z),$$

which represents the negative work done by all the forces. The internal actions and reactions balance and do no work, and the amount of work done by the remaining 'internal' forces is equal to the decrease $-\delta V$ in the potential energy. The amount done by the resistances is $-\delta H$, and if the work done by the remaining 'external' forces is δW, then

$$- \sum_{m} (X\,\delta x + Y\,\delta y + Z\,\delta z) = \delta V + \delta H - \delta W \qquad (33)$$

$$= \sum_{q} \frac{\partial V}{\partial q}\,\delta q + \sum_{q} \frac{\partial K}{\partial \dot{q}}\,\delta q - \sum_{q} Q\,\delta q. \qquad (34)$$

Dealing now with the other terms in (32),

$$m\ddot{x}\,\delta x = \sum_{q} \left(m\ddot{x}\,\frac{\partial x}{\partial q}\right)\delta q$$

$$= \sum_{q} \left\{\frac{d}{dt}\left(m\dot{x}\,\frac{\partial x}{\partial q}\right) - m\dot{x}\,\frac{d}{dt}\left(\frac{\partial x}{\partial q}\right)\right\}\delta q$$

$$= \sum_{q} \left\{\frac{d}{dt}\left(m\dot{x}\,\frac{\partial \dot{x}}{\partial \dot{q}}\right) - m\dot{x}\left(\frac{\partial \dot{x}}{\partial q}\right)\right\}\delta q,$$

using (8) and (11),

$$= \sum_q \left\{ \frac{d}{dt}\left[\frac{\partial}{\partial \dot{q}}(\tfrac{1}{2}m\dot{x}^2)\right] - \frac{\partial}{\partial q}(\tfrac{1}{2}m\dot{x}^2) \right\} \delta q, \tag{35}$$

and similarly for y and z. Then adding for all particles, and noting that

$$\sum_m \tfrac{1}{2}m(\dot{x}^2+\dot{y}^2+\dot{z}^2) = T, \tag{36}$$

we have

$$\sum_m m(\ddot{x}\,\delta x + \ddot{y}\,\delta y + \ddot{z}\,\delta z) = \sum_q \left\{ \frac{d}{dt}\left(\frac{\partial T}{\partial \dot{q}}\right) - \frac{\partial T}{\partial q} \right\} \delta q. \tag{37}$$

Collecting results,

$$\sum_q \left\{ \frac{d}{dt}\left(\frac{\partial T}{\partial \dot{q}}\right) - \frac{\partial T}{\partial q} + \frac{\partial V}{\partial q} + \frac{\partial K}{\partial \dot{q}} - Q \right\} \delta q = 0. \tag{38}$$

This must be true for any *arbitrary* small displacement, that is, independently of the values of the δq, and the only way in which this can be ensured is the vanishing, separately, of all the co-efficients. Hence we obtain the celebrated equations of motion due to Lagrange,

$$\frac{d}{dt}\left(\frac{\partial T}{\partial \dot{q}_1}\right) - \frac{\partial T}{\partial q_1} + \frac{\partial V}{\partial q_1} + \frac{\partial K}{\partial \dot{q}_1} = Q_1,$$

$$\frac{d}{dt}\left(\frac{\partial T}{\partial \dot{q}_2}\right) - \frac{\partial T}{\partial q_2} + \frac{\partial V}{\partial q_2} + \frac{\partial K}{\partial \dot{q}_2} = Q_2, \quad \text{etc.} \tag{39}$$

Since V is independent of the velocities, these results can be expressed more concisely in terms of the 'kinetic-potential', $\mathscr{L} = T - V$. A typical equation is

$$\frac{d}{dt}\left(\frac{\partial \mathscr{L}}{\partial \dot{q}}\right) - \frac{\partial \mathscr{L}}{\partial q} + \frac{\partial K}{\partial \dot{q}} = Q. \tag{40}$$

6.4. Examples of the use of Lagrange's equations

We now give a few examples of the use of Lagrange's equations, starting with simple ones where we are mainly concerned to show how to apply them, and that well-known results are readily reproduced by their aid. Subsequent examples show how they handle more complex systems, in which a direct application of Newton's laws is complicated.

(i) As a first example, let us consider a mass m controlled by a spring of stiffness s, with resistance proportional to the speed, with resistance coefficient r, acted on by a (varying) force $X = X(t)$. A suitable coordinate is the displacement x from the equilibrium position. Then

$$T = \tfrac{1}{2}m\dot{x}^2, \qquad \partial T/\partial \dot{x} = m\dot{x}, \qquad \partial T/\partial x = 0, \tag{41}$$

$$V = \tfrac{1}{2}sx^2, \qquad \partial V/\partial x = sx, \tag{42}$$

$$K = \tfrac{1}{2}r\dot{x}^2, \qquad \partial K/\partial \dot{x} = r\dot{x}, \tag{43}$$

$$\delta W = X\,\delta x, \tag{44}$$

and so the general formula gives

$$\frac{d}{dt}(m\dot{x}) + sx + r\dot{x} = X,$$

or

$$m\ddot{x} + r\dot{x} + sx = X. \tag{45}$$

(ii) *Simple pendulum*: mass m at the end of a string of length l, under gravity. We neglect resistance, and there are no external forces if we take account of gravity through the potential energy. The angle θ which the string makes with the vertical is a convenient coordinate.

$$T = \tfrac{1}{2}ml^2\dot{\theta}^2, \qquad \partial T/\partial \dot{\theta} = ml^2\dot{\theta}, \qquad \partial T/\partial \theta = 0, \tag{46}$$

$$V = mgl(1 - \cos\theta), \qquad \partial V/\partial \theta = mgl\sin\theta. \tag{47}$$

By the formula,

$$\frac{d}{dt}(ml^2\dot{\theta}) + mgl\sin\theta = 0,$$

or

$$l\ddot{\theta} + g\sin\theta = 0. \tag{48}$$

(iii) *The double pendulum.* We have already seen in section 6.2 that

$$T = \tfrac{1}{2}\{(M+m)a^2\dot{\theta}^2 + 2mab\dot{\theta}\dot{\phi}\cos(\phi-\theta) + mb^2\dot{\phi}^2\}, \tag{49}$$

$$V = (M+m)ga(1 - \cos\theta) + mgb(1 - \cos\phi). \tag{50}$$

Here,

$$\frac{\partial T}{\partial \dot{\theta}} = (M+m)a^2\dot{\theta} + mab\dot{\phi}\cos(\phi-\theta). \tag{51}$$

In deriving this, everything else except $\dot{\theta}$ explicitly occurring has been assumed constant, but in the next step, differentiating with respect to $t, \dot{\theta}, \dot{\phi}, \theta$, and ϕ are *all* to be considered as functions of t, so

$$\frac{d}{dt}\left(\frac{\partial T}{\partial \dot{\theta}}\right) = (M+m)a^2\ddot{\theta}+mab\ddot{\phi}\cos(\phi-\theta)-mab\dot{\phi}(\dot{\phi}-\dot{\theta})\sin(\phi-\theta).$$

(52)

Similarly, $\qquad \dfrac{\partial T}{\partial \dot{\phi}} = mab\dot{\theta}\cos(\phi-\theta)+mb^2\dot{\phi},$ (53)

$$\frac{d}{dt}\left(\frac{\partial T}{\partial \dot{\phi}}\right) = mab\ddot{\theta}\cos(\phi-\theta)-mab\dot{\theta}(\dot{\phi}-\dot{\theta})\sin(\phi-\theta)+mb^2\ddot{\phi}. \quad (54)$$

Also,

$$\frac{\partial T}{\partial \theta} = mab\dot{\phi}\dot{\theta}\sin(\phi-\theta), \quad \frac{\partial T}{\partial \phi} = -mab\dot{\phi}\dot{\theta}\sin(\phi-\theta), \quad (55)$$

$$\frac{\partial V}{\partial \theta} = (M+m)ga\sin\theta, \quad \frac{\partial V}{\partial \phi} = mgb\sin\phi. \quad (56)$$

Collecting terms, we find for the θ equation,

$$(M+m)a^2\ddot{\theta}+mab\ddot{\phi}\cos(\phi-\theta)-mab(\dot{\phi}^2-\dot{\phi}\dot{\theta})\sin(\phi-\theta)-$$
$$-mab\dot{\phi}\dot{\theta}\sin(\phi-\theta)+(M+m)ga\sin\theta = 0,$$

or, simplifying,

$$(M+m)a^2\ddot{\theta}+mab\ddot{\phi}\cos(\phi-\theta)-mab\dot{\phi}^2\sin(\phi-\theta)+$$
$$+(M+m)ga\sin\theta = 0. \quad (57)$$

For the ϕ equation, similarly,

$$mab\ddot{\theta}\cos(\phi-\theta)-mab(\dot{\theta}\dot{\phi}-\dot{\theta}^2)\sin(\phi-\theta)+mb^2\ddot{\phi}+$$
$$+mab\dot{\phi}\dot{\theta}\sin(\phi-\theta)+mgb\sin\phi = 0,$$

or, simplifying,

$$mab\ddot{\theta}\cos(\phi-\theta)+mb^2\ddot{\phi}+mab\dot{\theta}^2\sin(\phi-\theta)+mgb\sin\phi = 0. \quad (58)$$

We will not proceed any further with these equations, but if the reader wishes really to appreciate the advantage of Lagrange's equations, let him derive the equations just given in an elementary manner by use of the tensions P and S in the strings, and the acceleration components of M and m which are, for M, $a\ddot{\theta}$ perpendicular to OM and $a\dot{\theta}^2$ along MO, and for m these accelerations compounded with the relative accelerations $b\ddot{\phi}$ perpendicular to Mm and $b\dot{\phi}^2$ along mM.

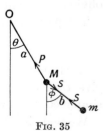

Fig. 35

It is, however, worth while examining a little more closely what happens when we approximate for the case of *small* oscillations, and showing in particular that, in this case, we may obtain correct results much more speedily by making the approximations in the energies.

Firstly, let us use the exact equations. In these, if θ and ϕ are small, so are $\dot{\theta}$ and $\dot{\phi}$, and $\ddot{\theta}$ and $\ddot{\phi}$. Moreover, as $\phi-\theta$ is small, $\cos(\phi-\theta) \doteqdot 1$ (with error of second order) and

$$\sin(\phi-\theta) \doteqdot \phi-\theta, \quad \sin\theta \doteqdot \theta, \quad \sin\phi \doteqdot \phi.$$

If we neglect any term in which there are products of two or more small quantities, and put $\cos(\phi-\theta) = 1$, we have

$$(M+m)a^2\ddot{\theta}+mab\ddot{\phi}+(M+m)ga\theta = 0, \tag{59}$$

$$mab\ddot{\theta}+mb^2\ddot{\phi}+mgb\phi = 0, \tag{60}$$

which are the *linear* differential equations for the *small* oscillations. (We shall see in the next chapter how the modes of vibration may be deduced from such equations.)

Secondly, let us first make the corresponding approximations in the energies. We find, however, that here we must *retain* terms of the second order in the small quantities (which are the largest variable terms) and discard terms of higher order. To the second order, the term $2mab\dot{\phi}\dot{\theta}\cos(\phi-\theta)$ becomes simply $2mab\dot{\theta}\dot{\phi}$, and the terms $(1-\cos\theta)$ and $(1-\cos\phi)$ become respectively $\frac{1}{2}\theta^2$ and $\frac{1}{2}\phi^2$. Hence

$$T = \tfrac{1}{2}\{(M+m)a^2\dot{\theta}^2+2mab\dot{\phi}\dot{\theta}+mb^2\dot{\phi}^2\}$$
$$= \tfrac{1}{2}Ma^2\dot{\theta}^2+\tfrac{1}{2}m(a\dot{\theta}+b\dot{\phi})^2, \tag{61}$$

which could have been written down at once upon using the obvious approximation $(a\dot{\theta}+b\dot{\phi})$ for the velocity of m.

The potential energy becomes

$$\tfrac{1}{2}(M+m)ga\theta^2+\tfrac{1}{2}mgb\phi^2. \tag{62}$$

It can now be readily verified that these simplified energies give rise, upon application of the Lagrange method, to the simplified equations above.

We shall, in later chapters, consistently make this approximation of small motions in the energies, and we shall find that the kinetic energy reduces to a homogeneous quadratic function of the velocities, with *constant* coefficients, and the potential energy to a quadratic function of the coordinates, again with *constant* coefficients.

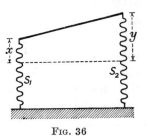

(iv) *Bar supported by two springs.* We make, at once, the approximations for small motions, as in (13) and (16) above, where we found, in terms of the displacements x and y of the ends,

Fig. 36

$$T = \tfrac{1}{6}m(\dot{x}^2 + \dot{x}\dot{y} + \dot{y}^2), \qquad V = \tfrac{1}{2}s_1 x^2 + \tfrac{1}{2}s_2 y^2, \tag{63}$$

whence we derive the equations

$$\tfrac{1}{6}m(2\ddot{x} + \ddot{y}) + s_1 x = 0, \qquad \tfrac{1}{6}m(\ddot{x} + 2\ddot{y}) + s_2 y = 0. \tag{64}$$

Again, we postpone the deduction of the modes and pulsatances until the next chapter.

(v) Finally, let us consider the system —the 'skeleton' of a one-armed governor —illustrated in Fig. 37. It represents a wheel, of moment of inertia I, which can rotate about a vertical axis, acted on by a (variable) torque G about the axis. A light bar of length l, pivoted at a distance a from the axis, can rotate about the pivot but remains in a meridional plane; it carries a mass m at its free end. Convenient coordinates are the angle θ turned

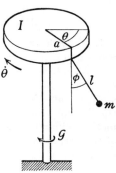

Fig. 37

through by the wheel, and the angle ϕ which the bar makes with the vertical. Neglecting the energies of the rod, we have

$$T = \tfrac{1}{2}I\dot{\theta}^2 + \tfrac{1}{2}m\{l^2\dot{\phi}^2 + (a + l\sin\phi)^2\dot{\theta}^2\},$$

$$V = mgl(1 - \cos\phi), \qquad \delta W = G\,\delta\theta. \tag{65}$$

Consequently, using Lagrange's equations,

$$\frac{d}{dt}\{I\dot{\theta} + m(a + l\sin\phi)^2\dot{\theta}\} = G,$$

$$ml^2\ddot{\phi} - ml\cos\phi(a + l\sin\phi)\dot{\theta}^2 + mgl\sin\phi = 0. \tag{66}$$

Looking carefully at these equations, we see that they represent well-known mechanical principles. The left-hand side of the first is the time rate of change of the moment of momentum about the vertical axis, and this should be equal to the torque applied about that axis. The second is—apart from a factor l—the equation of motion of m in the direction perpendicular to the rod. The second term may be recognized as the component in that direction (expressed by the factor $\cos\phi$) of the centripetal acceleration $m(a+l\sin\phi)\dot\theta^2$, and the term $mg\sin\phi$ is the component of the weight.

It may have been noticed in the above examples that the term $\partial T/\partial\dot q$ is the *momentum* corresponding to q if q is a displacement, and the *moment of momentum* corresponding to q if q is an angle. For any choice of q, $\partial T/\partial\dot q$ will be termed the '*generalized momentum*' corresponding to the coordinate q.

EXERCISES ON CHAPTER VI

1. Write down the kinetic and potential energies for the motion of a compound pendulum, and deduce the equation of motion.

2. A uniform bar AB of mass m is pivoted at A and has a mass M attached at B. The length of the bar is a. It is supported by a spring of stiffness s attached at C, distant c from A, so that it is horizontal in the equilibrium position. Find by the Lagrange method the equation of motion taking (a) the displacement x at B, (b) the angular deflexion θ of the bar, as coordinate. Show that both equations lead to the same pulsatance of free vibration.

3. Two masses M and m are connected by a string passing over a pulley of radius r and moment of inertia I. By Lagrange's method find the acceleration in the motion.

4. A uniform rod of mass m and length $2a$ slides in a vertical plane with its ends on a smooth vertical wall and a smooth floor respectively. If θ is the angle made with the vertical at any time, show that

$$d^2\theta/dt^2 = 3g\sin\theta/4a.$$

5. A uniform rod of mass m and length $2a$ has one end attached to a light ring which slides on a smooth horizontal wire. If at any time x is the displacement of the ring and θ the angle between the rod and the vertical, show that

$$dx/dt + a\cos\theta\,.\,d\theta/dt = \text{const.,}$$
$$4a\,d^2\theta/dt^2 + 3\cos\theta\,.\,d^2x/dt^2 + 3g\sin\theta = 0.$$

6. A light string of length $2a$ has a mass m attached at its mid-point and a mass M at one end. The other end is attached to a fixed support, and the system oscillates under gravity in a vertical plane. If θ and ϕ are the inclinations to the vertical of the upper and lower halves of the string respectively, show that

$$(M+m)\,d^2\theta/dt^2+M\cos(\phi-\theta)\,d^2\phi/dt^2-M\sin(\phi-\theta)(d\phi/dt)^2+$$
$$+(M+m)g\sin\theta/a = 0,$$
$$d^2\phi/dt^2+\cos(\phi-\theta)\,d^2\theta/dt^2+\sin(\phi-\theta)(d\theta/dt)^2+g\sin\phi/a = 0.$$

7. A rod of length $2a$ and mass m is falling in a vertical plane with its lower end on a smooth floor. If θ is the angle it makes with the vertical at any time, show that

$$(1+3\sin^2\theta)\,d^2\theta/dt^2+3\sin\theta\cos\theta(d\theta/dt)^2 = 3g\sin\theta/a.$$

8. By writing the kinetic energy of a particle moving in a plane in terms of polar coordinates, show that the radial and transverse components of the acceleration are

$$d^2r/dt^2-r(d\theta/dt)^2 \quad \text{and} \quad rd^2\theta/dt^2+2(dr/dt)(d\theta/dt).$$

9. Two pulleys, of moments of inertia H and I, are mounted at the ends of a light shaft of torsional rigidity CJ and length l, free to rotate in smooth bearings. A (variable) torque G acts on the pulley H. If θ and ϕ are the angles turned through by H and I respectively, write down the kinetic energy, the strain energy (potential energy) of the shaft, and the work differential dW due to G. Hence derive equations of motion. Deduce that

(a) if $G = 0$, $H\dot{\theta}+I\dot{\phi} = $ constant,

(b) if $G = 0$, and $\theta-\phi = \gamma$, $lHI\ddot{\gamma}+CJ(H+I)\gamma = 0$,

(c) if $G = \hat{G}\sin\beta t$, then for the *maintained* vibration,

$$\theta/(CJ-Il\beta^2) = \phi/CJ = G\sin\beta t/\beta^2(HIl\beta^2-CJH-CJI).$$

10. In a moving-coil loud-speaker the current i in the coil exerts a mechanical force Ai on the diaphragm. Show that the inclusion of a term Aix added to the kinetic-potential $\mathscr{L} = T-V$ will take account of this electro-mechanical interaction. (Cf. Ch. IV, Ex. 13.)

Taking $2\mathscr{L} = L\dot{q}^2+m\dot{x}^2+2A\dot{q}x-sx^2$, and a dissipation function K such that $2K = R\dot{q}^2+r\dot{x}^2$, where L and R are the self-inductance and resistance of the coil, m, s, and r the effective mass, stiffness, and resistance coefficient of the diaphragm, q a charge such that $i = \dot{q}$, and x the displacement of the diaphragm, deduce the equations of motion for an e.m.f. $E\sin\beta t$ applied to the coil. Obtain formulae for x and q, and the effective impedance of the coil circuit as modified by the reaction of the speaker.

VII

SYSTEMS WITH SEVERAL DEGREES OF FREEDOM: NORMAL MODES

7.1. Introduction

IF one examines a system with two or more degrees of freedom oscillating freely after being disturbed from its equilibrium position, it will at first sight appear that the motion is so complicated that any simple description of it seems impossible. If confirmation of this statement is necessary, it is easily obtained by rigging up a simple double pendulum—two masses on a string, suspended by one end.

Mathematical analysis, however, indicates the existence, for such systems, of *simple* modes of vibration, in which all particles *'keep step'* or, more precisely, in which *all* particles execute simple harmonic oscillations with the *same* pulsatance. Such modes will be termed 'normal modes of vibration'.

In the case of very simple, symmetrical systems the existence of such modes is easy to predict. Consider, for instance, the case

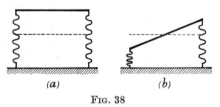

(a)   (b)

FIG. 38

of a uniform bar supported at the ends by equal springs. Clearly a purely up-and-down translational mode is possible, and if m is the mass and s the stiffness of each spring, the pulsatance ω_1 is given by $\omega_1^2 = 2s/m$. But equally clearly, a 'see-saw' purely rotational vibration is also possible, with the ends moving equally in opposite directions. The pulsatance ω_2 of this mode is given by $\omega_2^2 = 6s/m$ (cf. Ch. I, Ex. 6). Hence $\omega_2 = \omega_1 \sqrt{3}$, so that the pulsatances (periods, frequencies) are incommensurable. Now these two modes are, in this case, the *only* normal modes, and *every* motion of the system must be compounded from them. But, owing to the incommensurability of the periods, the *resultant* motion is *not periodic*.

If the springs are not equal, or if the mass-centre of the bar is not central, these two simple motions—up-and-down and see-saw—will *not* be normal modes. But if the springs are not very unequal there will be a normal mode which is nearly up-and-down —mainly translational but with a small rotational component —as indicated in Fig. 39 *a*. There will also be another mode,

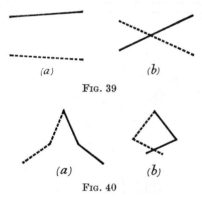

(a)   (b)

Fig. 39

(a)   (b)

Fig. 40

mainly rotational but with a small translational component, as in Fig. 39 *b*.

Similarly, with a double pendulum, there are two normal modes, with extreme positions as indicated in Fig. 40.

The above rests on no detailed reasoning, and the conclusions are only qualitative. The succeeding sections of this chapter will show how to obtain the values of the pulsatances, and the configurations, in these modes, but the mathematics will not be very intelligible unless the facts above described are recognized—one must know the sort of thing one is looking for to have much chance of finding it.

The essential property of a normal mode is that in it all points of the system move harmonically with the *same pulsatance*. Various points differ only in the *amplitude* of their motion and the instantaneous ratio of the *displacements* of two points is also the ratio of their amplitudes. Thus the *amplitude ratios* characterize the mode.

7.2. Pulsatances and amplitude ratios of normal modes

As an example of methods and results we consider the case of two pulleys on a shaft (Fig. 41).

Let $2I$ and $3I$ be the moments of inertia, CJ the torsional

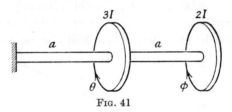

FIG. 41

rigidity of the shaft, and a the length of each segment. As coordinates we choose the rotations θ and ϕ of the two pulleys.

$$T = \tfrac{1}{2}3I\dot{\theta}^2 + \tfrac{1}{2}2I\dot{\phi}^2, \tag{1}$$

$$V = \frac{CJ}{2a}\theta^2 + \frac{CJ}{2a}(\phi-\theta)^2$$

$$= \frac{CJ}{2a}\{2\theta^2 - 2\theta\phi + \phi^2\}. \tag{2}$$

The equations of motion are

$$3I\ddot{\theta} + \frac{CJ}{a}(2\theta-\phi) = 0,$$

$$2I\ddot{\phi} + \frac{CJ}{a}(\phi-\theta) = 0. \tag{3}$$

These are, of course, two linear simultaneous differential equations with constant coefficients for θ and ϕ, which could be solved by standard methods to give θ and ϕ explicitly as functions of t. For our purpose, however, our first concern is the pulsatances of the normal modes, and secondly the amplitude ratios corresponding to the two normal pulsatances. These can be found more expeditiously by a method which starts by taking the existence of normal modes for granted.

In any normal mode, with pulsatance ω, let $\hat{\theta}$ and $\hat{\phi}$ be the amplitudes. Then, since the pulleys 'keep step', and vibrate harmonically with pulsatance ω, we may put†

$$\theta = \hat{\theta}\cos(\omega t + \epsilon), \quad \phi = \hat{\phi}\cos(\omega t + \epsilon). \tag{4}$$

From these formulae we have

$$\ddot{\theta} = -\omega^2\hat{\theta}\cos(\omega t + \epsilon) = -\omega^2\theta, \quad \ddot{\phi} = -\omega^2\hat{\phi}\cos(\omega t + \epsilon) = -\omega^2\phi. \tag{5}$$

Substituting these values in the above equations, and collecting terms in θ and ϕ ,we have

$$\left(\frac{2CJ}{a} - 3I\omega^2\right)\theta - \frac{CJ}{a}\phi = 0,$$

$$-\frac{CJ}{a}\theta + \left(\frac{CJ}{a} - 2I\omega^2\right)\phi = 0. \tag{6}$$

The first of these gives

$$\frac{\phi}{\theta} = \frac{2CJ/a - 3I\omega^2}{CJ/a}, \tag{7}$$

and the second,

$$\frac{\phi}{\theta} = \frac{CJ/a}{CJ/a - 2I\omega^2}. \tag{8}$$

These are consistent only for those values of ω which give the same value of the displacement ratio ϕ/θ, and the condition for this is

$$\frac{2CJ/a - 3I\omega^2}{CJ/a} = \frac{CJ/a}{CJ/a - 2I\omega^2}, \tag{9}$$

or‡

$$(2CJ/a - 3I\omega^2)(CJ/a - 2I\omega^2) - (CJ/a)^2 = 0. \tag{10}$$

This is the *pulsatance equation*. Simplified, it reads

$$6I^2\omega^4 - 7I\omega^2 CJ/a + (CJ/a)^2 = 0,$$

or

$$(6I\omega^2 - CJ/a)(I\omega^2 - CJ/a) = 0. \tag{11}$$

Hence there are *two* pulsatances which can correspond to normal modes, ω_1 and ω_2, such that

$$\omega_1^2 = CJ/6aI, \quad \omega_2^2 = CJ/aI. \tag{12}$$

---

† The cosines could both be replaced by sines. Direct opposition will appear as a *negative* amplitude.

‡ It may be seen that (10) is equivalent to the statement that the determinant of the coefficients in (6) must vanish.

From (7) or (8) we deduce, corresponding to each value of ω, an 'amplitude ratio' ϕ/θ $(= \hat{\phi}/\hat{\theta})$:

$$\begin{aligned} \text{if } \omega = \omega_1, \quad \phi/\theta = 3/2; \\ \text{if } \omega = \omega_2, \quad \phi/\theta = -1. \end{aligned} \tag{13}$$

We have now obtained all the information which we have sought. In the slower normal mode the pulsatance is

$$\omega_1 = \sqrt{(CJ/6aI)},$$

and the angular displacement of the outer pulley is at every instant 1·5 times that of the other, and in the *same* sense. In the faster mode the pulsatance is $\omega_2 = \sqrt{(CJ/aI)}$, and the angular displacements are at all instants equal but in *opposite* senses. The diagram indicates the angular displacement along the shaft, in the extreme positions, in the two cases.

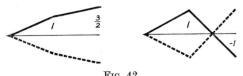

FIG. 42

Note that in the faster mode there is a *node* on the shaft, that is, a point of no motion (additional to the fixed end).

From these results we may write down a general formula for the displacements as functions of time. Suppose that α is the amplitude of the motion of $3I$ in the first mode, then that of $2I$ is $1·5\alpha$. Consequently,

$$\theta_1 = \alpha \sin(\omega_1 t + \epsilon_1), \quad \phi_1 = 1·5\alpha \sin(\omega_1 t + \epsilon_1). \tag{14}$$

Similarly, if β is the amplitude of $3I$ in the second mode, that of $2I$ is $-\beta$, and so

$$\theta_2 = \beta \sin(\omega_2 t + \epsilon_2), \quad \phi_2 = -\beta \sin(\omega_2 t + \epsilon_2). \tag{15}$$

If these motions are executed together, we have

$$\begin{aligned} \theta = \alpha \sin(\omega_1 t + \epsilon_1) + \beta \sin(\omega_2 t + \epsilon_2), \\ \phi = 1·5\alpha \sin(\omega_1 t + \epsilon_1) - \beta \sin(\omega_2 t + \epsilon_2). \end{aligned} \tag{16}$$

7.3. System with three degrees of freedom

Although the previous example illustrates all the fundamental principles, there are certain points of technique, and some generalizations of results, which can be illustrated only by a consideration of systems with more than two degrees of freedom. As an example we consider the case of three equal masses, m, equally spaced on a string of length $4a$ fixed at its ends, and stretched by a tension P.

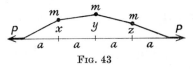

FIG. 43

Let x, y, and z be the *small* transverse displacements. Then

$$T = \tfrac{1}{2}m\dot{x}^2 + \tfrac{1}{2}m\dot{y}^2 + \tfrac{1}{2}m\dot{z}^2 = \tfrac{1}{2}m(\dot{x}^2 + \dot{y}^2 + \dot{z}^2), \qquad (17)$$

$$V = \frac{P}{2a}\{x^2 + (y-x)^2 + (z-y)^2 + z^2\}$$

$$= \frac{P}{2a}\{2x^2 - 2xy + 2y^2 - 2yz + 2z^2\}. \qquad (18)$$

The Lagrangian equations of motion are

$$m\ddot{x} + \frac{P}{a}(2x - y) = 0,$$

$$m\ddot{y} + \frac{P}{a}(-x + 2y - z) = 0, \qquad (19)$$

$$m\ddot{z} + \frac{P}{a}(-y + 2z) = 0.$$

If ω is the pulsatance of a normal mode,

$$\ddot{x} = -\omega^2 x, \quad \ddot{y} = -\omega^2 y, \quad \ddot{z} = -\omega^2 z, \qquad (20)$$

and inserting these we derive

$$(2P/a - m\omega^2)x \qquad\quad -(P/a)y \qquad\qquad\qquad = 0,$$

$$-(P/a)x + (2P/a - m\omega^2)y \qquad\quad -(P/a)z = 0, \quad (21)$$

$$-(P/a)y + (2P/a - m\omega^2)z = 0.$$

These homogeneous equations are consistent only if the determinant of the coefficients vanishes (see below), but the structure of the normal modes and the values of the pulsatances may here be deduced by elementary methods which are perhaps more instructive.

The first and last of these equations suggest that $x = z$. That *may* happen, but a more careful consideration indicates that it need not if the coefficient of x or z vanishes. In this case, $y = 0$, and the second equation then gives $z = -x$. The condition for this is

$$2P/a - m\omega^2 = 0. \tag{22}$$

This actually gives the 'second' pulsatance, ω_2, and we have, for this mode,

$$\omega_2^2 = 2P/am, \qquad x_2 : y_2 : z_2 = 1 : 0 : -1. \tag{23}$$

Returning to the case $x = z$, we have, from the first and last of the equations (21),

$$x = \frac{P/a}{2P/a - m\omega^2} y = z, \tag{24}$$

and now the use of the second equation leads to

$$\left\{ -\frac{(P/a)^2}{2P/a - m\omega^2} + (2P/a - m\omega^2) - \frac{(P/a)^2}{2P/a - m\omega^2} \right\} y = 0,$$

so that, multiplying by $2P/a - m\omega^2$, and discarding the possibility $y = 0$ which has already been noticed and examined,

$$(2P/a - m\omega^2)^2 - 2(P/a)^2 = 0,$$

or $\qquad\qquad m^2\omega^4 - 4m\omega^2 P/a + 2(P/a)^2 = 0. \tag{25}$

Calling the roots of this quadratic in ω^2, ω_1^2 and ω_3^2, we readily find

$$\omega_1^2 = (2 - \sqrt{2})P/am = 0{\cdot}586... (P/am), \tag{26}$$

$$\omega_3^2 = (2 + \sqrt{2})P/am = 3{\cdot}414... (P/am). \tag{27}$$

For each of these modes (with the appropriate value of ω^2),

$$y = \frac{2P/a - m\omega^2}{P/a} x, \tag{28}$$

so that

$$x_1 : y_1 : z_1 = 1 : \sqrt{2} : 1, \tag{29}$$

$$x_3 : y_3 : z_3 = 1 : -\sqrt{2} : 1. \tag{30}$$

The displacement ratios in the three modes are now clear, and extreme configurations are indicated in Fig. 44. We may note that in the second mode there is *one* (internal) node, and in the third mode *two* (internal) nodes.

In the general motion, let $\hat{\alpha}$ be the amplitude of the first component, in x, $\hat{\beta}$ that of the second, and $\hat{\gamma}$ that of the third. Then

$$x = \hat{\alpha}\sin(\omega_1 t+\epsilon_1)+\hat{\beta}\sin(\omega_2 t+\epsilon_2)+\hat{\gamma}\sin(\omega_3 t+\epsilon_3),$$
$$y = \hat{\alpha}\sqrt{2}\sin(\omega_1 t+\epsilon_1) \qquad\qquad -\hat{\gamma}\sqrt{2}\sin(\omega_3 t+\epsilon_3), \quad (31)$$
$$z = \hat{\alpha}\sin(\omega_1 t+\epsilon_1)-\hat{\beta}\sin(\omega_2 t+\epsilon_2)+\hat{\gamma}\sin(\omega_3 t+\epsilon_3).$$

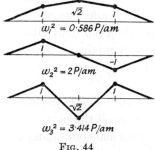

FIG. 44

These can also be written

$$x = \alpha+\beta+\gamma,$$
$$y = \alpha\sqrt{2} -\gamma\sqrt{2}, \quad (32)$$
$$z = \alpha-\beta+\gamma.$$

Since x, y, and z are determined by α, β, and γ, the three latter may be used as coordinates to specify the configuration of the system. In terms of them we can also calculate the energies, and the result is of considerable theoretical importance. First,

$$V = \frac{P}{2a}\{2(\alpha+\beta+\gamma)^2-2(\alpha+\beta+\gamma)\sqrt{2}(\alpha-\gamma)+$$
$$+4(\alpha-\gamma)^2-2\sqrt{2}(\alpha-\gamma)(\alpha-\beta+\gamma)+2(\alpha-\beta+\gamma)^2\}$$
$$= \frac{P}{2a}\{4(2-\sqrt{2})\alpha^2+4\beta^2+4(2+\sqrt{2})\gamma^2\}, \quad (33)$$

in which only square terms survive. Secondly,

$$T = \tfrac{1}{2}m\{(\dot{\alpha}+\dot{\beta}+\dot{\gamma})^2+2(\dot{\alpha}-\dot{\gamma})^2+(\dot{\alpha}-\dot{\beta}+\dot{\gamma})^2\}$$
$$= \tfrac{1}{2}m\{4\dot{\alpha}^2+2\dot{\beta}^2+4\dot{\gamma}^2\}, \quad (34)$$

where, again, only square terms survive.

Applying Lagrange's equations to these,

$$4m\ddot{\alpha} + 4(2-\sqrt{2})P\alpha/a = 0,$$
$$2m\ddot{\beta} + 4P\beta/a = 0, \qquad (35)$$
$$4m\ddot{\gamma} + 4(2+\sqrt{2})P\gamma/a = 0.$$

The three coordinates α, β, γ are thus separated, and the equations lead separately to the three pulsatances already discovered.

Such coordinates are called *normal coordinates*. We may describe the corresponding (normal) vibrations as 'uncoupled', and we can recognize 'coupling' between coordinates by the presence of product terms in *one or other* (or both) of the energies.

It would clearly be very simple to deal with systems having several degrees of freedom if the normal modes could be recognized at sight, so that normal coordinates could be chosen at the outset. Except for the simplest systems, having very few components, and possessing a high degree of symmetry, the immediate choice is rarely possible. In the example of this section, for instance, the configuration of the second mode can be guessed, and (after some experience) the configurations of the other two modes can be sketched, but the *exact numerical value* of the amplitude ratios in these modes cannot be found without calculation. In the absence of symmetry very little indeed can be predicted, and normal modes are to be discovered only as a result of calculations of the kind which we have exhibited in this and the previous section.

7.4. Some effects of coupling

Suppose we inter-connect (i.e. *couple*) two equal systems, what is the effect upon the pulsatance? The answer depends upon the system and upon the nature of the coupling.

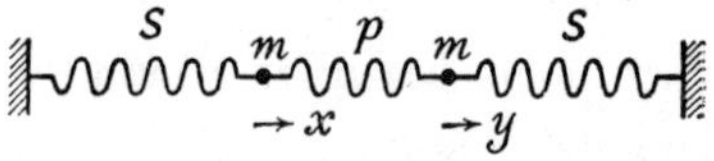

FIG. 45

As a simple instance consider two equal masses m controlled by springs of equal stiffness s, and coupled by a spring of stiffness

p, as indicated in the diagram. Then, if x and y are the displacements (in the same direction) of the two masses, we have

$$T = \tfrac{1}{2}m\dot{x}^2 + \tfrac{1}{2}m\dot{y}^2, \tag{36}$$

$$V = \tfrac{1}{2}sx^2 + \tfrac{1}{2}sy^2 + \tfrac{1}{2}p(y-x)^2. \tag{37}$$

The resulting Lagrange equations are

$$m\ddot{x} + sx + p(x-y) = 0,$$
$$m\ddot{y} + sy + p(y-x) = 0. \tag{38}$$

Substituting $\ddot{x} = -\omega^2 x$, $\ddot{y} = -\omega^2 y$, we derive

$$(s+p-m\omega^2)x - py = 0,$$
$$-px + (s+p-m\omega^2)y = 0. \tag{39}$$

Eliminating the ratio x/y gives

$$(s+p-m\omega^2)^2 - p^2 = 0, \tag{40}$$

whence $\quad\quad\quad\quad m\omega^2 = s \quad$ or $\quad s+2p,$

and $\quad\quad\quad\quad \omega_1^2 = s/m, \quad \omega_2^2 = (s+2p)/m. \tag{41}$

For the amplitude ratios,

$$\text{(i)} \quad y_1/x_1 = 1, \quad \text{i.e.} \quad y_1 = x_1, \tag{42}$$

and in this mode the coupling spring is unstretched;

$$\text{(ii)} \quad y_2/x_2 = -1, \quad \text{i.e.} \quad y_2 = -x_2, \tag{43}$$

so that the masses move in opposition and the extension of the coupling spring is *twice* the displacement of either mass (and hence the $2p$ in the formula for ω_2^2 in (41)).

In the above there is no 'inertia' coupling—no term in $\dot{x}\dot{y}$ in T—and the spring coupling is evidenced by a term in xy in V. A system with inertia coupling between the masses, variable in the way that p is variable in the above example, is not so easy to construct practically, but the effect can be investigated by the insertion of a term in $\dot{x}\dot{y}$ in T. Let us take

$$T = \tfrac{1}{2}m(\dot{x}^2 + 2\beta\dot{x}\dot{y} + \dot{y}^2), \tag{44}$$

$$V = \tfrac{1}{2}s(x^2 + y^2), \tag{45}$$

which describe a system of equal masses and springs with an

inertia coupling coefficient β. The above methods lead to the pulsatance equation

$$(s-m\omega^2)^2-m^2\beta^2\omega^4 = 0, \tag{46}$$

giving

$$\omega_1^2 = s/m(1+\beta), \qquad y_1/x_1 = 1; \tag{47}$$

$$\omega_2^2 = s/m(1-\beta), \qquad y_2/x_2 = -1. \tag{48}$$

7.5. Lagrange's pulsatance determinant†

The method of determining the pulsatances of the normal modes of vibration of a system with several degrees of freedom —say n—leads to a set of n homogeneous linear equations in the n coordinates. The elimination of the ratios of these coordinates is equivalent to finding the condition that this set of equations is consistent. It is shown in books on algebra that this condition is the vanishing of the determinant of the coefficients. This determinant constitutes a concise formulation of the equation giving the pulsatances of the normal modes. In practice, however, the expansion of a determinant of order higher than the third is little, if any, less laborious than the process of elimination. If the configurations of the modes are required as well as the pulsatances, something equivalent to the elimination process is necessary to determine the amplitude ratios, however the equation for the pulsatances is obtained and solved. The general form of the determinant is worth knowing, however, and methods exist of obtaining numerical results without first expanding the determinant.

The general forms of the energies for small displacements are

$$T = \tfrac{1}{2}\{a_{11}\dot{q}_1^2+2a_{12}\dot{q}_1\dot{q}_2+2a_{13}\dot{q}_1\dot{q}_3+\ldots+2a_{1n}\dot{q}_1\dot{q}_n+$$
$$+a_{22}\dot{q}_2^2+2a_{23}\dot{q}_2\dot{q}_3+\ldots+2a_{2n}\dot{q}_2\dot{q}_n+\ldots+a_{nn}\dot{q}_n^2\}, \tag{49}$$

$$V = \tfrac{1}{2}\{c_{11}q_1^2+2c_{12}q_1q_2+2c_{13}q_1q_3+\ldots+2c_{1n}q_1q_n+$$
$$+c_{22}q_2^2+2c_{23}q_2q_3+\ldots+2c_{2n}q_2q_n+\ldots+c_{nn}q_n^2\}. \tag{50}$$

The equation corresponding to q_1 is

$$a_{11}\ddot{q}_1+a_{12}\ddot{q}_2+a_{13}\ddot{q}_3+\ldots+a_{1n}\ddot{q}_n+$$
$$+c_{11}q_1+c_{12}q_2+c_{13}q_3+\ldots+c_{1n}q_n = 0, \tag{51}$$

† This section may without loss be omitted on a first reading.

or, when the pulsatance ω of a normal mode is introduced,

$$(c_{11}-a_{11}\,\omega^2)q_1+(c_{12}-\omega^2 a_{12})q_2+(c_{13}-\omega^2 a_{13})q_3+\ldots+$$
$$+(c_{1n}-\omega^2 a_{1n})q_n = 0. \quad (52)$$

The other equations can be written down by replacing the first suffix by $2, 3, \ldots, n$ in turn. The determinant of the coefficients, equated to zero to give the pulsatance equation, is

$$\begin{vmatrix} c_{11}-a_{11}\,\omega^2 & c_{12}-a_{12}\,\omega^2 & c_{13}-a_{13}\,\omega^2 & . & . & . & c_{1n}-a_{1n}\,\omega^2 \\ c_{21}-a_{21}\,\omega^2 & c_{22}-a_{22}\,\omega^2 & c_{23}-a_{23}\,\omega^2 & . & . & . & c_{2n}-a_{2n}\,\omega^2 \\ c_{31}-a_{31}\,\omega^2 & c_{32}-a_{32}\,\omega^2 & c_{33}-a_{33}\,\omega^2 & . & . & . & c_{3n}-a_{3n}\,\omega^2 \\ . & . & . & . & . & . & . \\ c_{n1}-a_{n1}\,\omega^2 & c_{n2}-a_{n2}\,\omega^2 & c_{n3}-a_{n3}\,\omega^2 & . & . & . & c_{nn}-a_{nn}\,\omega^2 \end{vmatrix}$$
$$= 0. \quad (53)$$

The rules for the expansion of determinants make it clear that this is an equation of the nth degree in ω^2 which will therefore have n roots (values of ω^2). It can be shown that, because T and V are essentially positive (in mathematical parlance *positive definite* quadratic forms), all the values of ω^2 are positive.

It can also be shown that the problem of simultaneously reducing T and V to sums of squares, that is, squares of n distinct linear combinations of the original coordinates, leads to the same equation, whose solution is a necessary step for the reduction.

It is outside the scope of this book to describe numerical methods for the solution of polynomial equations. Special numerical methods applicable to vibration problems will be given in Chapters IX and XV.

EXERCISES ON CHAPTER VII

1. A light string of length $3a$ is fixed at its ends and stretched by a tension P; it has masses m at its points of trisection. Find the pulsatances of the two normal modes of vibration, and the amplitude ratios corresponding to those pulsatances.

2. A string of length $2a$ hanging from a fixed point has masses m at its centre and lower end. Find the pulsatances and amplitude ratios for the two normal modes of vibration.

3. A mass m hangs at the end of a spring of stiffness s. From this mass an equal mass is suspended by a spring, also of stiffness s. Find the

pulsatances and amplitude ratios of the normal modes of vertical vibration. (U.L.)

4. A shaft of total length $4a$, fixed at each end, has pulleys of moments of inertia I and $3I$ at points distant a from the ends. Show that the equation for the pulsatances of the normal modes of torsional vibration is $3\omega^4 - 6\sigma\omega^2 + 2\sigma^2 = 0$, where $\sigma = CJ/aI$.

5. A uniform bar of mass m is supported by springs of stiffness $8s$ and $3s$ at its ends. Find the pulsatances of the two normal modes, and sketch the configurations of the system vibrating in these modes. Choose normal coordinates, and express the energies in terms of these, showing that these new expressions lead to the same pulsatances.

6. Masses B, C, D, of magnitude $2m$, $2m$, m, respectively, are hung from a fixed point A by three equal springs AB, BC, CD, each of stiffness s. Determine the pulsatances of the normal modes of vertical vibration. (U.L.)

7. Two bars, AB, BC, of equal mass are freely jointed together at B, and the system is supported by equal springs at A, B, and C, so that in equilibrium ABC is straight. Find the pulsatances of the three normal modes, and sketch the corresponding configurations.

8. Masses $3m$, $4m$, $3m$ are attached to the points of quadrisection of a light string of length $4a$, fixed at its ends, and stretched by a tension P. Find the pulsatances and amplitude ratios of the three normal modes; choose normal coordinates, verifying that the energies reduce to sums of squares, and that they lead to the same pulsatances.

9. A uniform bar of mass $3m$ and length $6a$ is pivoted at its mid-point, and a mass m is hung from one end by a string of length $8a$. Find the pulsatances of the normal modes of small oscillation under gravity, and the ratio of the angular deviations of string and rod for each mode. (U.L.)

10. A uniform bar of mass M and length $2a$ is freely pivoted about a horizontal axis through its centre perpendicular to its length, and is controlled by a spring which tends to restore it to its horizontal position of equilibrium, applying a torque G per unit angular deviation. From the ends of the bar are hung equal masses m by means of equal light springs of stiffness s. Show that the pulsatance of one normal mode of vibration of the system is $\sqrt{(s/m)}$, and that the others are roots of the equation

$$3sG - \omega^2\{sMa^2 + 3m(G + 2a^2s)\} + Mma^2\omega^4 = 0. \qquad \text{(U.L.)}$$

11. A table of mass M is suspended so that it can execute horizontal vibrations controlled by a spring of stiffness S. A small mass m rests on the table, on which it can slide with negligible friction, and to which it is attached by a spring of stiffness s. Find the equation which determines the pulsatances of the normal modes of vibration, and show that if squares and higher powers of (m/M) are neglected, the squares of the pulsatances are

$$\frac{S}{M}\left(1 - \frac{m}{M}\right) \quad \text{and} \quad \frac{s}{m}\left(1 + \frac{m}{M}\right). \qquad \text{(U.L.)}$$

12. Two diaphragms of effective mass m and stiffness s close the ends

of a tube of length l and sectional area A. Find the effect of the elasticity of the air (coefficient of volume elasticity K) upon the free pulsatances.

13. A light elastic bar, length l, flexural rigidity EI, clamped at one end, has a mass M of considerable moment of inertia Mk^2 attached to the other end. Express the energies in terms of the deflexion and slope at the 'M' end, and deduce the pulsatances of the two normal modes of vibration.

14. n masses, m, are attached at distances a apart to a light string of length $(n+1)a$ fixed at its ends and stretched by a tension P. If, in any normal mode of vibration with pulsatance ω, the displacement of the rth mass is y_r, show that

$$y_{r+1}+y_{r-1} = 2(1-ma\omega^2/2P)y_r.$$

Show that all the conditions are satisfied if $y_r = y_1 \sin r\phi/\sin\phi$, where $\cos\phi = 1-ma\omega^2/2P$, and $\sin(n+1)\phi = 0$. Apply these results to the case $n = 3$, determining pulsatances and configurations for the normal modes.

VIII

SYSTEMS WITH SEVERAL DEGREES OF FREEDOM: MAINTAINED VIBRATIONS

8.1. Introduction

THE maintained vibrations of a system with several degrees of freedom exhibit characteristics which might be expected as a natural extension of those already discussed for simple systems with but one degree of freedom. In particular they have large amplitudes, limited only by dissipative forces, at the pulsatances corresponding to free undamped vibrations, and respond at other frequencies in a manner almost unaffected by small damping. In the case of systems of several degrees of freedom, however, certain other properties emerge—such as the existence of 'anti-resonance', in which one part of the system may have zero motion at certain frequencies. It is also convenient to distinguish between vibrations executed in response to an applied external *force* of given magnitude, and vibrations due to the prescribed *motion* of some point or member of the system. For example, with two pulleys on an elastic shaft, we may consider torsional vibrations due to a periodic torque $\hat{G} \sin \beta t$ acting on the pulley A, with the end C of the shaft fixed, or alternatively the end C may be made to execute an angular oscillation of amount (say) $\hat{a} \sin \beta t$. Of course, in the second case, there must be a force applied to maintain the motion of C, but one can have mechanisms and a power supply which will 'automatically' maintain a displacement and supply the necessary force: for example, a crank and connecting rod can maintain a vibration of given amplitude and frequency if the rotation of the crank is maintained by a motor whose speed can be regulated. There is a slight difference in mathematical technique as applied to the two cases, which we shall now illustrate.

8.2. Vibration due to an external force

We consider the example already mentioned, with pulleys of moment of inertia $3I$, $2I$, at the centre and one end of a shaft of torsional rigidity CJ, and length $2a$, fixed at the other end. We

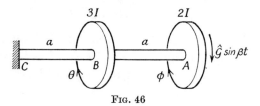

FIG. 46

suppose a periodic torque $G = \hat{G}\sin\beta t$ to act on the pulley A. If θ and ϕ denote the angular displacements of the pulleys, then

$$T = \tfrac{1}{2}\{2I\dot{\phi}^2 + 3I\dot{\theta}^2\}, \tag{1}$$

$$V = \frac{CJ}{2a}\{(\phi-\theta)^2 + \theta^2\}, \tag{2}$$

$$\delta W = G\,\delta\phi. \tag{3}$$

The equations of motion then become

$$2I\ddot{\phi} + \frac{CJ}{a}(\phi-\theta) = G = \hat{G}\sin\beta t, \tag{4}$$

$$3I\ddot{\theta} + \frac{CJ}{a}(2\theta-\phi) = 0. \tag{5}$$

Now for the *maintained* vibration, the system moves 'in step' with pulsatance β, so that

$$\ddot{\phi} = -\beta^2\phi, \qquad \ddot{\theta} = -\beta^2\theta. \tag{6}$$

Hence

$$\left(\frac{CJ}{a} - 2I\beta^2\right)\phi - \frac{CJ}{a}\theta = \hat{G}\sin\beta t, \tag{7}$$

$$-\frac{CJ}{a}\phi + \left(\frac{2CJ}{a} - 3I\beta^2\right)\theta = 0. \tag{8}$$

Solving these two equations for ϕ and θ, we find

$$\phi = \frac{(2CJ/a - 3I\beta^2)}{(CJ/a - 6I\beta^2)(CJ/a - I\beta^2)}\,\hat{G}\sin\beta t, \tag{9}$$

$$\theta = \frac{CJ/a}{(CJ/a - 6I\beta^2)(CJ/a - I\beta^2)}\,\hat{G}\sin\beta t, \tag{10}$$

H

or, considering amplitudes,

$$\hat{\phi} = \frac{\hat{G}}{I} \left| \frac{(2CJ/aI - 3\beta^2)}{(CJ/aI - 6\beta^2)(CJ/aI - \beta^2)} \right|, \tag{11}$$

$$\hat{\theta} = \frac{\hat{G}}{I} \left| \frac{CJ/aI}{(CJ/aI - 6\beta^2)(CJ/aI - \beta^2)} \right|. \tag{12}$$

Examining these formulae we note that they make the response formally infinite when $\beta^2 = CJ/6aI$, and when $\beta^2 = CJ/aI$, and, upon reference to Chapter VII, equation (12),

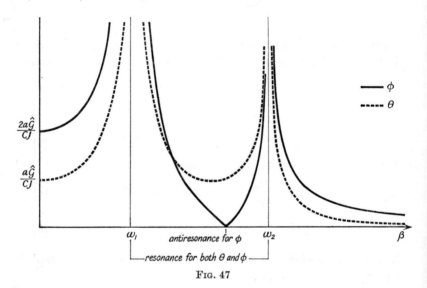

Fig. 47

we note (as expected) that the values of β concerned are in fact the pulsatances ω_1 and ω_2 of the two normal modes of free vibration. In practice, damping would be present, and would limit the amplitudes, but clearly if dangerously large vibrations are to be avoided, pulsatances near to resonance with any normal mode must be avoided.

We also note another rather remarkable fact, namely, that for one value of β, given by $2CJ/aI - 3\beta^2 = 0$, $\hat{\phi}$ becomes zero. Thus although a periodic force is acting upon the pulley A, it causes (at this one pulsatance) no motion at all in A. The pulley B oscillates, however, with amplitude $\hat{G}a/CJ$, in *opposition* to the external torque G, so that when the steady vibration has been built up, the resultant torque on A vanishes. It does so for just this one pulsatance, and this is an example of 'anti-resonance'. It indicates a possibility of producing 'dynamically rigid' bodies at certain frequencies. It is profitable to examine further this pulsatance, and a little thought or working-out will verify the fact that it is the pulsatance for the free vibrations of B when A and C are fixed.

Fig. 47 shows the response curves—using amplitudes, plotted positively—for the system so excited.

8.3. Vibration due to a prescribed motion

We now consider the same pulleys and shaft when the end C is constrained to have an angular displacement $\alpha = \hat{\alpha}\sin\beta t$.

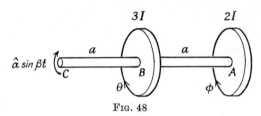

FIG. 48

Using θ and ϕ as before for the angular displacements of the pulleys, the energies are

$$T = \tfrac{1}{2}(3I\dot{\theta}^2 + 2I\dot{\phi}^2), \tag{13}$$

$$V = (CJ/2a)\{(\theta-\alpha)^2 + (\phi-\theta)^2\}. \tag{14}$$

The Lagrangian equations for θ and ϕ are

$$3I\ddot{\theta} + CJ(-\alpha+2\theta-\phi)/a = 0, \tag{15}$$

$$2I\ddot{\phi} + CJ(\phi-\theta)/a = 0. \tag{16}$$

The first may be rewritten

$$3I\ddot{\theta} + CJ(2\theta-\phi)/a = (CJ/a)\alpha = (CJ/a)\hat{\alpha}\sin\beta t. \tag{17}$$

Again, in the maintained vibration, the system moves 'in step' with pulsatance β, so that $\ddot{\theta} = -\beta^2\theta$, $\ddot{\phi} = -\beta^2\phi$, and the equations become

$$(2CJ/a - 3\beta^2)\theta - (CJ/a)\phi = (CJ/a)\hat{\alpha}\sin\beta t, \tag{18}$$

$$-(CJ/a)\theta + (CJ/a - 2\beta^2)\phi = 0. \tag{19}$$

Solving these for θ and ϕ we obtain

$$\theta = \frac{(CJ/aI)(CJ/aI - 2\beta^2)}{(CJ/aI - 6\beta^2)(CJ/aI - \beta^2)} \, \hat{\alpha} \sin \beta t, \tag{20}$$

$$\phi = \frac{(CJ/aI)^2}{(CJ/aI - 6\beta^2)(CJ/aI - \beta^2)} \, \hat{\alpha} \sin \beta t, \tag{21}$$

or
$$\theta = \left| \frac{1 - 2aI\beta^2/CJ}{(1 - 6aI\beta^2/CJ)(1 - aI\beta^2/CJ)} \right| \hat{\alpha}, \tag{22}$$

$$\phi = \left| \frac{1}{(1 - 6aI\beta^2/CJ)(1 - aI\beta^2/CJ)} \right| \hat{\alpha}. \tag{23}$$

Again we see that the amplitudes become formally infinite at the pulsatances corresponding to the normal modes of free vibration. This time the pulley B exhibits anti-resonance, but A does not. The corresponding pulsatance, given by $\beta^2 = CJ/2aI$, may be recognized as that of the pulley A when B is fixed.

As regards the torque which must be applied at C in order to induce the prescribed motion, this may be found by forming the equation of motion corresponding to the coordinate α. This coordinate contributes nothing to the kinetic energy, but, if G is the torque to be applied at C, we have

$$\delta W = G \, \delta \alpha. \tag{24}$$

Consequently, the Lagrangian equation for α is

$$(CJ/a)(\alpha - \theta) = G, \tag{25}$$

that is,
$$G = (CJ/a)\left\{ 1 - \frac{(CJ/aI)(CJ/aI - 2\beta^2)}{(CJ/aI - 6\beta^2)(CJ/aI - \beta^2)} \right\} \alpha$$

$$= \frac{(CJ/a)\beta^2(6\beta^2 - 5CJ/aI)}{(CJ/aI - 6\beta^2)(CJ/aI - \beta^2)} \, \hat{\alpha} \sin \beta t. \tag{26}$$

Of course, the torque becomes formally infinite at resonance with either of the normal modes. There is a pulsatance for which the torque vanishes, viz. when $\beta^2 = 5CJ/6aI$. This can be interpreted physically, for it is the pulsatance of free vibrations of A and B on the shaft joining them, with C free, and hence no torque in BC

8.4. The coupling of equal systems; 'double-humped' response curve

So far we have neglected friction and damping in our discussion of maintained vibrations of systems with several degrees of freedom. Its inclusion will have effects like those already noted for systems with one degree of freedom, especially in the rounding-off into a 'hump' of any infinity of the response curve.

We consider two equal masses, m, each controlled by a spring

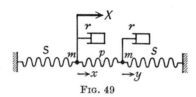

FIG. 49

of stiffness s and subject to a resistance proportional to the speed, with resistance coefficient r, and coupled by a spring of stiffness p. Let x and y be the displacements of the masses (in the same sense) and let a force $X = \hat{X}e^{j\beta t}$ act on the first mass. Then the equations of motion will be

$$m\ddot{x}+r\dot{x}+(s+p)x-py = \hat{X}e^{j\beta t}, \tag{27}$$

$$-px+m\ddot{y}+r\dot{y}+(s+p)y = 0. \tag{28}$$

Since in the *maintained* vibrations, x and y both vary as $e^{j\beta t}$,

$$\dot{x} = j\beta x, \quad \ddot{x} = -\beta^2 x; \qquad \dot{y} = j\beta y, \quad \ddot{y} = -\beta^2 y,$$

so that
$$(s+p-m\beta^2+jr\beta)x-py = \hat{X}e^{j\beta t}, \tag{29}$$

$$-px+(s+p-m\beta^2+jr\beta)y = 0. \tag{30}$$

Solving these for x and y, we obtain

$$x = \frac{s+p-m\beta^2+jr\beta}{(s-m\beta^2+jr\beta)(s+2p-m\beta^2+jr\beta)} \hat{X}e^{j\beta t}, \tag{31}$$

$$y = \frac{p}{(s-m\beta^2+jr\beta)(s+2p-m\beta^2+jr\beta)} \hat{X}e^{j\beta t}. \tag{32}$$

The amplitude responses are

$$\hat{x} = \hat{X} \sqrt{\frac{\{(s+p-m\beta^2)^2+r^2\beta^2\}}{\{(s-m\beta^2)^2+r^2\beta^2\}\{(s+2p-m\beta^2)^2+r^2\beta^2\}}}, \qquad (33)$$

$$\hat{y} = \hat{X} \frac{p}{\sqrt{\{(s-m\beta^2)^2+r^2\beta^2\}\{(s+2p-m\beta^2)^2+r^2\beta^2\}}}. \qquad (34)$$

The amplitude response curves are plotted in Figs. 50 and 51

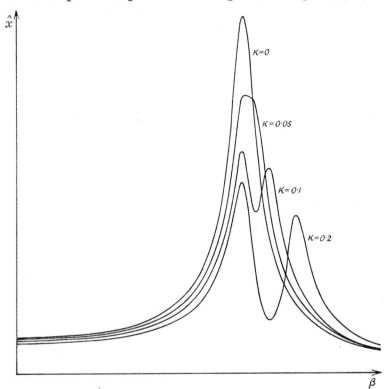

FIG. 50. Typical amplitude-response curves for the driven mass in the system of Fig. 49.

for a value of r equal to one-twentieth of the critical damping (for the uncoupled system). If ω is the resonant pulsatance for the uncoupled system, so that $\omega^2 = s/m$, this means that $r = m\omega/10$. Several values of p are used, and these are best specified by the 'coupling coefficient', which is here the ratio of p to $(s+p)$, that is, of the coefficients of x and y in equation (27) or (28). (For unequal systems, the definition of coupling co-efficient is more complex.) If the systems are uncoupled, $p = 0$; if coupling is complete, p must be infinite. Thus the coupling coefficient

$$\kappa = p/(s+p)$$

takes values between 0 and 1, and when $p = s$, $\kappa = 0.5$.

For $p = 0$ the $\hat{x}$-response curve has a single hump. As p increases the hump first broadens and then develops a double hump.

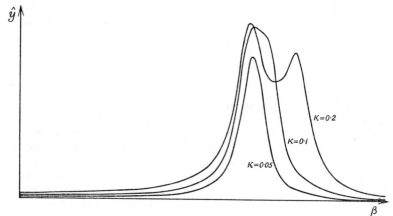

FIG. 51. Typical amplitude-response curves for the coupled mass in the system of Fig. 49.

The broadening of the peak of the response curve when two equal systems (i.e. systems which when uncoupled have the same resonant frequency, and are thus *tuned*) are coupled is a notable feature of vibration theory, and the electrical analogue will be familiar to all who have studied the behaviour of a pair of tightly coupled tuned circuits.

EXERCISES ON CHAPTER VIII

1. A light string AB of length $3a$ is fixed at B and has masses m attached at the two points of trisection. It is stretched by a tension P, and the end A is made to execute transverse vibrations with amplitude α and pulsatance β. Obtain formulae for the amplitudes of the motion of the two masses.

2. Draw with the same axes the graphs of the amplitude response for the masses in Ex. 1 for the values $P = 10^6$ dynes, $m = 10$ gm, $a = 10$ cm, and α as the unit, for a range of β from 0 to 300.

3. A uniform girder of mass M carries a machine at $1/4$ of its length from one end. The ends are supported by springs of stiffness s. The machine is slightly out of balance and exerts when running with angular velocity β, a vertical force $F \sin \beta t$ on the girder. Neglecting the mass of the machine, find the motions of the two ends of the girder.

4. Masses $3m$ and m are attached to the centre and one end of a string of length $2a$, attached to a support at the other end, and hanging freely. If the support is made to execute horizontal vibrations with amplitude α and pulsatance β, find the motions of the two masses.

5. Two equal systems, of mass m and stiffness s, are coupled by a spring of stiffness S. One mass is acted on by a periodic force $F \sin \beta t$. Find the amplitude of the vibration of each mass, and hence show

(a) that there is resonance if $\beta^2 = s/m$ or $(s+2S)/m$;

(b) that there is anti-resonance for the mass acted upon when $\beta^2 = (s+S)/m$.

Explain how the force $F \sin \beta t$ is equilibrated in (b).

6. A shaft of length $2a$ and torsional rigidity CJ is mounted on frictionless bearings. It carries pulleys of moment of inertia $2I$ and I respectively at the mid-point and at one end. The other end is subjected to a periodic twist of angular amplitude α and pulsatance β. Find the amplitude of the forced vibration of each pulley. (U.L.)

7. A uniform bar of mass m is supported by springs of stiffness s and $2s$ at the ends. A periodic force of peak value F and pulsatance β acts on the bar at its mid-point. Find a formula for the amplitude of vibration of the mid-point of the bar. (U.L.)

8. Two pulleys of equal moment of inertia I are attached at X and Y to a uniform shaft XYZ of torsional rigidity CJ fixed at Z; $XY = a = YZ$. A torque of maximum value G and pulsatance β acts on the pulley at X. Show that the maximum angular velocity of the pulley at Y, in the steady state, is $\sigma \beta G / I(\sigma^2 - 3\sigma\beta^2 + \beta^4)$, where $\sigma = CJ/aI$. (U.L.)

9. Two uniform rods, AB, BC, each of mass m, are freely jointed at B, and supported at A, B, and C by three springs of stiffness s, $2s$, and $3s$, respectively, so that the rods are in a horizontal line. The mid-point of AB is given a small periodic vertical motion of amplitude α and pulsatance β. Find the displacements at A and C at any time t. (U.L.)

10. Two equal vibrating systems, of mass m, resistance coefficient r, and stiffness s, are resistance-coupled, the coupling coefficient being γ. One system is acted upon by a periodic force of maximum value F and pulsatance β. Show that the velocity-response curve for the other system has but a single peak, at a pulsatance corresponding to the undamped free pulsatance of either system. (U.L.)

11. Two equal mechanical systems, whose constants are m, r, and s, are coupled by means which produce (a) a term $\gamma s x y$ in V, (b) a term $\delta r \dot{x} \dot{y}$ in K. Find in each case the amplitude responses due to a force of peak value F and pulsatance β acting on the first system.

12. Plot response curves for **Ex.** 11 (a), taking $m = 1, r = 1, s = 100,$ and $\gamma = 0{\cdot}5$.

13. Two mechanical systems, whose (vector) mechanical impedances are Z_1 and Z_2, are coupled by a mutual impedance Z_m. Show that the impedances which give the response to a periodic force acting on the first system are $Z_1' = Z_1 - Z_m^2/Z_2$ and $Z_2' = Z_m - Z_1 Z_2/Z_m$.

IX

RAYLEIGH'S PRINCIPLE AND OTHER APPROXIMATE METHODS

9.1. Introduction

WE showed, in Chapter II, that in any simple vibrating system the maximum (or mean) kinetic energy was equal to the maximum (or mean) potential energy. In Chapter III it appeared that a small degree of damping had a very small effect on the period of a vibrating system, and, in Chapter IV, that the resonant frequency was indeed that with which the system would vibrate if there were no dissipation. Later, in Chapter VIII, we saw that, in a system with several degrees of freedom, the normal modes were uncoupled, and that each behaved essentially as does the simple vibration of a system with one degree of freedom. The equality of the energies therefore subsists for any normal mode of a system with several degrees of freedom, and, in principle, the energy method remains available for the determination of resonant frequencies of such systems. The only difficulty is that each normal mode of vibration is associated with a corresponding configuration, specified by a set of amplitude ratios, and the energies cannot be exactly specified without knowledge of these amplitude ratios. The principle to which Rayleigh's physical intuition led him—and which has been amply substantiated by mathematical arguments—is that a reasonable approximation to these amplitude ratios gives, especially for the slowest mode, a good approximation to the pulsatance of the mode, and a good approximation to these amplitude ratios gives a very good approximation to the pulsatance. For many systems a reasonable approximation to the configuration is readily guessed, especially for the slowest mode, and so a good approximation to the slowest pulsatance can be found. For the avoidance of resonance this may be adequate. Methods exist for refining the approximation systematically, and, in theory, there is no limit to the accuracy which may be obtained by such methods of successive approximation. Such methods also yield information about the pulsatances of higher modes. It is to these, and to cognate matters, that the present chapter is devoted.

9.2. A simple example

We commence with a simple example of the principle in operation, applied to a system with three degrees of freedom,

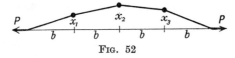

FIG. 52

namely that consisting of three masses m attached to the points of quadrisection of a light string of length $4b$ which is stretched by a tension P (Fig. 52). If x_1, x_2, x_3 are the amplitudes of the vibrations of the three masses respectively, and ω is the pulsatance of a normal mode, the maximum potential energy is

$$V = P[x_1^2+(x_2-x_1)^2+(x_3-x_2)^2+x_3^2]/2b, \qquad (1)$$

and the maximum kinetic energy is

$$T = m\omega^2(x_1^2+x_2^2+x_3^2)/2. \qquad (2)$$

To proceed we must guess the amplitude ratios for the slowest mode. The configuration will be somewhat as in Fig. 53.

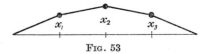

FIG. 53

Symmetry shows that $x_3 = x_1$, and x_2 lies between x_1 and twice x_1, since the configuration in the slowest mode is here convex.†
At a rough guess, $x_2 = 3x_1/2$, so (in integers) we choose as a reasonable approximation to the amplitude ratios $(2:3:2)$. With this approximation, equating T and V gives

$$\omega^2 = (10/17)(P/mb) = 0 \cdot 5882 \dots P/mb. \qquad (3)$$

In this case the theory of Chapter VII leads to the value

† For the slowest mode the restoring forces must be relatively weak, and this demands that the relative departure from straightness be as small as possible.

$(2-\sqrt{2}) = 0\cdot5858\ldots$ for the numerical coefficient, so that the error is less than $0\cdot4$ per cent. Here the correct solution gives the central amplitude as $\sqrt{2} = 1\cdot4142\ldots$ times the others, so that our approximate value is in error by about 6 per cent.

In this example the two extreme guesses $(1:1:1)$ and $(1:2:1)$ both lead to the numerical coefficient $\frac{2}{3} = 0\cdot667\ldots$. This is not good—but is still *much* better than the approximation to the modal configuration! One point which this experiment has shown is that all the approximations to the pulsatance are in excess of the true value. It will be seen later that this is always the case for the slowest mode, and it follows that of two approximations to the pulsatance of that mode it is the smaller which is the more accurate.

9.3. Some theory

We shall demonstrate the validity of Rayleigh's principle with reference to a system with three degrees of freedom, of which the above system is typical, but extension to systems with any finite number of degrees of freedom is immediate.

It was shown in Chapter VII that there are in such a system three normal coordinates, in terms of which potential and kinetic energies both reduce to sums of squares. If we denote the coordinates by α_1, α_2, and α_3, we may write

$$2T = a_1 \dot{\alpha}_1^2 + a_2 \dot{\alpha}_2^2 + a_3 \dot{\alpha}_3^2, \tag{4}$$

$$2V = c_1 \alpha_1^2 + c_2 \alpha_2^2 + c_3 \alpha_3^2, \tag{5}$$

where, if ω_1, ω_2, and ω_3 are the pulsatances of the three modes, respectively, such that $\omega_1 < \omega_2 < \omega_3$,

$$\omega_1^2 = c_1/a_1, \quad \omega_2^2 = c_2/a_2, \quad \omega_3^2 = c_3/a_3. \tag{6}$$

If we now assume a fictitious constrained mode in which all coordinates vary in phase, with pulsatance ω, equating maximum potential and kinetic energies gives for ω the value ω^*, where

$$\omega^{*2} = (\omega_1^2 a_1 \alpha_1^2 + \omega_2^2 a_2 \alpha_2^2 + \omega_3^2 a_3 \alpha_3^2)/(a_1 \alpha_1^2 + a_2 \alpha_2^2 + a_3 \alpha_3^2). \tag{7}$$

An immediate deduction from (7) is that ω^{*2} must always lie between the greatest and least of ω_1^2, ω_2^2, and ω_3^2—that is, ω^* is greater than ω_1 but less than ω_3.

If the assumed mode approximates to one of the normal modes, the corresponding α will be large compared with the others, so that ω^{*2} and the square of the pulsatance of the dominant mode will differ by quantities of the order of the *squares* of the small normal coordinates. This shows that the approximation to the pulsatance is of much greater accuracy than the approximation to the modal configuration.

The result just demonstrated may be expressed by saying that ω^{*2} is stationary for variations of the mode near any normal mode, and that the stationary value is a minimum at the slowest mode, and a maximum at the quickest mode.

9.4. Improvement of the approximation

The method by which improved values of the pulsatance may be obtained will be exemplified in connexion with the three-mass system already used, but, again, the possibility of extension to other systems should be obvious.

The method can be best explained in terms of two simple ideas. The first is that the system would be in equilibrium under the action of the reversed mass-accelerations and the restoring forces, and in particular we consider the special case where the system is in one of its extreme positions in a normal mode. The mass-accelerations are then proportional to the amplitudes. The other principle is that, in any elastic or 'stiff' system, a small redistribution of forces causes a change in the displacement which is relatively small. One has only to consider how little difference there is in the shape of a girder bent by a central concentrated load and by a uniformly distributed load to realize the truth of this statement.

To maintain the steady maximum displacement will require outward forces F_1, F_2, and F_3 at the three masses respectively. The equations of equilibrium—assuming displacements small, of course, and retaining only terms of the first order—will then be

$$F_1 = (P/b)(2x_1 - x_2),$$
$$F_2 = (P/b)(-x_1 + 2x_2 - x_3), \qquad (8)$$
$$F_3 = (P/b)(-x_2 + 2x_3).$$

We need to solve these equations for the x's in terms of the F's. This is not difficult by ordinary algebra, but can also be simply done by considering the effect of the three F's acting separately, as in Fig. 54, and adding the results. We obtain

$$x_1 = (b/4P)(3F_1+2F_2+F_3),$$
$$x_2 = (b/4P)(2F_1+4F_2+2F_3), \tag{9}$$
$$x_3 = (b/4P)(F_1+2F_2+3F_3).$$

Hence, if $(x_1)_1$, $(x_2)_1$, and $(x_3)_1$ are a first approximation to the

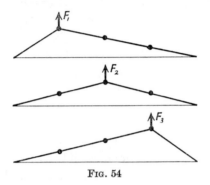

Fig. 54

amplitudes, putting $F_1 = m\omega^2(x_1)_1$, $F_2 = m\omega^2(x_2)_1$, and $F_3 = m\omega^2(x_3)_1$ we shall get a second approximation, to be denoted by suffix 2 outside the brackets. Actually, since only ratios of amplitudes are relevant, we may omit the dimensional parameters—contained in the non-dimensional factor $m\omega^2b/P$ —and write

$$(x_1)_2 = [3(x_1)_1+2(x_2)_1+(x_3)_1]/4,$$
$$(x_2)_2 = [2(x_1)_1+4(x_2)_1+2(x_3)_1]/4, \tag{10}$$
$$(x_3)_2 = [(x_1)_1+2(x_2)_1+3(x_3)_1]/4.$$

Another point about this iterative process is that, apart from the omitted factor, the F's are the forces corresponding to the $(x)_2$'s, from which it follows that the potential energy corresponding to the $(x)_2$'s is given by

$$2V_2 = (P/m\omega^2b)[F_1(x_1)_2+F_2(x_2)_2+F_3(x_3)_2]$$
$$= (P/b)[(x_1)_1(x_1)_2+(x_2)_1(x_2)_2+(x_3)_1(x_3)_2]. \tag{11}$$

Also, $\qquad 2T_2 = m\omega^2[(x_1)_2^2 + (x_2)_2^2 + (x_3)_2^2].$ $\qquad$ (12)

Equating the kinetic and potential energies gives

$$\omega^{*2} = \frac{P[(x_1)_1(x_1)_2 + (x_2)_1(x_2)_2 + (x_3)_1(x_3)_2]}{bm[(x_1)_2^2 + (x_2)_2^2 + (x_3)_2^2]}. \qquad (13)$$

9.5. Successive approximation and iteration

Actually there is much more information to be gained from each pair of successive approximations, and from a systematic sequence of iterative approximations of this type. The theory is most simply demonstrated in terms of the normal coordinates, although (as will be shown in the continuation of the foregoing example) it is not necessary to find these normal coordinates explicitly.

Moreover, in dealing with any specific system, where numerical results are required, the essential part of the process is numerical, and the inclusion throughout of the dimensional factors can be avoided, thus diminishing the writing and concentrating upon the arithmetic.

Let us denote by $(\alpha_r)_s$ the sth approximation to α_r, the amplitude of the rth normal mode in the assumed vibration. Also, let the coefficients in the energies be non-dimensionalized by writing

$$a_1 = a\tilde{a}_1, \quad a_2 = a\tilde{a}_2, \quad ..., \qquad (14)$$

$$c_1 = c\tilde{c}_1, \quad c_2 = c\tilde{c}_2, \quad ..., \qquad (15)$$

where a and c are dimensional and the quantities carrying tildes are all pure numbers. Then we shall find that, if ω is the pulsatance of the corresponding assumed mode,

$$2V = c(\tilde{c}_1 \alpha_1^2 + \tilde{c}_2 \alpha_2^2 + ...) = 2c\tilde{V}, \qquad (16)$$

$$2T = a\omega^2(\tilde{a}_1 \alpha_1^2 + \tilde{a}_2 \alpha_2^2 + ...) = 2a\omega^2\tilde{T}. \qquad (17)$$

The Rayleigh approximation then gives

$$\omega^{*2} = (c/a)(\tilde{V}/\tilde{T}). \qquad (18)$$

Since we know that

$$\omega_1^2 = c_1/a_1 = (c/a)(\tilde{c}_1/\tilde{a}_1), \qquad (19)$$

with similar formulae for the squares of the other normal pulsatances, we see that ω^* will be a good approximation to ω_1 if $\alpha_2, \alpha_3,...$ are small compared with α_1.

In the iterative process we shall concentrate upon the purely numerical quantities $\tilde{V}$ and $\tilde{T}$, and shall obtain approximations to ω_1^2 in the form $(c/a)\lambda$, where λ is an appropriate ratio of these quantities which is approximately equal to $\tilde{c}_1/\tilde{a}_1$.

Reverting now to the process of successive approximation commenced in the last section, we obtain the amplitudes in the second approximation by applying forces equal to the reversed mass-accelerations in the first. Since the normal modes are uncoupled, this leads to the simple relations

$$\tilde{c}_1(\alpha_1)_2 = \tilde{a}_1(\alpha_1)_1, \quad \tilde{c}_2(\alpha_2)_2 = \tilde{a}_2(\alpha_2)_1, \quad \ldots . \tag{20}$$

We have, from the first approximation,

$$2\tilde{T}_1 = \tilde{a}_1(\alpha_1)_1^2 + \tilde{a}_2(\alpha_2)_1^2 + \ldots, \tag{21}$$

$$2\tilde{V}_1 = \tilde{c}_1(\alpha_1)_1^2 + \tilde{c}_2(\alpha_2)_1^2 + \ldots, \tag{22}$$

giving the approximation

$$\lambda_{11} = \tilde{V}_1/\tilde{T}_1. \tag{23}$$

Again, using (20), we have

$$\begin{aligned}
2\tilde{V}_2 &= \tilde{c}_1(\alpha_1)_2^2 + \tilde{c}_2(\alpha_2)_2^2 + \ldots \\
&= \tilde{a}_1(\tilde{a}_1/\tilde{c}_1)(\alpha_1)_1^2 + \tilde{a}_2(\tilde{a}_2/\tilde{c}_2)(\alpha_2)_1^2 + \ldots \\
&= (c/a)[(\tilde{a}_1/\omega_1^2)(\alpha_1)_1^2 + (\tilde{a}_2/\omega_2^2)(\alpha_2)_1^2 + \ldots].
\end{aligned} \tag{24}$$

It thus follows that, when the first terms in the expressions for $\tilde{T}_1$ and $\tilde{V}_2$ dominate, $\quad \lambda_{12} = \tilde{T}_1/\tilde{V}_2 \tag{25}$

is also an approximation to $\tilde{c}_1/\tilde{a}_1 = \omega_1^2 a/c$. Moreover, since $\omega_2, \omega_3, \ldots$ are greater than $\omega_1, \lambda_{11} > \lambda_{12} > \tilde{c}_1/\tilde{a}_1$, as is easily shown. Thus λ_{12} yields a better approximation to ω_1^2 than λ_{11} does.

It may similarly be shown that the approximation given by

$$\lambda_{22} = \tilde{V}_2/\tilde{T}_2 \tag{26}$$

is better still, and so on for each further iteration.

It is worth noting that an alternative formula for $\tilde{V}_2$ is

$$2\tilde{V}_2 = \tilde{a}_1(\alpha_1)_1(\alpha_1)_2 + \tilde{a}_2(\alpha_2)_1(\alpha_2)_2 + \ldots . \tag{27}$$

The virtue of this formula is that both $\tilde{T}$ and $\tilde{V}$ can thus be calculated from the one set of coefficients, the $\tilde{a}$'s. It may be shown that this feature subsists even for non-normal coordinates if either T or V reduces to a sum of squares.

Reverting to the numerical example of three equal masses on a taut string, which we left at the end of the preceding section, we have
$$2T = m\omega^{*2}(x_1^2 + x_2^2 + x_3^2), \tag{28}$$
so that
$$2\tilde{T} = x_1^2 + x_2^2 + x_3^2, \tag{29}$$
and
$$2V = 2P(x_1^2 - x_1 x_2 + x_2^2 - x_2 x_3 + x_3^2)/b, \tag{30}$$
or
$$2\tilde{V} = 2(x_1^2 - x_1 x_2 + x_2^2 - x_2 x_3 + x_3^2). \tag{31}$$

The formulae for iteration are
$$(x_1)_{r+1} = [3(x_1)_r + 2(x_2)_r + (x_3)_r]/4,$$
$$(x_2)_{r+1} = [2(x_1)_r + 4(x_2)_r + 2(x_3)_r]/4, \tag{32}$$
$$(x_3)_{r+1} = [(x_1)_r + 2(x_2)_r + 3(x_3)_r]/4,$$
with
$$\omega^{*2} = \lambda P/mb. \tag{33}$$

Starting with $(x_1)_1$, $(x_2)_1$, $(x_3)_1 = (2, 3, 2)$, we find, for the successive values of $(x_1)_r$, $(x_2)_r$, $(x_3)_r$,

$$r = 1: \qquad 2 \qquad 3 \qquad 2$$
$$r = 2: \qquad 3{\cdot}5 \quad 5 \quad\; 3{\cdot}5$$
$$r = 3: \qquad 6 \qquad 8{\cdot}5 \quad 6$$

From these, we derive
$$2\tilde{V}_1 = 10, \quad 2\tilde{T}_1 = 17, \quad 2\tilde{V}_2 = 29, \quad 2\tilde{T}_2 = 49{\cdot}5, \quad 2\tilde{V}_3 = 84{\cdot}5,$$
$$2\tilde{T}_3 = 144{\cdot}25, \quad \dots .$$

Finally, from these,
$$\lambda_{11} = 0{\cdot}58824\dots, \quad \lambda_{12} = 0{\cdot}58620\dots, \quad \lambda_{22} = 0{\cdot}58586\dots,$$
$$\lambda_{23} = 0{\cdot}58580\dots, \quad \lambda_{33} = 0{\cdot}58579\dots$$

and, judging by the rate of convergence, the last of these would seem to be correct to five places of decimals. The true value is in fact $\lambda = 2 - \sqrt{2} = 0{\cdot}585786\dots$.

9.6. The next mode

The sequence of approximations to which the procedure just illustrated leads enables still more information to be extracted, for from any three successive approximations to ω_1—carried to enough figures—an approximation to the pulsatance of the mode of next higher frequency is accessible.

Suppose that the iteration has proceeded so far that the effect of the third and higher modes is negligible, and that (dropping the brackets and outer suffixes as not necessary here) α_2/α_1, although small, is not zero. Then it follows, on expanding in powers of α_2 and terminating at terms of the first degree in α_2,

$$\tilde{T}_1'/\tilde{V}_2 = (a/c)\omega_1^2[1+(a_2\,\alpha_2^2/a_1\,\alpha_1^2)(1-\omega_1^2/\omega_2^2)+...]. \qquad (34)$$

Similarly,

$$\tilde{V}_2/\tilde{T}_2' = (a/c)\omega_1^2[1+(a_2\,\alpha_2^2/a_1\,\alpha_1^2)(\omega_1^2/\omega_2^2)(1-\omega_1^2/\omega_2^2)+...]. \qquad (35)$$

This shows that the 'errors' in the series of successive approximations to ω_1^2 are approximately in geometric progression, with common ratio $(\omega_1/\omega_2)^2$—and the same must be true of their *differences*, which can be calculated. Hence, from the ratio of two successive differences, and the approximation already obtained for ω_1^2, an estimate of ω_2^2 can be found.

In our numerical instance, the approximation gives

$$\omega_1^2/\omega_2^2 = (17/29-58/99)/(10/17-17/29)$$
$$= 17/99.$$

Using the best value of ω_1^2 so far obtained, namely $58/99$, this leads to the approximation

$$\omega_2^2 = 58/17 = 3{\cdot}412.... .$$

Actually, however, this is not the second, but the *third* pulsatance, for, since the system is symmetrical, the modes of odd order will be symmetrical and the even modes antisymmetrical. As our guessed modal configuration and all the iterates derived from it are symmetrical, it follows that in our arithmetic α_2 *is* zero, so that our process here leads to ω_3^2. The exact value is $(2+\sqrt{2}) = 3{\cdot}4142....$. In view of the absence of the second mode, and since there are only three modes, this result is strikingly accurate—more so than can in general be expected.

The process can be extended, in theory, to higher modes, but, when decimals and not rational fractions are used, the accuracy diminishes for the higher modes, and since the small differences involved in the calculations entail the loss of the leading figures, very many decimals may be needed.

We also point out that the above estimate of ω_3 is too low—it lies between the greatest and least of the normal pulsatances, as was proved earlier.

For our simple symmetrical system, the modes are known to be alternately symmetrical and antisymmetrical, so that the second mode is here skew. The amplitude ratios can, therefore, be none other than $(1:0:-1)$, and, since this is exact, the Rayleigh quotient yields an exact value of the pulsatance. For this set of amplitude ratios,

$$2V = 4Px_1^2/b, \qquad 2T = 2m\omega_2^2 x_1^2 \qquad (36)$$

and equating these gives the correct value,

$$\omega_2^2 = 2P/mb. \qquad (37)$$

9.7. A closer approximation

The result of a sequence of successive approximations is a set of energies, which we may represent by $\tilde{V}_r$, $\tilde{T}_r$, and from which we can deduce a sequence of approximations to the square of the lowest pulsatance, which we may denote by

$$\omega_{2r}^{*2} = (c/a)\tilde{V}_r/\tilde{T}_r, \qquad \omega_{2r+1}^{*2} = (c/a)\tilde{T}_r/\tilde{V}_{r+1}. \qquad (38)$$

Now the differences between these and the exact value of ω_1^2 will be dominated, according to the theory of iterative approximations, by a term which varies from one to the next in geometrical progression. Hence, if iteration has proceeded so far that the other terms in the 'error' are negligible,

$$(\omega_1^2-\omega_{2r-1}^{*2})/(\omega_1^2-\omega_{2r}^{*2}) = (\omega_1^2-\omega_{2r}^{*2})/(\omega_1^2-\omega_{2r+1}^{*2}),$$

or $\qquad \omega_1^2 = (\omega_{2r-1}^{*2}\omega_{2r+1}^{*2}-\omega_{2r}^{*4})/(\omega_{2r-1}^{*2}-2\omega_{2r}^{*2}+\omega_{2r+1}^{*2}).$ $\qquad (39)$

This formula is due to Aitken, and, if calculations are made in decimals, they need to be carried to many figures. If, however, as in many of the approximate calculations of this type, results are obtained as rational fractions, a high accuracy is accessible with reasonably small numbers. Reverting to the above example, a better approximation to ω_1^2 is

$$(10/17 \cdot 58/99 - 17^2/29^2)/(10/17 - 2 \cdot 17/29 + 58/99)$$

$$= 1393/2378 = 0{\cdot}58578637..., $$

which is a much closer approximation to $(2-\sqrt{2})$ than any so far obtained in this chapter.

Having obtained a good approximation to any normal pulsatance, we can obtain an equally good approximation to the modal configuration from the equations of motion—in which, of course, the modal assumption $\ddot{x} = -\omega^2 x$ has been incorporated.

EXERCISES ON CHAPTER IX

1. Find, by the energy method, the pulsatances of the normal modes of transverse vibration of two equal masses m, attached to the points of trisection of a light string of length $3a$ stretched by a tension P.

2. A string of length $3a$ and mass m per unit length is stretched between two fixed points by a tension P, and carries two equal masses M at the points of trisection. Assuming that M is large compared with am, so that the portions of the string are (approximately) straight during transverse vibration, determine the kinetic and potential energies in each of the two normal modes, and deduce that the squares of the pulsatances are

$$6P/a(6M+5ma) \quad \text{and} \quad 6P/a(2M+ma). \qquad \text{(U.L.)}$$

3. Find, by the energy method, the pulsatance of the slowest mode of transverse vibration of three masses, $3m$, $4m$, and $3m$, attached to the points of quadrisection of a string of length $4a$ stretched by a tension P, using the (correct) amplitude ratios $2:3:2$.

4. Examine, for the system of Ex. 3, the effect of assuming amplitude ratios $1:\gamma:1$ and choosing γ to give maximum or minimum pulsatance.

5. For the system of three equal masses at the points of quadrisection of a string, considered in the text, obtain an approximation to the lowest pulsatance taking amplitude ratios $3:4:3$. Does a comparison of the result with that obtained for $2:3:2$ in the text suggest amplitude ratios likely to lead to a better approximation?

6. A uniform rod of length $2a$ and mass M is attached to two fixed points, distant $2(l+a)$, by two strings of length l and (small) mass m per unit length, stretched to a tension P. Assuming that the portions of the string are (approximately) straight during transverse vibration, indicate the configurations of the two normal modes of vibration of the rod and use the energy method to find approximations to the pulsatances. (U.L.)

7. A string of length $3a$ hangs from a fixed point, and to it are attached three equal masses, m, at points distant a, $2a$, and $3a$ from the fixed end. Using the energy method, find approximations to the pulsatance and configuration of the slowest normal mode of vibration under gravity.

8. Pulleys of moment of inertia I, $2I$, and $3I$ are attached to points distant a, $2a$, and $3a$ respectively from the fixed end of a shaft with torsional rigidity CJ. Using the energy method, find approximations to the pulsatance and amplitude ratios of the slowest normal mode of torsional vibration.

X

ELECTRO-MECHANICAL ANALOGIES

10.1. Introduction

WE have already noted, in the earlier chapters, a close analogy
between electrical and mechanical vibrating systems, in which
the electrical quantities inductance, resistance, capacitance,
charge, current, and voltage are analogous to the mechanical
quantities inertia, resistance (coefficient), stiffness, displacement, velocity, and force, respectively. With appropriate
modifications in meaning, the mechanical system may have linear
or angular displacement. The basis of these analogies is, as usual,
the formal similarity of the mathematical equations embodying
the results of the separate and independent investigation of the
properties of these physically diverse systems. The analogies
thus amount to no more than a change in the meaning to be
attached to the symbols in the equations, and in this sense they
teach us nothing new. There are, however, at least two good
reasons for becoming familiar with such analogies. They enable
knowledge relating to one class of system to be utilized in
connexion with another, and, possibly more important, they
enable the behaviour of one type of system to be simulated, and
thus explored, by means of an analogue. The possibility and
simplicity of the use of variable inductance, resistance, and
capacitance components in electrical circuits, and the convenience, sensitivity, and accuracy of electrical measuring instruments has resulted in the use of electric circuit analogies as tools
in many mechanical design problems. It therefore seems worth
while to devote a little space to the examination of the electro-
mechanical analogies for vibrating systems more complex than
those so far dealt with, and especially for coupled systems.

10.2. Connected systems

If we consider complex systems as built up of their elements,
our first task is to consider the mechanical connexions which are

analogous to the well-known electrical connexions known as 'series' and 'parallel'. To do this we must consider what property or quantity is common or conserved in each of these electrical arrangements.

Firstly, if two elements of an electric circuit are in series, they pass the *same current*. Now current is analogous to velocity, so that the corresponding mechanical elements must be so connected that they move with the *same velocity*. This will also mean that they must be so connected that they always have the same displacement, relative to their respective equilibrium positions. Again, if two branches of an electrical circuit are in parallel, they are subject to the *same voltage*. In an analogous mechanical system, therefore, the corresponding elements must be subject to the *same force*.

Alternatively to these physical considerations, the formulae for the energies and the dissipation function can be used to indicate the topology of an electrical circuit analogous to a mechanical system, or conversely.

Since there is usually scope for choice of coordinates in a mechanical system, it follows that the electrical analogue of a particular mechanical system is not necessarily unique.

We proceed to exemplify methods and results in a few simple cases.

10.3. Some simple examples

As a first example we consider two equal particles of mass m, controlled separately by springs of stiffness s_1, and coupled by a spring of stiffness s_2, as represented in Fig. 55 (a). In accordance with the foregoing we expect the analogous circuit to consist of two inductances, $L_1 = m = L_2$, and three capacitances, $C_1 = 1/s_1 = C_3$, and $C_2 = 1/s_2$.

Using x and y to denote the displacements of the masses from their equilibrium positions, the differential equations are

$$m\ddot{x} + s_1 x + s_2(x-y) = 0,$$
$$m\ddot{y} + s_1 y + s_2(y-x) = 0. \tag{1}$$

The currents analogous to $\dot{x}$ and $\dot{y}$ pass through the inductances

L_1 and L_2 respectively. The terms in s_2 show that the corresponding capacitance C_2 must be fed by a current $(\dot{x}-\dot{y})$, and so must be a 'shunt'. Hence, one mesh of the two-mesh analogue must contain L_1, C_1, and C_2, while the other must contain L_2, C_3, and C_2. The resulting circuit, with C_2 the only common branch, is the 'ladder network' indicated in Fig. 55 b. (This may alternatively be drawn as a 'T-network' by putting C_1 alongside L_1 and C_3 alongside L_2.) If q_1 and q_2 denote the charges on C_1

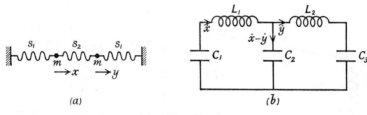

(a)   (b)

Fig. 55

and C_3 respectively, so that the charge on C_2 is q_1-q_2, and the currents through L_1 and L_2 are $\dot{q}_1$ and $\dot{q}_2$ respectively, the differential equations for the circuit are

$$L_1\ddot{q}_1+q_1/C_1+(q_1-q_2)/C_2 = 0,$$
$$L_2\ddot{q}_2+q_2/C_3-(q_1-q_2)/C_2 = 0. \tag{2}$$

The formal similarity with (1) demonstrates the completeness of the analogy.

The alternative method of constructing or verifying the analogy is by means of the energies. The kinetic energy, T, and the potential energy, V, of the mechanical system are given by

$$2T = m\dot{x}^2+m\dot{y}^2,$$
$$2V = s_1x^2+s_2(x-y)^2+s_1y^2. \tag{3}$$

The corresponding electrodynamic and electrostatic energies are given by

$$2T = L_1\dot{q}_1^2+L_2\dot{q}_2^2,$$
$$2V = q_1^2/C_1+(q_1-q_2)^2/C_2+q_2^2/C_3, \tag{4}$$

and, again, the formal similarity is evident.

Analogies between masses controlled by springs and pulleys on shafts have been noted in previous chapters, whereby it will be recognized that there is a similar circuit analogy to two pulleys on a shaft.

As an example showing that the analogous circuit depends on the choice of coordinates, as well as on the form of the mechanical system, we consider a uniform bar of mass m and length $2a$ supported at the ends by springs of stiffnesses s_1 and s_2, so that it can make transverse oscillations in a plane. Two systems of

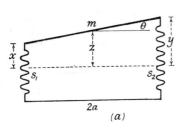 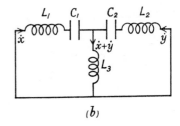

Fig. 56

coordinates naturally present themselves, namely the 'geometrical' ones, the displacements at the ends, and the 'dynamical' ones, the displacement of the mid-point and the angular deflexion.

Let x and y be the displacement of the ends. The energies are then given by

$$2V = s_1 x^2 + s_2 y^2,$$

$$2T = m[(\dot{x}+\dot{y})/2]^2 + (ma^2/3)[(\dot{x}-\dot{y})/2a]^2 \qquad (5)$$

$$= m(\dot{x}^2 + \dot{x}\dot{y} + \dot{y}^2)/3$$

$$= m[\dot{x}^2 + (\dot{x}+\dot{y})^2 + \dot{y}^2]/6.$$

Examination of these shows that the analogous circuit can be constructed of an inductance $L_1 = m/6$ and a capacitance $C_1 = 1/s_1$ in one mesh, with an inductance $L_2 = m/6$ and a capacitance $C_2 = 1/s_2$ in another, with a common shunt inductance $L_3 = m/6$. This is indicated in Fig. 56.

The alternative coordinates are the central deflexion z and the angular deflexion θ. In terms of these, the energies are

$$2V = s_1(z+a\theta)^2 + s_2(z-a\theta)^2$$
$$= 2s_1 z^2 + (s_2-s_1)(z-a\theta)^2 + 2s_1(a\theta)^2, \qquad (6)$$
$$2T = m\dot{z}^2 + m(a\dot{\theta})^2/3.$$

From these it appears that the currents in the meshes are to be $\dot{z}$ and $a\dot{\theta}$, with, in the first mesh, series inductance $L_1 = m$ and capacitance $C_1 = 1/2s_1$, in the second mesh series inductance $L_2 = m/3$ and capacitance $C_2 = 1/2s_1$, with a common shunt capacitance $C_3 = 1/(s_2-s_1)$, as indicated in Fig. 57. (This is

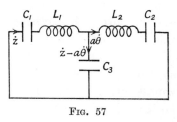

FIG. 57

valid only if (s_2-s_1) is positive, but if this is negative, the correct result is obtained by the interchange of s_1 and s_2.)

The same analogues may be obtained by means of the equations of motion, after suitable rearrangement. In terms of x and y these are

$$m(\ddot{x}+\ddot{y})/2 + s_1 x + s_2 y = 0,$$
$$(ma^2/3)(\ddot{x}-\ddot{y})/2a + s_1 xa - s_2 ya = 0. \qquad (7)$$

These can be rearranged, so that the terms $s_1 x$ and $s_2 y$ occur separately, one in each equation, that is,

$$(m/6)[\ddot{x}+(\ddot{x}+\ddot{y})] + s_1 x = 0,$$
$$(m/6)[\ddot{y}+(\ddot{x}+\ddot{y})] + s_2 y = 0. \qquad (8)$$

Alternatively, the equations of motion are, in terms of z and θ,

$$m\ddot{z} + s_1(z+a\theta) + s_2(z-a\theta) = 0,$$
$$ma^2\ddot{\theta}/3 + s_1 a(z+a\theta) - s_2 a(z-a\theta) = 0, \qquad (9)$$

or,

$$m\ddot{z} + 2s_1 z + (s_2-s_1)(z-a\theta) = 0,$$
$$ma\ddot{\theta}/3 + 2s_1 a\theta + (s_1-s_2)(z-a\theta) = 0. \qquad (10)$$

The technique of these rearrangements, both of the energies and the equations of motion, is to express these in terms of the variables, and either their sum or their difference. The point here is that the current in a shunt must be the sum or difference of the other currents at the junction, so that the existence of such terms in the energy may be represented by a shunt in the analogous circuit.

So far we have only considered non-dissipative mechanical systems, so that the electrical circuits are purely reactive. In many mechanical systems friction is unwanted, and minimized, but in some cases vibration dampers are a feature of the design, and the resistance is often viscous, and so proportional to speed, and then an electrical resistance is a valid analogue. We illustrate this by means of a simple, if somewhat artificial, example.

A mass m_1 is supported by a vertical leaf spring of stiffness s_1 so that it can execute small horizontal vibrations. On its horizontal surface rests a mass m_2 attached to a fixed point by a horizontal spring of stiffness s_2 and coupled to another mass, m_3, by a horizontal spring of stiffness s_3. Between m_1 and m_2 there is viscous friction with coefficient r_1, while m_3 rests on a fixed support, sliding thereon with viscous friction, coefficient r_2.

Let the displacements of the masses be x_1, x_2, and x_3 respectively. Then the equations of motion are

$$m_1\ddot{x}_1 + r_1(\dot{x}_1 - \dot{x}_2) + s_1 x_1 = 0,$$
$$m_2\ddot{x}_2 + r_1(\dot{x}_2 - \dot{x}_1) + s_2 x_2 + s_3(x_2 - x_3) = 0, \qquad (11)$$
$$m_3\ddot{x}_3 + r_2\dot{x}_3 + s_3(x_3 - x_2) = 0.$$

From the foregoing it should now be clear that an analogue to this is a branch containing an inductance $L_1 = m_1$ and a capacitance $C_1 = 1/s_1$ in series, a shunt resistance $R_1 = r_1$, followed by a branch containing an inductance $L_2 = m_2$ and a capacitance $C_2 = 1/s_2$ in series, a shunt capacitance $C_3 = 1/s_3$, and finally a branch containing inductance $L_3 = m_3$ and resistance $R_2 = r_2$ in series. The mechanical system and its electrical analogue are indicated in Fig. 58.

The above results may be obtained alternatively by consideration of the energies and the dissipation function. These are given by

$$2T = m_1\dot{x}_1^2 + m_2\dot{x}_2^2 + m_3\dot{x}_3^2,$$
$$2V = s_1 x_1^2 + s_2 x_2^2 + s_3(x_3 - x_2)^2, \qquad (12)$$
$$2K = r_1(\dot{x}_2 - \dot{x}_1)^2 + r_2\dot{x}_3^2.$$

It remains to say a few words about maintained vibrations in systems such as those considered in this section. An alternating force in the mechanical system is simulated in the circuit analogy by an alternating electrical force—a.c. voltage—applied in the appropriate mesh. Transients can be investigated by connecting a battery (to represent a constant force) or an alternator (to

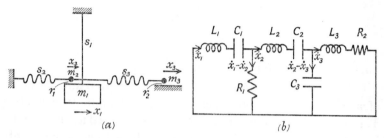

FIG. 58

represent an oscillatory force) in the appropriate branch, with a switch.

If we consider the bar on two springs, discussed earlier in this section, the vibration maintained by the action of a transverse force $F \cos \beta t$ acting at a point of trisection of the bar can be simulated by the inclusion of appropriate alternating e.m.f.s

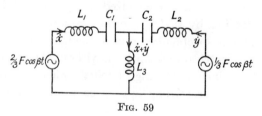

FIG. 59

in the appropriate branches. For example, the force is equivalent to $2F/3 . \cos \beta t$ and $F/3 . \cos \beta t$ acting at the ends respectively, so that the analogue requires the insertion of these a.c. voltages in the respective branches of Fig. 56 (b), as indicated in Fig. 59. Alternatively, the force may be regarded as an equal force at the mid-point, together with a couple of moment $Fa/6 . \cos \beta t$. Since the current corresponding to θ is $a\dot{\theta}$, it follows that the a.c. voltage to be included in the θ-branch of Fig. 57 is $F/6\,.\,\cos\beta t$, while that in the z-branch is $F\cos\beta t$. These results are indicated in Fig. 60.

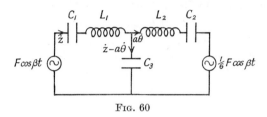

FIG. 60

10.4. Some further remarks

Other electrical terms and ideas can be imported into the field of mechanical vibrations, such as impedance, admittance, etc. These allow concise description of some mechanical features, and, in addition, have contributed to research and development of certain devices in the field of mechanical vibrations.

One important instance of this was in the development of gramophone pick-ups. It will be seen later that the transmission of vibrations from one medium to another is governed by a quantity which is analogous to an impedance, and that transmission is the more complete the more nearly the 'transmission impedances' are 'matched'. This is a principle which the electrical engineers have recognized and exploited for years, but its application, by analogy, to the gramophone pick-up was responsible for a spectacular improvement, even prior to the advent of the electrical pick-up, and, without the careful design based on this principle, the high fidelity which is displayed by our modern sound-recording apparatus would not have been achieved.

In such ways, although analogies teach us nothing essentially new, they do enable us to attack problems by methods which are new to the class of problem under attack, and permit the exploitation of knowledge in fields other than those in which it was discovered, with considerable effect in appropriate places.

To conclude the chapter we give a table in which the more important correspondences between electrical and mechanical terms and quantities are listed.

Electro-mechanical equivalents

| Electrical | Mechanical | | General |
	Translational	Rotational	
quantity, q	displacement, x	rotation, θ	coordinate, q
current, $i = \dot{q}$	velocity, $v = \dot{x}$	angular velocity, $\omega = \dot{\theta}$	$\dot{q}$
$di/dt = \ddot{q}$	acceleration, $\dot{v} = \ddot{x}$	angular acceleration, $\dot{\omega} = \ddot{\theta}$	$\ddot{q}$
inductance, L	mass, m	moment of inertia, I	inertia coefficient, a
resistance, R	resistance coefficient, r	resistance coefficient, r	resistance coefficient, b
capacitance, C	flexibility (reciprocal of stiffness), $1/s$	flexibility (reciprocal of stiffness), $1/s$ $(= l/CJ)$	reciprocal of the stiffness coefficient, $1/c$
voltage (e.m f.), E	force, F	torque, G	generalized force, Q
series	same displacement	same rotation	same coordinate
parallel	same force	same torque	same force
mutual inductance, M			coupling coefficient, a_{12}
transformer	lever, hydraulic ram	gear	
electrokinetic energy, $T = L\dot{i}^2/2$ $(M\dot{i}_1\,\dot{i}_2)$	kinetic energy, $T = mv^2/2$	kinetic energy, $T = I\omega^2/2$	kinetic energy, $T = a\dot{q}^2/2$ $(a_{12}\,\dot{q}_1\,\dot{q}_2)$
electrostatic energy, $V = Cq^2/2$	potential energy, $V = sx^2/2$	potential energy, $V = s\theta^2/2$	potential energy $V = cq^2/2$
dissipation function, $K = R\dot{i}^2/2$	dissipation function, $K = rv^2/2$	dissipation function, $K = r\omega^2/2$	dissipation function, $K = b\dot{q}^2/2$
impedance, $Z = E/\dot{i}$	impedance, $Z = F/v$	impedance, $Z = G/\omega$	impedance, $Z = Q/\dot{q}$

EXERCISES ON CHAPTER X

1. Each of two equal masses m is controlled by a spring of stiffness s, and they are coupled by a dash-pot with resistance coefficient r (i.e. the resistance is r times the relative velocity of the masses). Find an equivalent electric circuit, using the displacements of the masses as coordinates.

If one of the masses is acted upon by a periodic force of peak value F and pulsatance β, show that the peak velocities of the masses are $F\sqrt{(r^2+X^2)}/X\sqrt{(4r^2+X^2)}$ and $Fr/X\sqrt{(4r^2+X^2)}$, respectively, where $X = m\beta - s/\beta$.

2. A pulley of moment of inertia I is mounted at the end of a shaft of length a and torsional rigidity CJ clamped at the other end. An equal pulley mounted on an equal shaft is coupled to the first by a friction clutch which exerts a torque proportional to the relative angular velocity, with resistance coefficient r. A periodic torque of peak value G is applied to the free end of the second shaft. Indicate diagrammatically an analogous electric circuit in which currents correspond to the angular velocities of the pulleys, stating the values of the various circuit parameters. (U.L.)

3. A uniform shaft $PQRS$ has pulleys of moment of inertia A, B, and C at Q, R, and S; the torsional rigidity is CJ and the lengths $PQ = a$, $QR = b$, and $RS = c$. The system, supported in frictionless bearings, is set in motion by a periodic torque G applied at P. Show that the equivalent electric circuit has shunt capacitances a/CJ, b/CJ, c/CJ and series inductances A, B, C with voltage G applied across the first element, a/CJ, and with the end of the last element, C, short-circuited.

4. A number of masses, m, are attached at equal intervals a along a string stretched by a tension P. Show that the analogous electric circuit is a set of inductances m in series, shunted by capacitances a/P. (This is a low-pass filter circuit, the cut-off pulsatance being ω, where $\omega^2 = 4P/ma$.)

5. A series of equal uniform bars AB, BC, CD,..., each of mass m, freely pivoted at B, C,..., are supported by springs of stiffness s at the points A, B, C,.... Find, in terms of the displacements α, β, γ,... of A, B, C,..., the analogous electric circuit.

6. Specify a mechanical system of pulleys on a shaft analogous to a circuit containing a capacitance C in series with two parallel branches each containing an inductance L and a capacitance C. (U.L.)

7. A mass M is controlled by a spring of stiffness S. To it is attached a mass m by a spring of stiffness s. The relative motion of M and m is resisted by a friction damper which exerts a force proportional to the relative velocity of the masses, the resistance coefficient being r. A periodic force acts on the mass M. Construct an equivalent electric circuit, in which currents are analogous to the absolute velocities of the masses, indicating clearly the values of the parameters of the circuit in terms of those of the mechanical system. (U.L.)

8. A uniform bar PQ of mass $9m$ is pivoted at P and supported from above at Q by a light spring RQ of stiffness $2s$ so that in equilibrium PQ is horizontal. From Q hangs a mass m at the end of a light spring QS of stiffness s. The rotation of PQ is resisted by a friction damper which exerts the equivalent of a force at Q proportional to the velocity of Q, with resistance coefficient r. The support R is caused to oscillate vertically with amplitude α and pulsatance β. Design an analogous electrical network, in which the velocities of Q and S are represented by currents in two of the meshes, indicating clearly the values of all electrical quantities. (U.L.)

9. A platform of mass M is mounted on springs of stiffness S so that it can make vertical oscillations. A dash-pot on the platform contains oil and a piston of mass m supported by a spring of stiffness s, the resistance coefficient for the piston being r. Show that if a periodic force of pulsatance β acts on the platform, the vector impedance of the platform is

$$Mj\beta + r + \frac{S+s}{j\beta} - \frac{(r+s/j\beta)^2}{mj\beta + r + s/j\beta}.$$

Indicate the equivalent electric circuit. (U.L.)

10. A coil of mass m is supported so that it can move freely in the direction of its axis in a uniform magnetic field, so that a mechanical force αi acts upon the coil when a current i flows through it. If L and R are the total self-inductance and resistance of the circuit which includes the coil, and an e.m.f. $E\sin\beta t$ is applied to this circuit, show that the peak value of the current is

$$\frac{E}{\sqrt{\{R^2 + (L\beta - \alpha^2/m\beta)^2\}}}$$

and find the amplitude of the motion of the coil.

What is the electrical equivalent of the effect of the inertia of the coil? (U.L.) (Cf. Ch. VI, Ex. 10.)

XI

WAVE PROPAGATION

11.1. Introduction

WE now come to consider vibrations and vibratory disturbances in continuous systems. Although, of course, according to atomic theory all systems are microscopically discrete, and not continuous, the distances between molecules are so small that in a portion of matter 'physically' small—too small to be seen with the naked eye—there is an enormous number of molecules, and the general behaviour in no way reflects its molecular structure. For ordinary 'macroscopic' processes, we may regard solids, liquids, and gases as sensibly continuous, for example, such systems as a vibrating pianoforte string, a telephone diaphragm or a drum-head, or a bell, and the air through which the sound waves they produce travel to reach us.

As far as such a picture is admissible, a bounded (finite) continuous system has an infinite number of degrees of freedom. (Actually, if N is the number of particles—atoms, electrons— the number is at least $3N$, which, for any vibrating system we are likely to consider here, is very large indeed!)

The structureless continuous system into which we imagine real matter to be 'smoothed out' will show all the macroscopic properties of the real material. In the real system disturbances of atoms affect neighbouring atoms, which in turn affect others, and so disturbances are *propagated*, and the continuous system also has this property. We find that this property is associated with the restoring forces called into play when a particle is disturbed from its equilibrium position, and the inertia of the particle. Indeed, *propagation* of disturbances is associated with *vibrations* of the particles. The *disturbances* move large distances, but the particles only move quite *small* distances from their equilibrium positions. For example, in a case where the facts are clearly visible, namely the case of water waves on a pond, we see the *waves* advancing, but floating objects, like the actual water particles, bob up and down, with perhaps a small, hardly noticeable, sideways motion.

We shall find that a large number of physically different systems behave very similarly, and that the equations governing their behaviour are identical in form. In the next section we build up from first principles the equations for a few typical systems.

11.2. The differential equation of wave propagation

First let us consider what is probably the simplest and certainly the most easily visualized case, namely a stretched string. This

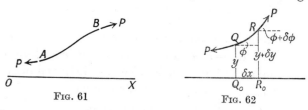

Fig. 61   Fig. 62

may be a piano or violin string, or a cable supporting part of a bridge being built out from the ends. In the latter case the relation between tension and speed of propagation can be used to estimate the tension, and hence the safety of the structure.

Let OX be the equilibrium position of the string, of mass m per unit length, stretched by a tension P, and let AB represent the displaced position of a portion of the string. Then, if we measure x from a suitable origin on OX, the point Q on AB which was originally at Q_0, the point x on OX, will have a transverse displacement, and this we shall call y. We are going to suppose that y is small, and that the inclination ϕ of the tangent at any point Q to OX is so small that the error made by taking $\cos\phi = 1$ is negligibly small. Then the displacement component parallel to OX is also negligible to the same order of approximation. Also, to this order of approximation, $\sin\phi$, ϕ, and $\tan\phi = \partial y/\partial x$ are equal. (The use of partial derivatives is essential, since y depends on both x and time t, and these are independent in the sense that we can consider *any* point at *any* instant. The value of ϕ is an 'instantaneous' value, obtained, so to speak, from a snapshot of the string, that is, the derivative of y with respect to x which gives us $\tan \phi$ must be taken with t constant.)

Consider the forces acting on the element between x and $x+\delta x$ in the displaced position. The transverse component of the force acting on the 'near' end is

$$-P \sin \phi = -P \frac{\partial y}{\partial x} \tag{1}$$

to our order of approximation. This is the *transmitted* (transverse) force, that is, the (transverse) force which the portion on the left of Q exerts upon the portion to the right, thus

$$\text{transmitted force} = -P \frac{\partial y}{\partial x}. \tag{2}$$

The resultant force on the element QR is the (numerical) difference between $-P \, \partial y/\partial x$ at the ends; this is instantaneous, so that, again, a partial x-derivative will be involved in evaluating the increment, which is, to the first order,†

$$\delta(P \, \partial y/\partial x) = P(\partial^2 y/\partial x^2) \, \delta x, \tag{3}$$

and which, when positive, acts in the direction of increasing y.

This resultant force produces an acceleration, in acting on the mass, $m \, \delta x$, of the element. For the element, x does not vary, so the acceleration is the second *partial* t-derivative. Hence Newton's law of motion gives us

$$P(\partial^2 y/\partial x^2) \, \delta x = m \, \delta x(\partial^2 y/\partial t^2), \tag{4}$$

or

$$\partial^2 y/\partial x^2 = (m/P)\partial^2 y/\partial t^2. \tag{5}$$

This is the equation which governs the displacement and the propagation of transverse disturbances, but before examining its solution and the meaning thereof, we will show that equations of the same form arise in other cases.

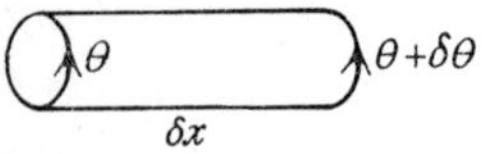

Fig. 63

Our next example is torsional displacements on a (circular) shaft. If θ is the twist at any point x, C the shear modulus, J the polar second moment of the section, then we have the

$$\text{transmitted torque} = -CJ \, \partial\theta/\partial x. \tag{6}$$

† The student should convince himself that higher-order terms do not affect the limit.

The resultant torque on the element is

$$\delta(CJ\,\partial\theta/\partial x) = CJ(\partial^2\theta/\partial x^2)\,\delta x \qquad (7)$$

(if the shaft is uniform, so that C and J are constant). This resultant torque produces the angular acceleration $\partial^2\theta/\partial t^2$ in the element. If ρ is the density of the material of the shaft, the moment of inertia of the element is $\rho J\,\delta x$. Consequently the equation of motion is

$$CJ(\partial^2\theta/\partial x^2)\,\delta x = \rho J\,\delta x(\partial^2\theta/\partial t^2), \qquad (8)$$

or

$$\partial^2\theta/\partial x^2 = (\rho/C)\partial^2\theta/\partial t^2, \qquad (9)$$

which is identical in form to (5) above.

Thirdly, we consider longitudinal disturbances on a bar. Let A be the sectional area of the bar, and denote by u the displacement of any point of a section initially at a distance x along the bar from a convenient origin. As displaced, the segment initially between x and $x+\delta x$ will lie between $x+u$ and $x+\delta x+u+\delta u$ so that its length will be $\delta x+\delta u$, the increase in length δu, the strain $\delta u/\delta x$, or in the limit $\partial u/\partial x$. If E is Young's modulus for the material, the stress will be $E\,\partial u/\partial x$, and thus the force $EA\,\partial u/\partial x$, so, taking into account the sense, we have

$$\text{transmitted force} = -EA\,\partial u/\partial x. \qquad (10)$$

The resultant force on the element will be

$$\delta(EA\,\partial u/\partial x) = EA(\partial^2 u/\partial x^2)\,\delta x. \qquad (11)$$

This produces an acceleration $\partial^2 u/\partial t^2$ in a mass $\rho A\,\delta x$ (ρ being the density of the material), so that

$$EA(\partial^2 u/\partial x^2)\,\delta x = \rho A\,\delta x(\partial^2 u/\partial t^2), \qquad (12)$$

or

$$\partial^2 u/\partial x^2 = (\rho/E)\partial^2 u/\partial t^2, \qquad (13)$$

again of the same form.

For liquid or gas in a (rigid-walled) tube, the same argument stands if only Young's modulus E is replaced by the bulk modulus K.

Finally, for an electric cable or transmission line, with distributed inductance and capacitance L and C per unit length respectively, well insulated and with negligible resistance, it is easy to show, by considering the voltage drop and current leakage in an element of the cable, that the voltage v and current i at any point at any time satisfy the equations

$$\partial v/\partial x = -L\,\partial i/\partial t, \qquad \partial i/\partial x = -C\,\partial v/\partial t. \qquad (14)$$

It follows that $\qquad \partial^2 v/\partial x^2 = LC\,\partial^2 v/\partial t^2, \qquad (15)$

and that i satisfies a similar equation.

The equations (5), (9), (13), and (15) are all of the form

$$\partial^2 y/\partial x^2 = (1/c^2)\partial^2 y/\partial t^2, \qquad (16)$$

the values of c^2 being P/m, C/ρ, E/ρ (or K/ρ for a liquid or gas), and $1/LC$ respectively. We shall now consider the general solution of this equation, known as the wave equation.

11.3. Solutions of the wave equation

It may readily be verified that a general solution of the wave equation $\qquad \partial^2 y/\partial x^2 = (1/c^2)\partial^2 y/\partial t^2 \qquad (17)$

is $\qquad\qquad y = f(x-ct)+g(x+ct), \qquad (18)$

where f and g are *any* (twice differentiable) functions. Let us consider first $\qquad y_1 = f(x-ct). \qquad (19)$

It should be clear that y_1 is the same at (x_2, t_2) as at (x_1, t_1) provided that $\qquad x_2-ct_2 = x_1-ct_1, \qquad (20)$

or $\qquad\qquad (x_2-x_1)/(t_2-t_1) = c. \qquad (21)$

This last statement corresponds to passage from x_1 at time t_1 to x_2 at time t_2 *with velocity* c. Hence (19) corresponds to some 'disturbance', whose form is given by the function f, *propagated* in the positive x-direction with velocity c.

By a similar argument,

$$y_2 = g(x+ct) \qquad (22)$$

corresponds to a disturbance propagated in the negative x-direction with velocity c. The general solution thus represents disturbances—waves—propagated with speed c. The most general solution represents the compounding or superposition of two independent disturbances, one propagated in each direction.

For some purposes it is convenient to write the general solution in the form

$$y = f(t-x/c)+g(t+x/c). \tag{23}$$

Experience will show which form, (18) or (23), is best suited for use in any case and the choice will depend upon the data of the problem, and will be exemplified in the next section.

11.4. Initial and end conditions

There are several ways in which wave motions may be initiated or maintained. If we consider the case of a stretched string, the motion may be initiated by drawing the string aside and letting it go (an idealization of the method of playing a harp), it may have a portion set in motion (as by the hammer of a pianoforte), or the motion of one point may be maintained (as in the case of the violin by a complicated mechanical sequence of 'stick and slip' between bow and string). The last form is the simplest—for a long string—since the two sections of the string on the two sides of the point being moved act independently. In the case of the torsional waves on a shaft, the first method can clearly be achieved by twisting the shaft and letting go, and the third by constraining one end to perform torsional oscillations. In the analogous electrical transmission line, the equivalent of the third method is to apply a varying voltage to one end. The case in which the vibration is maintained is the simplest and will be considered first.

Taking the system on one side only of the driving (or sending) point, and choosing the x-coordinate to be zero at this point and elsewhere positive, then (until reflections return from the distant end) only the wave transmitted in the positive direction exists, that is,

$$y = f(t-x/c). \tag{24}$$

At the driving point we are given the displacement, say

$$y = F(t) \quad \text{when } x = 0. \tag{25}$$

Putting $x = 0$ in (24) and using (25) gives

$$f(t) = F(t), \tag{26}$$

so that the solution of the problem is

$$y = F(t-x/c), \tag{27}$$

which represents the fact that the displacement of the driving-point at time t is that of the point distant x at an instant x/c later.

If, instead of (24), we had written

$$y = f(x-ct), \tag{28}$$

then, instead of (26) we should find

$$f(-ct) = F(t), \tag{29}$$

which is not so easy to interpret. But we have

$$y = f(x-ct) = f\{-c(t-x/c)\}$$
$$= F(t-x/c)$$

by (29), reproducing (27).

The conclusion is that if the data of the problem involve functions of time, it is convenient to have the functions in terms of a time, and to use the forms in terms of $(t-x/c)$ or $(t+x/c)$.

Similar arguments suggest that when the data involve functions of x (as below) the forms in $(x-ct)$ and $(x+ct)$ are likely to prove the more convenient.

These other cases, in which the motion ensues from an initial displacement or velocity (which may vary from point to point), must be treated together.

Let the initial displacement be

$$y = F(x) \quad \text{when} \ t = 0, \tag{30}$$

and the initial distribution of velocity be

$$\partial y/\partial t = G(x) \quad \text{when} \ t = 0. \tag{31}$$

In view of what has just been said, the convenient form to assume for y is

$$y = f(x-ct)+g(x+ct). \tag{32}$$

Applying the condition (30) for initial displacement gives

$$F(x) = f(x)+g(x), \tag{33}$$

which must be *identically* true for *all* (relevant) values of x, and gives one equation for the determination of f and g.

To apply the condition (31), we first differentiate (32) partially with respect to t, deriving

$$\partial y/\partial t = -cf'(x-ct)+cg'(x+ct). \tag{34}$$

Now using (31) we obtain

$$G(x) = -cf'(x) + cg'(x). \tag{35}$$

This, like (33), is to be identically true for all values of x, and consequently we may integrate with respect to x. This gives

$$\int G(x)\,dx = -cf(x) + cg(x). \tag{36}$$

It is convenient to write

$$\int G(x)\,dx = cH(x), \tag{37}$$

so that

$$H(x) = -f(x) + g(x). \tag{38}$$

We can now solve (33) and (38) for $f(x)$ and $g(x)$, obtaining

$$f(x) = \tfrac{1}{2}\{F(x) - H(x)\},$$
$$g(x) = \tfrac{1}{2}\{F(x) + H(x)\}, \tag{39}$$

so that

$$\begin{aligned}
y &= f(x - ct) + g(x + ct) \\
&= \tfrac{1}{2}\{F(x - ct) - H(x - ct) + F(x + ct) + H(x + ct)\} \\
&= \tfrac{1}{2}\{F(x - ct) + F(x + ct) + H(x + ct) - H(x - ct)\} \\
&= \tfrac{1}{2}\left\{ F(x - ct) + F(x + ct) + (1/c) \int_{x-ct}^{x+ct} G(z)\,dz \right\}. \tag{40}
\end{aligned}$$

The meaning of this result, as far as it involves F, is easy to see. The initial displacement divides into two equal halves, which are propagated in opposite directions.

The other terms may be best thought of in terms of H; initially equal and opposite values are propagated one in each direction.

11.5. Reflection: simple cases

Since any medium in which waves are propagated ultimately comes to an end it is natural to inquire what happens to a wave upon reaching such an end. In this section we examine in detail two very simple typical instances: (i) a transverse wave travelling along a stretched string coming to a fixed end of the string, (ii) a torsional wave travelling along a uniform shaft, coming to a free end. More complicated examples, such as those involving a 'load' (a mass attached to the string, or a pulley mounted on the shaft), or a change of medium, will be dealt with in section 11.8.

It is convenient to let the incident wave travel in the positive x-direction, so that in the first case mentioned the transverse displacement due to the incident wave may be represented by

$$y_i = f(t-x/c). \tag{41}$$

The effect of the end must be to give rise to a reflected wave travelling in the other direction, so that we may represent the displacement due to the reflected wave by

$$y_r = g(t+x/c). \tag{42}$$

Hence the resultant transverse displacement, which is the sum of these, will be given by

$$y = f(t-x/c)+g(t+x/c). \tag{43}$$

To determine how g depends on f, we have to apply the condition at the fixed end. This is conveniently taken as $x = 0$, so that

$$y = 0 \quad \text{when} \quad x = 0, \quad \text{for all } t. \tag{44}$$

Inserting this in (43), we have, for all values of t,

$$0 = f(t)+g(t), \tag{45a}$$

or $$g(t) \equiv -f(t). \tag{45b}$$

Consequently the formal solution of the problem is

$$y = \underset{\text{incident} \atop \text{wave}}{f(t-x/c)} - \underset{\text{reflected} \atop \text{wave}}{f(t+x/c)}. \tag{46}$$

It is easy to interpret this equation. The reflected wave has the same form as the incident wave (same f), but is reversed in sense, the incident wave undergoing a phase change of 180° on reflection. One can picture the process by imagining a virtual continuation of the string, in which an inverted wave travels, the two crossing at the fixed point. The case of a triangular wave is exhibited in Fig. 64, in which are drawn successive positions of the real and virtual waves, incident in thin continuous lines, reflected in dotted lines, where they differ from the resultant, and this last is given by the thick continuous line.

In the case of torsional waves on a shaft encountering a free end, we have for the twist θ the same expression as in (43) above, namely

$$\theta = f(t-x/c)+g(t+x/c). \tag{47}$$

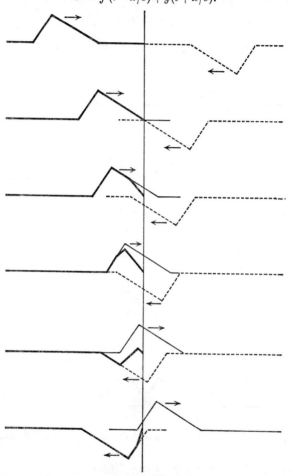

FIG. 64. Triangular wave on a stretched string: reflection at a fixed end.

The condition at a free end is that there is no transmitted torque, that is, by (6),

$$-CJ\,\partial\theta/\partial x = 0 \quad \text{at } x = 0, \quad \text{for all } t. \tag{48}$$

Applying this condition to (47) yields

$$0 = -(1/c)f'(t)+(1/c)g'(t), \tag{49 a}$$

that is, $g'(t) \equiv f'(t).$ (49 b)

This is true for all values of t, so that we may integrate, obtaining

$$g(t) = f(t),$$ (50)

any constant of integration being absorbed into g.

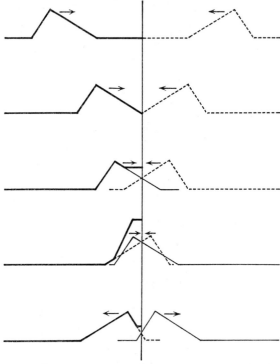

Fig. 65. Triangular wave on a shaft: reflection at a free end.

Hence $\theta = f(t-x/c)+f(t+x/c).$ (51)

The meaning of this is very similar to the former: the wave is reflected without change of form, and (this time) without change of sense (or phase). The history of the reflection is shown in Fig. 65, with the same methods of denoting the incident, reflected, and resultant waves as were used in Fig. 64.

The analogues of 'fixed' and 'free' ends in other cases of wave propagation will be evident, and the simple laws of reflection without change of form, and with or without change of sense (phase), apply to them all.

11.6. Progressive waves: transmission impedance: energy

The purpose of this section is to examine certain general properties of waves, and the media in which they are propagated. The example is that of torsional waves on a shaft, but the analogues in other cases are readily found, and some are given in the exercises.

A progressive torsional wave transmitted on a shaft is given by

$$\theta = f(t-x/c), \tag{52}$$

where $c^2 = C/\rho$ as in § 11.2. The angular velocity is

$$\dot{\theta} = \partial\theta/\partial t = f'(t-x/c). \tag{53}$$

The transmitted torque (cf. equation (6) above) is given by

$$-CJ\,\partial\theta/\partial x = (CJ/c)f'(t-x/c). \tag{54}$$

From equations (53) and (54) we see that the *velocity* is proportional to the transmitted torque (and *not*, as might have been expected, the acceleration). Now in the electrical analogy the ratio of force to velocity is that of e.m.f. to current, a ratio which the electrical engineer calls impedance. It is therefore convenient to call the ratio of transmitted torque to angular velocity (and the analogous quantity in other cases) the *transmission impedance*. In the present case,

$$\text{transmission impedance} = (-CJ\,\partial\theta/\partial x)/(\partial\theta/\partial t)$$
$$= CJ/c = \rho Jc, \tag{55}$$

where, to get the last result, we have used the fact that $C = \rho c^2$.

In the electrical analogue a purely real impedance corresponds to an electrical resistance, which, in its turn, is associated with a dissipation of energy. In the system we are considering (or in the idealized form of it which our equations represent), there is no true dissipation of energy, so that at first the parallel seems quite misleading. But energy *does* disappear from any portion of the shaft, after the wave has passed. In other words, energy is not dissipated, but is *propagated* or *transmitted*. (Subsequently we shall meet complex values of impedance, with a component corresponding to electrical reactance, and associated with change of phase.)

A similar quantity is encountered in connexion with all wave propagation; in acoustics it has been termed the 'radiation resistance', but the term transmission impedance is more general and is to be preferred.

The foregoing results suggest the desirability of examining the energetics of wave propagation.

In the case of the shaft, the moment of inertia of a small element of length δx is (as we have seen) $\rho J\,\delta x$, so that its kinetic energy is

$$\delta T = \tfrac{1}{2}\rho J\,\delta x(\partial\theta/\partial t)^2. \tag{56}$$

The potential energy of the same element is given by equation (20) of Chapter II, on writing δx for l and $\partial\theta/\partial x$ for θ/l, and is

$$\delta V = \tfrac{1}{2}CJ(\partial\theta/\partial x)^2\,\delta x. \tag{57}$$

But from (52),

$$\partial\theta/\partial t = f'(t-x/c), \quad \partial\theta/\partial x = -(1/c)f'(t-x/c), \tag{58}$$

so that, using $C = \rho c^2$,

$$\delta T = \tfrac{1}{2}\rho J\,\delta x f'^2(t-x/c) = \delta V. \tag{59}$$

From this it follows that if δE is the energy instantaneously associated with the element δx,

$$\delta E = \delta T + \delta V \tag{60}$$

$$= 2\delta T = 2\delta V$$

$$= \rho J\,\delta x f'^2(t-x/c). \tag{61}$$

If the energy per unit length is denoted by ϵ, then

$$\epsilon = \delta E/\delta x$$

$$= \rho J f'^2(t-x/c). \tag{62}$$

The fact that the potential and kinetic energies per unit length are equal is in some ways similar to the result that the maximum potential and kinetic energies of a simple vibrating system are equal, and can be made the basis of a determination of wave speeds similar to that of pulsatances given in Chapter II.

It is now natural to inquire how the energy is maintained and propagated, and to do this we consider the activity of the transmitted torque at any point. This is

$$-CJ(\partial\theta/\partial x).(\partial\theta/\partial t) = (CJ/c)f'^2(t-x/c)$$

$$= \rho Jcf'^2(t-x/c) \tag{63}$$

$$= c\epsilon. \tag{64}$$

In (63) we see the combination ρJc—the transmission impedance —again, while (64) shows that the rate of working at any point is exactly equal to the rate of energy transmission, at speed c, at the point.†

11.7. Simple harmonic waves

So far we have been able to deal with wave propagation without specifying any particular wave form, but in many important practical cases we shall be concerned with simple harmonic waves having a definite pulsatance (frequency). It seems desirable to repeat, for this important type of wave, the argument of the last section, and to record the special results in terms of the amplitude and pulsatance of the wave.

Still considering torsional waves on a shaft, denoting the (angular) amplitude by α and the pulsatance by ω, we take as the formula for the twist

$$\theta = \alpha\sin\omega(t-x/c). \tag{65}$$

Corresponding to this we have

$$\text{angular velocity} = \partial\theta/\partial t = \omega\alpha\cos\omega(t-x/c), \tag{66}$$

$$\text{transmitted torque} = -CJ(\partial\theta/\partial x) = (CJ\omega\alpha/c)\cos\omega(t-x/c), \tag{67}$$

and the ratio of these yields the previous value $CJ/c = \rho Jc$ for the transmission impedance.

The kinetic energy per unit length is

$$\tau = \tfrac{1}{2}\rho J(\partial\theta/\partial t)^2 = \tfrac{1}{2}\rho J\omega^2\alpha^2\cos^2\omega(t-x/c), \tag{68}$$

and the time average of this (over a number of complete periods) is

$$\bar\tau = \tfrac{1}{4}\rho J\omega^2\alpha^2. \tag{69}$$

† That waves and energy should be propagated at the same speed is *not* obvious; it is, in fact, *not true* if wave speed depends on pulsatance, that is, if the medium is dispersive.

The potential energy per unit length is

$$v = \tfrac{1}{2}CJ(\partial\theta/\partial x)^2 = \tfrac{1}{2}(CJ\omega^2\alpha^2/c^2)\cos^2\omega(t-x/c) \qquad (70\,\mathrm{a})$$

$$= \tfrac{1}{2}\rho J\omega^2\alpha^2\cos^2\omega(t-x/c)$$

$$= \tau. \qquad (70\,\mathrm{b})$$

Hence, also,

$$\bar{v} = \bar{\tau}. \qquad (71)$$

Again, $\epsilon = \tau+v$, and so

$$\bar{\epsilon} = \bar{\tau}+\bar{v}$$

$$= \tfrac{1}{2}\rho J\omega^2\alpha^2. \qquad (72)$$

Finally, the activity of the transmitted torque is

$$-CJ(\partial\theta/\partial x).(\partial\theta/\partial t) = (CJ\omega^2\alpha^2/c)\cos^2\omega(t-x/c). \qquad (73)$$

The average activity across the section, or the *power trans-mitted*, is thus

$$\tfrac{1}{2}CJ\omega^2\alpha^2/c = \tfrac{1}{2}\rho Jc\omega^2\alpha^2 \qquad (74\,\mathrm{a})$$

$$= c\bar{\epsilon}. \qquad (74\,\mathrm{b})$$

11.8. Reflection and transmission

Simple cases of reflection, where the medium terminates, have been considered in section 11.5, but in other cases, where the medium changes, or where the system has a 'load' at some point, there is (partial) transmission as well as (partial) reflection. It would be possible to illustrate the methods and results by means of torsional waves, but it is perhaps desirable to change the system, although it is to be emphasized that complete analogies exist between the various possible systems. In this section we use transverse waves on a stretched string.

In some problems of this type the result depends upon the wave form, that is, upon the pulsatance, and it is generally safer to assume a simple harmonic incident wave. If the pulsatance appears in the results, an arbitrary wave $f(t-x/c)$ would have led to difficulty. If the result is independent of pulsatance, an arbitrary wave form could have been used.

If m is the mass per unit length, and P the tension, the wave speed c is given by

$$c^2 = P/m, \qquad (75)$$

and (cf. Ex. 10, below) the transmission impedance is

$$R = mc. \tag{76}$$

The first problem we shall consider is that of change of medium, with one portion of the string having mass m_1 per unit length, the other having mass m_2 per unit length. The tensions must be the same, but the wave speeds and the transmission impedances differ. Explicitly,

$$c_1^2 = P/m_1, \qquad\qquad c_2^2 = P/m_2, \tag{77}$$

$$R_1 = m_1 c_1, \qquad\qquad R_2 = m_2 c_2. \tag{78}$$

It is convenient to have the incident wave travelling in the portion labelled by the suffix 1, and proceeding in the positive direction; it is also convenient to let the origin of x be at the junction. To allow for possible change of phase we use the complex exponential rather than the sine or cosine.

The transverse displacement in the incident wave is represented by
$$\alpha e^{j\omega(t-x/c_1)}.$$

The reflected wave travels in the negative direction in portion 1, and so can be denoted by
$$\beta e^{j\omega(t+x/c_1)}.$$

The transmitted wave travels in the positive direction in portion 2, and so can be represented by
$$\gamma e^{j\omega(t-x/c_2)}.$$

Hence the transverse displacements y_1 and y_2, in portions 1 and 2 respectively, are given by

$$y_1 = \alpha e^{j\omega(t-x/c_1)} + \beta e^{j\omega(t+x/c_1)}, \tag{79}$$

$$y_2 = \gamma e^{j\omega(t-x/c_2)}. \tag{80}$$

To determine β and γ we need two conditions, and these must represent what happens at $x = 0$. The first is purely geometrical —the fact that the displacement is the same for both portions at the junction, that is,

$$y_1 = y_2 \quad \text{when } x = 0, \quad \text{for all } t,$$

so that (cancelling the common factor $e^{j\omega t}$)

$$\alpha + \beta = \gamma. \tag{81}$$

The second condition is dynamical, expressing the continuity of the transmitted force at the junction, that is,

$$P \, \partial y_1/\partial x = P \, \partial y_2/\partial x \quad \text{when } x = 0, \quad \text{for all } t,$$

so that (again cancelling $e^{j\omega t}$)

$$-\omega P\alpha/c_1 + \omega P\beta/c_1 = -\omega P\gamma/c_2,$$

whence
$$m_1 c_1(\alpha-\beta) = m_2 c_2 \gamma,$$

or
$$R_1(\alpha-\beta) = R_2\gamma. \tag{82}$$

Solving (81) and (82) we derive

$$\beta/\alpha = (R_1 - R_2)/(R_1 + R_2), \qquad \gamma/\alpha = 2R_1/(R_1 + R_2), \tag{83}$$

which are the *reflection* and *transmission coefficients* respectively.

We note that these are independent of the pulsatance, and that they are not complex. We infer that they apply to all wave forms, and that no phase change (other than $180°$ if $R_2 > R_1$) occurs. We also note that they are entirely determined by the (ratio of) the transmission impedances.

The results previously obtained for terminated systems are included in (83). Corresponding to a fixed end, R_2 is infinite, so that $\beta/\alpha = -1$, which means reflection with reversal. The case of a free end corresponds to $R_2 = 0$, giving $\beta/\alpha = 1$, which means reflection without reversal.

The question of energy is important. The average energy per unit length for the three waves is

$$\begin{aligned}
&\text{incident} && \tfrac{1}{2}m_1 \omega^2\alpha^2, \\
&\text{reflected} && \tfrac{1}{2}m_1 \omega^2\beta^2, \\
&\text{transmitted} && \tfrac{1}{2}m_2 \omega^2\gamma^2.
\end{aligned}$$

The incident energy travels at speed c_1, so the rate at which energy approaches the junction is

$$\tfrac{1}{2}m_1 \omega^2\alpha^2 c_1 = \tfrac{1}{2}R_1 \omega^2\alpha^2. \tag{84}$$

The rate at which energy leaves the junction is, by the same argument,

$$\tfrac{1}{2}m_1\omega^2\beta^2 \cdot c_1 + \tfrac{1}{2}m_2\omega^2\gamma^2 \cdot c_2 = \tfrac{1}{2}R_1\omega^2\beta^2 + \tfrac{1}{2}R_2\omega^2\gamma^2$$

$$= \tfrac{1}{2}\omega^2\alpha^2\,\frac{R_1(R_1-R_2)^2+4R_2R_1^2}{(R_1+R_2)^2}$$

$$= \tfrac{1}{2}\omega^2\alpha^2 R_1. \tag{85}$$

It is thus clear that all the energy is accounted for.

The fractions into which the incident energy is divided are as follows:

$$\frac{\text{reflected energy}}{\text{incident energy}} = \frac{R_1\beta^2}{R_1\alpha^2} = \frac{(R_1-R_2)^2}{(R_1+R_2)^2}, \tag{86}$$

$$\frac{\text{transmitted energy}}{\text{incident energy}} = \frac{R_2\gamma^2}{R_1\alpha^2} = \frac{4R_1R_2}{(R_1+R_2)^2}. \tag{87}$$

We note that if $R_2 = R_1$, there is *no* reflected energy, and *all* the energy is transmitted. The necessity of equalizing, or *matching*, impedances to obviate reflection is well known in electrical engineering.

We now consider the effect of a concentrated mass M at a point of the string. It is convenient to let the point at which M is attached be $x = 0$. As before, on the left of M we have incident and reflected waves, and the resultant transverse displacement is given by

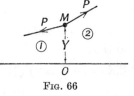

FIG. 66

$$y_1 = \alpha e^{j\omega(t-x/c)} + \beta e^{j\omega(t+x/c)}. \tag{88}$$

On the right of M we have the transmitted wave, in which the displacement is

$$y_2 = \gamma e^{j\omega(t-x/c)}. \tag{89}$$

If we denote by Y the displacement of M we must have the (geometrical) condition

$$(\alpha+\beta)e^{j\omega t} = Y = \gamma e^{j\omega t}. \tag{90}$$

The dynamical condition is the equation of motion of M under the influence of the transverse components of the tension on the two sides, namely

$$M\ddot{Y} = \{P\,\partial y_2/\partial x - P\,\partial y_1/\partial x\}_{x=0}, \tag{91}$$

or, using (88), (89), and (90),

$$(j\omega)^2 M\gamma = P(j\omega/c)(\alpha-\beta-\gamma), \tag{92}$$

whence, using the fact that $P = mc^2$, we derive

$$\alpha-\beta = \gamma(1+j\omega M/mc). \tag{93}$$

Solving (90) and (93) we obtain

$$\beta/\alpha = (-j\omega M/2mc)/(1+j\omega M/2mc), \quad \gamma/\alpha = 1/(1+j\omega M/2mc). \tag{94}$$

These complex ratios indicate phase differences between the

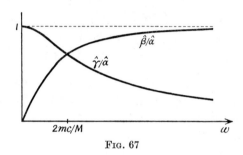

Fig. 67

three waves, and their moduli give the physical amplitude ratios, so that

$$\hat{\beta}/\hat{\alpha} = (\omega M/2mc)/\sqrt{\{1+(\omega M/2mc)^2\}}, \quad \hat{\gamma}/\hat{\alpha} = 1/\sqrt{\{1+(\omega M/2mc)^2\}} \tag{95}$$

and, if $\omega M/2mc = \tan \theta$, γ lags behind α by θ, and β lags behind α by $(\tfrac{1}{2}\pi+\theta)$.

Since it is evident from (95) that

$$\hat{\beta}^2+\hat{\gamma}^2 = \hat{\alpha}^2, \tag{96}$$

we conclude that the sum of the energies of the reflected and transmitted waves is equal to that of the incident wave. We also see, by (90), that $\hat{\gamma}$ is the amplitude of the motion of M, and that its vibration lags by θ behind that of the incident wave.

Fig. 67 shows how the relative amplitudes depend on the pulsatance of the incident wave.

If M is very large its position is practically fixed, and by letting M tend to infinity we recover the relation $\beta = -\alpha$ corresponding to a fixed end.

EXERCISES ON CHAPTER XI

1. Find the velocities of longitudinal and torsional waves in steel. ($E = 30,000,000$, and $C = 12,000,000$ lb wt/sq. in., density $0 \cdot 28$ lb/cu. in.)

2. A steel wire, 30 ft long, is stretched by a tension of 500 lb wt; the diameter is $0 \cdot 1$ in. Find the velocity of transverse waves and the frequency of the fundamental mode of transverse vibration.

3. A long, stretched string has the portion between $x = a$ and $x = -a$ displaced, so that the displacement at $x = 0$ is b and the portions on either side are straight. Plot the shape of the string at times $a/4c$, $a/2c$, $3a/4c$, a/c, and $2a/c$ after being released from rest, c being the velocity of wave propagation.

4. If one of the waves in Ex. 3 subsequently arrives at a fixed end, plot the shape of the string at the same intervals after the arrival of the wave at this end.

5. If a string of mass m per unit length stretched by a tension P is damped by a frictional force per unit length, r times the velocity, construct the partial differential equation of motion. Show that, if r^2 is neglected, the solution may be written in the alternative forms
$$y = e^{-\alpha t}[f(x-ct) + F(x+ct)],$$
or
$$y = e^{-\alpha x/c}g(x-ct) + e^{\alpha x/c}G(x+ct),$$
where $\alpha = r/2m$.

6. If the portion of the string of Ex. 3 between $x = a$ and $x = -a$ is given an initial velocity v, plot the form of the string at the same instants.

7. Describe and sketch the propagation of an initial displacement as in Ex. 3 on the string of Ex. 5.

8. Find the 'transmission impedance' (defined as force/particle velocity) for longitudinal waves in a bar of sectional area A, density ρ, and Young's modulus E.

9. Repeat Ex. 8 for transverse waves on a stretched string, using the definition (transverse component of force)/(transverse velocity).

10. A shaft undergoes a sudden change of section, the polar second moments of the sections being J_1 and J_2 respectively. Find the ratios of the amplitudes of the reflected and transmitted waves to that of an incident wave approaching the junction from side 1.

11. A long shaft (C, J, ρ) has a flywheel of moment of inertia I at one point. Find the effect of the flywheel upon torsional waves of pulsatance β, expressing the amplitudes of the reflected and transmitted waves as fractions of that of the incident wave. Sketch a graph showing the variation of these with β, taking $I = 0 \cdot 2 J c \rho$.

Also verify that the sum of the energies of the reflected and transmitted waves is equal to the energy of the incident wave.

12. Torsional waves are transmitted with speed c along a shaft of density ρ and polar moment of inertia J. The motion of the end of the

shaft is resisted by a torque proportional to the angular velocity, with resistance coefficient r. Determine the ratio of the amplitude of the reflected wave to the incident; show that it is independent of pulsatance, and that r can be chosen so as to absorb completely the incident energy. (U.L.)

13. If the flywheel in Ex. 11 is at the end of the shaft, show that the amplitudes of incident and reflected waves are equal, but that there is a change of phase of 2ϕ, where $\tan\phi = \beta I/Jc\rho$.

14. If the flywheel in Ex. 13 is also controlled by a spring which exerts a torque $\lambda\theta$ for a twist θ, show that a similar result holds, but with

$$\tan\phi = (\beta I - \lambda/\beta)/Jc\rho.$$

15. Calculate the 'transmission impedance' for the string of Ex. 5.

16. One end of a portion of a uniform cylindrical shaft, of length l, is constrained to execute an angular oscillation $\theta = \alpha \sin \beta t$, while the other end is free. Show that the angular amplitude of the free end is $\alpha \sec(\beta l/c)$, where c is the velocity of torsional waves, and that the torque necessary to maintain the vibration is

$$\rho c J \beta \alpha \sin \beta t \tan (\beta l/c),$$

where J is the polar second moment of the section, and ρ the density of the material of the shaft. (U.L.)

XII

SOUND

12.1. Introduction

SOUND, be it speech, music, the song of birds, thunder, or the roar of traffic or aircraft, is the medium whereby much information about the outside world reaches our ears, and thence our brain. That sound is transmitted as a pressure disturbance propagated through the air is a matter of general knowledge. In this chapter we shall concentrate on the transmission of sound through gases, although the transmission through liquids involves no different principles. It is also a matter of experience that sound can be transmitted through solids, but in solids there are two types of disturbance, sufficiently well described by their names, compressional and distortional, which are transmitted with different speeds. This difference of speed is the basis of the science of seismology, but its explanation would demand from the reader a deeper knowledge of the theory of elasticity in solids than is postulated, so that, apart from an occasional brief reference, it will not be considered in this chapter.

12.2. Physical properties of gases and liquids

The properties of a fluid essential for the transmission of sound are the possession of mass, the possibility of exerting and transmitting a pressure, and a mechanism whereby changes of mass distribution and changes of pressure are interdependent.

The quantity used as a measure of mass is the *density*, defined as the mass per unit volume. Possible units are pounds per cubic foot, or kilograms per cubic metre, but, for most scientific purposes, density is expressed in grammes per cubic centimetre.

Pressure is a force distributed over a surface, and it is measured by the force exerted per unit area. (This of course is, strictly speaking, *average* pressure, just as mass per unit volume is *average* density, but we take it for granted that we deal, generally, with surface elements or volume elements so small that the variations in density or pressure therein are irrelevant to the purpose in hand.) In the English-speaking world the pound weight per square inch is very frequently used as a unit, but for scientific purposes the metric unit, the dyne per square centimetre, is adopted. Meteorologists use the unit called a bar, which is an approximate average of the atmospheric pressure at the surface of the earth, but which, providentially, can be taken as 10^6 dynes per square centimetre.

The ability of a fluid to propagate a disturbance depends on the existence of a relationship between small changes of pressure and small changes of volume. This relationship is expressed in terms of a modulus of volume elasticity, or a 'bulk modulus', as it is called. Like all moduli of elasticity, this is defined as the ratio of an increment of stress to the corresponding increment of strain. In this case the increment of stress is clearly the increment of pressure, which we shall denote by δp. The corresponding increment of strain will be the fractional increase of volume— but it is more convenient to express it in terms of the increase in density. Indeed, it is desirable to introduce a quantity which is, essentially, the fractional increase in density. This is termed the 'condensation', and will be denoted by s. If ρ is the density, and ρ_0 the equilibrium density (the suffix 0 being consistently used to indicate equilibrium values), the definition of s is implied in the equation

$$\rho = \rho_0(1+s), \tag{1 a}$$

or, alternatively,

$$\delta\rho = \rho - \rho_0 = \rho_0 s. \tag{1 b}$$

In what follows we shall assume that δp and s are small quantities whose squares are negligible.

Since δp is the increment of stress and s is the increment of strain, it follows from the definition of K, the bulk modulus of elasticity, that

$$\delta p = p - p_0 = Ks. \tag{2}$$

In the case of a liquid the value of K must be measured experimentally—or inferred from the measured speed of sound. In the case of a gas—at least the 'perfect' gas of thermodynamic theory, to which the air approximates very closely at ordinary atmospheric pressures and temperatures—K is calculable in terms of other thermodynamic quantities.

The equation of state for such a gas is

$$p = RT\rho, \tag{3}$$

where T is the temperature and R the gas constant. From this it follows that, for an isothermal change,

$$\delta p = RT\delta\rho = RT\rho_0 s,$$

whence
$$K = RT\rho_0 = p_0. \tag{4}$$

In the propagation of sound, however, the changes of pressure and density take place so rapidly that they are adiabatic, and not isothermal. The relation between p and ρ for such a change is known to be
$$p = A\rho^\gamma, \tag{5}$$

where γ is the ratio of the specific heats of the gas, C_p/C_v. From this
$$\delta p = \gamma A\rho_0^{\gamma-1}\delta\rho = \gamma A\rho_0^\gamma s,$$

whence
$$K = \gamma A\rho_0^\gamma = \gamma p_0. \tag{6}$$

The adiabatic elastic modulus is greater in the ratio γ than the isothermal. That it should be greater is evident when one notes that the temperature is increased by compression, when this is so rapid that there is no time for any appreciable amount of heat to be conducted away, with the result that differences of pressure are enhanced. A similar argument applies to rarefaction.

12.3. Plane waves of sound

Ordinary sources of sound, such as the human voice, musical instruments, radio loud-speakers, gunshot, jet aircraft, or even a thunderstorm, are localized, and the sound which they emit is attenuated as it spreads. This attenuation is an inessential feature of sound transmission, which masks the fundamental simplicity of the process and of the mathematical equations which describe it. We therefore consider first the propagation of sound in one dimension, say in a tube or at a great distance from a localized source, where this attenuation does not occur.

Let x be distance measured in the direction of propagation. Then all the physical quantities related to the propagation will be functions of x and of the time t. Let u denote the displacement of the particles in the x-direction. Consider an element between two planes whose original coordinates are x and $x+\delta x$. Then their coordinates at some instant during the propagation will be $x+u$ and $x+u+\delta x+\delta u$ respectively. The distance between the planes, originally δx, will now be $\delta x+\delta u$. We shall assume that the motion is small, which is tantamount to assuming that δu is small compared with δx, or that $\partial u/\partial x$ is small. The amount of matter, per unit area of cross-section in the element, is conserved during the motion, so that

$$\rho_0\,\delta x = \rho_0(1+s)(\delta x+\delta u),$$

or
$$1 = (1+s)(1+\partial u/\partial x).$$

Since both s and $\partial u/\partial x$ are small, it follows that

$$s = -\partial u/\partial x, \tag{7}$$

and, from this and (2), that

$$\delta p = -K\,\partial u/\partial x. \tag{8}$$

The force per unit area acting on the element is equal to the difference of pressure between the faces, that is, $\partial(\delta p)/\partial x\,.\,\delta x$, and it acts in the negative x-direction. The mass per unit area of cross-section, upon which this force acts, is $\rho_0\,\delta x$. The equation of motion is, consequently,

$$\rho_0\,\delta x\,.\,\partial^2 u/\partial t^2 = -\partial(\delta p)/\partial x\,.\,\delta x,$$

or
$$\rho_0\,\partial^2 u/\partial t^2 = -\partial(\delta p)/\partial x. \tag{9}$$

Combining this with (8) it follows that—provided the gas is initially uniform, so that K is a constant—

$$\partial^2 u/\partial t^2 = (K/\rho_0)\,\partial^2 u/\partial x^2. \tag{10}$$

This we recognize as a particular form of the wave equation, showing that sound waves are propagated with a speed c given by
$$c^2 = K/\rho_0. \tag{11}$$

The general solution of (10), corresponding to waves propagated in the positive x-direction, is

$$u = f(x-ct). \tag{12}$$

Corresponding to this we have

$$s = -f'(x-ct), \tag{13}$$

$$\delta p = -Kf'(x-ct), \tag{14}$$

and, since $\partial u/\partial t = -cf'(x-ct)$, the transmission impedance for this form of wave is

$$(\delta p)/(\partial u/\partial t) = K/c = \rho_0 c = \sqrt{(K\rho_0)}. \tag{15}$$

It is, again, real, and represents non-dissipative propagation of energy.

The density of the kinetic energy (kinetic energy per unit volume), τ, is given by

$$2\tau = \rho_0(\partial u/\partial t)^2 = \rho_0 c^2 f'^2. \tag{16}$$

The potential energy density v is given by

$$2v = Ks^2 = Kf'^2. \tag{17}$$

We see that $\tau = v$, and consequently the total energy density ϵ is given by

$$\epsilon = \tau + v = 2\tau = 2v = Kf'^2. \tag{18}$$

12.4. Sinusoidal sound waves

A complex sound wave can be analysed by electronic devices, as it apparently is by the basilar membrane in the ear, into harmonic constituents, and musical and speech sounds can be synthesized with fair accuracy from pure tones properly blended. It is therefore of some interest to examine and record the properties of a pure tone, or a sinusoidal sound wave. The important quantities which define it are the amplitude of the particle motion, the pulsatance, and the phase. The last has little significance in many connexions, and we shall take the wave to be expressed in terms of its particle displacement by

$$u = a \sin \omega(t-x/c), \tag{19}$$

where a is the amplitude, and ω the pulsatance. From this,

$$\delta p = (K/c)\omega a \cos \omega(t-x/c) = \rho_0 c\omega a \cos \omega(t-x/c). \tag{20}$$

The local energy density is

$$\epsilon = 2v = 2\tau = \rho\omega^2 a^2 \cos^2\omega(t-x/c) \tag{21}$$

(where we have dropped the zero subscript to ρ as no longer necessary). The mean energy density is obtained by averaging this over a period, and is

$$\bar{\epsilon} = \rho\omega^2 a^2/2. \tag{22}$$

The activity, A—rate of doing work—per unit area is given by

$$A = \delta p\, \partial u/\partial t = (K/c)\omega^2 a^2 \cos^2\omega(t-x/c)$$
$$= \rho c\omega^2 a^2 \cos^2\omega(t-x/c),$$

and the mean activity per unit area—the mean rate of power transmission per unit area—is

$$\bar{A} = \rho c\omega^2 a^2/2 = c\bar{\epsilon}. \tag{23}$$

Here, as in the last chapter, we see that the power transmission is at the rate necessary to maintain the energy supply. We shall return to this point when we consider sources of sound and spherical sound waves.

The energy density is a measure of the intensity of a sound, and the equation (22) shows how the intensity depends, for a pure tone, on the three quantities ρ, ω, and a which characterize the wave and the medium through which it is being propagated. The fact that it depends on the square of the amplitude is to be expected, but its dependence on the square of the pulsatance (or frequency) is also important. It may be emphasized here that (22) gives a basis for physical measurements, but that our subjective judgement as to the relative loudness of sounds of different pitch is affected by the frequency response characteristics of the human ear.

12.5. Atmospheric acoustics

It is outside the scope of this book to pursue this topic of sound very deeply into regions more appropriate to a treatise on physics, and to such books we refer the reader for detail greater than we shall give. But the treatment of the subject would be incomplete without some account of sound waves in the atmosphere, the basis of our hearing, and some reference to the numerical values of relevant physical quantities.

A formula for the speed of sound, equivalent to $c^2 = K/\rho$, was obtained by Newton. In working out the value of K for air, however, he assumed isothermal conditions, and arrived at the

result—correct for that assumption—that $K = p$. Inserting
the numerical values, Newton obtained a value for the speed of
sound which was less, by about 20 per cent., than the value which
was known from experiment. Much later, Laplace adduced the
considerations which we have given at the end of section 12.2
to show that the adiabatic coefficient of elasticity should be used.
As already seen, this leads to the result $K = \gamma p$, and, since for
air the value of γ is very near to 1·4, the discrepancy is removed.

At sea-level, at a temperature of 15° C (59° F), the pressure
and density of (dry) air are 10^6 dynes per sq. cm. and 0·00122
gm per c.c. respectively, and $\gamma = 1\cdot4$. From these it follows that
the speed of sound in such air is $3\cdot39\,.\,10^4$ cm per sec, or 1,110
ft/sec, or about 750 m.p.h.

From the equation of state for a perfect gas—to which the
air closely approximates in this connexion—it follows that

$$c^2 = \gamma RT, \tag{24}$$

so that the speed varies as the square root of the absolute
temperature. It follows that as between summer and winter,
and, indeed, in the troposphere, the speed differs from its
average value by only a few per cent.

For different gases, at the same pressure and temperature, the
speed of sound varies inversely as the square root of the density.
In hydrogen, therefore, it will be nearly four times that in air,
at the same pressure.

12.6. Change of medium: transmission and reflection

We have in the last chapter had instances of the effect upon a
train of waves of some change in a property or properties of the
medium through which the waves are being propagated. The
results there obtained are of quite general application, but it may
nevertheless be of service to show how these results do, in fact,
arise in a different context.

Suppose that a train of plane waves, proceeding in the positive
direction in a medium with density ρ_1 and bulk modulus K_1,
encounters, at $x = 0$, an interface, and that the corresponding
physical quantities for the region of positive x are ρ_2 and K_2.

We represent the incident wave train by $u = f(t-x/c_1)$ where the argument of the function has been chosen so that, at $x = 0$, it is independent of the medium. There will be a reflected wave in the first medium, which will be represented by $g(t+x/c_1)$, and, in the second medium, a transmitted wave which will be represented by $h(t-x/c_2)$. Hence, in the respective media, we have

$$u_1 = f(t-x/c_1)+g(t+x/c_1), \qquad (25\,\text{a})$$

$$u_2 = h(t-x/c_2). \qquad (25\,\text{b})$$

The conditions to be satisfied at the interface are the continuity, across it, of the displacement and the pressure. The first of these gives

$$f(t)+g(t) = h(t). \qquad (26)$$

The second requires that, at $x = 0$,

$$K_1\,\partial u_1/\partial x = K_2\,\partial u_2/\partial x,$$

or, on substituting and using the relation $K = \rho c^2$,

$$\rho_1 c_1[f'(t)-g'(t)] = \rho_2 c_2 h'(t). \qquad (27)$$

From these it follows, after integrating (27), that

$$h(t) = [2\rho_1 c_1/(\rho_2 c_2+\rho_1 c_1)]f(t), \qquad (28\,\text{a})$$

$$g(t) = [(\rho_2 c_2-\rho_1 c_1)/(\rho_2 c_2+\rho_1 c_1)]f(t). \qquad (28\,\text{b})$$

The transmission and reflection coefficients here, as in the previous chapter, involve the physical constants only through the ratio of the transmission impedances.

It is easy to verify that the rate at which energy leaves the interface is equal to its rate of arrival in the incident wave.

These results may be applied to show the difficulty in transmitting sound from one medium to another—say from air to water or to the walls of a room: if $\rho_2 c_2/\rho_1 c_1$ is small and, as is usually the case, c_2/c_1 is moderate, little *energy* is transmitted although the transmitted *amplitude* will be nearly twice that of the incident wave.

12.7. Sound waves in three dimensions

Let us now consider the propagation of sound in three dimensions. Denote by (u, v, w) the components of the particle displacement in the x-, y-, and z-directions. The equations of motion are then—as in (9)—

$$\rho\partial^2 u/\partial t^2 = -\partial(\delta p)/\partial x,$$
$$\rho\partial^2 v/\partial t^2 = -\partial(\delta p)/\partial y, \tag{29}$$
$$\rho\partial^2 w/\partial t^2 = -\partial(\delta p)/\partial z.$$

It is also convenient to introduce the dilatation, Δ, which is the proportional increase in volume. It follows from the definition that

$$1+\Delta = (1+\partial u/\partial x)(1+\partial v/\partial y)(1+\partial w/\partial z),$$

or, since the partial derivatives are all small quantities whose products are negligible,

$$\Delta = \partial u/\partial x+\partial v/\partial y+\partial w/\partial z. \tag{30}$$

Differentiating the equations of (29) with respect to x, y, and z, respectively, and adding, we derive

$$\rho\partial^2\Delta/\partial t^2 = -\nabla^2(\delta p), \tag{31}$$

where ∇^2 represents the Laplacian operator,

$$\partial^2/\partial x^2+\partial^2/\partial y^2+\partial^2/\partial z^2.$$

Moreover, from the definitions of s and Δ it follows that

$$(1+s)(1+\Delta) = 1,$$

or, since s and Δ are small,

$$s = -\Delta. \tag{32}$$

Finally, since $\delta p = Ks$, it follows that

$$\partial^2\Delta/\partial t^2 = (K/\rho)\nabla^2\Delta = c^2\nabla^2\Delta, \tag{33}$$

which is the equation governing the propagation of waves in three dimensions.

The discussion of certain aspects of fluid motion can be considerably simplified by the introduction of a 'velocity potential', whose partial derivatives are the (negative) components of the fluid velocity. If this velocity potential be denoted by ϕ, the equations defining ϕ are

$$\partial u/\partial t = -\partial\phi/\partial x, \quad \partial v/\partial t = -\partial\phi/\partial y, \quad \partial w/\partial t = -\partial\phi/\partial z. \tag{34}$$

From this definition and that of Δ it follows that

$$\partial\Delta/\partial t = -\nabla^2\phi. \tag{35}$$

The equation of motion in the x-direction can be written in the form

$$\rho\partial^2\phi/\partial x\partial t = \partial(\delta p)/\partial x,$$

along with similar equations in the other two directions, and integrating these with respect to the space coordinates yields

$$\rho\partial\phi/\partial t = \delta p. \tag{36 a}$$

Since $\delta p = -K\Delta$, it follows that

$$\partial\phi/\partial t = -c^2\Delta. \tag{36 b}$$

It also follows that ϕ satisfies the same wave equation as Δ, that is, that

$$\partial^2\phi/\partial t^2 = c^2\nabla^2\phi. \tag{37}$$

12.8. Spherical sound waves

We do not propose to embark on an examination of the general solution of (37), but shall confine ourselves to the case of spherical waves, where ϕ is a function of the radial distance

$$r = \sqrt{(x^2+y^2+z^2)}$$

and t only. It is known that, in such a case,

$$\nabla^2\phi = \partial^2\phi/\partial r^2+(2/r)\partial\phi/\partial r = (1/r)\partial^2(r\phi)/\partial r^2. \tag{38}$$

The equation for ϕ then becomes

$$\partial^2(r\phi)/\partial t^2 = c^2\partial^2(r\phi)/\partial r^2, \tag{39}$$

of which the general solution is

$$r\phi = f(t-r/c)+g(t+r/c). \tag{40}$$

The terms on the right-hand side represent diverging and converging waves respectively. In general, (40) makes ϕ infinite at $r = 0$, and then the origin must be excluded from the region over which the solution is applied.

Let us examine the diverging wave represented by

$$\phi = (1/r)f(t-r/c). \tag{41}$$

The particle velocity is

$$\dot{u} = -\partial\phi/\partial r = f'(t-r/c)/cr+f(t-r/c)/r^2. \tag{42}$$

Since the area of the surface of a sphere of radius r is $4\pi r^2$, the rate of increase of volume of fluid instantaneously within the sphere is $4\pi r^2\dot{u}$. Equation (42) shows that this tends, as r tends to zero, to the finite limit $4\pi f(t)$. We may regard this as a rate of creation or injection of fluid at a *source*, and so as a measure of the *strength* of the source. We may therefore say that the potential (41) is due to a source of strength $4\pi f(t)$ situated at the origin.

We also have

$$\delta p = \rho \partial\phi/\partial t = \rho f'(t-r/c)/r. \qquad (43)$$

It is seen that $\delta p/\dot{u}$ is no longer a constant—the transmission impedance now has a reactive component—but that, as r increases, the ratio does approach the value ρc appropriate to a plane wave. The additional term in the transmission impedance is due to the attenuation consequent upon the spreading of the waves. Further detail depends on the nature of the source, and is simple only for the sinusoidally varying source, to which we now devote our attention.

12.9. Sinusoidally varying source

Let the strength of the source be $S \sin \omega t$, where S is a constant, so that

$$\phi = (S/4\pi r)\sin \omega(t-r/c), \qquad (44)$$

$$\delta p = (\rho \omega S/4\pi r)\cos \omega(t-r/c), \qquad (45)$$

$$\dot{u} = (\omega S/4\pi c r)\cos \omega(t-r/c)+(S/4\pi r^2)\sin \omega(t-r/c). \qquad (46)$$

The activity over the surface of a sphere of radius r, concentric with the source, is

$$A = 4\pi r^2 . \delta p . \dot{u},$$
$$= (\rho \omega^2 S^2/4\pi c)\cos^2\omega(t-r/c)+$$
$$+(\rho \omega S^2/4\pi r)\cos \omega(t-r/c)\sin \omega(t-r/c).$$

The average value of the second term is zero, so that the average activity—the rate of power transmission across the sphere—is

$$\bar{A} = \rho \omega^2 S^2/8\pi c. \qquad (47)$$

This is independent of the radius of the sphere, as one would expect, and is the power of the source.

Some of the formulae relating to the sinusoidal source—especially that for the transmission impedance, but *not* those concerning energy or power—can be simply deduced by the use of an imaginary exponential instead of the explicit sine or cosine. For example, if we write

$$\phi = (S/4\pi r)e^{j\omega(t-r/c)}, \tag{48}$$

then $$\qquad\qquad \delta p = j\omega\rho(S/4\pi r)e^{j\omega(t-r/c)}, \tag{49}$$

and $$\qquad \dot{u} = (j\omega/c + 1/r)(S/4\pi r)e^{j\omega(t-r/c)}. \tag{50}$$

The transmission impedance is

$$\delta p/\dot{u} = \rho c/(1 - jc/\omega r). \tag{51}$$

We see that, as r tends to infinity, this tends to the value ρc appropriate to a plane wave.

12.10. Propagation along a tube of variable section

Instances such as the megaphone, the horn of a gramophone, and the musical instruments of the woodwind and brass families, indicate that interesting phenomena are associated with the propagation of sound in tubes of variable sections. The main features will emerge if we neglect the surface effects of viscosity, and also assume that the variation in sectional area is so slow that the waves may be regarded as plane, normal to the centre line of the tube.

Let x be measured in the direction of propagation, and let u be the particle displacement. If $A = A(x)$ is the cross-sectional area at a point x, the net rate of inflow into an elementary slice of thickness δx is $\partial(A\partial\phi/\partial x)/\partial x \,.\, \delta x$, and, since the volume of the slice is $A\delta x$, the rate of increase of the condensation is

$$\dot{s} = (1/A)\partial(A\partial\phi/\partial x)/\partial x. \tag{52}$$

Remembering that $\delta p = Ks = \rho\partial\phi/\partial t$, we obtain the differential equation for the velocity potential,

$$\begin{aligned}\partial^2\phi/\partial t^2 &= (c^2/A)\,.\,\partial(A\partial\phi/\partial x)/\partial x \\ &= c^2[\partial^2\phi/\partial x^2 + (1/A)\partial A/\partial x\,.\,\partial\phi/\partial x]. \end{aligned} \tag{53}$$

If we consider the conical tube—the simple megaphone—we have $A = kx^2$, where k is a constant, so that $(1/A)\,.\,\partial A/\partial x = 2/x$, and the equation is effectively the equation (39) for spherical waves which we have already studied.

The reason why a megaphone increases the power of the voice is that, in the first place, this is distributed through a smaller solid angle, but, even more, by restricting the freedom of the issuing air, it increases the impedance confronting the source, and hence the power output for given motions of the vocal organs.

12.11. The exponential horn

In the gramophone the conical horn of the early days has been superseded by a horn more like that of the brass musical instruments, namely, with a 'flare', that is, a sectional area which increases more rapidly as it becomes greater. An instance of such a horn, for which a simple mathematical treatment exists, is the 'exponential horn', in which

$$A = A_0 e^{mx}, \tag{54}$$

and

$$(1/A)\partial A/\partial x = m, \tag{55}$$

so that

$$\partial^2\phi/\partial t^2 = c^2(\partial^2\phi/\partial x^2 + m\partial\phi/\partial x). \tag{56}$$

A simple solution of this equation exists for sinusoidal waves. If we put $\phi = X(x)\sin\omega t$,

$$X'' + mX' + (\omega^2/c^2)X = 0. \tag{57}$$

The solution of this is

$$X = Be^{\mu_1 x} + Ce^{\mu_2 x}, \tag{58}$$

where

$$\mu_{1,2} = -m/2 \pm \sqrt{(m^2/4 - \omega^2/c^2)}. \tag{59}$$

If $m^2 > 4\omega^2/c^2$, both roots are negative and real, so that there is attenuation of the sound. For smaller values of m or larger values of ω, the surd becomes imaginary, so that the transmission is now attenuated by an amplitude factor $e^{-mx/2}$, which is due to the expansion of the tube. The speed of propagation is $c_\omega = c/\sqrt{(1 - m^2c^2/4\omega^2)}$. The exponential horn therefore acts as a high-pass filter, with cut-off pulsatance $mc/2$.

EXERCISES ON CHAPTER XII

1. Find the velocity of sound in air at N.T.P. (0° C, barometer 76 cm, density of mercury 13·6 gm/cm³, density of air 0·00129 gm/cm³, $\gamma = 1·40$), and at 20° C.

2. Find the velocity of compressional waves in water. ($K = 2·135 \times 10^{10}$ dynes/cm².)

3. If, in a plane sound wave in a gas, the amplitude is a, the pulsatance

ω, the density of the gas ρ, and the wave velocity c, determine the peak excess pressure and the rate of energy propagation per unit area. (U.L.)

4. Calculate the radiation resistance per sq. cm. for (a) air at N.T.P., (b) water, (c) steel.

5. Using the results of Ex. 4, calculate the percentage of the amplitude of a wave transmitted from air to (a) water, (b) steel.

6. If the rate of transmission of energy in a sound wave in air is one milliwatt per sq. cm., find the peak value of the excess pressure, and the maximum particle velocity and displacement, at 50, 250, and 1,000 cycles/sec.

7. A piston closing one end of a long tube of sectional area A makes simple harmonic oscillations of amplitude α and pulsatance ω. Find (a) the instantaneous, (b) the average, rate at which work is being done on the air in the tube (on one side of the piston only), and hence calculate the damping coefficient for the piston. If the piston has mass 2 gm/cm², find the decay factor for its free oscillations.

8. A sound wave travelling along a tube comes to a point where the section area changes from A to B. Find the fractions of its energy reflected and transmitted, and verify that there is no loss.

What result is indicated when B is very large? Can this result be accepted?

9. A uniform tube is closed at one end. At the other a piston moves with amplitude α and pulsatance ω. Show that the particle velocity at a distance x from the closed end may be represented by

$$j\omega\alpha e^{j\omega t}\sin(\omega x/c)/\sin(\omega l/c),$$

and the excess pressure at the piston by

$$-\omega\alpha\rho_0\, ce^{j\omega t}\cot(\omega l/c),$$

where ρ_0 is the average density of the air and c the velocity of sound.

Find also the acoustic (transmission) impedance at the piston. (U.L.)

10. A sound wave travelling along a tube of sectional area A is incident upon a piston of mass m filling the tube and controlled by a spring of stiffness s; the pulsatance of the wave is ω and the amplitude of the particle motion a. Show that the reflected wave has an amplitude equal to that of the incident wave, but that there is a phase lag of 2ϕ, where $\tan\phi = X/R$, $X = m\omega - s/\omega$, $R = A\rho c$. Show also that the vibration of the piston lags by ϕ behind that of the incident wave, and that its amplitude is $2Ra/\sqrt{(R^2 + X^2)}$.

11. A long uniform tube has at one point a branch of the same sectional area, of length l, closed at the other end. Examine the effect of the branch upon sound waves travelling along the tube. Show that there is no transmitted wave for a series of special frequencies, and give a physical explanation of the phenomenon. (This device is known as the Quincke filter.)

12. A uniform tube A divides into two branches B and C of equal section, which join further on at D, but are of different lengths. Prove

that a simple harmonic sound wave in A will be completely reflected at D if the difference between the lengths of B and C is an odd multiple of the half wavelength. (U.L.)

13. A plane sound wave travelling along a tube of constant cross-section A encounters a diaphragm of effective mass m and stiffness s. Show that the ratio of the amplitude of the transmitted to the incident wave is given by

$$\frac{2\rho cA\omega}{\sqrt{\{(m\omega^2-s)^2+4\rho^2c^2A^2\omega^2\}}}$$

and that the lag in phase is $\tan^{-1}(m\omega^2-s)/2\rho cA\omega$, where ω is the pulsatance, c the wave velocity, and ρ the density. (U.L.)

14. If the intensity of sound at a distance of 100 cm from a source is 10 micro-watts per sq. cm., what must be the strength and power of the source (a) at 50 cycles/sec, (b) at 1,000 cycles/sec?

15. If P is the peak excess pressure at a distance R from a point source of strength S and pulsatance ω, show that the peak velocity there is

$$P\sqrt{(c^2+\omega^2R^2)}/\rho c\omega R,$$

where ρ is the density of the gas, and c is the velocity of sound. (U.L.)

16. Calculate the peak excess pressure, and particle velocity, at a distance of a metre from a point source of sound of strength 20 c.c./sec, in air of density $0\cdot00128$ gm/c.c., in which the velocity of sound is 330 m/sec, the frequency being 1,000/sec. (U.L.)

17. Write down the formula for the velocity potential in sound waves due to a point source of strength S and pulsatance ω. Deduce formulae for the peak values of the excess pressure and the particle velocity, at a distance r from the source.

If the peak value of the excess pressure at a distance of 100 cm from a point source of sound of frequency 500 cycles/sec is 1 dyne/cm^2, find the peak particle velocity and the strength of the source. Take the density as $0\cdot0012$ gm/c.c., the mean pressure as 10^6 dynes/cm^2, and $\gamma=1\cdot4$. (U.L.)

18. If spherical waves converge to a focus and then diverge again, show that the formula for the velocity potential must be

$$\phi=(A/r)\sin\omega t\sin(\omega r/c),$$

and express this as the sum of converging and diverging waves.

19. A sphere surrounded by air makes small radial oscillations, the radial motion being $\alpha\sin\omega t$. Obtain expressions for (a) the velocity potential, at a distance r from the centre, (b) the excess pressure at the surface of the sphere, (c) the average rate at which the sphere is emitting energy as sound.

20. If in Ex. 19 the diameter of the sphere is 2 cm, and $\alpha=0\cdot01$ cm, find, at both 50 and 1,000 cycles/sec, the strength of the equivalent source, the maximum excess pressure at the surface, and the (average) rate of emission of energy.

XIII

SIMPLE FINITE CONTINUOUS SYSTEMS

13.1. Introduction

In Chapter XI we considered continuous systems, and constructed partial differential equations governing their motion. We saw that a form of general solution of the equation corresponded to the propagation of waves in the system, and examined the effect of a termination or a discontinuity of the medium in producing reflected waves. If we have to deal with a finite portion of a continuous system, terminated at both ends, a sequence of successive reflections will take place, and thus introduce a periodicity, depending upon the dimensions of the system, into the motion.

Clearly many of the systems which produce audible vibrations —sound—are of this type, such as the strings of a piano or a violin, the columns of air in organ pipes and wind instruments, the stretched skin of a drum, bells, and many others. We know that in these cases the phenomenon is not quite so simple as the above might suggest, for there is not merely one periodicity, but many—a 'fundamental' note and many 'harmonics'.

Another way of thinking of a continuous system is of a large number of particles connected together. Thus we may obtain an idea of how a continuous taut string might be expected to vibrate from what we know of the system consisting of a number of masses attached along its length to a light taut string. The number of degrees of freedom, and hence the number of normal modes, is equal to the number of masses. Proceeding to the limit in order to consider a continuous system, it is clear that we must expect an infinite number of degrees of freedom, each with its normal mode and normal pulsatance. Just as the normal pulsatances for a system with several degrees of freedom were determined from the (algebraic) pulsatance equation, we shall expect some corresponding equation for the normal pulsatances of continuous systems. But if it is to have an infinite number of roots, it cannot be just a polynomial. Finally, just as the shape or configuration of the system with several degrees of freedom vibrating in a normal mode was given by a set of amplitude ratios, the configuration of a continuous system must be given by the specification of the displacement at all points, and this can be done only by a continuous function of position, to be termed a 'normal function'.

The problem of the present chapter is thus to determine, for continuous systems, the pulsatances, and the functions specifying the configurations, corresponding to the normal modes.

13.2. Transverse vibrations of a taut string

One of the simplest continuous systems, both to visualize, and to examine mathematically, is a uniform taut string with its ends fixed, such as a piano or a violin string.

Let m be the mass per unit length, P the tension, and l the length. If y is the transverse displacement at time t at distance x from one end, then y is governed by equation (16) of Chapter XI, namely,

$$\partial^2 y/\partial x^2 = (1/c^2)\partial^2 y/\partial t^2, \tag{1}$$

where $c^2 = P/m$. We seek solutions of this equation representing normal modes. They must satisfy the end conditions

$$y = 0 \quad \text{when } x = 0 \text{ and when } x = l. \tag{2}$$

In a normal mode, all particles move with the same pulsatance, and in phase (or in direct opposition), but the amplitude varies from point to point. If Y is this amplitude, and ω is the pulsatance, we may write

$$y = Y \sin \omega t, \tag{3}$$

in which Y is *a function of x only*. Hence

$$\partial^2 y/\partial x^2 = (d^2 Y/dx^2)\sin \omega t, \tag{4}$$

$$\partial^2 y/\partial t^2 = -\omega^2 Y \sin \omega t. \tag{5}$$

Substituting these in equation (1), and dividing through by $\sin \omega t$ (the ability to cancel the time factor shows that (3) represents a possible vibration, with Y independent of t),

$$d^2 Y/dx^2 = -(\omega^2/c^2)Y. \tag{6}$$

The general solution of this is

$$Y = A\sin(\omega x/c) + B\cos(\omega x/c), \tag{7}$$

where A and B are constants. It remains to make this solution satisfy the end conditions. When $x = 0$, $y = 0$ (for all values of t) and hence $Y = 0$, so that we must have $B = 0$. In order that y (and hence Y) may also vanish when $x = l$, we must have

$$A\sin(\omega l/c) = 0. \tag{8}$$

It is clear that we must also have $A = 0$ (and so zero deflexion) *unless*

$$\sin(\omega l/c) = 0. \tag{9}$$

This is the pulsatance equation, giving the values of ω corresponding to normal modes. For $\sin(\omega l/c)$ to vanish, $\omega l/c$ must be zero or an integral (positive or negative) multiple of π. Zero gives no vibration, and negative values of ω do not give results essentially different from those obtained from the corresponding positive values, so that the normal pulsatances are given by

$$\omega l/c = n\pi, \tag{10}$$

where n is any positive integer. If we denote the nth pulsatance, in order of magnitude, by ω_n, we have

$$\omega_1 = \pi c/l, \quad \omega_n = n\pi c/l = n\omega_1, \tag{11}$$

so that the pulsatances are integral multiples of the lowest, or *fundamental*, pulsatance. The frequency of the fundamental is

$$f_1 = \omega_1/2\pi = c/2l, \tag{12}$$

which is clearly, by elementary ideas of wave velocity, the number of times a disturbance can travel to and fro along the string in unit time. The other frequencies, those of the *harmonics*, are integral multiples of f_1. The period T_1 of the fundamental is

$$T_1 = 1/f_1 = 2l/c, \tag{13}$$

and the period of the nth harmonic is

$$T_n = 2l/nc = T_1/n, \tag{14}$$

so that the periodic times form a *harmonic* series. It was, of course, the discovery—by experiment—that the notes which are used in the simple (and almost universal) musical scale have frequency ratios expressible by simple rational fractions (2:1 for the octave, 3:2 for the fifth, etc.), which led to the use of the adjective 'harmonic' in these connexions.

The configuration, or, as it is often briefly termed, the *mode*, corresponding to the fundamental is given by

$$Y_1 = A_1 \sin(\omega_1 x/c) = A_1 \sin(\pi x/l), \tag{15}$$

where A_1 is a constant. Remembering that Y represents the amplitude of the motion at the point x—simple harmonic motion in so far as our assumption of small motion and neglect of damping are legitimate—we see that the actual value of the amplitude is not determinate, but that the ratio of the amplitudes of any two points is definite, and that the *shape* of the deflected string at any moment is one arch of a sine wave. For this particular mode the greatest amplitude is at the mid-point of the string, where it is actually A_1. The function which gives the ratio of the displacement at the point x to that at some standard point, and which thus gives the shape of the deflected string (in any mode), is termed the *normal function* † corresponding to the mode. We write

$$\phi_1 = \sin(\pi x/l). \tag{16}$$

Similarly, for the nth harmonic, the deflexion is given by

$$\begin{aligned} Y_n &= A_n \sin(\omega_n x/c) \\ &= A_n \sin(n\pi x/l), \end{aligned} \tag{17}$$

so that the deflected shape is n arches of a sine wave, and there are $(n-1)$ points of zero displacement, or *nodes*, equally spaced along the string. The corresponding normal function is

$$\phi_n = \sin(n\pi x/l). \tag{18}$$

In Fig. 68 are plotted the graphs of the first few normal functions, and their negatives (dotted), which represent the extreme displacements in the corresponding normal vibration. These forms can be seen, on account of the persistence of vision, in actual strings, although it is not easy to excite pure higher harmonics without some device which enables them to be maintained (e.g. with a steel wire, electrically).

† Other names are *characteristic function*, and *eigenfunction*.

The complete formula for the displacement y at any point x at any time t, in the nth mode, is

$$y_n = A_n \sin(n\pi x/l)\sin(n\pi ct/l). \tag{19}$$

Using a result from elementary trigonometry, we can write this

$$y_n = \tfrac{1}{2}A_n\{\cos n\pi(x-ct)/l - \cos n\pi(x+ct)/l\}, \tag{20}$$

which shows that the *standing wave* represented by (19) can be

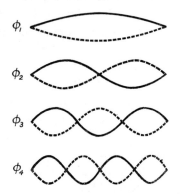

FIG. 68. Normal modes of a stretched string.

regarded as the resultant of two equal and opposite progressive waves travelling in opposite directions.

Finally, the complete motion of which the string is capable is the sum or resultant of the normal modes. Taking account of possible phase differences between the various modes, the general formula for the displacement is

$$y = \sum_{n=1}^{\infty} A_n \sin(n\pi x/l)\sin(n\pi ct/l + \epsilon_n). \tag{21}$$

The values of the coefficients depend upon the way in which the motion is caused, and their determination in particular cases will be considered later (see section 13.8).

13.3. Some other simple systems

There are analogues of the results of the last section in a number of other simple systems. For example, a length of shaft fixed at both ends can execute torsional vibrations in which the twist θ satisfies an equation formally identical with (1) and boundary conditions formally identical with (2). The same is true for the longitudinal vibrations of an elastic bar fixed at both ends, or of a column of air in a pipe closed at both ends. In the case of these systems, however, other end conditions are possible, notably that one or both ends may be 'free' (in the last case, open). The occurrence of different end conditions modifies the detail of the results, but not the method of obtaining them, or their general nature. We illustrate by means of the torsional vibrations of a shaft of length l fixed at one end and free at the other.

The differential equation governing the twist θ is

$$\partial^2\theta/\partial x^2 = (1/c^2)\partial^2\theta/\partial t^2, \tag{22}$$

where $c^2 = C/\rho$, as in equation (9) of Chapter XI. If the fixed end is taken to be $x = 0$, the end conditions are

$$\theta = 0 \quad \text{when } x = 0,$$
$$CJ\,\partial\theta/\partial x = 0 \quad \text{when } x = l. \tag{23}$$

Using Θ to denote the angular amplitude of the vibration at any point in a normal vibration of pulsatance ω, we write

$$\theta = \Theta \sin \omega t \tag{24}$$

and, substituting in (22), find

$$d^2\Theta/dx^2 = -(\omega^2/c^2)\Theta, \tag{25}$$

which has the general solution

$$\Theta = A \sin(\omega x/c) + B \cos(\omega x/c). \tag{26}$$

The first of the end conditions (23) shows that $\Theta = 0$ when $x = 0$, whence we conclude that $B = 0$. The second necessitates that $d\Theta/dx = 0$ when $x = l$, that is,

$$(\omega A/c)\cos(\omega l/c) = 0, \tag{27}$$

so that, if A is not to be zero, ω must this time satisfy the pulsatance equation

$$\cos(\omega l/c) = 0. \tag{28}$$

For this, $\omega l/c$ must be an odd multiple of $\frac{1}{2}\pi$, that is, if ω_n is the pulsatance of the nth mode,

$$\omega_n l/c = (2n-1)\pi/2, \tag{29}$$

or
$$\omega_n = (2n-1)\pi c/2l = (2n-1)\omega_1, \qquad (30)$$

with
$$\omega_1 = \pi c/2l, \qquad (31)$$

the pulsatance of the fundamental. The main difference between this and the preceding example is that here only odd harmonics occur.

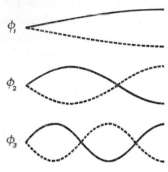

The nth normal function is

$$\phi_n = \sin(2n-1)\pi x/2l. \qquad (32)$$

The forms of the first few are given in Fig. 69. It is to be noted that the nth mode has again $(n-1)$ internal nodes.

The case of two free ends can exist in a length of shaft (freely supported in bearings), in a (supported) bar, and in a pipe open at both ends. The results are given in Ex. 3 below.

FIG. 69. Normal modes of a fixed-free shaft.

13.4. More complex systems

We now consider cases in which there is a combination of continuous and discrete masses. Typical examples are a taut string with a mass attached, when the mass of the string is not negligible compared with the added mass, and a pulley on a shaft, when the inertia of the shaft must be considered.

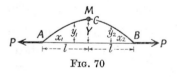

FIG. 70

Let us first consider the case of a mass M attached to the midpoint C of a string AB of length $2l$, fixed at its ends, and stretched by a tension P. If y_1 is the transverse displacement at a point in the segment AC, distant x_1 from A, then, with $c^2 = P/m$, the differential equation satisfied by y_1 is

$$\partial^2 y_1/\partial x_1^2 = (1/c^2)\partial^2 y_1/\partial t^2. \qquad (33)$$

We seek a normal mode, and we may write, if ω is the pulsatance of the mode,
$$y_1 = Y_1 \sin \omega t, \qquad (34)$$

so that
$$d^2 Y_1/dx_1^2 = -(\omega^2/c^2)Y_1. \qquad (35)$$

Hence $$Y_1 = A_1\sin(\omega x_1/c) + B_1\cos(\omega x_1/c). \qquad (36)$$

But when $x_1 = 0$, $y_1 = 0$, that is, $Y_1 = 0$, and hence $B_1 = 0$, so that

$$y_1 = A_1\sin(\omega x_1/c)\sin\omega t. \qquad (37)$$

For the segment BC, measuring x_2 from B, and denoting the transverse displacement by y_2, we obtain, similarly,

$$y_2 = A_2\sin(\omega x_2/c)\sin\omega t. \qquad (38)$$

It is now necessary to consider conditions at C, that is, the equation of motion of the mass M. Denote its displacement by Y; then we have

$$Y = \hat{Y}\sin\omega t.$$

The force acting on M is the resultant of the tension in the two strings attached to M, that is, a restoring force of magnitude

$$P(\partial y_1/\partial x_1)_{x_1=l} + P(\partial y_2/\partial x_2)_{x_2=l} \qquad (39)$$

$$= P(\omega/c)(A_1+A_2)\cos(\omega l/c)\sin\omega t. \qquad (40)$$

Hence,

$$-(P\omega/c)(A_1+A_2)\cos(\omega l/c)\sin\omega t = M\ddot{Y} = -\omega^2 M\hat{Y}\sin\omega t, \qquad (41)$$

so that $$P(A_1+A_2)\cos(\omega l/c) = \omega c M\hat{Y}. \qquad (42)$$

But we also have, since

$$(y_1)_{x_1=l} = \hat{Y} = (y_2)_{x_2=l}, \qquad (43)$$

$$A_1\sin(\omega l/c) = \hat{Y} = A_2\sin(\omega l/c),$$

or $$A_1 = \hat{Y}/\sin(\omega l/c) = A_2. \qquad (44)$$

Substituting these values and dividing by $\hat{Y}$, we find

$$2P\cot(\omega l/c) = \omega c M. \qquad (45)$$

We get, finally, a rather better form if we substitute for P its value mc^2, and derive

$$\cot(\omega l/c) = \tfrac{1}{2}\omega M/mc. \qquad (46)$$

(We note the occurrence of the quantity mc—the transmission impedance; ωM is a quantity of the same dimensions, and is evidently the mechanical impedance of M at pulsatance ω; the factor $\tfrac{1}{2}$ is due to a sharing of the action among the two segments of the string.)

The equation we have derived is, again, the pulsatance equation, and its roots give the set of normal pulsatances. The structure of the equation is less simple than that of the equations which appeared in the two preceding paragraphs, in the sense that we cannot immediately write down its roots 'by inspection', but this circumstance should not be allowed to obscure the fact that in all fundamental essentials it is exactly analogous.

To solve the above pulsatance equation, we need numerical values of m, M, l, and c, and must then find the roots by trial and error. In this process one will need to use tables of cotangents, and the angle $\alpha = \omega l/c$, so that a formula in terms of α will be more convenient. Substituting $\omega = c\alpha/l$, we have

$$\cot \alpha = M\alpha/2ml = \kappa\alpha, \tag{47}$$

where $\kappa = M/2ml$ is the ratio of the mass M to the total mass of the string.

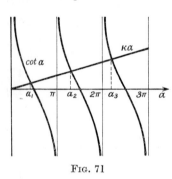

FIG. 71

The roots of the equation are conveniently located (roughly) by means of a graph, in which $\cot \alpha$ and $\kappa\alpha$ are drawn (only positive values of ω, and so α, are needed), and intersections give the required roots. We see that there is one root between 0 and $\frac{1}{2}\pi$, another between π and $\frac{3}{2}\pi$, and so on, in an infinite sequence; and the large roots are seen to approach integral multiples of π. If α_n is one of the roots, the corresponding pulsatance ω_n is given by

$$\omega_n = \alpha_n c/l = \sqrt{(P/m)} \cdot \alpha_n/l. \tag{48}$$

This sequence is *not* harmonic—the higher roots are *not* exact integral multiples of a fundamental—for any (finite) value of κ.

We give in the table below some values of α_n for small n and various values of κ.

If κ is either very small or very large, it is possible to approximate formally to the roots.

(i) If κ is large, that is, M is large compared with the mass of the string, we see that there is a small root. But when α is small

$$\cot \alpha \sim 1/\alpha, \tag{49}$$

so that $\qquad\qquad 1/\alpha \sim M\alpha/2ml,$

or $\qquad\qquad\qquad \alpha^2 \sim 2ml/M,$

and $\qquad\qquad \omega^2 = c^2\alpha^2/l^2 \sim 2mc^2/Ml = 2P/Ml, \qquad (50)$

which agrees with the elementary result obtained (cf. Ch. I, Ex. 1) by neglecting entirely the inertia of the string. A second

TABLE. *Roots of* $\cot\alpha = \kappa\alpha$

κ \ n	1	2	3	4
0·1	1·429	4·306	7·228	10·200
0·2	1·314	4·034	6·910	9·893
0·5	1·077	3·644	6·578	9·630
1	0·860	3·426	6·437	9·529
2	0·653	3·292	6·362	9·477
5	0·433	3·204	6·315	9·446
10	0·311	3·173	6·299	9·435

approximation may be obtained by using another term of the series for $\cot\alpha$,

$$\cot\alpha \sim 1/\alpha - \alpha/3, \qquad (51)$$

so that $\qquad\qquad 1/\alpha - \alpha/3 \sim M\alpha/2ml,$

$$\alpha^2 \sim 2ml/(M+2ml/3),$$

$$\omega^2 \sim 2P/(M+2ml/3)l, \qquad (52)$$

which shows that the effective mass of the string is one-third of its actual mass, and agrees with the result derived from the energy method and the assumption that the two segments of the string remain straight. (See Ch. II, Ex. 1.) Larger roots involve practically no motion of M, and consequently the inertia of the string is no longer negligible.

(ii) κ is small, that is, a small mass attached to the string. In this case,

$$\alpha \sim \pi/2,$$

$$\omega \sim \pi c/2l, \qquad (53)$$

which is the result when M is entirely neglected. A second approximation is

$$\alpha = \pi/2 - \eta, \qquad (54)$$

where η is small. With this, $\cot\alpha = \tan\eta$, or, as η is small,

$$\eta \sim (M/2ml)(\pi/2-\eta),$$

so that

$$\eta \sim M\pi/2(2ml+M),$$

$$\alpha \sim \tfrac{1}{2}\pi\{1-M/(2ml+M)\} = \pi ml/(2ml+M),$$

and

$$\omega \sim \sqrt{(Pm)\pi/(2ml+M)}. \tag{55}$$

Another simple—and in some ways technically more important —example is the case of a pulley on a shaft, when the inertia of the shaft is taken into account.

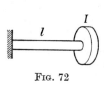

FIG. 72

Let the shaft have length l, polar second moment of section J, density ρ, shear modulus C, and let the pulley have moment of inertia I. Then, if θ is the angular displacement of the shaft at a point distant x from the fixed end, and $C/\rho = c^2$,

$$\partial^2\theta/\partial x^2 = (1/c^2)\partial^2\theta/\partial t^2. \tag{56}$$

Now, for a normal mode, we put

$$\theta = \Theta \sin \omega t, \tag{57}$$

where Θ depends upon x only. Then

$$\frac{d^2\Theta}{dx^2} = -(\omega^2/c^2)\Theta, \tag{58}$$

and

$$\Theta = A \sin(\omega x/c) + B \cos(\omega x/c).$$

But $\theta = 0$ when $x = 0$, so $B = 0$. Consequently

$$\theta = A \sin(\omega x/c)\sin \omega t. \tag{59}$$

The torque acting on the pulley is then

$$-CJ(\partial\theta/\partial x)_{x=l} = -(CJ\omega/c)A \cos(\omega l/c)\sin \omega t.$$

Also the displacement Θ_1 of the pulley is

$$\Theta_1 = A \sin(\omega l/c)\sin \omega t, \tag{60}$$

so that

$$I\ddot\Theta_1 = -I\omega^2 A \sin(\omega l/c)\sin \omega t.$$

Thus the equation of motion for the pulley becomes

$$-I\omega^2 A \sin(\omega l/c)\sin \omega t = -(CJ\omega/c)A \cos(\omega l/c)\sin \omega t,$$

whence

$$\cot(\omega l/c) = \omega cI/CJ = \omega I/\rho Jc. \tag{61}$$

This equation becomes formally identical with that in the preceding example, on putting

$$\alpha = \omega l/c, \tag{62}$$

$$\kappa = I/\rho l J, \tag{63}$$

and κ is here the ratio of the moment of inertia of the pulley to that of the shaft treated as (what it is *not*!) a rigid body.

So far, in this section, we have concentrated upon the determination of the normal pulsatances, since this is the most important practical aspect of this type of problem. But in these cases, too, there are normal functions which give the configurations in the modes, and they depend upon the roots of the pulsatance equation. For the case of the pulley at the end of a shaft, let α_n be the nth positive root of the pulsatance equation

$$\cot \alpha = \kappa\alpha \, ;$$

then, by (59) and (62), we see that the corresponding normal function is

$$\phi_n = \sin(\alpha_n x/l). \tag{64}$$

The first few are shown in Fig. 73. Comparing them with those for the shaft alone, Fig. 69, the difference is that the last quarter-wave is here incomplete, becoming a very small fraction for the higher modes. The number of internal nodes agrees, however, with that for the shaft alone.

Fig. 73. Normal modes of a shaft with pulley attached.

13.5. Initial conditions

The preceding sections of this chapter have shown how solutions can be obtained to problems where only the pulsatances of the free vibrations, and possibly the corresponding displacement configurations, are required. In some cases, however, we need to trace the motion subsequent to its initiation by some disturbance, such as, say, the plucking of a violin string, or the blow of the hammer on a pianoforte wire. The general idea which leads to the solution of such problems is quite simple. The differential equations are linear and homogeneous, so that the sum of a set of solutions is also a solution. In other words, any solution is obtained by the superposition of the normal modes, in suitable proportions.

To formulate this in mathematical language, let $\phi_n(x)$ be the normal function associated with the pulsatance ω_n. Then the most general vibration which the system can execute is given by

$$y = \sum (A_n \cos \omega_n t + B_n \sin \omega_n t)\phi_n(x). \tag{65}$$

By putting $t = 0$ in y and $\partial y/\partial t$ derived from (65), we see that the A_n are associated with initial displacement, and the B_n with initial velocity, and, in fact, the initial displacement, $y_0(x)$, is given by

$$y_0(x) = \sum A_n \phi_n(x), \tag{66}$$

and the initial velocity $\dot{y}_0(x)$ is given by

$$\dot{y}_0(x) = \sum \omega_n B_n \phi_n(x). \tag{67}$$

To determine the coefficients in (66) or (67) necessitates the expansion of a known function of x as a series of multiples of the normal functions. In the special case of the taut string, these normal functions are the sines of multiples of $(\pi x/l)$, so that the expansion is obtained as a Fourier series. The property, whereby the coefficients can be determined one by one, is, in fact, a special case of the more general rule applying to all expansions in terms of normal functions of this type. Before giving the solution of the two particular problems posed above, it seems desirable to demonstrate the general rule for determining the coefficients in such expansions, and, first of all, the important property of the normal functions upon which the method rests.

13.6. Orthogonality of the normal functions

The property of the set of cosines and sines on which the ability to determine the coefficients of a Fourier series one by one rests, is that the integral of the product of any two members of the set over a period (and, in some cases, over a half or quarter period) vanishes identically. The same property holds for the normal functions of any uniform finite continuous system, the range of integration being that corresponding to the system. For a system extending from $x = 0$ to $x = l$, this means that

$$\int_0^l \phi_m(x)\phi_n(x)\,dx = 0. \qquad (68)$$

This applies to all the systems so far dealt with, namely systems with normal functions satisfying the equation

$$d^2\phi/dx^2 + (\omega/c)^2\phi = 0$$

and various conditions at the ends $x = 0$ and $x = l$. A more general result holding for non-uniform systems, such as would be typified by a bar of variable cross-section executing torsional or longitudinal oscillations, is equally easy to obtain; this we now do. The differential equation will assume the form

$$d[p(x)\,d\phi/dx]/dx + \lambda q(x)\phi = 0, \qquad (69)$$

where $p(x)$ represents a variable distributed stiffness, $q(x)$ represents a variable distributed inertia, and λ is some multiple of ω^2. The end conditions will be taken in their most general form,

$$a_0\phi + b_0\,d\phi/dx = 0 \quad \text{at } x = 0,$$
$$a_1\phi + b_1\,d\phi/dx = 0 \quad \text{at } x = l. \qquad (70)$$

Let ϕ_m and ϕ_n be the solutions of (69) satisfying the conditions (70) for the values λ_m and λ_n respectively of λ. Then

$$d(p\,d\phi_m/dx)/dx + \lambda_m q\phi_m = 0, \qquad (71\,\text{a})$$
$$d(p\,d\phi_n/dx)/dx + \lambda_n q\phi_n = 0. \qquad (71\,\text{b})$$

Multiply (71 a) by ϕ_n and (71 b) by ϕ_m, subtract, and integrate over the range $(0, l)$. This yields

$$\int_0^l \{\phi_n\,d(p\,d\phi_m/dx)/dx - \phi_m\,d(p\,d\phi_n/dx)/dx\}\,dx +$$
$$+ (\lambda_m - \lambda_n)\int_0^l q\phi_m\phi_n\,dx = 0. \qquad (72)$$

The first integral can be completely integrated by parts (the integral after this process vanishing identically), yielding

$$[p(\phi_n\,d\phi_m/dx - \phi_m\,d\phi_n/dx)]_0^l.$$

N

Applying the boundary conditions to this, it is found to vanish, so that

$$(\lambda_m - \lambda_n) \int_0^l q\phi_m\phi_n \, dx = 0,$$

or, if $\lambda_m \neq \lambda_n$,

$$\int_0^l q\phi_m\phi_n \, dx = 0. \tag{73}$$

Pairs of functions satisfying this condition are said to be *orthogonal*, with respect to the weighting factor q in the range 0 to l. Since by (69) $q\phi_m$ is proportional to the distributed restoring force in the mth mode, (73) implies the vanishing of the work done by this force acting through the displacement in the nth mode—the important physical aspect of orthogonality.

In the special case of constant q, (73) reduces to the form (68).

13.7. Expansion in series of normal functions

We now return to the problem of (66) and (67), the expansion of a given function in a series of multiples of the normal functions. The orthogonal property of these normal functions, expressed by (73), enables the coefficients to be determined one by one, for if we multiply $f(x)$ by, say, $q(x)\phi_m(x)$ and integrate over the range, all the terms except that containing $\phi_m(x)$ will vanish.

Thus, if

$$f(x) = A_1\phi_1(x) + A_2\phi_2(x) + \dots, \tag{74}$$

multiplying by $q(x)\phi_m(x)$ and integrating from 0 to l yields

$$\int_0^l q(x)\phi_m(x)f(x) \, dx = A_m \int_0^l q(x)\phi_m^2(x) \, dx, \tag{75}$$

so that A_m is determined as the ratio of the two integrals.

The actual normal functions are not determined completely by the differential equation and the boundary conditions—they are indeterminate to the extent of a multiplicative constant. The use of (75) is greatly simplified if the normal functions are scaled—'normalized'—so that

$$\int_0^l q(x)\phi_m^2(x) \, dx = 1,$$

and this is often—but by no means always—done.

A simple example of (75) is given by the Fourier sine series, where the (un-normalized) normal functions are

$$\phi_m(x) = \sin(m\pi x/l). \tag{76}$$

With these functions, and, of course, $q(x) = 1$,

$$\int_0^l \phi_m^2(x)\, dx = l/2.$$

It follows that

$$A_m = (2/l) \int_0^l f(x)\sin(m\pi x/l)\, dx. \tag{77}$$

We now apply these results to two examples connected with the taut string.

13.8. Examples

Our first example will be that of a plucked, taut string. If the central point is drawn aside by a distance Y, and l is the length of the string, the initial form is given by

$$y_0(x) = \begin{cases} 2Yx/l & (0 < x < l/2), \\ 2Y(l-x)/l & (l/2 < x < l). \end{cases} \tag{78}$$

In the present case, $\phi_m(x) = \sin(m\pi x/l)$, so that

$$\int_0^l y_0(x)\sin(m\pi x/l)\, dx = A_m \int_0^l \sin^2(m\pi x/l)\, dx = A_m l/2. \tag{79}$$

To evaluate the first integral, we must divide the range into two parts, according to (78). The symmetry properties of the given deflexion and the normal functions about the mid-point show that in this case the even harmonics give no contribution, and that the contribution from any odd harmonic can be obtained by doubling the integral from 0 to $\frac{1}{2}l$. This gives, for an odd value of m, say $2r+1$,

$$2 \int_0^{l/2} (2Yx/l)\sin[(2r+1)\pi x/l]\, dx = (-)^r 4lY/(2r+1)^2\pi^2,$$

so that

$$A_{2r+1} = (-)^r 8Y/(2r+1)^2\pi^2. \tag{80}$$

Finally, the subsequent displacement of the string is given by

$$y = (8/\pi^2)Y \sum \sin[(2r+1)\pi x/l]/(2r+1)^2 . \cos[(2r+1)\pi ct/l].$$

(81)

The amplitudes of the harmonics vary inversely as $(2r+1)^2$, that is, in the ratios $1:1/9:1/25:....$ Since the energies are in the ratio of the squares of the amplitudes, we see that the fundamental dominates very markedly. This will be compared with the result of the next example.

For the next example we shall give a somewhat idealized account of the effect of the initiation of a vibration of a string by the impact of a hammer—for simplicity, at the mid-point.

The hammer strikes the string, and the impact causes a small portion of the string, say between $x = \frac{1}{2}l-\delta$ and $x = \frac{1}{2}l+\delta$, to start moving with velocity v. We shall consider the limiting case where δ tends to zero, for, although we could work out the less idealized case, the effect of the finite length of contact is insignificant. What *is* significant is the impulse, J, imparted to the string by the hammer blow. If, as usual, m denotes the mass per unit length of the string, we shall have

$$J = 2m\delta.v.$$

(82)

The rest of the work depends on the use of (67). Therein, $\dot{y}_0$ is to be zero, except between $\frac{1}{2}l-\delta$ and $\frac{1}{2}l+\delta$. Again—in our special case—symmetry shows that only the odd harmonics survive. On multiplying (67) by the normal function

$$\sin[(2r+1)\pi x/l]$$

and integrating from 0 to l, the right-hand side gives

$$(2r+1)\pi c/l . B_{2r+1}.\tfrac{1}{2}l = (2r+1)\pi c B_{2r+1}/2.$$

To evaluate the other side we note that $\dot{y}_0$ exists only in the short range δ on either side of the mid-point. The value of the integral is therefore 2δ times the average value of $\phi_{2r+1}(x)$ in that interval multiplied by v. Since δ is to tend to zero, we may use, as the *ultimate* average, the value of $\phi_{2r+1}(x)$ at the mid-point itself, namely $\sin(2r+1)\pi/2 = (-1)^r$. Hence

$$(2r+1)\pi c B_{2r+1}/2 = (-)^r 2v\delta = (-)^r J/m,$$

so that $\qquad\qquad B_{2r+1} = (-)^r 2J/(2r+1)\pi mc.$

(83)

The formula for the subsequent deflexion is easily written down.

In this case we note that the amplitudes of the harmonics are in the ratios $1:1/3:1/5:...$, and the energies in the ratio $1:1/9:1/25:...$, so that the fundamental does not predominate so much as when the string is plucked.

It is interesting to note here the occurrence in the denominator of the combination mc, which we have met before, as the transmission impedance of the string.

13.9. Maintained vibrations

We conclude the chapter by a short account of maintained vibrations of finite continuous systems. What we have so far learned should give us a fair idea, qualitatively, of what is to be expected when one of these systems is maintained in vibration by some applied periodic force. This may be applied to one or more points in the system, or distributed over some portion or the whole of its length. In the absence of friction we shall expect infinities in the frequency response curve at the frequencies corresponding to the normal modes.

Let us consider a uniform shaft, of length l, clamped at $x = 0$, and maintained in torsional vibration by a periodic torque $Q \sin \beta t$ applied at the free end. Let C, J, ρ, c have their usual meanings, and assume that the twist is given by $X(x)\sin \beta t$. Inserting this in the partial differential equation of wave motion, we have

$$d^2X/dx^2 + (\beta/c)^2 X = 0, \tag{84}$$

of which the general solution is

$$X = A \cos(\beta x/c) + B \sin(\beta x/c). \tag{85}$$

Since X must vanish at $x = 0$, we must have $A = 0$. At the other end, the torque $CJ \, \partial\theta/\partial x$ must be equal to the applied torque, so that

$$CJ(\beta/c)B \cos(\beta l/c) = Q,$$

that is,

$$B = (Qc/CJ\beta)\sec(\beta l/c). \tag{86}$$

The twist can be written down. It is clear, on recalling the pulsatance equation for the fixed-free shaft, namely $\cos(\omega l/c) = 0$, that the vibration becomes mathematically infinite whenever β coincides with one of the normal modes of free vibration. In practice, of course, friction (not included in our equations) will limit the vibration. It may also be noted that, using the fact that $C = \rho c^2$, the combination $\rho c J$ occurs in the denominator. Indeed, an understanding of the idea of transmission impedance will enable the occurrence of the expression $Q/\beta \rho c J$ to be predicted.

EXERCISES ON CHAPTER XIII

1. A steel pianoforte wire, 40 cm long and 1 mm thick, is stretched by a tension of 70 kg wt, and the density of the steel is $7 \cdot 8$ gm/cm³. Find the frequency of the fundamental.

2. What value of the tension in Ex. 1 would make the frequency 465?

3. Find the normal pulsatances of a uniform cylindrical bar in longitudinal vibration, (a) clamped at both ends, (b) clamped at one end and free at the other, (c) free at both ends. Repeat for the torsional vibrations of a shaft, and the acoustical vibrations of a pipe, under analogous end conditions.

4. A mass of $0 \cdot 15$ lb is attached to the mid-point of a wire of length 30 in. and mass $0 \cdot 01$ lb/in., fixed at the ends and stretched by a tension of 50 lb wt. Find the lowest frequency of transverse vibration.

5. A string is composed of portions of length l_1 and l_2 and of mass m_1 and m_2 per unit length respectively. It is fixed at the ends and stretched by a tension P. Show that the pulsatances of the normal modes of transverse vibration are given by $c_1 \tan(\omega l_1/c_1) + c_2 \tan(\omega l_2/c_2) = 0$, where $c_1^2 = P/m_1$ and $c_2^2 = P/m_2$.

6. A flywheel of moment of inertia I is fixed to the centre of a shaft of length l clamped at the ends. Show that the frequency f of torsional oscillations is given by $\theta = \pi f l \sqrt{(\rho/C)}$, if θ is a root of the equation $\cot \theta = I\theta/i$, where i is the moment of inertia of the shaft, taken as rigid.

7. A bar of length l, sectional area A, density ρ, and Young's modulus E, has one end clamped and a mass M attached at the other. Find the equation from which the frequencies of longitudinal oscillations can be determined.

8. A shaft of length l has flywheels of moments of inertia I_1 and I_2 at its ends. Show that the free torsional oscillations have frequencies given by $\cot \phi = (I_1 I_2 \phi^2 - i^2)/(I_1 + I_2)i\phi$, where i is the moment of inertia of the shaft, if rigid, and $\phi = 2\pi f l \sqrt{(\rho/C)}$.

9. A tube containing air has one end rigidly closed, and the other end is stopped by a plug of mass M which can move without friction in the

tube. If the length of the tube filled with air is l, show that the pulsatance, ω, of free vibrations is given by

$$\frac{\omega l}{c}\tan\frac{\omega l}{c}=\frac{M'}{M},$$

where c is the velocity of sound in the enclosed air, and M' is the total mass of this air. (U.L.)

10. Show that the pulsatances ω of the free radial vibrations of air contained in a rigid spherical vessel of radius a are given by the roots of the equation $\tan(\omega a/c) = \omega a/c$, where c is the velocity of sound.

11. Using the result of Ex. 10, and solving the equation (by trial), obtain the frequency of the slowest mode of vibration of the air contained in a sphere of radius 10 cm.

12. Two rods, AB, BC, each of length l, and of cross-section S and S' respectively, are joined at B so that ABC is straight. If A is fixed and C is free, show that the pulsatances of the normal modes of longitudinal vibration are given by

$$\tan\frac{\omega l}{c}\tan\frac{\omega l}{c'}=\frac{Sc\rho}{S'c'\rho'},$$

where c and c' are the wave velocities, and ρ and ρ' the densities of the materials, respectively. (U.L.)

13. A string of length l and mass m per unit length, stretched by a tension P, is acted on by a transverse force $F\sin\beta t$ at a point dividing it into segments of lengths a and b. Find expressions for the forced vibration in each segment.

14. A tube of length l is closed at one end and subject to a pressure $p_0\sin\beta t$ at the other. Show that the particle displacement at a distance x from the closed end is

$$(p_0/\rho c\beta)\sin(\beta x/c)\sec(\beta l/c)\sin\beta t,$$

where ρ is the density of the air and c the speed of sound.

15. If in Ex. 13 there is also damping, of coefficient $r = 2\alpha m$ (cf. Ch. XI, Ex. 5), and $a = b$, show that the mid-point vibration amplitude is

$$\frac{F}{2mc}\sqrt{\left\{\frac{\cosh(\mu l/c)-\cos(\lambda l/c)}{(\lambda^2+\mu^2)\{\cosh(\mu l/c)+\cos(\lambda l/c)\}}\right\}},$$

where λ^2, $\mu^2 = \beta[\sqrt{(\beta^2+4\alpha^2)}\pm\beta]/2$. Show also that if α tends to 0, this reduces to the value obtained in Ex. 13 for this case.

16. One end of a portion of a uniform cylindrical shaft, of length l, is constrained to execute an angular oscillation $\theta = \alpha\sin\beta t$, while the other end is free. Show that the angular amplitude of the free end is $\alpha\sec(\beta l/c)$, where c is the velocity of torsional waves, and that the torque necessary to maintain the vibration is

$$\rho cJ\beta\alpha\sin\beta t\tan(\beta l/c),$$

where J is the polar second moment of the section, and ρ the density of the material of the shaft. (U.L.)

17. Verify that, if ϕ_m and ϕ_n are two different normal functions for the torsional vibrations of a shaft clamped at one end and free at the other, they satisfy the orthogonality condition

$$\int_0^l \phi_m \phi_n \, dx = 0.$$

18. If the free end of the shaft in Ex. 17 is twisted through an angle θ_0 and the shaft is let go, find the amplitudes of the harmonics in the resulting vibration.

XIV

VIBRATIONS OF BEAMS AND WHIRLING OF SHAFTS

14.1. Introduction

In the vibrations of a tuning-fork, or of a bridge, the stiffness is due to the 'elasticity' of the material of which the fork or the girders is made. The laws of the vibrations of such bodies are of scientific and technical importance, and will be found also to have a close connexion with the phenomenon known as the whirling of shafts, where, at some critical speeds, a straight shaft shows a tendency to rotate in a bent form, a tendency which leads to dangerous situations and is to be avoided. It is with such matters that this chapter is concerned. We must commence with a résumé of the statical theory of the bending of thin elastic beams or rods, in the form used by physicists and engineers.

14.2. Elements of beam theory

We consider the bending of a long, thin, elastic beam or rod due to transverse loads, and, in the first place, restrict ourselves to the case where all the loads are in one plane. This elementary theory is associated with the names of Euler and Bernoulli. We also confine ourselves to the case where the centre-line of the unstressed beam is straight.

If we consider a section of the beam normal to the centre line, then there act across this section a 'bi-force' and a 'bi-moment', termed respectively the shearing force and the bending moment. We use the terms bi-force and bi-moment because, if the two portions into which the section separates the beam are separately regarded, then equal and opposite forces and moments act on the two portions across the section. For these stress resultants some sign convention is necessary, and there is no universally accepted agreement on this. The one we shall adopt is that which is most convenient in dealing with the bending of horizontal beams under gravity loads. Measuring x from left to right, and the deflexion y *down*wards, regarding *down*ward loads as positive, and taking the cantilever clamped (*encastré*) at the left-hand end and loaded at the other end as the 'all-positive' case, that is, that for which the deflexion, load, shearing force (S), and bending moment (M) are all regarded as positive, the governing equations (as demonstrated in texts on elasticity, or strength of materials, or theory of structures) are

$$dM/dx = -S, \qquad (1)$$

$$dS/dx = -w, \qquad (2)$$

where w is the intensity of the distributed load per unit length.

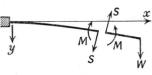

FIG. 74

The convention is exhibited in Fig. 74. It is also shown in the books just referred to that the effect of the bending moment is to produce a proportional curvature. For small deflexions the curvature is d^2y/dx^2,

and, if E is Young's modulus of elasticity for the material, and I the second moment of the area of the section about the 'neutral axis', then

$$M = EI\,d^2y/dx^2. \qquad (3)$$

From (1) and (2) it follows that

$$w = d^2M/dx^2, \qquad (4)$$

and, combining (3) and (4),

$$w = EI\,d^4y/dx^4. \qquad (5)$$

Occasionally it is necessary to express the shearing force in terms of the deflexion, and the result is seen to be

$$S = -EI\,d^3y/dx^3. \qquad (6)$$

A concentrated load at any point of the beam introduces a jump discontinuity into the shearing force, and hence into the corresponding derivative of the bending moment, the slope, and the deflexion.

We shall be dealing only with finite lengths of bar, beam, or shaft, so there will be conditions to be satisfied at the ends. In the commoner cases an end may be:

(a) clamped (fixed, *encastré*), the displacement y and the slope dy/dx both vanishing there;

(b) simply supported (or pinned), the displacement y and the bending moment M both vanishing there;

(c) free, the bending moment M and the shearing force S both vanishing there.

(The other three conceivable combinations of the four possible vanishing quantities seldom come into question.)

14.3. Transversely vibrating bars

The fundamental equation of motion for a stiff elastic bar is readily derived from the considerations of the last section by an application of d'Alembert's principle, that the system would be in statical equilibrium under the action of the loads and the reversed mass-accelerations. Suppose that the mass per unit length of the bar is m. Then, in any transverse vibration, this corresponds to a distributed mass-acceleration of intensity $m\partial^2 y/\partial t^2$. The required equation of motion is therefore

$$EI\partial^4 y/\partial x^4 = -m\partial^2 y/\partial t^2. \qquad (7)$$

If we consider a normal mode of vibration, with pulsatance ω, we may, as usual, write $\partial^2 y/\partial t^2 = -\omega^2 y$, so that the differential equation for the configuration of the mode at any time is

$$EId^4 y/dx^4 = m\omega^2 y. \qquad (8)$$

The elasto-dynamic properties of the bar are thus characterized by the single parameter m/EI, and the vibrations by the parameter $m\omega^2/EI$. The latter we shall denote by α^4, so that the equation for the configuration becomes

$$d^4 y/dx^4 = \alpha^4 y. \qquad (9)$$

It is clear that m and I, and consequently α, may vary along the bar. Such variation makes no fundamental difference in principle, but it leads to the necessity for mathematical functions whose properties have not always been fully studied, and whose values are not yet tabulated. We shall therefore restrict ourselves almost entirely to bars of uniform cross-section, for which α is a constant. The strategy of this chapter follows the same pattern as that of the last. The general solution of (9) will contain four constants, and the two conditions at each end of the beam will lead to the elimination of three of these, and to a transcendental equation from which the permissible values of α, and hence of the pulsatances, are to be determined. Corresponding to each value of α so determined, the constants of integration have a definite set of ratios, which determine the configuration of the corresponding normal mode.

14.4. The pinned-pinned bar

As a first example let us consider a uniform bar of length b pinned at both ends, or, what is equivalent, a uniform girder simply supported at its ends.

We first need the general solution of (9). Using D to denote the differential operator d/dx, the auxiliary equation is $D^4 = \alpha^4$, of which the solutions are $D = \pm\alpha$ and $D = \pm j\alpha$. Corresponding to the first pair of values of D we could use $e^{\alpha x}$ and $e^{-\alpha x}$, but it is more convenient to use the hyperbolic functions $\cosh \alpha x$ and $\sinh \alpha x$—which in any case would introduce themselves. Similarly, for the second pair of solutions it is most convenient to use the trigonometric functions rather than the imaginary exponentials. We therefore write the general solution of (9) in the form

$$A \cosh \alpha x + B \sinh \alpha x + C \cos \alpha x + D \sin \alpha x \qquad (10)$$

(where D is now an arbitrary constant, and not the differential operator).

The end conditions to be satisfied are the vanishing of y and of $M = EI d^2y/dx^2$ at $x = 0$ and at $x = b$. Since $y = 0$ at $x = 0$,

$$A + C = 0. \qquad (11)$$

Since $d^2y/dx^2 = 0$ at $x = 0$,

$$\alpha^2 A - \alpha^2 C = 0. \qquad (12)$$

From (11) and (12) it follows that both A and C must vanish.

Taking account of this, the vanishing of y at $x = b$ leads to the equation
$$B \sinh \alpha b + D \sin \alpha b = 0. \tag{13}$$
The vanishing of d^2y/dx^2 at $x = b$ yields
$$\alpha^2 B \sinh \alpha b - \alpha^2 D \sin \alpha b = 0. \tag{14}$$
From (13) and (14) it follows that $B \sinh \alpha b$ and $D \sin \alpha b$ must both vanish. Since $\sinh \alpha b$ does not vanish for any non-zero real value of its argument, it follows that B must vanish. If then D were also to vanish, there would be no vibration. It follows that the condition to be satisfied by the normal modes is
$$\sin \alpha b = 0. \tag{15}$$
The solutions of this are known to be
$$\alpha b = n\pi, \tag{16}$$
where, for our present purpose, n can be any positive integer. The configuration in the nth mode is thus given by
$$y = D \sin(n\pi x/b), \tag{17}$$
and the corresponding pulsatance, determined by
$$\alpha^4 b^4 = m\omega^2 b^4/EI = n^4\pi^4,$$
is given by
$$\omega_n{}^2 = n^4\pi^4 EI/mb^4. \tag{18}$$
The pulsatances, or frequencies, do not form a complete harmonic sequence, although they are all integral multiples of the fundamental frequency.

The configurations all have constrained nodes at the ends of the bar, and the nth mode has also $(n-1)$ internal nodes, equally spaced along its length.

The normal configurations have the same form as those of a stretched uniform string (see Fig. 68), but the frequency spectrum is very different and much more sparse. This is reflected in the difference in quality between the note of a string and of a bar caused to vibrate transversely.

14.5. The clamped-free bar

As the next example we consider the clamped-free bar, of which the prong of a tuning-fork is an instance. We revert to (10) and apply the appropriate end conditions. Let $x = 0$ be the clamped end, and again let the length be b. At $x = 0$, $y = 0$, so that

$$A + C = 0, \quad \text{or} \quad C = -A. \tag{19}$$

At $x = 0$, $dy/dx = 0$, so that

$$\alpha B + \alpha D = 0, \quad \text{or} \quad D = -B. \tag{20}$$

At $x = b$, $M = 0$, or $d^2y/dx^2 = 0$, whence, using (19) and (20),

$$\alpha^2 A(\cosh \alpha b + \cos \alpha b) + \alpha^2 B(\sinh \alpha b + \sin \alpha b) = 0. \tag{21}$$

Finally, at $x = b$, $S = 0$, or $d^3y/dx^3 = 0$, whence

$$\alpha^3 A(\sinh \alpha b - \sin \alpha b) + \alpha^3 B(\cosh \alpha b + \cos \alpha b) = 0. \tag{22}$$

Eliminating the ratio of A to B yields, after a little reduction,

$$\cosh \alpha b \cos \alpha b + 1 = 0. \tag{23}$$

This is the equation giving the normal pulsatances. A plot of $\cos \theta$ against $-1/\cosh \theta$ shows that there is an infinity of roots, and that the large positive ones are alternately greater and less than odd multiples of $\frac{1}{2}\pi$, and approximate more closely to these as θ increases. Their numerical values must be found by some method of successive approximation, and the early values are 1·875, 4·694, 7·855, 10·995,.... .

If we denote these values of αb by $\theta_1, \theta_2, ...$, the pulsatances are given by

$$\omega_n^2 = \theta_n^4 EI/mb^4. \tag{24}$$

There is now no harmonic relation between the fundamental and the overtones.

Having determined the value of α for a mode, we can find the ratio of B to A, and thence the configuration associated with the mode. It is again found that the nth mode has $(n-1)$ internal nodes.

Results for some of the other combinations of end conditions are given in the exercises at the end of the chapter.

14.6. The effect of an added mass

It is clear from general principles that the addition of a concentrated mass at the free end of the bar of the last section will, by increasing the inertia without affecting the elastic stiffness, slow down any mode of vibration in which the added mass does in fact move—in this special case, all modes.

Let M be the added mass (the context will make the risk of confusion with bending moment unlikely). Then the first three end conditions of the preceding section still hold, but the shearing force no longer vanishes when $x = b$—it has to be of the right magnitude to produce the acceleration of M. Careful consideration of the sign convention shows that we must have

$$S = -M\,\partial^2 y/\partial t^2 = M\omega^2 y$$

at the end, that is,

$$EId^3y/dx^3 = -M\omega^2 y, \qquad (25)$$

or, using the value of y and the results of (19) and (20),

$$\alpha^3[A(\sinh \alpha b - \sin \alpha b) + B(\cosh \alpha b + \cos \alpha b)]$$
$$= -(M\omega^2/EI)[A(\cosh \alpha b - \cos \alpha b) + B(\sinh \alpha b - \sin \alpha b)]. \qquad (26)$$

Using the ratio of A to B given by (21), and remembering that $\omega^2/EI = \alpha^4/m$, we find, after a little reduction,

$$\cosh \alpha b \cos \alpha b + 1 = (M\alpha/m)(\cosh \alpha b \sin \alpha b - \sinh \alpha b \cos \alpha b), \qquad (27)$$

or, if we put $\alpha b = \theta$,

$$\cosh \theta \cos \theta + 1 = (M\theta/mb)(\cosh \theta \sin \theta - \sinh \theta \cos \theta). \qquad (28)$$

The roots of this equation must be found by some numerical process, for any given value of M/mb, and from any root the corresponding value of ω is derived, and also, if desired, the configuration of the corresponding mode. If M is zero, we have the case of the preceding section, and if M tends to infinity, the results tend to those for a clamped-pinned bar.

14.7. Whirling of shafts

It has been found that shafts, initially straight, carrying a torque between bearings, with or without pulleys or other similar loads, will, at certain speeds of rotation, 'whirl', that is, rotate in a bent configuration about the initially straight axis. This is highly undesirable, and it is important to be able to design a shaft with its attachments so that the speeds at which this phenomenon of whirling occurs should be sufficiently removed from those at which the machine is designed to run.

If y is the deflexion of the centre-line of the shaft from its equilibrium straight position, at any point x, then the equivalent elastic restoring force must be equal to that necessary to produce the centripetal acceleration. Considering an element of the shaft, this leads to the fundamental equation for whirling,

$$EI d^4 y/dx^4 = m\omega^2 y, \tag{29}$$

where E, I, and m have their previous significance and ω is the angular velocity of rotation of the shaft. This has exactly the same form as (8), so that there is a close connexion between the pulsatances of transverse vibration and the whirling speeds. Indeed, whirling may be regarded as a resonance phenomenon, with the shaft free to vibrate in two dimensions, and its circular whirl can be thought of as the resultant of two perpendicular vibrations. The conditions at a free end are the same as those for a vibrating shaft. It is customary to class bearings in which the shaft runs as 'short' or 'long', the former imposing practically no restrictions on the angular deflexion of the shaft, and being analogous to simple supports, and the latter preventing angular deflexion, and being analogous to clamps at the ends of beams.

It follows that to every problem on the vibration of a bar there is a corresponding one on the whirling of a shaft. In particular, the analysis of section 14.4 shows that the lowest whirling speed of a shaft between short bearings is given by

$$\omega^2 = \pi^2 EI/mb^4, \tag{30}$$

and that the deflexion is proportional to $\sin(\pi x/b)$.

14.8. Orthogonality of solutions

It may be worth while to show again from the equations that the solutions corresponding to different modes are 'orthogonal', or (cf. p. 178) what is dynamically equivalent and more significant, that the forces corresponding to one mode do no work in the displacement corresponding to another mode.

Let u and v denote the displacements in two modes, and let the values of α corresponding to the modes be denoted by α and

β respectively. Then the forces are proportional to d^4u/dx^4 and d^4v/dx^4 respectively. We therefore need to show that

$$\int_0^b v(d^4u/dx^4)\,dx = 0, \qquad \int_0^b u(d^4v/dx^4)\,dx = 0. \qquad (31)$$

To prove this, consider the difference

$$\int_0^b (v\,d^4u/dx^4 - u\,d^4v/dx^4)\,dx \qquad (32)$$

of the two integrals. Integrating by parts twice in succession yields

$$[v\,d^3u/dx^3 - u\,d^3v/dx^3]_0^b - [dv/dx\,.\,d^2u/dx^2 - du/dx\,.\,d^2v/dx^2]_0^b +$$
$$+ \int_0^b (d^2v/dx^2\,.\,d^2u/dx^2 - d^2u/dx^2\,.\,d^2v/dx^2)\,dx.$$

The integral vanishes identically. The integrated parts will be found to vanish at each limit for every set of boundary conditions which can exist for a vibrating bar or whirling shaft, as the student should confirm by carrying out the detail of the substitution. Hence the integral (32) vanishes—for any two different functions u and v satisfying the same boundary conditions.

But, since u and v both satisfy the differential equation, the integral is equal to

$$\int_0^b (\alpha^4 - \beta^4)uv\,dx.$$

Hence, if α and β differ, it follows that

$$\int_0^b uv\,dx = 0. \qquad (33)$$

This expresses the orthogonality of the solutions, and, on applying the differential equation again, leads to (31), which we set out to demonstrate.

EXERCISES ON CHAPTER XIV

1. A steel bar 15 in. long, 0·5 in. wide, and 0·1 in. thick is supported at the ends. Taking $E = 3 \times 10^7$ lb wt/in.² and the density as 0·28 lb/in.³, find the frequencies of the two slowest modes of transverse vibration.

2. Calculate the frequencies of the two slowest modes of transverse vibration of a steel strip 1 in. wide and $\frac{1}{8}$ in. thick, clamped at one end, when the free length is 1 ft.

3. Obtain the equations giving the pulsatances of the free lateral vibrations of a uniform bar in the cases (a) clamped-clamped, (b) clamped-supported.

4. Find, correct to four figures, the roots of the equations in Ex. 3 (a), (b), corresponding to the fundamental and the first overtone.

5. If a bar of length b is pinned at one end and has a concentrated mass M at the other, show that the pulsatance ω of a normal mode of transverse vibration is given by a root of the equation

$$\frac{2M}{mb} = \frac{\coth \alpha b - \cot \alpha b}{\alpha b},$$

where $\alpha^4 = m\omega^2/EI$. (U.L.)

6. For a uniform bar of length b, flexural rigidity EI, and mass m per unit length, clamped at one end and having a mass M attached at the other, show, using section 14.6, eqn. (28), that when mb/M is small, the slowest mode is given approximately by $\omega^2 = 3EI/Mb^3$—which is the result of the simple theory neglecting the inertia of the bar. Show also that the second approximation is $\omega^2 = 3EI/b^3(M + 33mb/140)$. (Cf. p. 25, eqn. (58).)

7. A uniform bar (m, b, EI), clamped at one end, has the other constrained to execute a vibration of amplitude A and pulsatance β. Show that the amplitude of the maintained vibration, at distance x from the clamped end, is

$$A\frac{(\sinh \alpha b + \sin \alpha b)(\cosh \alpha x - \cos \alpha x) - (\cosh \alpha b + \cos \alpha b)(\sinh \alpha x - \sin \alpha x)}{2(\cosh \alpha b \sin \alpha b - \cos \alpha b \sinh \alpha b)},$$

where $\alpha^4 = m\beta^2/EI$.

8. A uniform girder (m, b, EI) is clamped at one end and pivoted at the other end where it carries a load of moment of inertia H about the pivot. Show that the pulsatances of the modes of free lateral vibration are given by the equation

$$\frac{mb^3}{H} = \frac{\theta^3(1 - \cosh \theta \cos \theta)}{\cosh \theta \sin \theta - \sinh \theta \cos \theta},$$

where $\theta^4 = m\omega^2 b^4/EI$.

Show also that when mb^3/H is small, a first approximate solution for the slowest mode is given by $\omega^2 = 4EI/bH$, and a second approximation by $\omega^2 = 4EI/b(H + mb^3/105)$. Verify these values by simple theory.

XV

APPROXIMATE METHODS FOR CONTINUOUS SYSTEMS

15.1. Introduction

THE exact analysis of the preceding chapter has shown that the determination of the normal frequencies and modes of vibration of continuous systems leads to transcendental equations which, even in the simpler cases of uniform systems, are laborious to solve. In the case of more complex systems, even the functions in terms of which the partial differential equation of motion can be solved may not have been studied and tabulated. For such problems, then, some form of approximate method is almost essential, if numerical results are desired.

In earlier chapters, and especially in Chapter IX, we have seen how Rayleigh's principle, based on the energies, can yield surprisingly accurate approximations to the normal pulsatances if reasonable approximations to the modes are used. We have seen also that there exist methods of successive approximation which allow systematic improvement of the modes, with consequent improvement in the pulsatances. The present chapter will, therefore, contain very little new in principle, and deals with the limiting form, for a system with an infinite number of degrees of freedom, of the results obtained in Chapter IX for systems with a finite number of degrees of freedom. The most obvious feature will be the replacement of the sums of that chapter by integrals.

15.2. The vibrating taut string

We commence with the classical example of the uniform taut string, of length l and of mass m per unit length, fixed at its ends and stretched by a tension P.

If y denotes the transverse displacement of the vibrating

string at distance x from one end, the energies T and V will be given by

$$2T = \int_0^l m\omega^2 y^2\, dx, \tag{1}$$

$$2V = \int_0^l P(dy/dx)^2\, dx. \tag{2}$$

Equating these, for a suitable approximate formula for y, will give an approximation to the lowest pulsatance, corresponding to the fundamental normal mode.

As a guide to the construction of a suitable approximation to the displacement formula we have only the end conditions, namely that y must be zero when $x = 0$ and $x = l$, along with the qualitative requirement that, in the fundamental mode, there is no internal node. The simplest polynomial which satisfies these conditions is

$$y = kx(l-x). \tag{3}$$

With this approximation, we derive

$$2T = m\omega^2 \int_0^l k^2 x^2 (l-x)^2\, dx = m\omega^2 k^2 l^5/30,$$

$$2V = P \int_0^l k^2 (l-2x)^2\, dx = Pk^2 l^3/3.$$

Equating these we find the approximation

$$\omega^2 = 10P/ml^2.$$

(We note that, as could have been anticipated, the scaling factor k in (3) has disappeared, and could have been omitted from the start.)

We already know that in the exact result the numerical coefficient is $\pi^2 = 9 \cdot 86960\ldots$, so that our first approximation is only about $1 \cdot 3$ per cent too great. For some purposes, however, such an accuracy is inadequate, and we proceed to show how closer approximations may be systematically sought and obtained. The essence of the process is a routine of successive approximation to the true displacement formula. It is also desirable to present an alternative formulation of the principle.

15.3. Successive approximation

As a basis for the improvement of the approximation to the deflexion formula, we need the differential equation, and, since the final quantity we seek is only the numerical coefficient in the formula for the pulsatance, it is convenient to make this differential equation non-dimensional. In the present case, if we use l as the unit of length, and write

$$\lambda = ml^2\omega^2/P, \tag{4}$$

the differential equation becomes

$$d^2y/dx^2 + \lambda y = 0. \tag{5}$$

Recognizing that, in the genesis of the equation, the second derivative stems from the restoring forces, and the other term from the reversed mass-accelerations which would be in equilibrium with these restoring forces, and invoking the principle already used in the process of successive approximation in Chapter IX, as well as noting that the factor λ is, for the process of improving the displacement formula, not essential, we expect that, if y_1 is a first approximation, a better approximation will be obtained by choosing y_2 such that

$$d^2y_2/dx^2 = -y_1 \tag{6}$$

and determining the constants of integration so as to satisfy the end conditions.

In the case we have considered, discarding the non-essential factor k, this gives

$$d^2y_2/dx^2 = -x(1-x) = -x+x^2.$$

The integral of this is

$$y_2 = Ax+B-x^3/6+x^4/12.$$

Determining the constants of integration, A and B, so as to make y_2 vanish when $x = 0$ and $x = 1$, we find that $A = 1/12$, $B = 0$, so that

$$y_2 = (x-2x^3+x^4)/12$$
$$= [x(1-x)+x^2(1-x)^2]/12. \tag{7}$$

To exploit fully this improved approximation, and further ones which can be obtained by repeating this process, an alternative formulation of Rayleigh's principle is convenient. This we now undertake.

15.4. An extension of Rayleigh's principle

If we multiply the differential equation (5) by y and integrate over the range, we obtain

$$\lambda \int_0^1 y^2 \, dx = - \int_0^1 y(d^2y/dx^2) \, dx \qquad (8\,\text{a})$$

$$= [-y \, dy/dx]_0^1 + \int_0^1 (dy/dx)^2 \, dx, \qquad (8\,\text{b})$$

and the integrated part vanishes on account of the end conditions. In its final form this repeats the result given by Rayleigh's principle. But for our present purpose it is better to use the intermediate form (8a), which gives

$$\lambda = - \int y(d^2y/dx^2) \, dx \bigg/ \int y^2 \, dx. \qquad (9)$$

This is an accurate result for the accurate displacement formula, but it gives, for an approximate displacement formula, the Rayleigh approximation. Putting y_2 for y, and therefore $-y_1$ for d^2y/dx^2, and denoting (for a reason which will become clear later) the resulting quotient by λ_{22}, we have

$$\lambda_{22} = \int y_1 y_2 \, dx \bigg/ \int y_2^2 \, dx. \qquad (10)$$

Similarly, multiplying the differential equation by d^2y/dx^2 and integrating, we derive the result

$$\lambda = - \int (d^2y/dx^2)^2 \, dx \bigg/ \int y(d^2y/dx^2) \, dx, \qquad (11)$$

which is accurate, and also the approximation λ_{12} given by

$$\lambda_{12} = \int y_1^2 \, dx \bigg/ \int y_1 y_2 \, dx. \qquad (12)$$

It is thus possible to obtain, from two successive members of the sequence of approximations, two different approximations to λ. Of these, since y_2 is a closer approximation to the true deflexion than y_1, we should expect λ_{22} to be closer than λ_{12}, and, as all these approximations lie between the greatest and least of the true values (cf. p. 108), they are all too great, so that $\lambda_{12} > \lambda_{22}$.

A third approximation, y_3, can be obtained from y_2 in the same way as y_2 was obtained from y_1. Thence two further approximations to λ, λ_{23} and λ_{33}, in descending order of magnitude, and of increasing accuracy, can be derived.

We now apply these results to our special example of the taut string. To simplify the arithmetic, we take

$$y_1 = 12x(1-x),$$

$$y_2 = x(1-x)+x^2(1-x)^2.$$

From these it readily follows that

$$\int y_1^2\, dx = 24/5, \quad \int y_1 y_2\, dx = 17/35, \quad \int y_2^2 dx = 31/630,$$

$$\lambda_{12} = 168/17 = 9{\cdot}8823..., \qquad \lambda_{22} = 306/31 = 9{\cdot}87097...,$$

the last of which is in error by only $1{\cdot}4$ parts in $10{,}000$.

The techniques developed in the earlier chapter (Chapter IX) enable us to derive, from any three consecutive members of the sequence of approximations to λ, both a considerably more accurate approximation, and also an approximation to the ratio of the first to the next normal pulsatance. (In our particular instance, however, since we start with a symmetrical mode, and the process continues to yield symmetrical formulae, the latter will be an approximation to the pulsatance of the next *symmetrical* mode, in this case the third.)

15.5. The general case

The foregoing was made particularly simple because of the constancy of the tension and the uniformity of the mass distribution. Varying tension is not easy to imagine—although, in the case of a stretched circular membrane (see section 15.6) the varying radius has the effect of multiplying the tension by a variable—but the case of variable mass distribution is by no means uncommon. If we suppose both to vary, so that $P = P_0 p(x)$ and $m = m_0 q(x)$, and the equation is made non-dimensional, it assumes the form (cf. Chapter XIII, equation (69))

$$(d/dx)[p(x)\,dy/dx]+\lambda q(x)y = 0. \tag{13}$$

The non-dimensional 'ghosts' of the energies are given by

$$2T = \int_0^1 q(x)y^2\,dx, \tag{14}$$

$$2V = \int_0^1 p(x)(dy/dx)^2\,dx. \tag{15}$$

Multiply equation (13) through by y and integrate over the range $(0, 1)$. This yields

$$\int_0^1 y(d/dx)\{p(x)\,dy/dx\}\,dx + \lambda \int_0^1 q(x)y^2\,dx = 0.$$

Integrating the first term by parts, and noting that the integrated part vanishes at both ends, it follows that

$$-2V + 2\lambda T = 0,$$

or $$\lambda = V/T, \tag{16}$$

so that Rayleigh's principle is recovered.

The formula for successive approximation will be

$$(d/dx)(p\,dy_{s+1}/dx) = -qy_s. \tag{17}$$

Multiplying (13) by the approximation y_s, and integrating over the range, gives

$$\int_0^1 y_s(d/dx)(p\,dy/dx)\,.dx + \lambda \int_0^1 qy_s y\,dx = 0. \tag{18}$$

Substituting y_s for y here, and using (17) (with s replaced by $s-1$), gives

$$\lambda_{ss} = \int_0^1 qy_{s-1}y_s\,dx \Big/ \int_0^1 qy_s^2\,dx. \tag{19}$$

Similarly, substituting y_{s+1} for y in (18), and using (17), gives

$$\lambda_{s,s+1} = \int_0^1 qy_s^2\,dx \Big/ \int_0^1 qy_s y_{s+1}\,dx. \tag{20}$$

Since y_{s+1} is presumably a better approximation than y_s, (20) may be expected to be a better approximation than (19). Similarly, $\lambda_{s+1,s+1}$ may be expected to be better than $\lambda_{s,s+1}$.

It should be noted that whereas the above method of derivation of (19) is identical with that of (10), for the simple differential equation (5), the method of derivation of (20) differs from and supersedes that of (12) for the same equation, which could not be carried through for the more general differential equation (13).

From the systematic sequence of approximations described above, the methods outlined in Chapter IX for discrete systems can be applied to enhance the accuracy of λ and to provide estimates of the higher normal pulsatances.

15.6. The taut circular membrane

As a simple example of the foregoing let us consider the uniform membrane of mass m per unit area, stretched by a uniform tension P and attached at its edge to a rigid circular ring of radius a. In the fundamental mode the displacement will be symmetrical about the centre. If y is the transverse displacement at radius r from the centre, the resultant force acting on a ring of radius r and width δr is $\delta(2\pi r P \, dy/dr)$, and the mass of the ring is $2\pi m r \, \delta r$. The equation of motion is, therefore,

$$2\pi m r \, \delta r \, \ddot{y} = \delta(2\pi r P \, dy/dr),$$

and, after putting, for a normal mode, $\ddot{y} = -\omega^2 y$, and cancelling the factor 2π, the equation of motion yields

$$d(P r \, dy/dr)/dr + m\omega^2 r y = 0. \tag{21}$$

The boundary conditions are, firstly that the deflexion vanishes at the edge, and secondly that there can be no conical point at the centre, that is, that dy/dr vanishes there. The simplest formula which satisfies these two conditions is

$$y = k(a^2 - r^2), \tag{22}$$

where k is a constant. For this displacement the energies are given by

$$2T = 2\pi m\omega^2 \int_0^a k^2(a^2 - r^2)^2 r \, dr = \pi m\omega^2 k^2 a^6/3,$$

$$2V = 2\pi P \int_0^a 4k^2 r^3 \, dr = 2\pi P k^2 a^4,$$

and equating these gives

$$\omega^2 = 6P/ma^2. \tag{23}$$

The exact solution of this case is known, in terms of the first zero of the Bessel function $J_0(x)$, whose value is 2·4048..., compared with the value from (23), namely $\sqrt{6} = 2\cdot4495...$, the error being somewhat less than 2 per cent.

To improve this by successive approximation, we shall find non-dimensional expressions simpler to use, so we choose the radius as the unit of length. Putting $y_1 = k(1-r^2)$, the equation for the second approximation, y_2, is

$$(d/dr)(r\,dy_2/dr) = -ry_1 = k(-r+r^3).$$

Hence $\qquad r\,dy_2/dr = A+k(-r^2/2+r^4/4).$

The condition at the centre shows that A must be zero. Integrating again yields

$$y_2 = B+k(-r^2/4+r^4/16).$$

The condition that y_2 vanishes when $r = 1$ now gives $B = (3/16)k$. Finally, to clear of fractions, we take $k = 16$, so that

$$y_1 = 16(1-r^2), \qquad y_2 = 3-4r^2+r^4.$$

From these, in addition to the approximation $\lambda = 6$ already obtained, we obtain two more approximations to λ, by putting $s = 1$ in (20), and $s = 2$ in (19), with x replaced by r and $q(r) = r$.

The integrals concerned are

$$\int_0^1 ry_1^2\,dr = 128/3,$$

$$\int_0^1 ry_1y_2\,dr = 22/3,$$

$$\int_0^1 ry_2^2\,dr = 19/15.$$

From these values we find the approximations

$$\lambda_{12} = 64/11 = 5\cdot8182... = (2\cdot4121...)^2,$$

$$\lambda_{22} = 110/19 = 5\cdot7895... = (2\cdot4061...)^2.$$

The true value of λ is $(2\cdot4048...)^2$, so that the percentage errors in the frequency are 0·3 and 0·05.

15.7. Beams and shafts

The fundamental differential equation governing both the vibration of beams and the whirling of shafts is, as was seen in the previous chapter,

$$(d^2/dx^2)(EI\,d^2y/dx^2) = m\omega^2 y, \qquad (24)$$

where allowance has been made for variation in the flexural rigidity, EI, as well as in the mass per unit length, m.

As before, we multiply by y and integrate over the relevant range. From the first term we get, on integrating by parts twice,

$$\int y(d^2/dx^2)(EI\,d^2y/dx^2)\,dx$$
$$= [y(d/dx)(EI\,d^2y/dx^2) - dy/dx\,.\,EId^2y/dx^2] +$$
$$+ \int EI(d^2y/dx^2)^2\,dx.$$

The integrated terms vanish as a result of the end conditions, for free, supported, or clamped ends. We therefore derive the special form of Rayleigh's principle appropriate to beams and shafts, namely

$$\int EI(d^2y/dx^2)^2\,dx = \int m\omega^2 y^2\,dx. \qquad (25)$$

It is worth noting that in the second integral, $m\,dx$ represents the mass of an element of the shaft, so that if a concentrated mass M is attached to a point of the shaft, its contribution to the right-hand side will be $MY^2\omega^2$, where Y is the amplitude at the point of attachment.

15.8. The clamped-free bar

The example chosen to illustrate this is the uniform bar, of mass m per unit length, flexural rigidity EI, and length b.

The end conditions are that y and dy/dx vanish at $x = 0$, and d^2y/dx^2 and d^3y/dx^3 vanish at $x = b$. The simplest polynomial satisfying these conditions is

$$y_1 = k(6b^2x^2 - 4bx^3 + x^4). \qquad (26)$$

From this we calculate the two energies in (25), finding

$$2V = 144EIk^2b^5/5,$$
$$2T = 104m\omega^2b^9/45,$$

so that, equating these, we find

$$\omega^2 = 162EI/13mb^4.$$

The numerical value of the coefficient is $12 \cdot 462 \ldots = (1 \cdot 879 \ldots)^4$. This compares with the exact value $(1 \cdot 875 \ldots)^4$ already found as the solution of the equation

$$\cosh \theta \cos \theta + 1 = 0.$$

Methods of successive approximation can be applied to this case, but it is hoped that enough has already been said, and enough examples given, to enable the reader to carry out such a process, and also to apply the method to non-uniform bars. The connexion between the transverse vibrations of bars and the whirling of shafts has also been made clear, and the same methods are therefore available for calculating approximations to whirling speeds.

EXERCISES ON CHAPTER XV

1. Using the four conditions (two at each end) to be satisfied by the displacement formula for the transverse vibrations of a clamped-clamped bar, deduce the simplest algebraic displacement formula, and use it to find an approximation to the pulsatance of the fundamental.

2. A stretched string (m, l, P) has a mass M attached to its mid-point. Obtain approximations to the pulsatance of the fundamental (a) when M is small, using $y = c \sin(\pi x/l)$, (b) when M is large, assuming the two portions of the string to be straight. Which is better when $M = ml$?

3. A uniform rod of length $2l$ and mass m per unit length is freely supported at each end, and carries at its mid-point a concentrated mass M. Find an approximate displacement formula for transverse vibrations, satisfying the conditions that the deflexion and bending moment vanish at both ends, and use this formula to obtain an approximation to the frequency of the fundamental. (U.L.)

4. Two equal particles of small mass M are attached to the points of trisection of a uniform string of length $3a$ and mass m per unit length, fixed at its ends and stretched by a tension P. Find, by the energy method, the pulsatance of the fundamental mode of transverse vibration due to the particles, using as approximate displacement formula that which is accurate in the absence of the particles. (U.L.)

5. A string of length l fixed at its ends and stretched by a tension P has mass per unit length which varies according to the formula $m(1-x^2/l^2)$, x being the distance from the centre. Construct an approximate deflexion

formula which makes the deflexion at the ends and the slope at the centre vanish, and use it to obtain an approximation to the pulsatance of the gravest mode of transverse vibration. (U.L.)

6. A string of length $2l$ is slightly thicker in the middle than at the ends, the mass per unit length m being given by $m = m_0\{9 + \cos(\pi x/2l)\}/10$, x being measured from the mid-point. Find, assuming $y = c\cos(\pi x/2l)$, an approximation to the fundamental frequency.

7. Using the deflexion formula (26) of section 15.8, obtain an approximation to the fundamental frequency of transverse vibration of a strip of uniform thickness t and length l, tapering uniformly in width from a at the clamped end to zero at the other, the density of the material being ρ.

8. A conical bar of length l is fixed at its base and performs torsional vibrations. If ls denotes distance measured from the vertex, show that $\theta = k(1-s^2)$ is an approximate deflexion formula satisfying the end conditions, and use this formula to show that if ω is the pulsatance of the fundamental, then $l^2\omega^2 < 22.5c^2$, where c is the velocity of torsional waves. (U.L.)

XVI

NON-LINEAR SYSTEMS

16.1. Introduction

IN the preceding chapters we have been dealing, except on very rare occasions, with systems which are called 'linear'. This adjective, as applied here, is a case of 'transferred epithet', for it refers rather to the graphs which represent the relation between restoring force and displacement, and, to a lesser extent, to that representing the relation between resistance and velocity, which are *straight* lines. Systems where these relationships are more complex, where the differential equation of motion contains terms which involve squares or products of displacement or velocity, or, indeed, any terms in which x or any of its derivatives occur to a degree not simply the first, or involve products, are termed 'non-linear'. In general the mathematical treatment is more difficult, and this is so, mainly, because the principle of superposition no longer holds—the sum of two or more separate solutions is no longer a solution. Each problem must therefore be treated as a whole. There is no longer any P.I. to be added to a C.F.—and the latter does not exist.

There are, however, so many types of non-linearity that it is not possible to give general methods at attempting to solve the equations for non-linear systems, nor is it possible to make general statements about the form or nature of the vibrations of such systems.

In recent years much attention has been given to non-linear systems of all sorts, and certain general methods of attack have been developed. It will be possible for us, within the compass of this book, to deal only with some of the simpler instances and methods, and we disclaim any pretence of giving more than a short treatment of a few particular cases by relatively simple and unsophisticated methods. It is hoped, however, that some of the important facts will emerge, and that some of the more fruitful methods will be exemplified.

16.2. The simple pendulum

We commence with what is probably the oldest vibrating system to be studied scientifically. Galileo is credited with having observed the isochronism of the pendulum by observing the swings of a chandelier in Pisa cathedral—timing them against his pulse. The way in which the pendulum speeded up so that it took no longer over long swings than it did over short ones seemed to Galileo mysterious and miraculous, and was not explained until the laws of motion had been more fully formulated and their consequences more thoroughly explored. Nor, strictly speaking, is Galileo's finding, in its crude form, strictly accurate. The speeding-up over the longer swings *does* occur—but not enough to compensate *completely* for the greater distance to be covered. But that is just what the precise mathematical formulation of the problem shows.

If m is the mass of the bob, l the length of the string (the mass of which is neglected), and θ the angular deflexion from the vertical at time t, and if the resistance of the air is neglected, the equation of motion is

$$mld^2\theta/dt^2 = -mg\sin\theta. \tag{1}$$

If we use the abbreviation $\omega^2 = g/l$, we may write this in the simple form

$$d^2\theta/dt^2 = -\omega^2\sin\theta. \tag{2}$$

If we make the approximation appropriate to small angles, this reverts to the simple linear equation $d^2\theta/dt^2 = -\omega^2\theta$ already studied in much detail in the early chapters.

To study equation (2) without making that simplifying approximation, we make use of the result which has served us on previous occasions, here in the form

$$\ddot{\theta} = (d/d\theta)(\tfrac{1}{2}\dot{\theta}^2), \tag{3}$$

whence

$$(d/d\theta)(\tfrac{1}{2}\dot{\theta}^2) = -\omega^2\sin\theta. \tag{4}$$

Integrating, and using the condition that $\dot{\theta}$ vanishes at the end of the swing, where $\theta = \alpha$ (say), it follows that

$$\tfrac{1}{2}\dot{\theta}^2 = \omega^2(\cos\theta - \cos\alpha). \tag{5}$$

(By using the approximation $\cos\theta = 1 - \frac{1}{2}\theta^2 + ...$, and similarly for $\cos\alpha$, we recover the simple form characteristic of the linear system, $\dot\theta^2 = \omega^2(\alpha^2 - \theta^2)$.)

It may be well here to emphasize that equation (5) is essentially the 'ghost' of the energy equation again. For, multiplying through by ml^2, it can be written in the form

$$\tfrac{1}{2}m(l\dot\theta)^2 = mgl(\cos\theta - \cos\alpha), \tag{6}$$

in which the left-hand side is the kinetic energy, and the right-hand side the loss of potential energy in falling from the extreme position in the swing.

To proceed further with the integration it is convenient first to use the formula $\cos\theta = 1 - 2\sin^2\tfrac{1}{2}\theta$, and similarly for $\cos\alpha$. This gives

$$\dot\theta^2 = 4\omega^2(\sin^2\tfrac{1}{2}\alpha - \sin^2\tfrac{1}{2}\theta). \tag{7}$$

Taking the square root, separating the variables, and integrating, it follows that

$$2\omega t = \int d\theta/\sqrt{(\sin^2\tfrac{1}{2}\alpha - \sin^2\tfrac{1}{2}\theta)}. \tag{8}$$

The integral in (8) is not in the table of elementary standard forms with which the student is expected to be familiar. It is termed by the mathematician an 'elliptic integral'—for a similar form arises in the problem of finding the length of an arc of an ellipse. Some approximate—formal or numerical—method is therefore necessary in order to evaluate it. Since in the important cases, $\sin\tfrac{1}{2}\alpha$ is going to be small, it is desirable to take advantage of this fact. To do so we write

$$\sin\tfrac{1}{2}\theta = \sin\tfrac{1}{2}\alpha\sin\phi, \tag{9}$$

whence $\qquad \tfrac{1}{2}\cos\tfrac{1}{2}\theta\,d\theta = \sin\tfrac{1}{2}\alpha\cos\phi\,d\phi,$

and since, from (9), $\cos\tfrac{1}{2}\theta = \sqrt{(1 - \sin^2\tfrac{1}{2}\alpha\sin^2\phi)}$, (8) gives

$$\omega t = \int d\phi/\sqrt{(1 - \sin^2\tfrac{1}{2}\alpha\sin^2\phi)}. \tag{10}$$

In the vertical position we note that $\theta = 0$, and consequently $\phi = 0$. At the outer end of the swing $\theta = \alpha$, so that $\sin\phi = 1$, and consequently $\phi = \tfrac{1}{2}\pi$. The time which elapses during this part of the motion is one-quarter of the periodic time, T, of the vibration. It follows that

$$\omega T = 4 \int_{0}^{\frac{1}{2}\pi} d\phi/\sqrt{(1-\sin^2 \tfrac{1}{2}\alpha \sin^2\phi)}. \tag{11}$$

This is a standard form of elliptic integral, and tables of values of these integrals, usually in terms of the 'modulus', $k = \sin\tfrac{1}{2}\alpha$, exist.

For our purpose—and, indeed, as a basis for computing the tables which exist—we note that good approximations are possible for at least the smaller values of k by expansion of the square root in series, followed by termwise integration. The result will be found to be

$$\omega T = 2\pi(1 + k^2/4 + 9k^4/64 + ...). \tag{12}$$

This shows that the longer the swing—that is, the greater the value of α, and therefore of k—the longer is the time T taken over the complete vibration. But the increase is, for small values of α, proportional to the square of k, so that it is not surprising that Galileo did not, with his not particularly accurate 'pulse' clock, notice this ! Indeed, if the swing on either side is as great as 60°, so that $k = \tfrac{1}{2}$, the increase is only about some 7 per cent.

The above investigation, and its results, are typical of systems with a small degree of non-linearity, when the effects of damping are neglected. There is usually an equation of energy, or its equivalent, and the periodic time is to be obtained to a good degree of approximation by some form of series expansion.

16.3. The phase plane

The existence of a first integral of the equation of motion—the energy equation or its equivalent—gives us a powerful tool with which to explore the properties of non-linear systems. This tool has been used to considerable effect in recent years for the study of such systems. Before we apply the method to the unfamiliar cases, however, we shall be well advised to gain understanding of what it can do, and how it does it, by applying it to our well-known examples of the behaviour of linear systems.

The essential element in this approach is the recognition that a relation between *velocity* and displacement may be accessible while that between *time* and displacement is much more complex—as in the case of the simple pendulum treated in the last section. We therefore try to discover how much information can be wrung out of the simpler relation.

Since graphical representation can be of considerable value in facilitating a grasp of the relationship between quantities which it pictures, it is of value to represent the relationship between displacement and velocity by means of curves, often called *trajectories*, in a plane in which the coordinates are *displacement* and *velocity*. That is to say, we denote by y the velocity—or some convenient multiple of it—and then the energy equation is represented by some curve in the (x, y) plane. This plane is termed the *phase plane*. Let us see what the curve becomes in the simplest case, that of the linear undamped system.

The differential equation is

$$\ddot{x} + \omega^2 x = 0. \tag{13}$$

The first integral of this is

$$\dot{x}^2 + \omega^2 x^2 = \text{const.}$$

If we represent $\dot{x}$ by y, the curve in the phase plane will be an ellipse. By using a multiple of $\dot{x}$ instead of $\dot{x}$ itself—measuring y on a different scale—this is transformed into a circle, which is a simpler figure. We therefore put $\dot{x} = \omega y$, and also, so as to be able to remove a factor ω^2, put the constant equal to $\omega^2 a^2$. The equation then becomes, on cancelling the common factor,

$$y^2 + x^2 = a^2, \tag{14}$$

which we recognize as the equation of a circle. This is shown in Fig. 75. As the motion of the physical system continues, the representative point at (x, y) travels round the curve. The essential periodicity of the motion is an immediate inference from the fact that the trajectory is closed.

Another fact which we might hope to gain from our phase-plane curve is the value of the periodic time. The result is contained—as far as it can be given—in the relations

$$dt = dx/\dot{x} = dx/\omega y. \tag{15}$$

An approximation to the period can therefore, in any case, be obtained from the graph by numerical or graphical integration, with ordinates y measured from the graph, to an accuracy depending on that of the measurement or calculation and of the integration formula employed.

We note from (15) that, with the above choice of axes, the

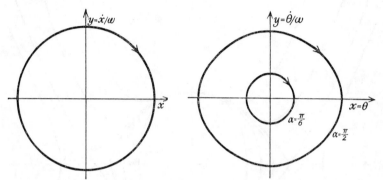

FIG. 75. Phase-plane trajectory
for simple harmonic motion.

FIG. 76. Trajectories for a
simple pendulum.

circle is described clockwise by the representative point. The x- and y-axes may be interchanged to secure the more conventional counter-clockwise description of the path if this is desired, but the nature of the information conveyed is not thereby altered.

Let us now apply the same technique to the case of the simple pendulum. Writing x in place of θ and ωy in place of $\dot{\theta}$, equation (5) becomes

$$y^2 = 2(\cos x - \cos \alpha). \tag{16}$$

The graphs of this relation between x and y are shown in Fig. 76 for two values of α, namely $\frac{1}{6}\pi$ and $\frac{1}{2}\pi$ radians. Since again the trajectories are closed, the motion is seen to be periodic. The curves are, however, no longer circles, so that the determination of the periodic time is not simple.

Another instance of an equation representing a non-linear system which is, for small amplitudes, very nearly linear, can be constructed on its own merits, or by considering the approximation to $\sin \theta$ using the first two terms of the series expansion. This suggests that we add, as a very simple type of non-linearity, a small term in x^3 to the usual equation of motion, that is, we write

$$\ddot{x} = -\omega^2(x-2\mu x^3). \tag{17}$$

Integrating this by the usual substitution (cf. (3)), writing

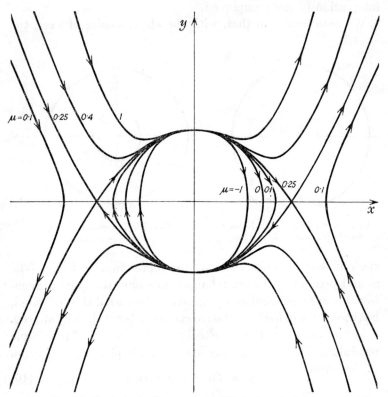

FIG. 77. Trajectories for a system with cubic restoring force.

$\dot{x} = \omega y$, and choosing an appropriate value of the constant of integration, we obtain the relation

$$y^2 + x^2 - \mu x^4 = a^2. \tag{18}$$

Some curves obtained from (18) are given in Fig. 77, for $a = 1$ and several values of μ. (Actually this exhibits all the possibilities, since the curves are similar if the value of μa^2 is the same, that is, a change of a and μ such that μa^2 is unchanged merely alters the size, but not the shape, of the curve in the phase plane.)

When $\mu = 0$, the trajectory is a circle of radius a, corresponding to a simple harmonic motion. For negative values of μ the trajectories are ovals lying within this circle, touching it at the points $(0, \pm a)$. In the critical case when $4\mu a^2 = 1$, the trajectory reduces to the pair of parabolas $y = \pm(a - x^2/a)$. These intersect in nodes on the x-axis, at $x = \pm a\sqrt{2}$, which correspond to points of unstable equilibrium.

For values of μ between 0 and $1/4a^2$, closed ovals between the circle and the two parabolas are possible trajectories, which correspond to periodic vibrations. But other possible trajectories for such values of μ, and all trajectories for $\mu > 1/4a^2$, are situated outside the lenticular region between the parabolas, and extend to infinity. They correspond to conditions which allow the body to 'escape' from the centre of force. Physically, this results from the fact that if $x^2 > 1/2\mu$ the force becomes repulsive, and provided the body has sufficient energy, the representative point will be in this outer region, and the body will eventually be repelled indefinitely, without return.

Formally, $y = a$ when $x = 0$, and the amplitude of a periodic motion is determined by the solution of the equation given by $y = 0$, or

$$\mu x^4 - x^2 + a^2 = 0, \qquad (19)$$

which is a quadratic in x^2. The roots are real only if

$$4\mu a^2 < 1.$$

To determine the periodic time, when the motion is periodic, we use the result

$$t = \int dx/\sqrt{(a^2 - x^2 + \mu x^4)}. \qquad (20)$$

The limits of the integral, to determine the quarter-period, are zero and the smaller positive real root of equation (19).

16.4. A damped system

Before proceeding further it is desirable to study the effect of damping on the trajectories in the phase plane. We do this first for the simplest case. We again put $\dot{x} = \omega y$, and so that we may remove a factor ω^2, we also write $\alpha = \omega\gamma$. The equation then

becomes
$$y\, dy/dx + 2\gamma y + x = 0. \tag{21}$$

This equation is of what is termed the 'homogeneous' type of first-order differential equations and in consequence assumes a simpler form in terms of the ratio of y to x as the dependent variable. To achieve this we put $y = xv$, so that

$$dy/dx = x\, dv/dx + v.$$

Inserting this in equation (21) yields

$$xv(x\, dv/dx + v) + 2\gamma xv + x = 0,$$

or
$$xv\, dv/dx + v^2 + 2\gamma v + 1 = 0.$$

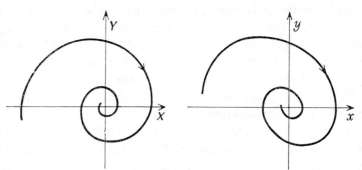

FIG. 78. Phase-plane spiral for a simple system with slight damping.

Separating the variables,

$$dx/x + v\, dv/(v^2 + 2\gamma v + 1) = 0. \tag{22}$$

Putting $u = v + \gamma$, this becomes

$$dx/x + (u - \gamma)\, du/(u^2 + 1 - \gamma^2) = 0. \tag{23}$$

Integrating gives

$$\log x + \tfrac{1}{2}\log(u^2 + 1 - \gamma^2) - \gamma/\sqrt{(1 - \gamma^2)}\,.\tan^{-1}\{u/\sqrt{(1 - \gamma^2)}\} = A. \tag{24}$$

The meaning of this relation is most easily seen if, noticing that $u = (y + \gamma x)/x$, we put

$$y + \gamma x = Y, \quad x\sqrt{(1 - \gamma^2)} = X, \quad 2\gamma/\sqrt{(1 - \gamma^2)} = \lambda. \tag{25}$$

In terms of these new symbols, (24) becomes

$$\log(X^2 + Y^2) - \lambda \tan^{-1}(Y/X) = A. \tag{26}$$

This is the equation of an equiangular spiral in the (X, Y) plane. It is traversed clockwise, so that (X^2+Y^2) steadily decreases and the representative point approaches the origin asymptotically. The corresponding path in the (x, y) plane is obtained by applying the distortion represented by the transformation (25)

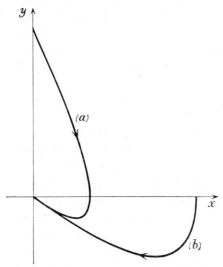

FIG. 79. Trajectories for a simple system with heavy damping.

of the equiangular spiral in the (X, Y) plane, and the two diagrams are shown in Fig. 78. The ellipse or circle of the phase-plane representation of the undamped vibration is replaced by the spirals which represent a damped vibration. Spirals will also be a feature of the representation of other dissipative non-linear systems.

The above holds only if γ is less than unity—that is, for relatively lightly (less than critically) damped systems. If γ is greater than unity, the denominator in (22) has real factors, and, if these are $(v-\mu_1)$ and $(v-\mu_2)$, we must replace (22) by

$$dx/x+\{\mu_1/(v-\mu_1)-\mu_2/(v-\mu_2)\}\,dv/(\mu_1-\mu_2) = 0. \qquad (27)$$

The integral of this is

$$\log x+\{\mu_1\log(v-\mu_1)-\mu_2\log(v-\mu_2)\}/(\mu_1-\mu_2) = A. \qquad (28)$$

In terms of x and y this becomes

$$\mu_1 \log(y - \mu_1 x) - \mu_2 \log(y - \mu_2 x) = A \qquad (29)$$

or

$$(y - \mu_1 x)^{\mu_1} / (y - \mu_2 x)^{\mu_2} = B. \qquad (30)$$

In the above, $\qquad \mu_1, \mu_2 = -\gamma \pm \sqrt{(\gamma^2 - 1)}, \qquad (31)$

so that (if γ is positive) both μ_1 and μ_2 are negative. Typical (x, y) trajectories are shown in Fig. 79. The curve (a) represents the non-oscillatory return to the equilibrium position of a system projected from the equilibrium configuration. The curve (b) represents the return of the system from a displaced position to the equilibrium position.

16.5. van der Pol's equation

In some oscillatory systems there is a source of power which increases with the amplitude of vibration. Certain electrical circuits, such as feed-back circuits controlled by valves, have this property. To exhibit the main features of the behaviour of such systems by a mathematical treatment, van der Pol invented an equation known now by his name. He introduced a form of damping which is negative for small amplitudes but becomes positive for sufficiently large amplitudes. The magnitude of the damping term is to be independent of the sign of x, and the simplest form is a multiple of $(x^2 - 1)\dot{x}$, if we take as the unit the critical amplitude for which the total damping vanishes. The equation can then be written

$$\ddot{x} + 2\alpha(x^2 - 1)\dot{x} + \omega^2 x = 0. \qquad (32)$$

Making the usual substitutions, $\dot{x} = \omega y$, $\alpha = \omega\gamma$, this becomes

$$y \, dy/dx + 2\gamma(x^2 - 1)y + x = 0. \qquad (33)$$

A formal integral of this is not known, but the run of the trajectories can be found graphically by the method of isoclinals. An 'isoclinal' is a curve along which the gradient of all the trajectories which cross it has the same value, that is, it is the locus of points where dy/dx has some specified value. Denote dy/dx by m; then the equation of the isoclinal corresponding to the gradient m is

$$y + x / \{m + 2\gamma(x^2 - 1)\} = 0. \qquad (34)$$

If the curves represented by (34) are drawn for a set of values of m, as in Fig. 80, the trajectories can be sketched in with fair accuracy, and their general form determined. This is done in the figure.

In the region of the phase plane near the origin, the trajectories

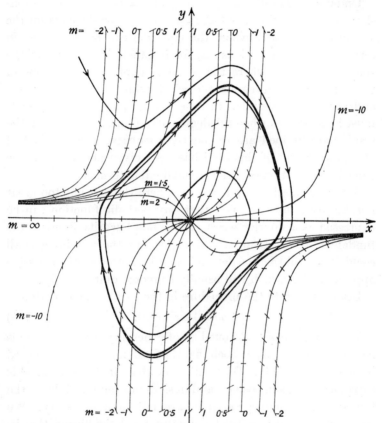

FIG. 80. Trajectories and limit-cycle for van der Pol's equation.

are spirals, very similar to those in the case of the linear system, but traversed in the outward direction. These spirals, however, do not expand indefinitely, but approach asymptotically a closed curve, known as the *limit cycle*, which corresponds to a periodic, but not sinusoidal, oscillation. The trajectories outside the limit cycle are also spirals, which extend to infinity, but spiral round the limit cycle and approach it asymptotically. In all cases the system settles down to a periodic oscillation represented by the limit cycle.

16.6. Periodic vibrations

Undamped non-linear systems can execute periodic (non-sinusoidal) vibrations, but the period of these depends on the amplitude. In cases where the equation can be integrated in terms of known functions, as, for instance, in the case of the simple pendulum where the result is expressible in terms of tabulated elliptic integrals, the relationship between amplitude and period is accessible. In other cases approximate methods must be used, and when the degree of non-linearity is small, the results so obtained are frequently adequate. One method of attaining results of this kind has been given above, when the equation of motion contains a small cubic term.

A general method, satisfactory where there is not too great non-linearity, uses the fact that any periodic function can be expressed as a Fourier series. If the non-linearity is small, the fundamental will dominate this series, and the remaining small coefficients will then be determinable by a process of successive approximation which will usually converge quite rapidly.

Let us illustrate the procedure in the case of the equation

$$\ddot{x}+\omega^2(x+\mu x^3) = 0. \tag{35}$$

We may suppose, without loss of generality, that the time is measured from such an epoch that the fundamental is represented by a sine term only. Trial will show that, if the term in x^3 is expanded, terms in cosines, and in sines of even multiples of the fundamental angular variable, are not here necessary. We suppose first that only the third harmonic is significant, that is, we write

$$x = a_1 \sin \beta t + a_3 \sin 3\beta t + ..., \tag{36}$$

where a_3/a_1 is small. Substituting this in equation (35), and neglecting higher harmonics, we find, after some reduction, that

$$-\beta^2 a_1 \sin \beta t - 9\beta^2 a_3 \sin 3\beta t - ... + \omega^2 a_1 \sin \beta t + \omega^2 a_3 \sin 3\beta t + ... +$$
$$+ \mu\omega^2\{a_1^3(3 \sin \beta t - \sin 3\beta t)/4 + 3a_1^2 a_3(2 \sin 3\beta t - \sin \beta t - ...)/4 +$$
$$+ 3a_1 a_3^2(\sin \beta t - ...)/2 + a_3^3(3 \sin 3\beta t - ...)/4...\} = 0. \tag{37}$$

Equating to zero the coefficients of $\sin \beta t$ and $\sin 3\beta t$ gives two equations from which β^2 and a_3 can be obtained in terms of a_1. These are

$$-\beta^2 a_1 + \omega^2 a_1 + \mu\omega^2(3a_1^3 - 3a_1^2 a_3 + 6a_1 a_3^2)/4 = 0, \qquad (38)$$

$$-9\beta^2 a_3 + \omega^2 a_3 + \mu\omega^2(-a_1^3 + 6a_1^2 a_3 + 3a_3^3)/4 = 0. \qquad (39)$$

If we further approximate, using the fact that a_3 is small compared with a_1, these become

$$\beta^2 = \omega^2(1 + 3\mu a_1^2/4), \qquad (38\,a)$$

$$(9\beta^2 - \omega^2)a_3 = -\mu\omega^2 a_1^3/4. \qquad (39\,a)$$

Using the approximation $\beta^2 = \omega^2$ in (39 a), we obtain, to the first order in the small quantity μ,

$$a_3 = -\mu a_1^3/32. \qquad (39\,b)$$

(38 a) and (39 b) may be regarded as the initial terms in the expansions of β^2 and a_3 in powers of μ. Further terms could be obtained by further use of (38) and (39).

The method could also be extended to take into account the fifth and higher harmonics.

16.7. Maintained vibrations

So far we have considered only the free vibrations which non-linear systems can execute. Of considerable practical importance, however, in both mechanical and electrical systems, is the response of a system to some external continuous disturbance, and, more especially, the response to periodic disturbing forces. The fundamental question in this connexion is the magnitude—or amplitude, although the vibration is not, in general, sinusoidal—of the resulting oscillation. Other circumstances, such as the phase lag, and the wave-form, are also of interest in many cases.

The obvious method—and it is effective in cases of small non-linearity—is to express the resulting disturbance as a Fourier series. We exemplify the method first in the case of the non-dissipative system just studied, to which is applied a sinusoidal disturbing force. The differential equation can be written

$$\ddot{x} + \omega^2(x + \mu x^3) = f \sin \beta t. \qquad (40)$$

Trial will again show that in this case, with only odd powers of x, only odd sine harmonics are necessary. We therefore write

$$x = a_1 \sin \beta t + a_3 \sin 3\beta t + \dots . \qquad (41)$$

Substituting in the equation, and neglecting all but the dominant terms (on the assumption that μ, and hence a_3, are both small), we have

$$(\omega^2 - \beta^2)a_1 \sin \beta t + (\omega^2 - 9\beta^2)a_3 \sin 3\beta t + \dots$$
$$+ \mu\omega^2\{a_1^3(3 \sin \beta t - \sin 3\beta t)/4 + \dots\} = f \sin \beta t. \qquad (42)$$

Equating coefficients of $\sin \beta t$ and $\sin 3\beta t$ yields

$$(\omega^2 - \beta^2)a_1 + 3\mu\omega^2 a_1^3/4 = f, \qquad (43)$$

$$(\omega^2 - 9\beta^2)a_3 - \mu\omega^2 a_1^3/4 = 0. \qquad (44)$$

(43) is an equation for a_1, and a first approximation when μ is small is $f/(\omega^2 - \beta^2)$—the result for the linear equation. Using this approximation in the small μ term, a second approximation is

$$a_1 = f/(\omega^2 - \beta^2) - 3\mu\omega^2 f^3/4(\omega^2 - \beta^2)^4 \dots . \qquad (45)$$

From (44), using the first approximation to a_1, we derive

$$a_3 = \mu\omega^2 f^3/4(\omega^2 - \beta^2)^3(\omega^2 - 9\beta^2) \dots . \qquad (46)$$

The maximum displacement occurs when $\beta t = \frac{1}{2}\pi$, and then

$$x_{\max} = \{f/(\omega^2 - \beta^2)\}\{1 - \mu\omega^2 f^2(\omega^2 - 7\beta^2)/(\omega^2 - \beta^2)^3(\omega^2 - 9\beta^2)\}. \qquad (47)$$

This shows, to the first order in μ, the reduction of amplitude due to the extra x^3 term in the expression for the restoring force. It should be noted that the approximations made are not valid unless ω^2 differs significantly from both β^2 and $9\beta^2$.

It is possible to extend the solution obtained in this manner to higher powers of μ, and also to include higher harmonics. This involves more labour but no additional principles.

16.8. Sum and difference tones

Perhaps the most important result which has emerged in the last section is that the effect of a disturbing force which is sinusoidal contains harmonics as well as the fundamental—the response to a pure tone is not pure. It is natural to ask what

will be the response to a combination of tones. To discover this
we examine the solution of the equation

$$\ddot{x}+\omega^2(x+\mu x^2) = f\sin\beta t+g\sin\gamma t. \tag{48}$$

(Here, for simplicity, we have used an x^2 term, which is simpler
than the x^3 term which complete antisymmetry would demand.)

The solution must, of course, contain terms in $\sin\beta t$ and $\sin\gamma t$.
We must, however, consider the effect of such terms through
the contribution they also make via the x^2 term. If

$$x = a\sin\beta t+b\sin\gamma t,$$

$$x^2 = a^2\sin^2\beta t+2ab\sin\beta t\sin\gamma t+b^2\sin^2\gamma t$$

$$= a^2(1-\cos 2\beta t)/2+ab\{\cos(\beta-\gamma)t-\cos(\beta+\gamma)t\}+$$

$$+b^2(1-\cos 2\gamma t)/2. \tag{49}$$

It is clear that, in order that the equation may be satisfied, terms
of all the kinds in (49) must be contained in x. They will, in
their turn, give rise to other terms, and it will easily be found that
x must contain terms in $(m\beta+n\gamma)t$, for all positive and negative
integral values of m and n, including zero. In addition to the
harmonics of βt and γt, terms with these other pulsatances,
known as combination tones, must be present in the response.
We notice that there is a constant term, which corresponds to a
displacement of the centre of the swing, and the most important
terms contain 'sum' and 'difference' pulsatances. One can go
further into details, and actually obtain an approximate formal
solution with as many terms as desired, but the labour of this
increases rapidly with the number of terms included. If the
restoring force contains also terms in higher powers of x, a similar
situation arises.

The important and quite general conclusion is that non-
linearity in the system produces impurity in the response.

16.9. Energy methods

We have had occasion to see, in previous chapters, the power
of energy methods for several purposes. It may be surmised
that their use will lead to means of obtaining some information
concerning non-linear systems. In particular, where these are

dissipative, and a vibration is maintained in a 'steady state' by some external source of energy, the work done per cycle by that source must supply the energy dissipated and the overall balance per cycle may be calculated on the basis of a plausible approximation to the motion. But the equation of energy is only *one* equation, and can, therefore, yield only *one* independent result. Where more than one relation is sought, the equation of energy needs to be supplemented by other considerations. Sometimes these can be given a physical meaning, but in other cases the appropriate method is most easily attained by use of mathematical techniques applied to the governing equation of motion.

As an example we take van der Pol's equation (section 16.5, eqn. (32)) as applied to a self-oscillatory valve circuit, viz.

$$\ddot{x}+2\alpha(x^2-1)\dot{x}+\omega^2 x = 0. \tag{32 bis}$$

The non-linear term here represents the possibility of drawing energy from the battery when the current is below the threshold, taken here as the unit of x. We assume that α/ω is small. The problem is to determine the amplitude and pulsatance of the self-maintained oscillation.

Assume that $x = A \sin\beta t$ is an approximate solution. Insert this into the equation, and integrate over a cycle. The term in α gives zero contribution, and we have

$$-\beta^2\pi A+\omega^2\pi A = 0,$$

or

$$\beta^2 = \omega^2, \tag{50}$$

so that the pulsatance is—as might have been foreseen from former experience—that of the corresponding undamped system. Integrating now with respect to x, over a complete cycle, the first and third terms give no contribution, since they return to their original value. The resulting relation is

$$\int \dot{x}\, dx = \int x^2\dot{x}\, dx. \tag{51}$$

The meaning of this equation is that the work done by the battery in the 'feed-back' is equal to the energy dissipated, per cycle. Again inserting the approximation $x = A \sin\omega t$, we obtain

$$\pi A^2 = \pi A^4/4, \tag{52}$$

whence $A = 2$. On the basis of this simple approximation, the amplitude of the self-maintained oscillation is twice the threshold value at which the damping term changes sign.

It must be clearly understood that the result here obtained —that $x = 2 \sin \omega t$—does *not* satisfy the differential equation exactly, but only 'on the average'.

16.10. Slowly varying amplitude and phase

Finally, we shall outline a method which can be used when a small degree of non-linearity is present, in stiffness or dissipation, or both. In such a case we assume that the amplitude and phase are slowly varying functions of time. The governing equation is

$$\ddot{x} + \omega^2 x + g(x, \dot{x}) = 0. \tag{53}$$

We assume that

$$x = a \sin \theta = a \sin(\omega t + \phi). \tag{54}$$

Then

$$\dot{x} = \dot{a} \sin \theta + a(\omega + \dot{\phi}) \cos \theta, \tag{55}$$

and, since we can arbitrarily choose one relation between a and ϕ —the differential equation giving us only one—we may postulate that the value of $\dot{x}$ is represented by the same expression as it would be in a sinusoidal oscillation, that is, $\dot{x} = \omega a \cos \theta$, so that

$$\dot{a} \sin \theta + a\dot{\phi} \cos \theta = 0. \tag{56}$$

It now follows that

$$\ddot{x} = \omega \dot{a} \cos \theta - a\omega(\omega + \dot{\phi}) \sin \theta, \tag{57}$$

and, substituting in the differential equation, there results a second relation between $\dot{a}$ and $\dot{\phi}$, namely

$$\omega(\dot{a} \cos \theta - a\dot{\phi} \sin \theta) + g(x, \dot{x}) = 0. \tag{58}$$

Solving (56) and (58) for $\dot{a}$ and $\dot{\phi}$ gives

$$\omega \dot{a} = -g(x, \dot{x}) \cos \theta,$$
$$\omega a\dot{\phi} = g(x, \dot{x}) \sin \theta. \tag{59}$$

These equations are true at every instant—but are even more difficult to solve *exactly* than the original equation. However, on the assumption that $g(x, \dot{x})$ and, consequently, $\dot{a}$ and $\dot{\phi}$ are all small, we may obtain useful and approximately true information by integrating over a cycle. In particular the changes Δa and $\Delta \phi$ in amplitude and phase in any cycle are given by

$$\omega^2 \Delta a = - \int_0^{2\pi} g(a \sin \theta, \; \omega a \cos \theta) \cos \theta \, d\theta,$$

$$\omega^2 a \Delta \phi = \int_0^{2\pi} g(a \sin \theta, \; \omega a \cos \theta) \sin \theta \, d\theta.$$

(60)

ANSWERS

Note: (1) *Numerical answers are usually given correct to about* 3 *significant figures.*

(2) *Where* formulae *for pulsatance are asked for, the value of* ω^2 *is given in these answers unless otherwise indicated.*

CHAPTER I

1. $2P/Ma$. 2. $3EI/Ml^3$. 3 (a) $48EI/Ml^3$; (b) $192EI/Ml^3$.
4. CJl/Iab. 5. $\gamma pA^2/mV$. 6. $6s/m$. 7. $\gamma pA/lV\rho$; $47/\text{sec}$, approx.
8. $3 \cdot 12/\text{sec}$. 9. $24 \cdot 2$ gm; $4 \cdot 10 \times 10^{-8}$ cm. 10. $7 \cdot 7/\text{sec}$.

CHAPTER II

1. $2P/(M+2ma/3)a$. 2. $CJ/l(I+I')$, with $I' = \pi r^4 l\rho/6$.
3. $6EI/(M+M')l^3$, where $M' = 34ml/35$.
4. (a) sa^2/Ml^2; (b) correction for bar, $m/3$. 6. (a) P/ma; (b) $3P/ma$.

CHAPTER III

1. $1003/\text{sec}$; $0 \cdot 1$ approx. (base e); about 7. 2. $0 \cdot 004$ farad. 3. $0 \cdot 014$.
4. $d^2x/dt^2 + 0 \cdot 693 \, dx/dt + 9 \cdot 990x = 0$.
5. $4,941$ dynes/cm; $11 \cdot 16$ dynes/cm/sec.
6. $11,540$ dynes; 150 dynes.

CHAPTER IV

1. (a) $\hat{x} = 100/\beta^2$, $\hat{\dot{x}} = 100/\beta$; (b) $\hat{x} = 10^{-4}$, $\hat{\dot{x}} = 10^{-4}\beta$; (c) $\hat{x} = 1/\beta$, $\hat{\dot{x}} = 1$.
2. $1,007$, 926 per sec.
3. $\hat{x} = 1,000/Z$, $\hat{\dot{x}} = 1,000/\beta Z$, $Z = \sqrt{\{7,000^2 + (8 \times 10^7/\beta - 2\beta)^2\}}$.
4. (a) $1,007$, 0 per sec; (b) $1,007$, $1,006$ per sec.
5. $0 \cdot 000885$ cm; $2 \cdot 224$ cm/sec; $8 \cdot 28 \times 10^{-4}$ watt.
6. (a) $0 \cdot 150$ in.; (b) $0 \cdot 030$ in. 8. $0 \cdot 126$, $0 \cdot 563$, $0 \cdot 118$, and $0 \cdot 024$ in.
9. $1 \cdot 34$, 165, and $0 \cdot 331$ cm.
10. (a) $1 \cdot 41 \times 10^8$ dynes; (b) $1 \cdot 38 \times 10^8$ dynes; (c) $1 \cdot 07 \times 10^8$ dynes.
12. $15 \cdot 8$, $1,580$, and $15 \cdot 8$ milliwatts.

CHAPTER V

1. $a \cos \omega t$, where $\omega^2 = s/m$. 2. $(v/\omega)\sin \omega t$.
3. $a \cos \omega t + (v/\omega)\sin \omega t$.
4. $ae^{-\alpha t}\{\cos \mu t + (\alpha/\mu)\sin \mu t\}$, $(v/\mu)e^{-\alpha t}\sin \mu t$, where $\alpha = r/2m$, $\mu^2 = \omega^2 - \alpha^2$.
5. $(F/s)\cos \omega t$. 6. $Fe^{-\alpha t}\{\cos \mu t + (\alpha/\mu)\sin \mu t\}/s$.
7. (a) $(F/s)\{1 - e^{-\alpha t}[\cos \mu t + (\alpha/\mu)\sin \mu t]\}$;
(b) $F\{(\omega^2 - \beta^2)\sin \beta t - 2\alpha\beta \cos \beta t +$
$+ \beta e^{-\alpha t}[2\alpha \cos \mu t - (1/\mu)(\omega^2 - \beta^2 - 2\alpha^2)\sin \mu t]\}/m\{(\omega^2 - \beta^2)^2 + 4\alpha^2\beta^2\}$.

8. $F(\sin \omega t - \omega t \cos \omega t)/2s$.

9. (a) $F(1-\cos \omega t)/s$; (b) $F\{\cos \omega(t-t_1)-\cos \omega t\}/s$.

10. (a) $\beta F\{\sin \omega(t-2\pi/\beta)-\sin \omega t\}/\omega(s-m\beta^2)$;

 (b) $-\beta F\{\sin \omega(t-\pi/\beta)+\sin \omega t\}/\omega(s-m\beta^2)$.

CHAPTERS I TO V

1. 2,000 dynes/cm/sec; $e^{-1} = 0\cdot368$ cm. 4. $9\cdot08$/sec; $0\cdot0150$ in.

6. Divides length in ratio $I_2 : I_1$; $\omega^2 = CJ(I_1+I_2)/lI_1 I_2$.

CHAPTER VI

2. $\omega^2 = sc^2/a^2(M+m/3)$.

3. $(M-m)g/(M+m+I/r^2)$.

10. Vector displacement $x = EAe^{j\beta t}/(s+j\beta r-m\beta^2)Z$,

$i = j\beta q = Ee^{j\beta t}/Z$;

vector impedance $Z = R+j\beta L+j\beta A^2/(s+j\beta r-m\beta^2)$.

CHAPTER VII

1. P/am and $3P/am$; $1:1$ and $1:-1$. 2. $(2\pm\sqrt{2})g/a$; $(-1\mp\sqrt{2}):1$.

3. $(3\pm\sqrt{5})s/2m$; $(-1\mp\sqrt{5}):2$. 5. $8s/m$ and $36s/m$; $1:4$ and $3:-2$.

6. s/m and $\{1\pm\frac{1}{2}\sqrt{3}\}s/m$.

7. $(3\mp\sqrt{3})s/m$ and $3s/m$; $1:1\pm\sqrt{3}:1$ and $1:0:-1$.

8. $P/6ma$, $2P/3ma$, P/ma; $2:3:2$, $1:0:-1$, $1:-1:1$.

9. $g/12a$ and $g/2a$; $3:4$ and $-1:2$.

11. $Mm\omega^4-(Ms+mS+ms)\omega^2+Ss = 0$. 12. s/m and $(s+2kA/l)/m$.

13. $k^2\omega^4-2\mu(l^2+3k^2)\omega^2+3\mu^2l^2 = 0$, where $\mu = 2EI/Ml^3$.

14. $(2\mp\sqrt{2})P/ma$ and $2P/ma$; $1:\pm\sqrt{2}:1$ and $1:0:-1$.

CHAPTER VIII

1. $P\alpha(2P-ma\beta^2)/D$ and $P^2\alpha/D$, where $D = (P-ma\beta^2)(3P-ma\beta^2)$.

3. Amplitudes, $(6s+M\beta^2)F/D$ and $(18s-5M\beta^2)F/D$, where
$$D = 2(2s-M\beta^2)(6s-M\beta^2).$$

4. Amplitudes, $4g(g-a\beta^2)\alpha/D$ and $4g^2\alpha/D$, where $D = (2g-a\beta^2)(2g-3a\beta^2)$.

6. $\sigma(\sigma-\beta^2)\alpha/D$ and $\sigma^2\alpha/D$, where $\sigma = CJ/aI$, $D = \sigma^2-4\sigma\beta^2+2\beta^4$.

7. $(9s-m\beta^2)F/(24s^2-12ms\beta^2+m^2\beta^4)$.

9. $(432s^2-156sm\beta^2+10m^2\beta^4)\alpha/D$ and $2m\beta^2(6s-m\beta^2)\alpha/D$, where
$$D = 324s^2-108sm\beta^2+7m^2\beta^4.$$

11. (a) $F\sqrt{\{(s-m\beta^2)^2+r^2\beta^2\}}/D$ and $F\gamma s/D$, where
$$D^2 = [\{s(1+\gamma)-m\beta^2\}^2+r^2\beta^2][\{s(1-\gamma)-m\beta^2\}^2+r^2\beta^2].$$

 (b) $F\sqrt{\{(s-m\beta^2)^2+r^2\beta^2\}}/D_1$ and $F\delta r\beta/D_1$, where
$$D_1^2 = [(s-m\beta^2)^2+r^2(1+\delta)^2\beta^2][(s-m\beta^2)^2+r^2(1-\delta)^2\beta^2].$$

CHAPTER IX

1. P/am and $3P/am$. 3. $P/6am$.

4. $P(2-2\gamma+\gamma^2)/am(3+2\gamma^2)$. Max., P/am; min., $P/6am$. (These are correct; see Ch. VII, Ex. 8.)

5. $10P/17am$ in both cases. Intermediate configuration $5:7:5$ is suggested, and gives $58P/99am = 0.58586...P/am$. Compare with true coefficient $2-\sqrt{2} = 0.58579...$.

6. $6P/l(3M+2ml)$ and $6P/l(M+2ml)$.

7. Recurrence relations for displacements x, y, z (in order from the top):
$$x_{n+1} = (x_n+y_n+z_n)/3, \qquad y_{n+1} = (2x_n+5y_n+5z_n)/6,$$
$$z_{n+1} = (2x_n+5y_n+11z_n)/6.$$
$\omega^2 = 0.41577...g/a$; ratios $0.25489...:0.58423...:1$. (3-figure ratios $0.255:0.584:1$ suffice to give ω^2 correct to at least 5 figures.)

8. Recurrence relations for angular displacements x, y, z (in order from fixed end):
$$x_{n+1} = x_n+2y_n+3z_n, \qquad y_{n+1} = x_n+4y_n+6z_n,$$
$$z_{n+1} = x_n+4y_n+9z_n.$$
$\omega^2 = 0.080452...CJ/aI$; ratios $0.39522...:0.75864...:1$. (3-figure ratios $0.395:0.759:1$ suffice to give ω^2 correct to at least 5 figures.)

CHAPTER X

1. Fig. 81.   2. Fig. 82.

5. A ladder network with shunt arms L_1, series arms (C, L) in series, where $L_1 = m/6$, $L = m/3$, $C = 1/s$. This is a band-pass filter, with cut-off pulsatances $\sqrt{(s/m)}$ and $\sqrt{(3s/m)}$.

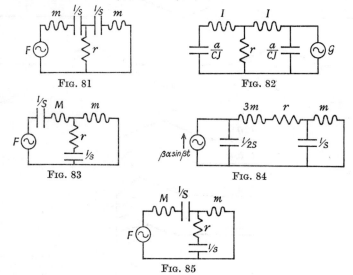

FIG. 81   FIG. 82

FIG. 83   FIG. 84

FIG. 85

6. Two equal pulleys I at points of trisection of shaft $(C', J, 3a)$, where
$$I = L, \quad C'J/a = 1/C.$$

7. Fig. 83.   8. Fig. 84.   9. Fig. 85.

10. $\hat{x} = E\alpha/\beta\sqrt{\{m^2\beta^2R^2+(m\beta^2L-\alpha^2)^2\}}$. Electrical equivalent of inertia m is capacitance m/α^2.

CHAPTER XI

1. 16,900 and 10,700 ft/sec.   2. 780 ft/sec; 13 cycles/sec.
3. Fig. 86.   4. Fig. 87.   6. Fig. 88.
7. Similar to Fig. 86, but ordinates of partial waves reduced in ratio $e^{-\alpha t}$.

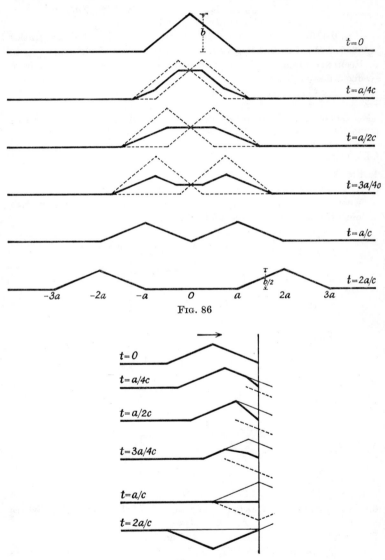

FIG. 86

FIG. 87

8. $A\sqrt{(E\rho)} = Ac\rho.$ 9. $\sqrt{(Pm)} = mc.$

10. $(J_1 - J_2)/(J_1 + J_2),$ $2J_1/(J_1 + J_2).$

11. $\beta I/\sqrt{(4\rho^2 J^2 c^2 + \beta^2 I^2)},$ $2\rho Jc/\sqrt{(4\rho^2 J^2 c^2 + \beta^2 I^2)}.$

12. $|\rho Jc - r| : (\rho Jc + r).$ No reflection if $r = \rho Jc$ (matching condition).

15. $mc(1 + \mu/j\beta),$ if μ^2 is negligible.

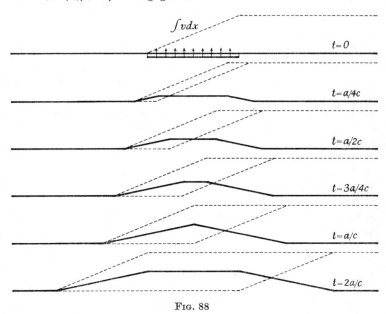

FIG. 88

CHAPTER XII

1. $331{\cdot}7$ m/sec; $343{\cdot}7$ m/sec. 2. $1{,}461$ m/sec.

3. $\delta p = \rho c \omega a$; mean rate $\tfrac{1}{2}\rho c\omega^2 a^2.$

4. (a) $42{\cdot}8$ gm/cm^2/sec; (b) $1{\cdot}461 \times 10^5$ gm/cm^2/sec;
   (c) $3{\cdot}987 \times 10^6$ gm/cm^2/sec.

5. (a) $0{\cdot}059$ per cent.; $0{\cdot}00215$ per cent.

6. 925 dynes/cm^2; $21{\cdot}6$ cm/sec; $0{\cdot}0688$, $0{\cdot}0138$, and $0{\cdot}0034$ cm.

7. Average rate, $\rho c A \omega^2 a^2/2$; damping coefficient $A\rho c$; decay factor, $e^{-10\cdot 7t}.$

8. $(B-A)^2/(B+A)^2$ and $4AB/(B+A)^2.$ With B infinite these suggest no energy is radiated from an open end. This is not correct.

9. $j\rho_0\, c \cot(\omega l/c).$

11. Transmission coefficient at pulsatance ω is

$$2\cos(\omega l/c)/\sqrt{[1 + 3\cos^2(\omega l/c)]}.$$

14. (a) $2{\cdot}87 \times 10^5$ c.c./sec; $1{\cdot}26$ watts; (b) $1{\cdot}43 \times 10^4$ c.c./sec, $1{\cdot}26$ watts.

16. $0{\cdot}128$ dynes/cm^2; $0{\cdot}00303$ cm/sec.

17. $0{\cdot}0245$ cm/sec; 333 c.c./sec.

18. $-(A/2r)\cos\omega(t+r/c) + (A/2r)\cos\omega(t-r/c).$

19. If $\theta = \omega\{t-(r-a)/c\}$, then

(a) $\phi = \omega\alpha ca^2(c\cos\theta+\omega a\sin\theta)/(c^2+\omega^2 a^2)r$,

(b) $\delta p = \rho\omega^2\alpha ca(\omega a\cos\omega t-c\sin\omega t)/(c^2+\omega^2 a^2)$,

(c) power $= 2\pi\rho ca^4\omega^4\alpha^2/(c^2+\omega^2 a^2)$.

20. 39·5 and 790 c.c./sec; 1·273 and 509 dynes/cm²; 0·238 erg/sec and 3·67 milliwatts.

CHAPTER XIII

1. 418·5/sec.   2. 86·4 kg. wt.

3. $\omega l/c = n\pi$, $\pi(2n-1)/2$, $n\pi$, with $c^2 = E/\rho$, C/ρ, or K/ρ.

4. 15·85/sec.   7. $\cot\theta = M\theta/m$, $m = $ mass of bar, $\theta = 2\pi f l\sqrt{(\rho/E)}$.

11. 2,380/sec.

13. $(F/\rho c\beta)\sin(\beta b/c)\sin(\beta x/c)\mathrm{cosec}(\beta l/c)\sin\beta t$, in segment a; corresponding formula in segment b.

18. $8\theta_0/\pi^2(2n-1)^2$.

CHAPTER XIV

1. 40·9 and 163·5/sec.

2. 28·4 and 178·2/sec.

3. (a) $\cosh\theta\cos\theta = 1$;   (b) $\tanh\theta = \tan\theta$ $(\theta = \alpha b)$.

4. (a) $\theta = 4·730, 7·853$;   (b) $\theta = 3·927, 7·069$.

CHAPTER XV

1. $y = kx^2(b-x)^2$; $\omega^2 = 504EI/mb^4$.

2. (a) $\omega^2 = \pi^2 P/l(ml+2M)$; (b) $12P/l(ml+3M)$. When $M = ml$, ω^2 given by (b) is smaller, therefore better.

3. With origin at centre,
$$y = k(5l^4-6x^2l^2+x^4); \quad \omega^2 = 2304EI/(375M+7936ml/21)l^3.$$

4. $\omega^2 = \pi^2 P/9a(ma+M)$.   5. $280P/27ml^2$.

6. $15\pi^3 P/2m_0\, l^2(27\pi+8)$.   7. $35Et^2/8\rho l^4$.

BIBLIOGRAPHY

WE append a short list of books which may be consulted by the student who wishes to increase his knowledge of the topics dealt with in this book.

RAYLEIGH, LORD, *Theory of Sound*, Macmillan (2nd ed., 1894) ; reprinted by Dover, 1945.

This is a classic treatise, and covers the whole range of the theory of vibrating systems.

LAMB, H., *Dynamical Theory of Sound*, Arnold (2nd ed., 1925).

A more elementary approach to some of the topics dealt with by Rayleigh.

CRANDALL, I. B., *Theory of Vibrating Systems and Sound*, Macmillan (1927).

This has a rather more technological approach, at a fairly advanced level.

TEMPLE, G., and BICKLEY, W. G., *Rayleigh's Principle*, Oxford Univ. Press (1933) ; reprinted by Dover, 1956.

MINORSKY, N., *Introduction to Non-linear Mechanics*, J. W. Edwards (1947).

An advanced mathematical treatment of non-linear vibration and other problems.

MORSE, P. M., *Vibration and Sound*, McGraw-Hill (2nd ed., 1948).

A fairly advanced mathematical treatment.

STOKER, J. J., *Non-linear Vibrations*, Interscience (1950).

A somewhat more elementary treatment than Minorsky's, dealing with both mechanical and electrical systems.

TIMOSHENKO, S., *Vibration Problems in Engineering*, Van Nostrand (3rd ed., 1954).

A standard treatise for the use of engineers.

DEN HARTOG, J. P., *Mechanical Vibrations*, McGraw-Hill (4th ed., 1956).

This book illustrates the theory with a wide variety of technological examples.

INDEX

Acoustics, atmospheric, 154–5.
Activity, 50, 141, 142, 154, 159.
Adiabatic gas law, 151, 155.
Amplitude, critical, 216.
  decay factor, 32, 33.
  of maintained vibration, 41–43, 45–48, 98, 100, 102–3, 181.
    in non-linear systems, 219–20.
  of oscillation, 8, 48.
    in non-linear systems, 216, 218–19, 222–4.
  of waves, 141, 153, 154, 156.
  ratios, in normal modes, 84, 86, 88, 91, 92, 106–8, 110, 113, 115, 116.
    in vibrating string, 167.
    in wave transmission, 144, 146.
  iterative process for, 109–13.
  response, 41–43, 45–47, 98, 100, 102–3, 181.
  slowly varying, in non-linear system, 223–4.
Analogies, electro-mechanical, 5, 48–49, 117 ff., 139.
  use in design, 124.
Anti-resonance, 99, 100.
Approximation to normal pulsatance, 107–9, 113–15,
  improvement of, 109–13, 115.
  in continuous systems, 195 ff.
Argand diagram, 12–13.
Atmospheric acoustics, 154–5.
Attenuation of sound, 151, 159, 161.

Backlash, effect of, 65.
Ballistic instrument, 34.
Bar, longitudinal waves in, 131.
  Rayleigh's principle for, 203–4.
  vibrations of, longitudinal, 169, 177.
    non-uniform, 177.
    strain energy of, 19.
    transverse, 187–91.
Beam, bending of, 185–7.
  Rayleigh's principle for, 203.
  strain energy of, 20.
  See also Bar.
Bending moment, 185–7.
Bulk modulus, 150, 155.

Cantilever, 3, 20.
  effective mass of, 24–25.
Capacitance, 5, 125.
Characteristic function, see Normal function.
Circle diagram, 44.
Circuit analogues, 119–24.
  oscillatory, 5.
  self-oscillatory, 216, 222.
Circular membrane, vibrations of, 201–2.
Complementary function, 54, 55, 58, 206.
Complex quantities, 8, 11–14.
Condensation, 150, 160.
Continuous systems, finite, 164 ff.
  waves in, 128 ff.
Converging wave, 158.
Coordinates, 10, 67–69, 120, 125.
  normal, 89–90, 108, 111.
Coupling, between coordinates, 90.
  coefficient, 102, 125.
  of systems, 90–92, 101–3, 104, 105.
Critical amplitude, 216.
  damping, 34–35.
Cubic restoring force, 212–13.
Current, 5, 118, 125.

d'Alembert's principle, 74, 109, 187, 197.
Damped systems, 27 ff., 37–44, 58–60, 62–63, 122, 213–16, 222–3.
Damped vibrations, 27, 29–36, 213–16.
Dampers, vibration, 122.
Damping, critical, 34–35.
  exponential, 30–35.
  large, 33–34.
  negative, 216.
  small, 29–33.
Decay factor, amplitude, 32, 33.
  energy, 36.
Decrement, logarithmic, 32.
Degrees of freedom, 10, 68, 128, 164.
Density, of fluid, 149.
  energy, 140, 141, 142, 153–4.
Dilatation, 157.
Discontinuity, reflection at, 142–6, 155–6.

Dissipation function, 73, 76, 81, 122, 125.
    coupling term in, 104.
    of energy, 35, 222.
Diverging wave, 158–9.
Dynamic stiffness, 50.

Ear, human, 153, 154.
Effective mass, of cantilever, 24–25.
    of spring, 24.
    of vibrating string, 173.
Eigenfunction, see Normal function.
Elasticity, bulk modulus of, 150, 155.
Electric cable, waves in, 131–2.
    circuits, 4–5, 216, 222.
    as analogues, 117–24.
Electrical connexions, 118.
    impedance, 49, 125.
Electrodynamic energy, 17, 119, 125.
Electro-mechanical analogies, 5, 48–49, 117 ff., 139.
    equivalents, table of, 125.
    interaction, 81.
Electrostatic energy, 21, 119, 125.
    loud-speaker, 66.
End conditions, 136, 137, 143–4, 165–6, 169, 171, 174, 177, 181, 187, 188, 190, 191, 193, 196, 197, 201, 203.
Energies, non-dimensionalized, 111, 200.
    use of, for analogue determination, 119–22.
Energy, decay factor, 36.
    density, 140, 141, 142, 153–4.
    dissipation of, 35, 222.
    electrodynamic, 17, 119, 125.
    electrostatic, 21, 119, 125.
    equation of, 22, 207–8, 209, 210, 212, 222.
    kinetic, see Kinetic energy.
    method for pulsatance, 22–25, 106 ff., 195 ff.
    methods, for non-linear systems, 221–4.
    potential, see Potential energy.
    strain, 19–20.
    transmission of, 139–41, 156, 159.
        balance in, 144–5, 146, 156.
Equilibrium position, 1, 2, 3, 11.
    as datum for potential energy, 17.
Exponential damping, 30–35.
    horn, 161.

Feed-back, 216, 222.
Filter, band-pass, 227.
    high-pass, 161.
    low-pass, 126.
    Quincke, 162.
Flexibility, 125.
Force, 125.
    restoring, 1, 109, 171, 197, 212.
    transmitted, 130, 131, 144.
Fourier series, 176, 179.
    for non-linear periodic vibration, 218–20.
Freedom, degrees of, 10, 68, 128, 164.
Frequency, 6, 11, 166.
    effect of damping on, 32, 33.
    spectrum, 189.
    See also Pulsatance.
Friction, 2, 27–29, 35, 73, 122.
    effect on frequency, 32, 33.
Fundamental mode, 167.
    pulsatance, 166, 170, 181, 189, 190.
        in non-linear system, 218–19.
    tone, 164.

Gas laws, 151, 155.
    perfect, 150–1, 155.
Gramophone, 66, 124, 161.

Harmonic series, 166.
Harmonics, 164, 166, 167, 170, 180, 181, 189, 190.
    in non-linear system, 218–19, 220, 221.
Hooke's law, 4.
Horn, exponential, 161.
    sound waves in, 160.

Impedance coupling, 105.
    effective, 81.
    electrical, 49, 125.
    matching, 124, 145.
    mechanical, 49, 125, 171.
    transmission, 139, 141, 143, 153, 156, 159, 160, 171, 182.
Impulse, elements of continuous force, 61.
    on stretched string, 180–1.
Incident wave, 136, 142, 156.
Inductance, 5, 125.
Inertia, 2, 11.
    coupling, 91.
    system dominated by, 46.
    variable, distributed, 177.

Initial conditions, 6, 34, 55, 57, 58–59,
    60, 61, 63, 134, 175–6, 179.
Integral formula for response, 62, 63.
Isochronous vibrations, 9.
Isoclinal, 216.
Isothermal changes, 151, 154.
Iteration process for normal modes,
    109–13.
    in continuous systems, 197, 200,
    202.

Kinetic energy, 16, 35, 70–71, 92,
    106 ff., 125, 140, 141, 153, 196,
    200, 201, 203.
    as sum of squares, 89, 108, 112.
Kinetic-potential, 75, 81.

Lagrange's equations, 75.
    examples of use, 75–80, 84, 87, 90,
    91, 92, 100.
Laplacian operator, 157.
    for case of spherical symmetry,
    158.
Limit-cycle, 217.
Linear force law, 4, 17, 18.
Logarithmic decrement, 32.
Longitudinal vibrations of bar, 169,
    177.
    waves, in bar, 131.
    in transmission line, 131–2.
Loud-speaker, 52, 66, 81, 161.

Maintained vibrations, 37 ff.
    in continuous systems, 181–2.
    in coupled systems, 101–3.
    in multiple systems, 96 ff.
    with prescribed force, 97–99.
    with prescribed motion, 99–100.
    in non-linear systems, 219–21.
Mass, effective, of cantilever, 24–25.
    of spring, 24.
    of vibrating string, 173.
Matching, of impedances, 124, 145.
Mechanical connexions, 118.
    impedance, 49, 125, 171.
Medium, change of, 143–5, 155–6.
Megaphone, 160–1.
Membrane, circular, vibrations of,
    201–2.
Mode, fundamental, 167.
Modes, normal, see Normal modes.
Modulus of volume elasticity, 150, 155.
Momentum, generalized, 80.

Multiple systems, 67, 70, 76–80.
    anti-resonance in, 99, 100.
    coupling in, 90–92, 101–3, 104, 105.
    maintained vibrations in, 96 ff.
    nodes in, 86, 88.
    resonance in, 98, 100.
    spring, see Spring systems, multiple.
    three-coordinate, normal modes in,
    86–90.
    two-coordinate, 82–86, 90–92.

Nodes, in multiple systems, 86, 88.
    in vibrating bar, 189, 190.
    in vibrating shaft, 170, 175.
    in vibrating string, 167.
Non-dimensionalized   differential
    equation, 197, 199.
    energies, 111, 200.
Non-linear systems, 206 ff.
    damped, 213–16.
    self-oscillatory, 216–18, 222.
    with small non-linearity, 223–4.
Non-uniform systems, 160–1, 177.
    Rayleigh's principle for, 199–202.
Normal coordinates, 89–90, 108, 111.
    functions, 165, 167, 170, 175.
    expansions in series of, 176, 178.
    orthogonality of, 176–8, 184, 192.
    modes, 82 ff.
    amplitude ratios in, 84, 86, 88, 91,
    92, 106–8, 110, 113, 115, 116.
    iteration process for, 109–13.
    Rayleigh's principle for, 106–9.
    higher, 113–15.
    of bar, 187 ff.
    of continuous systems, 164.
    of shaft, 169–70.
    with pulley, 174–5.
    of stretched string, 165–8, 195–9.
    with mass attached, 170–4.
    phases in, 85, 86, 89, 168.
    superposition of, 176.
    pulsatance, 82–83, 84–86, 88, 91,
    92–93, 164–6, 169–70, 172–4,
    175, 189, 190, 191, 196, 199,
    202, 204.
    improvement of Rayleigh's ap-
    proximation for, 109–13,
    115, 197–9.
    Rayleigh's principle for, 106–9,
    111–15, 195–6, 198–201.
Normalization, of normal functions,
    178.

Orthogonality, of normal functions, 176–8, 184, 192–3.
Oscillations, self-maintained, 216, 222.
  sinusoidal, 6–8.
  small, 78, 87, 92.
  superposition of, 57, 60.
Oscillatory circuit, 5, 216.

Parallel connexions, electrical, 118, 125.
Particular integral, 38, 54, 55, 56, 57, 58, 60, 206.
Pendulum, simple, 4, 9, 21, 76.
  with large swing, 207–9.
  double, 68, 70, 76–7.
  small oscillations of, 78.
  normal modes of, 83.
Perfect gas, 150–1, 155.
Period, 6, 11, 166, 209, 211, 213.
Periodic vibration, 6, 210, 211, 213, 217.
  series representation of, 218–19.
Phase, in maintained vibration, 43–44, 48.
  in normal modes, 85, 86, 89, 168.
  lag, 40, 43, 48, 146.
  of oscillation, 8.
  plane, 210.
  spirals, 214–15, 217.
  trajectories, 210 ff.
  response, 43–44.
  slowly varying, in non-linear system, 223–4.
Plane waves of sound, 151–3, 155–6.
Potential energy, 17, 35, 70, 92, 106 ff., 125, 140, 142, 153, 196, 200, 201, 203.
  as sum of squares, 89, 108, 112.
  coupling, 104.
Potential, velocity, 157–61.
  wave equation for, 158.
Power supplied in vibration, 50.
  factor, 51.
  transmitted in wave, 142, 154, 159, 160–1.
Pressure, 149.
  increment, 150, 151, 152, 153, 158, 159.
Progressive waves, 139, 168.
Propagation of waves, 128, 132, 152.
  along non-uniform tube, 160–1.
  in three dimensions, 157.
  velocity, 132, 152.

Pulsatance, 6, 10–11.
  cut-off, 126, 161, 227.
  determinant, 93.
  determination from energy, 22–25, 106 ff., 195 ff.
  effect on, of added mass, 11, 23–25, 173–4, 175, 190–1.
  of coupling, 90–92.
  of damping, 32–33.
  equation, 85, 88, 91, 92, 93, 164–5, 166, 169, 171, 189, 190, 191.
  approximate solution of, 172–4, 194.
  fundamental, 166, 170, 181, 189, 190, 218–19.
  in higher normal modes, 113–15.
  normal, see Normal pulsatance.
  of non-linear system, 222.
  of waves, 141, 144, 146, 153, 154.
  resonant, 40, 57, 98, 100, 182.

Quality, of tone, 189.

Radiation resistance, 140.
Rayleigh's principle, 106 ff.
  for continuous systems, 195 ff.
Reflected wave, 136, 143.
Reflection coefficient, 144, 146, 156.
  of waves, at discontinuity, 142–6, 155–6.
  at end, 135–9.
  in finite continuous systems, 164.
Representative point, in phase plane, 210.
Resistance, as internal force, 73.
  coefficient, 28, 125.
  electrical, 28, 125.
  frictional, 2, 27–29, 35, 122.
  radiation, 140.
  system dominated by, 45.
Resonance, 40, 43, 57, 98, 100, 182.
  in whirling, 192.
Response, amplitude, 41–43, 45, 46, 47, 181.
  double-humped, 102–3.
  of coupled systems, 101.
  of multiple systems, 98, 100.
  of non-linear systems, 219–21.
  phase, 43–44.
  to general disturbing force, 61–63.
  velocity, 40–41, 43, 44, 45, 46, 47.
Restoring force, 1, 109, 171, 197.
  cubic, 212.

Self-maintained oscillation, 216, 222.
Self-oscillatory circuit, 216, 222.
Series connexions, electrical, 118, 125.
Series, of normal functions, 176, 178.
  Fourier, 176, 179, 218–19.
Shafts, elastic, 4, 19.
  Rayleigh's principle for, 203–4.
  torsional vibrations in, 168–70,
    174–5, 177, 181–2, 184.
  waves in, 130–1, 137–8, 139,
    141–2.
  whirling of, 191–2, 204.
  with pulleys, 84–86, 97–100, 174–5.
Shearing force, 185–7.
Simple harmonic motion, 5–10.
  phase-plane trajectory of, 211.
  representation of, by complex num-
    bers, 8.
  geometrical, 7.
Simple harmonic wave, 141, 142–6.
Simple pendulum, see Pendulum,
  simple.
Simple systems, 2–5.
  continuous, finite, 164 ff.
  spring, 2, 11, 23–24, 76.
  with general disturbing force,
    61–63.
  with inertia dominant, 46.
  with negligible damping, 46.
  with resistance dominant, 45.
  with stiffness dominant, 45.
Sinusoidal oscillations, 6–8.
  sound waves, 153–4.
  source, 159–60.
Small oscillations, 78, 87, 92.
Sound, 149 ff.
  attenuation of, 151, 159, 161.
  plane waves of, 151–3, 155–6.
  waves, in air, 154–5.
  in three dimensions, 156–61.
  spherical, 158–9.
Source, strength of, 159.
  sinusoidally varying, 159–60.
Spherical sound waves, 158–9.
Spiral, for damped vibration, 30–31.
  in phase-plane, 214–15, 217.
Spring systems, multiple, 67, 70–71,
  79, 90, 101.
  electrical analogues of, 118–24.
  normal modes of, 82–83.
  simple, 2, 11, 23–24, 76.
Standing wave, 168.
Steady-state vibration, 37.

Stiffness, 2, 11.
  dynamic, 50.
  system dominated by, 45.
  variable, distributed, 177.
Strain energy, of bar, 19.
  of beam, 20.
  of cantilever, 20.
  of shaft, 19.
String, stretched, effective mass of,
  173.
  potential energy of, 21–22.
  struck by hammer, 180–1.
  transverse vibrations of, 165–8,
    170–4, 179–81, 195–9.
  waves on, 129–30, 136–7, 142–6.
  with mass(es) attached, 87–90,
    107–11, 113–16, 170–4.
Superposition, of impulse effects, 61.
  of normal modes, 176.
  of oscillations, 57, 60.
  of waves, 132.
  principle, 206.
Systems, damped, 27 ff., 37–44, 58–60,
  62–3, 122, 213–16, 222–3.
  multiple, see Multiple systems.
  non-linear, see Non-linear systems.
  simple, see Simple systems.

Tones, fundamental, 164.
  harmonic, 164.
  pure, 153.
  quality of, 189.
  sum and difference, in non-linear
    systems, 220–1.
Torque, transmitted, 130, 139, 141, 174.
Torsional vibrations of shaft, 168–70,
  177, 181–2, 184.
  with pulley attached, 174–5.
  waves in shaft, 130–1, 137–8, 139,
    141–2.
Trajectories, in phase-plane, 210 ff.
Transients, 53 ff.
  in damped systems, 58–60, 62–63.
  in undamped systems, 54–58, 61–62.
  due to general disturbing force,
    61–63.
Transmission coefficient, 144, 146,
  156.
  impedance, 139, 141, 143, 153,
    156, 159, 160, 171, 182.
  line, waves in, 131–2.
  of energy, 139–41, 144–5, 146, 156,
    159.

Transmitted force, 130, 131, 144.
torque, 130, 139, 141, 174.
wave, 143, 144, 145, 146.
Transverse vibrations of bar, 187–90.
with mass attached, 190–1.
vibrations of string, 165–8, 179–81, 195–9.
with mass attached, 170–4.
waves in string, 129–30, 136–7, 142–6.
Tuned systems, 103.

van der Pol's equation, 216–18.
energy method for, 222.
Velocity, as coordinate, 210.
of waves, 132, 152.
in air, 155.
in gas, 152.
in horn, 161.
potential, 157–61.
wave equation for, 158.
response, 40–41, 43, 44, 45, 46, 47.
Vibrating systems, essential properties of, 1.
damped, 27 ff., 37–44, 58–60, 62–3, 122, 213–16, 222–3.
multiple, see Multiple systems.
simple, see Simple systems.
Vibration dampers, 122.
Vibrations, damped, 27, 29–36, 213–16.
isochronous, 9.
maintained, see Maintained vibrations.
normal modes of, see Normal modes.
of bar, 169, 177, 187–91.
of particles, in waves, 128.
of shaft, 168–70, 174–5, 177, 181–2.
of stretched string, 165–8, 170–4, 179–81, 195–9.

periodic, 6, 210, 211, 213, 217.
steady-state, 37.
Viscous friction, 28, 73, 122.
Voltage, 5, 118, 125.

Wave, converging, 158.
diverging, 158–9.
incident, 136, 142, 156.
progressive, 139, 168.
reflected, 136, 143.
simple-harmonic, 141, 142–6.
standing, 168.
transmitted, 143, 144, 145, 146.
triangular, 136–8.
virtual, 136.
Wave equation, 130–2, 152.
in three dimensions, 157–8, 160.
solutions of, 132–3, 152, 158.
Waves, 128 ff.
initiation of, 133.
longitudinal, in bar, 131.
in transmission line, 131–2.
propagation of, 128, 132, 152.
in three dimensions, 156–61.
reflection of, 135–9, 142–6, 155–6, 164.
sound, in three dimensions, 156–61.
plane, 151–3, 155–6.
sinusoidal, 153–4.
spherical, 158–9.
torsional, in shaft, 130–1, 137–8, 139, 141–2.
transverse, in stretched string, 129–30, 136–7, 142–6.
velocity of, 132, 152, 155, 161.
with end condition prescribed, 133.
with initial conditions prescribed, 134–5.
Whirling of shafts, 191–2, 204.
Work, 17.
differential, 71–73, 76, 79.

PRINTED IN GREAT BRITAIN
AT THE UNIVERSITY PRESS, OXFORD
BY VIVIAN RIDLER
PRINTER TO THE UNIVERSITY

I reasoned. I could listen, rapt once more, to the problems of facing Fazal Mahmood on coconut matting.

This cheerful and unaffected demeanour of his had been mentioned without fail by the scores of people I talked to about him. Let one last voice speak for all, the aforesaid Baroness Heyhoe-Flint. 'I remember playing against him for England Ladies versus an Old England XI. Some ex-Test players were a little arrogant and patronising when they played against us. But not Tom. He played properly, if a little within himself, and never overstepped the mark, taking advantage. And afterwards, he'd talk endlessly about cricket, holding his audience in the palm of his hand. It all seemed so easy and effortless to those of us transfixed. Just like his batting, really.' As a eulogy of a man's life, you'd be hard pressed to beat that.

Some rage against the dying of the light; others face up to it with more stoicism. Either way, it cannot be much fun knowing that your memory is fading, your energy diminishing and your hinterland shrinking. Tom Graveney is like any other man; he finds the limitations of old age irksome. Who wouldn't yearn to be out there one last time, in the middle, batting for England, at your physical and skilful peak, rather than pushing a Zimmer frame down the corridor?

But he was headed for Jackie's room and he did not begrudge the effort; he had been absent from the marriage for long periods of time during his playing days and there was now ample time to repay her loyalty. 'Mr Graveney,' a nurse once interrupted us. 'Your wife is calling for you.' He pulled himself upright. 'Some things never change,' he remarked cheerfully. 'Tell her I'm on my way.' Then he looked at me and winked. 'Eventually,' he uttered *sotto voce*.

But it is my opinion that he copes better than most. His natural outlook is generally sunny and his mood cheerful, that has to be said. *How are you, Tom? Not so good, I hear.* 'Quite a lot better, actually.' *Are you eating enough?* 'Oh, I'm packing it away.' His spare frame might hint that 'packing it away' would not have been the first phrase to spring to mind but his warm and companionable nature seems impregnable. No doubt, during the long nights, he has his dark moments but in the same way that a batsman never betrays his innermost doubts and fears, his outward demeanour remains determinedly sanguine.

My belief is that his year's presidency of MCC was tough on his constitution but good for his soul. He could so easily have finished up as an embittered ex-player, bemoaning his bad luck and unsympathetic handling by those in authority. A surprising number do. By his own admission, he should have played more Test matches and his relatively modest record against Australia remains inexplicable. And he never made any money out of the game, either when he was playing or afterwards. The two visits to the head beak's office at Lord's on disciplinary charges rankled at the time and left scars. Of course, there was much about his career to reflect on with satisfaction and pride but still…we all feel that we could have done better if we had our time again.

For him, the honour of the MCC presidency was not so much that it put him in touch again with the game at the highest level but that it was MCC who had asked him. It was as if all the aggravation and tension in his dealings with the masters of the game had been washed away.

MCC had changed. And so had he. After all, as he said to me earlier, what is the point in harbouring grudges when you are in your 80s? At this stage in his life, he believes that all that could have been done has been done. And if there are one or two loose ends, life is too short now to bother about them. His year as president allowed him to sign off with dignity and fulfilment. Almost as good as scoring a hundred. At Lord's – where else?